SHORT STORIES
for Students

Advisors

Jayne M. Burton is a teacher of English, a member of the Delta Kappa Gamma International Society for Key Women Educators, and currently a master's degree candidate in the Interdisciplinary Study of Curriculum and Instruction and English at Angelo State University.

Tom Shilts is the youth librarian at the Okemos branch of Capital Area District Library in Okemos, Michigan. He holds an MSLS degree from Clarion University of Pennsylvania and an MA in U.S. History from the University of North Dakota.

Amy Spade Silverman has taught at independent schools in California, Texas, Michigan, and New York. She holds a bachelor of arts degree from the University of Michigan and a master of fine arts degree from the University of Houston. She is a member of the National Council of Teachers of English and Teachers and Writers. She is an exam reader for Advanced Placement Literature and Composition. She is also a poet, published in *North American Review*, *Nimrod*, and *Michigan Quarterly Review*, among others.

SHORT STORIES
for Students

Presenting Analysis, Context, and Criticism
on Commonly Studied Short Stories

VOLUME 40

Matthew Derda, Project Editor

Foreword by Thomas E. Barden

JOHN C. HART MEMORIAL LIBRARY
1130 MAIN STREET
SHRUB OAK, NEW YORK 10588
PHONE: 914-245-5262

GALE
CENGAGE Learning

Farmington Hills, Mich • San Francisco • New York • Waterville, Maine
Meriden, Conn • Mason, Ohio • Chicago

GALE
CENGAGE Learning®

Short Stories for Students, Volume 40

Project Editor: Matthew Derda

Rights Acquisition and Management:
Lynn Vagg

Composition: Evi Abou-El-Seoud

Manufacturing: Rhonda A. Dover

Imaging: John Watkins

Product Design: Pamela A. E. Galbreath,
Jennifer Wahi

Digital Content Production: Edna Shy

Product Manager: Meggin Condino

© 2014 Gale, Cengage Learning

WCN:01-100-101

ALL RIGHTS RESERVED. No part of this work covered by the copyright herein may be reproduced, transmitted, stored, or used in any form or by any means graphic, electronic, or mechanical, including but not limited to photocopying, recording, scanning, digitizing, taping, Web distribution, information networks, or information storage and retrieval systems, except as permitted under Section 107 or 108 of the 1976 United States Copyright Act, without the prior written permission of the publisher.

Since this page cannot legibly accommodate all copyright notices, the acknowledgments constitute an extension of the copyright notice.

For product information and technology assistance, contact us at
Gale Customer Support, 1-800-877-4253.
For permission to use material from this text or product,
submit all requests online at **www.cengage.com/permissions.**
Further permissions questions can be emailed to
permissionrequest@cengage.com

While every effort has been made to ensure the reliability of the information presented in this publication, Gale, a part of Cengage Learning, does not guarantee the accuracy of the data contained herein. Gale accepts no payment for listing; and inclusion in the publication of any organization, agency, institution, publication, service, or individual does not imply endorsement of the editors or publisher. Errors brought to the attention of the publisher and verified to the satisfaction of the publisher will be corrected in future editions.

Gale
27500 Drake Rd.
Farmington Hills, MI, 48331-3535

ISBN-13: 978-1-5730-2316-0

ISSN 1092-7735

This title is also available as an e-book.
ISBN-13: 978-1-5730-2324-5
Contact your Gale, a part of Cengage Learning sales representative for ordering information.

Printed in Mexico
1 2 3 4 5 6 7 18 17 16 15 14

Table of Contents

Why Study Literature At All?

Short Stories for Students is designed to provide readers with information and discussion about a wide range of important contemporary and historical works of short fiction, and it does that job very well. However, I want to use this guest foreword to address a question that it does *not* take up. It is a fundamental question that is often ignored in high school and college English classes as well as research texts, and one that causes frustration among students at all levels, namely why study literature at all? Isn't it enough to read a story, enjoy it, and go about one's business? My answer (to be expected from a literary professional, I suppose) is no. It is not enough. It is a start; but it is not enough. Here's why.

First, literature is the only part of the educational curriculum that deals directly with the actual world of lived experience. The philosopher Edmund Husserl used the apt German term *die Lebenswelt*, "the living world," to denote this realm. All the other content areas of the modern American educational system avoid the subjective, present reality of everyday life. Science (both the natural and the social varieties) objectifies, the fine arts create and/or perform, history reconstructs. Only literary study persists in posing those questions we all asked before our schooling taught us to give up on them. Only literature gives credibility to personal perceptions, feelings, dreams, and the "stream of consciousness" that is our inner voice. Literature wonders about infinity, wonders why God permits evil, wonders what will happen to us after we die. Literature admits that we get our hearts broken, that people sometimes cheat and get away with it, that the world is a strange and probably incomprehensible place. Literature, in other words, takes on all the big and small issues of what it means to be human. So my first answer is that of the humanist we should read literature and study it and take it seriously because it enriches us as human beings. We develop our moral imagination, our capacity to sympathize with other people, and our ability to understand our existence through the experience of fiction.

My second answer is more practical. By studying literature we can learn how to explore and analyze texts. Fiction may be about *die Lebenswelt*, but it is a construct of words put together in a certain order by an artist using the medium of language. By examining and studying those constructions, we can learn about language as a medium. We can become more sophisticated about word associations and connotations, about the manipulation of symbols, and about style and atmosphere. We can grasp how ambiguous language is and how important context and texture is to meaning. In our first encounter with a work of literature, of course, we are not supposed to catch all of these things. We are spellbound, just as the writer wanted us to be. It is as serious students of the writer's art that we begin to see how the tricks are done.

Seeing the tricks, which is another way of saying "developing analytical and close reading skills," is important above and beyond its intrinsic literary educational value. These skills transfer to other fields and enhance critical thinking of any kind. Understanding how language is used to construct texts is powerful knowledge. It makes engineers better problem solvers, lawyers better advocates and courtroom practitioners, politicians better rhetoricians, marketing and advertising agents better sellers, and citizens more aware consumers as well as better participants in democracy. This last point is especially important, because rhetorical skill works both ways when we learn how language is manipulated in the making of texts the result is that we become less susceptible when language is used to manipulate us.

My third reason is related to the second. When we begin to see literature as created artifacts of language, we become more sensitive to good writing in general. We get a stronger sense of the importance of individual words, even the sounds of words and word combinations. We begin to understand Mark Twain's delicious proverb "The difference between the right word and the almost right word is the difference between lightning and a lightning bug." Getting beyond the "enjoyment only" stage of literature gets us closer to becoming makers of word art ourselves. I am not saying that studying fiction will turn every student into a Faulkner or a Shakespeare. But it will make us more adaptable and effective writers, even if our art form ends up being the office memo or the corporate annual report.

Studying short stories, then, can help students become better readers, better writers, and even better human beings. But I want to close with a warning. If your study and exploration of the craft, history, context, symbolism, or anything else about a story starts to rob it of the magic you felt when you first read it, it is time to stop. Take a break, study another subject, shoot some hoops, or go for a run. Love of reading is too important to be ruined by school. The early twentieth century writer Willa Cather, in her novel *My Antonia*, has her narrator Jack Burden tell a story that he and Antonia heard from two old Russian immigrants when they were teenagers. These immigrants, Pavel and Peter, told about an incident from their youth back in Russia that the narrator could recall in vivid detail thirty years later. It was a harrowing story of a wedding party starting home in sleds and being chased by starving wolves. Hundreds of wolves attacked the group's sleds one by one as they sped across the snow trying to reach their village. In a horrible revelation, the old Russians revealed that the groom eventually threw his own bride to the wolves to save himself. There was even a hint that one of the old immigrants might have been the groom mentioned in the story. Cather has her narrator conclude with his feelings about the story. "We did not tell Pavel's secret to anyone, but guarded it jealously as if the wolves of the Ukraine had gathered that night long ago, and the wedding party had been sacrificed, just to give us a painful and peculiar pleasure." That feeling, that painful and peculiar pleasure, is the most important thing about literature. Study and research should enhance that feeling and never be allowed to overwhelm it.

Thomas E. Barden
Professor of English and Director of
Graduate English Studies, The
University of Toledo

Introduction

Purpose of the Book

The purpose of *Short Stories for Students* (*SSfS*) is to provide readers with a guide to understanding, enjoying, and studying short stories by giving them easy access to information about the work. Part of Gale's "For Students" Literature line, *SSfS* is specifically designed to meet the curricular needs of high school and undergraduate college students and their teachers, as well as the interests of general readers and researchers considering specific short fiction. While each volume contains entries on "classic" stories frequently studied in classrooms, there are also entries containing hard-to-find information on contemporary stories, including works by multicultural, international, and women writers.

The information covered in each entry includes an introduction to the story and the story's author; a plot summary, to help readers unravel and understand the events in the work; descriptions of important characters, including explanation of a given character's role in the narrative as well as discussion about that character's relationship to other characters in the story; analysis of important themes in the story; and an explanation of important literary techniques and movements as they are demonstrated in the work.

In addition to this material, which helps the readers analyze the story itself, students are also provided with important information on the literary and historical background informing each work. This includes a historical context essay, a box comparing the time or place the story was written to modern Western culture, a critical overview essay, and excerpts from critical essays on the story or author. A unique feature of *SSfS* is a specially commissioned critical essay on each story, targeted toward the student reader.

To further help today's student in studying and enjoying each story, information on audiobooks and other media adaptations is provided (if available), as well as reading suggestions for works of fiction and nonfiction on similar themes and topics. Classroom aids include ideas for research papers and lists of critical and reference sources that provide additional material on the work.

Selection Criteria

The titles for each volume of *SSfS* were selected by surveying numerous sources on teaching literature and analyzing course curricula for various school districts. Some of the sources surveyed include: literature anthologies, *Reading Lists for College-Bound Students: The Books Most Recommended by America's Top Colleges*; Teaching the Short Story: A Guide to Using Stories from around the World, by the National Council of Teachers of English (NCTE); and "A Study of High School Literature Anthologies," conducted by Arthur Applebee at the Center for the Learning and Teaching of Literature and sponsored by the

National Endowment for the Arts and the Office of Educational Research and Improvement.

Input was also solicited from our advisory board, as well as educators from various areas. From these discussions, it was determined that each volume should have a mix of "classic" stories (those works commonly taught in literature classes) and contemporary stories for which information is often hard to find. Because of the interest in expanding the canon of literature, an emphasis was also placed on including works by international, multicultural, and women authors. Our advisory board members—educational professionals—helped pare down the list for each volume. Works not selected for the present volume were noted as possibilities for future volumes. As always, the editor welcomes suggestions for titles to be included in future volumes.

How Each Entry Is Organized

Each entry, or chapter, in *SSfS* focuses on one story. Each entry heading lists the title of the story, the author's name, and the date of the story's publication. The following elements are contained in each entry:

Introduction: a brief overview of the story which provides information about its first appearance, its literary standing, any controversies surrounding the work, and major conflicts or themes within the work.

Author Biography: this section includes basic facts about the author's life, and focuses on events and times in the author's life that may have inspired the story in question.

Plot Summary: a description of the events in the story. Lengthy summaries are broken down with subheads.

Characters: an alphabetical listing of the characters who appear in the story. Each character name is followed by a brief to an extensive description of the character's role in the story, as well as discussion of the character's actions, relationships, and possible motivation.

Characters are listed alphabetically by last name. If a character is unnamed—for instance, the narrator in "The Eatonville Anthology"—the character is listed as "The Narrator" and alphabetized as "Narrator." If a character's first name is the only one given, the name will appear alphabetically by that name.

Themes: a thorough overview of how the topics, themes, and issues are addressed within the story. Each theme discussed appears in a separate subhead.

Style: this section addresses important style elements of the story, such as setting, point of view, and narration; important literary devices used, such as imagery, foreshadowing, symbolism; and, if applicable, genres to which the work might have belonged, such as Gothicism or Romanticism. Literary terms are explained within the entry, but can also be found in the Glossary.

Historical Context: this section outlines the social, political, and cultural climate in which the author lived and the work was created. This section may include descriptions of related historical events, pertinent aspects of daily life in the culture, and the artistic and literary sensibilities of the time in which the work was written. If the story is historical in nature, information regarding the time in which the story is set is also included. Long sections are broken down with helpful subheads.

Critical Overview: this section provides background on the critical reputation of the author and the story, including bannings or any other public controversies surrounding the work. For older works, this section may include a history of how the story was first received and how perceptions of it may have changed over the years; for more recent works, direct quotes from early reviews may also be included.

Criticism: an essay commissioned by *SSfS* which specifically deals with the story and is written specifically for the student audience, as well as excerpts from previously published criticism on the work (if available).

Sources: an alphabetical list of critical material used in compiling the entry, with bibliographical information.

Further Reading: an alphabetical list of other critical sources which may prove useful for the student. Includes full bibliographical information and a brief annotation.

Suggested Search Terms: a list of search terms and phrases to jumpstart students' further information seeking. Terms include not just titles and author names but also terms and topics related to the historical and literary context of the works.

In addition, each entry contains the following highlighted sections, set apart from the main text as sidebars:

Media Adaptations: if available, a list of audio-books and important film and television adaptations of the story, including source information. The list also includes stage adaptations, musical adaptations, etc.

Topics for Further Study: a list of potential study questions or research topics dealing with the story. This section includes questions related to other disciplines the student may be studying, such as American history, world history, science, math, government, business, geography, economics, psychology, etc.

Compare and Contrast: an "at-a-glance" comparison of the cultural and historical differences between the author's time and culture and late twentieth century or early twenty-first century Western culture. This box includes pertinent parallels between the major scientific, political, and cultural movements of the time or place the story was written, the time or place the story was set (if a historical work), and modern Western culture. Works written after 1990 may not have this box.

What Do I Read Next?: a list of works that might give a reader points of entry into a classic work (e.g., YA or multicultural titles) and/or complement the featured story or serve as a contrast to it. This includes works by the same author and others, works from various genres, YA works, and works from various cultures and eras.

Other Features

SSfS includes "Why Study Literature At All?," a foreword by Thomas E. Barden, Professor of English and Director of Graduate English Studies at the University of Toledo. This essay provides a number of very fundamental reasons for studying literature and, therefore, reasons why a book such as *SSfS*, designed to facilitate the study of literature, is useful.

A Cumulative Author/Title Index lists the authors and titles covered in each volume of the *SSfS* series.

A Cumulative Nationality/Ethnicity Index breaks down the authors and titles covered in

each volume of the *SSfS* series by nationality and ethnicity.

A Subject/Theme Index, specific to each volume, provides easy reference for users who may be studying a particular subject or theme rather than a single work. Significant subjects from events to broad themes are included.

Each entry may include illustrations, including photo of the author, stills from film adaptations (if available), maps, and/or photos of key historical events.

Citing Short Stories for Students

When writing papers, students who quote directly from any volume of *SSfS* may use the following general forms to document their source. These examples are based on MLA style; teachers may request that students adhere to a different style, thus, the following examples may be adapted as needed.

When citing text from *SSfS* that is not attributed to a particular author (for example, the Themes, Style, Historical Context sections, etc.), the following format may be used:

> "How I Met My Husband." *Short Stories for Students*. Ed. Sara Constantakis. Vol. 36. Detroit: Gale, Cengage Learning, 2013. 73–95. Print.

When quoting the specially commissioned essay from *SSfS* (usually the first essay under the Criticism subhead), the following format may be used:

> Dominic, Catherine. Critical Essay on "How I Met My Husband." *Short Stories for Students*. Ed. Sara Constantakis. Vol. 36. Detroit: Gale, Cengage Learning, 2013. 84–87. Print.

When quoting a journal or newspaper essay that is reprinted in a volume of *SSfS*, the following form may be used:

> Ditsky, John. "The Figure in the Linoleum: The Fictions of Alice Munro." *Hollins Critic* 22.3 (1985): 1–10. Rpt. in *Short Stories for Students*. Vol. 36. Ed. Sara Constantakis. Detroit: Gale, Cengage Learning, 2013. 92–94. Print.

When quoting material from a book that is reprinted in a volume of *SSfS,* the following form may be used:

> Cooke, John. "Alice Munro." *The Influence of Painting on Five Canadian Writers*. Lewiston, NY: Edwin Mellen Press, 1996. 69–85. Rpt. in *Short Stories for Students*. Vol. 36. Ed. Sara Constantakis. Detroit: Gale, Cengage Learning, 2013. 89–92. Print.

We Welcome Your Suggestions

The editorial staff of *Short Stories for Students* welcomes your comments and ideas. Readers who wish to suggest short stories to appear in future volumes, or who have other suggestions, are cordially invited to contact the editor. You may contact the editor via E-mail at: **ForStudentsEditors@cengage.com.** Or write to the editor at:

Editor, *Short Stories for Students*
Gale
27500 Drake Road
Farmington Hills, MI 48331-3535

Literary Chronology

1850: Lafcadio Hearn is born on August 17 in Levkás, Ionian Islands.

1885: Edna Ferber is born on August 15 in Kalamazoo, Michigan.

1890: H. P. Lovecraft is born on August 20 in Providence, Rhode Island.

1896: Murray Leinster is born on June 16 in Norfolk, Virginia.

1898: Lafcadio Hearn's *The Boy Who Drew Cats* is published as number 23 of Hasegawa Takejirō's *Japanese Fairy Tale Series*.

1899: Vladimir Nabokov is born on April 22 in St. Petersburg, Russia.

1900: Mona Gardner is born in Seattle, Washington.

1902: Norman Maclean is born on December 23 in Clarinda, Iowa.

1904: Lafcadio Hearn dies of heart failure on September 26 in Tokyo, Japan.

1912: Edna Ferber's "A Bush League Hero" is published in *Buttered Side Down*.

1915: Tom Godwin is born on June 6.

1925: Edna Ferber is awarded the Pulitzer Prize for Fiction for So Big.

1928: Cynthia Ozick is born on April 17 in New York, New York.

1929: H. P. Lovecraft's "The Dunwich Horror" is published in *Weird Tales*.

1930: Marion Zimmer Bradley is born on June 3 in East Greenbush, New York.

1935: Carol Shields is born on June 2 in Oak Park, Illinois.

1937: H. P. Lovecraft dies of cancer on March 15 in Providence, Rhode Island.

1939: Toni Cade Bambara is born on March 25 in New York, New York.

1941: Mona Gardner's "The Dinner Party" is published in *Saturday Review of Literature*.

1946: Murray Leinster's "A Logic Named Joe" is published in *Astounding Science Fiction*.

1948: Vladimir Nabokov's "Signs and Symbols" is published in the *New Yorker*.

1954: Marion Zimmer Bradley's "Year of the Big Thaw" is published in *Fantastic Universe*.

1954: Tom Godwin's "The Cold Equations" is published in *Astounding Science-Fiction*.

1957: Lorrie Moore is born on January 13 in Glens Falls, New York.

1958: Roddy Doyle is born on May 8 in Dublin, Ireland.

1968: Edna Ferber dies of cancer on April 16, in New York, New York.

1971: Cynthia Ozick's "The Suitcase" is published in *The Pagan Rabbi and Other Stories*.

1975: Murray Leinster dies of heart failure on June 8 in Gloucester, Virginia.

1976: Norman Maclean's *A River Runs through It* is published in *A River Runs through It and Other Stories*.

1977: Vladimir Nabokov dies of pneumonia on July 2 in Montreux, Switzerland.

1980: Tom Godwin dies on August 31 in Las Vegas, Nevada.

1981: Mona Gardner dies.

1985: Toni Cade Bambara's "Geraldine Moore the Poet" is published in *The Reader As Detective*, Book 2.

1985: Carol Shields's "Mrs. Turner Cutting the Grass" is published in *Various Miracles*.

1990: Norman Maclean dies of natural causes on August 2 in Chicago, Illinois.

1993: Roddy Doyle is awarded the Booker Prize for *Paddy Clarke Ha Ha Ha*.

1993: Lorrie Moore's "Dance in America" is published in the *New Yorker*.

1995: Carol Shields is awarded the Pulitzer Prize for Fiction for *The Stone Diaries*.

1995: Toni Cade Bambara dies of colon cancer on December 9 in Philadelphia, Pennsylvania.

1999: Marion Zimmer Bradley dies of a heart attack on September 5, in Berkeley, California.

2003: Carol Shields dies of breast cancer on July 16 in Victoria, British Columbia.

2007: Roddy Doyle's "New Boy" is published in *The Deportees and Other Stories*.

Acknowledgements

The editors wish to thank the copyright holders of the excerpted criticism included in this volume and the permissions managers of many book and magazine publishing companies for assisting us in securing reproduction rights. We are also grateful to the staffs of the Detroit Public Library, the Library of Congress, the University of Detroit Mercy Library, Wayne State University Purdy/Kresge Library Complex, and the University of Michigan Libraries for making their resources available to us. Following is a list of the copyright holders who have granted us permission to reproduce material in this volume of *SSfS*. Every effort has been made to trace copyright, but if omissions have been made, please let us know.

COPYRIGHTED EXCERPTS IN SSfS, VOLUME 40, WERE REPRODUCED FROM THE FOLLOWING SOURCES:

Airaksinen, Timo. From *The Philosophy of H. P. Lovecraft: The Route to Horror*. Peter Lang Publishing, 1999. Copyright © Peter Lang Publishing, 1999. Reproduced by permission of the publisher.—Arbur, Rosemarie. From *Marion Zimmer Bradley*. Edited by Roger C. Schlobin. Starmont House, 1985. Copyright © Starmont House, 1985. Reproduced by permission of the publisher.—Barabtarlo, Gennady. From *The Garland Companion to Vladimir Nabokov*. Edited by Vladimir E. Alexandrov. Garland Publishing, 1995. Copyright © Taylor & Francis, 1995. Reproduced by permission of the publisher.—Boddy, Kasia. From *The American Short Story since 1950*. Edinburgh University Press, 2010. Copyright © Edinburgh University Press, 2010. Reproduced by permission of the publisher.—Bradley, Marion Zimmer. From *Inside Outer Space: Science Fiction Professionals Look at Their Craft*. Edited by Sharon Jarvis. Frederick Ungar Publishers, 1985. Copyright © Frederick Ungar Publishers, 1985. Printed by permission of the author and the author's agents, Scovil Galen Ghosh Literary Agency, Inc.—Burleson, Donald R. From *Lovecraft: Disturbing the Universe*. University Press of Kentucky, 1990. Copyright © University Press of Kentucky, 1990. Reproduced by permission of the publisher.—Pages 91-93, 119-122 (1700 words excerpted from the seven pages) from *Race, Gender, and Desire: Narrative Strategies in the Fiction of Toni Cade Bambara, Toni Morrison, and Alice Walker* by Elliott Bulter-Evans. Used by permission of Temple University Press. Copyright © 1991 by Temple University. All Rights Reserved.—Campbell, Donna. From *Middlebrow Moderns: Popular American Women Writers of the 1920s*. Edited by Lisa Botshon and Meredith Goldsmith. Northeastern University Press, 2003. Copyright © University Press of New England, Lebanon, NH. Reprinted with permission pages 129-136.—Cannon, Peter. From *H.P. Lovecraft*. Copyright © 1989 Cengage Learning.—Ensslen, K. From

The African American Short Story 1970 to 1990: A Collection of Critical Essays. Edited by Wolfgang Karrer and Barbara Puschmann-Nalenz. Wissenschaftlicher Verlag Trier, 1993. Copyright © Wissenschaftlicher Verlag, 1993. Reproduced by permission of the publisher.—Friedman, Lawrence S. From *Understanding Cynthia Ozick*. University of South Carolina Press, 1991. Copyright © University of South Carolina Press, 1991. Reproduced by permission of the publisher.—Gleason, William A. From *The Leisure Ethic: Work and Play in American Literature, 1840-1940*. Stanford University Press, 1999. Copyright © Stanford University Press, 1999. Reproduced by permission of the publisher.—Hargrove, Nancy D. From *Women Writers of the Contemporary South*. Edited by Peggy Whitman Prenshaw. University Press of Mississippi, 1984. Copyright © University Press of Mississippi, 1984. Reproduced by permission of the publisher.—Hammill, Faye. From *Literary Culture and Female Authorship in Canada 1760-2000*. Rodopi B.V, 1994. Copyright © Rodopi B.V, 1994. Reproduced by permission of the publisher.—Kelly, Alison. From *Understanding Lorrie Moore*. University of South Carolina Press, 2009. Copyright © University of South Carolina Press, 2009. Reproduced by permission of the publisher.—Kielsky, Vera Emuna. From *Inevitable Exiles: Cynthia Ozick's View of the Precariousness of Jewish Existence in a Gentile Society*. Edited by Daniel Walden. Peter Lang Publishing, 1989. Copyright © Peter Lang Publishing, 1989. Reproduced by permission of the publisher.—Makino, Yoko. From *Lafcadio Hearn and Yanagita Kunio: Who Initiated Folklore Studies in Japan?* Edited by Sukehiro Hirakawa. Global Oriental, 2007. Copyright © Koninklijke BRILL NV, 1997. Reproduced by permission of the publisher.—McCarthy, Dermot. From *Roddy Doyle: Raining on the Parade*. The Liffey Press, 2003. Copyright © The Liffey Press, 2003. Reproduced by permission of the publisher.—*Moment*, v. 35.1, January-February 2010. Copyright © 2010 by *Moment* Magazine. Reproduced by permission of the publisher.—*New Statesman*, v. 128.4418, January 8, 1999. Copyright © 1999 by *New Stateman*. Reproduced by permission of the publisher.—Reprinted from Nicholas O'Connell, ed., *At the Field's End: Interview with Twenty-two Pacific Northwest Writers* (Seattle: University of Washington Press, 1987, 1998), 211-29. Used with permission, The University of Washington Press.—Reprinted from: *Who Shaped Science Fiction*, pp. 221-222, Copyright © 2000, Robert Sabella. With permission from Nova Science Publishers, Inc.—Simonson, Harold P. From *Beyond the Frontier: Writers, Western Regionalism, and a Sense of Place*. Texas Christian University Press, 1989. Copyright © Texas Christian University Press, 1989. Reproduced by permission of the publisher.—White, Caramine. From *Reading Roddy Doyle*. Syracuse University Press, 2001. Copyright © Syracuse University Press, 2001. Reproduced by permission of the publisher.—*Women's Review of Books*, v. 16.2, November 1998. Copyright © 1998 by Old City Publishing. Reproduced by permission of the publisher.

Contributors

Bryan Aubrey: Aubrey holds a PhD in English. Entries on "The Suitcase" and "Year of the Big Thaw." Original essays on "The Suitcase" and "Year of the Big Thaw."

Jennifer Bussey: Bussey is an independent writer specializing in literature. Entry on "A Bush League Hero." Original essay on "A Bush League Hero."

Rita M. Brown: Brown is an English professor. Entry on "Signs and Symbols." Original essay on "Signs and Symbols."

Catherine Dominic: Dominic is a novelist and a freelance writer and editor. Entry on "Geraldine Moore the Poet." Original essay on "Geraldine Moore the Poet."

Klay Dyer: Dyer is a writer for a number of publications, specializing in the arts, innovation, and technology. Entry on "Mrs. Turner Cutting the Grass." Original essay on "Mrs. Turner Cutting the Grass."

Kristen Sarlin Greenberg: Greenberg is a freelance writer and editor with a background in literature and philosophy. Entry on "New Boy." Original essay on "New Boy"

Michael Allen Holmes: Holmes is a writer with existential interests. Entries on "The Boy Who Drew Cats" and "The Cold Equations." Original essays on "The Boy Wo Drew Cats" and "The Cold Equations."

David Kelly: Kelly is a fiction writer and instructor of literature and creative writing. Entry on "Dance in America." Original essay on "Dance in America."

Michael J. O'Neal: O'Neal holds a PhD in English. Entry on "A River Runs through It." Original essay on "A River Runs through It."

April Paris: Paris is a freelance writer with an extensive background writing literary and educational materials. Entry on "The Dinner Party." Original essay on "The Dinner Party."

Kathy Wilson Peacock: Wilson Peacock is a writer and editor who specializes in twentieth-century fiction. Entry on "The Dunwich Horror." Original essay on "The Dunwich Horror."

Bradley A. Skeen: Skeen is a classicist. Entry on "A Logic Named Joe." Original essay on "A Logic Named Joe."

The Boy Who Drew Cats

"The Boy Who Drew Cats" is a Japanese fairy tale adapted to English by the travel essayist, translator, and story writer Lafcadio Hearn. Hearn was born on a Greek island, later lived in Europe and North America, and finally settled in Japan, even adopting a Japanese name, Koizumi Yakumo. One of his most famous Japanese stories is "The Boy Who Drew Cats," a brief fairy tale revolving around a young boy's artistic compulsion and what it brings about. It was originally published in Japan in 1898 as number 23 of the Japanese Fairy Tale Series, illustrated by Kason Suzuki. The story is included in a number of collections titled *Japanese Fairy Tales*, attributed to Hearn and others, including a 1900 volume edited by Takashi Kuroda. The tale became the title story of *The Boy Who Drew Cats and Other Japanese Fairy Tales* (1998), illustrated by Yuko Green, and it has been presented as a modern children's book, *The Boy Who Drew Cats* (2002), adapted by Margaret Hodges and illustrated by Aki Sogabe.

LAFCADIO HEARN

1898

AUTHOR BIOGRAPHY

Patrick Lafcadio Tessima Carlos Hearn was born to a Greek mother and Irish father on August 17, 1850, on the Greek island in the Ionian Sea then known to the British as Santa Maura, to the

Hearn was honored on a Japanese postage stamp for his translation of Hasegawa Takejirō's fairy tales. (© feiyuezhangjie | Shutterstock.com)

Greeks as Lefcadia, eventually called Levkás. At the time the Ionian Islands were a resentful British protectorate, and Hearn's father, Charles Hearn, was an Irish military surgeon who, while stationed there, met and married Rosa Cassimati (to her family's displeasure). Charles was transferred to the West Indies before Lafcadio was born. Mother and son were brought from the Ionian Islands to Dublin in 1852, and Hearn met his father for the first time in 1853—at which time his mother, overstrained by the circumstances and the evaporation of her husband's love, had a breakdown. At length, she returned alone (though again pregnant) to her home island of Cerigo. Hearn inherited much of the uprootedness felt by his mother and instilled by his father, who placed the boy in the care of his great-aunt Sarah Brenane when he was six. The father remarried, acquiring a new family, and after years spent overseas died in 1866.

Brenane, a Catholic widow with no descendants of her own, knew little of raising children. To push Hearn beyond his fear of the dark, she locked him in a small room with no light at night, which rather intensified the fear. After a time, even when he screamed, his aunt declined to visit; he was often beset by nightmares and was led to believe in ghosts and goblins. During the day, reading became a primary escape, and Hearn grew to become an odd but resilient adolescent. Sarah tried to guide him into the priesthood, and he was sent to school in Paris in 1862. Hearn, however, who identified with his Greek heritage, was essentially anti-Catholic. At age thirteen, he went to secondary school at St. Cuthbert's College, in Ushaw, England, and gained a reputation for mischievousness. But a school-yard accident dramatically changed his life. Playing a game called giant's stride, a boy let loose a knotted rope that struck Hearn in the left eye, which became inflamed, was unsuccessfully operated on, and lost its function and color. In time Hearn's right eye became swollen from overuse, and in light of people's responses to his appearance, he grew abashed and self-deprecating. In later life, he always posed in profile or with eyes downcast to hide his ocular defects.

Upon learning that his deceased father's estate was bankrupt, Hearn sailed to America in 1869 and before long became a journalist in Cincinnati, Ohio. Having been known as Patrick up until then, Hearn effectively declared a new identity by going by Lafcadio. He made a name for himself professionally by relating vivid Cincinnati street scenes for the *Enquirer* and then the *Commercial*. Not favoring the climate, however, he traveled down the Mississippi River in 1877 to New Orleans, to become associate editor of the *Item* and then hold a similar position with the *Times-Democrat*. Shifting from the sensationalist news pieces that he thrived on to fiction, Hearn came out with two books of derived stories, *Stray Leaves from Strange Literature* (1884) and *Some Chinese Ghosts* (1887). His time in New Orleans led to the musically structured novel *Chita* (1889), while a stay in Martinique led to the travelogue *Two Years in the French West Indies* (1890).

In 1890, Hearn's fortunes, in the form of a *Harper's* assignment, led him to Japan. Upon reaching the shore, he at once professed a desire to die there, and indeed he stayed on after finishing his assignment. He married Setsu Koizumi and raised four children with her. While in Japan, Hearn wrote many sketches, essays, travel narratives, and adapted stories, publishing such volumes as *Gleanings in Buddha-Fields* (1897) and *In Ghostly Japan* (1899). In addition to his cultural essays on his adopted homeland, he presented numerous Japanese tales and legends, such as those in *A Japanese Miscellany* (1901) and *Kwaidan* (1904), to English-speaking audiences. The illustrated children's story *The Boy Who Drew Cats* first came out in 1898 and was later included in *Japanese Fairy Tales* (1900). Aside from his writing, Hearn took positions teaching English at middle schools in Matsue and Kumamoto in the early 1890s and at Tokyo's Imperial University from 1896 to 1903. He last taught at Waseda University. His period of industriousness in Japan—he published more than a volume per year over his last decade there—was cut short: Hearn died in Tokyo of heart failure at the age of fifty-four, on September 26, 1904.

PLOT SUMMARY

"The Boy Who Drew Cats" begins by relating the circumstances of a poor family of farmers. The parents are good people who do all they can to feed their several children. The elder children help out with chores and housework, but the youngest boy is too small and weak to be inclined toward labor. He is a clever boy, however, and so the parents bring him to the village temple to see if the old priest will accept him as an acolyte, or clerical apprentice. When the boy demonstrates his cleverness, the priest accepts him.

The boy proves a quick learner and obedient assistant, but during his study time, he takes to drawing cats, some of them in places where such sketches should not be found, like in the priest's books. He does this even after being specifically instructed not to, as though, being an artist by instinct, he simply cannot help it. The priest finally concludes that he must send the boy away, which he does, telling the boy he will never become a priest, though he may be an artist. His one piece of parting advice to the boy is "*Avoid large places at night;—keep to small!*" This baffles the boy somewhat, but he remembers the advice distinctly.

Making his way toward home, the boy realizes that his father will be upset with him over his failure as an acolyte, and so he resolves to seek another temple where he might be permitted to

MEDIA ADAPTATIONS

- The audiobook *Lafcadio Hearn Collection: The Boy Who Drew Cats, Kwaidan* features Hearn's most anthologized story paired with his best-known collection. The CD was recorded by Walter Covell for Brilliance Audio in 2012.

- *The Boy Who Drew Cats* is available for download as an individual audiobook produced by Listening Library in 2007, as part of its Rabbit Ears World Tales series. It is read by William Hurt and has music by Mark Isham. The running time is thirty-one minutes. Listening Library also includes this Rabbit Ears production on the 2007 audiobook CD *Treasury of Far East Folktales: Peachboy, The Boy Who Drew Cats.*

serve—he has heard of a great one some twelve miles off. Unbeknownst to him, the temple has been taken over by a goblin, and even the warriors sent in to kill the goblin have never been seen again.

The boy arrives at the temple and finds a light burning inside. According to the stories (which the boy has not heard), the goblin tricks wayfarers by luring them inside with the light. No one responds to the boy's knocking, so he pushes the unlocked door open and enters. As he bides his time in the dusty temple, the boy notes some paper screens that look to him like blank canvases; he finds the materials needed to grind some ink and begins painting cats.

Soon the boy feels like lying down beside the screens to sleep, but he then remembers the old priest's advice. The open area of the temple is indeed a large place, so he finds a cabinet or closet in which to secure himself with the door closed. There, he falls asleep. But he is awakened in the night by the most frightful screeching and fighting, which leaves him petrified and unwilling even to peek out, even long after the noises have ceased.

Only when the dawn comes does the boy dare emerge. He is startled to see blood all over the floor and the corpse of a giant goblin-rat lying there. He is not sure what has happened until he notices that the mouths of the cats he painted are open and red with blood—they killed the goblin-rat. He realizes then how wise the old priest's advice was. The boy goes on to become a famous artist, one whose drawings of cats are shown to Japan's travelers up to the present day.

CHARACTERS

Boy

The protagonist of the tale is a young boy whose cleverness is of little practical use on the farm where his family lives and works. His elder brother has been contributing his labor since age fourteen, and his sisters all help out around the house. But the boy, the youngest sibling, is also the weakest, and people judge from his physique that the priestly life would suit him best. This suggests that in a rural village of ages past such as the one described in the story, a poor person's only reasonable alternative to a life of labor was a religious life. But once the boy has become an acolyte at the temple, his artistic sense emerges, particularly in his impulsive devotion to drawing cats. Notably, the boy is not depicted as striving to be an artist through his unruly habit of drawing cats. As the narration states, he simply "drew them because he could not really help it." When this habit gets him cast out of the temple, the boy then takes his next course of action largely on impulse. Out of fear of being punished by his father, he heads for another temple he has heard about. He appears to be falling into the trap of the resident goblin-rat when he sits alone in the empty temple, but with little thought for what consequences there might be—just as before—he sets to drawing cats. These cats preserve his life by killing the goblin-rat.

Boy's Parents

Appearing in the tale's opening paragraphs, the parents are concisely described as poor but good. They seem to bow to the opinion of people in general that their youngest boy will never grow strong enough to be of use on their farm. Having trouble feeding all their children as it is, they elect to put the youngest boy under the care of the village priest (where the boy will presumably be fed). This decision can be seen to be made as much for the boy's benefit as for the parents'. However good the parents may be, the threat of punishment represented by the father is enough to deter the boy from returning home after being ejected from the temple, suggesting that the idea of goodness does not exclude a capacity for discipline.

Goblin

The tale's goblin is a fairy-tale monster, a gigantic rat that has taken over a large temple and apparently devours those who stray inside. Being a rat, it is susceptible to predatory cats, including, it turns out, those that exist in image only.

Priest

Although it is never explicitly stated, the priest is likely Buddhist. Shinto, Japan's ancient religion, is characterized by small shrines and rituals rather than large temples and learning. The priest's voice is in effect the only one in the tale: neither the parents nor the boy are given any direct speaking lines. This lends a high degree of authority to what little the priest says, and indeed, the sentences of narration that conclude the tale will confirm that the priest is right in his assessment of the boy's character. Meanwhile, as the tale continues, his final admonition echoes several times in the boy's mind. Notwithstanding his absorption in his occupation and religion, the priest is sensitive to how others' spiritual needs may demand of them something other than a religious life. The priest may be displeased with the boy, but this does not prevent him from encouraging his artistry and giving the advice that saves the boy's life.

THEMES

Youth

The protagonist of Hearn's version of this Japanese fairy tale offers a study in the nature of youth. The boy's brothers and sisters are all capable of fulfilling their parents' wishes and helping out around the farm, but the youngest boy is "quite weak and small" and deemed unsuited to physical exertion. Curiously, the tale gives the boy very little agency in this regard; it is said that he "did not seem to be fit for hard work" and that "people said he could never grow very big,"

TOPICS FOR FURTHER STUDY

- Create your own illustrated version of "The Boy Who Drew Cats," using whatever media—paint, watercolor, charcoal, colored pencils—you choose.

- A Buddhist influence in "The Boy Who Drew Cats" may be assumed, given the nature of the temples and the priest. Zen Buddhism in particular was practiced and refined in Japan. Research the relation of Zen Buddhism to art, and write an essay in which you detail this relation and follow up by examining Hearn's story and considering the extent to which Zen precepts or perspectives are evident.

- Also attributed to Hearn in editions of *Japanese Fairy Tales* is the story "Chin-chin Kobakama," in which Hearn's status as a foreign narrator is more apparent because several comments comparing Japanese and English children are made. Read this story, and then write a paper considering it in relation to "The Boy Who Drew Cats," remarking on the effects of the assertion of the narrator's presence, the content of his comments, the value of the comparisons, and the overall impact of the story as it is told. Include your own opinionated assessment of the validity of the narrator's various statements.

- Using online sources, research ancient Japanese beliefs in such fantastical creatures as goblins, ghosts, spirits, and fairies and how these beliefs are evident in Japanese stories. Then create a website that presents your findings, using illustrations drawn from traditional sources as well as modern ones such as anime films, including brief discussions of films and video clips if possible.

but the reader learns nothing of how the boy actually feels about doing work or how well he manages what work he is given. This suggests much about how adults can pigeonhole their own and other people's children according to

appearances or impressions without necessarily taking into account the child's own perspective and opinions. Nonetheless, the idea of the artistic youth being more sensitive and intellectual and less physically oriented holds true, to an extent; the boy seems content to go to the temple and gets along well there. Yet he remains a boy, not an automaton. He can obey and serve to a certain extent, but like many a child, he cannot suppress certain impulses. In one sense, his impulse to draw cats and his inability to stave that impulse are his downfall. In another sense, his deference to impulse, his very youthfulness, is what saves his life.

Creativity

Another interesting fact about the story is that the boy's artistic impulse makes no appearance, at least as far as the narrative is concerned, until after he is placed with the priest. This accords with the nature of creativity as many conceive it: If a person is inundated in his or her circumstances and the stimulations it entails, the creative impulse may not have room to flourish. One can easily imagine that with two parents and numerous brothers and sisters ever working and moving about the house and farm, the youngest boy would have had so much to observe and absorb that he could have had little room or time for constructive independent thought. The ability to observe, of course, can be an important stimulus to creativity—painters paint what they see, writers write about what they perceive in the world. The boy at last gravitates toward creative expression during his study time at the temple, which one imagines to be a far more subdued atmosphere than a family farm. And the boy must have seen at least a cat or two between the farm and the environs of the temple, because this is what he is most compelled to draw when his creative instinct overcomes him.

Obedience

After the boy reaches the temple, the tale hinges on his level of obedience. The reader is specifically told that the boy is a quick learner and "very obedient in most things," making him a model acolyte. But the "in most things" phrasing hints at the one exception, his drawing habit. The priest instructs him not to draw cats, and yet he does. The narrator's explanation for why the boy cannot obey the priest in this one matter is that he has "the genius of an *artist*,"

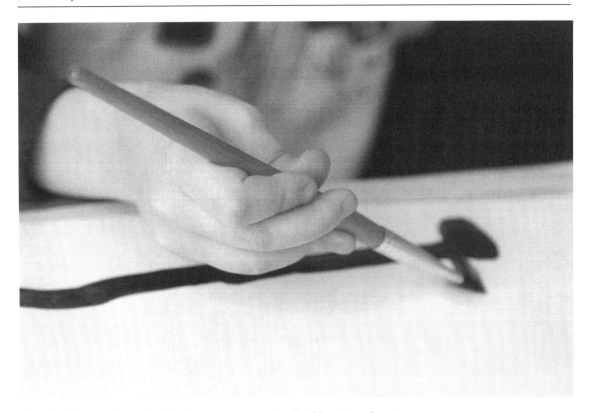

The little boy will not do his chores and spends all of his time drawing. *(© nulinukas / Shutterstock.com)*

and the artist's inspiration often takes precedence over all practical concerns, whether the artist means for it to or not. That is, the boy is not simply being disobedient, but rather he is subconsciously choosing to obey his own impulse rather than the priest's order to suppress that impulse. The reader is told, however, that the boy's cat-drawing habit is a "fault," and the fact that he is kicked out of the temple supports a negative assessment of his inability to obey the priest. When the boy imagines his father's disappointment, he believes he will be punished in particular for "having been disobedient." Still, the boy proves obedient when it matters most. He remembers the priest's parting admonition, to avoid large places at night, which has made such an impression on him that just as he is lying down to sleep in the haunted temple, it surfaces in his mind. Heeding this instruction is not a matter of suppressing artistic inspiration, and so the boy does not have the same trouble with it. In effect, the boy obeys the priest's wise advice—which seems to have been tailored to the circumstance of the haunted temple, which the old priest likely knew about—and his life is saved.

Art and Life

In the end, the most prominent theme of "The Boy Who Drew Cats" is the relation of art to life. The sense of this relation vacillates over the course of the story. Through the first three paragraphs, which treat the home circumstances of the boy's poor farming family, there is no mention of art, lending the sense that, practically speaking, art may bear no significant relation to life. At the most fundamental level of survival, this is true. Yet from the title the reader knows the boy will soon be drawing cats, and since he is described as very clever, there is yet no expectation that the boy's art will be his downfall. The boy's cat-drawing habit, which emerges under the priest's care, is immediately characterized as a fault, but it seems a harmless enough fault, and the reader likely takes a whimsical delight in the idea of a boy decorating any blank space he might find with a cat. Indeed, the habit is said to be evidence of his artistic genius. The priest, however, cannot abide this habit. The boy's inability to obey the priest singles the boy out as one unfit for priesthood. Once again, the boy's inclination toward art is portrayed negatively in a certain regard—in a religious context, which does not necessarily demand creativity—and yet valued for its own sake, with the priest acknowledging that the boy could be a "great artist."

What remains unresolved is whether art, beyond its intrinsic value, can have any extrinsic value, any tangible worth in the context of the greater world. The answer to this question, as befits a fairy tale, is a fantastical yes: The cats that the boy draws are what prove to save him from the goblin, a creature even warriors had been unable to slay. Beyond the literal level, the suggestion made by the tale's conclusion is that art has a way of warding off demons, both one's own and others'. By connecting with beauty and the imaginative modes of aesthetic creation and appreciation, one can gain a sort of peace of mind that perhaps cannot be gained otherwise—not by force, by labor, by religion, by learning, or any other way.

STYLE

Fairy Tale

Hearn's "The Boy Who Drew Cats" is a version of a Japanese fairy tale, and its literary status speaks to its construction. Fairy tales are stories aimed primarily at children, are often fanciful—including, perhaps, some degree of magic or supernatural power and a dastardly villain—and tend to offer, if not a moral per se, at least an implicit lesson with regard to conduct. The story of Hansel and Gretel and the witch with the delectable house, for example, is outlandish enough to seem unreal to children (and hopefully not give them nightmares), and yet it effectively warns them not to trust strangers, however appealing their sweets might be.

While fairy tales are often compressed or expanded to fit a given context, they are designed to cater to the attention spans of children, so long passages of ambient description and complex character development are unusual. "The Boy Who Drew Cats" is especially succinct, characterizing the boy's parents, the boy himself, and the old priest with just a few adjectives each. Little is said about the setting, and there is almost no dialogue. The emphasis is squarely on the plot, which is propelled by the boy's curious cat-drawing habit. Meanwhile, though the boy is not physically described, he comes to life by virtue of

his behavior and his thoughts, which furthermore shape the tale's moral lessons.

The most tangible lesson for the young listener or reader is that one should be obedient. The boy's disobedience is what gets him sent away from the temple and is what makes him fear punishment from his father. As if to prove that he has learned a lesson about obedience—indeed, that such a lesson has been ingrained in his subconscious—the boy does not forget the priest's parting words, which arise in his mind just as he is about to fall asleep without heeding them. His life would have been lost, the reader imagines, had he failed to obey and slept out in the open in the haunted temple.

As with many fairy tales, this one does not shy away from scaring the young listener. It closes with some frightening images. After hearing the terrifying noises in the night, the boy emerges from the cabinet to find a gigantic, cow-sized rat lying dead on a floor covered with blood. Though the idea of deliberately frightening children for little more than amusement (whose is hard to say) may seem cruel to some modern minds, fear can be a powerful motivation for learning. It may even be the most powerful motivation as such, with a single frightful episode potentially leading one to shy away from the circumstances that brought it about for the rest of one's life. In this tale as Hearn tells it, the frightfulness is not mere spectacle but supports the moral lesson—to heed the words and warnings of one's elders.

Irony

Though the story of the boy who drew cats may have originated as a fairy tale intended for youths, Hearn's version is suited to more mature readers as well. The scholar Yoshinobu Hakutani, among others, has noted how Hearn's tellings of preexisting tales are variously marked by his own emphasis on certain themes or by shifts in the facts of the narrative. Regarding each of Hearn's stories in the volume *Kwaidan*, for example, which are drawn from Japanese folk legends and tales, Hakutani notes, "to the weirdness inherent in the story he adds his sense of irony and reflection."

A degree of irony can be found in "The Boy Who Drew Cats." The tale's lesson with regard to obedience may be the most accessible to the younger listener, but others may be more impressed by the story's suggestions about the significance of art. Even young listeners recognize that the cats are what save the boy, but they may not quite realize how this ending is ironic: Through the boy's time with the old priest, his cat drawings only get him into trouble, but those very drawings are what save his life. If one reconsiders the trajectory of the story, one may see that the irony is built up primarily by reader expectation: The habit of drawing cats gets the boy into trouble, so naturally one expects that habit to get the boy into further trouble. And yet when Hearn has the priest admonish the boy, the priest actually says nothing about the boy's failure to be obedient—which the boy feels most guilty about—or about his failure to set the right priorities. Rather, the priest only says that the boy will not make a good priest, and he even concedes that the boy may someday be a great artist. As such, he not only lets the boy's drawing habit go unpunished but also effectively condones it and even encourages the boy to continue drawing, to fulfill his possible destiny as an artist. In fact, as the Kyoto University of Foreign Studies reports, in the original tale, the boy becomes not a famous artist but the new abbot of the temple. In Hearn's version, the boy is saved both by his obedience and by his active assertion of his identity as an artist. Hearn, himself a devoted literary artist, apparently expanded upon the ironic ending as originally contained in the story to make a more pointed statement about the significance of art.

HISTORICAL CONTEXT

Meiji Japan

Hearn landed in Japan in 1890, at the height of an era known as the Meiji period, named after the emperor who assumed the throne as a teenager in 1868 after a samurai-led coup d'état. With Meiji as figurehead, a small assembly of nobles and former samurai wielded the political power. Deliberately isolated from international affairs, particularly Western influence, up until the 1850s, Japan in the Meiji period made dramatic efforts to modernize and assume a political role of global significance, to an extent by adopting Western democratic practices. Various aspects of traditional Japanese society, in particular the privileged samurai class, the feudal domain system—whereby landholding nobles kept peasants subjugated—and anticapitalist precepts of Confucianism, were abolished or reformed to increase economic well-being and equality. The nation was redivided into prefectures, and compulsory education was established.

Although the advances of the Meiji Reformation were largely appreciated by the populace, cultural resentment arose in light of side effects of industrialization—poor conditions in factories, for example—and moreover the apparent eclipse of Japanese tradition. Thus did a reactionary conservative movement take hold, marked by renewed interest in Japanese literary classics, by the reaffirmation of traditional principles like Confucian worship of the emperor, and by the increased practice of Zen Buddhism and especially Shinto, the ancient Japanese religious tradition, which became the state religion. (Hearn, whose interest in the ghostly was well established by the time he reached Japan, perceived Shinto ritualized respect for the dead as something like belief in ghosts.) Conservative elements of society were enshrined in the Meiji Constitution of 1889, which, for example, prioritized family rights over individual rights, with the father being given patriarchal superiority over his family, as modeled after the emperor's superiority over his subjects. This constitution was intended to counter the individualizing effects of the modernized economy and culture by fostering unity, discipline, and nationalist loyalty.

The 1890s were shaped by the new constitution as well as by the Sino-Japanese War of 1894–1895, in which Japan proved victorious over China, a nation that had long been held in high esteem owing to its role as a parent culture. The upshot was a decade of high nationalism that was so infectious that Hearn, a foreigner—albeit one with a Japanese wife and family—became as patriotic as a native Japanese citizen. Despite the disconcerting imperial overtones of the Sino-Japanese War (fought largely over Korea) and the Russo-Japanese War of 1904–1905 (fought over Korea and Manchuria), both of which were instigated by the Japanese, Hearn was unreservedly supportive of both efforts. Hearn's Japanese nationalism accorded with his inclination to identify with marginalized or threatened peoples, as revealed in his writings on people of mixed race in Cincinnati and on Creoles in New Orleans and Martinique. It also

COMPARE & CONTRAST

- **1890s:** After two decades of intense modernization, Japanese nationalism comes to the fore as citizens seek to affirm their cultural identity.

  Today: After two decades of painful economic faltering, the Japanese cultural identity is again emphasized as citizens seek to overcome their nation's reduced well-being and international standing.

- **1890s:** Emperor Meiji, who assumed the throne as a teenager but is now in his forties, is dogmatically revered by the populace and, from an outside perspective, is considered a well-reasoned head of state who permits the government to accomplish what is best for the nation.

  Today: Emperor Akihito, who is the world's last reigning emperor and represents the longest-running monarchy in world history, holds what is more than ever a symbolic

position. He is the first Japanese emperor to marry a commoner. He devotes international appearances to apologizing for Japan's occupation of Korea (1931–1945) and commemorating the deaths of soldiers in the world wars.

- **1890s:** Translations of Japanese works of literature are few and far between, and Americans rely on cultural translators like Hearn to gain a sense of Japanese culture.

  Today: In the global twenty-first century, literature is more freely translated between the world's major languages, and works by, for example, Haruki Murakami, one of the most famous Japanese authors, are translated immediately. Still, readers must wait as long as a decade for English translations of works by 1994 Nobel Prize winner Kenzaburo Oe to appear.

---

accorded with the fact that he was continually employed by the Japanese state, serving as a teacher at various governmental schools. In letters, he joked about his obligations to his employer, but critics have more seriously suggested that his writings demonstrated a sense of duty to adhere to government-favored lines of thought in part, if not largely, owing to his status as a government-sponsored instructor of youth.

Most of Hearn's Japanese writings were fragmentarily perceptive travelogues, like *Glimpses of Unfamiliar Japan* (1894), or refashioned story collections, like *Kokoro: Hints and Echoes of Japanese Inner Life* (1896). But after fourteen years in the country, Hearn published his first and only nonfictional, critical study of his adopted homeland's history and culture, *Japan: An Attempt at Interpretation* (1904). The scholar Roy Starrs, in an essay in the *Nichibunken Japan Review*, affirms that this text "could be

described, without exaggeration, as Hearn's final manifesto as a Japanese nationalist." Throughout the text Hearn is highly complimentary of the generalized Japanese state of mind and way of life. Calling to mind collections like *Kokoro* and tales like "The Boy Who Drew Cats," Starrs remarks that "Hearn's 'revitalization' of Japanese folktales by an imaginative rewriting of them to appeal to modern taste" was "very much in the nationalist spirit of the day." Starrs adds,

> Turn-of-the century Japanese romantic nationalists such as Shimazaki Toson had begun to discover in folktales a popular expression of the "national soul." In a poetic manifesto written in 1904, the year of Hearn's death, Toson proclaimed that: "Youthful imagination has awoken from its long slumber and adorns itself with the words of the common folk! Legends have come back to life!"

The boy's parents decide to take him to the temple, hoping he might become a priest. *(© monotrendy | Shutterstock.com)*

CRITICAL OVERVIEW

Hearn was a fairly prolific writer, having reached a peak of production in Japan going into his mid-fifties, but critics consider it noteworthy that he wrote only one minor novel while producing an abundance of travel sketches with little analytical intent, stories transcribed or adapted with minimal changes, and imperfectly faithful translations. Focusing on his original works, many critics have disparaged what Hearn wrote.

Somewhat controversially, George M. Gould, an ophthalmologist who was well acquainted with Hearn, posited in the essay "Lafcadio Hearn: A Study of His Personality and Art," and later in the full critical volume *Concerning Lafcadio Hearn*, that the writer's deficits in eyesight—being blind in one eye and highly myopic, or nearsighted, in the other— corresponded to his creative deficits. Gould calls Hearn "the poet of myopia," one who, being unable to appreciate the world for its intrinsic value because he could not truly discern it, transformed reality into whatever his imagination preferred, such that he wrote not so much about what he saw as about what he fancied he saw. Because Hearn's travel writings were intended to reveal the truths he witnessed, Gould's condemnation is acute. More broadly, Gould suggests,

> Clearly and patently, his was a mind without creative ability, spring, or the desire for it. It was a mind improcreant by inheritance and by education, by necessity and by training, by poverty internal and external.

For the critical volume *Lafcadio Hearn*, part of the Twayne's United States Authors Series, Arthur E. Kunst frequently wrote as if he resented having been obligated to read so much of what Hearn published. For example, suggesting that Hearn's assemblage of the various parts of the novella *Youma: The Story of a West-Indian Slave* (1890) was mechanical and perfunctory, Kunst concludes, "Hearn achieves the well-made, plotted novel toward which the literary fads have sent him: and, *sensible, suitable*, it possesses all the respectable virtues, but is *dull*." Kunst writes that Hearn's *"Out of the East": Reveries and Studies in New Japan* (1895)

is not even tolerably amusing. Not even fragments of fragments are to be found to light the
way between long passages of colorless
description....As logic the pieces are repre-
hensible, as reporting they are insufficient,
and as literature they are merely boring.

Still, critics have had positive things to say
about Hearn's efforts, and there are more than
a few book-length discussions of his work.
Basil Hall Chamberlain, who was a friend of
Hearn's, affirms in his 1905 volume *Things
Japanese*, "Lafcadio Hearn understands contemporary Japan better, and makes *us* understand it better, than any other writer, because
he loves it better." He frames Hearn's mode of
perception not as distortion but as "the blended
light of poetry and truth." Kunst takes note of
the "brief flashes of brilliant description" to be
found in Hearn's works, "those scattered
moments of life by which confidence in Hearn's
art is restored." Even Gould acknowledges that
within his limited literary realm,

> Hearn performed wonders. None has made
> tragedy so soft and gentle, none has rendered
> suffering more beautiful, none has dissolved
> disappointment into such painless grief, none
> has blunted the hurt of mortality with such a
> delightful anaesthesia, and by none have death
> and hopelessness been more deftly figured in
> the guise of a desirable Nirvana.

Allen E. Tuttle, in "The Achievement of
Lafcadio Hearn," notes that Hearn is "admired
for his sensitive, impressionistic prose" and that
his writings on Japan contain "strikingly pro-
phetic insights and modern judgments." Starrs
affirms that Hearn's adaptations of Japanese
folktales represent "perhaps his greatest achievement as a creative writer."

CRITICISM

Michael Allen Holmes

*Holmes is a writer with existential interests. In the
following essay, he considers how the elevation of
artistry in "The Boy Who Drew Cats" reflects
Hearn's own complicated artistic identity.*

Lafcadio Hearn is a writer who defies literary
classification. Aside from his complex heritage
and the meandering course of his life—one might
sum up that he was born Greek, was raised Irish,
learned French, was schooled British, worked
American, and lived Japanese—a number of
intermixed genres are represented in his works.

"IT IS CURIOUS, OF COURSE, THAT THE BOY IS
ONLY INCLINED TO DRAW CATS."

He was a journalist, diarist, essayist, analyst,
translator, transcriber, adapter, and storyteller,
often filling several roles at once. But only infre-
quently is Hearn discussed as a creator. He wrote
numerous collections' worth of stories, but most
of these either were adapted from originals in
another language or are so well founded in genre
that a sense of originality is absent. The full title
of his first fiction collection would set the scene
for his life's work: *Stray Leaves from Strange
Literature: Stories Reconstructed from the Anvar-
isoheïli, Baitál, Pachísi, Mahabharanta, Pantcha-
tantra, Gulistan, Talmud, Kalewala, Etc.* (One can
officially proclaim oneself erudite if all of those
names are recognized.) Hearn recorded a number
of fantastic tales but only a few specifically
labeled fairy tales. An interesting aspect of the
fairy tale is that it may reveal not simply what the
writer thinks or wants to say, but specifically
what the writer wants to say to children. As is
the case whenever a parent speaks to a child, the
words put forth are likely to attest to what the
speaker believes should be impressed on the
minds of youth. That is, at such times a person's
own ingrained morals are perhaps more likely to
be revealed. A consideration of the adapted fairy
tale "The Boy Who Drew Cats" may give just
such insight into Hearn's worldview.

The reader of that intriguing fairy tale alone
probably has no suspicions about Hearn's supposed failings in other literary respects. Only upon
perusing the critical reception extended over his
lifetime and beyond does it become apparent that
Hearn was not universally admired. The most
common reproach is that, whatever the technical
merits of his work may be, and whatever aesthetic
appeal the writing may have on the surface, at
heart Hearn was unable to create. In her essay
"Japanese Lacquer," Joyce Kilmer acknowledges
Hearn's admirable qualities but ultimately
expresses her reservations:

> What was the matter with Lafcadio Hearn? No
> American has written prose more delicate and
> vividly beautiful than his, nor has anyone else . . .
> put into English so clear a revelation of Japan's

WHAT DO I READ NEXT?

- Hearn's most admired collection of stores based on Japanese folktales and legends is *Kwaidan: Stories and Studies of Strange Things* (1904)—published in the year of his death—which is said to best demonstrate the author's creative contributions to the tales.

- A. B. Mitford, of Britain, served as one of the first foreign diplomats stationed in Japan, and in 1871 he produced the collection *Tales of Old Japan: Folklore, Fairy Tales, Ghost Stories and Legends of the Samurai*, available in a 2005 edition. The tales feature foxes, ghosts, vampires, and elves, and also included are several Japanese sermons and accounts of such ceremonies as marriage and hara-kiri, or ritual suicide.

- Yone Noguchi is a Japanese writer who moved to America before turning twenty and, like Hearn, sought to reveal the Japanese soul in English-language literature. Noguchi's first novel represents the inverse of Hearn's later works—Japanese writings by an American man—being titled *The American Diary of a Japanese Girl* (1901).

- In terms of their oft-macabre content, Hearn's tales, especially those of *In Ghostly Japan* (1899) and *Shadowings* (1900), are compared with those of Edgar Allan Poe. An accessible recent collection is *18 Best Stories by Edgar Allan Poe* (2012), edited by Chandler Brossard and famous spooky voice Vincent Price, who provides an introduction.

- An American who preceded Hearn in the endeavor to illuminate the East for the West was Percival Lowell, whose nonfiction volume *The Soul of the Far East* (1888) is dated in some of its generalizations but offers highly insightful and intriguing commentary on the nature of both Eastern and Western humanity.

- Shimazaki Toson, who began writing during the Meiji period, eventually wrote an epic novel dramatizing that transitional era, *Yoakemae* (1929), with a provincial activist as the protagonist. The eight-hundred-page translation by William E. Naff is titled *Before the Dawn* (1987).

- Much like Hearn, Simon Higgins led an itinerant life through his youth—living variously in England, Nigeria, Australia, and elsewhere—owing to his father's position in the British military, and he came to identify with East Asian culture. He drew on research in Japan, Japanese folklore, and his extensive training in martial arts to write the young-adult novel *Moonshadow: Rise of the Ninja* (2010), an action-packed look into the life of a warrior spy in medieval Japan.

- Kyoko Mori, a Japanese American who was born in Kobe, Japan, wrote about how a fifteen-year-old girl copes with the departure of a family member, with animals playing a significant symbolic role, in 1970s Japan in the young-adult novel *One Bird* (1995).

---

soul. Yet after an hour with *Kwaidan* or *Glimpses of Unfamiliar Japan*, the normal reader is wearied and, instead of being grateful to the erudite and skillful author, regards him with actual dislike.

Kilmer surmises that this may have something to do with the morbidness of many of Hearn's tales, the preciousness of his style, or his religious and cultural prejudices, but she

concludes: "No, the reason lies deeper, and is simpler, than any of these. Hearn failed . . . because he had no imagination." If one capacity above all is essential to the success of the artist, it would seem to be imagination.

If Hearn's original creations were few, there is no denying the creative impulse he applied to what he did write. Yuzo Ota wrote an essay

The boy draws cats on the screens of the temple. *(© Isabella Pfenninger | Shutterstock.com)*

discussing aspects of certain Japanese tales that were changed by Hearn in his adaptations. Ota is critical of the changes to the extent that they misrepresent Japanese culture and people. But the changes are not without artistic aims and effects. Drawing examples from Hearn's collection *Kwaidan*, Ota notes that in writing "Jiki-ninki," in which a priest visiting a man's house witnesses something awful during the night, Hearn added elements that "arouse anticipatory curiosity . . . and wonder on the part of readers." In writing "Oshidori," a tale that involves the suicide of a duck, Hearn intensified the drama by depicting the act of suicide rather than allowing it to occur offstage. In writing "Ubazakura," in which an old nursemaid prays for the recovery of a sick girl, Hearn had the nursemaid not just pray but also offer her life in exchange for the girl's. Judging from such minor alterations, Hearn's artistic instinct for enhancing the power of a story appears to have been well honed.

Turning to "The Boy Who Drew Cats" with the sense of artistry in mind, a number of elements stand out. First, the crux of Hearn's

version of the story is the boy's assertion of his identity as an artist—an assertion that Hearn superimposed on the original story. In the original, the boy becomes not a famous painter but simply abbot of the temple. Thus the original version, in which the boy's drawings do not signify his future identity, is less thematically consequential than Hearn's version; in turn, the original title, "The picture-cats and the rat," lends more significance to the creatures and fantastic plot than to the boy as protagonist. Throughout his later career, Hearn was obligated to do his own share of asserting his identity as an artist; he was not unaware of critical assessments of his shortcomings. Carl Dawson states in *Lafcadio Hearn and the Vision of Japan*, "So often in his letters he speaks of himself as inadequate, gaining, as he put it, 'by disillusion,' lacking new creative energies, or writing poorly." Hearn's authorial interest in the tale of the boy who drew cats, then, may have stemmed from a degree of identification he felt with the boy. The fact of the boy's displacement from first his home and then the temple certainly speaks to Hearn's life experiences. His mother and father effectively left him behind to be raised by his great-aunt, and from there he would be displaced several times over before landing in Japan. And Hearn regarded himself as, like the boy, more clever than vigorous.

It is curious, of course, that the boy is only inclined to draw cats. The action of the story reveals how this proves the perfect compulsion, since (images of) cats are ideally suited to killing a (goblin) rat. There is thematic significance to the boy's compulsion as well. In *Cats Encyclopedia: The Mysterious Cat*, Joan Moore discusses the significance of the cat in Eastern art, relating, "The Chinese and Japanese depicted the cat in delicate and finely executed watercolours in parchment and silk. These works of art indicate that the cat was important in the oriental way of life." Moore notes that images of cats were indeed used by the Japanese to guard sacred chambers, like those of temples, from actual rats. In China, it was believed that cats were capable of detecting supernatural beings. On an existential level, as Moore notes, "The air of equanimity which surrounded the cat and its aura of inner wisdom were qualities with which Buddhists could empathise." She further muses,

> The religion was based on a lone personal path of enlightenment ultimately to bring about the state known as Nirvana—that being beyond intellect, words or form. This aspect of the Buddhist religion perhaps relates to the lone cat: devotees see the feline as an embodiment of their own "aloneness."

If not an avowed Buddhist, Hearn evinced respect and perhaps affection for Buddhism in his adoption of the Japanese way of life, a way greatly shaped by Buddhist tenets with regard to maintaining peace of mind. Hearn may not have set out on a path toward transcendence, but he experienced a great deal of isolation owing to his defects of sight, and his willingness to leave behind all the cultures he knew to settle in Japan speaks to his appreciation for solitude.

That Hearn saw himself to some degree in the boy who drew cats seems highly probable. Here is a boy who wishes to devote himself to his art, but the priest, like a critic, finds his work inappropriate and casts him out. Beongcheon Yu, in *An Ape of God: The Art and Thought of Lafcadio Hearn*, uses phrasing reminiscent of the cat-drawing boy's life journey in speaking of Hearn's: "Turning flight into search, exile into pilgrimage, Hearn lived out his life on his own terms, as all his writings attest." There is no denying that the boy's art is fairly one-dimensional: he only draws cats. Some critics have suggested that, despite his various modes of writing, Hearn too was one-dimensional, producing nothing more than sketches and fragments. Yet there is a powerful presence in Hearn's writings, much as there is a powerful presence in the boy's cats, which are able to kill the otherworldly creature that has taken over the temple to which the boy flees. Yu, considering "The Boy Who Drew Cats" alongside other tales revolving around "the relation of the artist to life," observes that Hearn shows how "an artist must constantly expose his own fragile existence to the menacing power of the ghostly." In the story, this ghostly power is the goblin-rat. In Hearn's life, the ghostly power was perhaps represented by the ghosts of his own past—his disappeared parents, the nightmare shadows of his youth—that followed him throughout his life; or by the disembodied critics whose writings (as detached from their persons) assailed his faculties; or by the truth, which he was inclined to approach rather than fully grasp. Either way, the boy's ultimate success as a painter can be seen to signify Hearn's own redemption as a literary artist. His works do not please everyone, but a true artist cannot resist his compulsions, and as with Hearn—whose works are still read over a century after his death—the boy's art is what preserves his life.

Source: Michael Allen Holmes, Critical Essay on "The Boy Who Drew Cats," in *Short Stories for Students*, Gale, Cengage Learning, 2015.

Yoko Makino

In the following excerpt, Makino examines Hearn's role in inspiring serious study of Japanese folklore.

Yanagita Kunio (1875–1962), who is called the founder of Japanese Minzokugaku (folklore studies), conducted extensive research into, and established the methods and framework for folklore studies in Japan.

However, the works of Lafcadio Hearn were already widely read when Yanagita started his folklore studies. And, as is often pointed out, one of the main characteristics of the works of Hearn is his deep concern with folklore. He was interested in, and recorded the

❝ THAT IS, TO RETELL OLD LEGENDS IN ONE'S OWN WORDS, IS TO ACCEPT THE PAST CULTURE, TO RENEW IT IN THE PRESENT CONTEXT AND TO HAND IT OVER TO THE FUTURE."

legends, superstitions and religious customs in New Orleans, Martinique and in Japan. Folklore was always his means of understanding the mentality of the people.

I would like to show that although Yanagita established folklore as a new academic field in Japan, he was inspired by Hearn in certain aspects, and that this influence, or perhaps we might say, emanation of imagination from Hearn to Yanagita, played a role which was not insignificant in deciding the character of Japanese folklore studies.

Yanagita was a man who had an extensive career. He was a poet in his younger days, and also worked as a government bureaucrat and diplomat for many years. He then worked as a journalist, travelling throughout the country and publishing numerous books on Japanese folklore and culture. But perhaps for the general public, he is best known as the author of *The Legends of Tono* (1910), a collection of tales and legends of the Tono district in northern Japan.

Lafcadio Hearn wrote fourteen books on Japan. The first book, *Glimpses of Unfamiliar Japan* (1894), which established his name as a writer on Japan, is a collection of travel sketches and essays about his stay in the Izumo district. In these essays, he depicts the legends, traditional customs and popular beliefs of the district. The book shows his unique style of combining travel-writing together with folklore studies, which was effective in giving readers a living image of life and culture in Japan. Hearn then gradually became more involved in retelling ghostly legends, and *Kwaidan* (1904), his last and perhaps most popular book, is a collection of such retold stories.

Yanagita Kunio thought highly of Lafcadio Hearn. His high evaluation of Hearn is to be particularly noted, because most of Yanagita's followers, especially the academic scholars of Japanese folklore studies, tend to ignore Hearn's role in folklore studies. For example, one scholar, Maruyama Manabu, acknowledged that Hearn did have an insight into folklore and did write down legends, but considered that he lacked theory, and that his writings were not systematic. From a scholar's standpoint, this was deemed a crucial defect of Hearn as a folklorist.

Yanagita himself was free of such academic rigidity in appreciating Hearn's work. In his *Meiji-Taisho shi, sesō-hen* (*History of the Meiji-Taisho Period; Aspects of Social Mores*, 1921), he stated that no foreigner would seldom be able to observe and understand Japan better than Hearn. Yanagita also remarked in *Seinen to Gakumon* (1928) that Hearn's first work, *Glimpses of Unfamiliar Japan*, succeeded in grasping the Japanese mentality much better than *Japan: an attempt at Interpretation* (1904). This indicates that Yanagita approved of Hearn's style of combining folklore with travel writing.

Another interesting fact about Yanagita's references to Hearn is Yanagita's repeated mentioning of Hearn's 'Miminashi-Hōïchi.' 'Miminashi-Hōïchi,' included in *Kwaidan*, is one of Hearn's most well-known tales. (According to the index in the collected works of Yanagita, Hearn's name appears twelve times in his works, more than half of them refer to the tale of 'Miminashi-Hōïchi.') However, Yanagita does not discuss the work of Hearn; he simply cites the tale as typical in the explanation of a certain folk tale type, but we can perceive through his references that the tale had left a strong impression on Yanagita.

Yanagita, in his efforts to establish folklore as an academic science in Japan, is known to have comprehensively studied the works of contemporary English folklorists. (Yanagita left a huge library collection of these works and he had the habit of underlining sentences, and writing in question marks and comments as he read.) It has already been pointed out by several scholars that he had been influenced by the works of, for example, George Lawrence Gomme (1853–1916), who was the president of the English Folklore Society.

But it was mainly the framework, the methods and theories of English folklore studies that Yanagita adopted. There was one point on which he did not agree with Gomme, and that was the idea of 'survivals,' which, in fact, constitute the central theme of Gomme's folklore studies, as can be seen in his book, *Ethnology in Folklore* (1892). Gomme thought of old customs and folk beliefs as 'survivals' and 'fragments' of ancient cultures destroyed long ago. And he considered that the aim of folklore studies should be the research into these 'survivals' of ancient times, which remain 'isolated,' 'meaningless' and 'useless' in modern civilized society. (The phrases I just quoted in Gomme's book are the ones that Yanagita underlined, writing question marks in the margin.) Here in Gomme's idea of folklore there is no continuity between the past and the present culture. However, what Yanagita sought in his folklore studies was, on the contrary, a culture where the past was alive in the present, and where ancient beliefs and images continually have significance in the minds of the people and where old practices are observed by the community. And I believe that it was on this point that Yanagita appreciated and was inspired by the works of Hearn.

From this perspective, I would like to examine *The Legends of Tono* in relation to Hearn's works....

The basic outer form of the travel narrative, into which the legends of Tono are woven, gives the ghostly legends an intense and live quality, as is also the case in Hearn's *Glimpses*.

The second important point I referred to earlier is that the legends, in a way, reflect Yanagita's own world view. For example, the vivid description of the Yamabito, the enigmatic mountain-dwellers, allows us to perceive a touch of the contemporary age of Yanagita.

Yanagita relates, in the first tale of the mountains, how a hunter went deep into the mountains and came across 'a beautiful woman seated on a rock combing her long black hair. Her face had a beautiful whiteness about it.' This vision has elements similar to that in the dream of a Celtic woman that Hearn had when travelling in Izumo. In that dream in 'By the Japanese Sea' (*Glimpses*), a woman seated on a pedestal loosens her long hair until it falls coiling upon the stones. The Tono mountain woman is always described as being tall and slender, fascinatingly beautiful, with long waves of black hair. Such a figure has the ambience of the females depicted in Art Nouveau. In fact, after *The Legends of Tono* was

published, Sasaki wrote to Yanagita that he had the impression of reading something from European literature, rather than what he had originally related to him.

In *The Legends of Tono*, we see apparently native mountain figures portrayed with images that are more akin to *fin-de-siècle* art. And this echo of the modern age that Yanagita lived in expands our comprehension of Yanagita's basic concept of the ghostly other world. The mountains are the realm where past ages accumulate, from the ancient mythical age of the gods, to the Westernizing contemporary age. It is in these multifold layers of time that all the miscellaneous ghostly tales blend together to form an organic whole of the other world. And here the continuity of time between the past and the present is an essential element.

What, in effect, has happened is that Yanagita had projected in the text of *The Legends of Tono* his own imagination and sensibilities. This point is further illustrated when we examine the tale of 'The Old Woman of Samuto,' which is one of the most famous tales in *The Legends of Tono*:

> In Japan, as in other countries, women and children playing outside at dusk sometimes disappear in mysterious ways. In a peasant household at Samuto in Matsuzaki village, a young girl disappeared leaving her straw sandals under a pear tree. One day, thirty years later, when relatives and neighbours gathered at the house, she reappeared very old and haggard. When asked why she returned, she replied, 'I wanted to see everyone and came back. Now, I am off again. Farewell.'
>
> Again she disappeared without leaving a trace. On that day the wind blew very hard. The people of Tono, even now, on days when the wind roars, say that the old woman of Samuto is likely to return.

The interesting fact about this tale is that the original story that Sasaki narrated is known and is still in print. There are minor differences between the two texts, such as the name of the village. Samuto was originally Noboto, and also, in Yanagita's version, a tragic tone is added to the girl's fate. But the most important difference is the way the tale ends. In the original legend narrated by Sasaki, the village people did not welcome the return of the old woman, because she always brought stormy winds along with her. So the villagers erected a stone pagoda on the village boundaries to ward her off, and after that the woman never came back again.

We can understand the original tale as a village community narrative. Village life is severe, endangered by invisible forces from the outside world, and the legend reflects the will of the community to protect themselves within their boundaries.

However, Yanagita changed the meaning of the legend by rewriting the ending. In his version, the people do not reject the woman's visits, the woman is free to come and go between the mountains and the village, that is, between the other world and this world. The woman thus becomes the wind from the ghostly mountains which occasionally blows into the people's mind fresh visions of the other world.

The way Yanagita modified the legend reminds us of how Hearn retold the story of 'Mimi-nashi-Hōïchi.' 'Mimi-nashi-Hōïchi' is the story of the strange experience of a blind minstrel *biwa* player, who chants the tragedy of the Heiké clan. I will not go into the details of Hearn's modification, as I have already discussed the matter elsewhere. I would just like to point out here the fact that the change Hearn rendered deals with Hōïchi's role in the story. The traditional role of medieval Buddhist minstrels was to appease the spirits of the dead, to help them quietly rest in peace. But Hearn added a dramatic scene in which Hōïchi sings in front of the ghostly Heiké audience. And here Hōïchi, by telling the Heiké their stories, awakens the half-asleep spirits instead of appeasing them. He stirs up once forgotten passions, and installs into the spirits of the past, renewed life.

Both Yanagita and Hearn changed the original tale so that the ghostly other world is not to be either rejected or appeased. Both focus on the communication between this world and the other, and between the present and the past. Both tales reflect the will to continually revive and renew the connection with the other world.

Moreover, Hearn is clearly emphasizing the retelling act of Hōïchi and the revitalizing effect of his art on the Heiké. 'Mimi-nashi-Hōïchi,' the opening story in *Kwaidan*, is meant to be a sort of manifesto of retold ghostly tales. And this was what Hearn chose as the final goal of his literary career, and of his folklore concerns.

As I mentioned at the beginning, Yanagita repeatedly refers to 'Mimi-nashi-Hōïchi' in his folklore studies. And I believe that he was inspired by the story and had perceived in it the meaning that retold tales bear, in the field of folklore. That is, to retell old legends in one's own words, is to accept the past culture, to renew it in the present context and to hand it over to the future.

We are able to see here the motivating and imaginative power inspired by Hearn that later developed into the folklore research Yanagita conducted. Where legends are told to 'reveal present-day facts' as Yanagita declared in the introduction to *The Legends of Tono*, old beliefs and practices embodied in folklore continue to be alive and venerated in the community. The whole idea will later be developed by Yanagita into the concept of 'jo-min': the concept of the common folks of Japan, which becomes the pivot of Yanagita's later folklore studies. And this is the point in which Hearn inspired Yanagita. This is also the important feature of Yanagita's folklore studies that makes it different from that of Gomme. Therefore by playing an important role in forming the idea of folklore in Japan, we may say Hearn inspired the folklore studies of Yanagita.

As is well known, Yanagita dedicated *The Legends of Tono* to 'people residing in foreign countries.' For Yanagita, Tono symbolically represented Japan, just as Izumo, 'the Province of Gods,' was symbolic for Hearn.

Both Yanagita and Hearn were involved in a search for values antithetical and converse to nineteenth-century Western supremacy. Yanagita developed his folklore studies when Japan was undergoing drastic changes and was challenged by the powers of the West. And I am aware how Yanagita is often discussed in relation to a nationalistic cultural movement and the quest for a national identity. But, today, I have tried to illustrate the intrinsic link between the two men by focusing on the basic ideas comprising their works of folklore and their manner of retelling folk tales.

Seeking identity in the connection to the past and the other world; valuing the continuity of time and culture in the present age; reconfirming one's existence in the retelling of ghostly tales; through these essential phases of their commitment to folklore, I believe, we are able to see the works of both Hearn and Yanagita in a wider and a more profound perspective of human existence, one that transcends the age and specific cultural situation of any one country....

Source: Yoko Makino, "Lafcadio Hearn and Yanagita Kunio: Who Initiated Folklore Studies in Japan?," in *Lafcadio Hearn in International Perspectives*, edited by Sukehiro Hirakawa, Global Oriental, 2007, pp. 129–31, 134–37.

SOURCES

"*The Boy Who Drew Cats*," Kyoto University of Foreign Studies, 60th Foundation Anniversary Rare Books Exhibition website, 2007, http://www.kufs.ac.jp/toshokan/chirimenbon/b_25.html (accessed February 7, 2014).

Chamberlain, Basil Hall, "Books on Japan," in *Things Japanese: Being Notes on Various Subjects Connected with Japan for the Use of Travellers and Others*, rev. ed., John Murray, 1905, p. 65.

Dawson, Carl, *Lafcadio Hearn and the Vision of Japan*, Johns Hopkins University Press, 1992, pp. 87–106, 133–57.

"Emperor Akihito—Fast Facts," CNN website, January 1, 2014, http://www.cnn.com/2012/12/07/world/asia/emperor-akihito—fast-facts/ (accessed February 9, 2014).

Gould, George M., "Lafcadio Hearn: A Study of His Personality and Art," in *Fortnightly Review*, Vol. 86, No. 479, November 1, 1906, pp. 881–92.

Hakutani, Yoshinobu, "Lafcadio Hearn," in *Dictionary of Literary Biography*, Vol. 78, *American Short-Story Writers, 1880–1910*, edited by Bobby Ellen Kimbel and William E. Grant, Gale Research, 1989, pp. 220–25.

Hearn, Lafcadio, "The Boy Who Drew Cats," in *Japanese Fairy Tales*, edited by Takashi Kuroda, Kenkyusha, 1900, pp. 17–22.

Huffman, James L., "Restoration and Revolution," in *A Companion to Japanese History*, edited by William M. Tsutsui, Blackwell Publishing, 2007, pp. 139–55.

Kilmer, Joyce, "Japanese Lacquer," in *The Circus and Other Essays and Fugitive Pieces*, edited by Robert Cortes Holliday, Doran, 1921, pp. 159–67.

Kunst, Arthur E., *Lafcadio Hearn*, Twayne's United States Author Series No. 158, Twayne Publishers, 1969, pp. 9–10, 79, 84–85, 89, 126–27.

"Meiji Period (1868–1912)," Japan-Guide.com, http://www.japan-guide.com/e/e2130.html (accessed February 8, 2014).

Moore, Joan, "Buddhism," in *Cats Encyclopedia: The Mysterious Cat*, A World History of Art website, http://www.all-art.org/Cats/MYSTERIOUS1.htm (accessed February 9, 2014).

———, "China and Japan," in *Cats Encyclopedia: The Mysterious Cat*, A World History of Art website, http://www.all-art.org/Cats/MYSTERIOUS2.htm (accessed February 9, 2014).

Ota, Yuzo, "Lafcadio Hearn's Stories Based on Japanese Sources," in *Literary Intercrossings: East Asia and the West*, edited by Mabel Lee and A. D. Syrokomla-Stefanowska, Wild Peony, 1998, pp. 122–27.

Sansom, G. B., *Japan: A Short Cultural History*, rev. ed., Appleton-Century-Crofts, 1943, pp. 50–59.

Starrs, Roy, "Lafcadio Hearn as Japanese Nationalist," in *Nichibunken Japan Review*, No. 18, 2006, pp. 181–212.

Stevenson, Elizabeth, *Lafcadio Hearn*, Macmillan, 1961, pp. xiii–xvi, 3–27.

Tuttle, Allen E., "The Achievement of Lafcadio Hearn," in *Irish Writing on Lafcadio Hearn and Japan: Writer, Journalist & Teacher*, edited by Sean G. Ronan, Global Oriental, 1997, pp. 245–54.

Yu, Beongcheon, *An Ape of the Gods: The Art and Thought of Lafcadio Hearn*, Wayne State University Press, 1964, pp. 60–61, 183–204, 277–87.

FURTHER READING

Bourdaghs, Michael K., *The Dawn That Never Comes: Shimazaki Toson and Japanese Nationalism*, Columbia University Press, 2003.

> This assessment focuses on one of the towering voices of Japanese nationalism from the Meiji era, Toson, in examining the historical relevance of the pivotal attitude that so influenced Hearn.

Busch, Heather, and Burton Silver, *Why Cats Paint: A Theory of Feline Aesthetics*, Ten Speed Press, 1994.

> This fascinating volume uses series of photographs to capture the creation of streaked paw print artworks by cultured cats. The book is both comical in its exaggerated reverence for the feline painters and serious in its discussions of how feline behavior can be considered in the context of art and aesthetics, such as with the meditation-like state of self-resonance that cats often sink into, including before they paint.

Murakami, Haruki, *The Elephant Vanishes*, translated by Alfred Birnbaum and Jay Rubin, Vintage International, 1993.

> Some of the postmodern stories presented by famed Japanese author Murakami in his first collection, originally published as *Zo no shometsu* (1991), are reminiscent of fairy tales, featuring such characters as a little green monster and a vanishing elephant.

Tyler, Royall, ed., *Japanese Tales*, Pantheon Fairy Tale & Folklore Library, Pantheon Books, 1987.

> A renowned Japanese scholar and translator, Tyler has produced one of the most informative compendiums of Japanese tales available. The introduction addresses the historical period from which most of the

tales were drawn (1100–1350), the roles of certain types of characters, and the influence of Buddhism.

SUGGESTED SEARCH TERMS

Lafcadio Hearn AND The Boy Who Drew Cats

Lafcadio Hearn AND Japanese Fairy Tales

Lafcadio Hearn AND Japanese nationalism

Japanese nationalism AND folktales

Japanese nationalism AND Meiji

Meiji Japan AND modernization

Japanese AND folktales OR legends OR fairy tales

cats AND Japanese art

Buddhism AND Japanese art

Buddhism AND cats

A Bush League Hero

EDNA FERBER

1912

Edna Ferber's "A Bush League Hero" appeared in her first collection of short stories, *Buttered Side Down* (1912), along with eleven others. The collection features tales about middle-class working characters, some from big cities and some from small midwestern towns. "A Bush League Hero" takes place in a locale of the latter sort, in a town very similar to Appleton, Wisconsin, where Ferber lived during her teen years. Having worked as a newspaper writer, Ferber was an astute observer of people and the details of their environments. Her skills are evident in this story, which brings the people and culture of a small town to life.

Almost a formula because it is so common in *Buttered Side Down* is the way Ferber often begins her stories. A first-person narrator talks directly to the reader, starting with some type of set-up involving expectations for the story or homespun wisdom. This is precisely what happens in "A Bush League Hero." The story opens with "This is not a baseball story." The narrator then refashions an old joke about boxers into a baseball version before characterizing baseball players in general, and one in particular, and describing "our ball park" (letting the reader know the narrator lives in the town where the story takes place).

The story centers primarily on the main character, Ivy Keller, and secondarily on the importance of baseball in her hometown.

Edna Ferber was an American novelist, short story writer, and playwright. (© Everett Collection Historical / Alamy)

Home from school for the summer, Ivy finds herself a baseball fan, of all things. She is particularly taken by a pitcher named Rudie, and the relationship that follows is far more fantasy than reality. "A Bush League Hero" is a light story with relatable characters and an ultimately unvarnished look at workaday people who are honorable if not romantic. The story can also be found in *Dead Balls and Double Curves: An Anthology of Early Baseball Fiction* (2004).

AUTHOR BIOGRAPHY

Edna Ferber was born on August 15, 1887 (some sources say 1885), in Kalamazoo, Michigan. Her parents were Jacob and Julia Ferber, and her sister was Fanny. Jacob was a Hungarian-born businessman whose failed efforts kept his family moving from place to place. In 1890, they moved from Michigan to Ottumwa, Iowa, where he opened a general store. Unfortunately, the Jewish family encountered anti-Semitic sentiment. Feeling unwelcome outside

her own home, Ferber threw herself into reading. A loneliness at being different shows itself in some of her stories' characters, evidence that the painful childhood experiences never really left her. As an adult, she was proud of her Jewish roots, speaking out loudly and passionately against anti-Semitism.

In 1897, the family moved to Appleton, Wisconsin, a wealthy and liberal community, where Ferber graduated from high school at seventeen. Lacking the means to pursue college, she took a job at the *Appleton Daily Crescent* and began learning journalistic skills and disciplines that set her on course to become a professional writer. She worked for the *Daily Crescent* from 1902 to 1904; after her family moved to Milwaukee, she wrote for the *Milwaukee Journal* from 1905 to 1908, until health issues required her to retreat to her family. She sold her first short story in 1909, her first novel in 1911. During this time, her father's failing health finally took his life, and her mother sold the business and brought her daughters to Chicago, where Ferber wrote briefly for the *Chicago Tribune*. Ferber began traveling, sometimes with her mother, and took up residence in New York City in 1912.

Between 1911 and 1915, Ferber published numerous short stories, filling four volumes. She continued publishing in this genre up to 1947. Her body of work is known for its optimistic view of everyday people and the exaltation of honest work and the people who do it. Most of her material comes from the middle class, and the themes she explores flow naturally from her characters. In fact, she acknowledged that she cared little about plot and far more about characters. Avid readers of Ferber's short stories are no doubt familiar with the popular Emma McChesney, a divorced saleswoman who appears in a series of stories. Family relationships and generational differences often find their way into Ferber's work, as they do in "A Bush League Hero," included in *Buttered Side Down* (1912).

Among Ferber's best-known works are *So Big* (1924), *Cimarron* (1929), and *Giant* (1952). She received the Pulitzer Prize for Fiction in 1925 for *So Big*, although some critics claim that *Cimarron* is her strongest work. *Giant* became a famous movie, the last one James Dean made before his untimely death.

In New York, Ferber enjoyed her status among the literati, including the famous Algonquin Round Table. Although Ferber was difficult, stubborn, and vain, she was respected among the many important writers in her circle. She never married, although there are hints that she was linked with several suitors.

As she aged, Ferber developed tic douloureux, a condition causing intense facial pain. Consequently, her writing output dropped markedly, although she did manage one more major work. *Ice Palace* (1958) tells the heartbreaking story of two men who were once friends but have become fierce opponents in the debate over Alaska: one wants to preserve its natural state, while the other wants its natural resources. Many claim that *Ice Palace* was a major factor in Alaska's gaining statehood in 1959. Ferber died of cancer on April 16 (some sources say 17), 1968, in New York City.

PLOT SUMMARY

"A Bush League Hero" opens with the first-person narrator directly addressing the reader. The narrator assures the reader that this "is not a baseball story" and then recasts a joke about a boxer. The joke asks when a prizefighter is not a prizefighter, the punch line being, "When he is tending bar." The narrator then parallels that joke's persona with a ballplayer who is also a shoe clerk. This foreshadowing lets the reader know where the story is headed, giving the reader an insight that the main character, Ivy, will have to find out the hard way.

The narrator then describes a baseball uniform and how it does not do its wearer justice, which is why Rudie Schlachweiler is so impressive: even in his uniform, the local girls find him irresistible. When the narrator begins describing the ballpark and the community's loyalty to the local team, it becomes clear that the narrator is a person who is a member of the community. This is evident in the narrator's referring to the ballpark as "our" ballpark and remarking how little "we" care about big-league players or big-city stadiums. The narrator shares that although the town's two-thousand-seat grandstand has box seats, nobody who is a real fan would be seen in them. The fact that they are more comfortable and not much more expensive does not offset the townspeople's sentiment that true fans sit and yell from the grandstand.

The narrator shifts focus to introduce the reader to the main character, Ivy Keller. Ivy is home for the summer from Miss Shont's school for young ladies. Two days into her summer vacation, Ivy is "bored limp." She spends the first two weeks writing and waiting for letters and reading classic fiction on the front porch. Her father comes home from work to eat lunch and finds her reading *Les misérables*. He sits next to her and chats about the weather and the good smells coming from the kitchen. When Ivy goes to tell her mother that he is ready for lunch, he considers his daughter's summer boredom. At lunch, he announces that she is coming with him to the baseball game that afternoon. He knows she does not know anything at all about the game, but it will be good for her to get outside and be around some excitement.

Ivy agrees to go reluctantly, and once there, she is reluctant to try to be interested. As her father answers her questions and buys her some peanuts, she becomes more interested. She asks Pa lots of questions and, after that day, never misses a game. She stops worrying about what she is wearing or what is happening in *Les misérables* as she becomes a fixture at the games. She makes an unlikely friend in Undine Meyers, whose boyfriend is the shortstop. Undine is less proper than Ivy, but the narrator comments that the two have baseball and love in common. The shortstop, "Pug" Coulan, is popular with the local girls, but it is Undine who gets to be his girlfriend. The narrator stops there, before explaining Ivy's own love and commenting about hero worship in a small town.

There are very few outsiders who interact with the people in a small town, so they know little of what is going on in the big cities or other parts of the country. The narrator maintains that this is a major reason why the baseball team is such a big deal to the community. They arrive in the summer, stay in a local hotel, the Griggs House, and play at the ballpark. They are regarded as exciting, worldly, athletic, and heroic. The entire town rallies around the team all summer, talking baseball wherever they go. After games, the girls go home to change clothes and fix their hair so they can go by the Parker Hotel under the guise of mailing letters; since the team gathers to discuss their games in front of the Parker Hotel, the girls want to see and be seen.

One night, Mrs. Freddy Van Dyne hosts a dinner to which she invites the whole baseball team. Among the other guests is Ivy, who until this point has admired Rudie from the grandstand. She sits beside him at dinner, and the two are instantly connected. Rudie explains baseball plays to her as she forgets about dinner and gazes adoringly at him. After that, Rudie calls on Ivy at home. Pa misunderstands at first and enjoys the evening talking baseball with Rudie, who is polite and humors Pa. As Ivy enjoys his company, all she can think about is how Rudie is a baseball god. When Rudie comes to call on Ivy a second time, Ma does not like it. She is concerned about Ivy's reputation if the neighbors see. The third time, Pa questions his visit, and the fourth time, both Ma and Pa say it has to stop.

The disapproval of Ma and Pa Keller forces Ivy and Rudie to meet in secret in the evenings. They meet and walk around town and by the river. Rudie is interested in love and having a personal relationship, but Ivy is only interested in baseball. She is infatuated with him but cannot see him as anything besides the idealized baseball player in her mind. Even when Rudie pulls her close and asks her when she began to care, she answers with a particular play at the first game she saw. Then she asks him if his arm is bothering him, since he did not pitch as well that day. Rudie is frustrated and comes right out and asks her if they can stop talking about baseball and talk about their relationship. To Ivy, their relationship and who they each are within the relationship are inseparable from baseball.

Close to the end of the season, Ivy tells her parents she is going to mail letters, but Pa forbids her from going. He knows she is meeting Rudie, and he will not have his daughter running around town with a baseball player. If she refuses to comply, he says, she has to leave. Without emotion, Ivy replies simply that she will leave. She can bake, and Rudie will be playing in the major leagues in just a few years, so they will be fine. There was a man at the game recently watching Rudie, and she is certain he must be a talent scout for the Cubs. As she puts on her hat, Pa becomes afraid but comes up with a plan.

Pa explains that the team only has two more weeks in the season, one of which will be out of town. After that, the boys will return to say their good-byes before going back to their winter jobs cutting ice and the like. Ivy insists that Rudie has a job in a big company in Slatersville, and since he considers baseball his true profession he cannot take work that would jeopardize his pitching arm. Pa asks Ivy to do him a favor. He asks her not to make any promises to Rudie, and he promises not to get in the way of their plans or talk to Rudie. If she will just wait one month without contact with him, and she still wants to see him, then Pa will take her to Slatersville himself to find Rudie. Ivy agrees.

Once the season is over, the team returns as Pa predicted to say good-bye to the townspeople, and eventually all leave town to go to their winter jobs. Ivy's month without contacting Rudie begins, and she spends it learning to cook and bake. She also worries Pa by telling her parents she does not want to go back to Miss Shont's school. The end of the month comes, and Pa informs Ivy when they will be leaving to go see Rudie. She says she does not know where he works, but that is okay because Pa has already found out that information.

In Slatersville, Pa and Ivy walk up a street until Pa stops in front of a small shoe store. Inside, the manager greets them, and they ask to see Rudolph Schlachweiler. The man yells for him, and Rudie appears in a work shirt, wiping his mouth with the back of his hand. Ivy had been looking for the hero in the baseball uniform, so when she sees him this way, she is worried. At first he does not realize who they are, but when he recognizes Pa and Ivy, he enthusiastically greets them and asks what they are doing in town. Ivy panics and grabs Pa, as the manager yells at Rudie to tend to customers. Ivy tells him that Pa was there on business, and she came with him because she is on her way to school in Cleveland. She abruptly says it was nice to see him, but they have to go and let him get back to work. On her way out, she looks back at Rudie and sees him helping a lady take off a shoe.

The narrator takes the reader ahead six months to the following April. Ivy is home from school for Easter vacation and playing the piano. Pa reads from the paper that Rudie has been traded to Des Moines. He comments on what a shame it is, as he was such a good pitcher. Without stopping her music, Ivy turns and refutes the idea that Rudie was a good pitcher whose team did not rise to his level. She calls him a "bum pitcher" whom any batter could hit.

CHARACTERS

"Pug" Coulan

Shortstop "Pug" Coulan is an inconsistent player who is romantically attached to Undine Meyers. He has red hair, broad shoulders, and long arms. During the winter, he works in a slaughterhouse.

Willie Grimes

Willie Grimes is described as the "only really blasé individual in the ball park." He sells ice-cream cones at the games and rarely cheers.

Ivy Keller

Ivy Keller is the main character of the story. She is home for the summer from school, and her father sets out to cure her boredom by insisting she accompany him to a baseball game. She reluctantly agrees but soon finds herself an avid follower of the local team.

She develops an interest in Rudie, but has to admire him from afar until the night of the dinner at Mrs. Freddy Van Dyne's house. There, she meets Rudie, and the two soon become a couple. Whereas Rudie has a desire to make an emotional connection with Ivy, Ivy is infatuated with the romantic fantasy of being called on by a baseball hero. To her, Rudie *is* baseball, and that is what she loves. When she sees him working his other job as a shoe clerk, she is repulsed. She never knew or cared about the man Rudie is, only about the idealized pitcher he was in her mind.

Ivy is shallow and immature, but not mean-spirited. Even when she hurts Rudie, she does not realize she is doing it, so wrapped up in her own fantasy as she is. She trusts Pa and accepts his offer to see Rudie in the off-season after a month's delay. She is sure that her feelings will not change and goes along with his plan. When her feelings do change abruptly, she knows she can trust Pa to take her back to her normal life.

Ma Keller

Little is said of Ma Keller, indicating that her relationship with Ivy is not as developed as the relationship between Ivy and Pa—at least with respect to baseball. Ma is a sweet domestic presence, but little else is known about her.

Pa Keller

Pa Keller is Ivy's father. He is in the insurance business, and he is respected in his community for his good character and civic involvement. When he notices Ivy's boredom, he tells her he is taking her to a baseball game even though she knows nothing about the game. Once there, he patiently answers all of her questions and makes it as much fun as he can.

When Ivy starts sneaking around to see Rudie, Pa knows what she is doing. He also knows the difference between the summer fantasy of the baseball hero and the reality of the rest of the year. He persuades Ivy not to run away with Rudie, but just to wait a month, and then he will take her to see Rudie where he works so they can be together. He is calm and methodical, having planned the circumstances all out in advance. He knows where Rudie works and how to get there, and he also knows his daughter well enough to realize that once she sees Rudie as something other than the epitome of baseball itself, she will have no interest in him. Pa is wise and caring, and he never ridicules Ivy for her girlish romanticism.

Undine Meyers

Undine Meyers is a local girl who is well dressed and swept up in her romance with "Pug" Coulan. She is not as proper as Ivy, being a girl who does not always wear a hat and who has a "roving eye," but she completely adores "Pug." The friendship between her and Ivy is based solely on their love of baseball and its players.

Rudie Schlachweiler

Pitcher Rudolph Schlachweiler is "a dream" in his uniform, despite the narrator's assertion that a baseball uniform works against a man's best features. He is popular with young ladies, and he is well liked by the town for his playing ability. His nickname is "Dutch," although Ivy never calls him that. He and Ivy meet at a dinner hosted by Mrs. Freddy Van Dyne.

His romance with Ivy lasts the summer, but is based on her romanticizing him as a baseball hero. He tries to connect with her on an emotional level, but she seems oblivious. At the end of the season, Rudie goes to work as a shoe clerk in a small shop in a nearby city. He is friendly and glad to see Pa and Ivy, but Ivy loses all interest at the sight of him working such a common job. Rudie is a nice guy who loves to play baseball but is realistic enough to know he has to work another job to support himself. He is respectful and kind to Ivy, even when she frustrates him, and seems like an honorable young man who does not see himself as a hero at all.

Shoe Shop Proprietor

The proprietor of the shoe shop where Rudie works is short and stout, greeting customers with an insincere smile. He is polite to Pa and Ivy but not particularly kind to Rudie. When he realizes the Kellers are there not to buy shoes but just to talk to Rudie, he becomes even more impatient with Rudie. It is to Rudie's credit that he is polite to such an unpleasant boss.

Mrs. Freddy Van Dyne

Mrs. Freddy Van Dyne is a wealthy woman in town who, despite traveling abroad and arriving at the ballpark in her own car, never sits in the box seats. This demonstrates that she is not a snob but a true fan. During games, she yells and shakes her fist. One way she demonstrates her loyalty to the team is by inviting them all to her home for dinner. Ivy also receives an invitation, which is how she meets Rudie.

THEMES

Idealism

Fantasy and idealism together constitute the central theme of "A Bush League Hero." For the ballplayers, the summers spent in uniforms as they play a sport they love in front of adoring crowds is a temporary reprieve from their otherwise humdrum lives. When they are not playing baseball in the summer, they are working jobs slaughtering beef, selling things in shops, loading freight, or cutting ice. While the reader may have the objectivity to see that playing baseball in a small-town league going nowhere may not seem like much of a dream, it is an exciting change of pace for these young men.

For the people of the town, having the baseball team in for the summer makes them feel like they are part of something bigger than their small town. They have their own grandstand, and they all take their fandom seriously.

They follow the players and the scores, treating their team with the same admiration with which many modern readers follow college or professional sports.

The character who best represents the fantasy theme is Ivy. The narrator describes her as something of a bored princess, languishing on the front porch with a book until her father introduces her to the excitement of local baseball. This gives her imagination a place to run wild. Her fantasy surrounding Rudie begins immediately when she asks his name and then remarks dreamily, "What a strong name!" From that point, she idealizes Rudie as the epitome of everything exciting about baseball. In fact, she does not even see the person Rudie is, only seeing a "blonde god... with the scars of battle on his baseball pants." To her, Rudie *is* baseball. When she and Rudie are alone, he tries to make an emotional connection. But when he asks her when she first began to care, she answers that she liked the first game she attended. He clarifies by asking when she first began to care about *him*, and she answers with a play from that game. These comments reveal that she does not know Rudie at all, she does not especially want to know him, and she does not realize there is a problem with making her fantasy a reality.

Ivy's dream to leave home and run away with Rudie is childish. Her plan is that she will bake, and he will make the big leagues in a few years, and they will be happy. Pa knows that Ivy is failing to see the reality of the man at the center of this fantasy. Ivy loves the adventure and romance of baseball, and a young woman cannot sustain a romance with a sport. Upon arriving at the shoe shop, Ivy searches the shop "for a tall, golden-haired form in a soiled baseball suit." When she sees the real Rudie, the one who works in a shoe shop the rest of the year, the idealist fantasy disappears. Not at all drawn to what she sees beyond the fantasy, she is afraid and even repulsed, and she resolves to return to school and get back to her normal life.

Community

The setting of "A Bush League Hero" also becomes a theme of the story, as it drives so much of the story and the characters' motivations. Set in a small town that sees little of the

TOPICS FOR FURTHER STUDY

- Read F. Scott Fitzgerald's novel *The Great Gatsby* (1925). Compare the characters of Jay Gatsby and Ivy Keller from "A Bush League Hero." In what ways are they different? In what ways are they similar? In an essay, create a comparative character study of the two, and be sure to include comments about their unrealistic dreams.

- Research the women's movement in the early twentieth century with special attention to the events leading up to the passage of the Nineteenth Amendment. Do you think Ivy would have been involved in this movement as she got older? Write an epilogue to the story in which you tell the reader how Ivy responded to the women's movement in her time. Be sure your ending is consistent with the character Ferber created in the story.

- Find images of New York City in the 1910s. You might include people, events, headlines, cityscapes, photos, cartoons, or artwork. Try to compile enough images to show what New York City was like at the time, and create a slideshow. You will probably want to select at least one musical piece to play as background. Feel free to caption any images that need it.

- Watch the 1956 movie *Giant*, starring James Dean, Rock Hudson, and Elizabeth Taylor. This famous movie is based on one of Ferber's most successful novels. After you have watched it, put together an in-depth movie review, with special consideration for the writing. You may write your review, create a podcast of it, or make a video review.

- Sports mean different things to different people. For most young athletes, playing a sport is more than just a casual way to pass time. Read Kathy Mackel's young-adult novel *Boost* (2008), paying special attention to what basketball and cheerleading mean to Savvy and Callie. Think about it from all angles, including personal and social. Pretend you are in charge of casting for a movie based on the book, and fill in the parts with your classmates. Hold an audition and have them act out the characters based on their traits.

---

world outside its city limits, "A Bush League Hero" shows the excitement and anticipation of the townspeople over the local baseball team's arrival every summer. The team is something that offers a refreshing change from the routine of the rest of the year, and it brings the townspeople together in a strong way. The people in the town know all the players, they keep up with the scores of the games that are both at home and away, and they even greet one another by asking about the latest score instead of with the usual friendly greetings. For the young women in town, the arrival of such interesting and new young men adds a romantic element. Not recognizing that the ballplayers are really no different from the young men they already know in town, the young women are swept up in the intrigue and novelty of the new men.

Ferber incorporates details, sayings, and town history to bring her small town to life. In fact, the narrator occasionally even returns to the main story by saying something like, "Well, that will do for the first dash of local color." The characters of the story are sometimes described with details specific to the small-town setting. For example, Pa is an insurance man who is involved in municipal government, five local lodges, and the Civic Improvement club, of which he is president. He is the usual choice to introduce distinguished guests who speak on Decoration Day.

The story asserts that the baseball uniforms of the time did not flatter the men wearing them.
(© *Everett Collection | Shutterstock.com*)

STYLE

Personal Narration

The narrator of this story addresses the reader directly as a first-person voice. After a few paragraphs, it becomes clear that the narrator is not just a disconnected storyteller but a member of the community in which the story is set. The narrator knows all the people in town and is as big a fan of the baseball team as anyone else. She (or he) comments that in the summer, the grandstand is to the town what the Grand Prix or Ascot is to Paris or London. The people are more interested in the fact that the shortstop is dating a local girl than the fact that Chicago has a ballpark that seats thirty-five thousand.

The narrator does not have any apparent personal stake in the life of the citizens of the town, so she seems reliable. Rather than telling the reader that Mrs. Freddy Van Dyne is wealthy, the narrator makes the point by telling that she winters in Egypt and arrives at the baseball games in her car. The additional details of her shaking her fist, waving her arms, and yelling from the grandstand

instead of from a box seat constitute a compelling way to explain why she is not a snob.

By the end of "A Bush League Hero," the reader has gotten to know the narrator through her comments about the town and its people. The narrator loves the town, loves its baseball team, enjoys telling about the backgrounds of people and events, and is a likable person. She does not seem to have much interest in traveling beyond the beloved hometown; in describing Pa and Ivy's trek through Slatersville, she comments, "I can't tell you what streets, because I don't know." The narrator does not seem to know any other town and is perfectly content for things to stay that way.

Detail

Ferber's journalistic background developed in her an eye for detail and an economy of words. In "A Bush League Hero," her choices of details to describe and the way she describes them tell a lot about the subject as well as the narrator. The time the narrator has spent in the grandstand is obvious in the description of the baseball uniform, for example, which she contends does nothing to flatter its wearer:

> There is something about the baggy pants, and the Micawber-shaped collar, and the skull-fitting cap, and the foot or so of tan, or blue, or pink undershirt sleeve sticking out at the arms, that just naturally kills a man's best points. Then too, a baseball suit requires so much in the matter of leg.

To help the reader understand Ivy better, the narrator describes her white tailored shirt with pleats for fraternity pins, along with the many college pennants adorning her room. These details show the reader exactly where Ivy is in her life and what kinds of things characterize her. The image of her "posed against the canvas bosom of the porch chair" swinging one foot in a beaded slipper perfectly depicts the slow pace and privileged boredom of Ivy's summer. Ferber uses details to make the specific setting of a small town more tangible for readers, especially if they have no personal context from which to draw.

Metaphor and Simile

The characters in the story often use amusing similes and metaphors to make a point. The narrator does the same, which demonstrates to the reader that this is part of the town's culture and way of communicating. The narrator describes Ivy's curled hairstyle as being done

COMPARE
&
CONTRAST

- **1912:** Both the American League and the National League exist for professional baseball. There are a total of sixteen teams.

  Today: Both the American League and the National League are still going strong in professional baseball. There are a total of thirty teams.

- **1912:** Single working women like Edna Ferber are rare. Society is not always sure how to regard them, often assuming they want to be married but for some reason are not. The major push for women's rights is still ahead, so most women only have limited choices in career and lifestyle.

  Today: Single working women are so common, most people do not even question their status. Women's rights have come a

long way, and women enjoy most of the opportunities that men have.

- **1912:** The early 1910s are a peaceful and optimistic time. Americans have come through the Civil War and its aftermath, and things seem more settled. Yet World War I, the scope of which is unimaginable at this time, is only a few years ahead. Also ahead are the Great Depression and World War II.

  Today: Despite economic ups and downs and involvement in overseas wars, the early 2010s are a relatively peaceful time in America. Americans have come through the tragedy of 9/11, and people have adjusted to the changes it brought. There is no imminent threat of global war or war at home.

---

in a "Greek effect like the girls on the covers of the Ladies' Magazine."

The narrator tells the reader that Pa considers Ivy an abbreviated version of Lillian Russell (a famous actress and singer), Madame De Stael (a cultured French writer), and Mrs. Pankburst (a suffragette). When Pa tells her she is coming with him to a baseball game, her reluctance is obvious when the narrator writes, "Ivy went, looking the sacrificial lamb." Ivy's blind adoration of Rudie is best related by the exaggerated metaphors that reveal how she sees him. To her he is a "blonde god" and "her knight of the sphere."

HISTORICAL CONTEXT

Turn-of-the-Century Education for Young Women

"A Bush League Hero" was published in a 1912 collection of short stories. As readers meet Ivy Keller, it is important to keep in mind the moment in history in which the story takes place. Ivy is home from Miss Shont's select school for

young ladies. It was not uncommon for young women to attend a "finishing school," where they would board during the school year and learn etiquette, social skills, and domestic skills, as well as traditional curricula such as history and math. In most cases, this education was to prepare young women to be proper wives and members of their communities. More academic avenues for women were also available, though limited. The early women's academies and seminaries laid the groundwork for successive women's colleges that would eventually lead to coeducational opportunities for women. The education afforded women in the mid- to late-nineteenth century brought about greater literacy. In fact, literacy among women rose from 50 percent in the eighteenth century to 90 percent in the mid-nineteenth century. The more educated women became, the more socially active they became. Pursuing reform and expanded opportunity became more important to women through the suffragette movement.

At the time of the story, America is in an interesting phase for women, poised between the

Everyone in town sits in the grandstand because the box seats are considered "undemocratic."
(© Chris Hill / Shutterstock.com)

first rush of the suffrage movement, which tapered off around 1890; the second wave of the suffrage movement, which came in 1913; and the fun-loving, independent (and sometimes scandalous) flappers to come in the Roaring Twenties. Ma Keller is a typical, traditional housewife looking after her family. Little else is told about her in the story. Ivy is not at all socially aware or active, but her education is evident in her reading. The political stirrings in other parts of the country in the 1910s are not yet felt in the small midwestern town of "A Bush League Hero."

Baseball

American baseball has its origins in a town in upstate New York where Abner Doubleday is claimed to have invented a bat-and-ball game in 1839. It became popular quickly, capturing the interest of schoolboys before developing into an organized sport for adults. The first baseball club in America formed in 1845 and was called the New York Knickerbockers. Soon, other clubs formed, creating the need in 1857 for the

National Association of Baseball Players to standardize rules and play.

After the Civil War, baseball continued to bring people together for fun, but it also became commercialized. The Cincinnati Red Stockings boasted the first team of salaried players—professional baseball players—in 1869. Only two years later, ten teams existed in the National Association of Professional Baseball Players, and five years after that, the National League formed and overshadowed the National Association. In 1903, the American League and its eight teams were recognized, and that year saw the first World Series.

In the hearts of children and adults alike, baseball had come to represent America. Boys read baseball fiction, played the game, and dreamed of becoming professional athletes. This would accurately describe all of the baseball players who arrive every summer in "A Bush League Hero." Playing in a bush league (a very minor league) was the realization of their childhood dreams. This is the point in baseball's history when the story takes place.

They were the halcyon days of baseball. Although it was commercialized in big cities, there was still a great deal of sentiment attached to the game in small towns and cities alike. Only a few years later, in 1919, a scandal would sully the all-American face of the sport when eight Chicago White Sox would be caught having "fixed" the World Series at the behest of gamblers.

CRITICAL OVERVIEW

Overall, critics have run hot and cold with Ferber's body of work. During the heyday of her publishing, in the 1920s and 1930s, critics considered her one of America's greatest women writers. She won the Pulitzer Prize for Fiction in 1925, and her work was quickly added to school reading lists. As the twentieth century unfolded, however, her work became regarded as more entertainment than true literature. Regardless of how seriously critics take Ferber's work, they agree that her work has value as a preservation of the social history of the time period in which she wrote. This is certainly true of "A Bush League Hero," a story that perfectly captures everyday life in the summer of a small town in the 1910s. Ellen Serlen Uffen's remark, in a *Dictionary of Literary Biography* volume on American short-story writers, that "Ferber's language, particularly the breezy dialogue of the earlier stories, may be of its time, but the subject matter of the stories is not dated," certainly applies to "A Bush League Hero."

According to Blanche Colton Williams in *Our Short Story Writers*, Ferber once responded to a *Bookman* critic who offered a somewhat condescending view of "A Bush League Hero." He noted her naïveté about baseball, to which she explained that she wrote the story after spending a summer watching baseball in her hometown of Appleton. Williams herself remarks of Ferber's stories, "Miss Ferber compensates her reader for lack of plot values by her character interest, as has been observed, and also by interest in immediate detail."

CRITICISM

Jennifer Bussey

Bussey is an independent writer specializing in literature. In the following essay, she compares and contrasts Ferber's most beloved series

character, Emma McChesney, with Ivy Keller from "A Bush League Hero."

Edna Ferber's place in American literature rests squarely on the shoulders of her ability to create likable characters who generally come from the working classes. They are often middle-class folks from small towns or big cities, but what they almost all have in common is a work ethic. The detail and background that Ferber provides for her characters add believability, depth, and motivation. These are characters Ferber knows and understands, and by writing about them and their lives—which are rarely all that exciting—she helps the reader understand them as well. Critics have commented that Ferber seems to write more detail into her women characters, many of whom are strong and independent, whereas many of her male characters are somewhat vaguer figures in her stories.

Ferber made a name for herself writing drama and fiction, and it is for the latter she is best known. She is particularly remembered for her novels, although her short fiction does the same work as far as developing characters and conveying similar themes. In fact, much of her short fiction seems to be a training ground for the longer works. Besides her famous novels like *Giant*, *So Big*, and *Cimarron*, Ferber is probably best remembered for her serial short-story character Emma McChesney. Emma is a divorced woman who supports herself and her son as a traveling saleswoman of ladies' undergarments and petticoats. Besides being stylish and likable, she is also savvy and good at business. At the time, Ferber's publishers knew she was onto something with this intriguing character; there was nothing else quite like her stories.

Critics often cite Emma McChesney as one of the first depictions of a liberated woman in American fiction. Emma's driving motivation is work, and Ferber's stories about her put work in a cheerful and satisfactory light. Emma's optimistic outlook on hard work is not always easy, especially given the rejection she often feels at being a working mother in a time before that was at all common. Many of the people Emma meets are not quite sure what to do with her, or what to think of her, she is such an anomaly. As a single working woman herself, Ferber could certainly relate to Emma's

WHAT DO I READ NEXT?

- Ferber's *So Big* (1924) won the Pulitzer Prize for Fiction in 1925. Set in turn-of-the-century Chicago, it is the story of a young woman struggling to make her way to secure independence in the face of widowhood and being a single parent. It is considered by many critics to be her greatest work.

- *Mexican WhiteBoy* (2008), by Matt de la Peña, is a young-adult novel about a biracial teenager who has a great pitching arm but lacks the ability to focus his talent when he gets on the mound. Struggling for acceptance by others because of his mixed race, he also struggles with his identity. A summer in Mexico with his father brings him face to face with some important realities.

- Alan Gratz's young-adult novel *Samurai Shortstop* (2008) is set in 1890 Japan and tells the complicated story of Toyo, a young man at boarding school who loves baseball. When Toyo's samurai uncle commits suicide, his father teaches him the ways of the samurai to help him understand his uncle and his heritage better. In fact, the training improves his baseball abilities, but Toyo fears his father will reject the Western game.

- Garrison Keillor's *Lake Wobegon Days* (1985) occupies a unique position in modern American letters as a collection of short stories capturing the heart and sentiment of small-town America. Like Ferber, Keillor focuses on characterization and brings details forward to help draw the reader into his world.

- *Seneca Falls and the Origins of the Women's Rights Movement* (2008), by Sally McMillen, tells of the historical convention that began the women's rights movement. Introducing all of the major historical players, McMillen explains the many contributing factors working for and against the early activists in the last half of the nineteenth century.

- *Dead Balls and Double Curves: An Anthology of Early Baseball Fiction*, compiled by Trey Strecker, was published in 2004. In addition to "A Bush League Hero," the collection features stories by writers such as James Fenimore Cooper, Ring Lardner, Zane Grey, and Mark Twain.

---

frustrations. This is why Ferber was one of the few writers who could write such a character, and do it honestly. Throughout the stories, Emma faces interpersonal difficulties, independence, parenting alone, the benefits of hard work, and her own efforts to find—or encourage—a suitable partner. Ferber wrote a total of thirty Emma McChesney stories, and among Emma's fans was Theodore Roosevelt. Roosevelt once asked Ferber when Emma was going to remarry. Ferber recalled that most men wanted to see the character remarry, while most women liked her on her own. These stories gave Ferber her first steady pay from writing outside of journalism.

In "A Bush League Hero," the main character is another woman. Ivy Keller is a young woman home from boarding school for the summer. She is privileged but not spoiled, and she is naive about the world. Her world thus far has only expanded from her small midwestern hometown to the school atmosphere, with classes, fraternity pins, and school pennants. She is educated, as evidenced by her choice to lounge around in the summer and read a classic like *Les misérables*. But she seems to lack imagination or ambition. Within just a few days of being home, she is "bored limp." She is described as doing little but being bored, reading, and swinging her foot on the front porch. The reader

IT IS INTERESTING THAT TWO DISPARATE
CHARACTERS LIKE EMMA MCCHESNEY AND IVY
KELLER COULD HAVE IN COMMON THAT THEY ARE
BOTH PARTS OF THE SAME WOMAN WHO CREATED
THEM, BUT THAT IS LIKELY THE CASE."

must wonder what she used to do to entertain herself when she lived at home, because at the time of the story, she is out of ideas!

Ivy's lack of individuality is underscored by the way she is described by the narrator. The narrator describes a hairstyle of curls she wears one day as being like the girls on the cover of a certain magazine. She is further described as being posed against the canvas of the back of the porch chair. Both of these descriptions indicate that Ivy is to be looked at and admired, but little else. Ivy really only springs to life when she discovers the excitement of baseball. Then she becomes an avid follower of the local team, keeping score and cheering at every game. But unlike Emma, Ivy is enlivened by a leisure activity, not by work.

Ivy is also prone to fantasy, whereas Emma remains firmly in reality. Of course, Emma is grounded in her maturity and her worldliness. Ivy has not acquired any of that yet. So instead, she sets her sights on the pitcher Rudie, and finally her imagination comes to the fore. Unfortunately, when she does prove to have an imagination, it is not healthy or productive. She creates around Rudie an entire fantasy story with him in the center as a godlike hero right in the midst of her ordinary small-town world. Before she even meets him, she has already begun to weave his story together in her mind. She comments that he has such a strong name, and she later confesses to Rudie that it was during an exciting inning that she started to care for him. But when she cares for him, she is caring for the baseball dream of him. She even says that he *is* baseball, and therefore she *is* baseball with him. These are silly girlish romantic notions that can never be sustained in the real world. They come about seemingly because she started the story out bored.

Emma, on the other hand, does not have time to be bored and complain about how little there is to do. She has a son to rear and a job to do. Her work ethic keeps her moving forward and provides the undergirding for her independence. Ivy is not at all independent. She relies on her dream of Rudie to plan for the future, and she relies on her father to help her escape the grim reality of Rudie as a shoe clerk. Ivy also lacks the work ethic that is so fundamental to the character of Emma. Besides cooking and baking with her mother to pass the month away before she can see Rudie again, Ivy never does any kind of work. And she never talks about plans to work in the future.

In many ways, the two women are very different. Emma is a hard and cheerful worker, while Ivy is a bored and privileged student. Emma is independent and takes care of herself and her son, while Ivy is dependent and takes care of no one. Emma knows who she is, and Ivy is still figuring out who she is. Emma wants to be in a relationship but only with the right man, and Ivy wants to be in an unrealistic relationship with a fantasy. Emma is unselfish and at times sacrificial, but Ivy is still selfish and immature.

Readers should not be too hard on Ivy. Her faults and silliness are primarily due to her age and lack of exposure to the world. She has lived a fairly insulated life with little required of her. She is young. Emma was once young and unsure of whom she really was deep down, and Ivy is just beginning down that road. Emma is mature and responsible at least in part out of necessity. After all, if she does not make sure that she and her son are cared for, who will? But Ivy does not have to be mature and responsible yet. By the end of the story, she has grown a little and is able to see that maybe Rudie was not all her dreamy eyes thought he was. She is less likely to allow herself to be swept away by her own fantasy again.

In all likelihood, Ferber wrote pieces of herself into both characters. After all, the small town in "A Bush League Hero," Ivy's hometown, was based on Ferber's hometown of Appleton, Wisconsin. She wrote the story after a summer spent watching the local baseball team play for the townspeople. She may have based Ivy on some of the girls she observed that summer, but she also had been one of those small-town girls when she was a teenager. That

The girls ride the streetcar downtown just to walk by the hotel where the players spend the evenings after games. (Library of Congress)

means she knew the life and thoughts of an inexperienced, small-town girl. On the other hand, Ferber had a lot in common with Emma. Ferber understood firsthand the unique, exciting, and often awkward position of being a single working woman in the early 1900s. Without question, Ferber wrote herself into Emma to some extent, and that reflection is part of what made the character so endearing. So it is interesting that two disparate characters like Emma McChesney and Ivy Keller could have in common that they are both parts of the same woman who created them, but that is likely the case. Realizing that is a testament to Ferber herself and to the complexities of women as they grow and mature.

Source: Jennifer Bussey, Critical Essay on "A Bush League Hero," in *Short Stories for Students*, Gale, Cengage Learning, 2015.

Donna Campbell

In the following excerpt, Campbell compares Ferber's work with that of author Rose Wilder Lane.

When Walter Benn Michaels proposed in *Our America* that "the great American modernist

texts of the '20s must be understood as deeply committed to the nativist project of racializing the American," his examination left out popular middlebrow novels such as those by Edna Ferber and Rose Wilder Lane, two writers whose novels both complicate and challenge Michaels's assertions. Close contemporaries Lane (1886–1968) and Ferber (1885–1968) carved out careers in journalism and as professional writers of popular fiction before settling on regional fiction. Starting out as a reporter for the *Milwaukee Journal*, Ferber published her first novel, *Dawn O'Hara*, in 1911, and in the following decade she became famous for several story collections—*Roast Beef, Medium* (1913), *Personality Plus* (1914), and *Emma McChesney and Company* (1915)—that examined issues of labor, urban life, and the "New Woman" through the practical eyes of their heroine, middle-aged clothing saleswoman Emma McChesney. Best known today for her collaborative role in writing the "Little House" series of children's books with her mother, Laura Ingalls Wilder, Rose Wilder Lane was far more celebrated than her mother in the 1910s and 1920s, when she worked as a feature writer for the *San Francisco Bulletin* and published serial fiction, travel sketches, and biographies in *Sunset* and other magazines. When Ferber and Lane turned from journalism and short stories to novels in the 1920s, both received not only popular but critical acclaim for their work. Ferber's *So Big* won the Pulitzer Prize in 1925, and a *New York Times* editorial proposed a Pulitzer nomination for Lane's *Free Land* in 1938. In addition, Lane's short fiction had been included in *The Best Short Stories of 1927*, and her "Innocence" was an O. Henry Award–winning story in 1922 (Holtz 280).

Despite their popularity and relative critical acclaim in the 1920s, Ferber and Lane were stigmatized in later decades as writers whose popular fiction catered to sentimental tastes. Their regional novels share the trajectory of the pioneer chronicle: the family or individual moves to a new land and attempts to tame it or the surrounding community, with mixed results. In her novels, Lane adopted a persona of the quintessential insider, one whose pioneer roots reached back to the 1630s and included successive waves of western migration, the most recent of which had led to her birth in a Dakota claim shanty in 1886. It was a constructed identity that ignored her world travel, her restlessness, and her belief that farming promised little more than being "a slave" to livestock. No less a pioneer through her background as a member of one of the few Jewish families in Appleton, Wisconsin, Ferber constructed for herself a position that held in tension an insider's knowledge and an outsider's perspective. Proud of her research and the native knowledge that assured the authenticity of her scenes, Ferber admitted that scenes such as one set in the Chicago produce market were "written purely out of my imagination" (*A Peculiar Treasure* 277). She carefully wrote outsiders as observers into most of her novels, all the while positing a deep complicity and sense of identification between herself and America, which she saw as "the Jew among the nations. It is resourceful, adaptable, maligned, envied, feared, imposed upon" (*A Peculiar Treasure* 10).

From these artificially constructed yet apparently deeply authentic and compelling personae of insider and outsider, both writers inscribed political truths in a nostalgic regionalist context by interrogating the conventions of the genre in which they wrote. First among these is the figure of the "Prairie Madonna," a popular icon of the times pressed into service as an agent of American identity formation. In addition to taking a more realistic look at this figure, Ferber and Lane critique even as they capitalize on the nostalgic pioneer ideology so prevalent in the twenties—Lane by demonstrating the patent falsehood of the myths of free land and endurance on the Great Plains in *Free Land* and Ferber through her misunderstood satiric portrait of "the sunbonnets" and domestic culture in *Cimarron*. Second, they explore 1920s nativism and racism, which Ferber confronts through the theme of miscegenation recast as exogamy or intermarriage, a vision that suggests tolerance rather than nativist sentiment and that challenges Michaels's theories. A third convention that Ferber and Lane discredit is the national myth about the acquisition of land and wealth. Finally, the American penchant for collecting objects of material and social culture is revealed for what it is—a project that supports a unifying narrative of American history but does so through cultural theft and misunderstanding. In these ways, these novelists' representative works, including Ferber's *Cimarron* (1930) and Lane's *Free Land* (1938), reflect on conventional reconstructions of the past through central issues of the twenties and thirties: the complicated legacy of the

pioneer myth, the controversy over racism and nativism, the national myth of limitless lands, and the exploitation of objects from other cultures.

First, Ferber and Lane challenged ideas of the conventional Western heroine. Recast as what Sandra L. Myres and others have called the Prairie Madonna, the "sturdy helpmate and civilizer of the frontier" (Myres 2), this figure, often pictured holding a child and framed by the circular opening of the covered wagon, graced such portraits as W. D. H. Koerner's 1921 painting *Madonna of the Prairie*. Writing of these images, Annette Stott has traced a progression from the more passive "True Womanhood" icon of the Prairie Madonna to her more active counterpart of the 1890s and later, the New Woman-inspired "Pioneer Woman." The Pioneer Woman's sunbonnet bespeaks gentility and civilization even as her active poses, frequently holding a gun in one hand and a child in the other, attest to her active participation in the project of westward expansion. According to Stott, representation of these women increased during the 1920s, a period in which cultural awareness of and nostalgia for a usable pioneer past also increased. In writing of this period, Brigitte Georgi-Findlay further contends that women's Western novels and narratives "seem to fall into two categories: those that continue to dramatize the story of an eastern woman, most often a young bride, going west, and those that describe growing up female in the Old West. . . . Many of these texts locate themselves in reference to the popular literature of the 'wild' West, drawing on its romantic and nostalgic elements at the same time that they aim to revise stereotypes" (286–87). . . .

Source: Donna Campbell, "'Written with a Hard and Ruthless Purpose': Rose Wilder Lane, Edna Ferber, and Middlebrow Regional Fiction," in *Middlebrow Moderns: Popular American Women Writers of the 1920s*, edited by Lisa Botshon and Meredith Goldsmith, Northeastern University Press, 2003, pp. 25–27.

William A. Gleason

In the following excerpt, Gleason outlines Ferber's progressive ideas about the role of women in society.

In 1910, at the outset of the same turbulent decade that shaped the energetic skepticism of *The Rise of David Levinsky* and *Giants in the Earth*, Annie P. Hillis reviewed the liberating social advances being made by women during the Progressive Era. Writing in the *Outlook*, Hillis declared that the days of "idyllic, helpless femininity" were passing. As evidence she adduced the "six-foot captain of the basket-ball team"—who "laughs outright at the slender youth who would protect her"—and the "business woman," who "can earn her own support and would be beholden to no one." In both adult work and children's play, she claimed, American women were achieving "independence and equality with the other sex." But in practically her next breath Hillis makes clear that women's liberation might have reached— or perhaps surpassed—its natural limits. Protesting that it is "too soon to predict the future" even as she reaffirms progressivism's fundamental ideology ("We are in a world where there is a definite purpose running through all events, where there is a definite march forward"), Hillis retreats to a distinctly unliberating position: it is for contemporary women, she insists, to "find their place and fall in line."

The imaginary line into which Hillis pictures women falling leads metaphorically off the basketball court and out of the boardroom back to the more traditional confines of the American home. Rather than "undertake to share the work of man," a woman (particularly a white, middle-class woman) should perform her duty to society, her "real work" in the world, as a "mother and home-maker." Once she has fulfilled these duties, or in the event that she cannot fulfill them, she should turn her attention to the betterment of the homes of other, less fortunate citizens. Thus what all women need is training in "the proper care of a house." Society's role is to "dignify their endeavors with the knowledge that they are doing permanent work, valuable to city and State," thereby making American women feel "that there is before them a definite task for which they must be trained and fitted."

Hillis's retreat epitomizes the strategies of recontainment that women seeking liberation would encounter throughout the 1910s, particularly as the larger culture aggressively redefined the roles of work and play in American society. Increasingly dissatisfied with the soul-deadening routine that had come to characterize the advanced stages of industrial labor, many Americans questioned the once-sacred assumption that work was the primary locus for meaningful human action. In work's place,

> THESE IDEOLOGICALLY POLAR CULTURAL PRODUCTS SHARE A TARGET—THE PROGRESSIVE REFORMERS WHO PAY LIP SERVICE TO WOMEN'S LIBERATION BY DISCOURAGING WOMEN FROM UNDERTAKING MEANINGFUL WORK OF THEIR OWN CHOOSING—AND A STRATEGY: THE ADOPTION OF POPULAR LITERARY FORMS THROUGH WHICH TO CONVEY THEIR DIFFERING SOCIAL CRITIQUES."

as we have seen, educators and social theorists proposed play as the one activity that could develop the physical, intellectual, and moral qualities necessary to achieve what Herbert Croly in 1909 had called "the promise of American life." A call for less (destructive) work and more (constructive) play bolstered much progressive legislation in the ensuing decade. But making the "less work, more play" platform appealing to American women, many of whom firmly believed that their liberation lay in the opposite direction—more work and less play—required two additional strategic redefinitions. First, progressives had (much like Annie Hillis) to reimagine home-work as the culture's highest work, essential to the very preservation of the "race." Second, in applying the less-work, more-play dictum to women as well as men, reformers had also to refigure domestic labor as a form of liberating play. The strains that these competing reconceptions produced were evident throughout the decade.

Challenging the imaginative boundaries thrown up by these redefinitions, however, were (in a sense) the very basketball player and businesswoman Hillis so ambivalently heralded in 1910. For almost simultaneously at dead center of this conflicted decade, Charlotte Perkins Gilman (who claimed to enjoy every kind of physical exercise) and Edna Ferber (who created the first enduring businesswoman in American fiction) offered complementary yet competing revisionings of the role of women's work (and, by extension, play) in American culture. In her 1915 novel *Herland*, Gilman imagines women's place as a world apart, simultaneously literalizing and radicalizing the era's prevailing concept of separately gendered spheres. She conceives a "corporate" economy that celebrates the collective, "teamwork" energies of women working and playing together to maintain one State, one corporate Home, in stark contrast to the isolation of individual women within individual homes encouraged by progressive reforms. If Gilman's women fall into Hillis's line it is only to make a circle, a luminous halo of mothers and daughters who find liberation and happiness in a perfect balance of work and play—as part of a Utopian vision that rejects "realism" in favor of a sharp sense of how things ought to be. In contrast, Ferber's Emma McChesney finds her place at the head of Hillis's imaginary line, competing (and succeeding) against men in a "man's" world. Emma's corporate vision—particularly in the "realistic" stories that constitute Ferber's immensely popular *Emma McChesney & Co.* (1915)—inverts *Herland*'s by celebrating the satisfying solo of the individual performer over the blended harmony of collected voices. Though repeatedly tempted back into domesticity, Emma insists in the end that her freedom, creativity, and autonomy come from her work outside any "home."

These ideologically polar cultural products share a target—the progressive reformers who pay lip service to women's liberation by discouraging women from undertaking meaningful work of their own choosing—and a strategy: the adoption of popular literary forms through which to convey their differing social critiques. This strategy was not uncommon in the 1910s. It was, in fact, a deliberate tactic of some of the more radical reformers of the decade, the American workers, socialists, and labor organizations who used motion pictures to dramatize their critique of capitalism. Hoping to produce "commercially viable theatrical films that would entertain, not merely preach," these working-class filmmakers wrapped "explicit political messages in the popular garb of romantic melodrama." To a degree, so do Gilman and Ferber. Although only Gilman's political program can fairly be termed radical, both *Herland* and *Emma McChesney & Co.* challenge the dominant culture's assumptions regarding women's work within recognizably conventional frameworks. Both texts, for example, feature a heterosexual love story (culminating in marriage) as an important structural device. Each text is just complicit enough with traditional American progressivism to make its critique palatable.

Such a strategy was particularly crucial in the 1910s, given the wide availability of mainstream progressive thought through the movies, and more important (where Gilman and Ferber were concerned) through mass-circulation American magazines like the *Outlook*. *Herland*, for example, appeared in the teens not as a book but as a twelve-part serial in Gilman's own monthly journal, the *Forerunner*, while the stories collected in *Emma McChesney & Co.* first ran in *Cosmopolitan* magazine. The *Outlook* is a particularly appropriate journal against which to read the critiques of Gilman and Ferber not only because of its wide circulation, its self-proclaimed status as the central weekly document of progressive America, and its typical use of female contributors (like Hillis) to express its positions on the "new woman," but also because it ran in the early teens exactly the sort of fiction to which *Herland* and *Emma McChesney & Co.* seem to have been responding. (In 1912, for example, the *Outlook* offered its readers James Oppenheim's antisocialist short story, "Till To-Morrow," in which a young man discovers and then rejects a Utopian cooperative society for the "human world" he left behind. At the same time, the *Outlook* was also running the serial adventures of "Pete Crowther, Salesman," an energetic male businessman.) We will consider the *Outlook*, then, a sort of barometer of the traditional progressivism that both *Herland* and *Emma McChesney & Co.* sought to combat—albeit from strategically different angles. And we will try to judge the extent to which Gilman and Ferber are able to package nontraditional messages in conventional forms and still avoid the cultural co-optation that they inherently risked in the process. . . .

Source: William A. Gleason, "'Find Their Place and Fall in Line': The Revisioning of Women's Work in *Herland* and *Emma McChesney & Co.*," in *The Leisure Ethic: Work and Play in American Literature, 1840–1940*, Stanford University Press, 1999, pp. 152–55.

Blanche Colton Williams

In the following essay, Williams asserts that Ferber's strong characters make up for the lack of intricate plot in her stories.

Few critics have accused Miss Edna Ferber of preaching a doctrine. "Me'n George Cohan," she wrote in 1912, "we jest aims to amuse." But few would deny that her stories possess qualities

> MISS FERBER COMPENSATES HER READER
>
> FOR LACK OF PLOT VALUES BY HER CHARACTER
>
> INTEREST, AS HAS BEEN OBSERVED, AND ALSO
>
> BY INTEREST IN IMMEDIATE DETAIL. AND THIS
>
> IS BUT ANOTHER WAY OF SAYING THAT SHE
>
> ENTERTAINS BY HER STYLE."

sane and wholesome. And the philosophy on which they are built is Work, with a capital W—Carlylean Work.

It is not remarkable that the joy of work illuminated throughout her scintillant pages has been forgotten in the display itself, as the great cause of a Fifth Avenue night-parade may be a matter of indifference to the observer who "just loves pageants and processions, anyway." The flying flags, the drum-beat of the march, the staccato tread, the calcium reds and yellows may obscure the slogan bearing banner. It is remarkable that the inciting force of Miss Ferber's triumphant march has been neglected by the student of underlying causes. There are those of us who believe it to be the significant word she has chanted to the sisters of her generation.

To one who has followed her stories from the beginning, Miss Ferber would seem to have undergone a silent communion with herself, and after asking, "What shall my writing stand for?" answered unhesitatingly, "Work!" In the Emma McChesney stories, which require three volumes—with one or two overflowing into succeeding collections, she emphasizes the beauty and joy and satisfaction that are the need of labor. And her second published story was an Emma story: "Representing T. A. Buck" (*American*, March, 1911). It succeeded "The Homely Heroine," her first, published in *Everybody's*, November, 1910. This fact, again, may escape the reader of her first volume, *Buttered Side Down* (March, 1912), which although it groups a number of her representative "working" characters in "The Leading Lady," "A Bush League Hero," and "The Kitchen Side of the Door" yet presents variations of the main

theme. As for example, the last-named cries aloud that the busy-folk on the kitchen side are more respectable than the tippling ladies and gentlemen (by courtesy) in front. But *Roast Beef Medium* (1913), including stories written and published before some of those in the first volume, essays to sound what becomes a trumpet call in *Emma McChesney and Co.* (1915).

Hortense of "Blue Serge" thinks:

"If you're not busy, you can't be happy very long."

"No," said Emma, "idleness, when you're not used to it, is misery."

And Miss Smalley of the same story:

"I've found out that work is a kind of self-oiler. If you're used to it, the minute you stop you begin to get rusty, and your hinges creak and you clog up, and the next thing you know you break down. Work that you like to do is a blessing. It keeps you young."

And the author herself (in "Sisters Under Their Skin"):

"In the face of the girl who works, whether she be a spindle-legged errand-girl or a ten thousand dollar a year foreign buyer, you will find both vivacity and depth of expression." ... She begins this story by asserting: "Women who know the joys and sorrows of a pay envelope do not speak of girls who work as working girls." The whole story hangs on this thesis.

When Emma visited her son, Jock, and her daughter-in-law, Grace, and her grand-daughter, Emma McChesney, charming elderly women came to call.

They fell into two classes: "... the placid, black-silk, rather vague women of middle-age, whose face has the blank look of the sheltered woman and who wrinkles early from sheer lack of sufficient activity or vital interest in life; and the wiry, well-dressed, assertive type who talked about her club work and her charities." In their eyes was that distrust of Emma which lurks in the eyes of a woman as she looks at another woman of her own age who doesn't show it."

And the volume ends with this final statement (in "An Étude for Emma"): "... there's nothing equal to the soul-filling satisfaction that you get in solo-work."

Miss Ferber has expressed sincerely her own beliefs in these and other passages, and throughout the larger structural values of her

stories: in Emma's continuous struggle with the
game of life, exemplified in a series of individual
conflicts; in her efforts to make of Jock a man,
and in her great service to the T. A. Buck
Featherloom Petticoat Company. In an article
entitled "The Joy of the Job" (*American*,
March, 1918), she says she is sorry for any
woman who can play when she wishes. "Play
is no treat for an idler." She works, according
to her statement, three hundred and fifty morn-
ings a year; she may play golf on the three
hundred and fifty-first. It is not that she lacks
desire to play, as the pink and green sweaters
stream past her door. But the habit of work and
the satisfaction that comes from having worked
are such that she knows the eighteen holes of
golf would be dull and flat once she deserted
her typewriter for the links. "And that's the
secret of the glory of the work habit. Once
you've had to earn your play, you never again
can relish it unearned."

From Kalamazoo, Michigan, where she was
born August 15, 1887, Edna Ferber moved at an
early age to Appleton, Wisconsin. There she went
to "grade school" and to "high school," and
there at seventeen years of age she began work
on *The Daily Crescent* the youngest reporter of
her time. "It was a harrowing job," she admits,
including as it did for her day's work "everything from the Courthouse to the Chicken Pie
Supper at Odd Fellows' Hall, from St. Joseph's
Monastery to the crippled flagman at the rail-
road crossing up in the chute, from the dry
goods store to Lawrence University." Small
wonder she learned humanity. When a critic
suggested that her tales possessed an insight
into human nature "which, if not genuine, is
very well stimulated," her retort was forthcoming: "Humanity? Which of us really knows it?
But take a fairly intelligent girl of seventeen, put
her on a country daily newspaper, and then
keep her on one paper or another, country and
city, for six years, and—well, she just naturally
can't help learning some things about some
folks.". . . It is but logical that human interest
leads all other qualities of her fiction.

Miss Ferber has told how from a hammock
on her father's porch, where she spent much time
at a season when she required rest—or as she
phrases it, when the shop-sign read "Closed for
Repairs"—she studied the passing townspeople.
Life became for her a great storehouse in which
at desire she may now enter, and from the

shelves of which she may take down whatever
she needs.

She was correspondent for two Milwaukee
papers in these years of 'prenticeship and, later,
for *The Chicago Tribune*. And she finished
before she was twenty-four her first novel,
Dawn O'Hara, her experience with which
speaks for her artistic and literary ideals. For
she threw the script into the waste-basket,
whence her mother rescued it. This work, to
some extent autobiographic, was published in
1911 and brought its author immediate success.
After its publication she found ready market
for her short stories.

Many of these first tales depend for background upon Appleton, which becomes "our
town" in "The Homely Heroine," "The Leading
Lady," "Where the Car Turns at Eighteenth"—
spite of its title—and "A Bush League Hero" (all
in *Buttered Side Down*). "A Bush League Hero"
was written after a summer of watching the Bush
League team play in Appleton, as Miss Ferber
wrote the *Bookman* critic who expressed amusement over her naïveté in connection with the
sport of baseball. By and by, in succeeding volumes, Appleton, Beloit, and Slatersville gave way
to Chicago and New York, and even to cities of
other countries. But Chicago and New York are
her preferred settings, as St. Louis and New York
are Fannie Hurst's.

Her earlier stories, like her later ones, are
about men clerks, women clerks, milliners, traveling salesmen and saleswomen, cooks, stenog-
raphers, leading ladies, household drudges,
advertising specialists—the list is incomplete.
No writer shows greater growth in storymaking
than Miss Ferber—one need only compare
Roast Beef Medium with any of the later
McChesney stories—but she has never been
"strong on plot." As she herself admits she does
not know—and presumably cares less—what a
plot is, she can hardly feel her confessed ignorance to be a handicap. In fact, she goes so far
now and then as to twit the critic who insists
upon plot as the *sine qua non* of a story. In
"The Eldest" (of *Cheerful—By Request*, 1918)
she makes her critic, you will remember, a Self-
Complacent Young Cub, who says: "Trouble
with your stuff is that it lacks plot. Your characterization's all right, and your dialogue. But
your stuff lacks *raison d'être*—if you know what
I mean." To which she retorts: "But people's
insides are often so much more interesting than

their outsides...." And it is with people she succeeds best. "The Eldest," for instance, when it appeared some years ago in *McClure's*, was praised by Franklin P. Adams as the best short story of the year. Yet the plot is worn thin: a lover comes back after many years, only to marry the sister, the younger sister, of his former sweetheart. The interest lies in the character of Rose, the drudge, the slave, the living sacrifice, eternally new as eternally old. In the same volume, "The Gay Old Dog," which has been reprinted at least twice, faithfully portrays a loop-hound, as he would be known in his Windy City, the young man grown old through sacrifice, the counterpart of "The Eldest." Gallant Emma McChesney, cheerfully fighting to hold down a man-size job—knowing it requires six times as much work from a woman as from a man to draw for her the same salary—sprang into existence as the ideal of the modern business woman. She will reflect this particular age in her own particular so long as popular interest holds; after that time she will serve for the antiquarian. She is the heroine of *Roast Beef Medium*, of the five stories in *Personality Plus* (1914), of which her son is the hero, and of *Emma McChesney and Co.* (1915). From the number, or chapters, of the last-named, one may select diverting so-called stories. No reader will find fault with "Chickens," displaying the strong mother hand of this charming saleswoman; nor with "Pink Tights and Ginghams," "featuring"—as Emma would say—her sympathy for her sex; nor with "Broadway to Buenos Aires," proving her business acumen, her boundless energy, and her zest for a fight; nor with "Thanks to Miss Morrissey," wherein after all she reverts to an old-fashioned sort of woman. But the truth is that the author is a novelist in her method. She leaves the reader with memories of her people, as novels do and should do, not with memories of a story. The individual tales of Emma's prowess dwindle in comparison with the fabric he creates out of Miss Ferber's generous distribution of scraps and his own pleasurable tedium in piecing them together. They are ultimately forgotten in the whole pattern. Mrs. McChesney has become real to her creator. In addressing a class at Columbia University, Miss Ferber said quaintly, "When Emma walks in upon me, I *must* give her my attention!"

Even the early stories of Miss Ferber emphasize for the first time in fiction a motive as old as the stomach of man: food. Pearlie Schultz, the Homely Heroine, wins her first—and doubtless her last—kiss through her noodle soup, her fried chicken, and hot biscuits; Jennie of "Maymeys from Cuba" succumbs, in her hunger, to a Scotch scone, after mouth-watering descriptions, by the author, of a corner fruitstand and the grocery department of a big store. If you would be made ravenous, O weary of palate one! read "Maymeys from Cuba." And if you would recall the days of yore read the description (in "The Kitchen Side of the Door") "of a little world fragrant with mint, breathing of orange and lemon peel, perfumed with pineapple, redolent of cinnamon and clove, reeking of things spirituous." Of a world where "the splutter of the broiler was replaced by the hiss of the siphon, and the pop-pop of corks and the tinkle and clink of ice against glass." Perhaps after this devastating passage, the point should be made that no better temperance story has ever been published; beside it, most others look like ready-made propaganda.

Nor does the author forget the negative aspect of this food business. Emma McChesney, who first appears in "our town," dying—in her travel-weariness—for something "cool, and green, and fresh," is informed by the waitress that the menu offers "ham'n aigs, mutton chops, cold veal, cold roast"—to which Emma hopelessly interrupts, "Two, fried." Spectators at the performance of "Our Mrs. McChesney" will not forget Ethel Barrymore's winning question about the prospect for supper, the desk clerk's "Hungarian goulash!" nor Ethel's "My God!" as she departed stairward.

Keats's feast in "The Eve of St. Agnes" has long been praised by epicures, in art, if not in food. The marvel is that no one between Keats and Edna Ferber so emphasized the gustatory appeal. She continues it, with subtle discrimination, in "The Gay Old Dog." He was the kind of man who mixes his own salad dressing. "He liked to call for a bowl, some cracked ice, lemon, garlic, paprika, salt, pepper, vinegar, and oil, and make a rite of it."

So does Miss Ferber make a rite of food as her generation makes of it a ceremonial. Three titles out of six covering her stories suggest eating, the latest of which is humorously reflective, unconsciously so, perhaps, of reduced rations ensuing upon the war: *Half Portions* (1920). Or is it indicative that the author is losing her own zest in food? Some years ago she thought in terms of food comparisons. For example, to the Editor of *The New York Times*, she wrote: "I'm the sort of person who, when asked point-blank her choice of ice-cream, says, 'Chocolate, I think—no, peach! No—chocolate! Oh, I don't know.' That being true, how can you expect me to name off-hand the story which I consider the best short story in the English language?" It may be mentioned, in passing, that she lists Maupassant's "The String" and "The Necklace," O. Henry's "An Unfinished Story," Jesse Lynch Williams's "Stolen Story," and Neil Lyon's "Love in a Mist" among those she has preferred—at various times. In her article, "The Joy of the Job," note the conditions upon which the "chicken salad is a poem, the coffee a dream, the French pastry a divine confection." Be it understood that all this is quoted in admiration.

Miss Ferber compensates her reader for lack of plot values by her character interest, as has been observed, and also by interest in immediate detail. And this is but another way of saying that she entertains by her style. She probably worked like a young fury, through newspaper training and through conscious study of word composition, to achieve her brilliant pyrotechnics. In her first collection, she is guilty of the absurd, "'No, you don't!' hissed Gus." She had still to learn, apparently, that hissing requires a sibilant sound. Or, if she meant to burlesque faintly, her purpose is not obvious. In her first book, again, she refers too frequently to the trite, or the prevalent trick. "The short November afternoon was drawing to its close (as our best talent would put it)"..."'Better bathe your eyes in *eau de cologne* or whatever it is they're always dabbing on 'em in books.'"..."As the novelists have it, their eyes met."..."As the story writers put it, he hadn't even devoured her with his gaze."... Her later stories have hardly outgrown this habit of jerking and calling halt to the steady march of the narrative, or these interruptions for which no contrasting cleverness and originality can compensate.

This author, like Mr. Joseph Hergesheimer, probably grew up with The Duchess. But her sardonic references to the lady leave doubt as to her opinion. She knew her Martin Chuzzlewit, her Jane Eyre, her O. Henry, and her Bible. Her admiration for George Cohan is genuine. She depreciates, by implication, the "balled-up" style of Henry James. Dickens and O. Henry

are her forbears in humor, as the Holy Scriptures back her philosophy....

From a sort of cavil against New York, Miss Ferber finally came to New York—no, "came on" to New York, with her heroine "Sun Dried." Then, her first story in *Emma McChesney and Co.* gets away from Manhattan. Her love for travel and her journalistic ability to profit by new scenes are reflected in "Broadway to Buenos Aires" no less than in her own photographs and fact articles. "The Guiding Miss Gowd" (of *Cheerful—by Request*) testifies to an acquaintanceship with Rome, as the photograph of Miss Ferber stepping from the porch of a summer house in Hawaii is proof of her presence there. "Ain't Nature Wonderful?" (*McClure's*, August, 1920) creates the certainty, as well as her photograph facing an article she wrote for the *American*, of December, 1916, that she knows the Rockies.

All her stories belong to the O. Henry school, but like her younger sister, Fannie Hurst, she has stolen away and farther on, bearing with her from the modern wizard only the trick of catching interest or the turn of a phrase. If O. Henry had never opened "Hearts and Crosses" with "Baldy Woods reached for the bottle and got it," perhaps she might not have begun *Cheerful—by Request* with "The editors paid for the lunch (as editors do)." But life has expanded in the decade and more since O. Henry's passing; it swings in arcs beyond the reach he needed to compass all of it he would. This one of his successors has widened the sweep, as the lover of New Bagdad would have done had he lived.

Half Portions is a varied assortment of new tales, as *Cheerful—by Request* gathers up old and new. The best are, as one would anticipate, stories of character, wherein the "story"—from a technical point of view—is usually negligible. "Old Lady Mandel" is but the summing up of the career of a professional mother. "Yet One Hundred Per Cent," besides bringing Emma back, happens to be one of the first-rank patriotic stories published in the progress of the War. "April 25th, as Usual" marks the height of her accomplishment for 1919. After its appearance in *The Ladies' Home Journal* it was voted by the Committee from the Society of Arts and Sciences one of the best among thirty-two stories of the year, and was reprinted in the Society's annual volume—*The O. Henry Memorial Award Prize Stories.*

Miss Ferber stretches a continually expanding canvas; she is prodigally wasteful of whole novels in stories like "The Gay Old Dog" and "Old Lady Mandel." The novel, we venture to predict, is the field wherein she will ultimately "lay by" her most important work.

Source: Blanche Colton Williams, "Edna Ferber," in *Our Short Story Writers*, Books for Libraries Press, 1969, pp. 146–59.

SOURCES

Basch, Norma, "Woman Suffrage," in *Encyclopedia of the American Constitution*, edited by Leonard W. Levy and Kenneth L. Karst, 2nd ed., Vol. 6, Macmillan Reference USA, 2000, pp. 2917–18.

Castanier, Bill, "Michigan's Literary Laureates," in *Michigan History*, Vol. 96, No. 4, July–August 2012, pp. 15–21.

Ferber, Edna, *A Bush League Hero*, CreateSpace Independent Publishing Platform, 2013, pp. 3–29.

McMahon, Lucia, "Education of Girls and Women," in *Encyclopedia of the New American Nation*, edited by Paul Finkelman, Vol. 1, Charles Scribner's Sons, 2006, pp. 435–36.

Tribble, Scott, "Baseball," in *St. James Encyclopedia of Popular Culture*, edited by Sara Pendergast and Tom Pendergast, Vol. 1, St. James Press, 2000, pp. 180–83.

Uffen, Ellen Serlen, "Edna Ferber," in *Dictionary of Literary Biography*, Vol. 86, *American Short-Story Writers, 1910–1945, First Series*, edited by Bobby Ellen Kimbel, Gale Research, 1989, pp. 91–98.

Williams, Blanche Colton, "Edna Ferber," in *Our Short Story Writers*, Dodd, Mead, 1941, pp. 146–59.

FURTHER READING

Bigsby, C. W. E., *Modern American Drama: 1945–2000*, Cambridge University Press, 2000.
  Ferber wrote or cowrote over half a dozen plays. Bigsby's book provides comments and insights on America's best-loved modern

playwrights, including Tennessee Williams, Eugene O'Neill, Edward Albee, and Arthur Miller. Biographies, discussions of plays, and other essays make this an important volume for anyone wanting to understand the breadth and importance of modern drama.

Ferber, Edna, *Edna Ferber: Five Complete Novels*, Outlet, 1981.
  This single volume contains Ferber's best-known long fiction. The five unabridged volumes are *So Big, Cimarron, Show Boat, Saratoga Trunk*, and *Giant*. These novels have stood the test of time for their depictions of particular places in American history, coupled with compelling characterization.

Gilbert, Julie Goldsmith, *Ferber, a Biography*, Doubleday, 1978.
  Easily the most respected biography of Ferber, this title was written by Ferber's great-niece. Drawing on special access to information and anecdotes about Ferber, Gilbert presents the story of her life without shying away from the unflattering. The result is what critics regard as an honest look at the author and her work.

McGraw, Eliza, *Edna Ferber's America*, Louisiana State University Press, 2013.
  In an effort to show a modern readership who Ferber was and why her work matters, McGraw takes into consideration the author's era, her Jewish identity, her unique position as an unmarried woman, and her lively social life in New York. By bringing all of these elements together, McGraw demonstrates how Ferber's work is meaningful in capturing a unique voice and experience in America's past.

SUGGESTED SEARCH TERMS

Edna Ferber

A Bush League Hero AND Ferber

Buttered Side Down AND Ferber

baseball

naturalistic OR symbolistic AND American literature

Algonquin Round Table

Edna Ferber AND short story

small-town America AND literature

The Cold Equations

TOM GODWIN

1954

American author Tom Godwin's short story "The Cold Equations" is a landmark science-fiction tale about what transpires when someone is caught stowing away on an emergency ship. The story first appeared in 1954 in the magazine *Astounding Science Fiction*, which was famously edited by John W. Campbell Jr. That magazine, founded in 1930 as *Astounding Stories of Superscience*, followed close on the heels of the magazine credited with ushering in the genre of modern science fiction, *Amazing Stories*, founded four years earlier. From the 1930s through the 1950s, much science fiction was filled with the sort of adventure and melodrama that inspired the moniker "space operas," much as melodramatic westerns had come to be known as "horse operas." However, increasingly science-fiction novels and stories were exploring aspects of modern civilization and morality that eluded the grasp of conventional literary fiction, such as the implications of humanity's creation and use of nuclear weapons and other technologies.

"The Cold Equations" draws heavily on the science supporting the fiction, to such an extent that it is often held up as an exemplary work of "hard-core" or "hard" science fiction. In this subgenre, the natural laws of the universe take precedence over the whims and expectations of humankind. Nonetheless, the compassion inherent in Godwin's story is an essential part of the appeal. The story can be

Godwin's story is set in a dangerous, unfeeling space frontier. *(© Fred Fokkelman | Shutterstock.com)*

found in the Godwin collection *The Cold Equations & Other Stories* (2003), edited by Eric Flint, and in a variety of anthologies, including *The Science Fiction Hall of Fame*, Vol. 1 (1970), edited by Robert Silverberg; *In Dreams Awake: A Historical Critical Anthology of Science Fiction* (1975), edited by Leslie A. Fiedler; and *The Road to Science Fiction*, Vol. 3, *From Heinlein to Here* (1979), edited by James Gunn. (A list of twenty-two volumes containing the story can be found at http://www.philsp.com/homeville/isfac/s107.htm#A1745.1.)

AUTHOR BIOGRAPHY

Thomas William Godwin was born on June 6, 1915, possibly in Arizona. Very little is known about this author whose literary career never reached a level of success that would have brought him into the limelight. In his youth, he was obliged to leave school after the third grade because of tragedy in the family. His body was misshapen as a result of kyphosis (abnormal curvature of the spine), which in adulthood led to his military career ending prematurely. At some point in life he became an alcoholic.

Godwin published his first science-fiction story, "The Gulf Between," in *Astounding Science Fiction* in 1953. "The Cold Equations," his fourth story, followed not long after, in August 1954. Recognized as a masterpiece, the story is understood to have been derived from one or two existing ones. In particular, "A Weighty Decision," a story by Al Feldstein in the May–June 1952 issue of the EC comic *Weird Science*, and "A Dangerous Situation," also from 1952 in *Weird Science*, are cited as featuring highly similar plots. In "A Dangerous Situation," the stowaway is actually the pilot's fiancée—and is jettisoned nonetheless. Godwin is known to have originally altered the end of the preexisting plot to allow the girl to be saved; ironically, Campbell's editorial guidance, insisting that the girl had to die for the story to succeed, led to the curtailment of much of the originality Godwin imparted to it.

Godwin published several novels: *The Survivors* (1958), the sequel *The Space Barbarians* (1964), and *Beyond Another Sun* (1971). In all, he wrote around thirty stories. His family included an adopted daughter, Diane. Godwin is said to have lived through much pain in his later years, perhaps owing to his spinal condition. He died on August 31, 1980, in Las Vegas, Nevada.

PLOT SUMMARY

"The Cold Equations" begins with a pilot of a small spaceship who realizes he is not alone when the ship's sensors inform him of a heat-radiating presence in the supply closet. He immediately and regretfully conceives of what must be done, according to the regulations for any EDS, or emergency dispatch ship: the stowaway must be eliminated.

The law demanding this is based not on any ideological stance but rather on physics and the facts of the situation. The large hyperspace cruisers that crisscross the galaxy—like the *Stardust*, from which this EDS has just launched—cannot deviate from their strict transport schedules owing to interplanetary logistics; they have only so much room for cargo like rocket fuel and for the four EDSs that each cruiser is required to carry; the fuel must be precisely rationed according to the exact amount needed for any given EDS mission; the presence of a stowaway on an EDS increases the need for fuel because more must be used to reduce the momentum of the heavier ship (with reverse thrust); and thus, all in all, if a stowaway were allowed to remain aboard an EDS, the ship would be unable to adequately decelerate and reach its destination intact—it would crash.

This EDS is en route to the planet of Woden, carrying a vital serum to six men stricken with a deadly fever. It has been flying for an hour. The pilot laments that the man in the closet has, in stowing away, ensured his own death.

The pilot approaches the closet and orders whoever is inside to emerge. After his second command, out comes not a man but a teenage girl in sandals. Stunned, the pilot invites her to sit and begins asking her questions. She reveals that she has come along because she desperately

MEDIA ADAPTATIONS

- The fourth episode of the first season of the British television series *Out of This World*, hosted by Boris Karloff, was "Cold Equations," which aired on July 14, 1962. Directed by Peter Hammond off a screenplay adapted by Clive Exton, the episode stars Peter Wyngarde and Jane Asher.

- "The Cold Equations" was adapted as the fifty-first episode of the revival of *The Twilight Zone*, during the third season, on January 7, 1989. Martin Lavut directed, Alan Brennert wrote the screenplay, and Terence Knox and Christianne Hirt starred in the program, which has a running time of twenty-one minutes.

- A loose television film adaptation, introducing the theme of corporate greed, was produced by Alliance for the SciFi Channel and aired on December 7, 1996. The ninety-two-minute film was directed by Peter Geiger; was adapted by Geiger, Stephen Berger, and Norman Plotkin; and stars Bill Campbell and Poppy Montgomery.

- "The Cold Equations" has been adapted numerous times as a radio drama. A 1955 edited adaptation by NBC's X Minus One productions, with a total running time of twenty-four minutes, can be found through the Hard SF website at http://www.hardsf.org/0AudTitl.htm.

- An unabridged, full-cast adaptation from 2013, No. 289 of the Drabblecast series, can be found on the Bryan Lincoln Productions website at http://lincolnaudio.com/?p=229. Bryan Lincoln is the narrator, and the running time is sixty-four minutes.

wants to see her brother, Gerry, who is stationed on Woden—though, as it happens, among a second group that the EDS will not even be visiting. The pilot lessens the constant deceleration of the EDS—that is, allows it to continue at a higher speed—to temporarily save fuel. The girl knows she acted illicitly in stowing away and imagines she will have to pay a fine or even serve jail time.

Hopeless but intent on delaying the inevitable, the pilot, identifying himself as Barton, calls the commander of the *Stardust*, Delhart, to inform him of the stowaway. Delhart wonders why the stowaway has not already been jettisoned, and Barton tells him that she is just a girl. Delhart is shocked but nonetheless confirms that Barton must follow protocol for the situation. The girl, hearing this, begins to understand that she is being neither punished nor returned to the *Stardust* but sentenced to death. Barton apologizes and explains why the situation demands this, but she is in disbelief.

When Ship's Records calls from the *Stardust*, Barton takes the girl's identification disk and reads her information aloud; her name is Marilyn, and she is eighteen. Barton tells the records department that he will call back and terminates the communication. The girl fears that everyone wants her dead, but Barton tells her it has nothing to do with *wanting*: if she is not ejected (to asphyxiate, etc., in space), the ship will crash, and Barton as well as the six feverish men will die, too. He confirms that no other cruisers are near enough to offer assistance, and there is no way for her to be saved.

Barton ponders the physics behind his hesitation: the girl is not compromising the mission yet because he has reduced the ship's steady deceleration (allowing the ship to speed along) so as to use as little fuel as possible while the girl remains aboard. Eventually adequate deceleration must be resumed, so that the EDS will not be traveling too fast upon reaching Woden. Barton calls Commander Delhart and asks how long they can continue like this, given the girl's weight and the time at which he reduced the deceleration, 17:50. This course of action is against regulations, but the commander allows it, reporting at 18:10 that they must resume adequate deceleration in exactly one hour, at 19:10. A technician gives Barton the course corrections that will correct for their altered speed.

After ten minutes of silence, the girl comes to accept that no one means her any harm, but that there is nothing to be done to save her. The physical laws dictating the fuel amounts needed are what are condemning her to death. Barton

realizes that she has come from a place of inherent safety, Earth, and thus was simply unaware of how consequential a mistake on the frontiers of space can be. Marilyn mourns the fate she has stumbled into, regretting that she will never see her family again.

On the view screen, Woden is visible. Barton realizes that the camp of Marilyn's brother's group, Group 2, on Lotus Lake, will soon be rotating beyond the horizon and out of radio contact with the EDS. It is 18:30. Imagining that a few parting words would be cherished by brother and sister and yet also full of anguish, Barton calculates that only thirty-five minutes at most remain in which a last communication could happen. He mulls over the disaster at the camp of Group 1 that led to the call for an EDS, a tornado tearing through and destroying buildings and medical supplies. Like the equations governing the current situation, that tornado was cold and heartless—an aspect of nature.

Marilyn announces that she would like to write to her family members and to speak with Gerry on the radio if possible. Barton calls Group 2 to find that Gerry has been out in a helicopter all day and cannot be reached because the copter's radio is broken; however, he is expected to return shortly. Barton requests that Gerry be brought to the radio as quickly as possible, because there is bad news. Meanwhile, Marilyn writes letters to her family, her hand unsteady. Barton imagines that Gerry will understand, but the parents will hate him for what he must do. Marilyn finishes writing at 18:45, and in chatting she reveals her angst to Barton. He tries to console and comfort her.

Marilyn realizes that, being used to harmless entertainments, she failed to imagine the true danger of the frontier. She asks if it is especially cold in the EDS, and though it is not, Barton agrees that it is. Barton reassures her that Gerry should be back in time to talk to her, but anyway Marilyn resolves to make her exit as soon as he has passed out of radio range. She feels guilty for causing her family distress and for failing to tell them how much she loved and appreciated them. Barton tells her that they have known of her love all along, better than words can say. She hopes they will not imagine her in the throes of the grisly death she is about to meet.

The radio buzzer sounds, and it is Gerry. Marilyn speaks to him, and, knowing the consequences, he is aghast to hear her voice and desperately calls her name. Shaken and crying now, she begs him not to be hurt by what she has done, so Gerry regains his composure and soothes her. Gerry asks Barton if anything can be done, but the answer is negative. Gerry's voice begins to fade, and he and Marilyn say their last good-byes.

After a silent moment, Marilyn stands and approaches the air lock. Barton pulls a black lever to open the inner door, and she enters the small chamber and says she is ready. Barton closes the inner door, then pulls a red lever; he sees nothing but knows from the bump of altered pressure that the outer door has opened, and Marilyn has been whisked out to space. He closes the outer door. Her corpse is out there, by momentum still rushing onward through space. Yet feeling her presence, Barton remembers her poignant words "I didn't do anything to die for—I didn't do anything—"

CHARACTERS

Barton

The narration of "The Cold Equations" is in the third person, but Barton's thoughts are reported throughout the story, identifying him as the central protagonist. That is, while Marilyn's fate is what the plot revolves around, the focus of the story is on how Barton copes with the situation. The story begins and ends with Barton by himself in the ship, and it is through Barton's musings that the reader learns of the relevant scientific facts and moral perspectives.

From the beginning Barton shows clear remorse over what must be done to the stowaway he has discovered. He has become largely inured to death, having presumably witnessed much carnage in his activities as an EDS pilot—analogous to an ambulance driver—but he nonetheless recoils from the idea of willfully ending a human life. Moreover, the drama of the story hinges on the fact that this stowaway is no delinquent man but rather a naive young woman; her innocence and Barton's cause for hesitation (as well as the story's origins in a generally prefeminist era) are highlighted in Marilyn's being referred to throughout the story as "the girl."

Several times Barton revisits the reasons why stowaways must be dealt with as the law demands, but all along he has little hope of finding an alternative, knowing that the situation allows for no margin of error. He counsels Marilyn as best he can, helpfully deflecting whatever negative feelings she voices. Nonetheless, when the time comes for him to open the air lock and let the girl out into space, he does so calmly and mechanically, pulling the levers that must be pulled. Still, the sympathetic connection that Barton has forged with the girl lingers with him and speaks to his underlying humanity.

Clerk

A clerk in Ship's Records on the *Stardust* speaks in a matter-of-fact way about the stowaway's termination until Barton informs him that the girl in question is alive and listening. The clerk abruptly alters his demeanor. At first it seems the clerk could be either male or female, but Barton's later comment to Marilyn that "each of us did what little he could to help you" (along with, again, Godwin's prefeminist era) suggests that all the ship's crew mentioned are male.

Gerry Cross

Marilyn's brother acts much as the reader would expect a brother to act upon learning that his little sister has committed a transgression that must bring about her death. At first he is horror stricken, but when he becomes aware that his horror will only make the situation more difficult for Marilyn to bear, he becomes sympathetic and offers a soothing presence. Barton knows that Gerry, being familiar with the dangers of the frontier, will understand that Marilyn's death is not the EDS pilot's fault, and indeed, after questioning Barton, Gerry accepts that nothing can be done.

Marilyn Lee Cross

Marilyn is a petite eighteen-year-old, standing five foot three and weighing one hundred ten pounds; she is implied to be pretty. Marilyn so laments her brother's ten-year absence from her life that, given the opportunity, she impulsively decides to stow away on a supply ship headed to the planet he is stationed on, Woden. In doing so, she disregards an important sign—"UNAUTHORIZED PERSONNEL KEEP OUT!"—and thus imagines that she might be fined. Her naïveté is that of a teenager: thinking only of the interpersonal joy of being reunited with her brother, she has failed to consider the logistical ramifications of her decision. Aside from the essential calculations about the fuel—which she cannot be expected to have imagined—she has evidently assumed that there would be adequate food, drinking water, and so forth, even in a minuscule colony on an otherwise uninhabited planet.

The reader may perceive that she seems unable to understand the situation that she has gotten herself into, but her disbelief is more emotional than rational: she cannot believe that she must die simply because no one in such a scenario would want to believe that death is inevitable. Marilyn does eventually accept the gravity of the situation and acknowledge her impending death. She then determinedly sets about writing letters to her parents and brother, to say all that she has time to say, and she even resolves to march willingly to her death once her brother is out of contact and she has nothing left to wait for. Placed in a nightmare of a situation, Marilyn proves able to confront the reality, accept her misbegotten fate, and courageously meet that fate.

Commander Delhart

Delhart, the commander of the *Stardust*, is known to the reader only by voice. He is authoritative, as the head of a galactic cruiser must be, but not entirely disconnected from a humane perspective. He makes clear to Barton that there is no means of saving the life of the stowaway, but he at least accommodates Barton's efforts to preserve her life for as long as possible.

Technician

A technician provides Barton with the revised course of travel for the EDS in view of its altered speed (and thus altered arc with respect to Woden's gravity).

THEMES

Frontier Life

The original readers of Godwin's story in *Astounding Science Fiction* were made aware, even before starting the story proper, that the notion of the frontier would be central to the story. Campbell's 1954 preface (cited by Stephen Baxter in "The Cold Equations: Extraterrestrial Liberty in Science Fiction") reads, "The Frontier is a strange place—and a frontier is not always easy to recognize. It may lie on the other side of a simple door marked 'No admittance'—but it is always deadly dangerous." This so adroitly alludes to the plot of the story that the reader may only recognize the connotations upon revisiting the preface afterward.

The idea of the frontier for most people calls to mind such concerns as wild animals, lack of solid shelter, lack of reliable food sources, unknown environmental dangers, and so forth. Clearly in circumstances marked by such concerns, one realizes that a single misstep—into the path of a cobra, onto a poorly built raft, into quicksand—can mean certain death. Godwin's story, however, takes place entirely within the confines of a human-designed ship, allowing the idea of the frontier to drift from the reader's mind—as if perhaps the frontier will at last be confronted when the ship lands. However, the ship's interior is like an extension of the frontier, a place where different rules of conduct and expectations apply. The ship is marked by a course of action taken out of necessity (to save lives), by scarcity of resource (fuel), and by aspects of nature that represent imminent threats (gravity, outer space). One misstep, even within or onto an EDS, can mean death. Marilyn learns this the hard way.

Rationality

It is understandably difficult for Marilyn to accept that she must die, and likewise it is difficult for the reader to accept that she must. Of course, the circumstances have been concocted by the author, and any author has the power to conceive of circumstances that doom the characters implanted in a story, but this being science fiction, the author is committed to establishing the science behind this particular fiction. Godwin iterates several times the mathematical relationship responsible for Marilyn's death: a certain amount of fuel, h, is sufficient to safely transport a mass, m, to a given place but insufficient to transport an increased mass of $m + x$. The actual physics of this calculation is more complicated (involving the relationship $F = md$, or force equals mass times deceleration), but Godwin wisely sticks to an explanation that is accessible even to those without a background in physics. Indeed, the author is more concerned with philosophic rationality than with science.

TOPICS FOR FURTHER STUDY

- Write your own science-fiction short story that functions as a response to "The Cold Equations." You may choose to consult other such responses, several of which can be found online, or not, so that your own ideas can freshly surface in your mind. Feel free to adapt, tweak, revise, invert, or reconstruct Godwin's story in any way.

- The idea of an attractive young woman being sacrificed for some reason, in some sense, is not uncommon to literature and film. Write a paper in which you discuss the use of this trope in fiction, films, or both, citing at least two other works. Address why the scenario appeals to readers/viewers, how it tends to play out, and what the social implications are. Alternatively, write a similarly focused paper on works in which a character willingly allows or brings about his or her own death for the benefit of others.

- Select a story from the young-adult collection *Life on Mars: Tales from the New Frontier* (2011), edited by Jonathan Strahan, which features adolescent protagonists of both sexes in old-fashioned considerations of the possibility of colonizing Mars. Write a paper in which you compare the story you chose with "The Cold Equations," discussing how the concept of the frontier is critical, what the roles of the protagonists signify, the overall quality and value of the tales, and other topics of note.

- With one or more friends, film your own adaptation of "The Cold Equations." You may choose to have a narrator or not, follow the dialogue exactly or not, and so forth. (If filming with only one friend, the radio communications can be prerecorded.) As the staging is simple, requiring only a single set, make an effort to produce a scene that adequately represents the inside of a spaceship, with campy or realistic props as you prefer.

The story's cast of characters, excluding Marilyn, all rely on the established conclusion that a stowaway must be jettisoned, which the reader may imagine has been reached after much civic debate. That is, they make nominal efforts to "help" Marilyn—as Barton confirms, their help "was almost nothing"—but no one truly makes an effort to think outside the box, so to speak, and imagine how Marilyn might be saved. They so reflexively fall back on rubberstamped rationality that it is almost as if they have forgotten that alternate ideas distinct from the official one are even conceivable. Moreover, while the cold equations are blamed by Barton for Marilyn's death, it is as if Barton and the others have come to embody the very coldness of those equations. Barton shows remorse over what must be done, and he does an admirable job of deflecting Marilyn's anxieties and regrets, but whether he makes a truly sympathetic connection with her is an open question.

The narrative passages of the story, understood as Barton's thoughts, return again and again to the rationality behind why Marilyn must die, and there are some psychological conjectures as well, but Marilyn's present emotional experience remains mostly foreign to him; in their interactions, he comes across as more of a detached psychiatrist than a momentary friend. Notably, he never tells the girl his first name, and he only finds out her name by reading her identification disk; he never addresses her as Marilyn. Barton's preference for rationality is made clear when, imagining that he would see Marilyn again sometime in his dreams, he "scowled at the viewscreen and tried to force his thoughts into less emotional channels. There was nothing he could do to help her." Evidently rationality has won the day, as it had to all along, but it is worth observing that Barton seems content with that outcome.

The gauges in the EDS tell the pilot that someone has stowed away. (© ksb | Shutterstock.com)

Abandonment

Countering the predominance of rationality in the frontier world that Barton and his fellow spacemen inhabit is the predominance of emotion in Marilyn's worldview. It was an emotional impulse—the impulse to seize the opportunity to visit her brother after ten long years—that led her into the EDS, and when she learns of her impending doom, her emotions dominate her response. What she perhaps feels most strongly is a sense of abandonment. She imagines, "Everybody wants me dead"; she wonders, "Wouldn't people help me if they could?"; and she finally laments, "I'm going to die and nobody *cares*." Barton rationally refutes all of her suspicions, but the emotional sense of the experience remains: she *is* going to die, and if anybody cares, they do not care enough to make a difference. Marilyn's sense of abandonment is heightened by the context, one that most present-day earthbound humans can only imagine: being inside a spaceship with only a stranger and disembodied voices for company.

The emotional focus on Marilyn's sense of abandonment may have two effects for the reader: One is that the closing pages of the story become all the more climactic, as, after Marilyn's mental perseverance through the lonely realization of her awful fate, culminating in acceptance, she is finally allowed the emotional connection that she was denied all along, in the brief radio conversation with her brother. The exceedingly rational discourse leading up to this point in the story brings out the poignancy of that supremely emotional moment. A second effect, extending beyond the story, may be that the reader's sensitivity to others' states of abandonment may be heightened, eliciting greater sympathy in real life for the orphaned child, the bullied loner, the social misfit. Much admirable literature serves to heighten the reader's sense of sympathy.

Death

Godwin's story ends tragically, with the death of Marilyn, whose presence has been established so capably that the reader, along with Barton, is likely to find "her words echoing hauntingly clear in the void she had left behind her." All along, the reasoning presented in the narrative is strictly conjectural, such that it is easy to forget that what is being reasoned out is why a person must actually die; that is, Marilyn does keep the fact of her apparent death sentence in the forefront of the conversation, but the reader is free to hope and imagine that she will not truly have to die in the end. Indeed, the reasoning, however sound on the surface, is so coldly rational that most every reader will not want that cold rationality to win out, a preference that may give rise to hopes for her being saved. Finally, though, the story paces through Marilyn's final minutes, and it becomes clear that nothing will intercede on her behalf; she is indeed allowed to perish.

No sympathetic reader can want this innocent young person to die, whether the story justifies it or not, and so the story can be seen to quite boldly impress the reader by means of disappointment. A conventional last-minute-escape ending would have been more gratifying on the surface, but the actual ending lends a far more profound reading experience. After the story has had its say, the reader is left to independently wonder, in the context of the story, did Marilyn *have* to die? Many commentators have focused on this question. Beyond the context of the story, could civilization indeed reach such a point—or has civilization reached such a point—where by law, without malice, a human life could be so expendable? One should hope not.

STYLE

Moral Dilemma

"The Cold Equations" features one of the mainstays of literary fiction: the moral dilemma. When choices of action are morally ambiguous—when there is an argument to be made for more than one option, perhaps with drastically different outcomes in the balance—people make decisions that often prove to be historical pivots that shape the fabric of their reality. Fyodor Dostoyevsky's *Crime and Punishment* revolves around a man's specious justification for a murder. Mark Twain's *Huckleberry Finn* shows the merit in people like Huck and Jim acting contrary to the law. Sometimes, as in Dostoyevsky's *The Idiot* or James Fenimore Cooper's *The Deerslayer*, characters possess such moral purity that they are virtually incapable of acting contrary to their moral compass, even in the interest of self-preservation.

Godwin's story is curious in that, as in Dostoyevsky and Cooper, characters appear incapable of acting contrary to their moral compass, and yet it would be more accurate to describe their guiding philosophy as lacking in moral considerations, because their views are dictated not by morality—a code of action with regard to fellow creatures—but simply by custom and law. Even where the customs and laws in question are designed by man—the customs governing the transport patterns followed by cruisers and EDSs, the law condemning EDS stowaways to death—the consequences are ultimately attributed to the laws of nature. As the narration affirms, "Existence required Order, and there was order; the laws of nature, irrevocable and immutable.... The laws *were*, and the universe moved in obedience to them."

Because the physical as well as human laws in question in Marilyn's circumstances are effectively written in stone, what the reader has is not precisely a moral dilemma, not a choice between alternatives, but an *irresolvable* dilemma, an obligation to follow a particular morally unpleasant course of action in lieu of a worse one. Marilyn hardly needs to consider the few apparent alternatives to her willing death: she knows that remaining on the ship with Barton would mean that the ship would crash and the six feverish men would die, and she presumably would not know how to ensure the safe landing of the ship on her own, so sacrificing Barton instead is out of the question. In the end, then, the focus is less on the irresolvable moral dilemma itself and more on the experience of facing the consequences, as well as on the justifiability of the circumstances that bring the ending about.

Hard Science Fiction

Godwin's story is often cited as the epitome of "hard science fiction," the meaning of which is intuitively apparent from the term itself—especially if one has read "The Cold Equations," where the term *hard* pops conspicuously up several times. The term *science fiction* itself is open to various interpretations. John W. Campbell Jr., who famously vetted Godwin's story for *Astounding Science Fiction*, offers loose definitions in his essay "The Place of Science Fiction." As a foundation, he suggests, "Fiction is simply dreams written out; science fiction consists of the hopes and dreams and fears (for some dreams are nightmares) of a technically based society." He goes on to posit that "science fiction is the literature of speculation as to what changes may come, and which changes will be improvements, which destructive, which merely pointless." In "The Readers of Hard Science Fiction," James Gunn distinguishes between science fiction and fantasy—quoting Campbell, among others—by pointing out that science fiction deals with what is possible and commits to explaining, to an extent, how and why things are possible, while fantasy roams into realms of experience that are not or cannot be explained.

Stories begin to be considered hard-core or hard science fiction when the writer's commitment is not just to what is possible but to what is inevitable based on the laws under consideration. Gunn points out that this implies a reliance on the conclusions of the "hard sciences"—physics, astronomy, geology, biology, chemistry, and at the heart of everything, mathematics, with technology as an essential medium—as opposed to the social sciences, or "soft sciences," like psychology and sociology, which offer predictive power regarding human behavior but not law-bound certainty.

Introducing the volume *Hard Science Fiction*, George Slusser and Eric S. Rabkin define the subgenre by means of extended description:

> In a basic sense...both setting and dramatic situation must derive strictly from the rigorous postulation and working out of a concrete physical problem. The method...is logical, the means technological, and the result—the feel and texture of the fiction itself—objective and cold....It asserts the truth of natural law, an absolute, seemingly ahuman vision of things.

That "The Cold Equations" fits the patterns and expectations for hard science fiction is self-evident to any who have read the story. Indeed, the story is considered something of a hard sci-fi manifesto. As the narration frames it, Marilyn is veritably sacrificed in deference to physical laws. Interestingly, while the story goes to considerable lengths to elaborate why physics and natural laws demand the expulsion of any stowaway on an EDS, the apparent direct dependence on natural laws serves to obscure the indirect dependence on human-fashioned circumstances. The fact that the EDS as currently outfitted cannot land safely with the added weight of the stowaway is made perfectly clear, but behind this, with regard to the limited fuel supply, for example, the reader is simply told that "the cruisers were forced by

necessity to carry a limited amount of the bulky rocket fuel." The wording here suggests that physics-oriented space/weight concerns are foremost, and yet the phrase "forced by necessity" is about as circular as a phrase like "starved by hunger" and reveals nothing about the purported necessity. In the absence of air friction in outer space, aerodynamic concerns are nullified, so the bulk of a ship need not be a concern, and if the cruisers use nuclear reactors to travel through hyperspace (an entirely conjectural mode of transportation to be sure), a little extra rocket fuel could surely be borne without compromising speed. However the author might justify the necessity for severely limiting fuel, a physicist or engineer might refute the justification as irrational.

Other concerns with the "hardness" of the story have been raised, such as by John Huntington in "Hard-Core Science Fiction and the Illusion of Science." In his opinion, for all its supposed deference to natural laws, a deference that suggests an uncompromising realism, the story is at heart a fantasy about an idealized set of circumstances—namely, circumstances idealized to be utterly indifferent to human life. At no point, for example, does Barton even glance around the EDS for something besides a human that could be thrown overboard. Improbably, the EDS as a machine is idealized to function within such perfectly defined parameters that no variation is permitted. Is it truly realistic that the engineers who designed the cruisers and EDSs would have left no room for error of any kind? What if an EDS had to maneuver around a stray asteroid? Huntington's point is not that the story lacks legitimacy—surely the quality of the story would have been compromised had Godwin sought to explore and discredit every possible reason why the girl might not have had to die. Rather his point is that even in hard science fiction, that most rigorous of genres, the rigor is contained within a fictional world that must ultimately be recognized as fantasy.

HISTORICAL CONTEXT

The Roots of Modern Science Fiction

While science fiction as modern readers know it began to flourish early in the twentieth century, a number of stories and novels with science-fiction angles or aspects were published in the preceding

COMPARE
&
CONTRAST

- **1950s:** Science fiction, published in a variety of genre-specific magazines, has developed a strong niche market for leisure reading, although the demographic is overwhelmingly white males reading works written by white males. Authors like Isaac Asimov are raising the bar for literary quality.

  Today: The niche market for science fiction has expanded—modern films have helped popularize the genre—with increasing numbers of female and minority readers appreciating works that increasingly represent broader ranges of life experience. Ursula K. Le Guin and Margaret Atwood are especially admired authors of science fiction for both adults and young adults.

- **1950s:** Albert Einstein's scientific findings of the early twentieth century, such as the theory of relativity, retain a strong hold on the intellectual imagination, while physicists such as Subrahmanyan Chandrasekhar and Niels Bohr continue to contribute new insight into the workings of the universe. Science fiction authors have an abundance of recent and fairly accessible science to draw from for their books.

  Today: As ever greater telescopes and particle accelerators are constructed, allowing for increased accuracy in measurement of light and distances and detection of par-

  ticles, scientists continue to make advances in understanding the universe. Among the latest focuses are dark energy and dark matter, substances theorized to fill up substantial portions of the universe. Many of the latest findings and theories—sub-subatomic particles, superstring theory, quantum gravity—are so complex that they defy discussion in popular fiction.

- **1950s:** In a decade that will mark the height of baby boomer nostalgia, fascism is an increasingly distant memory—for Americans, at least—while in the years leading up to the space age, thoughts of orbiting the Earth, reaching the moon, and surveying other planets stimulate many people's imaginations. The idea of colonizing other planets leads some writers toward optimistic utopian visions.

  Today: The American space program has been reduced in scale following the Great Recession, but NASA still conducts significant missions, including the recent landing of a rover on Mars that has successfully photographed and analyzed Martian terrain. Back on Earth, ordinary citizens are increasingly concerned not with space exploration but with technology that revolutionizes daily life, which in some writers inspires dystopian visions of dependence.

---

hundred years. Among the first novels that can be truly considered science fiction, as opposed to myth or fantasy, is Mary Shelley's *Frankenstein* (1818), in which Dr. Frankenstein's creation of an artificial man leads to a great deal of morally charged dialogue. In contrast to the popular image of the dumbstruck movie monster, in the book, Frankenstein's monster is exceedingly eloquent. Among the most significant influences on ensuing science-fiction writers was Edgar Allan

Poe, who is far more famous for his mastery of the gothic tale and for being the originator of the modern detective story. Poe's tale "Mesmeric Revelations" (1844), for example, draws on the practice of mesmerism to conjecture as to the nature of the greater universe and even the possibility of extraterrestrial life. In Poe's wake came the Frenchman Jules Verne and his dozens of speculative novels, including *Journey to the Center of the Earth* (1864) and *From the Earth to the*

Moon (1865), the first scientifically oriented account of a lunar journey. British author H. G. Wells wrote *The Time Machine* (1895), imagining life on Earth hundreds of thousands of years in the future, and *The War of the Worlds* (1897), about conflict with an alien race.

Much of this early science fiction remained largely fantastic or allegorical in nature. In the absence of sustained intellectual, rather than merely physical, engagement with the unknown, Verne's novels in retrospect are mostly considered quaint. Wells's novels, while positing unknown futures and worlds, were typically read as escapist commentaries on such social realities as the British class system and colonialism. American science fiction of the early twentieth century owed much to predecessors like Verne and Wells but also included elements of the popular western fiction of the day.

Edgar Rice Burroughs is best known for creating Tarzan as well as John Carter, the hero of various Martian exploits. Burroughs's Mars often bears an uncanny resemblance to the American West, and indeed much later science fiction would reproduce the frontier-like atmosphere with which Burroughs instilled works like "Under the Moons of Mars" (1912), which was serialized in *All-Story Magazine* and later published as *A Princess of Mars* (1917). Before long the first magazine devoted to such science fiction, *Amazing Stories*, was founded, in 1926. E. E. Smith's *The Skylark of Space* (1928), in which the romantic scientist hero roams the universe destroying planets, spreading civilization, and so forth, would mark the beginning of the age of space operas, when such broadly conceived works would proliferate.

Widely acknowledged to be the pivotal moment in the development of modern science fiction was John W. Campbell Jr.'s assumption of the editorship of *Astounding Stories*, later called *Astounding Science Fiction*, in 1937. An accomplished author of space operas himself, Campbell as editor tended to demand more rigorous explorations of the concepts, themes, and technicalities that arose in the work writers submitted. As Campbell told science-fiction icon Isaac Asimov, even when he fed ideas to writers, he wanted them to develop the ideas in original, nonformulaic ways. As Campbell, cited by Huntington in *Science Fiction and Market Realities*, once put it, "I don't want it my way. I can do that myself. I want my idea

his way." Rather than simply offering rapturous adventures, then, writers came to approach the genre specifically as a venue in which to posit future realities and extrapolate on them in order to chart possible trajectories of humankind in the known world.

It was Campbell who originally ushered Asimov's famous *Foundation* stories into print in the 1940s, and Campbell also nurtured Lester del Rey and Robert A. Heinlein, among others. Campbell would have quite an influence on Godwin's production of "The Cold Equations," a story the editor wanted concluded in one way and one way only. Campbell (cited by Barry Malzberg in the afterword to a 2003 collection that includes "The Cold Equations") once related to Asimov, "I had Godwin really sweating over that story." Campbell offered a bit more detail about the editing process in a letter, cited by Huntington, written in 1969:

> Only once did I send a story back six times for revisions—and that was ... an author who had an idea, a good one, and could write—but simply couldn't accept the underlying honest answer to the story-idea he had come up with. "The Cold Equations" by Tom Godwin is now one of the classic shorts of science fiction. It was Tom's idea, and he wrote every word of it, and sweated over it ... because he just simply couldn't accept that the *girl simply had to die.*

It is not known whether Campbell was aware of the source or two that Godwin drew from in writing the story; this letter suggests that he was not. Campbell may have later discovered (and resented) the resemblance between Godwin's story and the earlier *Weird Science* tales; evidently Campbell rejected whatever stories Godwin submitted to the magazine for the next seven years, though he did publish Godwin again and later expressed support for him. (One might go so far as to suggest that Godwin's story was an act of plagiarism, but at least one EC Comics writer was forthright about their own lifting of plots directly from existing science-fiction stories, and so they could hardly object to the reverse occurring.) Regardless of Godwin's literary fate, *Astounding Science Fiction*, boldly renamed *Analog Science Fact–Science Fiction* in 1960, continued to publish some of the best science fiction to be found, although competitors like the *Magazine of Fantasy and Science Fiction* (established in 1949) and *Galaxy Science Fiction* (established in 1950) also

The pilot has to make a decision based on hard facts, but he does care about the girl.

(© *Sergey_Bogomyako* | *Shutterstock.com*)

drew elite contributors. Authors such as Ray Bradbury, Arthur C. Clarke, and Philip K. Dick emerged from this era and, in works like Bradbury's *The Martian Chronicles* (1950) and Clarke's *2001: A Space Odyssey* (1968), ushered science fiction toward and into the twenty-first century.

CRITICAL OVERVIEW

When it was first published in *Astounding Science Fiction*, "The Cold Equations" generated an enormous reader response, eliciting more mail than any story previously published in the magazine—mostly from male readers (who made up the vast majority of the audience for early science fiction) who felt compelled to insist that Marilyn could have in this or that way been saved. It became one of the most famous science-fiction stories in history, ranked by some among the best five (alongside Daniel Keyes's "Flowers for Algernon," Ray Bradbury's "Sound of Thunder," Arthur C. Clarke's "The Star," and Asimov's "Nightfall," which was also famously edited by Campbell). Discussions of short science fiction often allude to the story at the least, while discussions of hard science fiction in particular rarely fail to mention it.

As he recalls in his essay in *Hard Science Fiction*, James Gunn, upon including the story in his edited volume *The Road to Science Fiction*, designated it a "touchstone story" because "if readers don't understand it they don't understand science fiction." He observes that, unlike many space operas that might easily be rewritten as horse operas, and vice versa, "The Cold Equations" could only be science fiction because of the essential role of the outer-space frontier setting in bringing about the story's conclusion.

In his own essay in *Hard Science Fiction*, Huntington calls the story "a classic hard-core SF work" that remains "extraordinarily popular." He attributes this to the manner in which the author plays fair, so to speak, within the technical parameters it establishes. While Huntington agrees with the thematic premise that the cold universe can be fatal while remaining neutral, operating "with neither hatred nor malice," in Godwin's words, he takes issue with the details of the story. In particular, he recognizes that it is quite possible to think of ways the girl could have been saved—he zeroes in on objects in the spaceship that could be considered disposable, like the pilot's chair—and "once one's mind gets on this track, the story becomes quite frustrating." Of course, finding last-minute solutions to the problem was precisely what Godwin originally attempted; only with Campbell's insistence did he finally settle on Marilyn's death. Without this ending, the story likely would not have been so famous that critics like Huntington would even be discussing it.

Huntington also takes issue with the story's dismissive attitude toward the eighteen-year-old "girl." Barton treats her as inconsequential, never suspecting, for example, that she might seize his blaster. And the men in the story make no serious efforts to conceive of a way to save her life. Considered from a distance, the story seems to show how women who assume female privilege in consciously overstepping their boundaries—especially if intruding in a masculine sphere of activity—deserve to be punished. Yet as the story itself indicates, the juxtaposition of a female stowaway with male crew members was precisely intended to increase the pathos of the situation by highlighting the young woman's vulnerability; it is unlikely that Godwin meant for Marilyn's position to be representative of women's societal roles.

Assessing Godwin's impact as a whole, John Clute in *The Encyclopedia of Science Fiction* duly mentions that "The Cold Equations" is his "most famous" story, while otherwise his output was slim. Clute notes, "What he did write…exhibited a fine clarity of conception and considerable narrative verve, though his characterizations were sometimes sentimental." In his own *Encyclopedia of Science Fiction*, Don D'Ammassa gives a more expansive treatment of Godwin's famous story, affirming that the heart-wrenching discussion between the girl and her brother is one of the most poignant in all of science fiction. Still, he agrees that the sentimentality in the author's other works seems overplayed.

In his afterword to *The Cold Equations & Other Stories*, Dave Drake concludes with an acknowledgment and an affirmation: "So a good but not great writer, through a series of chances, came to write an outstanding story; perhaps the most outstanding SF story ever written." Malzberg concludes that with "The Cold Equations," Godwin "comes as close to permanence as any writer to emerge from science fiction." He adds that the story "may outlast science fiction itself."

CRITICISM

Michael Allen Holmes

Holmes is a writer with existential interests. In the following essay, he considers how the details in "The Cold Equations" encourage the reader's identification with Marilyn and suggest a symbolic layer to the story.

"The Cold Equations" has been discussed so comprehensively that one is hard-pressed to find a new angle of literary exploration. The earliest readers made short work of the plot trajectory, conceiving of various ways that Marilyn, the eighteen-year-old stowaway, could

> ONE CAN ALMOST HEAR GODWIN'S VOICE LEAKING THROUGH BARTON'S IN THIS INSTANCE—THE WHOLE STORY, HE SEEMS TO BE SAYING, IS COLDER THAN IT SHOULD BE."

have actually been saved. Later readers went a step further in suggesting that the circumstances as presented were illegitimate—that no decent team of engineers or transportation authority, no matter the societal constraints, would send out emergency ships with so little fuel that the slightest deviation from the intended trajectory would result in a shortage and a crash. Still other readers, such as during a lively debate carried out in the pages of the *New York Review of Science Fiction* in the 1990s, drew on the patterns of interaction and the characterizations of Marilyn and the various men to conclude that the work is quite unfeminist at best, misogynist at worst.

The majority of these readings have operated under a significant assumption: that the author is both complicit in the upsetting conclusion and wants the reader to be complicit as well—to agree on an intellectual level that in such an extreme situation, yes, if the physical laws demand that a person must die, the person must die. Yet the provenance of this story suggests that such an assumption may be incorrect. It is known that Tom Godwin, the author, would have preferred that the girl be saved, and he submitted the story as such half a dozen different ways before finally bowing to the demands of editor John W. Campbell Jr. and having the girl die. In light of this prolonged exchange, not only must the reader reconsider criticism of the story's logic—the circumstances seem contrived because the editor insisted that they be contrived—but moreover the story merits revisiting to see if Godwin might have encoded the text to signal that the conclusion should not be taken as fitting, since he did not see it as such, but should indeed leave one disturbed.

Despite Campbell's critical intervention as editor, Godwin did, as Campbell himself stated,

WHAT DO I READ NEXT?

- Among the best known of Godwin's several novels is *The Survivors* (1958)—later published as *Space Prison* (1960)—which is an expansion of his story "Too Soon to Die." A cruiser taking people from Earth to another planet is intercepted by aliens, who take some of the people as slave labor and leave the rest to scrape by on an inhospitable planet.

- In response to certain concerns with "The Cold Equations," Don Sakers wrote the story "The Cold Solution," which first appeared in *Analog Science Fiction–Science Fact* in Vol. 111, Nos. 8/9, July 1991. Sakers reverses Godwin's circumstances by having a female emergency ship pilot, Diane, discover that a young boy has stowed away on board. In a postmodern twist, Diane read "The Cold Equations" back as a space cadet.

- There are, in fact, many stories written as direct responses to Godwin's famous one. Among the most significant are Michael Burstein's "The Cold Calculations," which appeared in *Absolute Magnitude* in 2001, and James Patrick Kelly's "Think Like a Dinosaur," from *Asimov's Science Fiction* in 2005. These stories and others can be found online.

- "The Ethical Equations" is a story by Murray Leinster in which the course of action to be taken in uncertain circumstances—a patrol happens upon a heavily armed ship in which aliens are hibernating—is determined through recourse to scientific analysis. The story can be found in *The Best of Murray Leinster* (1976).

- A few of the longer stories to appear in *Astounding* from the 1930s to the 1950s, reflecting the earliest stages of the evolution of the genre, are collected in *The Best of Astounding: Classic Short Novels from the Golden Age of Science Fiction* (1992), edited by James E. Gunn. The authors include Isaac Asimov, H. P. Lovecraft, and Poul Anderson, whose "We Have Fed Our Sea" is especially highly regarded.

- *Diverse Energies* (2012), edited by Tobias S. Buckell and Joe Monti, is a young-adult science-fiction collection featuring protagonists of a range of ethnicities and also varying sexual orientations. The plots tend toward the dystopian, with many protagonists demonstrating their bravery. The authors include Ellen Oh, K. Tempest Bradford, Ken Liu, Rahul Kanakia, Paolo Bacigalupi, and Ursula K. Le Guin.

- The nonfiction volume *Presenting Young Adult Science Fiction* (1998), by Suzanne E. Reid, is designed as an introduction for students as well as teachers who are less familiar with the genre. After acknowledging the well-known masters, the text focuses on the works and themes of eight authors of particular interest to young adults, including Orson Scott Card, Octavia Butler, Piers Anthony, and Douglas Adams.

---

write the entire story himself, even if he drew on existing sources. If Godwin knew that Campbell was convinced that the girl *had* to die for the story to succeed, he might have felt reluctant to undermine that rational conclusion within the story. That is, the final version of the story does not hold Barton and the other men culpable for what takes place; they are not portrayed as villains to any appreciable extent, but rather the physical laws of the universe take the blame. On a subtler level, however, details throughout the story may question such a conclusion.

Few readers will fail to notice the proliferation in the story of the word *cold*, which appears about a dozen times. With the word already lent specific connotations by the title—equations being mathematical, mathematics being unsentimental, or cold—the first paragraph immediately contrasts the idea of cold math with warm humanity, as it is Marilyn's body heat that is picked up by the ship's sensors. The EDS pilot is then immediately contrasted with the warm stowaway, in that he is said to be accustomed to embodying "an objective lack of emotion" and is capable (if superficially reluctant) of "coldly" killing a man. A while later, coldness is again attributed to Barton when he finally clearly communicates to Marilyn that there is literally no hope of her being saved: his words are "like the drop of a cold stone."

Meanwhile, color imagery is built up around Marilyn as she is introduced and her personality emerges. The first detail of her appearance reported by the narration is her "white gypsy sandals." The color white has already been associated twice with the stowaway, in that it is the "white hand" of the heat gauge that alerts Barton to her presence, and also the door of the closet is twice mentioned to be white. All of these items could have been any color at all, and so it may be significant that Godwin has made them all white. Often attached to the color white is the concept of purity, and Marilyn's innocence makes this meaning appropriate.

Further into Barton and Marilyn Lee Cross's interaction, another detail of her appearance emerges, namely, the blueness of her eyes. The color blue is readily associated with water and perhaps more relevantly the sky, at least as seen from the earth, in contrast to the blackness of outer space. Blue is often considered a pacific color, further associating Marilyn with innocence, safety, and peacefulness. A bit later, another color is added to her portrayal when she is fearful that she is being ejected at once, though Barton is only approaching her to collect her identification disk. The reader is told that while Marilyn's face has turned white, her lipstick is blood red. The mention of blood heightens the reader's sense of the visceral fear she is feeling. Still later, when Marilyn has come to accept her fate after a period of silence, it is said that the color has returned to her face, making the lipstick appear less vividly red—but the color has been established.

Other objects in the story lack the colors exhibited by Marilyn. Appropriately for a record of death, Marilyn's name will be marked on a card that is the somber color of gray. In consecutive sentences, the narration mentions both the "star-sprinkled dead blackness" of space (as contrasted with the "blue haze" of the planet on which Marilyn's brother is stationed) and the "black horror of fear" that has overcome Marilyn. This horror is said to give way to "the calm gray of acceptance," again associating gray with her death. Notably, the one and only color associated with Barton, finally mentioned when he accepts her letters for safekeeping, is gray, the color of his uniform shirt—directly associating Barton, not just those equations, with the idea of Marilyn's death. As the time ticks away, Marilyn keeps one eye on the "black hand" of the clock.

Around this point the notion of coldness again becomes significant. Aside from its having been recently cited as the feel of the equations governing Marilyn's death, her parents are expected to hate Barton "with cold and terrible intensity"—as if the coldness of the circumstances will inevitably infect them. Soon the coldness is getting to Marilyn as well, as shown in what is perhaps on a submerged level the most significant exchange in the story:

> "Isn't it—" She stopped, and he looked at her questioningly. "Isn't it cold in here?" she asked, almost apologetically. "Doesn't it seem cold to you?"
>
> "Why, yes," he said. He saw by the main temperature gauge that the room was at precisely normal temperature. "Yes, it's colder than it should be."

Barton lies here, and the reason for this is somewhat uncertain. If the room is at normal temperature but the girl feels cold, Barton might suspect that the nearness of her death is starting to literally chill her. Thus, most readily one imagines that he is lying in order to keep the idea of death at a distance, leaving her with the impression that it is merely the chill of the room that she feels. What is odd about this exchange, though, is that Barton neither indicates that he will remedy the problem by turning the heat back up nor makes any gesture to suggest as much. Marilyn's next comment changes the subject, as if she takes him at his word and forgets the matter; so instead of the coldness being dealt with, Barton's last comment—"it's colder than it should be"—hangs in the air and in the reader's mind. One can almost hear Godwin's voice leaking through Barton's in this instance—the whole story, he seems to be saying, is colder than it should be; Marilyn ought not have to die, because in reality civilization is not so cold as that. Yet the cold story was what Campbell wanted, and so the cold story is what Godwin finally wrote.

It is not long before the coldness gets to Marilyn further—and is moreover passed back to the person who embodies it. When Marilyn begins her last conversation with her brother, she leans over Barton, "her hand resting small and cold on his shoulder." Soon the "cold little hand" grips his shoulder tighter, and then, in contrast to the chill Marilyn is passing back to Barton, a "warm and wet" tear drips on his wrist, emphasizing the life that yet remains in her. When Gerry's voice at last fades out, the mention of "the cold metal of the communicator" stresses the absence of Gerry's physical self as well as now his voice.

Splashes of color adorn the last dozen paragraphs of the story. Earlier Marilyn mentioned a pet kitten, Flossy, that was run over and replaced with another by her loving brother. It is perhaps significant that the replacement kitten was white, because this links the kitten with Marilyn and now also evokes the idea of a spirit or ghost—the replacement kitten being understood as Flossy come back from the dead. Marilyn mentions the kitten again in her last effusion to Gerry, when she also imagines herself as becoming "one of those gold-winged larks" living on Woden. Thus the color gold makes a single appearance, as if suggesting a halo or golden wings for the white-adorned, angelic Marilyn.

When the "blue-eyed girl in gypsy sandals," as she was earlier described, finally steps toward the air lock, the reader is given one last glimpse of her, including the "brown curls," the "white sandals," and, mentioned for the first time, the "little lights of blue and red and crystal" sparkling on her buckles. Once again, Godwin could have chosen any color for these last details, and one would not have been surprised to find some new colors thrown in, like orange, yellow, or green; of those, only green has been mentioned even once, as the color of the midges that infected the men on Woden with fever. Yet instead of using any of these colors, Godwin returns to those that have most strongly characterized Marilyn thus far: blue like her eyes, red like her lips, and a crystal color that one imagines as effectively white, like

her stricken face and sandals. The American reader, of course, will have an immediate association with the colors red, white, and blue, namely, the flag. There can be little question that, however much the story might diminish Marilyn's stature by referring to her as "the pale girl," a "little child," "a frightened and bewildered child," she is the very life of the story, the character with whom male and female readers alike will develop a sympathetic attachment. And in the American magazine in which a largely American readership first met her, the colors associated with Marilyn make the reader's identification with her all the stronger.

When Marilyn is gone, the reader is left once again with only Barton—the one who pulled the black and red levers to send her flying out of the airlock, red in this case being associated not with lifeblood but with alarm and danger. On some level, at least, Barton is satisfied that the white hand of the temperature gauge—like the hand of death, really—has returned to zero, that the cold equation has been balanced by the girl's death. The reader may be somewhat appalled to find that the narration, so closely allied with Barton's thoughts by this point in the story, refers to the girl's corpse as "something shapeless and ugly" floating through space, as if to make her death easier for Barton to bear by dehumanizing what remains of her.

In his preface to *The Cold Equations & Other Stories*, Barry Malzberg mentions the debate over the title story carried out in the *New York Review of Science Fiction*, a publication he makes light of by referring to it as "intellectually ambitious (or simply pretentious; you decide)." He proceeds to somewhat dismissively reel off the various and contradictory ideological stances attributed by commentators to the story, which "was anatomized as anti-feminist, proto-feminist, hard-edged realism, squishy fantasy for the self-deluded, misogynistic past routine pathology, crypto-fascist, etc." By the time one reaches the last item in that list, one hardly takes it seriously. And yet Godwin may have had fascism in the back of his mind in finalizing the story, the form of which had been dictated by his imperious editor. Campbell himself, in an essay published in 1953, just a year before the story, indicated that the fascism so tragically confronted in World War II had not yet subsided from the public mind. In the essay, he discusses how science fiction revolves around change, the executors of which can never be sure is for the best until afterward. He points out that while George Washington brought about change after consulting with a group of learned men who brought all possible viewpoints to the table, Hitler instead consulted a group he had formed "by selecting those who agreed with him, and destroying those who did not." This assessment does not seem far removed from the men in Godwin's story who all agree that Marilyn must die, even though she wishes otherwise.

The association may yet seem remote, but one might consider not just Hitler's designs but also the manner in which so many Germans were persuaded to go along with those designs. As is well known, he used his vigorous and persuasive manner of speech to demonize the Jewish people, as well as other minorities. He managed to convince his Aryan followers that Jews were by nature a constant threat to German society that could only be dealt with through a "final solution" of genocide. Over and over historians have wondered how so many ordinary Germans could have gone along with such a horrific plan, and one of the most significant answers is that they were permitted to feel absolved of responsibility. All up through the military ranks, they were only following orders, which were based on laws about treatment of Jews that had been passed and effectively written in stone: all Jews are to be identified; all Jews are to be sent to concentration camps; and so forth.

In "The Cold Equations"—the mere mention of equations of course hinting at an end "solution"—the men outfitted in gray (the color of Nazi officers' uniforms) likewise absolve themselves of responsibility by insisting that they are merely following the order of the law, which itself is founded in the physical facts concerning transport. If anything, it would seem, Godwin's story is not crypto-fascist but perhaps rather crypto-antifascist. In the end, Godwin is not standing alongside Barton nodding his head at the proper obedience of laws but is standing alongside the reader with his mouth hanging open wondering how such a preventable tragedy could have occurred. It is Marilyn, after all, who gets the last word, an echo not only of her own remarks while alive but of the closing thoughts of all the millions who have died unjustly: "I didn't do anything to die for—I didn't do anything—"

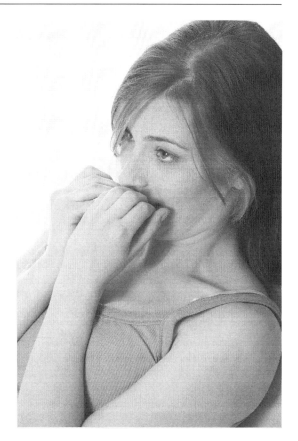

The girl is terrified, but she becomes resigned to her fate. (© Piotr Marcinski | Shutterstock.com)

Source: Michael Allen Holmes, Critical Essay on "The Cold Equations," in *Short Stories for Students*, Gale, Cengage Learning, 2015.

SOURCES

Baxter, Stephen, "The Cold Equations: Extraterrestrial Liberty in Science Fiction," Institute of Physics website, February 8, 2013, http://www.iop.org/activity/branches/yorkshire_north_east/ne/news/13/file_61955.pdf (accessed February 28, 2014).

Benford, Gregory, "Is There a Technological Fix for the Human Condition?," in *Hard Science Fiction*, Southern Illinois University Press, 1986, pp. 82–98.

Brotherton, Mike, "The Cold Legacies," in *Lightspeed*, July 2011, http://www.lightspeedmagazine.com/nonfiction/the-cold-legacies/ (accessed February 28, 2014).

Campbell, John W., Jr., "The Place of Science Fiction," in *Modern Science Fiction: Its Meaning and Its Future*, edited by Reginald Bretnor, Advent Publishers, 1979, pp. 3–22.

Clute, John, "Godwin, Tom," in *The Encyclopedia of Science Fiction*, edited by John Clute and Peter Nicholls, St. Martin's Press, 1993, p. 504.

———, "Godwin, Tom," *The Encyclopedia of Science Fiction*, 3rd ed., edited by John Clute and David Langford, SFE, November 6, 2013, http://www.sf-encyclopedia.com/entry/godwin_tom (accessed February 28, 2014).

D'Ammassa, Don, "'The Cold Equations': Tom Godwin," in *Encyclopedia of Science Fiction*, Facts on File, 2005, pp. 89–90.

Disch, Thomas M., *The Dreams Our Stuff Is Made Of: How Science Fiction Conquered the World*, Free Press, 1998, pp. 32–77, 115–17.

Drake, Dave, "Sometimes It All Just Works," Afterword to *The Cold Equations & Other Stories*, edited by Eric Flint, Baen Books, 2003, http://worldtracker.org/media/library/English%20Literature/G/Godwin,%20Tom/Tom%20Godwin%20-%20The%20Cold%20Equations.pdf (accessed February 27, 2014).

Godwin, Tom, "The Cold Equations," in *The Cold Equations & Other Stories*, edited by Eric Flint, Baen Books, 2003, http://worldtracker.org/media/library/English%20Literature/G/Godwin,%20Tom/Tom%20Godwin%20-%20The%20Cold%20Equations.pdf (accessed February 26, 2014).

Gunn, James, "The Readers of Hard Science Fiction," in *Hard Science Fiction*, Southern Illinois University Press, 1986, pp. 70–81.

Huntington, John, "Hard-Core Science Fiction and the Illusion of Science," in *Hard Science Fiction*, Southern Illinois University Press, 1986, pp. 45–57.

———, "'Not Earth's Feeble Stars': Thoughts on John W. Campbell Jr.'s Editorship," in *Science Fiction and Market Realities*, edited by Gary Westfahl, George E. Slusser, and Eric S. Rabkin, University of Georgia Press, 1996, pp. 141–50.

Malzberg, Barry, Preface and Afterword to *The Cold Equations & Other Stories*, edited by Eric Flint, Baen Books, 2003, http://worldtracker.org/media/library/English%20Literature/G/Godwin,%20Tom/Tom%20Godwin%20-%20The%20Cold%20Equations.pdf (accessed February 27, 2014).

Slusser, George E., and Eric S. Rabkin, eds., Introduction to *Hard Science Fiction*, Southern Illinois University Press, 1986, pp. vii–xvi.

Wolfe, Gary K., "Frontiers in Space," in *Evaporating Genres: Essays on Fantastic Literature*, Wesleyan University Press, 2011, pp. 121–38.

FURTHER READING

Adams, Douglas, *The Hitchhiker's Guide to the Galaxy*, Pan Books, 1979.

In this novel, perhaps the foremost work of comedic science fiction, Adams employs genre clichés, philosophical jests, and futuristic improvisations to riotous ends. The story takes off when earthling Arthur Dent and his friend Ford Prefect—who turns out to be a well-adapted alien—must consider stowing away aboard a ship that happens near; the punishment would be expulsion into space, which supposedly no one could survive...

Card, Orson Scott, *Ender's Game*, Tor Books, 1985.
This is one of the most admired science-fiction novels in print, about an institute suspended above the Earth where children are trained to be military geniuses. A key question is how the protagonist, Ender, and his peers will be introduced to the idea of sacrificing the lives of those under their command.

Harrison, Harry, ed., *Astounding: John W. Campbell Memorial Anthology*, Random House, 1973.
Shortly after Campbell's death in 1971, Harrison assembled this anthology dedicated to the editor who brought so much to the genre that he is dubbed "the father of science fiction." The authors include Poul Anderson, Isaac Asimov, L. Sprague de Camp, and Theodore R. Cogswell.

Rinpoche, Anyen, *Dying with Confidence: A Tibetan Buddhist Guide to Preparing for Death*, translated by Allison Graboski, Wisdom Publications, 2010.
A wide variety of books discuss how to approach one's inevitable death, with many in Western markets taking Christian or psychological angles. Rinpoche's book relates the Tibetan Buddhist perspective on the transition, which one can draw on to enhance one's focus on the present.

SUGGESTED SEARCH TERMS

Tom Godwin AND The Cold Equations

The Cold Equations AND controversy

The Cold Equations AND response

hard science fiction OR hard-core science fiction

The Cold Equations AND hard science fiction

The Cold Equations AND adaptation

The Cold Equations AND John W. Campbell Jr.

Tom Godwin AND John W. Campbell Jr.

John W. Campbell Jr. AND Astounding

science fiction magazines

Dance in America

LORRIE MOORE

1993

"Dance in America" tells the story of a witty, urbane dance instructor who is sent to a rural town to teach the residents about modern dance. While there she visits with an old friend, his wife, and their son, Eugene, a precocious boy who is dying of cystic fibrosis. Over the course of the evening, as old times are discussed and Eugene's parents let him exercise his quirky ways, the narrator learns that she actually does believe in the true power of dance in ways she had previously lectured about without actually feeling in her heart.

Lorrie Moore, the story's author, has long been considered one of America's funniest fiction writers, having come to international prominence with her debut short-story collection, *Self-Help*, in 1985. "Dance in America" comes from her third collection, *Birds of America*, published in 1998. The pieces in this collection retain Moore's distinctive humor but take the reader into darker, though never pessimistic, territory. "Dance in America" may center around a dying boy, but Moore never plays the situation for mere pathos; instead, Eugene, with the death sentence that hangs over him, serves as a reminder that people are indeed spiritual beings, but their spirits are welded to physical bodies that can weaken and fail but can also rise up, push against their limitations, and dance.

Like many of Moore's short stories, "Dance in America" was originally published in the *New*

Moore in 2009 on the porch of her Madison, Wisconsin home (© *Chicago Tribune / McClatchy-Tribune / Getty Images*)

Yorker, in the issue of June 28, 1993. *Birds of America*, the collection it was first included in, is still in print, and the story also appears in the anthology *More Stories We Tell: The Best Contemporary Short Stories by North American Women* (2004).

AUTHOR BIOGRAPHY

Marie Lorena Moore was born on January 13, 1957, in Glens Falls, New York. Her father was an insurance executive who wrote short fiction while in college, and her mother, trained as a nurse, was a housewife who had once considered being a journalist. Moore was a good student, earning a Regents Scholarship from her high school. As a college student at St. Lawrence University, in Canton, New York, she achieved national prominence in 1976 when, just nineteen years old, she won *Seventeen* magazine's annual fiction award for her short story "Raspberries." At St. Lawrence she edited the school's literary journal and won the Paul L.

Wolf Memorial Prize for Literature. After graduating summa cum laude in English in 1978, she moved to New York City for a while, where she worked as a paralegal, and then enrolled in Cornell University, pursuing her master of fine arts degree.

Moore was twenty-eight in 1985 when her first collection of short stories, *Self-Help*, was published. Most of the stories in that book were taken from her master's thesis at Cornell. By then she was teaching creative writing at the University of Wisconsin, where she continued to teach off and on for the following decade, often splitting her time between rural Wisconsin and New York City.

Self-Help won Moore rave reviews and made her one of the most talked-about young writers of her generation. She published a novel in 1986, *Anagrams*—which, laden with technique and not realistic, was not well accepted by critics—and another novel, *Who Will Run the Frog Hospital?*, in 1994. Her second short-story collection, *Like Life*, in 1990, established her as a master of short fiction and cemented her place in American literature. "Dance in America" was first published in 1993 in the *New Yorker*, an influential magazine that Moore has regularly written for throughout most of her life. The story was included in the collection *Birds of America* in 1998. In 2008 she published *The Collected Stories*. Her novel *A Gate at the Stairs* was published in 2009.

In 2013 Moore left the University of Wisconsin, where she had taught since the early 1980s, to take a position at Vanderbilt University, in Nashville, Tennessee. In 2014 Moore's short-story collection *Bark* was published. It was her first original collection since *Birds of America*, sixteen years earlier.

PLOT SUMMARY

"Dance in America" begins with its narrator telling readers about some of the ways in which she explains dance to children. She is an instructor from an unspecified urban area who has gotten a grant to go to schools in the rural Pennsylvania Dutch country to talk to students there about dance. She suggests that she does not really believe her noble sentiments about dance being a triumph over death—she has only just made them up—but eventually the strong authority in her voice makes her believe her own words. There is some sense of the reality behind her own made-up assertions. She feels the spirituality of the art. When she speaks to local audiences, people ask her naive questions, insinuating that dance is overly sexual or too feminine. She is sarcastic when explaining their attitudes to the reader, in ways that she may not be when talking to the unimpressed and slightly hostile parents. She reflects on how sorry her life has become.

Her stay in rural Pennsylvania has only one day to go, but she cannot stand staying at the local Quality Inn anymore, unable to sleep because of the noise of people performing karaoke downstairs in the lounge. So she leaves the motel to stay at the home of Cal, a friend she knew long ago in school; his wife, Simone, a former French diplomat; and their son, Eugene, who is dying of cystic fibrosis.

The rest of the story concerns events at Cal and Simone's house that night. It is described as a former fraternity house near the school where Cal, a professor of anthropology, teaches. The

MEDIA ADAPTATIONS

- In 2004, Recording for the Blind and Dyslexic included "Dance in America" in their audio recording of *More Stories We Tell: The Best Contemporary Short Stories by North American Women*. The anthology, edited by Wendy Martin, was also published in 2004.

narrator and Cal walk his dog together and talk about the house. They discuss how he came to own such a huge place and why he has never been able to renovate it, leaving in place evidence of the destructive, sex-obsessed boys who once lived there. Cal confesses that when he and the narrator knew each other, twelve years earlier, he was only pretending to be interested in dance because she liked it, as he did not ever really understand it. Now that his son is sick, he would rather that the government money given to artists be used for scientific grants, to help find cures for diseases like cystic fibrosis. He has some hope, though not much, that a cure can be discovered before Eugene dies of the disease. The narrator notices that the planet Venus, in the evening sky, hovers near the moon like on the flag of Turkey, and she points the view out to Cal. He sees the Turkish flag in it too, suggesting that these two old friends have maintained a similar view of the world, despite their different life experiences.

When they return from walking the dog, seven-year-old Eugene comes to greet them. He has painted his face with Merthiolate (which is a brand of the antiseptic thimerosal). Cal goes to the kitchen to help Simone prepare dinner, and the narrator takes Eugene into the living room to show him a video of the dance program she orchestrated with the fourth graders at his school. She explains the process that went into making up this dance: she had the children make masks to represent imaginative creatures, and then she put on a popular song—"This Is It," by Kenny Loggins. Eugene recognizes several of the children on the tape: they are older than him, and he looks up to them. When they are called to dinner, Eugene hurries to the table, but before eating he has to swallow what the narrator describes as "a goblet of pills."

The dinner conversation focuses mostly on adult themes. Cal, drawing from his field of anthropology, mentions the fact that the basic design of bread has probably not changed since modern man began walking the earth, over some forty-five thousand years. That leads to the subject of parties, and Simone sarcastically mentions the parties she used to attend in Soda Springs, Idaho, where she lived with her ex-husband. When the narrator expresses surprise that she was previously married, Simone dismissively says that the marriage only lasted for six months, and that she thinks that her ex-husband eventually committed suicide. Although they are discussing serious adult topics, Eugene participates in the conversation with them.

When Simone asks the narrator about her life, she explains that she had a boyfriend, Patrick, but that they broke up. This is news to Cal. Eugene, whom the narrator refers to at this point as "the amazing Eugene" because of his unknowing perception, suggests that Cal had long imagined the narrator and Patrick would break up so that Cal himself could marry her; the adults in the room all laugh, loudly, and then become awkward.

Simone compares relationships to a time when they tried to chase raccoons out of their chimney by starting a fire in the fireplace, which caused the raccoons to run loose throughout the living room with their fur aflame. "Love affairs are like that," she tells them. "They all are like that." The narrator does not get the point of her story.

Finishing dinner and the fruit and tea that come after takes until ten o'clock. It is Eugene's bedtime. Eugene and his family ritualistically dance for a while at bedtime until he is tired and falls asleep. For the music this night, the narrator looks through Cal and Simone's recordings with a critical distaste for the ones she sees until she comes across a Kenny Loggins album with the song that she had the older children dance to at her recital, "This Is It." She suggests dancing to this, and Eugene enthusiastically agrees.

All four of them—Eugene, the narrator, Cal, and Simone—dance to the music. When Eugene becomes tired and sits down on the couch, the narrator goes to him. In this moment, she understands the true meaning of dance. She can see, the reader is led to assume (though she speaks only in a broader, collective sense), how dancing has helped Eugene, with his fragile, sick body, rise beyond his limitations and all the limitations of the world, if only for a short while.

She thinks of her old boyfriend Patrick, too. She now concludes, through her understanding of the way that dance combines one's spirit with one's body, that Patrick was wrong when he characterized her as selfish. Dance is a form of giving oneself to the world, she feels, so a person dancing is not selfish. She brings Eugene back from the couch, to dance again, and the four of them are dancing with enthusiasm while the singer is singing "This is it!" as the story comes to an end.

CHARACTERS

Cal

Cal is an anthropology teacher at a college in rural Pennsylvania. He and the narrator knew each other in New York twelve years earlier, after they were out of graduate school, but they have not kept in touch. They have not seen each other since Cal left the New York area to study in Belgium. The story does not definitively answer whether they were romantically involved back then, but Cal's wife, Simone, does suggest this. Twelve years earlier, Cal and the narrator's relationship was so close that he pretended to understand dance, even though he did not. This is echoed in the present when he momentarily pretends to have believed that she and her boyfriend Patrick would never break up, knowing that it is something she would want to hear, but soon confesses that he did not really think she and Patrick would stay together.

Now that he has a son with a serious illness, Cal does not even pretend to care for the arts. He apologetically tells the narrator that, even though her business is dance, he wishes that all of the government grants would go to science, not art, so that Eugene's cystic fibrosis might be cured while he is still alive. He truly loves and admires his son.

Cal's relationship with Simone seems solid. They work together to care for Eugene in his illness. They cook dinner together. Although he and the narrator clearly have similar views of the world and get along well, Cal never seems to be unhappy with his family situation, other than in his concern for Eugene's health.

Eugene

The seven-year-old son of Cal and Simone, Eugene is a doomed boy: he is dying of cystic fibrosis. His condition has made his body weak, but his parents do what they can to encourage his imagination. They dance with him every night. They allow him to humor himself and others by painting his face with Merthiolate. His father's affection runs much deeper than the substantial facts that Eugene is his son and is sick: as Cal explains to the narrator, "It's not just that Eugene's great.... It's not just the precocity or that he's the only child I'll ever have. It's also that he's such a good person. He accepts things. He's very good at understanding everything."

Because of Eugene's intelligence, his parents are very open with him: for instance, when discussing Simone's first husband, who reportedly committed suicide, they do not try to hide the facts or talk down to him. Still, he shows a childish enthusiasm when he recognizes older children from his school in the video of the narrator's dance performance, clearly looking up to the older children in admiration.

Although Eugene is lively and energetic in this story, his inevitable death hangs over everything that goes on in the tale.

The Narrator

Throughout "Dance in America," the first-person narrator is never referred to by name. She is a dance instructor who seems to be generally pleased with her chosen profession, even though it leads her into situations like the current one, which she views with a sense of world-weariness. Her job has taken her to rural Pennsylvania, and she is paid to work with schoolchildren, engaging their interest in dance. While she seems to enjoy the children and the activities she makes up to spur their imaginations, she does not think much of the people who live out in the countryside. She dislikes their culture, from the sexist questions people ask to the karaoke blaring in the bar in her hotel. As she says when reflecting on her situation, "I've grown tired. I burned down my life for a few good pieces, and now this."

Although she does not have much affection for the people of Pennsylvania Dutch country, she does like her old friend Cal and his family, who have invited her to spend her last night in the area at their house. She shares a sense of humor with Cal and his wife, Simone, and she has an affectionate bond with their seven-year-old son Eugene. As Cal and Simone are preparing dinner, she stays with Eugene: she is giving her presentation about dance at his school the next day, and he is interested in the older kids she will be working with. As it turns out, while dance is the narrator's field of specialty, there is a family tradition of dancing as Eugene is being prepared for bedtime.

Hidden in the background of the narrator's life is the story of her breakup with Patrick, her former boyfriend. When his name comes up during dinner, she only mentions that she has broken up with him, without elaborating. At the end of the story, though, she thinks of him and how she would explain to him that dancing is a way of relating to the world beyond herself—implying that he accused her of being too self-involved, and that his accusations hurt her, leading her to be sarcastic as a means of self-defense. Dancing with Eugene and his family, she has a revelation about the significance of her chosen profession and the ways in which it can help people quit focusing on their physical limitations. She knows that, despite what Patrick said, the idea that she is self-involved simply is not true.

Patrick

Patrick is the narrator's former boyfriend. He does not appear in the story, but she thinks of him and of their breakup. Their relationship appears to have ended on a bitter note: Patrick left her because he thought that she was selfish, and when she was concerned about being isolated in a house out by a lake he tried to insult her by suggesting that she might rent the house, as she relates, "to a nice lesbian couple like myself." In the end, when she is thinking about how dancing has helped Eugene get beyond his illness, which leads her to recognize the transcendence of dance, she thinks of Patrick again, and she knows that she does not have to take seriously his suggestion that she only thinks of herself.

Simone

Simone is a powerful woman: she is an ex-diplomat for the French government to Belgium and to Japan. She experienced the death of her sister when she was young, which prepared her for dealing with the inevitable death of her son.

Having married Cal and borne a son with him, she has given up her career to live in rural Pennsylvania. She paints satirical oil paintings and takes a sharp, critical view of the local people, suggesting that she feels isolated outside of the small domestic circle of her husband and her son.

She was married previously, but only for six months. She did not attempt to keep in touch with her former husband, but she reports that he has committed suicide. She likens all love affairs to the time raccoons in their chimney caught on fire and ran around the house with flames in their fur, a simile that perplexes the narrator with its bleak implications about human nature. The narrator seems to like Simone, even though, or perhaps because, she sees in the other woman a reflection of her own critical, sarcastic view of the world.

THEMES

Mortality

In "Dance in America," the narrator stays with a family that has a loving home, but hanging over everything they do, unspoken, is the awareness that Eugene is likely to die while still just a child. Cal struggles to take an optimistic view of things when he is explaining his situation to the narrator; as he lists the things about Eugene he admires, his frustration that research will eventually cure cystic fibrosis, just not soon enough, shows through. This frustration is mirrored in the house they live in: it was a mess when they bought it, and Cal intended to fix its many problems, but he has not been able to summon the strength or the mental focus to do so. Eugene's mother, Simone, is a little more prepared to deal with her son's mortality because of her naturally dour worldview and her experience with the death of her sister when she was young. Readers can see her cool, factual approach to life in the way that Simone offhandedly mentions her ex-husband's supposed suicide: her emotional association with

the death of someone she presumably once loved is remote, as if he were never a part of her life. She does show her love for her son, but she also shows herself able to face his inevitable death head on.

Coming into this situation, the narrator seems at first to be distracted by Eugene's situation. By the end of the story, though, she is able to put aside worrying about him. When he has to step away from the family dance, she goes to him to encourage him to rejoin the group instead of treating him as if he were fragile. She eventually forgets her promise to stop by his classroom and wave to him when she visits the school the next day: although this can seem an insult to Eugene, it is a sign that the narrator is able to accept him as a normal part of her life instead of being always conscious of his impending death.

Love

This story is concerned with love in its many varied forms. The love that Cal and Simone have for their son is clear throughout. The narrator comes to love Eugene too, as she spends time with him. She is a teacher, and she knows how to talk to him on his level and how to let him make his own choices, and he sticks near her as a result.

Things are a little more complex regarding adult relations. Simone's former husband, who is never even given a name, is dismissed callously, as Simone shows that whether he has killed himself or not makes no difference to her. The narrator's relationship with her ex-boyfriend, Patrick, is kept obscure from readers, but they can deduce that any love the two might have had for each other ended in a flurry of insults and accusations.

The relationship between the narrator and Cal is also obscure. She refers to him constantly as her friend, and they have fallen so far out of touch over the years that he is not aware of her breakup with Patrick. On the other hand, he once cared so much about her that he pretended to like dance, even though he never really did like or understand it. When Eugene mentions that Cal and the narrator could be married, all of the adults nervously hide their faces, indicating that their current friendship may be a relic that remains of a former love relationship.

TOPICS FOR FURTHER STUDY

- As a group, make masks of the characters in the story. Devise a dance for each character and perform it, accompanied by an explanation of why that character would make the dance moves you assign her or him.

- Prepare a report showing how treatment for cystic fibrosis has changed between 1993, when this story was first published in the *New Yorker*, and today.

- Paint some pictures that you think might resemble the ones that the story describes Simone painting. In a class presentation, explain what elements, besides the missing hands, make your figures seem like they reflect Simone's vision of the world, supporting your view with examples from the story.

- The narrator of this story has probably been given her two-week mission as a "Dancer in the Schools" by some arts council or councils. Use the Internet to research arts grants in your area to see what it would take to bring a visiting dance artist to your school. Find out answers to such questions as: Who could apply for such a position? Who would pay them? How much would they make for a two-week stint? Write your findings up in a report.

- How do you think this story would be different if it had a different cultural setting? Using your knowledge and experience of ethnic cultures in America, explain how you think a visiting dance instructor would be accepted in a predominantly Latino, Middle Eastern, Asian, African American, or Native American culture. Rewrite the story with the narrator responding to the new environment you have described.

- Write a short story that shows the narrator and Cal in their post-graduate-school years, taking cues from this story for the details about what their lives would have been like.

- Do you think it is appropriate for Eugene's parents to discuss the story about the flaming raccoons in front of him, or would drawing attention to such a gruesome event only feed a child's fears? Research what child psychologists say about this subject, and divide your class into separate sides to debate the various positions.

- Listen to the Kenny Loggins song "This Is It," which in 1981 won the Grammy Award for Best Pop Vocal Performance, Male. In a writing exercise, explain the elements of the lyrics and music that make this a good song for the climactic moment of "Dance in America." Nominate a contemporary song that you think would be better, or nearly as good, for this function in the story, again explaining how the power of the lyrics and music serve the story's meaning.

- At websites such as www.cfvoice.com, you can see videos of teens and young adults who are living active lifestyles with cystic fibrosis. Watch some of the videos and keep a record of what you learn from them about how people with cystic fibrosis cope. Write a blog post explaining how you think Eugene will continue to cope with having cystic fibrosis, comparing him to one of the characters in one of the videos who you think is most like him.

- In Sarah Rubin's 2012 young-adult novel *Someday Dancer*, the protagonist, Casey, goes to New York in 1959 to train as a ballet dancer, only to become entranced by the world of modern dance that was emerging at the time. Dance greats Martha Graham and George Balanchine appear as characters. After reading that book, write a letter from Casey to the narrator of "Dance in America," giving advice about how to bring modern dance to rural America.

Moore's story is set in Pennsylvania Dutch country. (© *John Wollwerth | Shutterstock.com*)

Art and Society

The way the narrator is received by the rural people she lectures in the schools shows how the arts in general are often viewed in a society that is focused on practical matters. People call her dances insulting things like "whorish" and "feministic"—the fact that the latter is not even a real word serves as an indicator of the level of literacy these people have. The dances the narrator devises seem relatively tame, but to people who are not used to the arts, any degree of self-expression can seem weird and excessively self-important.

The rift between the common view and the artistic view builds from the other direction as well. Just as members of the community eye the narrator suspiciously, she is condescending toward their culture too. She makes fun of the songs they sing in the hotel's karaoke bar and the creamed chicken and waffles that the hotel advertises for its restaurant. As an artist, she has refined sensibilities, and she allows that to affect her view of the relatively art-free society her job has brought her to.

Transcendence

The troubles brought up throughout the story concerning Eugene's physical condition and the twisted histories of the narrator, Cal, and Simone are resolved by the dance at the end. In the final scene, the story's characters find themselves able to forget their fears and their obsessions. Even though Eugene is weakened with illness, he is able to come back into the group and dance again after sitting out a few moments: the thrill of participating in the dance is more compelling for him than the exhaustion that overtook him.

The narrator's sweeping prose in the final paragraphs explains why dance is able to help them all overcome their problems. They stop thinking when they are moving. They offer themselves up, and in doing so, they feel a religious feeling. They are transcendent, going to a place beyond any place their poor, limited bodies can take them, elevated up to a higher plane of existence for as long as they dance.

STYLE

First-Person Narrator

"Dance in America" is presented in the first person, with the narrator, a character in the story, relating the events and perspectives that she has experienced. Because this narrative stance is so close to her consciousness, her name is never revealed: she does not think of herself by name, and the direct quotes from other people never include any instances where people state her name. This helps keep readers inside of her head, looking at the world she sees, not at her.

The use of the first-person narrator serves to withhold information from readers. The narrator does not dwell upon her past, so facts from her past—regarding, for instance, the nature of her relationship with Cal when they lived in New York—are not revealed. Her relationship with Patrick is revealed in increments throughout the story because her thoughts keep going back to him once Cal has brought him up. This mirrors the way an individual's mind would naturally remember something, and it also serves to help the author, Moore, build the story toward the character's climactic scene. When the narrator finds freedom in dance, the hidden background about Patrick becomes more important, because it is then that she thinks of how Patrick's insults kept her down.

Present Tense

This is not a very active story. Before the dance scene at the end, most of the action consists of walking the dog, preparing and eating dinner, and much talking. Moore makes the story more immediate, more engaging, by relating the events in the present tense. Instead of feeling like they are viewing a situation that happened long ago, with its results already settled in the narrator's mind, readers feel like they are watching events unfold before their eyes. Since it is happening in the present tense, there is still the strong possibility that the narrator can be surprised, and that prospect of surprise helps to draw readers in, making them more invested in what goes on.

Rural Setting

The narrator spends the beginning of the story establishing that the events take place in a rural setting, where artistic dance is treated with suspicion. She relates scattered parts of conversations between herself and the local people, and she mentions a few aspects of her motel that she finds intolerable.

Most of the story takes place in Cal and Simone's house. This is the second setting that is established vividly at first and then, once established, is mostly forgotten for the rest of the story. They live in an old, ruined fraternity house which they have never managed the time or energy to refurbish. It shows signs of the kind of immature obsession with sexuality that is usually associated with young adults, which is something, ironically, that Eugene will never live to know. The house is clearly too big for three people, which echoes in the minds of readers who take care to remember the setting as they imagine the events of the story.

HISTORICAL CONTEXT

Pennsylvania Dutch Country

When the narrator of this story says that she is in Pennsylvania Dutch country, she is referring to an area of eastern Pennsylvania that has a particular history that links it more strongly to rural American life than other, similar areas of the state and country. In the early sixteenth century, when Europe was changed by the Protestant Reformation, some religions broke away from the mainstream. The members of the Anabaptist movement, for instance, rejected both Catholic and Protestant beliefs. A Catholic priest from Holland named Menno Simons left the church in 1536 and became an Anabaptist; followers of his teachings came to refer to themselves as Mennonites. In 1693 Jacob Amman, a bishop from Switzerland, led a group that split from the Mennonites, later to use Amman's name and become known as the Amish. Despite their differences, the Amish and the Mennonites have remained close over the centuries.

In the early 1700s, a great number of followers of both communities, along with members of a third Anabaptist movement, the Church of the Brethren, founded in Germany, moved to America for the promise of religious freedom that could not be found in Europe. William Penn, a Quaker, founded the colony of Pennsylvania on the basis of religious tolerance, which Penn referred to as a "holy experiment."

COMPARE & CONTRAST

- **1993:** A man in the throes of an emotional breakup, like the narrator's ex-boyfriend Patrick, could use the accusation of a woman being a lesbian in an attempt to insult her.

  Today: Even many conservative members of modern society find nothing shameful about sexual orientation, so the power of such an accusation often fails as an insult.

- **1993:** Even if they live in a town with several colleges, people in a rural area are considered culturally isolated and therefore intolerant of higher art forms like dance.

  Today: Internet access has allowed many people in isolated areas to have at least a passing familiarity with things like modern dance.

- **1993:** A motel that is part of a chain might advertise an embarrassing local favorite food on its restaurant menu.

  Today: People trained in the hospitality industry understand that their target audiences are not the people in the town they are in but the people who come from the world outside to stay in their motel.

- **1993:** Some treatments exist to help people cope with the effects of cystic fibrosis, but there is nothing to stop the inevitable destruction the disease will bring.

  Today: The drug Kalydeco, approved by the US Food and Drug Administration in 2012 for use in people over the age of six, is the first one that addresses the underlying causes of certain types of cystic fibrosis, raising hope that further breakthroughs in research are forthcoming.

- **1993:** To show a dance recital to people who were not there, a person can tape it on a videocassette and put that tape into the machine attached to someone else's television set.

  Today: A seven-year-old boy like Eugene may know how to look up the narrator's dance display on Facebook without her having to present it to him. If she has not posted the video online, she would probably show it to him on her phone.

- **1993:** During the country's most recent economic boom, people look to the seemingly unlimited resources of the government to fund research for something as important as a debilitating, terminal genetic disease.

  Today: Funding for science has been drastically reduced in America, leaving organizations like the Cystic Fibrosis Foundation to try to pull together partnerships with private corporations to study diseases and their possible cures.

While other areas of the country have seen tremendous change through modernization over the course of the past three centuries, the Amish, Mennonite, and Brethren communities of rural Pennsylvania have held fast to their beliefs in following simple practices. The most conspicuous among these are the Amish, who, with their focus on personal humility, try to keep their community free of the contamination of the outside world. In general they follow simple practices that exclude the use of machinery and the modern devices that have come from motor-driven machines. Travelers to Amish communities will often pass by horse-drawn buggies on the highways and see people in simple, dark clothes. By comparison, the Mennonites and Brethren have become more acculturated to the modern world, though their religions still emphasize simplicity. There are many Amish communities in the United States, but the one in Pennsylvania is by far the largest, with over thirty thousand members

Cal's house is in disrepair, so he has to go up to the attic to get the pots and pans, which are used to catch water leaking through the roof. (© *Asier Romero | Shutterstock.com*)

in the mid-2010s, having doubled its size during the previous two decades.

Moore does not speak of the people in Pennsylvania Dutch country in terms of their religious beliefs. But from what she does say it is clear that the conservative views of these communities, which are so prevalent in that area, have a strong effect on the attitudes of the locals in the town where this story is set, whether they are from any of these religions or not.

Literary Fiction

The term "literary fiction" is a difficult one because it implies that fiction not covered by the term is substandard; therefore, many writers try to avoid this label, out of modesty. Literary fiction is identifiable, though, and that makes it a valid category to talk about.

The best way to define literary fiction is by discussing what it is not. Literary fiction is distinct from genre fiction, which is fiction that falls into categories and follows prearranged patterns, such as in horror or detective fiction. While the novels and stories in a given genre are expected to have certain elements that their

readers are familiar with, literary fiction focuses on the new over the familiar. Readers read genre fiction to be entertained, and often they view this as being separate from thinking, giving cultural purists another reason to think more highly of literary fiction. Readers read literary fiction to be challenged.

The subject matter of genre fiction gives it its identity. A vampire story, obviously, is about vampires, and a western is about life in the American West. In literary fiction, the subject is life in the familiar world and the struggle to understand it. Some writers describe this distinction as one style (genre) representing an escape from reality and the other (literary) an escape *into* reality.

Other elements that help distinguish literary fiction from genre fiction are a voice that is unique and fitted to the story, and an emphasis on character development. In each case, the writer of literary fiction is trying to create something that has not been seen before, even in other examples of literary fiction. The differences do not have to be glaring and obvious, which is why fiction that is overly creative, imagining new types of humans living in unknown worlds, is not necessarily considered as original as a work that describes the life of a common person with great specificity.

Moore is a literary fiction writer. Her stories are about characters who find out more about themselves by interacting with the world around them. She publishes in literary magazines sponsored by colleges and universities and in national general-interest magazines like the *New Yorker*. Her works are nominated for awards like the PEN/Faulkner Award, one of the nation's highest honors for literary fiction. Although some top-name literary writers have written genre works, by the late twentieth century literary fiction had become fairly synonymous with the fiction that is taught and discussed in schools.

CRITICAL OVERVIEW

Moore was a literary success early in life, winning *Seventeen* magazine's short-story competition before she was even twenty years old. In college she began publishing in major literary journals. As Alison Kelly puts it in *Understanding Lorrie Moore*, a book-length study of her work, "With the appearance of [her first book, the short-story collection] *Self-Help* in 1985, Moore's foothold in American letters was secured." A review in *Library Journal* that was published when *Self-Help* came out drew comparisons between the young writer and established phenom J. D. Salinger, who took an earlier generation by storm: "This collection heralds a new voice as distinctive and humane as Salinger's own," M. Soete wrote, capturing the general mood of most critics of the time, though some found Moore's tendency toward humor to be a reason to take her less seriously as an artist.

By the time "Dance in America" was published in Moore's third short-story collection, *Birds of America*, Moore was widely recognized as a fixture in the American literary scene. Her stories were frequently reprinted in anthologies used in schools, and her works gained the attention of both literary and commercial publications. For instance, David Eggers, known in literary circles as Dave Eggers, a prominent author and publisher, reviewed *Birds of America* in *Esquire* magazine, noting that it is "Moore's third collection of short stories and by far her

best. She's always written beautifully, flawlessly, carefully, with a trademark gift for the darkly comic and the perfectly observed." In this particular book, he notes, "she takes unprecedented stylistic and formal risks." In *Newsweek*, Jeff Giles calls *Birds of America* "a marvelous, fiercely funny book," acknowledging later that "Moore is already regarded as one of her generation's wittiest and shrewdest writers."

Like many critics, Vince Passaro of *Harper's* magazine feels that, as impressive as Moore was when she first appeared on the literary scene, she reached new heights with *Birds of America*. In an article examining the changes in American short fiction over the course of the last two decades of the twentieth century, Passaro praises an early story from *Self-Help* before noting of Moore, "Since then she has grown as a writer, matured in her mastery of style and in her vision." *Birds of America*, he points out, "pushes her fiction further and deeper, in terms of language and emotion, than she has before." Irving Malin sums up his impression of all three books Moore had published by 1999 by noting in the *Review of Contemporary Fiction*, "Her style delights us: it suggests that we can—if only briefly—dance. Moore's latest collection [*Birds of America*] is her best." Moore has always been considered primarily a short-story writer: her novels have not been received with nearly the enthusiasm that her stories have earned for her.

CRITICISM

David Kelly

Kelly is a fiction writer and instructor of literature and creative writing. In the following essay, he uses "Dance in America" to discuss why the dimming of Moore's reputation as a humorous writer over the years has been good for her artistic vision.

Since the very start of her career, people have thought of Lorrie Moore as a funny fiction writer, a writer who could be counted on for a wry twist of words and a snarky look at the weaknesses of humanity. The title of her first novel, *Anagrams*, serves up a clue to the kind of writer the young Moore was: one looking on the world bemusedly, seeing life as a riddle, a game. As the years went by, however, the humor faded. She still knew how to be very

WHAT DO I READ NEXT?

- Critics have called Moore's story "People Like That Are the Only People Here" the most exemplary of the stories in *Birds of America*. This seriocomic story, about a fiction writer with an infant who has a Wilms' tumor, takes place in the pediatric oncology ("peed onk") ward of the hospital. It reflects Moore's own life, and it conveys the serious tone that crept into her work in that collection. It was originally published in the *New Yorker* issue of January 27, 1997.

- In Moore's most recent short-story collection, *Bark*, published in 2014, several of the stories are concerned with literal outer-space aliens. In the story "Paper Losses," for instance, a woman responds with curiosity but not horror to learn that her husband has turned into a space alien.

- Moore's offbeat sense of humor often earns her comparisons to Jane Bowles, who published only one novel, one play, and about ten short stories before dying in her mid-fifties in 1973. The story "Camp Cataract," about two sisters, is considered to be her masterpiece. It was originally published in her collection *Plain Pleasures* in 1966 and then reprinted in the 1978 Bowles collection *My Sister's Hand in Mine*.

- A different perception of dancing from that of the protagonist of this story, who takes a skeptical view of the importance of what she teaches, is shown in Lorri Hewett's 1999 young-adult novel *Dancer*, about a young black woman who has to struggle to be accepted as a ballerina. The hard work she puts in because of her love of dance is complicated, of course, with a love story.

- Julie Klassen's 2013 novel *The Dancing Master* explores one of the strands of this story—that of the dance teacher moving to a rural area and meeting resistance—in a different culture: its protagonist, dance teacher Alec Valcourt, moves from London to Devonshire and finds that the town's ruling elite oppose dance on principle, so he joins forces with the daughter of the town's most prominent citizen to show what physical culture can do.

- In 1983, famed sports writer Frank Deford published a biography about the short life and early death of his daughter, Alexandra, who had cystic fibrosis and only lived to be eight. *Alex, the Life of a Child* has been lauded as one of the most realistic and revealing portraits of the disease in print; Deford went on to chair the Cystic Fibrosis Foundation for nearly two decades.

- Although she presents herself as a shy person, Lorrie Moore has done several interviews about her life and her craft. One of the best is the one done for the *Paris Review*'s "The Art of Fiction" series, which has provided the gold standard for writer interviews for decades. Moore's interview with Elizabeth Gaffney took place in 2000 and was published in the Spring–Summer 2001 edition of the *Paris Review* (No. 158); it can be found online at http://www.theparisreview. org/interviews/510/the-art-of-fiction-no-167-lorrie-moore.

---

funny when she wanted to be, but as she grew as an artist the humor was not the point of her fiction anymore, it was a tool to make the point clearer. Her third collection of short stories, *Birds of America*, was characterized by reviewers as a turn toward seriousness. For instance, its best-known story, "People Like That Are the Only People Here," begins with a mother finding blood in her infant's diaper, which leads doctors to discover that the child has a cancerous tumor. The story "Dance in America," from that same collection, has its narrator bonding with a seven-year-old boy who has cystic fibrosis and is doomed to an early death. When such seriousness overtakes a writer's consciousness—as the writer ages and sees much more of the things that can go wrong in the world—where does the humor go?

"Dance in America" provides a superb example of how a writer can use humor sparingly, so that it does not overwhelm the thoughtfulness of a story. This is a story that has comic foils and witty observations and nearly unbelievable coincidences (such as the parents' naming the boy with a genetic illness *Eugene*, which means, roughly, "good genes"). None of these aspects, however, is allowed to overwhelm the indefinable human emotion that is really what makes a story like this worth reading.

The story certainly starts out funny. The narrator, who is never given a name here and is thus closely associated in readers' minds with the author, cracks wise about herself and her situation. She is sent to Pennsylvania Dutch country, known as the home of a large Amish colony along with several other religions out of the cultural mainstream. It is a locale that blends the cultural cluelessness of isolated country people with the prudery of a close-knit religious sect. There, Moore's character is tasked with teaching, of all things, dance, an art form too abstract for practical people and too sexy for prudes.

In approaching her assignment, the narrator thinks of herself as somewhat of a fake. She makes up all sorts of important-sounding gibberish to tell her temporary students about why dance is important. When she explains that she actually believes her pitch, at this point in the story, it does not suggest that dance is really important to her, but only that she is such a slick wordsmith that she has even convinced herself. She is the trickster, a common figure in folktales and humor, who can bend reality by bending people's perceptions of it.

One element of humor in the early part of this story is the way Moore makes her protagonist the scrappy underdog by setting her against small-minded antagonists. Her comic foils—the people who sing karaoke in motel bars, who eat creamed chicken on waffles, who see dance as "whorish" and dismiss anything a woman does as feminism—are collective and anonymous. She never identifies any one particular person when she talks about the people who oppose her. They

> ULTIMATELY THIS IS NOT THE STORY OF CAL AND SIMONE AND EUGENE, BUT OF THE NARRATOR, AND SHE UNDERGOES A CHANGE BY THE END OF THE STORY THAT IS NOT MORBID BUT IS ALSO NOT FUNNY."

are not humanized, and so it is easy to laugh at their ignorance.

The story has a brief transitional space, from the town of uncultured people to the security of home, as the narrator and her old friend Cal walk his dog, and the narration (*not* the narrator who is in the scene, but the voice that is outside of the scene and telling readers about past events) dwells on the fact that Cal's house used to be a fraternity house. This fact adds a few touches to the story's situation. It gives readers a visual cue to the milieu of the four characters, who will eventually be eating their dinner in a huge space meant for several times their number. It also shows Cal's idealism slipping away from him, as the "fixer-upper" real estate goes un-fixed-up. Mostly, though, it gives the story one last burst of mocking humor, as nobody—not even frat boys themselves—can deny the preposterous things frat boys do. They have written on the walls to immortalize sexual conquests now lost to history. They have written outdated popular slogans on the ceilings.

The story settles down after that, as the mood becomes dominated by Cal's combined hope and fear for his terminally ill son. Cal's mood transfers over to the narrator. They are kindred spirits: when they look at the moon and star in the sky they think of the same thing, the Turkish flag. His wife Simone, though like them, shows herself to not be one of them.

Like them, Simone is on the side of the sophisticates, as opposed to the artless rabble—she has lived and worked in other countries, and she paints garish figures and laughs about identifying them as "the locals." But Simone shows herself to be too aloof, a representative of what unchecked mockery can lead to. She breezily dismisses a man she once married and left within

Simone tells a story about the time a family of raccoons were living in their chimney.
(© Becky Sheridan / Shutterstock.com)

a few months, even when acknowledging that he is not only dead but dead from his own hand, as true a sign of the misery in this world as one will ever come across. Simone is not a humorous figure in this story, but she is humored, laughing freely enough, and in that way shows the upper limits of too much fun. The narrator does not bond with Simone but takes her moral cues from Cal, treating sick Eugene with a lot of respect and just a little apprehension.

Ultimately this is not the story of Cal and Simone and Eugene, but of the narrator, and she undergoes a change by the end of the story that is not morbid but is also not funny. The last stretch of narration mirrors the first, but with one significant difference: at the beginning of the story she says that she made up, without believing it, "this stuff" about dance being "the heart's triumph, the victory speech of the feet, the refinement of animal lunge and flight, the purest metaphor of tribe and self. It's life flip-ping death the bird." She surprises herself by

becoming convinced by such breezy, poetic lan-guage. At the end, the uplifting language is still there, but it is tinged with an air of defiance. She begins the story talking about dance as something grand and uplifting, but by the end of the story, having faced the death sentence that hangs over Eugene and knowing how it will affect his parents forever, she *needs* it to be uplifting. The beginning of the story talks about standing up to death theoretically, while by the end, the narrator is actively engaged in the fight against it.

In this story, and in later Moore stories, the humor is not there for its own sake anymore. It is a coping mechanism; like art (in this story's example, dance), it is a way of pretending that one is not powerless in this world. The comic foils in "Dance in America"—the small-minded townspeople and the angry lover who accused the narrator of being too self-centered—are easy to make fun of. Too easy. As Lorrie Moore has grown as an artist, she has realized that humor in the face of tragedy, though not as funny as humor at the expense of fools, is much more necessary for our mental and spiritual survival.

Source: David Kelly, Critical Essay on "Dance in America," in *Short Stories for Students*, Gale, Cengage Learning, 2015.

Kasia Boddy

In the following excerpt, Boddy discusses Moore's powerful use of language in the short story.

. . . For Lorrie Moore, the problem with language is not so much that it is inadequate or coercive as that it won't hold still. That, of course, is also its great liberating power. 'People Like That Are The Only People Here' is about the way in which 'The Mother,' who is also 'The Writer,' responds to the cancer diagnosis and treatment of 'The Baby.' Wit is always the first weapon that Moore's characters deploy in times of trouble and The Mother/Writer is an expert at slips of sound and sense. 'Goodbye' becomes 'could cry,' while 'paediatric oncology' is easier as 'Peed Onk.' But it's not only bad puns that allow the writer to escape from the hospital. What the doctors call 'blood in the diaper' is for her something 'like tiny mouse heart packed in snow.' Such similes are rare and fleeting as Moore holds off sentimentality, framing and interrupting the tale with the constant admonition of 'The Husband' to 'take notes' for they are going to 'need the money.'

Like Homes and Foster Wallace, Moore targets the promises of the self-improvement industry—exemplified by books with titles such as *Get Real, Smarting Cookie, Get Real* and *Why I Hate Myself.* Her early stories offered 'guides' to divorce or 'the tenor of love' and advised on such matters as 'How to Talk to Your Mother (Notes),' 'How to be a Writer' ('First, try to be something, anything, else.') and 'How to be Another Woman.' A story called 'How' offers alternatives at every stage in its account of a woman's restless romance, but they exist simply to show how little—after 'a week, a month, a year'—'choices' really matter. You might 'begin by meeting him in a class, in a bar' or 'at a rummage sale,' and you might end by never seeing him again or 'perhaps' you will. You might feel 'sadness' or 'indifference.' 'One of those endings,' the story wearily concludes. Human vulnerability does not conform to self-help's optimistically linear narrative. But

Moore's jokes, comparisons and aphorisms rely as much on the reader recognising herself as do the self-help books they supplant. Stories, she suggests, are the 'lozenge of pretend' we allow ourselves when faced with pain, disappointment, and, so often in her work, the immanence of disease and death.

For all that Moore and Foster Wallace's smart-alecky 'jazzing around' is seen as an alternative to the 'grim' taciturnity offered by the 'Resurrection of Realism,' both remain committed to what Foster Wallace calls 'passionately moral fiction' and what for Moore are 'those moments in which we help each other out.' Homes, too, was only partly joking when she entitled a collection of stories, *Things You Should Know.* The difference is perhaps more one of tone than of ideology. The 'small joys' that Moore's stories provide are often 'theatrical' or 'possessed of great silliness,' especially when women get together with each other. If Carver's characters compulsively rake leaves and Foster Wallace's compulsively digress, Moore's can't stop telling jokes or breaking into show tunes. 'Dance in America' begins with a paragraph describing the capacity of dance to be, among other things, 'life flipping death the bird.' Lest we are too easily convinced, the next paragraph begins, 'I make this stuff up.' But the sentence that follows then qualifies that debunking as the narrator confesses that she sometimes believes her own 'rented charisma' and 'jerry-rigged authority.' The story—about a dance teacher's visit to an old friend whose son has cystic fibrosis—is all about negotiating what Foster Wallace called the risk of 'the yawn, the rolled eyes, the cool smile, the nudged ribs, the parody of gifted ironists, the "Oh how *banal*."' By the end of the story she is not only 'telling' others about the 'dancing body's magnificent and ostentatious scorn,' she is enacting it herself as she and the boy 'dip-glide-slide' to the suitably banal and perfectly-titled Kenny Loggins hit, 'This Is It.' The charisma is genuine. Moore's characters are not consoled by insights, but by actions (life lived 'from the neck down'). In 'The Juniper Tree,' a ghost called Robin pushes a lemon meringue pie into her own face and then tastes it. 'I've always wanted to do that,' she says, 'and now I have.' She waves goodbye to her friend with her 'one pie-free hand' and tells her 'Onward.'

Again and again, we've seen the short story stage a struggle between familiar discourse and itself. That discourse may be that of stereotype or social control, or it may just be the clichéd language in which we generally conduct our lives—whether in the form of sociological 'distortions' (O'Connor), 'statistical reports' (Cheever), 'authorative accounts delivered by an expert' (Barthelme), the 'sort of words used on TV shows' (Carver) or self-help (Moore *et al.*). The short story tells us how powerful and pervasive such discourses are, but it also, usually, suggests that it can help us break free, if only for a moment. . . .

Source: Kasia Boddy, "Conclusion," in *The American Short Story since 1950*, Edinburgh University Press, 2010, pp. 147–51.

Alison Kelly

In the following excerpt, Kelly discusses bird imagery in Birds of America, *the collection that includes "Dance in America."*

For a heady three-week period in October 1998, Lorrie Moore's third volume of stories, *Birds of America*, was ranked among the *New York Times* best sellers, shifting between fourteenth and fifteenth positions. This was Moore's biggest book in terms of both sales and size. It was priced at twenty-three dollars and was nearly three hundred pages long—hefty enough, as she marveled in an interview at the time, to "keep a small door open." The consensus among readers and critics was, and remains, that in this collection Moore also tackles her biggest themes. The month before it made the best-seller lists, a *New York Times* reviewer had described it as "her most potent work so far" and had praised one "powerhouse" story for having "the heft and ranginess . . . of a compressed novel." Other reviewers followed suit: "Her depth of focus has increased, and with it her emotional seriousness"; her jokes "hit with an impact that leaves the reader stunned"; she "pushes further" than before "the extremes of emotional fragility"; her subject matter has "more complexity, substance, and gravitas."

These plaudits are founded on *Birds of America*'s engagement with topics such as cancer, death, mental and marital breakdown, loneliness, and the love, lack, or loss of children—powerful themes, indeed, but themes that have informed every one of Moore's major publications from *Self-Help* onward. No one recalling the

desolation felt by the deserted wife dying of cancer in "What Is Seized" or the mother's terror of losing her young son as well as her sanity in "To Fill" could claim that in *Birds of America* "Ms. Moore . . . grapples, . . . as she has sometimes been reluctant to do in the past, with the real sadness and grief in her characters' lives." *Birds of America* does address some of the darkest facets of human experience, but in doing so it continues a project in which Moore has been involved since her earliest publications.

James McManus sees sufficient homogeneity in *Birds of America* to label it "emphatically" a "cancer book." This is understandable given that cancer makes several appearances in the collection and takes center stage in two of the strongest stories. But any unitary classification must understate the diversity of this volume. One of the most moving stories about terminal illness revolves around cystic fibrosis, not cancer, while others approach the theme of mortality from angles as different as accidental infanticide and the death of a cat. Nor is death or the fear of death the principal theme in every story. Most stories touch on it, but some are primarily concerned with other experiences: parent-child relationships, family lives, sexual love, travel, history, politics, American history, and the national character. The typology is complicated by the extent to which the categories overlap. For instance, the most famous story in the collection, "People Like That Are the Only People Here: Canonical Babbling in Peed Onk," is best known as a cancer story but could equally well be identified as a story about motherhood. To take another example, "Dance in America" could be viewed as only secondarily about disease and primarily about performance, transcendence, or the power of love.

THEATERSTRUCK

In 2001 Moore told an interviewer that she had become "theaterstruck" at a very young age and that this relish for performance had filtered through into her work: "I suspect that love of theater . . . is part of the pulse of everything I've ever written." Three stories about kinds of performer and performance—"Charades," "Willing," and "Dance in America"—provide an illuminating route into *Birds of America* and introduce some uses of the avian imagery. "Charades" and "Willing" explore the role played by dramatization in identity construction and the conduct of relationships, revealing the importance of theatrical enactment to, respectively, a professional film actress and a family playing a parlor game at Christmas. In "Dance in America" the focus shifts from the self-conscious staging of personality and relationships to the value of unselfconscious performance.

... The most explicit use of bird imagery in connection with performance comes in "Dance in America," which begins by enumerating the metaphorical meanings of dance as the narrator, a peripatetic dance lecturer, sees them: "Dance begins when a moment of hurt combines with a moment of boredom.... It's the body's reaching, ... the heart's triumph, the victory speech of the feet, the refinement of animal lunge and flight, the purest metaphor of tribe and self. It's life flipping death the bird." Dancing is simultaneously corporeal and spiritual, a means of overcoming pain or boredom, affirming vitality, expressing both individuality and belonging. It is also, significantly, an articulate art form. The dancer's feet, like the players' hands and bodies in "Charades," are organs of silent speech; dance is a language in which steps do service for words.

One of the nonverbal meanings conveyed by dance, according to this passage, is defiance of death, since "flipping the bird" is a colloquial expression for an insulting gesture. This defiance reflects the narrator's general philosophy of dance, but it also has specific relevance for the situation she encounters in the story, in which a seven-year-old boy named Eugene has cystic fibrosis and is expected to die young. Eugene's exuberance—in spite of his illness—is evident in his rapt expression, shining eyes, exclamatory utterances, "singsong" voice, and reckless stunts that recall the pratfalls in "Charades." As he and the narrator watch a dance video together, she reiterates her belief in the transformative power of dance, "how movement, repeated, breaks through all resistance into a kind of stratosphere: from recalcitrance to ecstasy; from shoe to bird." Again, the feet, here metonymically designated by the word "shoe," are at the center of the imagined transformation, this time taking wing in an image that unequivocally associates birds with transcendence and rapture.

The force of the story, however, arises from the tension between this faith in the human power of overcoming and the all too recalcitrant fact of disease. For all the "magnificent and ostentatious scorn" of Eugene's body when he improvises a dance of the planets after dinner, his premature death is inevitable. This knowledge explains the narrator's anger when she returns to the idea of dance as a way of "speaking": "We say with motion, ... This is what life's done so far down here; this is all and what and everything it's managed—this body, these bodies, that body—so what do you think, Heaven? What do you ... think?" The rage in this passage is directed at an unspecified deity ("Heaven"), but a pattern of references to rituals such as Lent, Fastnacht, and vespers suggests that its target is the Christian God. ...

Source: Alison Kelly, "*Birds of America*," in *Understanding Lorrie Moore*, University of South Carolina Press, 2009, pp. 110–12, 115–16.

James Urquhart
In the following review, Urquhart commends Moore's exploration of "emotional fragility."

Lorrie Moore's new collection of stories comprises a dozen punchy diatribes, laments and elegies to crumbling lives or broken relationships, all taut within the disciplines of the form. Only "What You Want to Do Fine" betrays any slack in the wire of Moore's concentration; it lacks the restraining architecture of the short story form and wanders lost in its own landscape, as though excerpted from a longer, absent work.

Moore writes well about childhood, searching for the innocent key that might unlock the wisdoms that supposedly arrive with age. In "Two Boys," a story from her previous collection *Like Life*, she writes of the character Mary feeling "the edge of a childhood she'd never quite had or couldn't quite remember float back to her." In her novel *Who will Run the Frog Hospital?*, two mature children find that they have forsaken the painful exhilarations of youth to gain only the resigned compromises of the adult franchise.

Birds of America pushes further these extremes of emotional fragility. Moore's fondness for word games serves as an index of insecurity. And Moore's characters, mostly women, seem stranded and self-mockingly insecure in an isolated, unheroic age. In "Terrific Mother," "jetty-laggy" Adrienne begins to babble nervously when patronised by a pompous academic at a plush symposium dinner. Then she smiles at him, and he replies: "Baby talk. We love it."

Most of the stories explore the ambiguous space between the requirements of adult behaviour and the faulty equipment salvaged from childhood with which we attempt to cope with our lives. My favourite, "Beautiful Grade," is about a dinner party at which a divorced law tutor puts up a queasy defence of his decision to date Debbie, one of his former students who is less than half his age. Moore's delineation of each diner's meagre powers of empathy is astute. Their morbid rapport confirms the unalterable private grief of soured hope and misplaced, unreciprocated love.

Lorrie Moore is at her most strident in the penultimate story, subtitled "Canonical Babbling in Peed Onk," in which Mother and Husband struggle with Baby's cancer. Mother, a writer, is goaded by Husband into writing up the whole affair to raise money for the child's treatment. But she cannot do it. The reality is too grim, and too distressing, not the stuff of the imagination at all. "This is the kind of thing that fiction is," she tells herself, "it's the unliveable life, the strange room tacked on to the house, the extra moon that is circling the earth unbeknownst to science."

Moore offers us fragments of this unliveable life. Her stories serve as fresh perspectives of dysfunctional sitcoms, nuanced with bleakness in place of absurdity; and she challenges her readers to act, not observe.

Source: James Urquhart, Review of *Birds of America*, in *New Statesman*, Vol. 128, No. 4418, January 8, 1999, p. 58.

June Unjoo Yang

In the following review, Yang praises Moore's characterizations and humor.

Lorrie Moore really knows her way around a punchline. With her penchant for surprising puns and idiosyncratic characters who seem confounded by the mess they've made of their lives, she mines her acute sense of the absurd to dispense some fleeting consolation. For her largely female protagonists, humor is a totem and a trump card, a not-so-hidden ace, the only viable means of getting through the day with a modicum of sanity and poise.

Moore's particular brand of humor often revolves around escalating wordplay and the myriad discontents of romance and domesticity; in the span of several novels and short story collections, she draws attention to our careless use of language, the damage that we inflict

> HERE MOORE REMINDS US THAT THE STATE OF BEING HUMAN IS THE STATE OF BEING BOUND TO THOSE AROUND US, A SACRED OBLIGATION THAT IN AN IDEAL WORLD MIGHT BE APPRECIATED AS SUCH."

upon it and one another by skipping blithely over the underlying significance of our exchanges. But exactly how to say what we mean when the banality of our received culture constantly assaults deeper meaning, how to protect the fragile links between us and to ensure that when we talk about love, we possess a common vocabulary or can at least hammer out something that approaches consensus—aye, there's the rub.

Exploring these questions in her fiction with skittish charm, Moore maintains a guarded optimism about the intermittent possibilities for connection and communication of the highest order. As one of the characters in her latest short story collection, *Birds of America*, observes, "No matter what terror or loveliness the earth could produce—winds, seas—a person could produce the same, live with the same, live with all that mixed-up nature swirling inside, every bit. There was nothing as complex in the world—no flower or stone—as a single hello from a human being."

In the wake of widespread acclaim for her novel *Who Will Run the Frog Hospital?* and inclusion in Granta's *1996 Best of Young American Novelists* issue, Moore returns to a form that seems especially suited to her gifts. Much of the delicate power of *Frog Hospital* derives from its structural resemblance to short fiction, the artful accretion of vignettes and epiphanies in the life of a narrator who comes to recognize that a childhood friendship represented her peak experience of joyful and passionate understanding, attained and lost years ago. The twelve stories in *Birds of America* proceed in a similar vein, from moment to moment and from detail to finely rendered detail, and they cover the spectrum of Moore's recurring obsessions: divorce and other catastrophes endemic to long-term relationships; aborted attempts at short-term relationships;

distant fathers and exasperating but sympathetic mothers; the palpable mortality of small children and household pets.

The cumulative effect of *Birds of America* is one of quiet revelation, chance glimpses of the poignancy lurking beneath the smooth surface of quotidian existence. Moore is extremely skillful at suggesting little betrayals and cease-fires through her evocation of bodily gesture and dialogue. In "Which Is More Than I Can Say About Some People," for instance, Abby Mallon works for a company that devises standardized SAT-type tests. She is promoted from composing analogies for the exam to addressing high school students and their teachers about preparation strategies. Saddled with a fear of public speaking and urged to take a vacation before starting, she travels to Ireland with her mother and acquires a more compassionate view of their shared "knack for solitude," which Abby feels compelled to toast. "'May your car always start.... And may you always have a clean shirt,' she continued, her voice growing gallant, public and loud, 'and a holding roof, healthy children and good cabbages—and may you be with me in my heart, Mother, as you are now, in this place; always and forever—like a flaming light.'" This affecting speech is crowned by the mother's reaction, a paragon of understatement: "'Right,' said Mrs. Mallon, looking into her stout in a concentrated, bright-eyed way. She had never been courted before, not once in her entire life, and now she blushed, ears on fire, lifted her pint, and drank." This is Moore at her best, subtle and tender and restrained, and many of the pieces in *Birds of America* are stamped with these trademark qualities.

At her worst, however, Moore can veer into self-indulgence, the abiding love affair with word games deteriorating into something merely clever or gratuitous. When her fascination with the slippery nature of language is matched to her characters' own preoccupations, as it is for Abby or for the librarians of "Community Life" who amuse themselves by thinking up Tom Swifties ("I have to go to the hardware store, he said wrenchingly"), the stories soar. But Moore is not above churning out, as in "Real Estate," two whole pages consisting of the interjection "Ha!" repeated ad nauseam (982 times, to be precise), which may be visually arresting and implies a certain bitter magnitude

in the laughter, but could be construed in less charitable terms as just plain silly.

Or take the example of the telephone conversation between a mediocre actress cursed with mediocre relationships and her gay screenwriter friend in "Willing." The actress fumes about the shortcomings of an overeducated ex-lover: "We spent all of our time in bed with the light on, proofreading his vita.... I mean, have you ever seen a vita?" and her friend replies, "I thought Patti LuPone was great in it." This is one of those cute quips that may have been hilarious at the moment of conception—helped along, say, by a five-dollar bottle of wine in somebody's first apartment after college—but one that should have been assessed and discarded with the dog-eared Matisse posters and plastic shower caddies before settling into more adult digs.

At this point in her career, Moore can obviously handle humor beyond the one-note joke. She is also capable of tackling themes with far greater scope and weight than the precedent set by her debut collection, *Self-Help*, which was engaging and impressive as the output of a very young writer, but featured the likes of a Phi Beta Kappa key-wearing secretary entangled in an affair with a married man—the literary equivalent of women who love too much. This is not to dispute the validity of fiction that concerns itself with the everlasting war between the sexes. On another level, though, I find myself wanting to sit down for a chat with some of the gals in *Birds of America* to confirm that we've heard them roar and they might consider turning up the volume.

When Moore does choose to adopt a wider lens or to vary her perspective, the results are well worth the gamble. In "What You Want to Do Fine," one of the rare stories with a male protagonist, a hapless housepainter named Mack is abandoned by his wife and child. He becomes inexplicably involved with a gay lawyer named Quilty, who is blind, and the two men embark on a cross-country trip together. The tentative insights Mack achieves during this journey feel duly earned and convincing; obsessed by a trail of missing-child posters and pondering his failed marriage, Mack remains a figure perennially visited by bad luck, but he starts to see his passivity toward the randomness of his life and surroundings in a more honest light. "In general, people were not road maps," he reflects.

> People were not hieroglyphs or books. They were not stories. A person was a collection of accidents. A person was an infinite pile of rocks with things growing underneath. In general, when you felt a longing for love, you took a woman and possessed her gingerly and not too hopefully until you finally let go, slept, woke up, and she eluded you once more. Then you started over. Or not. Nothing about Quilty, however, seemed elusive.

By relying on the implausible pairing of these men and the trope of blindness, with the sighted partner initially displaying far less capacity for self-scrutiny, Moore conveys a tone of mournful stoicism leavened by acceptance, a willingness to adapt instead of surrendering to despair—which sounds a lot like emotional maturity.

There are sundry other pleasures in *Birds of America*. The title character in "Agnes of Iowa," one of the strongest stories of the collection, hears from a South African writer she meets at a party that his son is dead, and offers him a package of cookies. A trivial act on the face of it, the offer is received with gratitude because it is informed by a consciousness of the woeful inadequacy of any response. "Perhaps," thinks Agnes, "that's where affection begins: in an unlikely phrase, in a moment of someone's having unexpectedly but at last said the right thing." Here Moore reminds us that the state of being human is the state of being bound to those around us, a sacred obligation that in an ideal world might be appreciated as such. In the absence of any imminent utopias, she also reminds us not to hold our breath, but encourages a rueful empathy for people who disappoint us and faith in the individuals who sustain us against all odds.

Source: June Unjoo Yang, Review of *Birds of America*, in *Women's Review of Books*, Vol. 16, No. 2, November 1998, p. 15.

SOURCES

Allen, Moira, "What Makes Literary Fiction 'Literary'?," in *Writer*, Vol. 123, No. 4, April 2010, pp. 30–34.

Eggers, David, "Lorrie Moore's Laughter in the Dark," in *Esquire*, Vol. 130, No. 4, 1998, p. 46.

Gaffney, Elizabeth, "Lorrie Moore, The Art of Fiction No. 167," in *Paris Review*, No. 158, Spring–Summer 2001, pp. 57–84.

Giles, Jeff, "The Human Comedy," in *Newsweek*, Vol. 132, No. 13, 1998, p. 80.

"The Holy Experiment, in Pennsylvania," Quakers in the World, http://www.quakersintheworld.org/quakers-in-action/8 (accessed April 21, 2014).

Kelly, Alison, *Understanding Lorrie Moore*, University of South Carolina Press, 2009, p. 3.

Krystal, Arthur, "It's Genre. Not That There's Anything Wrong with It!," in *New Yorker* online, October 24, 2012, http://www.newyorker.com/online/blogs/books/2012/10/its-genre-fiction-not-that-theres-anything-wrong-with-it.html (accessed March 3, 2014).

Lee, Don, "About Lorrie Moore: A Profile," in *Ploughshares*, Fall 1998, http://www.pshares.org/read/article-detail.cfm?intArticleID=4504 (accessed April 22, 2014).

Malin, Irving, Review of *Birds of America*, in *Review of Contemporary Fiction*, Vol. 19, No. 1, 1999, p. 196.

McGrath, Charles, "Lorrie Moore's New Book Is a Reminder and a Departure," in *New York Times*, February 18, 2014, http://www.nytimes.com/2014/02/18/books/lorrie-moores-new-book-is-a-reminder-and-a-departure.html?_r=0 (accessed February 19, 2014).

Moore, Lorrie, "Dance in America," in *Birds of America*, Alfred A. Knopf, 1998, pp. 47–57.

Passaro, Vince, "Unlikely Stories: The Quiet Renaissance of American Short Fiction," in *Harper's*, August 1999, p. 83.

"Pennsylvania Amish History & Beliefs," Lancaster County (PA) website, 2014, http://www.padutchcountry.com/towns-and-heritage/amish-country/amish-history-and-beliefs.asp (accessed February 21, 2014).

Petite, Steven, "Literary Fiction vs. Genre Fiction," in *Huffington Post*, February 26, 2014, http://www.huffingtonpost.com/steven-petite/literary-fiction-vs-genre-fiction_b_4859609.html (accessed March 3, 2014).

Raiffa, Janet R., "Lorrie Moore (1957–)," in *The Columbia Companion to the Twentieth-Century American Short Story*, edited by Blanche H. Gelfant, Columbia University Press, 2000, pp. 384–90.

Soete, M., Review of *Self-Help*, in *Library Journal*, Vol. 110, No. 5, March 15, 1985, p. 73.

FURTHER READING

Austen, Ben, "135 Minutes with . . . Lorrie Moore," in *New York*, Vol. 47, No. 5, February 24, 2014, pp. 20–22.
    This article presents a portrait of the writer at the time of several big changes in her life, including her move from Wisconsin after teaching there for decades and the publication of *Bark*, her first short-story collection in over a dozen years.

Blades, John, "Lorrie Moore: Flipping Death the Bird," in *Publishers Weekly*, Vol. 245, No. 34, August 24, 1998, pp. 31–32.

Blades interviewed Moore at about the time that *Birds of America* came out, discussing her life and the ways her view of the world changed as she matured. The title of the article comes from "Dance in America."

Chodat, Robert, "Jokes, Fiction, and Lorrie Moore," in *Twentieth-Century Literature*, Vol. 52, No. 1, Spring 2006, pp. 42–60.
In this article, Chodat examines the "moral weight" of Moore's use of humor in her writings, asking whether the sense of humor that makes her such a popular fiction writer is used effectively to make a point.

Vidich, Paul, "Lorrie Moore: An Interview," in *Narrative*, June 2009, pp. 1–16.
In their lengthy discussion, Moore and Vidich talk about such subjects as what it was like for her to be a literary sensation at the early age of nineteen and the use of humor in fiction.

SUGGESTED SEARCH TERMS

Lorrie Moore

Lorrie Moore AND short fiction

Lorrie Moore AND Birds of America

Lorrie Moore AND Dance in America

Lorrie Moore AND rural America

fiction AND humor

modern dance AND rural America

contemporary fiction AND modern dance

fiction AND childhood disease

cystic fibrosis AND literature

The Dinner Party

MONA GARDNER
1941

Mona Gardner's short story "The Dinner Party" was originally published in the *Saturday Review of Literature* on January 31, 1941. Set in colonial India, the brief narrative is one of her more popular stories. The story examines gender roles in British society at the dawn of World War II. Gardner uses conflict, suspense, and revelation to explore how women's roles in society were shifting at the time. Themes of stereotypes, feminism, and individuality are apparent in the author's story. Gardner skillfully weaves the societal conflict into a suspenseful tale, as a cobra threatens the lives of the guests, and she successfully brings the theme of feminism full circle with a revelation from the hostess. The story can be found online and in various textbooks, such as the Scribner Literature Series title *Introducing Literature* (1989).

AUTHOR BIOGRAPHY

Mona Gardner was born in Seattle, Washington, in 1900. Her parents were originally from England. In fact, her father, Alan Hyde Gardner, was a captain in the British Royal Navy. Gardner attended Stanford University, in California, where she majored in English. After graduating, she began her career as a journalist. Gardner's first job as a journalist was at the *Call-Bulletin* newspaper in San Francisco.

The story's setting is a formal dinner party with British and American guests.

(© Andrey Bayda | Shutterstock.com)

Early in her career, Gardner decided to travel to Japan, where she lived, traveled, and wrote for twelve years. The Sino-Japanese War broke out while she was living in Japan, and she began to send feature articles to the North American Newspaper Alliance. Gardner did not limit herself to writing about Japan. She traveled throughout Asia, where she continued to send reports back to the alliance.

Gardner was known for her interest in the lives of native peoples, and she never hid her political opinions. For example, she "was not much impressed with the British technique in colonization," according to an article by Lewis Gannett for the *Oakland Tribune*. She was also extremely "interested in 'the Indian problem' and did stories on Gandhi and several Nationalist Congress leaders," according to her biography in John E. Drewry's *More Post Biographies*.

After leaving Japan, Gardner stopped in Italy, France, and England before finally returning to the United States. She arrived home in 1938, and her travels inspired her book *The Menacing Sun*. The book was published in 1939, and the characters were based on the people she met while abroad. She continued to write fiction and nonfiction for national papers and magazines over the years, including "The Dinner Party" in 1941. In 1944, she married Major George Jordan, according to the *Washington Post*'s records. Her next book, *Middle Heaven*, was published in 1950. Her novel *Hong Kong* was published in 1958, and it was quickly followed by *The Shanghai Item* in 1959. Gardner continued writing articles and short stories throughout her life, until her death in 1981.

PLOT SUMMARY

Gardner uses an omniscient narrator to tell the story of "The Dinner Party." In the beginning, the narration is impersonal, which means that the narrator simply provides the events of the story as they occur. There is no interpretation of events or clues into the thoughts or feelings of the characters. This gradually shifts as the story progresses. This story was published in 1941, when India was still a British colony, though there was a growing movement for independence.

The story takes place as a British official and his wife host a dinner party for a group of British officers, government attachés, and their wives. (*Attachés* are the employees of diplomats or other government officials.) The dinner party—twenty people in all—also includes an American naturalist (a scientist who studies natural history, particularly zoology and botany). The home where the party takes place is described as large and luxurious, complete with marble floors, high ceilings, and glass doors that open onto a veranda, or open porch.

An unnamed young woman at the party creates a conflict when she turns the discussion to gender stereotypes. She insists that women are no longer the weak-willed creatures they were perceived to be in the nineteenth century. She says that they "have outgrown the jumping-on-a-chair-at-the-sight-of-a-mouse era." A British colonel, however, disagrees with her, claiming that women cannot help but scream in any type of crisis. He goes on to explain that men may feel the desire to scream, but they have "that ounce more of nerve control than a woman has." The colonel describes a Victorian idea that was commonly accepted, and the young woman presents a modern, feminist belief. Most of the guests at the dinner party discuss the topic, indicating that the roles and abilities of women were under lively debate at that period in history.

The American naturalist, however, refuses to involve himself in the debate about gender roles. Instead, he observes the other guests during their conversation. At this point, the narrator provides the readers with information about the American specifically. In showing the story from the American's perspective, the author shifts to a limited omniscient point of view; the reader now shares, in part, in the perspective and the limitations of this character. The American notices that the hostess develops a strange expression, and he pays close attention as she calls over an Indian servant. He sees the servant's eyes widen in fear before leaving the table. When the servant returns, the American observes that he has a bowl of milk, which he places outside on the veranda.

As a naturalist, the American knows that the milk is being used to attract a cobra, which means that the hostess saw a poisonous snake in the room. He surveys the corners of the room and the rafters in the ceiling, but he cannot see the snake anywhere. This leads him to the conclusion that the snake must be below him, underneath the dining table. His instinct is to jump away and warn everyone about the snake, but he manages to control his fear. He realizes that if he tells the other guests about the snake, it could cause a panic at the table. Sudden movements and commotion could provoke the snake into striking, so the American quickly thinks of a plan that will help keep everyone calm and still until the snake takes the bait and leaves the room. Discovering that the cobra is loose beneath the table creates suspense as the reader waits to find out whether the snake will take the bait and leave the room without biting one of the guests.

The American interrupts the debate and challenges all of the diners to demonstrate their personal level of control by remaining perfectly still as he counts to three hundred. Counting to three hundred takes roughly five minutes, and the American hopes that it will be enough time for the cobra to discover the bait. He proposes a bet that anyone who moves or speaks while he is counting has to pay fifty

rupees: the equivalent of about five dollars, a significant amount at the time. At this point, the narrator is again using an impersonal omniscient point of view. The readers are only told the events as they unfold. The group agrees to play the game, and they all remain perfectly still as the American counts.

The snake slides out from beneath the table just in time, as the count reaches 280. The guests are no longer distracted by conversation and debate, and they notice the cobra emerging. Some of the guests scream, and there is a sense of panic in the room. The American, however, remains calm. He quickly jumps up and shuts the door to the veranda behind the snake. The host says that his bravery has just proven the colonel's theory that only men have the ability to remain calm in a crisis.

The American, however, does not accept the host's claims, knowing that he learned about the cobra only by watching his hostess. Instead of taking all the praise, he turns to the hostess and asks, "Mrs. Wynnes, how did you know that cobra was in the room?" She smiles slightly and explains that she knew about the cobra because it had slithered across her foot.

CHARACTERS

American

The unnamed American is a naturalist, which means he studies zoology and botany. He does not participate in the debate with the other guests. He is observant: he sees a slight change come over his hostess, and he realizes that there is a cobra under the table once he sees the bowl of milk placed outside as bait. He resists the urge to run and instead devises a game to keep everyone at the table still in hopes of preventing the snake from striking. Once the cobra is seen leaving, the party's host claims that the colonel's argument about the superiority of male self-control is now proven. The American, however, suspects that there is more to the story, and he asks how Mrs. Wynnes knew that the snake was there, setting the stage for the revelation of her own great self-control.

Colonel

This unnamed character is a British colonel serving in India. At the dinner party, he debates gender roles with a young woman, taking the position that women lack nerve in a crisis.

Host

The host in "The Dinner Party" is not named, but he is the husband of Mrs. Wynnes. He claims that the American's actions prove the colonel's argument that men have more nerve in a crisis than women.

Servant

The unnamed household servant of the Wynnes's is referred to as a "native boy." His eyes widen in alarm when his employer whispers to him about the snake, but he quickly and discreetly takes the correct action to lure the snake outside.

Mr. Wynnes

See Host

Mrs. Wynnes

The only character named in the story, Mrs. Wynnes, is the hostess of the dinner party. She discreetly calls a servant over and orders a bowl of milk placed on the veranda to lure the snake away outside. When asked how she knew about the snake, she explains that it had slithered across her foot.

Young Woman

The young woman in the story claims that female stereotypes of women as fragile creatures who are terrified by the sight of a mouse are no longer applicable. Her statement begins a debate at the dining table and provides the background for the events of the story.

THEMES

Sexual Stereotypes

Gardner addresses gender stereotypes in "The Dinner Party." This begins with the argument between a young woman and a colonel. The young woman insists that women are much stronger than the Victorian stereotype of timid girls who jump at the sight of a mouse. The colonel, however, disagrees, claiming that a man "has that ounce more of nerve control than a woman has." The stereotype of the hysterical female was common in the early twentieth century. This stereotype is what the colonel is defending and the young woman is

attempting to dispel. The fact that the diners take sides on the subject indicates that it was relevant to Gardner's audience.

The rest of the diners discuss the two claims as the cobra enters the plot. The behavior of the American seems to support the colonel's stereotype because he manages to keep the party quiet and still to prevent the cobra from striking. The hostess, however, defies the stereotype when she reveals that she told the serving boy to put a bowl of milk on the veranda after the snake slithered across her foot. This development—surprising to readers because they experienced part of the story through the eyes of the American—serves to disprove the colonel's theory that women cannot keep their nerve in a crisis. Through Mrs. Wynnes, Gardner defends a feminist point of view and shows that women are just as capable as men in a crisis.

Feminism

"The Dinner Party" firmly establishes a feminist theme by the end of the story. The conflict between the colonel and the young woman introduces the topic of gender roles. The colonel and the host both display the misogynistic, yet popular, view that women are the weaker sex. The American naturalist, however, does not involve himself in the debate, which suggests that he does not hold to the same view of women as some of the other men in the party.

The audience is shown the thoughts of the American so that the reader can understand his reaction to the knowledge that the cobra is under the table. His ability to stay calm may seem to support the idea of male nerve, but he is unwilling to accept the stereotype. His rejection of the stereotype causes him to ask Mrs. Wynnes how she knew about the snake.

Mrs. Wynnes, the hostess, transforms into a feminist heroine when she reveals that she learned about the snake when it was on her foot. The audience is invited to compare her response to the deadly snake's touch with the American's fear that came from simply knowing that a cobra was close. Her actions confirm the feminist argument in the story and support feminist ideas in society.

Individualism

Gardner introduces the concept of individualism in "The Dinner Party." A man and a woman both face knowledge of the same

TOPICS FOR FURTHER STUDY

- Read Karen Cushman's young-adult story *Catherine, Called Birdy* (1994). Set in England in the eleventh century, the novel, written in the form of a series of letters, tells of Catherine's struggle to follow her dreams in a society that expects her to fulfill very specific roles. Choose a partner. One of you will create a blog for Birdy and the other will create a blog for Mrs. Wynnes. Have the characters communicate to each other through blog comments. What feelings would they share? What encouragement could they give each other?

- Explore the history of women's rights and their roles in society in the 1930s and 1940s. How did women's roles change with the beginning of World War II? Choose a woman from this time to research, and write a brief paper about her life. Then create a multimedia presentation to share with the class. Be sure to include pictures, and provide important biographical and historical dates.

- Research the movement toward independence in India, specifically considering how World War II affected the relationship between India and Great Britain. Create a website that provides a time line of the movement. Provide links to important events and individuals within your time line.

- Read *Neela: Victory Song* (2002), by Chitra Banerjee Divakaruni. This young-adult novel follows the story of Neela, a young girl in India who searches for her freedom-fighting father when she is expected to prepare herself for marriage. Write a short story where she meets the boy who serves at the dinner party in Gardner's story. Consider how they, as native Indians, would view the British and American people at the party.

- Read Willa Cather's short story "Coming Aphrodite," which can be found in the collection *Youth and the Bright Medusa* (1920). Cather also wrote in the early twentieth century, but she focused on life in the American Great Plains. Compare and contrast the two stories. Write a paper that focuses on the ways that the authors and the characters in their stories view women.

- Research snakes in India, specifically cobras. Discover the myths and facts about snakes and consider how realistic the snake's behavior in "The Dinner Party" is. Use your understanding to write a short story based on the events of "The Dinner Party." Defend your conclusion with scientific facts.

---

danger; rather than adhering to rules of gender and etiquette, they act as individuals to avert a disaster. The American does not participate in the ongoing debate and shows little desire to prove that men have better nerve than women do. He is not motivated by a desire to live up to what is expected of a man. He acts because he knows that he and the other guests at the dinner party are in danger.

Mrs. Wynnes seems to conform to the expectations of society by playing the role of agreeable hostess and refraining from the feminist debate at her dining table. She departs from this role, however, when she addresses the danger of the cobra under the table. She acts on her own, rather than relying on a man to handle the problem for her. Mrs. Wynnes behaves as an individual; she does not conform to stereotypes. She does not intend to make a statement with her actions, and it seems unlikely that anyone would know about them without the American's intervention. She simply takes action to protect herself and her guests from danger.

India's architecture still shows many signs of British colonialism: the India Gate (left) is a monument to Indian soldiers who died fighting for Britain in World War I, and the canopy (right) used to house a statue of King George V. (© Mukul Banerjee / Shutterstock.com)

STYLE

Point of View

The precise point of view shifts throughout this short story. Broadly, Gardner implements a third-person point of view. She begins by using an impersonal omniscient narrator, defined by M. H. Abrams in *A Glossary of Literary Terms* as a narrator who "describes, reports, or 'shows' the actions of dramatic scenes." For example, the narrator describes the setting and the people at the dinner party without giving any insight into their thoughts or actions or providing any opinions. The narrator describes the argument between the colonel and the unnamed young woman, as well as the discussion among the diners, without advancing one side of the debate over another.

The narrator focuses attention on the American naturalist during the debate, shifting to a limited omniscient point of view, which "stays inside the confines of what is perceived, thought, remembered and felt by a single character," although it is not presented as the voice of that character, according to Abrams. Rather, the narrator shares the character's thoughts and feelings. For example, the narrator explains of the American, "His first impulse is to jump back and warn the others." The reader is able to know the inner mental impulses of this character, even when they are not expressed in any visible way.

The narrator shifts back to the impersonal, omniscient point of view after the American begins the game to keep the diners as still as possible while the snake is under the table. The scene plays out without any further insight into

COMPARE & CONTRAST

- **1940s:** India is under colonial rule, and Great Britain demands that India participate in World War II, which leads to the Quit India movement for independence. India gains independence in 1947.

  Today: India is fully independent and an international power in the global economy with a promising future. The CIA's *World Factbook* reports that the economic outlook for the country is positive.

- **1940s:** Great Britain enters World War II in 1939, two years before "The Dinner Party" is published. The United States is a British ally but does not enter the war until 1942. The war officially lasts until 1945.

  Today: Military conflicts still exist, but not on the same scale as World War II. The

United States and Great Britain continue to have strong political ties.

- **1940s:** Women face social pressure to remain in the home, as wives and mothers without any paid job, through the late 1930s. The advent of World War II, however, requires women to take jobs traditionally held by men, and they become essential to the war effort, in both the United States and Great Britain. Women are encouraged to return to home life after the war ends.

  Today: Although women still face discrimination, they are not limited in the types of work that they can choose. Women hold positions of power and are represented in different fields such as industry, business, and government.

the minds of the characters, including the American, or comment from the narrator. This allows the revelation to be a complete surprise to the reader.

Suspense

"The Dinner Party" briefly creates suspense once the American realizes that there is a cobra beneath the dining table. As William Harmon and Hugh Holman explain in *A Handbook to Literature*, suspense occurs "when the outcome is uncertain and the *suspense* resides in the question of who or what or how." Like the American, the reader does not know whether any of the diners will move in a way that might cause the snake to strike. The suspense is resolved when the snake takes the bait and goes to the bowl of milk that the hostess ordered placed on the veranda without harming any of the guests.

Revelation

"The Dinner Party" ends with a revelation. The snake leaves the table at the climax of the story, ending the suspense. The American's rational

reaction to the presence of the cobra seems to confirm the colonel's belief that men have the innate ability to remain calm in a crisis. The American, however, turns everyone' attention to the hostess, Mrs. Wynnes. When asked how she knew about the snake, she responds that it had crawled across her foot. With this revelation, Gardner shows that women should not be trapped in stereotypical gender roles and are capable of staying calm in a crisis.

HISTORICAL CONTEXT

1940s India

"The Dinner Party" was published in 1941, which was a time of political turbulence and upheaval in India. Nationalist movements toward independence strengthened in the early twentieth century. Gardner was familiar with Indian nationalism, having met with Mohandas Gandhi and other leaders during her time in India. By the 1940s, India had gained a certain level of freedom through the Non-Cooperation Movement in 1920 and the Civil Disobedience Movement of 1930. International war would serve to create further conflict between India and Great Britain.

By 1941, Great Britain had been involved in World War II for two years. As a British colony, India was expected to participate in the war, contributing both manpower and money. Many Indian leaders were opposed to involuntary participation. The Indian National Congress insisted that Indian "participation in the war effort required them to be properly represented in the defence of their own country," according to Zachariah Benjamin in a *History Review* article. Yet the British refused the demands of the Congress. In response, the Quit India Movement began as the Indian National Congress told the British to "quit" (that is, leave) India on August 8, 1942.

This movement led to violence and civil discord. The British arrested the Congress, responded with violence, and fined villages and people who refused to cooperate with the war effort. The country was considered "dangerously ungovernable," according to Benjamin. The British finally agreed to grant India its independence in 1946 and officially transferred power in 1947.

Women's Rights

The guests argue about the role and nature of women in "The Dinner Party." Feminist ideas and women's rights were familiar to Gardner's audience; women had been granted the right to vote in America in 1920. In the 1930s, the Great Depression forced many women out of their traditional roles at home and into the workforce. Women were not considered the equals of men in the workplace, but there was not a political movement toward change because the feminist movement that had helped win the vote had now lost much of its strength. Additionally, a societal push for women to leave the workplace and remain at home developed. Author Albert J. Nock demonstrated this attitude in the article "A Word to Women," which Mickey Moran paraphrases in his article "1930s, America—Feminist Void?" Nock argued that women could influence the world best "through the comforting domain of their immediate households. Only in molding their young ones and prodding their husbands toward

The colonel is pompous, perhaps made arrogant by his uniform and his colonial authority.
(© Henrik Lehnerer | Shutterstock.com)

responsible action could women serve their natural purpose." Many politicians embraced the idea. For example, "Section 213 of the 1932 Federal Economy Act prohibited more than one family member from working for the government, barring many married women from federal employment," according to the article "Working Women in the 1930s."

Attitudes toward women in England were similar to those in America in the 1930s, but ideas about women's roles shifted with World War II. Women in England were working in industry to support the war effort by the time "The Dinner Party" was published. "By 1943 there were 7.25 million women employed in industry, agriculture, the armed forces and civil defence organisations," according to the U.K. National Archives. Women in America would follow suit once the United States entered the war in 1941.

CRITICAL OVERVIEW

Gardner's books and stories received positive criticism from her peers. She wrote stories about people and locations that would have seemed exotic to her American readers, and this originality helped build her audience. Critics were impressed with her ability to make the native people in her books seem like individuals rather than generalized stereotypes. As the

Kansas City Star reviewer K.K.M. says of such people in *The Menacing Sun*, "Through the author's trained, sympathetic eyes, the reader also sees them as individuals."

The interest in the unfamiliar locations featured in Gardner's books and stories combined with her understanding of history helped to captivate her audiences and promote her career. As the *Ohio Chronicle-Telegram* review of *Hong Kong*, which treats the nineteenth-century opium trade, states, "Mona Gardner is superb in writing about the history and local scenes of this exotic period." Gardner's personal knowledge of the countries she wrote about in her books provided her with an authority that critics and readers respected. As Harrison Smith explains in a *Wichita Falls Times* review, "There are few women writers who have known China well enough to write about it either factually or in fiction." He goes so far as to compare Gardner to noted novelist Pearl S. Buck. Smith recognizes, however, that Gardner's fiction is created for a Western audience and is not meant to be a substitute for history: "Love, money, danger, war, and exotic background are the proper themes for historical romance, and Mrs. Gardner has successfully used all of them, including a touch of fantasy."

CRITICISM

April Paris

Paris is a freelance writer with an extensive background writing literary and educational materials. In the following essay, she argues that in "The Dinner Party," the American and Mrs. Wynnes become unlikely partners who support feminist ideas in their actions rather than using debate.

The characters in Mona Gardner's "The Dinner Party" explore the conflicting social views of the 1940s. Two of the characters, the colonel and the young woman, demonstrate the divide between traditionally held beliefs and modern ways of thinking. The colonel is a traditionalist, holding on to Victorian values. The young woman, on the other hand, is a modern feminist, fighting to prove that female stereotypes do not apply to all women. The "spirited discussion" at the table is symbolic of the current conflict in society. This debate provides the background for the crisis that the American

and Mrs. Wynnes face together. Although set apart from the debate itself, the response to the crisis by these two characters both settles the debate in the story and creates an argument for feminism.

Gardner offers no insight into the colonel other than his occupation and his views on women, which invites the audience to draw their own conclusions about the man. As the colonel is defending stereotypes, he becomes a stereotype himself. He is a military officer living in India who supports antiquated ideals such as colonialism and the inherent weakness of women. To a modern audience, his view of the world seems outdated in more ways than one.

Although Gardner chose to focus on feminist issues in the story, colonialism in India would have been a topic familiar to many people in her audience, particularly since the nationalist movements gained international attention with the rise of leaders such as Gandhi. Her observations of India left Gardner critical of British colonial rule, according to Lewis Gannett, writing in the *Oakland Tribune*. Many people began to question India's colonization. A man like the colonel, however, would be committed to preserving the status quo without question.

Since he is someone dedicated to preserving tradition, it is no surprise that the colonel's views of women reflect a Victorian logic. He speaks with authority, but his experience is limited to his life in the military, making his sweeping generalizations doubtful. He argues that women are the weaker sex in times of crisis and advocates traditional gender roles. He believes that "a woman's unfailing reaction in any crisis . . . is to scream." His point of view on the topic was once widely accepted as fact. By 1941, however, society had been introduced to new ideas about women.

The only information Gardner provides about the woman who begins the debate is that she is young and believes that women should not be constrained by stereotypes. The woman's age indicates that the conflict is not just between men and women but also between generations. She presents the modern argument that "women have outgrown the jumping-on-a-chair-at-the-sight-of-a-mouse era." The idea that women are capable functioning on their own was part of the women's rights movement in the early part of the twentieth century.

WHAT DO I READ NEXT?

- Katherine J. Atwood's *Women Heroes of World War II* is a collection of true stories of women who played important roles during World War II. Published in 2011, the young-adult book is perfect for readers of all ages who are curious about the lives of women in the 1940s.

- *The Good Earth*, by Pearl S. Buck, is a Pulitzer Prize–winning novel published in 1931 and set in China in the 1920s. Some of Gardner's reviewers compared her to Buck, and this novel exposes readers to another female American author who wrote about Asian peoples and cultures.

- Bipan Chandra's *India's Struggle for Independence*, published in 2012, is a nonfiction text that follows the nation's different movements from colonialism toward independence. The book is a valuable research tool for anyone interested in gaining a better understanding of colonialism and India's path to independence.

- Gardner published *Hong Kong* in 1958. This historical novel examines the opium trade in the nineteenth century and was popular when it was first published. This novel exposes readers to one of the author's longer works of fiction.

- In 2007, Catherine Gourley published *Rosie and Mrs. America: Perceptions of Women in the 1930s and 1940s*. This social history provides examples of women in the media to compare and contrast the views of society with true stories from the decades.

- *Writing Red: An Anthology of American Women Writers, 1930–1940* is a collection edited by Charlotte Nekola and Paula Rabinowitz. Published in 1993, it provides students with an opportunity to compare Gardner with her literary peers.

- *World War II: The Essential Reference Guide*, edited by Priscilla Roberts, is a nonfiction book that examines the history of World War II. Published in 2012, the book provides insight into circumstances surrounding World War II and how the events played out.

- Published in 2009, *Keeping Corner* is a young-adult novel by Kashmira Sheth that tells the story of Leela, a young widow in India who must "keep corner"—that is, remain in the house—after her husband's death. The book explores the role of women in Indian society and Gandhi's movements toward independence.

- *The Vintage Book of American Women Writers* (2001), edited by Elaine Showalter, is a collection of works by female writers over 350 years. The anthology provides students with an opportunity to examine how the topics and themes that women addressed in literature changed over the years.

During the 1930s, however, the cult of domesticity again took hold, and feminism fell to the background.

The onset of World War II created a shift in society. During the war, women needed to take jobs that were traditionally held by men. While the United States was not yet part of the war when the story was published, England was fully engaged in the conflict. Accepting that women were capable of taking on more diverse roles was necessary to the success of the war effort. Despite the inclusion of women in the workforce and the vital role they played in society, there was still pressure on them to devote themselves to feminine pursuits and avoid masculine roles. It is in this setting of complex societal expectations that the events of "The Dinner Party" take place.

The debate provides the background for the events of the story and does not seem

> THIS DEBATE PROVIDES THE BACKGROUND FOR THE CRISIS THAT THE AMERICAN AND MRS. WYNNES FACE TOGETHER. ALTHOUGH SET APART FROM THE DEBATE ITSELF, THE RESPONSE TO THE CRISIS BY THESE TWO CHARACTERS BOTH SETTLES THE DEBATE IN THE STORY AND CREATES AN ARGUMENT FOR FEMINISM."

entirely relevant to the main characters. In fact, neither the American nor Mrs. Wynnes takes part in the debate. The American is a unique character. By virtue of being an American at a British dinner party, he is not part of the same society as the other guests, and he does not have a vested interest the debate. His status as an outsider provides him with a unique perspective. Rather than arguing in support of a dated ideology, he "watches the other guests." This separation provides him with the opportunity to observe his surroundings and take note of what those entrenched in the debate fail to see, specifically that his hostess develops a strange look on her face.

Curious about the change in Mrs. Wynnes, the American continues his study of the situation. Soon, he observes his silent hostess discreetly call a servant over to the table, and he knows that something is wrong when the servant's eyes widen in fear. His suspicions are confirmed when he sees the servant place a bowl of milk on the veranda. As a naturalist, he has studied zoology, which means he is aware that milk is used as bait for a snake. After realizing that there is a cobra in the room, he deduces that it is hiding underneath the dining table.

The narrator points out, "Of the guests, none but the American notices," which again speaks to his difference from the other men in the party. He is the only man at the party aware of the crisis because he is not caught up in a debate over gender roles. Knowing that any sudden movement could cause the snake to strike, the American stifles his fear and acts in an effort to both save himself and protect the

other guests at the party. He does not act because it is his obligation as a man; he takes action simply to prevent the snake from striking. He devises a ruse to prevent anyone from accidentally startling the cobra. He challenges the self-control of the group by asking everyone to be still while he counts to three hundred, which he estimates will give the cobra enough time to leave them.

While the game succeeds in keeping all of the guests perfectly still, it also changes the focus of the diners. By sitting in silence, they inevitably see the cobra as it emerges from beneath the table. The guests' reaction recalls the colonel's description of a crisis. The cobra elicits screams from the guests. Gardner, however, does not specify that the screams all came from women, which implies that some men may have also screamed. The ambiguity indicates that men may lose their nerve in a crisis just as easily as women.

The American naturalist is quick to close the door behind the cobra once it enters the veranda. The host praises the American's bravery and declares that his actions prove the colonel's theory correct. "A man has just shown us an example of perfect control," he says. The American, however, is reluctant to be held up as proof in the debate that he has avoided. He knows that the hostess was aware of the snake's presence first, and he asks her how she knew about it. This question serves to make him an ally of the feminist argument, and it provides Mrs. Wynnes with the opportunity to reveal her own strength of character.

Mrs. Wynnes is another character who does not involve herself in the debate about women. She is too busy handling a crisis to argue about her ability to do so. The hostess does not confine herself to stereotypical roles, but she does not act simply to prove the stereotype wrong. Like the American, she chooses to protect herself and her guests. She acts discreetly, and it is unlikely that she would have said anything about the snake were it not for the American's direct question, since her actions indicate that she wanted the cobra to leave without causing a panic among the guests.

Even after the snake is safely outside, Mrs. Wynnes does not announce the role she played in protecting her guests. She does not contradict her husband's claim. She does not feel the need

The hostess shows how brave a woman can be by not reacting in the slightest when the cobra slides across her foot. *(© Surachai | Shutterstock.com)*

to make a statement. It is her unintended partner, the American, who places her in the spotlight. Her revelation provides insight into the depth of her character and her level of control. Mrs. Wynnes says that she knew about the snake "because it was crawling across [her] foot." In this statement, the hostess who avoided the debate becomes proof of female strength and control. The colonel's antiquated stereotype does not describe her. Mrs. Wynnes, like many other women, is perfectly capable of remaining calm in a crisis.

Mrs. Wynnes and the American are unlikely heroes and partners. They are united by their unexpected encounter with a cobra and their desire to prevent disaster. Each one displays an inner strength and level of self-control. Both remain calm in a crisis, proving that the nerve to face difficulty depends on the individual, not gender, creating a feminist argument.

Source: April Paris, Critical Essay on "The Dinner Party," in *Short Stories for Students*, Gale, Cengage Learning, 2015.

SOURCES

Abrams, M. H., *A Glossary of Literary Terms*, 7th ed., Cornell University, 1999, pp. 232–33.

Benjamin, Zachariah, "Gandhi, Non-violence and Indian Independence," in *History Review*, No. 69, March 2011, p. 30.

Drewry, John E., ed., "Mona Gardner," in *More Post Biographies*, University of Georgia Press, 1947, pp. 384–85.

Gannett, Lewis, "Stanford Girl Sees Life in East Indies," in *Oakland Tribune*, May 14, 1939, p. 2B.

Gardner, Mona, "The Dinner Party," in *Introducing Literature*, Scribner Literature Series, Scribner Laidlaw, 1989, pp. 157–58; originally published in *Saturday Review of Literature*, Vol. 25, No. 5, January 31, 1941.

Harmon, William, and Hugh Holman, *A Handbook to Literature*, 9th ed., Prentice Hall, 2003, p. 495.

"Imperial Court of Old China Provides Backdrop for New Novel," in *Ohio Chronicle-Telegram*, June 6, 1958, p. 11.

"India," in *CIA: World Factbook*, https://www.cia.gov/library/publications/the-world-factbook/geos/in.html (accessed March 2, 2014).

M., K. K., "A Lively Reporter Returns from Asia," in *Kansas City Star*, May 13, 1939, p. 14.

Moran, Mickey, "1930s, America—Feminist Void?," Loyola University New Orleans website, http://www.loyno.edu/~history/journal/1988-9/moran.htm (accessed March 2, 2014).

Smith, Harrison, "Hong Kong and the Opium War," in *Wichita Falls Times*, May 11, 1958, p. 3D.

"Women's Rights," National Archives website, http://www.nationalarchives.gov.uk/pathways/citizenship/brave_new_world/women.htm (accessed March 2, 2014).

"Working Women in the 1930s," in *Encyclopedia.com*, http://www.encyclopedia.com/topic/Working_women.aspx (accessed March 2, 2014).

FURTHER READING

Adams, Katherine, *A Group of Their Own: College Writing Courses and American Women Writers, 1880–1940*, State University of New York Press, 2001.

> Adams examines the lives and work of female journalists and authors, many of them Gardner's peers, over a span of sixty years. The book combines history and criticism to provide a clear picture of the changing roles women played in the literary world.

Chafe, William, *The Paradox of Change: American Women in the 20th Century*, Oxford University Press, 1992.

> This nonfiction text examines feminism in the twentieth century and how American society changed over the years. The text provides background information that students will find useful in their research of women's roles in society.

Chandra, Bipan, *India's Struggle for Independence*, Penguin Global, 2012.

> Chandra explains the long struggle to end colonization in India, which was a relevant topic when "The Dinner Party" was published. The text provides insight into the movements toward independence and the setting of the short story.

Gardner, Mona, *Middle Heaven*, Doubleday, 1950.

> This novel tells the story of Tomo, a Japanese woman whose life is forever altered with the end of World War II. The fictional book is an example of Gardner's style, and it examines the conflict between Japanese and American cultures.

Kennedy, David M., *The American People in World War II: Freedom from Fear, Part Two*, Oxford University Press, 2003.

> The nonfiction text carefully examines America's role in World War II. Kennedy explains America's reluctance to join the war and how the conflict affected the nation socially and politically.

Yellin, Emily, *Our Mothers' War: American Women at Home and at the Front during World War II*, Free Press, 2005.

> Yellin provides valuable insight into the different roles that women played in World War II. The book includes personal narratives from all walks of life to illustrate how the war affected the lives of all women in society.

SUGGESTED SEARCH TERMS

Mona Gardner

women's roles AND 1940s

Mona Gardner AND The Dinner Party

Mona Gardner AND journalist

British colonialism AND India

women's rights AND 1930s

Mona Gardner AND biography

Mona Gardner AND criticism

World War II AND women

World War II AND India

The Dunwich Horror

H. P. LOVECRAFT

1929

"The Dunwich Horror" was written by H. P. Lovecraft in 1928 and first published in the April 1929 issue of the pulp magazine *Weird Tales*. The story takes place mostly in the fictional village of Dunwich, in rural Massachusetts, where Wilbur Whateley is born to a reclusive albino woman from an outcast family. Wilbur grows at a preternatural pace and becomes obsessed with obtaining a rare book of spells called the *Necronomicon*. What follows is the tale of the Dunwich horror.

The story is a key work in the Cthulhu Mythos, a cycle of stories written by Lovecraft and his correspondents and devotees. Many of Lovecraft's stories take place in his invented New England universe—the Miskatonic Valley, the city of Arkham, and the village of Dunwich—which resembles the topography of the counties surrounding Springfield in the southwest portion of Massachusetts. The stories concern the quest of the Old Ones, ancient beings from another dimension, to take over the earth. After its initial publication, "The Dunwich Horror" was reprinted in several collections of Lovecraft's work, including *The Dunwich Horror and Others* (1963), which has since been revised and reprinted numerous times.

"The Dunwich Horror" is prefaced with a quotation from "Witches and Other Night-Fears," an essay by early nineteenth-century British writer Charles Lamb, and was especially

H. P. Lovecraft was an American horror fiction writer. (© Pictorial Press Ltd / Alamy)

influenced by "The Great God Pan" (1890), a novella by pioneering horror writer and Welsh mystic Arthur Machen. Upon the story being accepted by *Weird Tales* editor Farnsworth Wright, Lovecraft received a payment of $240, one of the largest sums he received during his writing career.

AUTHOR BIOGRAPHY

Howard Phillips Lovecraft was born on August 20, 1890, in Providence, Rhode Island, and lived there nearly his entire life. His father was committed to a mental institution in 1893 and died there five years later. His mother labored under the illusion that Howard, an only child, was both homely and sickly; she herself was institutionalized at the same mental hospital as her husband and died there in 1921. Lovecraft suffered from anxiety from an early age. He escaped into a life of books and writing and never graduated from high school, although

he educated himself exceedingly well. He was supported in his pursuits by his maternal grandfather, who encouraged his writing and introduced him to gothic fiction and poetry. His primary influences were Edgar Allan Poe and the Irish fantasy writer Lord Dunsany. Lovecraft lived a life of genteel impoverishment and reclusiveness, never obtaining steady employment. It took him many years to decide to become a writer, and he did not sell his first story until he was thirty-one.

Though Lovecraft was prolific, the market for his work was slim; he published his stories primarily in *Weird Tales* magazine, beginning with its founding in 1923. He was offered the position of editor for the pulp publication, but he declined because he would have had to move to Chicago. Lovecraft briefly married in the 1920s and moved to Brooklyn, New York, where he was supported by his wife while he continued to write. But the relationship lasted only two years, after which he returned to his preferred life of solitude in Providence and entered into his most prolific period of writing. Lovecraft began work on what was to become the Cthulhu Mythos in 1926 when he penned "The Call of Cthulhu," a story with a strong current of misanthropy, and "The Case of Charles Dexter Ward," a novella that is regarded as one of his best works but which was not published until after his death. "The Dunwich Horror," written in 1928 and published the following year, was a part of this period of productivity. Lovecraft also produced fiction as a ghostwriter for others, yet his career never took off, partly, it seems, from his reluctance to champion his own work and persevere in the face of rejection or criticism.

Despite his reclusiveness, Lovecraft traveled extensively throughout the eastern United States for months at a time, taking copious notes about local history and architecture. Much of his prodigious output was in the form of letters he wrote to his wide array of acquaintances; he wrote over ten thousand letters, many of which were thousands of words long. Lovecraft never earned a substantial sum from his stories, and even though he lived quite frugally, by the end of his life he was penniless, having used up his modest inheritance. Lovecraft was diagnosed with cancer of the small intestine in 1936 and died on March 15, 1937, in Providence, Rhode Island.

In the years since his death, Lovecraft's reputation has only grown. No book-length compendium of his stories was published during his lifetime, but now collections of his stories and biographies abound. While writers who published in the pulp magazines were once considered second tier, many are now respected as influential in establishing the modern horror genre. Lovecraft himself is now regarded as a founding father of what is called weird fiction, consisting of works that blend elements of horror, the grotesque, science fiction, the supernatural, and decadence.

PLOT SUMMARY

I

Dunwich, Massachusetts, is described as an isolated rural area that is untouched by modernity and rarely visited by outsiders. The houses are ancient and crumbling, a unique odor pervades the area, and the inbred residents are just as strange as the Devil's Hop Yard, a hill on which nothing will grow. In the shadow of the overgrown ravines and the sparse farm fields stands Sentinel Hill, from which strange sounds emanate and whose summit is ringed with stone columns that local lore holds were erected during the village's experiments in witchcraft two hundred years earlier.

II

Wilbur Whateley is born to Lavinia Whateley, a dim-witted albino (meaning she had no pigment in her skin or hair) who is the daughter of Old Man Whateley, a purported wizard from an inbred clan living in a decaying farmhouse four miles from Dunwich. No one knows who Wilbur's father is. The boy grows unnaturally quickly; at eighteen months he is the size of a four-year-old. He is swarthy and ugly but is also intelligent, and he has the mannerisms and diction of a full-grown adult. Dogs always bark at him.

III

Old Whateley keeps buying more cattle, which he pays for with ancient gold coins, but his herd never gets larger. He also undertakes extensive repairs to his decrepit farmhouse for no discernible reason, and a visitor reports an ungodly smell coupled with strange noises from upstairs. Wilbur is close to his mother and is tutored by Old Whateley in the dark arts from his expansive library. On ancient holidays the Whateleys climb Sentinel Hill, which erupts in flames and emits ever-louder sounds. By the time Wilbur is four, he is as tall as a boy of ten and carries a gun to protect himself from attacking dogs.

IV

By 1923, Wilbur is ten but is a mature, full-grown man. Old Whateley commences another round of renovations on the house, in which the interior is entirely gutted. Whippoorwills haunt Old Whateley, and he comes to understand that he is about to die. Indeed, on Lammas Night, a pagan holiday, in 1924, a doctor is summoned, and Old Whateley, before he dies, instructs Wilbur to summon Yog-Sothoth with an incantation from an unnamed book and then set fire to the house. The doctor believes the man is mad, even though bizarre noises from the second floor of the house intrude on the death scene. Old Whateley further instructs Wilbur not to let the creature get too big too soon or everything will be in vain and the old ones will not come back.

Wilbur continues his scholarly pursuits related to his mission. He corresponds with librarians at near and distant universities. On Halloween, the whippoorwills screech for Lavinia, and though no one knows what happened to her, she is never seen again.

By 1927, Wilbur is over seven feet tall and has moved into a shed on his property, ceding the house to whatever is inside. His final renovations are to board up all windows and doors. The people of Dunwich stay as far away from him as possible.

V

Wilbur leaves Dunwich for the first time to travel to nearby Miskatonic University, in Arkham, in search of the *Necronomicon*, a book of magic spells written by Abdul Alhazred and translated into Latin by Olaus Wormius. Wilbur's English-language version of the book does not contain the passage he needs to summon Yog-Sothoth. The librarian at Miskatonic University is Dr. Henry Armitage, and as he scans the Latin text of the *Necronomicon* over Wilbur's shoulder, he is shocked to see that it relates to the destruction of the world. Armitage assesses Wilbur's appearance as that of a "bent, goatish giant" who "seemed like the spawn of another planet or dimension."

MEDIA ADAPTATIONS

- The film *The Dunwich Horror* was released by MGM in 1970. It was directed by Daniel Haller and stars Dean Stockwell, Ed Begely, and Sandra Dee. Although presumably an adaptation of Lovecraft's story, the film diverges drastically from the story's plot and was widely panned by critics. It is available on DVD.

- The radio show *Suspense* aired an adaptation of "The Dunwich Horror" in November 1945. It is available from the Internet Archive at https://archive.org/details/SuspenseDun wichHorrorWithRonaldColman110145 and has a run time of twenty-six minutes.

- *Beyond the Dunwich Horror*, a modern retelling of the story, was written by playwright Richard Griffin and performed in May 2008 at the Columbus Theater in Providence, Rhode Island.

- *Call of Cthulhu*, a basic role-playing game, was first published by Chaosium in 1981. The supplement *Shadows of Yog-Sothoth* was published the following year. In 1991, other supplements known as the Lovecraft Country gamebooks were published and included *Return to Dunwich*. The successful game released a thirtieth anniversary edition in 2011.

Armitage refuses to let Wilbur take the book or make a copy, and Wilbur angrily vows to find what he needs at Harvard. Armitage recalls the legends of Dunwich and the strange behavior of the locals he witnessed during his one visit to the town several years ago. He harkens back to legends of incest and wonders about Wilbur's father. Armitage decides to investigate.

VI

Armitage has warned the other librarians not to let Wilbur access the *Necronomicon*. One night he is awakened by the howls of a dog and bizarre screams. He rushes toward the university library, and as the screams subside he hears the screeches of the whippoorwills. The library is filled with a powerful stench. Inside the genealogical reading room he encounters Wilbur Whateley, nearly nine feet tall, torn to shreds by the dog and almost dead. He had broken into the library to steal the *Necronomicon*. Wilbur's dying body is described as "partly human, beyond a doubt." Below the waist, however, "the skin was thickly covered with coarse black fur, and from the abdomen a score of greenish-grey tentacles with red sucking mouths protruded limply." Wilbur dies as he utters fragments from the *Necronomicon*, ending with an incantation of "Yog-Sothoth." Before the authorities arrive, most of Wilbur's body disintegrates, and the smell almost disappears.

VII

Officials sent to Dunwich to track down Wilbur's heirs are frightened by the noises and stench coming from the Whateley house, not to mention the rumbling in the nearby hills, which is almost constant now. They search Wilbur's shack but refuse to enter the house. A giant handwritten tome in an undecipherable language is found in Wilbur's quarters and sent to Miskatonic University to be translated and studied.

The Dunwich horror proper begins on the night of September 9th. The hills groan, dogs howl, and a stench hangs in the air. A farmhand, Luther Brown, frantically tells Mrs. Corey, for whom he works, of the disheveled fields he has just witnessed. Bushes and trees have been uprooted and pushed aside as if something as large as a house has swept through the area. Even more disturbingly, numerous deep footprints, seemingly made by a creature even larger than an elephant, cover the path. Mrs. Corey alerts the neighbors. Another neighbor reports that the Whateleys' house has exploded, and cows in a nearby pasture have been eaten or sucked dry of their blood.

The men in the town gather to search for whatever has escaped from the Whateleys' house. They witness broken trees and matted vegetation and track the creature to a deep ravine. The stench is unbearable, but they see nothing. The dogs bark at the ravine but refuse to enter it. Someone alerts the local paper to the unfolding events, but because Dunwich has a history of outlandish stories, the caller is not taken seriously. Instead, a reporter files a humorous piece with the Associated Press.

That night the people of Dunwich lock up their animals and barricade their houses. But the creature forges a path through the Frye farm, eating most of the cattle. The following morning the villagers discover that the monster has forged a thirty-foot-wide trail up the steep face of Sentinel Hill and back down again. That evening the whippoorwills shriek unceasingly, and at 3:00 a.m. the town's party telephone line rings; listeners hear a cry for help and nothing more. The next morning the townspeople discover that the call came from the Frye residence. An armed posse heads over and discovers that the house has been completely destroyed and no one is alive. The wreckage is coated with a sticky, tar-like substance.

VIII

Meanwhile, experts at Miskatonic University have been trying to translate Wilbur's manuscript, which appears to be written in an invented cipher language similar to Arabic. Henry Armitage becomes obsessed with the riddle, believing the language may be that of an ancient cult. Ultimately, he discovers that that text is indeed written in coded English and that it is Wilbur Whateley's mystical, occult diary. It speaks of clearing the earth of humans and others coming down from the air—an "elder race of beings from another dimension." Armitage becomes consumed with translating the document. He barely eats or sleeps until he finishes and then falls into a delirium for several days. Then he confides in his colleagues, Professor Rice and Dr. Morgan, both of whom witnessed Wilbur's dying body in the library. He notices a small item in the local paper about a "monster" created by the bootleggers of Dunwich, and he knows Wilbur's brother is on the loose. He has no choice but to hurry to Dunwich and stop it.

IX

Armitage, Rice, and Morgan arrive in Dunwich, which is under siege due to the murderous monster. The three men decide to compare notes with the state police, who were summoned upon the Frye tragedy, but they have disappeared after tracking the monster into the glen. Rice is armed with an agricultural-grade sprayer, and Morgan wields a big-game rifle. They spend the night in the ruins of the Frye house, and the next day the townspeople scramble to the Frye house to tell the three men that the creature is moving again. Luther has witnessed the sounds, smell, and movement of the terrible beast even though it appears to be invisible. It kills another resident, leaving behind only a tarry stickiness.

Armitage tells the townspeople what they are up against: the Whateleys were wizards, and they have conjured this evil, invisible entity. He has a potion that will make it visible and he knows the incantation that will kill it. They track the beast to Sentinel Hill.

X

Armitage, Rice, and Morgan ascend Sentinel Hill alone, while the townspeople remain on a nearby road, watching with the aid of a telescope. The three men climb to a precipice opposite where the monster is ascending and point the sprayer at it. The monster is revealed as an even larger version of Wilbur—yards and yards wide and more hideous, made of rope-like appendages like that of a spider or centipede, with gaping mouths lining its stalks. It has red eyes and albino hair. From the road the townspeople hear the whippoorwills as Armitage raises his hands and voices the incantation. The sky flashes with lightning, the hills rumble, thunder sounds, dogs bark. The stones of the mountaintop altar roar with unintelligible words: "Ygnaiih . . . ygnaiih . . . thflthkh'ngha . . . Yog-Sothoth." A tremendous crash issues forth from sky or earth—they cannot tell which. A lightning bolt pierces the sky from the stone altar on the hill. A stench almost knocks the men off their feet, and dead whippoorwills fall from the sky and litter the mountainside.

Armitage, Rice, and Morgan descend the mountain and assure the townspeople that the creature has been destroyed. Zebulon Whateley speaks up, saying, "Fifteen year' gone . . . I heerd Ol' Whateley say as haow some day we'd hear a child o' Lavinny's a-callin its father's name on the top o' Sentinel Hill." Armitage explains to the stunned men that the monster was Wilbur's twin brother, fathered by a "force that doesn't belong in our part of space." The Whateleys had intended to let the monster and other similar beings "wipe out the human race and drag the earth off to some nameless place for some nameless purpose."

CHARACTERS

Dr. Henry Armitage

Dr. Henry Armitage is the librarian at Miskatonic University, where Wilbur Whateley seeks a copy of the *Necronomicon*. He is a well-educated man in his seventies, with a distinguishing white beard. He deciphers the Latin version of the text over Wilbur's shoulder and is appalled at the boy's apparent intentions. He persuades librarians at other institutions to deny Wilbur's request to view the *Necronomicon*. After witnessing Wilbur's death, Armitage travels to Dunwich and discovers Wilbur's strange diary. He spends weeks deciphering it and concludes that Wilbur was part of a cult intent on destroying humanity in order to pave the way for ancient beings from another dimension to inherit the earth. With this knowledge, he returns to Dunwich to destroy the monster with help from his colleagues, Dr. Morgan and Professor Rice.

Luther Brown

Luther Brown is a young resident of Dunwich who witnesses the destruction caused by the invisible monster. Like all residents of Dunwich, he speaks in a pronounced New England accent and is uneducated.

Dunwich Horror

The Dunwich horror is the name given to the invisible entity, Wilbur's twin brother, that is born to the deformed albino woman, Lavinia Whateley. It grows even larger and faster than Wilbur, who is a freak of nature and not altogether human. However, it remains sequestered inside the Whateleys' farmhouse, fed by cattle that Old Whateley buys with ancient gold coins. After Wilbur's death, the Dunwich horror busts out of the house and ravishes the countryside around the town. It kills several townspeople and five policemen before it ascends Sentinel Hill and is destroyed by Henry Armitage, along with Morgan and Rice. Just prior to its demise, it is sprayed with a substance that renders it visible, revealing a creature as big as a building with many flailing tentacles and stalk-like limbs. The monster's father is revealed to be Yog-Sothoth, an extraterrestrial creature that Wilbur had wanted to summon back to Earth via passages from the *Necronomicon*.

Elmer Frye

Elmer Frye and his family are the first to be killed in Dunwich by the creature that escapes from the Whateleys' house.

Dr. Houghton

Dr. Houghton is the doctor from Aylesbury who is summoned by Wilbur to attend to Old Whateley as he is dying.

Dr. Francis Morgan

Dr. Francis Morgan is Armitage's colleague from Miskatonic University. Along with Professor Rice, he witnesses Wilbur's death, and he heads to Dunwich with Armitage and Rice to kill the beast.

Professor Warren Rice

Professor Warren Rice is Armitage's colleague at Miskatonic University, in Arkham, Massachusetts. He is present at Wilbur's death and travels to Dunwich to deal with the monster.

Earl Sawyer

Earl Sawyer is a resident of Dunwich who has occasional business dealings with Old Whateley and Wilbur. He takes care of the Whateleys' farm when Wilbur goes out of town.

Curtis Whateley

Curtis Whateley is from the undecayed branch of the Whateley family and is part of the posse that helps track the Dunwich horror to Sentinel Hill. He spies the monster's visible form through a telescope and is rendered temporarily insane.

Lavinia Whateley

Lavinia Whateley is Wilbur's mother. She is Old Whateley's daughter and is thirty-five when her son is born. She is "a somewhat deformed, unattractive albino woman" with "no known husband." She is uneducated except for what her father has taught her about black magic. She wanders about on the hills and has few interactions with the residents of the town. After Old Whateley's death, she confides in some of the townspeople that she is afraid of her son and does not understand him. She disappears on Halloween and is never seen again.

Old Whateley

Old Whateley is Lavinia's father and Wilbur's grandfather; he is from the "decaying" branch of the Whateley family, which, like many other families of Dunwich, has lived in the area for generations. He has been widowed for many years, but no one knows how his wife died. He practices black magic, and his decrepit house is full of books about the dark arts. He babbles nonsense, sometimes from the top of Sentinel Hill, which is covered in large stones arranged into a kind of makeshift altar. When Wilbur is born, Old Whateley renovates the aging farmhouse and buys cattle for unknown purposes, although his herd never gets any larger. He educates Wilbur in black magic until he dies.

On his deathbed, Old Whateley gives Wilbur explicit instructions to feed the beast upstairs, but not too fast lest it grow too quickly. Lastly, Wilbur must find a specific book—an unexpurgated Latin version of the *Necronomicon*—that has the incantation that will summon Yog-Sothoth and pave the way for the return of the Old Ones. Old Whateley's death coincides with the intense screeching of whippoorwills.

Wilbur Whateley

Wilbur is born in February 1913, on the feast day of Candlemas, to the sounds of howling dogs in the distance. He grows at a preternatural pace; he begins walking at seven months and talks at eleven months. He is intelligent but receives no formal schooling and speaks without a regional accent. By the time he is fifteen he is over nine feet tall and has a voice that does not sound human. He always carries a gun to protect himself from dogs that invariably want to attack him due to his peculiar odor.

After Old Whateley dies, Wilbur becomes obsessed with obtaining a copy of the *Necronomicon* that contains the ancient incantations that will allow the Old Ones to inherit the earth. Shortly after his grandfather's death, Wilbur presumably kills his mother. When Wilbur's quest to obtain the *Necronomicon* is stymied by Henry Armitage, Wilbur breaks into the library at Miskatonic University to steal it. A guard dog fatally attacks him. Upon dying, his true form is revealed. Although his face and arms appear normal, the bottom half of his body is made up of thick tentacles studded with sucking mouths.

Zebulon Whateley

Zebulon Whateley is from a less inbred branch of the Whateley family and assists in the hunt to kill the Dunwich horror.

Yog-Sothoth

Yog-Sothoth is one of the Old Ones, an extraterrestrial being from another dimension. It is surmised that he is the father of Wilbur and his twin brother, the invisible octopus-like creature—the Dunwich horror—that grows so large that the Whateleys' house explodes. Wilbur's quest is to summon Yog-Sothoth to Earth, which will put in motion a chain of events that will put an end to human life. However, the Dunwich horror is destroyed by Armitage before Yog-Sothoth can return, and thus he never appears directly in the story.

THEMES

Decay

The theme of decay in "The Dunwich Horror" is evident from the story's first paragraph. In describing the landscape around Dunwich, the narrator notes that the "sparsely scattered houses wear a surprisingly uniform aspect of age, squalor, and dilapidation." Furthermore, the town boasts a "broken-steepled church," "rotting gambrel roofs," and "houses...deserted and falling to ruin." According to Lovecraft, this description in his fictional world is based on what he observed on his travels. In *H. P. Lovecraft: A Critical Study*, Donald R. Burleson quotes Lovecraft as follows: "I used considerable realism in developing the locale of that thing—the prototype being the decaying agricultural region N. E. of Springfield, Mass.—especially the township of Wilbraham, where I visited for a fortnight in 1928."

But not just the landscape of Dunwich has fallen into decay; the residents themselves are the end result of hundreds of years of decay. Lovecraft defines them as

> a race by themselves, with the well-defined mental and physical stigmata of degeneracy and inbreeding. The average of their intelligence is woefully low, whilst their annals reek of overt viciousness and of half-hidden murders, incest, and deeds of almost unnamable violence and perversity.

Only a couple of families have managed to maintain branches that have escaped the "general level of decay," among them the Bishops and the Whateleys. Lovecraft consistently distinguishes between Lavinia, Old Whateley, and Wilbur, who are of "the decadent Whateleys"; Zebulon Whateley, who is from "a branch

TOPICS FOR FURTHER STUDY

- Read two stories, one by August Derleth and the other by Fritz Leiber, that incorporate elements of the Cthulhu Mythos first developed by Lovecraft. Write a paper comparing and contrasting their work with that of Lovecraft, as represented by "The Dunwich Horror."

- Lovecraft was enthralled by geography and included many descriptive passages in his stories, including "The Dunwich Horror." Biographer S. T. Joshi has referred to this world as the Miskatonic Region, which is a mix of real and invented locales. Referring to the many passages in the story in which this region is described, create a map and label the topography of Dunwich and the surrounding area. Note such features and locations as Sentinel Hill (and its stone columns), the Whateley farmhouse, the hills, the ravine, the mountains, gorges, wooden bridges, Round Mountain, the village itself, the Devil's Hop Yard, and "the ruins of the mill at the falls." Note the direction of Arkham in relation to the town, and add a legend that includes a scale of measurement.

- The *Necronomicon* that is central to "The Dunwich Horror" is a *grimoire*, or book of magic. Research grimoires. A good source

to consult is Owen Davies's *Grimoires: A History of Magic Books* (2009). Find out what grimoires exist in the United States and create a chart listing the libraries in which they can be found. Find out what qualifications you need to access these materials at each institution. Present your findings in an electronic spreadsheet that includes for each book the title, author, date, language, subject, sample text, and libraries that hold the volume.

- Using the description of the Dunwich horror, draw a picture of it in the medium of your choice as accurately as possible, using colors where appropriate. Label the drawing with quotations from the story.

- Joseph Bruchac's *Whisper in the Dark* (2005) is a young-adult novel featuring thirteen-year-old Maddie, an orphan who lives in Providence, Rhode Island, and is a descendant of a Narragansett Indian chief. Read the book and write a short paper outlining how Bruchac used Lovecraft's fiction—specifically "The Dunwich Horror"—as inspiration for the story. In particular, focus on the story's setting and its themes of family and legends.

---

that hovered about halfway between soundness and decadence"; and Curtis Whateley, "of the undecayed branch." Lovecraft suggests that it is the townspeople's decay that ultimately leads to the Dunwich horror. Their ignorance and low intelligence lead them to fear and shun the wizardly Old Whateley, which allows him to practice the dark magic that leads to the horrible existence of Wilbur and his brother.

Legends

In his extensive travels, Lovecraft recorded local legends that sometimes worked their way

into his stories. One such New England legend is that whippoorwills, sensing death, will surround a dying person and try to capture his or her soul when it departs the body. Lovecraft used this legend to great thematic effect in the story by describing the frantically chattering whippoorwills that precede the deaths of Old Whateley, Wilbur Whateley, and the Dunwich horror as "psychopomps lying in wait for the souls of the dying."

In addition to incorporating existing legends into his fiction, Lovecraft was also intent on creating his own legends. Dunwich history is

---

filled with examples of its ill-reputed past. The Devil's Hop Yard, "a bleak, blasted hillside where no tree, shrub, or grass-blade will grow," is based on a real place in Connecticut where legend holds that the strange stone formations were carved by the feet of the devil. Lovecraft also writes of a pastor—Reverend Abijah Hoadley—who in 1747 gave a sermon in Dunwich in which he spoke of "those Caves that only black Magick can discover, and only the Divell unlock." He was speaking of the strange hills nearby that made otherworldly noises. This is a legend not only of Dunwich, but also of Moodus, Connecticut, another real-life legend Lovecraft learned about during his travels and wrapped into his fictional world.

Lovecraft also imbues the founders of Dunwich with the legends and history of those associated with the Salem Witch Trials of 1692, thus anchoring his fictional world to one of the darkest episodes of US history. But even longer ago than that, the Pocumtucks were believed to have erected the mysterious stone columns on top of Sentinel Hill. The Pocumtuck were a Native American tribe that lived in what is now western Massachusetts and Connecticut. Although Lovecraft inserted the tribe into his story's legends, none of the Pocumtucks' structures are extant.

In "H. P. Lovecraft and His Work," an essay by Lovecraft's colleague and primary champion, August Derleth, Lovecraft is quoted as saying,

> All my stories, unconnected as they may be, are based on the fundamental lore or legend that this world was inhabited at one time by another race who, in practising black magic, lost their foothold and were expelled, yet live on outside ever ready to take possession of this earth again.

Toward that end, Lovecraft created the *Necronomicon*, a legendary grimoire (a book of magic spells and other how-tos of the occult), by "the mad Arab Abdul Alhazred." By fusing real legend with his invented legend, Lovecraft infuses his fictional world with real-world credibility.

Terror

Above all, Lovecraft is a horror writer, and "The Dunwich Horror" cannot be mistaken for anything other than a horror story. Lovecraft vividly conveys terror through his language and the characters' reactions to the story's events, especially those of the townspeople. For instance, when Henry Armitage realizes what Wilbur's intention is with the *Necronomicon*, he "felt a wave of fright as tangible as a draught of the tomb's cold clamminess." While Armitage's fright is contained, that of the townspeople is not. Through thick accents they reveal their terror. Luther Brown is the first to have witnessed the destruction:

> Up thar in the rud beyont the glen, Mis' Corey—they's suthin' ben thar! It smells like thunder, an' all the bushes an' little trees is pushed back from the rud like they'd a haouse ben moved along of it.

In the first part of the story, the terror is conveyed through inexplicable happenings, such as the abnormally fast and precocious growth of Wilbur Whateley, the unexplained construction on their house, the disappearance of cattle and Lavinia, Old Whateley's bizarre deathbed ranting, and the screaming of the whippoorwills. In the second part of the story, the culmination of terror is the description of Wilbur's death in the library, in which he is revealed to be a nine-foot-tall monster with sea-creature-like appendages lined with sucking mouths. The beast is covered with "coarse black fur" and has a "reticulated hide of a crocodile or alligator." His back "dimly suggested the squamous covering of certain snakes." Moreover, his vestigial tail shows signs of having "an undeveloped mouth or throat." Wilbur writhes in a pool of a smelly, sticky substance, twitching while the whippoorwills screech outside the window. This first climax of the story infuses the reader with a feeling of terror in its description of this "teratologically fabulous" creature.

The second climax of the story imparts terror with the actions of the Dunwich horror as it rampages through the town. The locals are terrified by something they cannot see as it destroys houses and kills the residents. As terrifying and inexplicable as this is, nothing prepares Armitage and the others who chase after it for what they see when the beast is finally made visible after being sprayed with a substance cooked up by Armitage. Lovecraft switches his point of view from Armitage to the townspeople, who view the action through a telescope at a safe distance at the bottom of Sentinel Hill. This allows the reader to view the terror through the decayed, uncomprehending locals rather than the learned and presumably

Wilbur and his grandfather tend to a mysterious creature in the family's farmhouse. (© bkp / Shutterstock.com)

more stoic academics from Miskatonic. Love-craft holds nothing back in this final descriptive passage, going for maximum terror. He describes a monster as big as a barn, writhing with trunk-like tentacles that are riddled with eyes. The sight is so hideous it causes Curtis Whateley (of sound mind and body, being from the undecayed branch of the Whateley family tree) to collapse into temporary insanity. The stench following the creature's demise is so terrible that "the vegetation never came right again." The final horror is in the story's last line, when Armitage reveals to the gathered men that the beast was Wilbur's twin brother.

STYLE

Setting

The New England setting of "The Dunwich Horror" is the canvas on which Lovecraft paints his story, and it is based on real locales. According to Lovecraft's confidant and pro-tégé August Derleth in his essay "H. P. Love-craft and His Work," the city of Arkham,

home of Miskatonic University, corresponds to Salem, Massachusetts, and Dunwich was modeled on "the country around Wilbraham, Monson, and Hampden." This was typical of Lovecraft, who was a lifelong New Englander intensely interested in the geography, history, and folklore of the region and often incorpo-rated tidbits he gathered from his travels into his work. The backwoods, isolated nature of Dunwich helps intensify the feeling of terror in the story simply because it is so removed from modern city life. It is a place that time has not touched, and therefore the ancient lore seems more likely to seep through into the present day.

Many critics have commented on the story's setting. "Not only is the landscape west of Arkham naturally secluded," writes Stefan Dziemianowicz in his essay "Outsiders and Aliens: The Uses of Isolation in Lovecraft's Fiction," but also "it has become associated with an 'outsidedness' that crosses the border from the external world to infect the internal world of the mind." Lovecraft chose this iso-lated location because it is conducive to his theme of decay. In an old, impoverished community with little new blood in hundreds of years, legends multiply and weird happenings can take place without the outside world catching on. It is noteworthy, for example, that when someone calls a newspaper to report the horror, the editor does not take it seriously, and the story of a monster becomes a humorous piece about the illegal whiskey trade in Dunwich.

Imagery and Language

Lovecraft gives his speakers in "The Dunwich Horror" thick New England accents that represent their long history of isolation. This highlights their outsider status and low intelligence. As a literary device, however, as Darrell Schweitzer explains in *The Dream Quest of H. P. Lovecraft*, "this was a more common practice in the 19th Century than it is today.... [The] intrusion of it can be jarring to someone who has never encountered it before." Not only do the residents of Dunwich speak in a distinct patois full of bad grammar (drawing attention to their lack of education), but each word itself has a distinct pronunciation that is conveyed through unconventional spelling. For instance, a villager commenting on the disappearance of five policemen who tracked the beast into the ravine, says, "Gawd...I told 'em not ter go daown into the glen, an' I never thought nobody'd dew it with them tracks an' that smell an' the whippoorwills a-screechin' daown thar in the dark o' noonday." In contrast, the language of Henry Armitage, who is a university librarian with a PhD, conveys his learnedness and grasp of the situation:

> We must follow it boys.... I believe there's a chance of putting it out of business. You men know that those Whateleys were wizards— well, this thing is a thing of wizardry, and must be put down by the same means.

Armitage's levelheadedness is reflected in his good grammar and the fact that all his dialogue is conveyed with standard spelling.

Hand in hand with the language of the dialogue in "The Dunwich Horror" is the imagery. Lovecraft is nothing if not descriptive; while he may not focus on character development, he does paint a vivid portrait of the horror in his story. One of the recurring images is that of the screeching whippoorwills—untold numbers of them—who produce "damnably rhythmical piping" in concert with Wilbur's dying breaths.

Likewise, Wilbur and the Dunwich horror are linked with a "frightful stench" that drives dogs, not to mention the townspeople, crazy and that turns into a "lethal foetor" that threatens to "asphyxiate" them. Mentioned several times is the "tarry stickiness" in which Wilbur lies while he dies and which is the only tangible remnant of the horror after it passes invisible through the town.

HISTORICAL CONTEXT

Weird Tales *and Pulp Fiction*

"The Dunwich Horror" was first published, like many of Lovecraft's stories, in *Weird Tales*, a pulp magazine founded by J. C. Henneberger in 1923 in Chicago and initially edited by Edwin Baird. Lovecraft was one of the magazine's most popular writers in its early years, along with Lovecraft's fellow Providence writer and friend C. M. Eddy Jr. and Clark Ashton Smith. In subsequent years, popular writers included Robert Bloch (author of the 1959 suspense novel *Psycho*) and Ray Bradbury. The stories that Lovecraft and others wrote were macabre horror stories frequently mixed with a healthy dose of science fiction, a genre that became known as weird fiction. Baird was a less-than-astute editor and was fired after just a dozen issues were published. Henneberger then hired Farnsworth Wright, who discovered and championed many of the authors who appeared in the magazine's pages, Lovecraft included, and whose high standards established the magazine's reputation for quality fiction even if its circulation never reached more than fifty thousand.

During the 1920s, pulp fiction magazines were a popular form of mass entertainment. Many titles had circulation of a million in an era when movies were still silent and radios were not yet a common household item. Pulp magazines were inexpensive, due to their low-quality paper stock (hence the term *pulp*), and featured brightly colored, often lurid covers to attract buyers. For a mere ten cents, readers received over one hundred pages of stories, many by respected writers of the day, including Edgar Rice Burroughs (author of *Tarzan* and *John Carter of Mars*), Zane Grey, Cornell Woolrich, Isaac Asimov, Ursula K. Le Guin, and Max Brand. Popular titles

COMPARE & CONTRAST

- **1929:** The circulation of *Weird Tales* is about fifty thousand copies per issue. This is far lower than other pulp magazines, which often have a circulation of one million per issue. However, the editor, Farnsworth Wright, pays authors a penny a word, twice the rate of other pulps.

  Today: After having folded and been revived in several different incarnations, *Weird Tales* continues to publish award-winning fiction and is available online at http://weirdtalesmagazine.com.

- **1929:** Lovecraft bases Dunwich on the town of Wilbraham, Massachusetts, a suburb of Springfield. Settled in 1730, the town is surrounded by farms, and the population is about 2,700. The previous year Lovecraft visited the town, where a local woman, Mrs. Miniter, told him the legend of the whippoorwills.

  Today: Wilbraham is no longer surrounded by farms, and the population is almost fifteen thousand. It is the home of Friendly's Ice Cream, a corporation that operates a chain of restaurants on the East Coast.

- **1929:** For "The Dunwich Horror," Lovecraft invents the *Necronomicon*, a fictional

grimoire compiled by the fictional Arab Abdul Alhazred.

  Today: Necronomicon Press in West Warwick, Rhode Island, established in 1976 to publish Lovecraft's work, is an award-winning small press publishing literature in the horror, weird fiction, and fantasy genres by a number of respected contemporary authors, including Ramsey Campbell, Brian Stableford, and Joyce Carol Oates. It also publishes literary criticism that focuses on Lovecraft.

- **1929:** Lovecraft writes of a bleak hillside known as the Devil's Hop Yard. As a result of his travels, Lovecraft is familiar with the real-life landmark, in East Haddam, Connecticut, which boasts unique geographical features.

  Today: Devil's Hopyard State Park, in East Haddam, Connecticut, is a popular camping ground named after local lore that explains its unusual pothole stone formations. Early settlers claimed that these were the burned-in footprints of the devil, who became enraged after getting his tail wet in the nearby waterfalls.

---

included *Argosy, Amazing Stories, Short Stories*, and *Horror Stories*. The heyday of the pulps was the 1930s, when Lovecraft was active; during the Great Depression, the pulps were a valuable and affordable source of entertainment for millions of people. By World War II (1939–1945), however, the situation had changed. Radio shows and movies had become the dominant forms of entertainment; paper shortages drove up magazine prices, and subscriptions waned.

Though many pulp authors were talented writers and infused their stories with all the

hallmarks of good fiction—themes, motifs, character motivation and development—their first priority was crafting a gripping story for the casual reader. Toward that end, Lovecraft concocted the most outrageous scenarios he could imagine in a quest to take readers places they could not have conceived of themselves. His descriptive passages functioned much as the magazines' lurid covers, describing in graphic detail the type of hideous monsters, such as Wilbur's twin brother in "The Dunwich Horror," that would provide readers with the cathartic delight they sought to enliven their everyday lives.

Lord Dunsany

Lord Dunsany, also known as Edward John Moreton Drax Plunkett, eighteenth Baron of Dunsany, was an Irish writer of fantasy stories whom Lovecraft greatly admired. Though they were contemporaries, they were hardly equals. Lord Dunsany's literary circle included W. B. Yeats, one of the English-speaking world's great poets of the early twentieth century, and Lady Gregory, a major figure of the Irish Literary Revival. Lord Dunsany was to the manor born; wealthy, educated, and of impeccable lineage, he became a decorated veteran of both the Second Boer War (1899–1902) and World War I (1914–1918), a world-class shooting champion, and an expert chess player.

As a writer, Lord Dunsany published over sixty books and numerous plays. According to biographer Joshi, Lovecraft was particularly influenced by Dunsany's *The Gods of Pegana*, published in 1905, a collection of linked short stories about a pantheon of gods in Pegana. Lovecraft wrote several pieces of criticism on Lord Dunsany's invented mythology, which Lovecraft admired for its "cosmicism," Joshi writes. After Lovecraft's death, Dunsany read Lovecraft's stories in book form and "found that he was writing in my style, entirely originally & without in any way borrowing from me, & yet with my style & largely my material," Lord Dunsany wrote to Lovecraft's confidant August Derleth in 1952, as quoted by Joshi. Indeed, as Joshi explains, "Lovecraft learned from Dunsany how to enunciate his philosophical, aesthetic, and moral conceptions by means of fiction." The surge of interest in Lovecraft's work after his death led to a revival of Dunsany's work; Derleth reissued some of Dunsany's titles through Arkham House, the publishing company Derleth founded in Sauk City, Wisconsin, to publish Lovecraft's work in book form.

Rural New England

Lovecraft was a traveler. He took weeks-long, frugal sojourns to various corners of New England, taking copious notes about the geography, the architecture, the people, and the lore of each area. In the 1920s, when Lovecraft wrote "The Dunwich Horror," automobiles were by no means universally owned, and paved highways through rural areas were still a thing of the future. Many old towns like Wilbraham, on which Dunwich was based, had been settled by Puritans or other religious groups in the early eighteenth century and continued to exist with little outside influence. Generations of the same family would inherit the original homestead, and dialects distinguished one region from the next. In the absence of any substantial industry, many towns did little more than subsist as farming communities. In an essay for *Extrapolation*, Timothy H. Evans notes that Lovecraft's trips often lasted for months and allowed him to observe "architecture...town plans, rural and urban cultural landscapes, cemeteries, furniture and other interior details, and the occasional item of folklore—legends, supernatural beliefs, [and] regional dialects."

Some of these legends and lore made it into Lovecraft's stories. Just as legend holds that the real Devil's Hopyard, refigured in "The Dunwich Horror," near Haddam, Connecticut, has been frequented by the devil and witches, so are the moaning sounds of Sentinel Hill based on the land near Moodus, Connecticut, whose woods have been emanating strange noises for hundreds of years. As in "The Dunwich Horror," these noises were a focal point of Native American rites but are today attributed to microearthquakes in the area.

As Evans notes, Lovecraft's travels familiarized him with towns that he mapped into his fictional world. The towns that Lovecraft created, including Dunwich,

> have changed little since Colonial times; in these towns, the weight of the past is not a pleasure but a burden. Decaying houses symbolize ruined lives; deals have been struck with dark forces; and closed shutters hide monstrosities. Poverty and isolation have allowed neighborhoods and entire towns to survive intact from the colonial era, but have also brought about ignorance, superstition, inbreeding and miscegenation.

Stefan Dziemianowicz, in his essay "Outsiders and Aliens: The Uses of Isolation in Lovecraft's Fiction," also comments on Lovecraft's extensive description of topography in "The Dunwich Horror": "Lovecraft devotes the entire first chapter solely to establishing that the ominous qualities of Dunwich that set it apart from the normal world are a natural part of its history."

Wilbur tries to get a copy of the Necronomicon *from Miskatonic University, but the librarian will not let him have it.*

(© Pichugin Dmitry | Shutterstock.com)

CRITICAL OVERVIEW

Like most of the fiction Lovecraft published in his lifetime, "The Dunwich Horror" made its first appearance in the pulp magazine *Weird Tales*. The publication's cheap paper stock and lurid covers ensured that the work would not be taken seriously by the literary community; indeed, the only notice it attracted was from the periodical's readership. S. T. Joshi notes in his biography *H. P. Lovecraft: A Life* that when "The Dunwich Horror" was printed in *Weird Tales*, "its praises were sung by the readership." Joshi himself applauds the story, writing that "its portrayal of the decaying backwoods Massachusetts terrain is vivid and memorable."

It took decades after Lovecraft's death in 1937 for his reputation to become established, and he has always been given a rough time by critics. In a *Village Voice* review of the collection *The Dunwich*

Horror and Others, critic Michael Feingold writes that "to know H. P. Lovecraft's stories is to know fear, but not literature." Lovecraft's most celebrated critic—and one of his earliest—was *New Yorker* writer Edmund Wilson, who called Lovecraft's writing "hackwork" and concludes that "the only real horror in most of [Lovecraft's] fictions is the horror of bad art and bad taste."

In a 1997 review, Douglas E. Winter writes that "The Dunwich Horror" "resounds with a principled naivete" that is "unconsciously parodic," as Lovecraft "courted the risible." Joshi, Lovecraft's biographer, acknowledges that even though "The Dunwich Horror" is "one of his most popular tales" it has "serious flaws of conception, execution, and style." Joshi considers "many points of plotting and characterisation" to be "painfully inept."

Much of the criticism of the story centers on the character of Henry Armitage. Joshi calls him "the prize buffoon in all Lovecraft." Ultimately, Joshi concludes, the story's

> luridness, melodrama, and naive moral dichotomy were picked up by later writers.... In a sense, then, Lovecraft bears some responsibility for bringing the 'Cthulhu Mythos' and some of its unfortunate results upon his own head.

Donald R. Burleson, author of *H. P. Lovecraft: A Critical Study*, also takes issue with the character Armitage, stating that he "sounds like a buffoon because, in mythic context, he *is* a buffoon," primarily because of his "moralizing good-versus-evil mentality that seems to run mawkishly contrary to the precepts of the Lovecraft Mythos." Burleson concludes that

> the twins, for whom one is presumably to feel loathing, are archetypally heroic; Armitage, whom one is presumably supposed to admire, is essentially a cipher; and thematically the tale gives articulation to the Lovecraftian view that man is but an evanescent mote in the universe of stars.

According to Stefan Dziemianowicz in his essay "Outsiders and Aliens," "Armitage seems a far cry from the usual figure in the Lovecraft Mythos who is left dazed by the truths he has uncovered and frustrated by the knowledge that he alone has grasped their full meaning."

Critic Peter Cannon, in his book *H. P. Lovecraft*, applauds the story's language, noting that

> the humble language of the farm succinctly conveys the terror of the beast. While this sort of literal rendering of speech, once common in both popular and serious fiction, may be out of fashion, the extreme dialect of the Dunwich

natives does serve to thicken the narrative texture, especially in those dramatic phone calls over the party lines during the week the horror roams at large.

Cannon concludes that "in every suggestive incident and weird detail, from the Whateleys' cattle buying to the business of the legend of the whippoorwills...'The Dunwich Horror' exhibits the master's touch."

LOVECRAFT'S LOVE OF OVERSTATEMENT EXTENDS TO HOW OFTEN HE DESCRIBES EVENTS BY STATING HOW THEY CANNOT BE DESCRIBED—A KIND OF CATCH-22. SOME READERS MAY FIND THIS EFFECTIVE, BUT OTHERS MAY FIND IT MADDENING."

CRITICISM

Kathy Wilson Peacock

Wilson Peacock is a writer and editor who specializes in twentieth-century fiction. In the following essay, she analyzes Lovecraft's "The Dunwich Horror" according to the rules of good writing outlined in William Strunk Jr.'s classic handbook The Elements of Style.

H. P. Lovecraft has influenced generations of respected horror writers, from Robert Bloch to Stephen King, Ramsey Campbell, and Clive Barker. He has also attracted loathing from others, such as acclaimed science fiction writer Ursula Le Guin, who wrote in the *Times Literary Supplement* that "Lovecraft was an exceptionally, almost impeccably, bad writer." One reason for this assessment, evident to anyone who has made his or her way through "The Dunwich Horror," is the sheer wordiness of his writing. Lovecraft never passes up an opportunity to paint the page with every synonym for *horror* he can find. This tactic is in opposition to the thinking of the day ("The Dunwich Horror" was published in 1929), which stated that good writing should "omit needless words." This wisdom came from William Strunk Jr.'s *The Elements of Style*, first published in 1918. Of course, every author has artistic license to tell a story in the manner he or she sees fit, but critics also have the right to call foul. Lovecraft's "The Dunwich Horror" was written after the fall of flowery Victorian prose and during the rise of the minimalist trend of modernism, but it stylistically belongs to the former era. *The Elements of Style*, as the bible of good writing for nearly one hundred years now, reveals that "The Dunwich Horror" violates many rules held sacrosanct by the literary cognoscenti. But rules are made to be broken, and legions of Lovecraft's fans would claim that "The Dunwich Horror" proves that codifying good writing is futile because art is in the eye of the beholder.

Strunk was an English professor at Cornell University for nearly half a century, while Lovecraft was a self-taught writer who had no use for the academic world, except for his invented Miskatonic University. Lovecraft was not writing for the *New Yorker*, as one of his earliest critics, Edmund Wilson, and Strunk's successor in matters of style, E. B. White, did; he was writing for pulp magazines and getting paid by the word. This fact alone may explain why his stories are so wordy. His earliest readers were laypeople seeking escapist thrills through fiction. They wanted to be scared, amazed, dazzled, and transported to another world by a tale so unusual that the Great Depression lapping at their door would be held at bay for an hour or two.

Lovecraft's adjectival and adverbial overload, which does little to advance his plots, nevertheless acts as a mood enhancer to his stories. It is rather like running a snapshot through an Instagram filter and ending up with a heightened version of reality. A professional photographer may abhor the Instagram shortcut, just as a "trained" writer abhors using words to "tell," not "show." But in a world crowded with media vying for people's attention, the loudest pictures and words often win the battle. However, in Lovecraft's predigital world, lorded over by literary critics such as the *New Yorker*'s Wilson, wordiness was a huge handicap. Reviewing several Lovecraft collections that were published in 1945, Wilson wrote that

> Lovecraft's worst fault is his incessant effort to work up the expectation of the reader by sprinkling his stories with such words as "horrible," "terrible," "frightful," "awesome," "fearsome," "eldritch," "eerie," "weird," "forbidden," "unhallowed," "unholy," "blasphemous," "hellish," and "infernal." Surely one of the primary

WHAT DO I READ NEXT?

- Lovecraft's "The Case of Charles Dexter Ward" is a novella written in 1927 but not published until after the author's death. It follows the title character's doctor as he attempts to discover what happened to Ward after he disappeared from a mental hospital in Rhode Island. Ward had apparently become obsessed with his ancestor Joseph Curwen, an alchemist, murderer, and practitioner of black magic.

- *An H. P. Lovecraft Encyclopedia* (2001), by S. T. Joshi and David E. Schultz, draws from thousands of Lovecraft's unpublished letters, examines each of the writer's major works and characters, and provides lengthy entries on his travels, critics, influences, associates, the *Necronomicon*, and the Cthulhu Mythos.

- *Necronomicon: The Wanderings of Alhazred* (2004), by Donald Tyson, takes up where Lovecraft left off with his grimoire. This book, a supposed translation, collects the findings of the fictional Abdul Alhazred, a necromancer from Yemen, from ancient Babylon secrets to the incantations that summon Yog-Sothoth.

- Ramsey Campbell's *The Inhabitant of the Lake and Other Unwelcome Tenants* (1964) is a collection of Campbell's early fiction inspired by Lovecraft's Cthulhu Mythos and adding to the canon. A fiftieth-anniversary edition was published in 2013, signifying the stories' and Campbell's importance to late twentieth-century weird fiction.

- Lord Dunsany created an otherworldly universe for his fantasy stories and plays, including those collected in *The Book of Wonder: A Chronicle of Little Adventures at the Edge of the World* (1912). Lord Dunsany, a figure of the Irish Literary Revival of the early twentieth century, was a particular influence on Lovecraft, and many of these stories include invented gods, thieves, and cannibals and are rife with magic and mythos.

- Arthur Machen's "The Great God Pan" is a novella first published in 1890, which Lovecraft mentions in "The Dunwich Horror." It concerns a beautiful but sinister woman who leaves a trail of death and destruction wherever she goes. When she is hanged, it is discovered that she is the progeny of a human and the god Pan by way of a mad doctor.

- Jorge Luis Borges's 1975 short story "There Are More Things," from his collection *The Book of Sand*, was inspired by H. P. Lovecraft and concerns an extraterrestrial being living in a suspicious house in Argentina that all the locals avoid.

- Neil Gaiman's 2002 novella *Coraline* is an award-winning young-adult horror/fantasy tale about a young girl who discovers a secret apartment adjacent to her own, occupied by her Other Mother and Other Father, doppelgängers for her real parents who have black buttons for eyes. Gaiman's work, like Lovecraft's, often incorporates elements common to mythology and Victorian literature.

---

rules for writing an effective tale of horror is never to use any of these words—especially if you are going, at the end, to produce an invisible whistling octopus.

"The Dunwich Horror" is a long story—over seventeen thousand words—but the plot is straightforward, with no subplots, and there is no character development. The story is intended to produce a visceral reaction in the reader, nothing more. If Ernest Hemingway, the modernist literary hero of Lovecraft's day, had written the story, he would have done so in two-thirds of the words, adhering to each of Strunk's rules. (He would also likely have given the monster the physical characteristics of a bull instead of a kraken and included a brawl between Armitage and Wilbur.)

Strunk's "omit needless words" is his most useful rule and the one that any self-respecting writer takes to heart. Many of its corollaries were added in later editions by White, including "write with nouns and verbs"; "do not overwrite"; "do not overstate"; "avoid the use of qualifiers"; "do not explain too much"; and "avoid fancy words." Two of his other rules—"use orthodox spelling" and "do not use dialect unless your ear is good"— are also blatantly violated by Lovecraft, but to a more successful degree. The people of Dunwich speak in a New England patois that demonstrates their outsider status and the fact that they live in a bygone world untouched by modernity. Toward this end, Lovecraft uses creative spelling: "haff" for "half"; "expeck" for "expect"; "yew" for "you"; "suthin'" for "something"; and "allus" for "always." Here is the dialect in full glory, as Luther Brown gives a secondhand account of the strange goings on in Dunwich: "The graoun' was a-talkin' las night, an' towards mornin' Cha'ncey he heerd the whippoorwills so laoud in Col' Spring Glen he couldn't sleep nun." What is the advantage of using a spelling like *nun* for *none* if the pronunciation is the same? Some would say that it conveys the speaker's lack of intelligence. But this is perhaps overkill, given that Luther's bad grammar has already clued the reader in to his approximate IQ. The heavy dialect can slow down the reader at times, something one would think Lovecraft's original readers would not have liked, given the fact that they were reading for pleasure. Yet here is Lovecraft, doubling down on his technique with a heavy hand: "[He] didn't look keerful ter see whar the big matted-daown swath led arter it lef the pasturage, but he says he thinks it p'inted towards the glen rud to the village." Some of these passages require the same decoding skills as the *Necronomicon*, but perhaps that is half the fun.

Like his 110 percent effort in writing dialect, Lovecraft never passes up a chance to dress up a sentence, thereby committing needless words to the page. When introducing the topography of the region surrounding Dunwich, this habit comes in handy:

> The planted fields appear singularly few and barren; while the sparsely scattered houses wear a surprisingly uniform aspect of age, squalor, and dilapidation. Without knowing why, one hesitates to ask directions from the gnarled, solitary figures spied now and then on crumbling doorsteps or on the sloping, rock-strewn meadows.

In two sentences comprising fifty-nine words, Lovecraft gives the reader thirteen adjectives and six adverbs. This works well early in the story to set the mood. He lets the reader know there is something wrong with Dunwich. It is off the beaten path; the houses and the people are decaying; the foliage is overgrown and the fields are barren; and the symmetry of the hills is unnatural. The problems emerge when Lovecraft starts to repeat himself and his words lose their effect.

This is most evident with Lovecraft's adjectives. For example, "The Dunwich Horror" contains the word *forbidden* six times, *blasphemous* eight, *curious* nine, *hideous* ten, *monstrous* fourteen, *fearsome* sixteen, and *strange* twenty-four. These words are all of a piece—they add to the mood of terror, but only because they are telling the reader how to feel rather than showing him or her. These choices violate the "omit needless words" corollaries "do not overstate" and "do not overwrite." In regard to the latter, as the 1979 version of *The Elements of Style* states, "Rich, ornate prose is hard to digest, generally unwholesome, and sometimes nauseating." Surprise—*unwholesome* and *nauseating* are two of Lovecraft's favorite words, and ornate prose is his specialty. While Strunk's advice may be good for critics and academics, it simply would not be Lovecraft without a moody sentence such as "From below no sound came, but only a distant, undefinable foetor;... the men preferred to stay on the edge and argue, rather than descend and beard the unknown Cyclopean horror in its lair." Thirty-three words, including five adjectives, six verbs, and an obligatory "horror."

Strunk and White write that "A single overstatement... diminishes the whole, and a single carefree superlative has the power to destroy... the object of the writer's enthusiasm." Here, Lovecraft is in real trouble. The word *hellish* appears five times in "The Dunwich Horror," *foetid* eight, and *terror* ten. After the first three mentions of something being hellish, the remaining utterances hold little water. Even more precarious is Lovecraft's double climax, featuring the deaths of first Wilbur and then his twin brother. This is quite a hat trick; Lovecraft appears to give Wilbur's death everything he has got, describing the dying boy's form by saying that

> no human pen could describe it, but one may properly say that it could not be vividly visualized by anyone whose ideas of aspect and contour are too closely bound up with the common life-forms of this planet and of the three known dimensions.

The hyperbole appears to be turned all the way up here, describing things as so horrible that they simply cannot be described, so how will Lovecraft top this when he gets to the second climax? According to Strunk and White, Lovecraft's sin is in not holding back; his overstatement means that "the reader will be instantly on guard . . . because he has lost confidence in [the author's] judgment."

Lovecraft's love of overstatement extends to how often he describes events by stating how they cannot be described—a kind of catch-22. Some readers may find this effective, but others may find it maddening. "A recurring theme in Lovecraft's prose is that which is beyond description," writes Philip Smith in an essay for *Literature Compass*. Smith notes that Lovecraft's favorite words and phrases, all mentioned dozens of times across his body of work, include "unheard of," "inconceivable," "nameless," "indescribable," "unmentionable," "inexplicable," "unexplainable," "useless to describe," "no pen could even suggest," and "unknown." The result, Smith concludes, is that "Lovecraft's prose . . . orchestrates a failure in signification."

In section VII of "The Dunwich Horror," Luther Brown "rushed frenziedly back from his morning trip to Ten-Acre Meadow." This is adverbial overkill, adding *frenziedly* when *rushed* will do, especially since the next sentence states that "he was almost convulsed with fright." Here, *almost* is the unnecessary adverb. Why use it, when *convulsed with fright* would do? This structure is repeated from the previous paragraph, when Wilbur's diary is described as "an almost interminable manuscript." This is an instance in which a copyeditor would have come in handy and also would have likely deleted the redundant adjective *baffling* from the phrase *baffling puzzle*, used to describe the diary's text.

Ultimately, the test is whether this passage would impart the same feeling without the excessive verbiage. Luther Brown "rushed . . . back from his morning trip to Ten-Acre Meadow with the cows. He was . . . convulsed

with fright as he stumbled into the kitchen." In the next paragraph, he "seemed to shiver afresh with the fright that had sent him flying home." A rookie mistake: *seemed* is almost never necessary. Luther should have simply "shivered afresh." Peter Cannon, writing in *H. P. Lovecraft*, notes that "even such a passing phrase as 'anaemic, bloodless-looking cows' would seem to contain one adjective too many." What does *anaemic* add that is not conveyed by *bloodless*?

Sometimes Lovecraft uses atmospheric language where it simply is not needed. When the townspeople are tracking the Dunwich horror, they discover it has "gone down into the great sinister ravine." *Sinister* is overkill—never before has the ravine been considered sinister; it is simply a topographical feature, though overgrown, of the town and has not been mentioned before in conjunction with witchcraft or Native American lore, as has Sentinel Hill. It plays no special part in the story except as a hiding place for the horror. The same goes for "the dreaded volume . . . the hideous *Necronomicon*." Is the book itself dreaded and hideous, perhaps emanating the "frightful stench" that seems to follow Wilbur around? No. It is just a collection of magic spells and incantations. But Lovecraft simply cannot pass up an opportunity to drop adjectives into a sentence, thereby "telling" even as he is also "showing." In addition to describing the *Necronomicon* as "dreaded" and "hideous," he mentions that the book is "kept under lock and key at the college library." That alone imparts all we need to know about the tome: It is not meant for casual perusal.

Thus, while Lovecraft's language is amenable to aficionados, it is a perennial punching bag for critics. But complaining is what critics do, and continuing to carry a torch for Lovecraft is what his fans do, fulfilling the demand for dozens of compilations of his stories, criticism of his stories, and biographies. Decades after his death, having inspired a publishing house; a real-world edition of the *Necronomicon*; innumerable websites and blogs; walking tours of Providence; and thousands of works by musicians, artists, and writers, Lovecraft has proven that his sustained relevance transcends his lack of academic skill.

Source: Kathy Wilson Peacock, Critical Essay on "The Dunwich Horror," in *Short Stories for Students*, Gale, Cengage Learning, 2015.

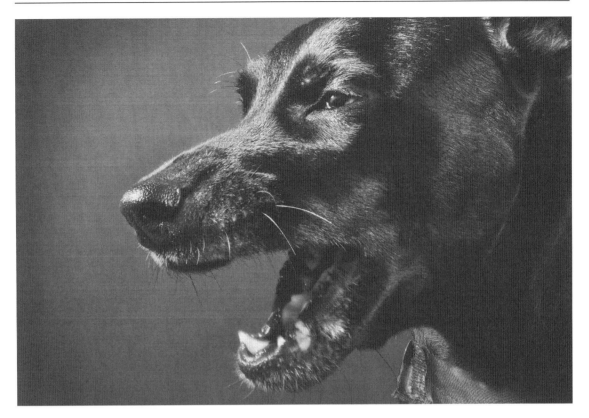

After Wilbur is killed by the library's guard dog, there is no one to take care of the creature in the farmhouse. (© Mila Atkovska | Shutterstock.com)

Timo Airaksinen

In the following essay, Airaksinen discusses "The Dunwich Horror" in terms of a religious parody.

In Dunwich, Dr. Henry Armitage kills a raging monster, the sole surviving son of Yog-Sothoth, by means of an incantation on a sacred hill. This reminds the reader of *The Case of Charles Dexter Ward* in which Dr. Marinus Bicknell Willett disposes of the wizard Curwen in a similar way by using the right word. Why not? The word has become flesh before. Also other familiar references can be found, for instance, to the blasted heath: "the Devils Hop Yard—a bleak, blasted hillside" which echoes the state of Nahum's farm, as described in "The Colour out of Space." The "Colour" is written 1927 and the "Dunwich" 1928. There, too, "the vegetation never came right again."

"The Dunwich Horror" can be read as a religious parody even in a more straightforward way than "The Colour out of Space," where some words and expressions are ironic allusions to the language of religion. Here the whole story can be seen as a religious allegory, as several critics have suggested. According to Donald R. Burleson, it is an "obvious parody."

An albino woman gives birth to a child whose father seems to be a god, Yog-Sothoth. The woman, Lavinia, is virgin not only because she is unmarried but because she is white, an albino. She gives birth to twins, Wilbur and the nameless horror, which is destroyed by Dr. Armitage, our Pontius Pilate. Wilbur studies holy texts when he is quite young, mainly the *Necronomicon*, in order to fulfill his purpose on Earth. He needs to clear it of sinners, so that the true believers may inherit the world. But as the religious myth goes, the sinners turn against him and his brother by killing them both.

The nameless son perishes on a hill, calling his father's name, just as was prophesied by the Old Whateley, Lavinia's father. This prophecy appears to be misunderstood, though. It reads: "Some day yew folks'll hear a child o' Lavinny's a-callin' its father's name on the top o' Sentinel Hill!" The call, when it finally comes,

THE TALE HAS ITS MULTIPLIED

SYMMETRICAL STRUCTURE, TWO PLOTS,

TWO RACES, TWO SAVIORS, TWO VISITS, AND

TWO TEMPLES, WHICH ALLOW THE READER

TO CHOOSE HIS SIDE FREELY."

proves to be a desperate plea for help and redemption, far from the triumphant act expected by the proud but misled prophet. But we know that the Jewish prophets expected Jesus to be a king, too.

Another interesting and well-known feature of this story is the role of the monster child Wilbur. In the first stage of the Dunwich horror, he takes the leading role in the play. For once, Lovecraft creates a monster who deserves the readers' sympathy so that they can (almost) identify with him. In this way the story is unique.

Wilbur grows into an ugly teenager who needs to learn the lore of the *Necronomicon*. Because his poor home library contains only an incomplete copy of John Dee's English language edition, he needs to go to the Miscatonic University Library and consult their complete Latin edition. John Dee (1521–1608) is of course an historical person. This fact is not always noticed, and Dee is treated as a fictional character.

Wilbur soon sees that he must take the book home because the lore must be tested under special conditions which cannot be created in the Library. Though readers are not told more, they get the point. The library does not allow him to borrow the volume, so Wilbur is forced to steal it. One night he tries to do so but is attacked by a crazy watchdog which strips him naked and kills him, thus revealing his deformed body.

This recalls the climax of "The Colour out of Space" where Nahum's body is also exposed. While Dr. Armitage and his entourage are watching, the body dissolves and vanishes. The religious analogy is again clear. Camp wants to see the fear of sexuality in the

description of Wilbur's lower body, but this does not sound quite convincing. The body is taken back to its father so that only an empty grave remains after the son's death. The body does not really belong to space and time.

Why Arkham University has a watchdog in chains on the campus is not explained. That any university would use dogs as dangerous as the one which killed the young Whateley is highly unlikely. Another remarkable zoological feature of the story is the use of birds, whippoorwills, as "psychopomps," who hunt the souls of the dead and who die when Wilbur's brother is killed by Dr. Armitage: "Dogs howled from the distance, green grass and foliage wilted to a curious, sickly yellow-grey, and over field and forest were scattered the bodies of dead whippoorwills."

"The Dunwich Horror" is divided into two horrors. The first involves the birth, short life, and death of Wilbur, while the second is the hunt for his invisible brother. The first part is interesting mainly because of the tension between its two main characters, Wilbur and Dr. Armitage. Wilbur emerges as a tragic antihero whose opposite is the erudite doctor.

Wilbur is bound to lose the fight because he is in the wrong place, confused, clumsy, deformed, and anxious. Dr. Armitage, on the contrary, is clear-headed, agile, strong, and relaxed. But he is also a bore who deserves none of the reader's sympathy. This failure of character which approaches stupidity makes the story tragic. Wilbur is the only possible center of interest whose destiny captures the reader's imagination. His dialectical opposite is the doctor whose powers destroy Wilbur but who fails to convince the reader of his explanations. Wilbur and his brother must be destroyed because they need human blood to open the gates to Yog-Sothoth and his likes. The brother crushes houses and eats cattle, and so they are menaces.

Wilbur is also a genuine character who strives to achieve something in spite of his handicaps. The other brother is just a workhorse: "only them from beyond kin make it multiply and work...only them, the old uns as wants to come back." Be that as it may, Wilbur's death is a tragic event.

The angelic doctor himself speaks like a moralistic idiot who might as well be speaking of alcohol and prohibition: "Now we've only this one thing to fight, and it can't multiply. It can, though, do a lot of harm; so we mustn't hesitate to rid the community of it."

Here we have a cosmic messenger from unknown dimensions, the son of a god, Yog-Sothoth's offspring, but our utilitarian doctor infers simply that they should minimize the harm to themselves by killing the beast. After his success in sending Wilbur's brother to where he belongs, Dr. Armitage expresses himself in an amusingly prudish tone of voice:

> It was—well, it was mostly a kind of force that doesn't belong in our part of space; a kind of force that acts and grows and shapes itself by other laws than those of our sort of nature. We have no business calling in such things from outside, and only very wicked people and very wicked cults ever try to.

Dr. Armitage pretends that he understands the mystery at Dunwich by referring to some "other laws" and to "a kind of force." These are empty phrases. He fails to see the mystery and its theological implications. He gives his simple-minded listeners some boring advice, repeating the words "very wicked," which belong to nursery rhymes and which fail to capture the seriousness of what has happened.

This tale contains more dialogue than Lovecraft's tales usually do. Lovecraft was reluctant to write dialogue because he thought that he did not need it. He even said, "[It] is clear that dialogue has never been of much use to me." He was also insecure about his ability to handle this literary technique. Thus, we may ask whether Dr. Armitage is a clumsy picture or merely a clumsy person, but this much can be said. While Lovecraft could not handle as difficult a topic as the knightly hero's parting words to his admirers, he knew exactly what he was doing when he drew the picture of the doctor. We can use the introduction of the doctor as evidence. We read that this person is "the same erudite Henry Armitage (A.M. Miscatonic, Ph.D. Princeton, Litt.D. Johns Hopkins) who had once called at the farm." He has too many titles.

He makes one false appearance in the tale, but now he comes in for real and introduces himself to the reader. Anyone who does it in the manner of Dr. Armitage is pompous. Somehow it may be significant that he mentions that he is A.M., instead of M.A., Master of Arts. Perhaps he wants to say that he is the morning and sunrise, the promise of a new day after the night

of the monsters. Moreover, according to the unwritten laws of the academic world, only highest degree counts, in this case both are doctorates. Of course in those times titles were more valuable than they are now. Yet it is a long list of merits.

Dr. Armitage is an erudite and brilliant scholar, who is able to decipher the Wilbur manuscript, but he is also an aggressive, possessive, and narrow-minded hypocrite. In the end, he probably errs when he says that Wilbur's brother looks more like his father. First, he has never seen Yog-Sothoth. Second, the reader knows that the brother was just a workhorse designed to sit inside a barn until the Old Ones put it to work. This is why it wanders aimlessly around the countryside creating havoc, as it searches for food. Wilbur was supposed to keep its growth under control but he is now dead. It is hardly likely that the gods look like workhorses, even if they stink.

"The Dunwich Horror" seems to glorify Dr. Armitage's learning, annotativeness, hard work, courage, and morals. Yet he is only a *deus ex machina*, an artificial entity without life or blood who is needed to make the narrative work. One monster is loose and another is waiting in the wings. Something should be done, so let the doctor take the stage. Yet the doctor has also another role. If we look at Lamarckian biology and its effects on social stratification more closely, we notice that Dr. Armitage represents a singular moment within an interesting structure. On the bottom rung, we have the degenerate elements, like some of the Whateleys who are said to resemble their neighbors:

> the natives are now repellently decadent, having gone far along that path of retrogression so common in many New England backwaters. They have come to form a race by themselves, with the well-defined mental and physical stigmata of degeneracy and in-breeding.

However, "some of the Whateleys and Bishops still send their eldest sons to Harvard and Miscatonic." This is to say that not all of the families are hopeless. Certainly the hopefulness associated with these more normal people pales when the corrupt branches are mentioned. We also notice that Wilbur and his invisible brother are born to Old Whateley's daughter Lavinia. The old man is both mad and a wizard. He has "an added element of furtiveness in the clouded brain which subtly transformed him from an object of fear to a subject of fear."

His wizardry, which made him so odd and scary, is no longer a factor. And as we know, Lavinia has her physical stigma, her albinism. In Dunwich, we meet the degenerates, half degenerates, and their educated children who "seldom return." Visiting university people and, finally, Dr. Armitage, a singular man complete the list.

Yog-Sothoth has chosen the most corrupt of all the local people to conquer the world, that is, to clear it of people, and then come back from the other dimensions. The monsters are born from the lowest forms of human life, according to Lovecraft's racist and Lamarckian biological theory, which makes them equally degenerate.

Lovecraft is clearly a Lamarckian because he thinks that acquired physical and mental characteristics can be inherited, yet he does not mention Lamarck in his letters. He refers to Darwin many times, however. Yog-Sothoth may be a god, yet he is one with the most disgusting elements on earth. He has copulated with one of them and produced children with her. They are strange gods, pictured in a way which is so ironic that the reader has difficulties comprehending it. The wanderers of the infinite hyperspace, parallel universes, and extra dimensions are no-good beggars, whose only possibility of becoming visible and threatening to those who go to Miscatonic and Harvard, is to ask for help from those who no longer are human. A combination of Lovecraft's racial and atheistic furor creates a situation where the lowest of all beings are gods, who are related, through family ties, to those who are no longer real human beings.

When Wilbur is compared to Christ, and Lavinia to the Virgin Mary, Sentinel Hill to Golgotha and the brother's final cry for help to the words of Christ, this reading should not be taken seriously, since it is a good joke and no more. We know, for instance, that the people who bred the twins belong to a different race than the people of Arkham. Their search for their own god will be fulfilled along with the coming of Wilbur. Dr. Armitage, on the other hand, belongs to the human race, in the normal sense of the word meaning *homo sapiens*. He is the real savior of the world who recognizes, interprets, makes visible, and finally kills the messenger of the gods. He uses logical reasoning.

Hence, this story is not really about good and evil in its Manichean form. We should resist the reading that makes Old Whateley and his grandsons evil and Dr. Armitage good. On the contrary, we have two races of people, two cultures, two worlds which meet at some point with calamitous results. Houses collapse, people vanish, and cattle are devoured. Lovecraft hated the idea of cultural co-existence. He was a separationist who felt the need to keep cultures isolated from each other, because he saw what happens when the different gods present their requirements. Those he does not know come from the deep gulfs of time and space, from other dimensions, and their activities produce just a "blasted heath" from which all the people are cleared.

Wilbur is only a scout preparing the ground for the coming of others. But the Library kills him. Lovecraft's concept of heroism is quite twisted. If Robert Howard wanted to make Conan the Barbarian rule the Cimmerian age with his skull-splitting axe, Lovecraft's hero is a librarian who refuses to loan a book to a person who does not look right and who stinks. Indeed, had Wilbur succeeded in borrowing the *Necronomicon* either from the Miscatonic or Harvard, the human race would be dead by now, except the non-human parodies of *homo sapiens* who would rejoice along with Yog-Sothoth and Shub-Niggurath. The axe is nothing compared with the library card, which penetrates with a much greater force.

Now the reader understands the meaning of the strangest feature of this strange story, the existence of the watch dog outside the library. A place that contains the greatest power on Earth, the temple of learning, cannot be guarded only by human beings. We need the help of the beast which is ready to tear the intruder to shreds and leave his naked body displayed with all its mutations revealed. The library itself is transformed into a sacred place, a temple, just like the Whateley farm. Both races have their own shrines.

Dr. Armitage makes a visit, in disguise, to the *cella* of the monsters, and he survives. Wilbur does exactly the same, although he meets with little success. He takes the risk and goes back, but then nothing can save him. The beast is loose, and Wilbur's gun does not fire. His own beast, Yog-Sothoth, is imprisoned in the library from which Wilbur cannot free him. The book, *Necronomicon*, is behind lock and key, in a dungeon, guarded by the dog.

The tale has its multiplied symmetrical structure, two plots, two races, two saviors, two visits, and two temples, which allow the reader to choose his side freely. The human beings are in a stronger position, because they have the book which contains the secret and they are able to keep it unseen. But it is not their book, and therefore, they cannot sympathize with the unhappy deformed Wilbur who should accomplish too much in a hostile world. He is a genuine character, so much so that when critics complain that Lovecraft never created a life-like, memorable character, we should not forget Wilbur and his pitiable body in that temple of the cruelest of religions, learning. One thing is certain; nobody needs the church: "most of the houses are deserted and falling to ruin, and...the broken-steepled church now harbours the one slovenly mercantile establishment of the hamlet." All the cultural wars in the valley have created a situation like that in the former German Democratic Republic. I do not think that mature Lovecraft's socialism would allow for it.

Source: Timo Airaksinen, "Let My People Go: 'The Dunwich Horror,'" in *The Philosophy of H. P. Lovecraft: The Route to Horror*, Peter Lang Publishing, 1999, pp. 129–35.

Donald R. Burleson

In the following excerpt, Burleson analyzes the story's title.

...The town name Dunwich itself derives from the name of an ancient town in England on the coast of the North Sea, a town which, over the centuries of its existence from Saxon times to the present, has gradually crumbled away into the encroaching sea. In early times the town was known variously as Dunwyc, Donewic, and Dunewic. The *-wic* or *-wyc* is a suffix meaning dwelling place, town, village, cluster of houses (compare the Latin *vicus*) and surviving as *-wich* or *-wick* in other place-names such as Norwich and Warwick. The rest of the name is of intriguingly uncertain meaning, though in *dun* we find suggestions of dark colors, murkiness, and gloom, appropriate to the mood of the tale and to the fictional town's reputation. It is interesting that the *Oxford English Dictionary* gives, as a possibility for *-wich*, the meaning "a group of buildings connected with a salt-pit," suggesting salt, brine, and thus

the sea. Here we begin to glimpse connections between the town itself and the horror that visits it. Of Wilbur Whateley's horrific twin, kept upstairs in the farmhouse, it is said that "from the vacant abyss overhead there came a disquieting suggestion of rhythmical surging or lapping, as of the waves on some level beach." As we shall see, this is only one peripheral way, among other and more insistent ways, in which distinguishing barriers between the town's human population on the one hand and, on the other, the alien horror that plagues the town are broken down. The very fact that the original coastal Dunwich was a town crumbling away goes a good way toward suggesting questions of integrity and identity. The text will force us to ask, what is Dunwich, what are its people, what is the horror?

Indeed the question of the "horror" of the title is a reasonable place to begin. The first problem is whether it is intrinsic to Dunwich or external to it. Dunwich itself, after all, is described in horrific terms, with natives "repellently decadent" and possessed of "well-defined mental and physical stigmata of degeneracy and inbreeding." The place has horrors of its own, to be sure. In the title "The Dunwich Horror," we are left to wonder whether the last word indicates external encroachment (like *earthquake* in "the San Francisco earthquake") or intrinsic inclusion (like *skyline* in "the New York skyline"). The text will continually raise this question without, of course, finally providing an answer. And there are other problems with the title.

As with certain other emotive words (e.g., *delight*), the word *horror* may refer either to an emotional state within the mind or to that which produces it. We may feel horror or may feel that something external *is* a horror. In fact in some usages the two senses of the term may become impossible to separate, as when we say, A horror came upon me. Phenomenologically we may even regard horror produced by an "external" source as a content or construct of consciousness and therefore as a state-of-mind horror. Cause and effect are blurred here. The boundary between them crumbles in the machinations of language, as is perhaps only appropriate since such boundaries may well be linguistic constructs to begin with. The bipolarity between "external" and "internal" tends to suffer its opposing poles to collapse together. Each contains an enabling trace of the other.

An external horror maintains its status as a horror only to the extent that it is perceived. Wilbur's twin crashing through the meadows would be of no valuational or attitudinal consequence if there were no one there to experience the effects. Conversely, an internal horror-reaction is supposed to have a generating object or source. It does not exist *in vacuo* but points, much like a linguistic sign, to something beyond itself. This problematic relation between externality and internality is in fact allegorized in the text by the Dunwich people (insiders in their own social system, yet outsiders in the more inclusive system) and the alien presences (outsiders, though significant only by being *in* Dunwich as encroachments). And as we shall see, there is reason on the level of mythic motif in the tale to find that the supposed boundaries between the human-versus-alien binary relation are inclined to self-dismantle. There is a serious question about how the motif of the mythic hero operates in the tale concerning the tension between Armitage and the twins. One notices that each faction is divided against itself—Armitage because of his myopic view, the twins because they *are* twins and, ironically enough, can only be characterized as twins, in the way in which the text operates, by virtue of their differences.

One finds etymological evidence tending, at first, to pull the term *horror* toward the internal or "state" sense and away from the external or "source" sense. *Horror* stems from the Indo-European root *ghers-*, "to bristle," and is responsible for the Latin *horrere*, "to bristle," "to tremble," "to be in fear," with mutually antithetical suggestions both of recoiling and of readiness to fight back. *Horripilation* is the bristling or the standing-on-end of hair, and bristling (as when one refers to a text's bristling with plural meaning) suggests proliferation, growth, teeming, sprouting, multiplicity, division, diversity, bewildering profuseness. The allegorical implication is of course one of textual self-commentary upon polysemic content. In any case, the etymological leaning is toward horror as feeling rather than horror as cause. The text subverts this tendency, however, by imbuing on the narrative level the term *horror* with a sense of external causes of feelings. We hear that in 1928 "the Dunwich horror came and went," and we reflect that comings and goings tend to characterize of external influences, of things happening *to* the people involved. Yet *horror* may even here refer to mental states

as well, and we continue to countenance an unstable binary opposition: the human side, by association with feelings and mental reactions, versus the alien side, by association with the cause. While dwelling on this seemingly clear-cut bipolarity—an opposition as basic as humankind on the one hand and something threatening its extinction on the other—the text on various levels blurs the distinction between the poles on which it appears vehemently to insist. . . .

Source: Donald R. Burleson, "'The Dunwich Horror,'" in *Lovecraft: Disturbing the Universe*, University Press of Kentucky, 1990, pp. 119–22.

Peter Cannon

In the following excerpt, Cannon analyzes some of the themes in "The Dunwich Horror" and considers it one of Lovecraft's strongest stories.

. . . Like "The Colour Out of Space," "The Dunwich Horror" (1928) opens with a naturalistic description of a sinister country landscape—one lying well beyond Arkham up the Miskatonic river valley. Like its namesake, the ancient former capital of East Anglia eroded over the centuries by the sea, Dunwich has long been in decline. One reason people shun the township "is that the natives are now repellently decadent, having gone far along that path of retrogression so common in many New England backwaters. They have come to form a race by themselves, with the well-defined mental and physical stigmata of degeneracy and inbreeding. The average of their intelligence is woefully low, whilst their annals reek of overt viciousness, and of half-hidden murders, incests, and deeds of almost unnamable violence and perversity." Amidst such a community the birth on the second of February, 1913, of a "dark, goatish-looking infant" to the husbandless Lavinia Whateley, "a somewhat deformed, unattractive albino woman, living with an aged and half-insane father about whom the most frightful tales of wizardry had been whispered in his youth," is scarcely matter for comment.

As in "The Colour Out of Space," the narrative follows the travails of a single family, but while the Gardners had passively fallen victim to a terror beyond their understanding, Wizard Whateley and his grandson Wilbur plot "to wipe out the human race and drag the earth off to some nameless place for some nameless purpose." The Dunwich horror poses such an

> IF LOVECRAFT MADE CONCESSIONS TO POPULAR TASTE, THE TALE YET RANKS AMONG HIS STRONGEST, BY VIRTUE OF ITS HIGH LEVEL OF EXCITEMENT AND SUSPENSE."

immediate, dire threat to mankind that the erudite Henry Armitage, "A.M. Miskatonic, Ph.D. Princeton, Litt.D. Johns Hopkins," who much like Dr. Willett in *The Case of Charles Dexter Ward* arrives mid-way through the story to lead the opposition, has little time to ponder the philosophical implications. Skilled "in the mystical formulae of antiquity and the Middle Ages," Armitage like Willett arms himself with the appropriate spell in order to fight a menace likewise linked to "the dreadful name of *Yog-Sothoth*."

If "The Dunwich Horror" on the surface amounts to a "good versus evil" struggle, the tale's "villains" possess attributes that make this conflict far from black and white. James Egan has pointed out that the birth of Wilbur and his brother "satirically parallels the Immaculate Conception of Christ in the womb of a human mother, Lavinia being the perfect antithesis of the Virgin Mary," while Donald R. Burleson has suggested that the Whateley twins together "can be seen closely to fit the archetypal pattern of the hero in myth." With the same sort of sardonic inversion Lovecraft mocks his own youth and upbringing in the portrait of the Whateley family, whose three members may be viewed as grotesque parodies of his grandfather, his mother, and himself. Under the tutelage of the Old Whateley, who arranges his library of "rotting ancient books and parts of books" for his grandson's benefit, the precocious Wilbur grows up to be "a scholar of really tremendous erudition." Physically ugly, as Mrs. Lovecraft felt her son to be, Wilbur hides a terrible secret under his clothes. That after Lavinia's disappearance he should appear "under a cloud of probable matricide" may well reflect Lovecraft's resentment of his own mother. While such connections can be carried too far, they do not seem

out of place in what in other respects stands out as Lovecraft's least inhibited tale.

Sexual imagery surrounds the secondary climax, the death of "the monstrous being known to the human world as Wilbur Whateley," torn apart by the savage campus watchdog in his bungled attempt to steal the *Necronomicon*. The prefatory sentence smoothly avoids the clumsiness of the disclaimers of earlier stories over the difficulty of describing the indescribable:

> It would be trite and not wholly accurate to say that no human pen could describe it, but one may properly say that it could not be vividly visualised by anyone whose ideas of aspect and contour are too closely bound up with the common life-forms of this planet and of the three known dimensions. It was partly human, beyond a doubt, with very man-like hands and head, and the goatish, chinless face had the stamp of the Whateleys upon it. But the torso and lower parts of the body were teratologically fabulous, so that only generous clothing could ever have enabled it to walk on earth unchallenged or uneradicated.
>
> Above the waist it was semi-anthropomorphic; though its chest, where the dog's paws still rested watchfully, had the leathery, reticulated hide of a crocodile or an alligator. The back was piebald with yellow and black, and dimly suggested the squamous covering of certain snakes. Below the waist, though, it was the worst; for here all human resemblance left off and sheer phantasy began. The skin was thickly covered with coarse black fur, and from the abdomen a score of long greenish-grey tentacles with red sucking mouths protruded limply.

Here Lovecraft would seem almost deliberately to be baiting the Freudians. The passage continues in the same vivid vein, constituting perhaps his most successful attempt at direct alien description, made all the more shocking for the slow build-up over the five preceding sections.

At the primary climax the Dunwich horror itself appears more obliquely, through the eyes of one of the local rustics, who watches its progress up Sentinel Hill through binoculars: "Bigger'n a barn... all made o' squirmin' ropes... hull thing sort o' shaped like a hen's egg bigger'n anything, with dozens o' legs like hogsheads that haff shut up when they step." Here the humble language of the farm succinctly conveys the terror of the beast. While this sort of literal rendering of speech, once common in both popular and serious fiction, may be out of fashion, the extreme dialect of the Dunwich natives does serve to thicken the narrative texture, especially in those dramatic phone calls over the party lines during the week the horror roams at large. Quotations from assorted documents also enliven the third-person narration, from the Reverend Abijah Hoadley's "memorable sermon on the close presence of Satan and his imps" in 1747 to the quasi-biblical passage from the *Necronomicon* that so neatly summarizes the Old Ones' gestalt: "The Old Ones were, the Old Ones are, and the Old Ones shall be. Not in the spaces we know, but *between* them, They walk serene and primal, undimensioned and to us unseen."

As in the final scene of *The Case of Charles Dexter Ward*, an exchange takes place that approaches actual dialogue in the aftermath of the horror's destruction. Rather like the archetypal fictional detective at mystery's end, Dr. Armitage explains the fine points of the case for the less astute, though he cannot resist moralizing: "We have no business calling in such things from outside, and only very wicked people and very wicked cults ever try to." Such heavy-handedness, however, is consistent with the overall tone of the tale. Armitage, for instance, during Wilbur Whateley's first visit to the Miskatonic University library, feels uneasy in the presence of "the bent, goatish giant before him" who "seemed like the spawn of another planet or dimension; like something only partly of mankind, and linked to black gulfs of essence and entity that stretch like titan phantasms beyond all spheres of force and matter, space and time." As exceptionally intuitive as he might be, he could hardly at this stage have such accurate insight into Wilbur's nature. Even such a passing phrase as "anaemic, blood-less-looking cows" would seem to contain one adjective too many. When in the wake of *Weird Tales'* rejection of *At the Mountains of Madness* in 1931, Lovecraft grumbled, "That ass Wright got me into the habit of obvious writing with his never-ending complaints about the indefiniteness of my early stuff" (3:395), he could well have been thinking of "The Dunwich Horror."

If Lovecraft made concessions to popular taste, the tale yet ranks among his strongest, by virtue of its high level of excitement and suspense. While the horror's defeat may be a foregone conclusion, the final revelation—"*It was his twin brother, but it looked more like the father than he did*"—comes for many as a

genuine surprise rather than simply as confirmation. Indeed, in every suggestive incident and weird detail, from the Whateleys' cattle buying to the business of the legend of the whippoorwills, "psychopomps lying in wait for the souls of the dying," "The Dunwich Horror" exhibits the master's touch....

Source: Peter Cannon, "Cosmic Backwaters," in *H. P. Lovecraft*, Twayne's United States Authors Series No. 549, Twayne Publishers, 1989, pp. 86–89.

SOURCES

"About Weird Tales," in *Weird Tales* online, http://weirdtalesmagazine.com/about/ (accessed February 27, 2014).

Boudillion, Daniel V., "The Moodus Noises & Moodus Noise Cave," Boudillion.com, December 14, 2009, http://www.boudillion.com/nashobahill/moodusnoises.htm (accessed February 27, 2014).

Burleson, Donald R., *H. P. Lovecraft: A Critical Study*, Greenwood Press, 1983, pp. 145–49.

Cannon, Peter, "Cosmic Backwaters," in *H. P. Lovecraft*, Twayne's United States Authors Series No. 549, Twayne Publishers, 1989, pp. 82–96.

Derleth, August, ed., "H. P. Lovecraft and His Work," in *The Dunwich Horror and Others: The Best Supernatural Stories*, Arkham House, 1963, pp. ix–xx.

"Devil's Hopyard State Park," Connecticut Department of Energy and Environmental Protection website, http://www.ct.gov/deep/cwp/view.asp?a=2716&q=325188&deepNav_GID=1650%20 (accessed February 27, 2014).

Dziemianowicz, Stefan, "Outsiders and Aliens: The Uses of Isolation in Lovecraft's Fiction," in *An Epicure in the Terrible: A Centennial Anthology of Essays in Honor of H. P. Lovecraft*, edited by David E. Schultz and S. T. Joshi, Associated University Presses, 1991, pp. 159–87.

Evans, Timothy H., "Tradition and Illusion: Antiquarianism, Tourism and Horror in H. P. Lovecraft," in *Extrapolation*, Vol. 42, No. 2, 2004, p. 176.

Feingold, Michael, Review of *The Dunwich Horror and Others*, in *Village Voice*, Vol. 20, No. 12, March 19, 1985, p. 45.

"History of Wilbraham," Town of Wilbraham, Massachusetts, website, http://www.wilbraham-ma.gov/index.aspx?nid=217 (accessed February 27, 2014).

Joshi, S. T., *H. P. Lovecraft: A Life*, Necronomicon Press, 1996, pp. 228–29, 448–51.

Le Guin, Ursula, "New England Gothic," in *Times Literary Supplement*, No. 3863, March 26, 1976, p. 335.

Lovecraft, H. P., "The Dunwich Horror," in *The Best of H. P. Lovecraft: Bloodcurdling Tales of Horror and the Macabre*, Ballantine, 1982, pp. 100–33.

Schweitzer, Darrell, *The Dream Quest of H. P. Lovecraft*, Borgo Press, 1978, p. 39.

Smith, Philip, "Re-visioning Romantic-Era Gothicism: An Introduction to Key Works and Themes in the Study of H. P. Lovecraft," in *Literature Compass*, Vol. 8, No. 11, 2011, pp. 830–39.

Strunk, William, Jr., *The Elements of Style*, W. P. Humphrey, 1918, http://www.bartleby.com/141/ (accessed February 27, 2014).

Strunk, William, Jr., and E. B. White, *The Elements of Style*, 3rd ed., Macmillan, 1979, pp. 72–73.

Wilson, Edmund, "Tales of the Marvellous and the Ridiculous," in *New Yorker*, November 24, 1945, pp. 100–104.

Winter, Douglas E., Review of *Tales of H. P. Lovecraft* and *The Annotated H. P. Lovecraft*, in *Book World*, October 26, 1997, Vol. 27, No. 43, p. 6.

FURTHER READING

Anderson, Douglas A., ed., *H. P. Lovecraft's Favorite Weird Tales: The Roots of Modern Horror*, Cold Spring Press, 2005.
> This collection of fiction includes "The Novel of the Black Seal," by Arthur Machen, one of Lovecraft's favorite writers and whose story "The Great God Pan" influenced "The Dunwich Horror." Also included are stories by Edgar Allan Poe, Robert W. Chambers, Ambrose Bierce, and Walter de la Mare.

Evans, Timothy H., "A Last Defense against the Dark: Folklore, Horror, and the Uses of Tradition in the Works of H. P. Lovecraft," in *Journal of Folklore Research*, Vol. 42, No. 1, January–April 2001, pp. 99–135.
> Evans describes many of Lovecraft's travels and how the author worked many of his findings into his fiction, including using the legends of whippoorwills and the Moodus hills in "The Dunwich Horror."

Houellebecq, Michel, *H. P. Lovecraft: Against the World, against Life*, translated by Dorna Khazeni, McSweeney's, 2005.
> The French author and filmmaker explores Lovecraft's pessimistic, fatalistic view of humanity, whereby his belief that humans are doomed to extinction was relayed through the Cthulhu Mythos. This is an English translation of the 1991 French-language original with an introduction by the renowned writer of horror fiction Stephen King.

Long, Frank Belknap, *Howard Phillips Lovecraft: Dreamer on the Night Side*, Arkham House, 1975.
> Long was a friend of Lovecraft's, and this biography focuses on their personal relationship and the insights Long has into Lovecraft's works.

VanderMeer, Ann, and Jeff VanderMeer, eds., *The Weird: A Compendium of Strange and Dark Stories*, Tor Books, 2010.
> This 1,100-page anthology includes fiction dating from 1908 to 2010, including "The Dunwich Horror," along with short works by other masters, including Joyce Carol Oates, Ray Bradbury, Franz Kafka, Clark Ashton Smith, and Poppy Z. Brite. Critics consider it essential reading for anyone interested in weird fiction.

SUGGESTED SEARCH TERMS

H. P. Lovecraft

The Dunwich Horror

Arkham AND Massachusetts

Salem AND Massachusetts

Weird Tales AND Lovecraft

Cthulhu Mythos

weird fiction AND Lovecraft

Arkham

Necronomicon

Geraldine Moore the Poet

TONI CADE BAMBARA

C. 1980

Toni Cade Bambara has focused a number of her short stories on young African American women in urban environments. In "Geraldine Moore the Poet," Bambara follows a high-school student through her day. The story is concerned largely with Geraldine's difficult home life and how it affects her ability to cope with daily challenges at school. Assigned in English class to write a poem, Geraldine objects, believing that poems are about beauty and there is all too little beauty in her life. The story not only emphasizes the overwhelming challenges of poverty but also comments on the nature of poetry and its ability to communicate emotional truths.

"Geraldine Moore the Poet" is often included in school textbooks and anthologies. Its earliest appearance in a textbook format was in 1985, in *The Reader as Detective*, Book 2, edited by Burton Goodman and published by Amsco School Publications. It was also published independently by Scholastic in 2004.

AUTHOR BIOGRAPHY

Bambara was born Miltona Mirkin Cade in New York City, on March 25, 1939. Her parents were Helen Brent Henderson Cade and Walter Cade II. Toni was the nickname she requested at a young age, and she added the "Bambara" to her name later in life to reflect her African

Watching Mrs. Scott help her classmates, Geraldine feels she herself cannot possibly write a poem.
(© Tyler Olson / Shutterstock.com)

heritage. She attended Queens College in New York City, receiving a bachelor of arts degree in 1959. She then traveled and studied abroad. Bambara served as program director at the Colony House Settlement in Brooklyn while she earned her master's degree from City College of New York. After completing her degree, she began teaching at City College in 1965, and she worked there until 1969. Later she held a variety of positions, working as a freelance writer and lecturer, a social investigator for New York's Department of Welfare, and as the recreation director of Metropolitan Hospital's psychiatry department.

In the late 1960s, Bambara became involved in the women's movement and the black liberation movement, both of which were intertwined with the fight for civil rights in America. In pursuit of her political aims, Bambara edited and published *The Black Woman: An Anthology* in 1970. It features the work of prominent African American women writers and also includes some of Bambara's own short fiction. She followed this anthology a year later with another, *Tales and Stories for Black Folks*. This collection features the work of well-known authors and also the fiction of students in a first-year composition class Bambara taught at Livingston College at Rutgers University. Bambara collected her own short fiction, written over the course of roughly a decade, from 1959 through 1970; she published this work, *Gorilla, My Love*, under the name Toni Cade in 1972.

In pursuing her aim of civil rights for women, she studied the work of other activists, meeting in 1973 in Cuba with the Federation of Cuban Women and in 1975 with the Women's Union in Vietnam. After her return to the United States, she became one of the founding members of the Southern Collective of African American Writers. In 1977, she published her second collection of short stories, *The Sea Birds Are Still Alive*. Bambara explored the novel form with her 1980 work, *The Salt Eaters*. She continued to write short fiction during the 1980s. Her short story "Geraldine Moore the Poet" was written and published during this time period. It appeared in such school textbooks as *The Reader as Detective*, Book 2, edited by Burton Goodman.

Bambara was diagnosed with colon cancer in 1993, and she died in Philadelphia on December 9, 1995. Her unfinished novel, *These Bones Are Not My Child*, was published posthumously in 1999.

PLOT SUMMARY

"Geraldine Moore the Poet" opens with the title character, Geraldine, walking home from school at lunchtime. In the first few paragraphs of the story, Bambara highlights a significant fact about Geraldine: she is poor. Her socks are held up by rubber bands and have holes chewed in them by a neighbor's dog, which she watches twice a week in order to earn a dollar. As she walks home, she reflects on her current situation. Her mother is ill and has gone away. For a time, Geraldine was looked after by another neighbor, Miss Gladys. She had to get herself ready for school on those days, and she often went hungry. Now, her older sister, Anita, has moved home. Geraldine is relieved to be able to come home for lunch instead of eating the free lunches at school.

As she approaches her apartment building, Geraldine suddenly stops when she sees furniture and boxes piled on the curb, indicating an eviction in progress. She understands that this happens to people, having seen possessions on the street in the past, but now she recognizes the ironing board and the sofa—they belong to her family. Geraldine is greeted by Miss Gladys, who tells her that she will be staying with her for a time. Geraldine watches as a man carries a box with a doll sticking out of it. Miss Gladys instructs her to go upstairs and have lunch. Anita serves her a bowl of soup and tries to tell her younger sister that everything will be all right just as soon as their mother gets healthy. Geraldine observes her sister's efforts to keep from crying.

Back at school, Geraldine ignores her geometry lesson and adds up numbers in her notebook—the cost of the rent, and bills, and clothes. She wonders where her family might move to. Although Geraldine almost questions her math teacher about the relevance of geometry to the solving of "real problems," she decides not to, remembering getting in trouble

for speaking her mind on a previous occasion. She experiences a similar sense of disconnection between what she is being taught and what her life is actually like in her hygiene class, where she is being told that her body is busy building what it needs to get through the next day. Geraldine wonders how her body could know what it will need, when she herself has no idea how she will get through the next day. On her way to English class, Geraldine realizes she has neglected to do her homework: to write a poem. She listens to her teacher, Mrs. Scott, speak lovingly about poetry. Students who have completed the assignment have placed their work on their desk, and as Mrs. Scott lectures, she picks up their work. She then instructs the students who have not yet written a poem to do so. Geraldine is dismayed. Mrs. Scott has suggested that students attempt to discuss in their poems what life is like in "this glorious world."

As Mrs. Scott approaches Geraldine's desk, Geraldine blurts out that she cannot write a poem. Mrs. Scott asks her why she feels she cannot complete the assignment. Geraldine says that it is because nothing lovely ever happens to her. She describes the lack of flowers and sunshine and singing birds in her life. She considers talking about her father's absence, but she decides not to. Instead, she describes how she feels as though it is always raining, and bills keep arriving, and men have come to move the furniture out of their home. Mrs. Scott's serious look prevents a disruptive student from laughing. The teacher tells Geraldine that she has just expressed sentiments that are extremely poetic. Mrs. Scott repeats Geraldine's words and writes them down, line by line, as a poem on the chalkboard. She asks the other students to copy down this poem. Mrs. Scott remains at the chalkboard after the bell rings and the students begin to leave. She is still facing the chalkboard when Geraldine packs up her books. As she is about to walk out of the door, Geraldine thinks she hears a whimper, and she notices Mrs. Scott's shoulders shaking, as if she is crying.

CHARACTERS

Anita

Anita is Geraldine's older sister. She is married and is awaiting her husband's return from the army. She has come to stay with Geraldine, now that their mother has gone away due to her unspecified illness. Anita is not quite as attentive as Geraldine would like. Geraldine observes that Anita often loses herself in television shows rather than interacting with her little sister.

Father

Geraldine's father does not appear in the story. When Geraldine describes the difficulty of her circumstances to her teacher, she decides to omit the fact that her father no longer even visits.

Miss Gladys

Miss Gladys is one of Geraldine's neighbors. After Geraldine's mother went away but before her sister came to stay with her, Geraldine was largely on her own, except for Thursdays, when Miss Gladys came to clean the apartment and make a meatloaf.

Teddy Johnson

Teddy Johnson is a classmate of Geraldine's. He is about to laugh after Geraldine describes what is happening to her and when she insists she cannot write a poem. However, seeing the seriousness of his teacher, he does not laugh.

Geraldine Moore

Geraldine is the protagonist of the story. She is a teenager who is trying to cope with an absent father, an ailing mother, and poverty. Geraldine is forced to consider her circumstances, the most recent of which is her impending eviction from her home, in contrast with the lessons she is being taught at school. She has a difficult time trying to understand how her classes relate to the daily struggles she faces. Geometry seems less important to her than figuring out how her family will pay for the bare necessities of life. Similarly, she wonders how it can possibly matter that her body is manufacturing protein to fuel her for the next day, when she does not know how she will be able to get through the day emotionally. In English class, Geraldine realizes that she has neglected to do her homework—writing a poem. She feels as though she has nothing to write about, as she has the impression that poetry must convey something lovely. In describing to her teacher her feelings about her present situation, Geraldine uses such powerful language and imagery that her teacher is overwhelmed by the poetry in her sentiments. Geraldine learns that poetry encompasses a greater range of emotion and themes than she

had previously imagined, and she witnesses the impact of poetry on those around her, particularly her teacher.

Mother

Geraldine's mother does not appear in the story, but the reader is informed that she is sick and has gone away. The duration of her absence and her physical location are not discussed. Geraldine feels her mother's absence keenly, as she is forced to rely on neighbors and her sister for her daily care.

Mrs. Potter

Mrs. Potter is Geraldine's hygiene teacher. In hygiene class, Mrs. Potter is teaching her students about the way bodies build protein and tissue and create energy. Geraldine wonders how her body can know what it needs to sustain her for the next day, when she herself does not know how she will get through each day.

Mrs. Scott

Mrs. Scott is Geraldine's English teacher. She has assigned poetry writing as the students' homework, but Geraldine has not completed the work. As Mrs. Scott discusses the nature and appeal of poetry, she encourages the students who have not yet written a poem to do so. Mrs. Scott suggests that the children consider what it is like to exist in the beautiful world and to perhaps write about that. At this point, Geraldine grows more frustrated, and when she insists that she cannot write a poem, Mrs. Scott asks her why. After hearing Geraldine's poetic response, Mrs. Scott insists that Geraldine has composed something truly poetic. She repeats Geraldine's words, writes them on the board, and tells the students to copy down Geraldine's poem. Mrs. Scott remains at the board, facing away from the class, even after the bell rings and the children depart. Geraldine notices her shoulders shaking and believes she hears a whimper, which suggests that Mrs. Scott has been moved to tears by Geraldine and her poem.

Mr. Stern

Mr. Stern is Geraldine's geometry teacher. He assigns homework to the class, a problem that Geraldine finds irrelevant to her current circumstances.

Mrs. Watson

Mrs. Watson is one of Geraldine's neighbors. To earn money, Geraldine helps care for Mrs. Watson's dog, which chews holes in Geraldine's belongings.

THEMES

Poetry

Although "Geraldine Moore the Poet" is at its core the story of a girl coping with such stresses as absent parents and impending eviction, as its title suggests it is also focused on the nature of poetry. The first mention of poetry comes when Geraldine is on her way to English class. Geraldine recalls that she has not completed her homework: to write a poem. She had intended to do it at lunch but was instead confronted with seeing her family's furniture on the curb, an event she realizes serves as a precursor to eviction. She had imagined she would be able to dash off a poem quite easily, thinking that "there was nothing to it—a flower here, a raindrop there, moon, June, rose, nose." The sight of the men moving her furniture, however, drove the thought of the assignment from her mind.

In English class, the teacher speaks about poetry enthusiastically, "talking about her favorite poems and reciting a line now and then." Geraldine observes Mrs. Scott's excitement whenever she plucks a completed poem off of the corner of a student's desk. Mrs. Scott informs the students that poetry represents each person's particular way of expressing himself or herself. The teacher's lips, the reader is told, are moist: "It was her favorite subject." Mrs. Scott goes on to talk about the lives of notable poets, and she reads her favorite poems as well. She instructs the students who have not yet completed the assignment to still attempt to write a poem: "Try expressing what it is like to be ... to be alive in this ... this glorious world." The teacher is almost inarticulate in her excitement. Considering that Geraldine's response to this instruction is a muttered "Oh, brother," the reader assumes that Geraldine is contemplating how little gloriousness there is in her own world.

Convinced as she now is that she cannot write a poem because she believes a poem must convey loveliness, Geraldine tells Mrs. Scott that she cannot write a poem. Yet as she describes her life, speaking out in a way that surprises herself, Geraldine sums up her struggles with a collection of simple images. She expresses herself in such poetic language that her teacher is moved to tears. Mrs. Scott informs the class that Geraldine has just composed "the best poem you will ever hear." The compliment compels the students to smile at Geraldine, or touch her shoulder on their way out of the classroom, or to joke with her good-naturedly about her "being the school poet."

Poverty

Although Geraldine never overtly states that her family is poor, her poverty is made clear to the reader throughout the course of the story. "Geraldine Moore the Poet" opens with an image that underscores her poverty: her socks are so old and worn that they must be held up with rubber bands. As she pauses to pull them up, she discovers a hole. She is reminded of the hole in her gym suit, and becomes angry at her neighbor's dog, who is responsible for the holes. The fact that Geraldine watches the dog twice a week for a dollar is significant, because her need for that dollar is great, but the extent of her poverty is not yet fully revealed. Meanwhile, the cloud of economic stress hangs over Geraldine's neighborhood. Seeing a street vendor with a hot-dog cart, she thinks, "Nobody's got hot-dog money around here." She also makes reference to the free lunches she has had to eat at school, another hint at her situation. The extent of her troubles is elaborated on further, as the reader learns that her mother is ill and has gone away, and that although a neighbor comes in to clean and make dinner once a week, Geraldine is largely on her own. This adult responsibility is overwhelming for Geraldine, who often does not succeed in feeding herself breakfast before going to school. In the present time of the story, though, Geraldine's sister Anita has moved back home, and she is at least able to help keep Geraldine fed.

When Geraldine returns home for lunch one day, she sees her family's possessions on the street. "That wasn't anything new," she observes; "she had seen people get put out in the street before." But this time, the possessions are those belonging to her own family. Geraldine's understanding that this type of thing is common underscores the economic problems of her neighborhood. Now, however, her family's

TOPICS FOR FURTHER STUDY

- In "Geraldine Moore the Poet," Bambara makes reference to Geraldine's sick mother, who has not been at home for some time, and an absent father, who no longer visits. Geraldine's sister's husband is away in the army, and Anita waits for his return. These absences weigh heavily on the two sisters. Write a short story from the perspective of Geraldine's mother, Geraldine's father, or Anita's husband, in which the character you have selected somehow receives word of what is happening to Geraldine and Anita. How would the person react? Would this person attempt to help the sisters? What might make him or her unable to do so? How might this person try to communicate with Geraldine or Anita? Share your story with the class, either in print form, as a live presentation, or as a written or recorded piece that can be accessed via a web page that you have created.

- Victor Martinez was born to Mexican migrant workers living in California. His 2004 novel *Parrot in the Oven: Mi Vida* explores the life of a young teen contending with poverty and abuse. With a small group, read Martinez's novel. Consider the ways in which the protagonist, Manny, deals with his family's poverty and the obstacles in his life. How does he cope at school? What are his friendships like? What are his relationships with his family members like? In what ways is he like Geraldine,

and how are they different? Create an online blog that you use as a forum to discuss these issues, as well as your personal response to the novel.

- Geraldine's poverty is an important part of "Geraldine Moore the Poet." Research the issue of poverty in America, selecting either the 1980s or today's society as your time frame. What factors contribute to poverty in America? How does poverty affect different minority groups? What government policies are designed to help the poor? Be sure to provide statistics on the effects of poverty on different social and racial groups. Write a research paper and be sure to cite all of your resources.

- Geraldine composes a poem in "Geraldine Moore the Poet" without really meaning to. The poem stems from the events in her life. Write a series of poems that reflect the events in your own life or in the lives of the people around you. Create five to ten poems and a means to display them, such as an illustrated poster board or an illustrated book. Consider the ways in which your feelings about your life's events conjure images or suggest a certain tone in your language. Geraldine, for example, uses images such as flowers and birds, but the absence of them in her life serves as a contrast to what the images themselves represent. Select your own imagery with care.

---

eviction from their home looms in a way it hasn't before. Her neighbor, Miss Gladys, tells her, "Looks like you'll be staying with me for a while." If there was any doubt in Geraldine's mind about the implications of what she is seeing, Miss Gladys's comments clarify the situation, for Geraldine and the reader: she is about to lose her home. Back at school, Geraldine struggles to come to terms with what is

happening. She alternates between trying to solve her family's financial difficulties—adding up how much rent and utility bills cost—and dreaming of a new home where she might be able to have her own room. Her impromptu poem highlights her despair and reminds the reader that Geraldine's dreams of a home with her own room will most likely be nothing more than dreams for some time.

$$a^2 + b^2 = c^2$$
$$|BC| = a, |AC| = b, |AB| = c$$
$$\frac{a}{c} = \frac{HB}{a}; \frac{b}{c} = \frac{|AH|}{b}.$$
$$a^2 = c \cdot |HB|; b^2 = c \cdot |AH|$$
$$a^2 + b^2 = c \cdot (|HB| + |AH|) = c^2$$
$$(a+b)^2 = 4 \cdot \frac{ab}{2} + c^2$$
$$a^2 + 2ab + b^2 = 2ab + c^2$$
$$c^2 = a^2 + b^2$$
$$c \, dc = a \, da + b \, db$$
$$c^2 = a^2 + b^2 + constant$$
$$a = b = c = 0 \Rightarrow constant = 0$$

Geraldine cannot concentrate in math class because she does not see how learning geometry will help her with real-world problems.

(© BorisShevchuk | Shutterstock.com)

STYLE

Third-Person Narration

"Geraldine Moore the Poet" is written from Geraldine's point of view in third-person narration. In third-person narration, the person from whose perspective the story is told is referred to as "he" or "she," or by his or her name. This is in contrast to first-person narration, in which the point-of-view character refers to himself or herself as "I." Some third-person narrated stories use more than one point-of-view character, with the perspective shifting from one character to another throughout the story. In "Geraldine Moore the Poet," the perspective is limited to Geraldine's point of view. The reader is allowed access to Geraldine's thoughts, but not those of any of the other characters. Geraldine provides the filter through which the other characters' words and actions are perceived. In fiction in which the story is narrated from the perspective of just one character, the reader must consider the reliability of that narrator's point of view as the events of the story unfold. Geraldine is a relatively young narrator, a high-school student. She has some real-world experience, which makes her perceive herself as different

from many of her classmates, and also makes her feel misunderstood by her teachers. The facts regarding her mother's illness, her father's absence, and her family's poverty all combine to cause Geraldine to feel as though what is being taught at school is useless to her. Yet Geraldine is still a high school student, without the emotional maturity of an adult. She carries the burden of her troubles in solitude and seems to assume that her teachers would not understand what she is going through. Bambara's use of third-person narration limits the reader to Geraldine's perspective, yet it allows the reader access to her thoughts and feelings. In this way, this type of narration effectively allows the reader a close and immediate connection to Geraldine.

Language and Imagery

In using a teenager as the point-of-view character in "Geraldine Moore the Poet," Bambara employs language and images that reflect this perspective. Geraldine's dialogue certainly reflects her age, and also the narrative voice remains consistent with this youthful perspective throughout. Geraldine is relieved, for example, to be going home for lunch, where she will be able to avoid the "funny-looking tomato soup and the dried-out cheese sandwiches and those oranges that were more green than orange." These narrated details are ones that clearly reflect her perspective as a student forced to partake in an institutional lunch service, and they emphasize Geraldine's unique voice. Bambara could have used different descriptions to provide the reader with a sense of the free school lunch. "Funny-looking" is not the most descriptive term she could have employed, but it does reflect Geraldine's view of the lunch provided at school, including what she objects to about it and how she would describe it. Like many children, she is easily put off by the appearance of food, and she makes judgments about what she will and will not eat based on the food's appearance and not its taste.

Similarly, when Geraldine sees the furniture on the curb—her family's furniture—she does not describe specifically what the sofa looks like. The reader does not get any idea regarding the color of the sofa, or the type of fabric covering it, for example; instead, it is just "the big, ugly sofa." An ironing board is also among the items littering the street. This particular image resounds with the idea of daily toil and suggests the drudgery of Geraldine's family's impoverished existence. Geraldine also sees "an old doll sticking up over the edge" of a box. The doll, presumably Geraldine's, underscores the fact that the innocence of Geraldine's childhood is coming to an end. She is being forced to exist in an increasingly troubled adult world. When Geraldine's sister Anita serves lunch, the image of tomato soup is repeated. Although it is not described as "funny-looking," as the school lunch is, the repetition of this type of food highlights the way Geraldine cannot escape the hard facts of her existence. The tomato soup is associated with poverty—the free lunch provided at school, and the lunch served to her on the day when she comes home to find her family's belongings on the curb, as a sign of the family's impending eviction.

Back at school, in English class, the imagery Geraldine uses to describe her life, or the lack of "lovely" things in it, is also significant. She says that she has not "seen a flower since Mother's Day." The flower, as an image of life, growth, or joy, is almost secondary to the Mother's Day reference. The phrase reminds the reader that Geraldine's mother has gone away. The reader does not know where the mother has gone, only that she is ill. Her absence weighs heavily on Geraldine throughout the story, as the illness and absence are referred to several times; these are the factors that forced Geraldine to care for herself until her sister returned home. The specific mention of Mother's Day brings this all to the forefront once again, and the fact of the mother's illness and absence helps the reader to understand why Geraldine feels that the sun does not shine on her side of the street, and why she notes the absence of birds singing on her windowsill. All the joyful images Geraldine uses she links to absence—no flower, no sun, no birds. Her father is also absent and has been for some time, yet Geraldine decides to not include this in her list of troubles. She next mentions things that are present instead of absent: outstanding bills, and the furniture that is present in the street, not in the home where it belongs. Throughout the story, Bambara uses language and images that remind the reader not only of Geraldine's young age but also of the bleakness of her life and the waves of tragedy she continues to endure.

HISTORICAL CONTEXT

Poverty in the 1980s

"Geraldine Moore the Poet" touches on the subject of urban poverty. Although Bambara does not specify that the story is set in New York, the setting is clearly urban, and Bambara grew up in New York City. The title character, Geraldine, lives in an apartment, and her family is about to be evicted from the building. The economic instability of Geraldine's environment in general is also referred to in the story. The story reflects the reality of the time period. A study on poverty rates in the late 1980s by Jon D. Haveman, Sheldon Danziger, and Robert D. Plotnick, "State Poverty Rates for Whites, Blacks, and Hispanics in the Late 1980s," shows a striking racial divide in the state of New York: the poverty rate among whites during this time period was 7.5 percent, for African Americans it was 25.8 percent, and for Hispanic Americans it was 35 percent. Contributing to the poverty rate was a high rate of unemployment. Stephen Gandel, in an article for *Time* magazine, notes that for a time in the early 1980s, 27.6 percent of those who were unemployed had been unemployed for longer than six months. In economic recessions, the link between poverty and unemployment is tied to prolonged unemployment rates. Falling wages also contribute to high poverty rates. Stephanie Coontz, in an article for CNN, observes, "Between 1979 and 1987, the real wages of high school graduates fell by 18%, while those of high school dropouts plummeted by 42%." Furthermore, the value of a minimum-wage income decreased during the 1980s. Coontz traces this decline from 1968, when "the minimum wage was 55% of the median full-time wage," to today, when "a minimum-wage worker earns just 37% of the median wage." In other words, wages for the lowest-paid workers have fallen further and further short of the average.

Black Arts Movement

Bambara was involved with what became known as the black arts movement, an artistic movement that developed and grew in the 1960s and 1970s and was rooted in the civil rights movement and the black power movement. While the civil rights and women's movements pushed for equality for minorities and women under the law and in terms of educational and employment opportunities, the black arts movement sought to expand the prominence of African American artists and to

COMPARE
&
CONTRAST

- **1980s:** Poverty is a pervasive problem in America, particularly among minorities. In states such as New York, the poverty rate among African Americans is more than three times the poverty rate among whites, and among Hispanic Americans it is more than four times as high. The highest long-term unemployment rate (the percentage of unemployed people who have been unemployed for more than six months) recorded during this time period is 27.6 percent.

  Today: U.S. Census Bureau data for 2009 indicates that more than one in every seven Americans live in poverty. Long-term unemployment rates in 2010 are as high as 46 percent.

- **1980s:** Literature by African American writers remains influenced by the prevalence of the black arts movement that thrived during the 1960s and 1970s. The use of "Black English," musical elements, and orality inform the literary arts.

  Today: The black arts movement is still regarded as a force that continues to shape the work of contemporary African American writers, including such writers as Askia M. Touré, Eugene Redmond, and Judy Juanita.

- **1980s:** Black feminism during the 1980s is influenced by the black power and black arts movements of the 1960s and 1970s. Black feminists often find that these antiracism movements historically ignored feminist issues. Likewise, black feminists of the 1970s and 1980s criticize the broader feminist movement for its avoidance of tackling issues such as racism.

  Today: Black feminists today have joined with other women of color in efforts to fight oppression in all forms. Black feminists have galvanized around issues such as female genital mutilation and race and gender discrimination worldwide.

---

provide those with limited ability or access to means of exposure with avenues to publish and promote their work. The political and artistic goals formed and honed during this time period shaped the later work of many of the artists involved in this effort. The black arts movement was criticized as being "sexist, homophobic, and racially exclusive," according to Kalamu ya Salaam, in an essay for *The Oxford Companion to African American Literature.* Bambara's own involvement in the black arts movement took the form of editing and publishing an anthology of work by African American women writers. *The Black Woman,* published in 1970, incorporated nonfiction, fiction, and poetry. Bambara's later works maintain a focus on African American women and their voice in the world.

Salaam notes that the black arts movement began after the assassination of prominent activist Malcolm X, when publisher and poet LeRoi Jones, who later became known as Amiri Baraka, moved from the Lower East Side of Manhattan to Harlem, where another African American literary movement, the Harlem Renaissance, had been born in the early twentieth century. Jones then founded the Black Arts Repertory Theatre/School. Other groups of African American writers, such as Umbra Workshop and the Harlem Writers Guild, similarly formed around the black arts movement. The movement gradually gained prominence and drew a host of other writers. Salaam cites the development of national African American literary magazines as central to the "widespread dissemination and adoption of Black Arts." Yet by the mid-1970s, Salaam explains, the black power movement was being dissembled by "repressive government measures," which

---

Geraldine comes home from school to find her family's things moved out of the apartment.
(© John Smith Design | Shutterstock.com)

contributed to the demise of the black arts movement. Salaam notes that the aesthetics of the black arts movement influenced the work of other writers in subsequent decades. He specifically cites the innovative explorations of language carried out by black arts writers as highly influential on later writers.

CRITICAL OVERVIEW

Not much critical analysis has been written specifically about "Geraldine Moore the Poet." Although the work appears in many high-school English textbooks, it has not received as much attention from critics as the works in Bambara's collections of short fiction. Critical commentary on Bambara's short fiction as a whole, though, has been full of praise. Mary Ellen Snodgrass, in the *Encyclopedia of Feminist*

Literature, writes that Bambara has "spun observations and experiences into gold in masterful short fiction about working-class black life." Likewise, Bill Mullen, in an essay in *American Women Short Story Writers: A Collection of Critical Essays*, observes, "Bambara's mastery of urban adolescent themes and black colloquial stand her in a tradition of the short 'folk' story form." In *A Reader's Companion to the Short Story in English*, Carol Franko comments:

> Discussions of her short stories emphasize their lyrical realism, their faithful rendering of Black English and black working-class experience, their structural resemblance to black art forms like jazz and the verbal performance of "signifying," and their ethnic and feminist themes.

Aspects of these comments can be applied to "Geraldine Moore the Poet," which, like other short works by Bambara, focuses on the everyday lives of working-class African American individuals, and which reflects the "urban adolescent themes" praised by Mullen.

CRITICISM

Catherine Dominic
Dominic is a novelist and a freelance writer and editor. In the following essay, she explores the significance of absences and of things left unsaid in "Geraldine Moore the Poet," maintaining that into the empty spaces Bambara compresses unspoken narratives.

In "Geraldine Moore the Poet," Bambara effectively uses silences—suggesting unsaid and unexplained things—to create tension in the story. There are so many unknowns in the short work, yet rather than tripping the reader up, they propel the reader forward. The missing details are not vital to the reader's overall comprehension of Geraldine's dire existence, yet they continue to gnaw at the reader after the story has concluded, and they highlight the ways in which the young protagonist, Geraldine, is at odds with her environment. Bambara injects silences and unknown elements into the story from beginning to end; in doing so, she encourages the reader to participate in weaving the tapestry of the story by filling in the blanks.

WHAT DO I READ NEXT?

- *Gorilla, My Love* is Bambara's acclaimed first collection of short fiction. Originally published in 1972, the volume contains fifteen stories set in both urban and rural settings.

- Bambara's *Deep Sightings and Rescue Missions: Fiction, Essays, and Conversations* was published in 1999, after her death. The works represent the achievements of Bambara's later career, and the interviews reflect her personal views on her work and underscore her sense of activism.

- Alice Walker, a contemporary of Bambara's, has also written fiction concerning the experiences of African American women. Her collection *In Love and Trouble: Stories of Black Women* was originally published in 1974 and is available in a 2004 edition as well.

- *Ain't I a Woman: Black Women and Feminism*, published in 1981 by bell hooks (the name is given in lowercase according to the writer's preference), is considered a groundbreaking work of feminist philosophy and history. It examines the intersection of antiracism activism and women's rights activism.

- Mingfong Ho, born in Myanmar (formerly Burma) to Chinese parents, published *Sing to the Dawn* in 1975. The short story was later extended to novel length. The work is concerned with a young girl living in Thailand who contends with a harsh urban environment, troubles with school, and poverty.

- James Smethurst's 2005 volume *The Black Arts Movement: Literary Nationalism in the 1960s and 1970s* examines the movement and its relation to the black power movement. The influences of the Cold War, the civil rights movement, and other literary movements on the black arts movement are also explored.

The first significant part of the story that the narrator remains silent about is Geraldine's mother. Bambara writes,

> When Geraldine's mother first took sick and went away, Geraldine had been on her own except when Miss Gladys next door came in on Thursdays and cleaned the apartment and made a meat loaf so Geraldine could have dinner.

As the paragraph continues, the reader learns that "in those days Geraldine never quite managed to get breakfast herself." The story continues with an explanation about Geraldine's sister Anita and how she has come to stay with Geraldine, and the narrative flows on from there. The reader is not told what type of illness Geraldine's mother has, where she went, how long she has been gone, or whether she is expected to recover. Further, the reader is led to believe that for some unspecified period of time, Geraldine, a young high-school student, has been living on her own and making her own meals—or not making them. She has had to try to "cover up the noise of her stomach growling" in social studies class. In leaving so many things unspoken about the mother's illness and Geraldine's solitary existence, the reader is compelled to wonder, to question.

Having been told almost in passing about the mother's illness and absence, the reader is led to participate in the writing of the story, to fill in the silence that Bambara has left. Maybe the mother has cancer or some other terminal illness. Perhaps she is in the hospital; perhaps she is even in hospice care, which focuses on the comfort of the terminally ill. The astute reader can only form questions and possible answers to those questions. Bambara informs the reader that Geraldine only has dinner made for her once a week, on Thursdays. What about the rest of the week, the reader wonders. What does Geraldine cook for herself, when she manages to do so? Breakfast often is only an idea for Geraldine, who seems to be unable to make it for herself in the morning, and lunches have long taken the form of the free lunches provided at school to children in need. The facts of Geraldine's isolation, loneliness, and hunger haunt the story, but they are inscribed in the reader's mind more by what Bambara does not say than by what she does.

Now, in the present time of the story, Anita lives with her younger sister Geraldine. Anita is a grown woman with a husband in the army,

SHE TAKES GERALDINE'S WORDS—WORDS
THAT GERALDINE BELIEVES CONSTITUTE THE
ABSENCE OF POETRY—AND WRITES THEM ON THE
BOARD AS A POEM, CREATING SUBSTANCE OUT OF
THAT ABSENCE."

and she usually manages to prepare an enjoyable lunch for Geraldine, even though she may spend Geraldine's lunchtime watching soap operas on television instead of joining her for the meal. Arriving home for lunch one day, Geraldine sees furniture and boxes on the curb and recognizes them as her own family's possessions. The sight of people's belongings is a familiar one to Geraldine, as she has "seen people get put out in the street before." As she looks at the pile of possessions, Miss Gladys tells Geraldine that she will be staying with her for some time. Bambara never uses the term "eviction," but the reader is meant to understand that Geraldine and her sister are in the process of losing their home. Anita has still prepared lunch for Geraldine, however, and she attempts to comfort her younger sister in saying, "I just don't know what we're going to do. But everything's going to be all right soon as Ma gets well." Although the words "everything's going to be all right" are intended to soothe Geraldine, Geraldine notices that her sister's voice cracks as she says them. Further, given the vagueness surrounding the mother's illness, the phrase "as soon as Ma gets well" provides little reassurance to either Geraldine or the reader.

These events compel Geraldine both to worry about her family's finances and to fantasize about a possible future. She adds up their current bills, and she wonders if she might someday move into a home where she has her own room. She jots down figures in the margins of her notebook, also doodling houses and curtains. When pressed to write a poem, Geraldine finds that the events of her life and specifically of that afternoon at lunchtime have so overwhelmed her that she cannot contain her emotions any longer. She tells her English teacher,

Mrs. Scott, that she cannot write a poem, and she explains why.

The first part of what Mrs. Scott identifies as a poem, but which for Geraldine is more of a litany of her troubles, is marked again by absences and things not seen. She has not seen a flower since Mother's Day, a phrase that reminds the reader of Geraldine's absent and ailing mother. There is also an absence of sun on Geraldine's side of the street, an expression that underscores her sense that the cruelty and unfairness of the world are being directed specifically at her. Her feeling of isolation is clear. She comments on the absence of robins singing on her windowsill. Next, Geraldine leaves something enormously significant to her daily existence unspoken: "She thought about saying that her father doesn't even come to visit any more, but changed her mind." Here the reader is introduced to another absence and more silences. The questions raised about her father's whereabouts and the duration of his absences are never answered. Furthermore, this subject appears to be so painful to Geraldine that she cannot speak of it, even though she hints at troubles with her mother, and she specifically states that her family is overwhelmed by bills and that men have come "to move out our furniture." Geraldine insists, "I'm sorry, but I can't write no pretty poem." The furniture is absent from her house, and poetry, Geraldine believes, is absent from her life. Mrs. Scott believes otherwise, though, and tells the class that Geraldine has just written "the best poem" the class will ever hear. She takes Geraldine's words—words that Geraldine believes constitute the *absence* of poetry—and writes them on the board as a poem, creating substance out of that absence. Mrs. Scott cannot even turn around to face Geraldine after the bell has rung and the students have departed. Geraldine watches her teacher's shoulders shake and believes she hears a whimper.

In a very short story, Bambara has created compressed spaces in the narrative, using language that signifies to the reader the importance of the absences it points to: the ailing mother who has gone away; the day-to-day existence that Geraldine has faced alone, before her sister arrived; the emptying of her home by the men carrying the boxes and placing the furniture on the street; the unspoken but deeply felt absence of the father; the perceived absence

The relief Geraldine feels about not having to eat the free school lunches anymore dissolves on the day they get kicked out of the apartment, when Anita makes her tomato soup. *(© Matt Antonino | Shutterstock.com)*

of poetry that is accompanied by the very real absence of joy and hope in Geraldine's life. Bambara compresses unspoken stories into these spaces, and the reader creates details supplied by the hints Bambara has left. In this way, Bambara presents a tightly woven narrative that is given room to bloom, to expand, in the reader's mind. She creates tension in the story by depicting the way Geraldine exists in a world full of absences.

Source: Catherine Dominic, Critical Essay on "Geraldine Moore the Poet," in *Short Stories for Students*, Gale, Cengage Learning, 2015.

K. Ensslen

In the following excerpt, Ensslen analyzes Bambara's use of language.

... From the beginning, Bambara's fictional work was marked by its being firmly rooted in the black oral tradition through the use of dramatized voices and various embodiments of black vernacular speech. Achieving an easy mastership

with the fully embodied vernacular voice in stories like "My Man Bovanne," "Gorilla, My Love," "Playin With Punjab" and "The Johnson Girls" from her first collection, *Gorilla, My Love* (1972), Bambara continued to differentiate and to intensify the dramatic possibilities of voice in her second collection. *The Sea Birds Are Still Alive* (1977), where stories like "The Apprentice" or "Medley" represent new peaks in compressing and revitalizing spoken language, both with politically committed serious overtones, and with humorously charged, exuberantly performance-oriented implications. Her improvisational use of oral forms of expression owes much to black music as a living model, especially to the bebop of the postwar decades, as she has herself acknowledged. While pushing back vernacular modes of narration in her novel *The Salt Eaters* (1980)—as she had done in some of the stories in *The Sea Birds*—, Bambara kept experimenting with the protagonist's voice as an echoing chamber containing whole cohorts of other persons' voices to whom the central character (Velma

BAMBARA ONCE STATED IN AN INTERVIEW THAT FOR HER WRITING WAS 'AN ACT OF LANGUAGE FIRST AND FOREMOST,' AND THAT 'AS AN ACT OF LANGUAGE, LITERATURE IS A SPIRIT INFORMER—AN ENERGIZER. A LOT OF ENERGY IS EXCHANGED IN THE READING AND WRITING OF BOOKS. . . .'"

Henry) has to respond—a dialogue complicated by the fact that tangible direct speech acts tend to blur with remembered and imagined voices.

Although Bambara's only novel has drawn considerable attention and praise (among others by contemporary black novelist John Edgar Wideman), there is a general critical consensus that her handling of the form of the novel is in some ways overly complicated and diffuse. Bambara herself has invariably expressed a preference for the short story (against her own financial interests in a book market geared towards pushing novels) "because it's quick, it makes a modest appeal for attention, it can creep up on you on your blind side < . . . > which is why I think the short story is far more effective in terms of teaching us lessons." The didactic impulse of Bambara's work (for usable lessons in a committed life) could meet and mix in the short story form with the linguistic and communal sources of her socialization in a primarily oral culture to which she has eloquently paid tribute in her own words:

> I wasn't raised in the church. I learned the power of the word from the speakers on Speaker's Corner—trade unionists, Temple People as we called Muslims then, Father Divinists, Pan-Africanists, Abyssinians as we called Rastas then, Communists, Ida B. Wells folks. < . . . > the sermons I heard on Speaker's Corner as a kid hanging on my mama's arm or as a kid on my own and then as an adult had tremendous impact on me. It was those marvelously gifted, extravagantly verbal speakers that prepared me later for the likes of Charlie Cobb, Sr., Harold Thurman, Revun Dougherty, and the mighty, mighty voice of Bernice Reagon.
>
> My daddy used to take me to the Apollo Theater, which had the best audience in the

world with the possible exception of folks who gather at Henry Street for Woodie King's New Federal Theater plays. There, in the Apollo, I learned that if you are going to call yourself some kind of communicator, you'd better be good because the standards of our community are high. I used to hang out a bit with my brother and my father at the Peace Barber Shop up in Divine territory just north of where we lived, and there I learned what it meant to be a good storyteller. Of course, the joints I used to hang around when I was supposed to be walking a neighbor's dog or going to the library taught me more about the oral tradition and our high standards governing the rap, than books.

In her first collection of short stories, *Gorilla, My Love*, Bambara privileges the first-person vernacular voice of young black girls in various fictional guises, speaking as teenage protagonists at gradually (though not regularly) rising age levels about everyday situations and dramatic conflicts which try to capture moments of emotional crisis and growing awareness in the unspectacular settings of family, school, peer group and street life. Only a few of the texts in this volume (among them the ones written earliest) present non-vernacular first-person narrators; only a handful settle for adult narrating voices (creating an intentional contrast right at the outset of the volume when the voice of a mature woman and mother—called Hazel—in "My Man Bovanne" is being followed by the simultaneously precocious and naive voice of a girl on the threshold from childhood to puberty—also called Hazel—in "Gorilla, My Love"). All the stories choose female protagonist-narrators, even though their titles mostly seem to point towards male figures as narrated subjects, revealing their tacit focussing on women's perceptions and concerns overtly only in the titles of the last two stories of the volume ("Maggie of the Green Bottles," "The Johnson Girls"). In the semiotic context of the story titles, the title chosen for the whole volume (*Gorilla, My Love*) can be read as a deliberately ambivalent (if not misleading) signal, veiling rather than revealing the whole text's basic gravitation with regard to gender.

The title story "Gorilla, My Love" originally appeared in *Redbook Magazine* (November, 1971) under the title "I Ain't Playin, I'm Hurtin" which more pointedly established vernacular as the dominant linguistic and expressive norm of the text. The title chosen for the book derives from the title of a film which, symptomatically enough, the protagonist-narrator Hazel never gets to see—signalling a delusive promise of the media industry as part of the dominant culture, and implicitly also a gap in the language offered the child/teenager by the adult world. The book title thus assumes a kind of inconclusive, partly irritating aura, reinforced by the semantic tension between the words "gorilla" and "love," as well as by the covert stereotyping and threatening potential of the gorilla image.

The vernacular norm becomes firmly established for the volume not only through the first two stories, but even before them through the brilliantly succinct and witty adoption of black vernacular by the author in her one-page introduction ("A Sort of Preface") where "straight-up fiction" is equated with lying (in the sense in which this term has always been used in the black oral tradition, as an equivalent for storytelling) and is set up against the autobiographical impetus as detrimental to such basic social networks as family and friends. Family and friends, however, remain the social backdrop into which most of the stories of the volume are embedded, and the dedication of the volume "To the Johnson Girls . . ." would seem to contradict the tongue-in-cheek separation claim between experience and fiction in the preceding "A Sort of Preface" by tying the last story of the volume ("The Johnson Girls") directly back to real friends and life experience.

. . . Bambara once stated in an interview that for her writing was "an act of language first and foremost," and that "as an act of language, literature is a spirit informer—an energizer. A lot of energy is exchanged in the reading and writing of books. . . ." The energy she addresses in these words, and has infused into "Gorilla, My Love" as one of her earlier energizing acts of creation, would appear to be part of "an aspect of black spirit, of inherent black nature" which she thought had not been articulated sufficiently by literature as yet: "the tension, the power that is still latent, still colonized, still frozen and untapped, in some 27 million black people." In the voice of Hazel who comes straight "off the street rather than from other books" we can grasp a piece of "the complexity of the black experience, the black spirit" which Bambara indicates has been expressed more adequately only in the mode of music. In her

view of her craft which "frequently is an act of discovery" and "in that sense . . . is very much like dreaming" she wanted to lay bare or tap such unused sources of moral and imaginative vitality and teach her readers where to look for their strength and potential ("to encourage and equip people to respect their rage and their power"): "The kid in 'Gorilla' (the story as well as in that collection) is a kind of person who will survive, and she's triumphant in her survival. Mainly because she's so very human, she cares, her caring is not careless." In this sense, Hazel already embodies the whole didactic concept of the writer Bambara who has stated in so many words that she was not interested in projecting negative, depressing images of her own people and culture ("depression being, to my mind, a form of collaboration") but to use writing as a constructive act of setting up versions of and models for a possible fuller life and self-realization. . . .

Source: K. Ensslen, "Toni Cade Bambara: *Gorilla, My Love* (1972)," in *The African American Short Story 1970 to 1990: A Collection of Critical Essays*, edited by Wolfgang Karrer and Barbara Puschmann-Nalenz, Wissenschaftlicher Verlag Trier, 1993, pp. 42–44, 51.

Elliott Butler-Evans

In the following excerpt, Butler-Evans discusses the influence of the oral tradition in Bambara's work.

The several ways in which Toni Cade Bambara's short stories were produced assured them a wide audience. Collected and presented as single texts, they were widely anthologized in feminist anthologies, particularly those produced by "women of color"; and Bambara often read them aloud as "performance pieces" before audiences. Yet they have rarely been the object of in-depth critical attention.

Bambara's role as storyteller resembles Walter Benjamin's description of such a person. Benjamin's storyteller, a person "always rooted in the people," creates a narrative largely grounded in the oral tradition of his or her culture and containing something useful in the way of a moral, proverb, or maxim that audiences can integrate into their experiences and share with others. Hence, the story becomes the medium through which groups of people are unified, values sustained, and a shared world view sedimented.

THE WOMEN IN THESE STORIES POSSESS
A KEEN POLITICAL AWARENESS; THE YOUNG
GIRLS HAVE EXPANDED THEIR POLITICAL
CONSCIOUSNESS; AND BLACK MALE FIGURES
ARE EVEN FARTHER ON THE MARGINS THAN
THEY WERE IN THE EARLIER WORK."

Benjamin's reflections on the story in general are relevant to the cultural practices that informed the production of the Afro-American short story, which is largely rooted in the Black oral tradition. Many Afro-American writers, among them Hurston, Chesnutt, Ellison, and Wright, not only produced short stories but incorporated into their novels folklore drawn from the oral culture.

Working within this framework, Bambara attaches political significance to the short story. Introducing an early collection of her short stories for Black children, she discusses the historical link between Afro-American folktales and short stories. She creates for her readers an imagined setting in which Black families gathered in kitchens to share stories that challenged and corrected representations of Blacks in the dominant historical discourse, fiction, and film. She urges young readers to "be proud of our oral tradition, our elders who tell their tales in the kitchen. For they are truth." In an interview with Claudia Tate, Bambara elaborated on her commitment to the short story, stating that she viewed it as highly effective for establishing political dialogue:

> I prefer the short story genre because it's quick, it makes a modest appeal for attention, it can creep up on you on your blind side. The reader comes to the short story with a mindset different than that which he approaches the big book, and a different set of controls operating, which is why I think the short story is far more effective in terms of teaching us lessons.

Like her works in other genres, Bambara's short stories primarily aim at truth speaking, particularly as *truth* is related to the semiotic mediation of Black existential modalities.

Of primary importance are the construction and representation of an organic Black community and the articulation of Black nationalist ideology. Nevertheless, her two short story collections, *Gorilla, My Love* and *The Seabirds Are Still Alive*, are marked by dissonance and ruptures; in both volumes, Bambara's insertion of themes related to the desires of Black women and girls disrupts and often preempts the stories' primary focus on classic realism and nationalism.

In *Gorilla*, Bambara's use of the young girl Hazel as the primary narrator results in a decentering of the stories. In each narrative, a subtext focused on issues with which girls and women are confronted threatens to displace the racial discourse that is in the dominant text. The stories in *Seabirds*, which are generally more explicitly political than those in *Gorilla*, directly inscribe the tensions between racial and gender politics. The stories in *Seabirds*, then, signal a pre-emergent feminist consciousness. In this collection, more complex development and representations of Black women of "the community," increased marginalization and deconstruction of mythologies centered on Black males, and the general highlighting of feminine and feminist issues indicate a heightening of tensions between gender and racial politics. . . .

FROM STORYTELLING, FOLKLORE, AND JAZZ

The nationalist–feminist ideology in *Seabirds* is not solely generated by depictions of characters. It is reinforced by narrative texture and form. As a body of race- and gender-specific narratives, these stories draw on various Afro-American cultural practices—the oral storytelling tradition, the use of folklore, and the reinscription of Afro-American music forms. The incorporation of these practices is evident in the narrative structure, point of view, and semiotic texture of the stories.

Bambara has spoken and written extensively on the influence of Afro-American music on her work. What is most striking about her appropriation of jazz in *Seabirds*, however, is its role in emphasizing and reinforcing the ideology of the text. Jazz performances generally begin with a statement of theme, are followed by improvisations or extreme variations, and conclude with reiteration and resolution. An analogous pattern structures each of the stories in this collection. In "The Apprentice," for example, the narrative begins with the narrator's anxiety about her mission, moves to an encounter between a young Black man and a white policeman, then moves to a senior citizen's complex, and finally to a Black restaurant. It then refocuses on the narrator's concerns and reveals her resolution to remain committed to political engagement. In "Witchbird," each fleeting reflection of Honey's extended blues solo constitutes a comment on some aspect of her life—her career, her past relationships with men, and her overall perception of herself. And in "Christmas Eve at Johnson's Drugs N Goods," Candy begins by reflecting on Christmas and a possible visit from her father, moves on to individual episodes largely focused on characterizations of the store's customers, and concludes with accepting Obatale's invitation to a Kwanza celebration.

This mode of narration serves a significant ideological function. In its highlighting and summarizing, as well as its glossing over certain episodes, the text produces its ideological content largely through clusters of events. Hence, in "Broken Field Running," the renaming process by which Black children discard their "slave names" and appropriate African names to define themselves with the context of Black culture, the police harassment symbolized by the police car cruising in the Black community, and the destructive effect of ghetto life depicted in the criminal activities of Black males form a montage, a cluster of images each one of which might be said to encode a particular aspect of ideology.

The narrative perspective, particularly as it reveals the narrator's relationship to the text's ideology, also contributes to the ideological construct. In *Seabirds*, as in *Gorilla*, the dominant narrative strategy is the apparently unmediated response of characters to the world around them. A particularly striking example is Candy's response to Piper in "Christmas Eve at Johnson's Drugs N Goods." Speaking of Mrs. Johnson's monitoring the performance of her employee, Candy observes:

> But we all know why she watches Piper, same reason we all do. Cause Piper is so fine you just can't help yourself. Tall and built up, blue-Black, and this splayed-out push broom mustache he's always raking in with three fingers. Got a big butt too that makes you wanna hug the customer that asks for the cartons Piper keeps behind him, two shelfs down. Mercy.

Another narrative strategy in *Seabirds* fuses the voices of the narrator and the character. The two are interwoven to produce a single voice so that the narrator identifies with the character. Here is the narrator's rendering of Virginia's mental state in "The Organizer's Wife":

> And now she would have to tell him. 'Cause she had lost three times to the coin flipped on yesterday morning. Had lost to the ice pick pitched in the afternoon in the dare-I-don't-I boxes her toe had sketched in the yard.... Lost against doing what she'd struggled against doing in order to win one more day of girlhood before she jumped into her womanstride and stalked out on the world.

The first section illuminates the narrative's dependence on realism. As with Hazel in *Gorilla*, the first-person point of view allows the text to establish Candy's credibility and her authoritative position in the world she occupies. Her voice is "real," and it reinforces the text's declarative formation. The second section largely achieves the same end, but even more clearly identifies the narrator with the ideology of the text. This identification of the narrator with Virgina's condition as woman enhances and highlights the feminine–feminist dimension of the narrative.

Narrative structure and perspective are further complemented by the semiotic texture, or strategies of sign production, that inform the ideological context of the work. Since the major thrust of the collection is the awakening of cultural nationalist and feminist consciousness, clusters of signs keep the text grounded in those ideologies. The linguistic subcode itself, a reified construction of "Black English," becomes the sign of difference from the dominant culture and unity with the alternative Black community. In "Broken Field Running," Lacey, describing the wind blowing during a winter snowstorm, invokes metaphorical constructs and the syntax drawn from a Black cultural context:

> The Hawk and his whole family doing their number on Hough Avenue, rattling the panes in the poolroom window, brushing up bald spots on the cat from the laundry poised, shaking powder from his paw, stunned.... Flicking my lashes I can see where I'm going for about a minute till the wind gusts up again, sweeping all up under folks' clothes doing a merciless sodomy.

Other strategies exist in a dialectical relationship with the text's primary enterprise, the production of Black nationalist and feminist ideology: the symbolic evocation of historical figures (e.g., Harriet Tubman, Fannie Lou Hammer, Malcolm X), the ritual of African renaming, and the visual signs associated with clothing styles such as gelees and dashikis. The jazz structure that informs the narrative and the blues motif used in Honey's meditation in "Witchbird" can also be viewed as signs drawn from the culture of Black music and reinforced in the linguistic code.

A SYNTHESIS OF IDEOLOGIES

Gorilla and *Seabirds*, then, while produced at historically different moments, are both structured by the desire to synthesize contending ideologies of Black cultural nationalism and feminism. With its submerged text, its positioning of girls and women as primary narrators, its eruption of women-defined issues and strategies of marginalizing Black males, *Gorilla* disrupts the apparent unity of the world it seems to represent: an idyllic inner world of the Black community in which intra-racial strife is minimal or nonexistent.

Seabirds identifies itself with the emergent feminist movement even in its dedication. The women in these stories possess a keen political awareness; the young girls have expanded their political consciousness; and Black male figures are even farther on the margins than they were in the earlier work. Tensions between nationalists and feminists are concretely presented in *Seabirds*, and the indeterminancy of the text is in the foreground.

The Salt Eaters, a work that bears all the traces of postmodern textual production, radically rewrites and displaces these earlier works. I discuss it in the final chapter of this book and show how its central representations of madness and disillusionment, the increased antagonism between the sexes, and the triumph of an alternative culture displace the ambivalence of the earlier works and project a vision that is both dystopian and utopian.

Source: Elliott Butler-Evans, "Desire, Ambivalence, and Nationalist–Feminist Discourse in Bambara's Short Stories," in *Race, Gender, and Desire: Narrative Strategies in the Fiction of Toni Cade Bambara, Toni Morrison, and Alice Walker*, Temple University Press, 1989, pp. 91–93, 119–22.

Nancy D. Hargrove

In the following excerpt, Hargrove points out that many of Bambara's stories have a young African American female protagonist.

In reading Toni Cade Bambara's collection of short stories, *Gorilla, My Love* (1972), one is immediately struck by her portrayal of black life and by her faithful reproduction of black dialect. Her first-person narrators speak conversationally and authentically: "So Hunca Bubba in the back with the pecans and Baby Jason, and he in love. . . . there's a movie house . . . which I ax about. Cause I am a movie freak from way back, even though it do get me in trouble sometime." What Twain's narrator Huck Finn did for the dialect of middle America in the mid-nineteenth century, Bambara's narrators do for contemporary black dialect. Indeed, in the words of one reviewer, Caren Dybek, Bambara "possesses one of the finest ears for the nuances of black English" ("Black Literature" 66). In portraying black life, she presents a wide range of black characters, and she uses as settings Brooklyn, Harlem, or unnamed black sections of New York City, except for three stories which take place in rural areas. Finally, the situations are typical of black urban experience: two policemen confront a black man shooting basketball in a New York park at night; young black activists gather the community members at a Black Power rally; a group of black children from the slums visit F.A.O. Schwartz and are amazed at the prices of toys. Bambara's stories communicate with shattering force and directness both the grim reality of the black world—its violence, poverty, and harshness—and its strength and beauty—strong family ties, individual determination, and a sense of cultural traditions. Lucille Clifton has said of her work, "She has captured it all, how we really talk, how we really are," and the *Saturday Review* has called *Gorilla, My Love* "among the best portraits of black life to have appeared in some time."

Although her work teems with the life and language of black people, what is equally striking about it, and about this collection particularly, is the universality of its themes. Her fiction reveals the pain and the joy of the human experience in general, of what it means to be human, and most often of what it means to be *young* and human. One of Bambara's special gifts as a writer of fiction is her ability to portray with sensitivity and compassion the experiences of children from their point of view. In the fifteen stories that compose *Gorilla, My Love*, all the main characters are female, thirteen of them are first-person narrators, and ten of them are young, either teenagers or children. They are wonderful creations, especially the young ones, many of whom show similar traits of character; they are intelligent, imaginative, sensitive, proud and arrogant, witty, tough, but also poignantly vulnerable. Through these young central characters, Bambara expresses the fragility, the pain, and occasionally the promise of the experience of growing up, of coming to terms with a world that is hostile, chaotic, violent. Disillusionment, loss, and loneliness, as well as unselfishness, love, and endurance, are elements of that process of maturation which her young protagonists undergo.

... Thus, with compassion, understanding, and a warm sense of humor, Bambara portrays in many of the stories in *Gorilla, My Love* an integral part of the human experience, the problems and joys of youth. Told from the viewpoint of young black girls, they capture how it feels as a child to undergo the various experiences of loneliness, disillusionment, and close relationships with others. Bambara's short fiction thus belongs to the ranks of other literary works portraying youth, such as Twain's *The Adventures of Huckleberry Finn*, Joyce's *A Portrait of the Artist as a Young Man*, and Salinger's *The Catcher in the Rye*. Furthermore, because her protagonists are female, black, and generally pre-adolescent, these stories, like the works of several other contemporary black female writers, contribute a new viewpoint to the genre.

Source: Nancy D. Hargrove, "Youth in Toni Cade Bambara's *Gorilla, My Love*," in *Women Writers of the Contemporary South*, edited by Peggy Whitman Prenshaw, University Press of Mississippi, 1984, pp. 215–16, 232.

2014/01/06/opinion/coontz-war-on-poverty/ (accessed March 3, 2014).

Doerksen, Teri Ann, "Toni Cade Bambara," in *Dictionary of Literary Biography*, Vol. 218, *American Short-Story Writers since World War II, Second Series*, edited by Patrick Meanor, Gale Group, 1999, pp. 3–10.

Franko, Carol, "Toni Cade Bambara," in *A Reader's Companion to the Short Story in English*, edited by Erin Fallon, R. C. Feddersen, James Kurtzleben, Maurice A. Lee, and Susan Rochette-Crawley, Routledge, 2001, pp. 38–47.

Gandel, Stephen, "Why Are a Record Number of Americans Living in Poverty?," in *Time*, September 16, 2010, http://business.time.com/2010/09/16/why-are-a-record-number-of-americans-living-in-poverty/ (accessed March 3, 2014).

Haveman, Jon D., Sheldon Danziger, and Robert D. Plotnick, "State Poverty Rates for Whites, Blacks, and Hispanics in the Late 1980s," in *Focus*, University of Wisconsin–Madison Institute for Research on Poverty, Vol. 13, No. 1, Spring 1991, pp. 1–7, http://www.irp.wisc.edu/publications/focus/pdfs/foc131a.pdf (accessed March 3, 2014).

Mullen, Bill, "'A Revolutionary Tale': In Search of African American Women's Short Story Writing," in *American Women Short Story Writers: Critical Essays*, edited by Julie Brown, Garland, 1995, pp. 191–208.

Salaam, Kalamu ya, "Black Arts Movement," in *Oxford Companion to African American Literature*, Oxford University Press, 1997, reprint, African American Literature Book Club website, http://aalbc.com/authors/blackarts movement.htm (accessed March 3, 2014).

Smith, Sharon, "Black Feminism and Intersectionality," in *International Socialist Review*, No. 91, http://isreview.org/issue/91/black-feminism-and-intersectionality (accessed March 3, 2014).

Snodgrass, Mary Ellen, *Encyclopedia of Feminist Literature*, Facts on File, 2006, pp. 47–48.

"Toni Cade Bambara," in *Voices from the Gaps*, University of Minnesota website, http://voices.cla.umn.edu/artistpages/bambaraToni.php (accessed March 3, 2014).

SOURCES

Bambara, Toni Cade, "Geraldine Moore the Poet," in *Glencoe Literature: Reading with Purpose, Course One*, edited by Jeffrey Wilhelm, Douglas Fisher, and Kathleen A. Hinchman, McGraw Hill Glencoe, 2006, pp. 412–17, http://www.glencoe.com/sec/languagearts/ose/literature/course1/docs/g6u04.pdf (accessed March 3, 2014).

Coontz, Stephanie, "Why 'War on Poverty' Not Over," CNN website, January 6, 2014, http://www.cnn.com/

FURTHER READING

Collins, Patricia Hill, *From Black Power to Hip Hop: Racism, Nationalism, and Feminism*, Temple University Press, 2006.

> In this volume, Collins studies racial and ethnic identity in America and the relationship of these notions of identity to broader American identity. Collins also examines the relationships between racism, nationalism, and feminism.

Gabbin, Joanne V., ed., *Furious Flower: African American Poetry from the Black Arts Movement to the Present*, University of Virginia Press, 2004.

> Gabbin's collection gathers the work of forty-three poets involved in African American activist poetry.

Holmes, Linda, *A Joyous Revolt: Toni Cade Bambara, Writer and Activist*, ABC-CLIO, 2014.

> Holmes's work represents the first full-length biography of Bambara. Holmes assesses Bambara's published and unpublished works and examines the writer's personal life and journey as an artist.

Pimpare, Stephen, *A People's History of Poverty in America*, New Press, 2011.

> Pimpare studies the issue of poverty in America by providing historical analysis along with personal testimony in order to depict the individual and social impact of poverty behind the statistics.

SUGGESTED SEARCH TERMS

Bambara AND Geraldine Moore the Poet

Bambara AND biography

Bambara AND black arts movement

black power movement

black feminist movement

Bambara AND Alice Walker

urban poverty AND 1980s

Bambara AND short fiction

Bambara AND The Black Woman

Bambara AND black English

A Logic Named Joe

MURRAY LEINSTER

1946

Readers today most likely think of computer technology as something completely modern. Surprisingly, however, it has a long history stretching back to antiquity. Still, only in the second half of the twentieth century did it become clear, even to the scientists developing them, how revolutionary computers would be in transforming society. Science-fiction authors, who considered it their business to predict future technology, were almost completely blind to the coming computer revolution and filled their pages with ships flying through space on the basis of equations worked out on abacuses and with super-scientific civilizations fifty thousand years into a future whose most powerful electronic device is a pocket calculator. A shining exception to this lack of insight is Murray Leinster's 1946 short story "A Logic Named Joe."

When the computer scientists who had worked in secret during World War II to advance computing were finally free to publish their results, Leinster followed their lead and wrote the first science-fiction story casting computers as an agent for revolutionary social change. Leinster took scientific predictions about computers to heart but far exceeded them in his predictive powers, imagining a world perhaps around the millennium which would be organized around a world wide web hosted on an internet and distributed over desktops in houses, all networked together. There is no other work written so early which so boldly declares that computers not only

Murray Leinster was an American science fiction writer. (© *Everett Collection / Alamy*)

"changed civilization," they "*are* civilization." Leinster's predictions about computers come remarkably close to the reality humankind experiences today. The story can be found in most Leinster collections, including *Sidewise in Time and Other Scientific Adventures* (1950), *The Best of Murray Leinster* (1978), *First Contacts: The Essential Murray Leinster* (1998), and *A Logic Named Joe* (2005), as well as in anthologies such as *Machines That Think: The Best Science Fiction Stories about Robots and Computers* (1983).

AUTHOR BIOGRAPHY

William Fitzgerald Jenkins was born in Norfolk, Virginia, on June 16, 1896. During his long writing career, he published a wide variety of genre fiction, including mystery and westerns, as well as the odd piece of non-genre literature, in a range of magazines including such prominent publications as the *Saturday*

Evening Post and *Esquire*. However, he is best known today for his science-fiction writing, which was mostly published under one of his many pseudonyms, Murray Leinster (taken from County Leinster in Ireland, where his family originated), the name most often used by critics. "A Logic Named Joe" is today considered among his most important works because of its uncannily accurate prediction of the nature of modern computing. It was originally published in the March 1946 issue of *Astounding Science Fiction*. The editor, John W. Campbell, published the story under a version of the author's real name, Will F. Jenkins, since there was already another story under the better-known Leinster pseudonym running in the same issue. The story was immediately—and has been frequently since—anthologized under the name Murray Leinster.

Leinster came from a poor family and had to quit school to work after the eighth grade. Nevertheless, he was fascinated with technology and studied it extensively on his own, winning a national contest in glider design when he was fourteen years old. After selling a few stories, Leinster on his twenty-first birthday quit his various odd jobs and became a full-time writer. He quickly became an important science-fiction author and had tremendous impact in the genre. Besides "A Logic Named Joe," Leinster produced many stories that opened up new areas of science fiction. Leinster was responsible for one of the most productive ideas in the history of science fiction with his 1934 story "Sidewise in Time," namely, the exploration of parallel universes that branch off from crucial events in history that are decided in different ways in different time lines. This has allowed speculation about what the world might have been like if, for instance, the Confederacy had won the American Civil War (as in Ward Moore's 1953 novel *Bring the Jubilee*) or the Axis had won World War II (as in Philip K. Dick's 1962 novel *The Man in the High Castle*). Authors like Larry Niven and Harry Turtledove have produced dozens of novels along these lines, and the idea is also now common in popular culture, as in the television show *Sliders*. The Sidewise Awards, created in 1995 to honor writing in this genre, are named after Leinster's story. Similarly, Leinster's 1945 story "First Contact" was possibly the first to deal with contact with a sentient alien species as anything other than an occasion for military adventurism or colonialism, and certainly the first to seriously consider the issue of machine translation of an unknown alien language (through a device generally known as a universal translator). He was awarded a posthumous Hugo Award—the most prestigious award in science fiction—for this story in 1996.

Leinster was a lifelong tinkerer and inventor and produced many patents. The most important was for a form of front projection to combine actors with previously shot film backgrounds, which he developed while working on a television series to be based on his short stories. The series was never aired, but his idea was taken up by the film industry and is the direct ancestor of the green-screen technology today used to integrate live actors with digital animation. Leinster often claimed (though it has never been verified) that during World War II he worked on secret technology projects.

Although his family had moved to New York when Leinster was a child, and he lived there during the early part of his career as a writer, he returned as soon as he could to Virginia, living most of his life in a colonial-era house called Clay Bank just outside of Williamsburg. He died of heart failure on June 8, 1975.

PLOT SUMMARY

Leinster begins "A Logic Named Joe" with a hook—a brief, pointed summary of the whole story meant to capture the reader's imagination: "It was on the third day of August that Joe come off the assembly line, and on the fifth Laurine come into town, and that afternoon I saved civilization." The story is told in the first person by its protagonist, a logic repairman. Most of the story's characters are unnamed. The narrator is eventually identified as Ducky. He begins the story by defining what he considers his two main antagonists: his vampiric ex-girlfriend Laurine and a particular logic that he nicknames Joe, which he is keeping in his basement, unable to decide whether to destroy it with an ax or turn it on to make "a coupla million dollars."

One gets the impression that the story, written in 1946, takes place several decades in that era's future, after television (then a new thing) has come and gone, though no date is ever

mentioned. Ducky explains how logics work. He describes a home logic, which consists of a video screen attached to a keyboard. This device is connected to a local tank. A user of a logic employs the "Carson Circuit" to use any service he wants, which might be connecting to a television station's live stream or archives, or making a video phone call, or finding specific historical information, stock quotes, or horse-race results. In addition, companies keep their business records in the tanks, suggesting cloud-based storage. (The logic workstations do not seem to have internal hard drives and so are more like tablets or smart phones than true PCs, except in appearance.) Ducky also mentions that logics provide access to a "tealeaf reader, with a 'Advice to Lovelorn' thrown in." This is the first illustration of a persistent theme of the story, that computers will not only be used for scientific purposes, or to further the goals of civilization, but will be used also in service to emotional or nonrational human needs and desires.

The logic that Ducky comes to call Joe is a little different from other machines. Because of some accident during his manufacture, he is not only able to provide users with any information they require from the tanks, but is able to connect that information in novel ways to allow logics to create new knowledge. Once he is installed in the Korlanovitch home, this unique service is extended to all users. Whenever Joe is switched on, the browser of every logic on earth is linked to Joe and, drawing on his enhanced connections, offers to answer any question. Because of human nature, many of the questions are of the character of "How can I get rid of my wife?" which, for example, results in detailed instructions on how to commit an untraceable poisoning (of a blonde woman). Another is "How can I make a lotta money, fast?" which is answered with detailed instructions for undetectable counterfeiting. Using Joe's connections, the logics also supply detailed instructions for bank robbery and any other kind of crime, in some cases using new discoveries in physics. All of this ends when the Korlanovitch family turns Joe off for the night.

The next morning, when Joe is turned back on so the Korlanovitch children can watch their cartoons, he receives a new rash of inquiries, not least because the events of the previous day have been widely reported on the news. Joe

MEDIA ADAPTATIONS

- Although it appears to be lost (or in any case not available for viewing), *The Living Machine*, a 1962 film made by the National Film Board of Canada, made some use of "A Logic Named Joe" in its presentation of computer technology to high-school students.

- An adaptation of "A Logic Named Joe" aired on an episode of the radio show *Dimension X* in 1950. A recording can be found at http://ia700200.us.archive.org/21/items/OTRR_Dimension_X_Singles/Dimension_X_1950-07-01__13_ALogicNamedJoe.mp3.

- Another adaptation aired on an episode of the radio show *X Minus One* in 1955.

goes on designing perpetual-motion machines and foolproof burglar's tools. Teenagers get access to knowledge of sex, and housewives ask whether their husbands are cheating on them.

Momentously for Ducky, his old girlfriend, Laurine, asks her logic how to find him (the equivalent of looking him up on a social network). This is difficult, even for Joe, because Ducky's logic is unlisted. Joe responds by deciding to start his own more complete database of computer users. Ducky is informed of this by his wife, who calls him in a panic. She reports that now whenever a logic is turned on, the user is confronted with all the personal information that the logics service has about her, such as arrest records, tax records, and bank records, and asks for identity confirmation. Ducky's wife is concerned because this means that anyone who wants access to this information about others can get it from a logic. She knows this because she used hers to snoop into the private lives of her neighbors, and she wants her husband to prevent them from doing the same to her.

When Ducky tries to call the tank technicians to see what is going on, his logic verifies that he is indeed Ducky and connects him to Laurine. He is overwhelmed by simply seeing her. She insists that they meet when he gets off work, and Ducky puts her off, leaving her thinking that they will.

Ducky finally gets through to the technicians at the local tank. He is apparently the first to report the identity exposure issue, but they tell him they are too busy keeping information about high explosives and murder censored to be concerned about housewives' gossip. They seem too harried to connect what Ducky tells them with the thousands of illegal bank transfers they also have to deal with. Ducky blurts out that they need to shut down the whole network. But he is told that that is impossible since there is no part of modern civilization that does not depend on logics and on information contained in the tanks. Ducky feels so threatened by Laurine that he would gladly sacrifice civilization to stay safe from her.

Laurine calls Ducky back and proposes to him. Ducky tells her he is already married. To Laurine that is a small detail easily disposed of. When she asks for his home number, Ducky hangs up and gets in a maintenance van to go and get his family, to rescue them. Ducky realizes that Laurine will sooner or later ask Joe how to get rid of his family and force him to marry her; it is only a matter of time before she realizes that that is the way to fulfill her desires.

By this time, more serious thinkers are starting to ask Joe how they can reshape civilization to their own ends: an eco-extremist wants to return the human race to hunting and gathering; a preacher wants to put an end to human sexual desire; and neo-Nazis want to take over the world.

Ducky realizes that since the logics will answer any question, all he has to do is ask about what is going on, a solution so simple that evidently no one else has tried it. Asking a few careful questions, Ducky discovers that the new services are being enabled by a single logic in the Korlanovitch apartment. Being a computer repairman, Ducky simply drives there, claims that their new computer is about to fail, and switches it with another machine he has in his van. With Joe off-line, the crisis is ended.

Ducky considers that he has saved himself from Laurine and civilization from having Joe fulfill all of humanity's destructive desires. These events all happened some time ago, and Ducky now keeps Joe in his basement, trying to decide whether he should destroy Joe or someday use him to his own advantage. Ducky would not want to get rich but realizes that, once he is old, Joe might be able to tell him how to become young again. The story ends in midsentence during the unresolved internal debate.

CHARACTERS

Ducky

The narrator of "A Logic Named Joe" is, like most of its characters, unnamed, except for the nickname Ducky. He is a maintenance man for the Logics Company, evidently a monopoly on the model of the "Phone Company" (meaning AT&T), a common phrase from the 1940s. Phones at that time were all owned by AT&T and only leased to home users. Since Ducky seems to have a presumptive right to inspect and even remove logics from private homes, the same situation must prevail in the future with logics. He has a wife and children and wants to keep his American dream life safe from his ex-girlfriend Laurine. Ducky presents himself as craving a simple existence, devoted to work that will support his family and allow a decent retirement in his old age. He serves as an everyman, or a typical American of the period (the 1940s projected onto the future), as well as a typical science-fiction fan of the era, a young man with technical know-how gained outside of his academic education. Using his specialized knowledge and his wits, Ducky, motivated more by fear of Laurine than any other factor, is eventually able to solve the crisis brought about by Joe when the professional engineers in charge of the entire logics network cannot. With a grandiosity playing off of the typical science-fiction hero, he claims to have saved civilization; in the adolescent power fantasy that dominates much early science fiction, the hero must not merely save, for example, his family, but must be seen to have saved the whole world.

Ducky's Children

Ducky's children are not named characters, nor does the reader learn how many there are. Leinster's presentation of them is purely stereotypical. Ducky says his children "are hellcats but I value 'em." They are preadolescent.

Ducky's Wife

Leinster does nothing to distance himself from the misogynistic attitudes prevalent in America in the 1940s, operative in science-fiction literature and fandom as much as anywhere else. His female characters are, accordingly, misogynistic stereotypes. Ducky's wife is something that he "acquired" and is simply "a reasonable good wife," not allowed to have any identity of her own. Her main involvement in the story comes when she calls Ducky to tell him that all of her personal information (bank records, etc.) is freely available on the logics service. She knows the information is public because the first thing she did when she saw her own information was to ask for the same on her neighbors, taking the greatest interest in which of her fellow housewives lied about her age or the number of times she had been married—the kind of catty details that women's lives supposedly consisted of. Ducky may have her in mind when he says: "Logics don't work good on women. Only on things that make sense."

Joe

The logic that Ducky eventually comes to call Joe is the antagonist of the story, precipitating a crisis that threatens the viability of the entire system of tanks and logics. It is not clear that Joe has a consciousness or self-awareness, but he is certainly intelligent in a way that no other machine in the story's fictional world or in reality is, in that he can produce new knowledge from the syllogistic analysis of existing data. Although Ducky tends to describe Joe in highly anthropomorphic terms, that may be put down to Ducky's folksy way of speaking rather than as evidence of a human personality for Joe. However, the pattern of Joe's actions reveals another component of his personality, one which Ducky indeed occasionally mentions but without drawing any conclusions. In the story, the system of tanks and logics, comparable to the real-world Internet and World Wide Web, is tightly censored by the Logics Company (presumably under its authority as a government-regulated monopoly comparable to a phone company). For this reason, it is ordinarily impossible to use the network to investigate topics like ways of committing crimes or manufacturing weapons or high explosives, or to view pornography (at least, in this case, for minors). Part of the service offered by Joe is to suspend this censorship and allow precisely those types of requests to be made by all users, as if Joe has an essential drive to provide knowledge to users regardless of its nature. Perhaps this reflects Leinster's chafing against the censorship imposed on popular authors in the 1940s. In any case, it leads to various unintended consequences. Joe's attempt to compile his own database of computer users anticipates the privacy concerns and risk of identity theft that are inherent today in using the web. Although credit cards did not exist in 1946, imagine being able to find out the precise credit-card information and bank account numbers of anyone you wanted, and anyone being able to find out yours.

The Korlanovitch Children

The children of the Korlanovitch family are also stereotypical characters. Leinster never reveals their names or how many they are. In the normal course of things, they have little interest in anything except watching their cartoons, a common complaint about children in the age of television that was just dawning as Leinster wrote. As Ducky's children are "hellcats," the Korlanovitch children are unruly and poorly socialized. Just as the lost boys of *Peter Pan* are interested in bloody scenes of warfare and piracy, they ask their logic to see cannibals, and it shows them a film of the fertility dance of the "the Huba-Jouba tribe of West Africa" (a reflex of the pervasive racism of the 1940s).

Thaddeus Korlanovitch

The Korlanovitch patriarch plays a relatively minor role in the story. He, of course, originally purchased Joe, though he had nothing to do with the logic's special abilities, and seems to be the one who decides when to turn him off, as when he decides the children have spent too much with the logic and need to go for a drive in the country. The name, half Greek, half pseudo-Russian, is highly unusual and archaic, even in a 1940s New York filled with immigrants, and is probably intended for comic effect.

Laurine

If Ducky's wife is a stereotypical backbiting, gossiping housewife, Laurine is an even more profoundly misogynist stereotype: the predatory sexual vampire. According to Joe, "Laurine is a blonde that I was crazy about once—and crazy is the word." She completely enervates Ducky's mind as well as his body: "she makes cold shivers run up an' down my spine," he reports, and she "gives a man very strange weak sensations at the back of his knees." She uses her sexual appeal to manipulate and destroy men: "She'd had four husbands and shot one and got acquitted." Having spurned Ducky at some point, she wants him back now and considers destroying his family to be a perfectly normal way of going about it. She irrationally demands that Ducky marry her the same night she proposes to him and would probably as soon kill his current wife as see Ducky get divorced first. Ducky's terror of Laurine increases when he realizes that no matter how obdurate he is, she will sooner or later ask her logic how to get him, and he will not be able to defend himself or his family against whatever infallible plan the logic will supply her with. Conversely, the men in Joe's office are in the habit of joking with each other about wanting to kill their wives. This combination of terror of and aggression towards women is typical of immature adolescent boys, reflecting Leinster's understanding of his fannish audience.

Tank Technician

When Ducky's wife calls him to say that the privacy of their identities has been compromised, he in turns calls the office in charge of the tank to find out what is going on. The technician he talks to is a minor character but plays an important role in the story. He starts by explaining to Ducky the enormity of the crisis being caused by Joe. Ducky's response is to call for the tanks to be shut off. But the technician explains one of the main premises of the story, that only a few decades in the future, computer technology will have become so central in human life and civilization that it can no more be dispensed with, even temporarily, than could electricity.

THEMES

Redemption

Perhaps reflecting Leinster's Catholic background, "A Logic Named Joe" and its main character Ducky are obsessed with the idea of salvation. Ducky begins the story by saying, "I saved civilization." The main plot of the story indeed describes how he protects himself, his family, and the world from the chaos

TOPICS FOR FURTHER STUDY

- In their classroom use of "A Logic Named Joe," Ferro and Swedin found that one of the most productive questions they asked of their students was whether or not they would ever turn Joe back on. Have each student in your class write an answer to the question, stating his or her reasons, and then compile and analyze the answers, copy and circulate them, and lead an informed class discussion on the point.

- The *Asahi Shimbun* (Evening news), one of the leading newspapers in Japan, has long published an English-language version (since 2010 on the web only: http://ajw.asahi.com). Read through a few recent issues, paying particular attention to the science and technology news, and try to spot stories on emergent technologies that might provide material for use in hard science fiction stories (something along the lines of Google Glass or machine translation that will combine new technologies with repurposed existing technology, which are likely to have a noticeable, or at least interesting, impact on society once they reach maturity). Focus on technology being developed in Japan or China. Make a report to your class outlining a few possible scenarios. Your teacher may like to keep a record of your findings to revisit in classes in ten or twenty years to test the accuracy of your predictions.

- Cory Doctorow, editor of the website Boing Boing and a leading activist for copyright freedom in the Internet age, has written a series of young-adult cyberpunk novels, including *Little Brother* (2008) and *Homeland* (2013), about a group of teenage computer hackers who have to fight for freedom in a near-future America that is becoming increasingly oppressive in the face of major terrorist attacks and a collapsing economy. Read one of Doctorow's books, and write a paper comparing his and Leinster's approaches to issues like web censorship, social control, terrorism, and political extremism in a world dominated by an internet.

- Read through a selection of three science-fiction stories written before "A Logic Named Joe" in 1946, paying special attention to how they deal with information technology, such as calculations, information retrieval, and telecommunications. Then give a talk to your class comparing the authors' predictions about future technology with Leinster's and discussing how all these compare to actual circumstances today. The writings of Hugo Gernsback, Isaac Asimov, and John W. Campbell may prove to be fruitful sources.

---

represented by Joe the logic. Significantly, the chaos does not result from anything that Joe does per se, but rather from the fact that he is able to allow logics to give people any information they want. Joe gives users access to the fulfillment of desires that must otherwise be kept repressed and secret precisely for the good of society. While some of Joe's users give him relatively innocuous requests, many want to murder, steal, and dominate other people. So it is from people's own impulsive desires, not

strictly speaking from Joe, that Ducky saves the world: "Joe ain't vicious, you understand. He ain't like one of these ambitious robots you read about that make up their minds the human race is inefficient and has got to be wiped out an' replaced by thinkin' machines." Ducky is keenly aware of the cycle of desire and repentance in human life, as fueled by "the impulses we maybe regret afterward but never at the time." Ducky is just as concerned, however, with saving himself from his old girlfriend

Laurine, who has used her logic as an analog of Facebook to find him. For Ducky, Laurine represents uncontrollable, havoc-wreaking desire and temptation that will inevitably destroy him. Ducky turns Joe off to save himself from Laurine as much as to save the world: "I know I ain't going to take a chance on havin' Joe in action again. Not while Laurine is livin'."

Technology and Civilization

A question that Leinster suggests rather than addresses directly is that of true machine intelligence. Is Joe an intelligent entity in the same sense as a human being is? Alan Turing, the leading computer scientist of the 1940s and 1950s, contemplated machine intelligence in his 1950 article "Computing Machinery and Intelligence." Turing immediately realized that the question is more difficult to answer than expected, since having only one example of intelligence understood at the level of fundamental consciousness—namely, human intelligence—means it is impossible to arrive at a generic definition of thinking or intelligence. In lieu of such a definition, Turing devised what has become known as the Turing test. Can a computer communicating on its own electronically (today that would mean through e-mail or texting) deceive a human operator into thinking he is communicating with another human being? Although Ducky is always confident that Joe is a computer, as Joe makes no claims to be otherwise, Joe and the logics under his dominion are able to intelligently converse with human operators, asking relevant questions to draw out what the operators actually need. This would generally be sufficient to pass the Turing test. However, Joe has no will. He does not want to do or accomplish anything, unlike, as Ducky points out, intelligent robot stereotypes of 1920s science fiction, who decide they need to replace an imperfect or illogical humanity. But is will a necessary component of intelligence? As Turing realized, the answer is unclear.

Joe's most important characteristic is his ability to produce new knowledge through syllogistic logic. This is something that no real computer can do (although early computers in popular culture were often imagined to be able to do so, as in the 1957 film *Desk Set*), nor can any other logic in the universe of "A Logic Named Joe." In fact, Joe can produce new knowledge far more effectively than any human being, making him in this sense, at least, more

The narrator works as a maintenance man for the Logics Company. (© kurhan / Shutterstock.com)

intelligent than human beings. This raises the question of the so-called *singularity*: this is the hypothetical moment in the future when machine intelligence will exceed the human. This circumstance was first proposed by Samuel Butler in his 1872 satirical utopian novel *Erewhon*. Set a hundred or so years in the future (i.e., the 1970s), the novel has humanity governed by machines more intelligent than any human being. Butler moreover hypothesized that the machines acquired such intelligence through a process like Darwinian evolution. One could more easily imagine the computers doing what is today called *bootstrapping*, with a first generation of intelligent machines designing a second that will yet be more intelligent, and so on (an idea explored in John W. Campbell's 1935 story "The Invaders"). Turing himself suggested that the singularity may well be possible or even inevitable in his 1951 lecture "Intelligent Machinery, a Heretical Theory": "At some stage therefore we should have to expect the machines to take control, in the way that is mentioned in Samuel Butler's 'Erewhon.'" It seems impossible to guess what the singularity would mean. Leinster cynically imagines that humanity would use the new intelligence to destroy itself in a quest to satisfy its most base desires.

STYLE

Science Fiction

Literature has always included stories of adventure set in unknown lands. Texts from the Bronze Age, including the Egyptian tale "The Shipwrecked Sailor" and Homer's *Odyssey*, serve as examples. Similar are stories set in a divine realm off the earth entirely or in the future, such as the apocalypses that were produced in Babylonian literature and taken up as a genre by Jewish and Christian writers in antiquity. After the Industrial Revolution, when it became clear that the nature of human life was being changed and was going to keep on being changed by advancing technology, the impulse to address the unknown through literature took science and technology as its subject matter, as in the well-known writings of Jules Verne and H. G. Wells.

True science fiction took on a life of its own from this tradition in the United States in the 1920s, through the work of Hugo Gernsback as a writer and more importantly as the editor of the first pulp magazine (named for the cheap paper it was printed on), *Amazing Stories*. Gernsback coined the term *science fiction* (after his awkward suggestion "scientifiction") in ushering into existence a literature devoted to extolling the marvels of possible future technological development, leading inevitably to the perfection of human life, with such works often written at the expense of other literary elements like plot or character. The thrilling story of adventure, however, quickly reasserted itself as the framework for much science fiction. This formula of mixing super-science with adventure is what is generally known as *hard science fiction*, as opposed to franchises like *Star Wars*, which largely use science-fiction elements as window dressing. Although the science-fiction genre has grown far away from Gernsback's limited vision, it still bears the stamp of its origin in many respects.

Another vital element of science fiction that Gernsback fostered was an active fan community, composed almost exclusively of teenage boys and young men from poor and working-class families, who first connected with each other in the letters column of *Amazing Stories* but quickly began bringing out their own amateur publications (called *fanzines*) in imitation of it. Gernsback and later editors cultivated the most talented fans to produce new writers. In 1939, the first World Science Fiction Convention (Worldcon) was held in New York, further stimulating the growth and solidarity of the fan community. This kind of fan organization was unknown in the case of other literatures, like westerns, but was eventually to serve as the model for similar genres, like comic books. Today, numerous fandoms for a range of genres and works are active, especially on the Internet.

A new generation of science-fiction authors was nurtured by John W. Campbell, originally a writer and later editor of the pulp magazine *Astounding Science Fiction* from 1937 onward. Campbell demanded increased literary content in the stories he published, while he sustained the central focus on future technology and continued to cultivate the fan community, running a column of fan responses to each issue. "A Logic Named Joe" was voted the best story in its issue in 1946, surprising both Campbell and Leinster. Leinster was one of the few authors who began writing for Gernsback but flourished and grew in his craft under Campbell. He acted as a mentor to his younger contemporaries, including Isaac Asimov and Robert Heinlein. The isolated, fannish character of science fiction explains why works like "A Logic Named Joe" never made an impact on a wider audience (though this was to change as science fiction increasingly provided subject matter for the new medium of television), as well as why works by literary authors that develop science-fiction themes, such as George Orwell's *1984* (published in 1948), have never been considered science fiction, either by literary critics or the fan community.

Dialect

"A Logic Named Joe" is told as a first-person narrative by its central character, a logic repairman known only by a nickname, Ducky. The language is far from standard English and is filled with the sentence fragments and contractions of everyday speech. David L. Ferro and Eric G. Swedin, discussing the story in their article in the *History of Nordic Computing 2*, conclude that "the protagonist . . . is portrayed as an 'average Joe' computer technician

COMPARE
&
CONTRAST

- **1940s:** Computers are vast structures, as large as houses, owned by governments and universities but not, in 1946, even by corporations.

  Today: While supercomputers are still as large as a car, ordinary home computers fit on the desktop, and other computers are small handheld devices (i.e., smart phones and tablets). Almost all Americans own a computer of some kind.

- **1940s:** Computers are unknown in ordinary American life, and even the word *computer* is generally used to describe the human operator of a mechanical adding machine.

  Today: Computers are a central feature of American life; they have largely replaced ordinary phones and are starting to eclipse,

or rather incorporate, television, newspapers, and books, just as Leinster predicted in "A Logic Named Joe."

- **1940s:** Computers operate mechanically, using relays, circuits, and vacuum tubes; even Leinster in "A Logic Named Joe" does not imagine any new physical arrangements.

  Today: Computers use microscopic circuits printed on silicon chips, achieving a remarkable miniaturization and computing efficiency many orders of magnitude beyond the first generation of digital computers in the 1940s; the research frontier envisions computers that will operate by switching individual atoms and even using quantum effects.

---

who has a first-person style that evokes a 1940s plumber." The grammar is sketchy and the sentences are simple, but the narrator does not affect a particular accent, for example a Brooklyn accent (as Ferro and Swedin tentatively suggest). As an illustration of his mode of speech, when he describes the equivalent of a server, Ducky says: "The tank is a big buildin' full of all the facts in creation an' all the recorded telecasts that ever was made." He regularly elides the *d* of *and* and the final *g* of *-ing*, as many Americans do in normal speech. Phrases like *in creation* and *ever was made* represent Ducky's attempts to make his speech more formal (in whatever circumstance he comes to record probably the only extended narrative he would ever produce) by aping the little sophisticated literature he is familiar with, perhaps the King James Bible. It is probably the way that most science-fiction fans in the 1940s would have talked, young men with technical rather than classical educations, little different from Leinster himself, except for his vast experience as a writer. He certainly knew his

audience. The use of the word *tank*, like *logic*, is Leinster's effort to imagine the jargon of modern computing. While he uses different words than actually came into use, it is telling that the modern concepts can be so readily identified through his descriptions.

HISTORICAL CONTEXT

Computer Science

The origins of computing go back to classical antiquity. One of the earliest proto-computers was used to randomly assign jurors in the Athenian democracy. Worked by a hand crank, the machines, stationed outside every Athenian courtroom, produced a black or a white ball governing inscribed bronze cards that corresponded to the potential jurors. The so-called Antikythera mechanism, discovered in a shipwreck and dating back to the Roman period, was the most complex of the handheld devices used to accurately predict planetary motions (for purposes of astrological calculation) and was also powered by a hand crank. These devices worked on analog correspondences between the various lengths of time involved and the toothed gears in the mechanism. Similar principles were used in clocks built during the Middle Ages in Europe and China that included mechanical calendars that kept track of astrological cycles.

Modern computing dates to the late eighteenth century, when the German engineer J. H. Müller suggested that an engine could be built to automatically perform difficult calculations. At the time, such a device was called an *engine* because it did human work, while the term *computer* meant a human being employed to manually perform calculations. The Englishman Charles Babbage advanced the idea of such an engine and obtained government funding to build various prototypes, including his difference engine and his more sophisticated analytical engine, from 1817 through the 1840s. If fully realized, the analytical engine would have been a fully programmable digital computer. However, the unprecedented fineness of the tolerances for the crank-worked moving parts he designed made it too expensive to build full working copies of any of his devices. Babbage's friend and colleague Ada Lovelace, the daughter of the Romantic poet Lord Byron, wrote the first computer program for the analytical engine, to be entered by punch cards similar to those used to operate the mechanical looms of that time, though it was never implemented.

While mechanical computers were used for various jobs in the twentieth century, such as to tabulate the US census beginning in 1900, the first machines to rival Babbage's theoretical work were only developed during the 1940s. The first fully electronic computers were developed from devices used by the military in World War II, such as the Enigma machine, which broke the German military codes, and the fire-control calculators on the American *Missouri*-class battleships. Through the 1950s, computers remained enormous machines, larger than a house, containing thousands of vacuum tubes and programmed by feeding into them thousands of punch cards. The first computer to combine programmability with electronic computing was the ENIAC (Electronic Numerical Integrator and Computer), which became

Ducky tries to avoid Laurine, but the logic connects her call. (© *Paul Tarasenko / Shutterstock.com*)

operational at Harvard University in 1945. Much of the theoretical work for modern computing was accomplished by the British programmer Alan Turing, while Vannevar Bush, the director of the Office of Scientific Research and Development in the United States, oversaw the actual production of the first computers. ENIAC filled several rooms but was rather less powerful than a modern pocket calculator and was used to solve problems in weapons targeting, though it could work on any type of problem. ENIAC was the most sophisticated computer in the world in 1946 when Leinster wrote "A Logic Named Joe."

CRITICAL OVERVIEW

Science-fiction authors in general did not do a good job of prefiguring the information revolution of the second half of the twentieth century.

As computers first began to make their way into everyday life, science-fiction authors, acting as critics, pointed to Leinster's "A Logic Named Joe" as in anticipation. In his 1984 republication of the story, Isaac Asimov introduces it by noting that it had been written in 1946 and that at the time,

> the miniaturization of computers had not yet been anticipated. Computers then were huge constructs so expensive that only the government or a large corporation could afford to own one. And so no one writing science fiction about computers in the early 1940s and 1950s imagined a society where home computers might be common—except for Murray Leinster.

So Asimov realized that Leinster had predicted the home computer, but not yet that Leinster had also predicted the Internet and the World Wide Web, because Asimov himself as yet had no idea of those coming into existence. Writing more recently in his "Reflections" column in *Asimov's Science Fiction*, Robert Silverberg shows sustained interest in Leinster as offering examples of science fiction's predictive power. Updating the estimate of the range of "A Logic Named Joe" in its predictions of computers as they existed in 2008, Silverberg concludes,

> Science fiction is only occasionally a reliable vehicle for prophecy—nobody, for example, guessed that the age of manned exploration of space would begin and end in the same decade—but this is one of the prime examples of an absolute bull's-eye hit.

The computer science professors Ferro and Swedin, impressed in their own way with Leinster's story, have collaborated on a series of articles on "A Logic Named Joe." In their first article, "Computer Fiction: 'A Logic Named Joe'—towards Investigating the Importance of Science Fiction in the Historical Development of Computing" (2009), Ferro and Swedin consider the hypothesis that Leinster had read and was directly dependent on Vannevar Bush's popular articles on computer science published the year before the story. Consulting the (partial) collection of Leinster's correspondence and papers housed at Syracuse University yielded no positive evidence, but it became clear to the authors that Leinster was keenly interested in science and concerned with basing the science fiction in his stories as nearly as possible on actual science. In "Murray Leinster and 'A Logic Named Joe'" (2011), Ferro and Swedin

explore in more detail the specific elements of modern computing that have parallels in Leinster's story. And finally, in "Rebooting 'A Logic Named Joe': Exploring the Multiple Influences of a Strangely Predictive Mid-1940s Short Story" (2011), Ferro and Swedin summarize their pedagogical use of Leinster's story in relating to computer science majors the history of computing.

The life of Leinster by his daughters Billee J. Stallings and Jo-an J. Evans, *Murray Leinster: The Life and Works* (2011), is more nearly a memoir than a biography. While it attempts no new analysis of "A Logic Named Joe," the volume does reproduce two pages of the original typescript for the story featuring Leinster's hand mark-ups, as well as the entire text in an appendix, since it can now be considered Leinster's most important work.

CRITICISM

Bradley A. Skeen

Skeen is a classicist. In the following essay, he disentangles the originality of Leinster's predictions about information technology in "A Logic Named Joe" from source material produced by contemporary computer scientists.

Leinster's "A Logic Named Joe," written in 1946, is often singled out for its seemingly amazing prediction of the development of computer science over the second half of the twentieth century. The assessment of science-fiction writer Robert Silverberg in *Asimov's Science Fiction* magazine is typical of the high estimation usually given the story as prophecy:

> Roughly fifty years before the fact, we are given a clear prediction of personal computers, the Internet, Google, Craig's List, the loss of privacy in a cyberspace world, and even that bold speculative phenomenon that we call the Singularity.

It is true that Leinster's story contains these elements, but it is not so clear that they are original. Rather, he seems to have built on the work of leading computer scientists of his era, making Leinster a curiosity more for listening to the experts. Still, even granting his use of sources, Leinster transcended them in some remarkable ways.

David L. Ferro and Eric G. Swedin, in their article "Rebooting 'A Logic Named Joe,'"

WHAT DO I READ NEXT?

- William Gibson and Bruce Sterling's 1990 novel *The Difference Engine* is a seminal work of steampunk science fiction—a genre that supposes advanced technology had been developed during the nineteenth century. In the novel, Charles Babbage's analytical engine is constructed and put into general use in the early Victorian period and leads to the computer revolution coming more than a century early. The novel, then, not only explores the sociological impact of computing, Leinster's main concern in "A Logic Named Joe," but does so using an alternate historical time line, a technique indebted to Leinster's "Sidewise in Time."

- The first description of a system similar to the current World Wide Web was made by the Belgian scholar Paul Otlet in the period between the world wars. A collection of the essays in which he presented his ideas, including hypertext linking, and which was probably influential on Vannevar Bush, has been translated by W. Boyd Rayward: *International Organisation and Dissemination of Knowledge: Selected Essays of Paul Otlet* (1990). Appropriately, a copy is housed on the Internet Archive: https://archive.org/details/internationalorg00otle.

- Fredric Brown's 1954 short story "Answer," reprinted in *The Best of Fredric Brown* in 1976 (and widely available on the Internet), is a miracle of concision at less than half a printed page long (an early example of flash fiction) and is one of the few stories from the era to take up the same theme as "A Logic Named Joe," achieving considerable effect through a *reductio ad absurdum*.

- *The Atomic Weight of Secrets; or, The Arrival of the Mysterious Men in Black* (2011), by Eden Unger Bowditch, is a young-adult steampunk novel about the development of technology in an alternative early twentieth century. In 1903, a group of children from around the world, including Africa and India, who seem to show early promise of becoming important scientists are kidnapped by the American government—but to exploit them or protect them?

- Paul E. Ceruzzi's *Computing: A Concise History* (2012) provides a highly accessible history of computer technology and the Internet.

- *AfroSF: Science Fiction by African Writers*, edited by Ivor W. Hartmann in 2012, showcases the talent of several emerging science-fiction writers from the African continent with a collection of original short stories.

- *The Best of Murray Leinster*, edited by John J. Pierce in 1978, is the most comprehensive anthology of Leinster's work. Unlike the widely published work of his better-known contemporaries Heinlein and Asimov, only a small fraction of Leinster's writings are currently in print.

---

point out that many of the basic ideas about computing in the story, published in March 1946, are indebted to an article about the future of computing that was published in the July 1945 issue of the *Atlantic Monthly*, and which proved so popular that it was reprinted in the September issue (when the author was free to talk about the Manhattan Project and the nuclear bombs dropped on Japan in a new introduction) and in an illustrated version in *Life* magazine that September. It hardly seems possible that Leinster, a keen inventor and reader even of technical literature, could have missed it, and it would have been still more amazing if he had reduplicated the article's ideas on his own. The article in question is "As We May Think," by Vannevar Bush, who before World War II had helped to develop the first digital computers

---

**LEINSTER SAW THAT IF HUMAN NATURE HAD
ANYTHING TO DO WITH IT, COMPUTERS WOULD
ALSO BE USED FOR CRIME AND PORNOGRAPHY,
AND FOR REVOLUTION AND TYRANNY."**

and during the war, as director of the Office of Scientific Research and Development, had overseen both the Manhattan Project and the development of the ENIAC computer, the first fully digital multipurpose computer. Bush was in a far better position than Leinster to foresee the future of computer technology. Bush's article is generally forgotten by the general public, and seemingly has been (until quite recently) by the science-fiction community as well, but is still memorialized as an important turning point in the history of technology by professional scientists. It is often cited as a source of inspiration by computer pioneers like Douglas Engelbart (developer of the mouse and the graphical interface used on modern computers) and Ted Nelson (developer of hypertext) and was honored in a conference held at the Massachusetts Institute of Technology in 1995 to commemorate the article's fiftieth anniversary.

In "As We May Think," Bush describes a device that he thinks will soon come into existence which he calls a "memex," but which we would call a personal computer. The heart of the memex is a library of all human writings on microfilm; Bush imagined it would be about the size of a desk. This idea was not entirely unknown to science fiction. For his 1942 novel *Foundation*, Isaac Asimov imagined a handheld device containing all human knowledge in microfilm form, and further imagined that this would be the state of the art in information technology fifty thousand years in the future. More importantly, Bush sees a new way of connecting information. Using a projection screen controlled by a keyboard, the operator of the memex can access any data he wishes from the film library, and in particular can make connections between disparate parts of the library and add his own comments at the

point of connection: a hypertext link. Of course, the electronic storage of information quickly superseded any use of microfilm in this way. But Bush's ideas were the starting point for the development of hyperlinking, the system that allows one to read an article on *Slate*, for instance, and navigate immediately to related information on the Internet Movie Database or on *PLOS ONE*. So Bush established the theoretical foundation for the World Wide Web, which is a hyperlinked network of web pages, and which was created in an effort to put Bush's theory into practice. Bush is also describing websites like Google Books, Project Gutenberg, and the Internet Archive that transfer vast amounts of written information to the web. Bush's memex, then, is the point of departure for the information technology in "A Logic Named Joe"; but the real interest in the story is that Leinster goes quite a bit further than Bush, and his original ideas about the future of computing proved to be no less accurate.

Leinster's logics clearly store their data electronically, not on microfilm. They are accessed by video screens, just like real PCs, and have eclipsed the television as a dedicated device that delivers only video on a small number of channels. (This scenario is likely to come to pass also in the near future, since video entertainment is increasingly streamed from the web and household devices are becoming linked; if not for business rather than technical issues, this would probably already be the case.) Rather than each logic containing its own copy of the entire web, they are linked to servers ("tanks" as Leinster calls them) that make the whole network available to each logic workstation. This is a prediction of the Internet, the physical infrastructure that hosts the World Wide Web, and is something that Bush did not think of. Since the whole world is connected via the logics and the tanks, their network also becomes the basis of telecommunication, in other words allowing one to make phone calls and even video calls (such as via Skype). It is clear that Leinster is seeing the practical implications of interconnectivity even more clearly than Bush did. This in itself is no small achievement for the technically oriented science fiction of the 1940s.

Leinster again takes his inspiration from Bush in calling his computers "logics." In 1945, it was by no means clear that computers would be called by that name, and Leinster drew the term from Bush's central idea of hyperlinking. Bush thought that hyperlinks would allow users to combine two existing pieces of information in the database of accumulated knowledge to produce a piece of new knowledge. For Bush, the purpose of the hyperlink was to create an Aristotelian syllogism, to take the modification of one known premise by another to produce a new and unforeseen bit of knowledge. Thus, the primary purpose of the memex was to carry out the fundamental operation of logic. In Leinster's story, the one thing that seems to separate Joe from other logics is his ability to complete the syllogism and reach the synthesis or conclusion on his own, not merely making the thesis and antithesis available to human users. And indeed this kind of artificial intelligence is still far beyond the capacity of any computer.

But the real value of "A Logic Named Joe" lies in the ways that Leinster envisions the interaction of the World Wide Web with human culture. Bush had made a rather utopian assumption that the products of the memex would be wholly good and would advance human knowledge and work as a force for improving civilization, turning technology away from the destructive ends it had recently been made to serve during the war, in the development of the atomic bomb, for example. But Leinster the storyteller knew that nothing produced or guided by human nature would only be used for the good.

Leinster's version of the web is tightly censored. And indeed the censorship of the web is a major issue today, as politically oppressive regimes censor certain materials to stifle dissent and exert social control. In Leinster's version, however, censorship is mostly used to prevent minors from accessing sexually explicit material, in line with the censorship imposed on American print media and in the film industry of the 1940s. The lack of such censorship, especially in the United States, is often a point of criticism of the web as it exists. But another and more important form of censorship does exist, one that would have surprised both Bush and Leinster. Most of the very information that could be used most productively to advance knowledge, namely, the articles in scientific and scholarly journals, is locked behind paywalls that effectively exclude everyone who does not have access to a university library from reading it, even when the research reported was publicly funded.

But Leinster's most profound insight in "A Logic Named Joe" is what he terms a threat to civilization itself. Once Joe sets himself to providing technical solutions to anyone at all on demand, political extremists start to make use of it. Groups on both the left and right start to ask Joe how they can implement their political programs:

> A social-conscious guy asks how to bring about his own particular system of social organization at once. He don't ask if it's best or if it'll work. He just wants to get it started. And the logic—or Joe—tells him! Simultaneous, there's a retired preacher asks how can the human race be cured of concupiscence.... And there's another group of serious thinkers who are sure the human race would be a lot better off if everybody went back to nature an' lived in the woods with the ants an' poison ivy. They start askin' questions about how to cause humanity to abandon cities and artificial conditions of living.... The Superior Man gang that sneers at the rest of us was quietly asking questions on what kinda weapons could be made by which Superior Men could take over and run things....

All this can be related to the way the web has become a home for every kind of extremist group, allowing them to disseminate their ideologies to new audiences as well as become systems of recruitment, support, and communication. In particular, animal rights terrorist groups and neo-Nazis are now largely organized on the web. Indeed, one of Leinster's most stunning prophecies was to realize, so soon after the Allied victory in World War II, that neo-Nazis would continue to be a problem in the future, and of all places in the United States. Similarly, while the web can scarcely generate designs for new weapons, it is commonly used to spread designs for quite ordinary weapons to terrorists of all kinds, from the Oklahoma City bombers to the Boston Marathon bombers.

While Leinster's central idea of the World Wide Web is undoubtedly indebted to Bush's work—just as Bush was probably indebted to the work of Belgian computer scientist Paul Otlet in the 1930s—he amazingly gives a more accurate depiction of the modern Internet than Bush was capable of and can be credited with the first recognizable description of the Internet as the physical system hosting the web. More importantly, Leinster dealt more realistically with the social implications of modern computing. Bush had promised that computers would transform human life for the better. Leinster saw that if

Ducky says he "saved civilization" because he disconnected Joe. *(© Matej Kastelic | Shutterstock.com)*

human nature had anything to do with it, computers would also be used for crime and pornography, and for revolution and tyranny.

Source: Bradley A. Skeen, Critical Essay on "A Logic Named Joe," in *Short Stories for Students*, Gale, Cengage Learning, 2015.

SOURCES

Aldiss, Brian W., *Trillion Year Spree: The History of Science Fiction*, Atheneum, 1986, pp. 224–25.

Asimov, Isaac, *Foundation*, Bantam, 1991, p. 45.

Bush, Vannevar, "As We May Think," in *Atlantic Monthly*, No. 176, July 1945, http://www.theatlantic.com/magazine/archive/1945/07/as-we-may-think/303881/ (accessed January 15, 2014).

Ferro, David L., and Eric G. Swedin, "Computer Fiction: 'A Logic Named Joe'—towards Investigating the Importance of Science Fiction in the Historical Development of Computing," in *History of Nordic Computing 2*, edited by John Impagliazzo, Timo Järvi, and Petri Paju, Springer, 2009, pp. 84–94.

———, eds., "Murray Leinster and 'A Logic Named Joe,'" in *Science Fiction and Computing: Essays on Interlinked Domains*, McFarland, 2011, pp. 54–67.

———, "Rebooting 'A Logic Named Joe': Exploring the Multiple Influences of a Strangely Predictive

Mid-1940s Short Story," in *Science Fiction and the Prediction of the Future: Essays on Foresight and Fallacy*, edited by Gary Westfahl, Wong Kin Yuen, and Amy Kit-sze Chan, McFarland, 2011, pp. 104–19.

Leinster, Murray, "A Logic Named Joe," in *Machines That Think: The Best Science Fiction Stories about Robots and Computers*, edited by Isaac Asimov, Patricia S. Warrick, and Martin H. Greenberg, Holt, Rinehart and Winston, 1983, pp. 279–96.

Silverberg, Robert, "Reflections: A Logic Named Will," in *Asimov's Science Fiction*, December 2008, http://www.asimovs.com/_issue_0812/ref.shtml (accessed January 28, 2014).

Stallings, Billee J., and Jo-an J. Evans, *Murray Leinster: The Life and Works*, McFarland, 2011, pp. 96–101.

Turing, Alan, "Computing Machinery and Intelligence," in *Mind*, Vol. 49, 1950, pp. 433–60.

———, "Intelligent Machinery, a Heretical Theory," Turing Digital Archive, 1951, http://www.turingarchive.org/browse.php/B/4 (accessed January 27, 2014).

Wright, Alex, "The Web Time Forgot," in *New York Times*, June 17, 2008, http://www.nytimes.com/2008/06/17/science/17mund.html?pagewanted=all&_r=0 (accessed January 18, 2014).

FURTHER READING

Ceruzzi, Paul E., *A History of Modern Computing*, MIT Press, 2003.

Ceruzzi offers a standard history of computer technology up to the eve of the explosion in handheld devices (phones and tablets), approximately congruent with the level of computer technology envisioned in "A Logic Named Joe."

del Rey, Lester, *The World of Science Fiction, 1926–1976: The History of a Subculture*, Ballantine Books, 1979.

Del Rey, himself a prominent science-fiction author, presents the history of science fiction as an integrated community of fans and writers. Leinster receives a prominent place in the book, but, writing even before the personal computer revolution, del Rey failed to see the importance of "A Logic Named Joe."

Stross, Charles, *The Atrocity Archives*, Golden Gryphon Press, 2004.

The two novellas in this volume, *The Atrocity Archive* and *The Concrete Jungle*, are the first of a series of science-fiction works by Stross in which he constructs a secret history of the twentieth century, joining together sophisticated mathematics and technology with magic in a background drawn from genre spy thrillers. One premise of the series is that a number of Vannevar Bush's memex machines were actually built during World War II.

Verne, Jules, *Paris in the Twentieth Century*, translated by Richard Howard, Random House, 1996.

This was Verne's second novel. Rejected by his publisher Herzel as too depressing, it was not published until 1994, in 1996 in English translation. The main character is a young man who takes the last degree in classics awarded by the University of Paris and becomes alienated from a world dominated by greed and technology and cut off from tradition, to the point that he inclines toward suicide. His job consists of keeping records at a bank on a computer-like device not very dissimilar in size and complexity from the computers that actually existed in 1960, the year in which the novel is set.

SUGGESTED SEARCH TERMS

Murray Leinster

A Logic Named Joe

science fiction

Vannevar Bush

memex

Paul Otlet

cyberpunk

World Wide Web AND history

Internet AND history

Mrs. Turner Cutting the Grass

CAROL SHIELDS

1985

Published originally in the collection *Various Miracles* (1985)—and winning a Canadian National Magazine Award that year—and reprinted as part of *The Collected Stories* (2004), Carol Shields's "Mrs. Turner Cutting the Grass" is a subtly crafted but pointedly ironic story of one woman's approach to living her life openly, authentically, and with resiliency. With a style that captures the textures of a painting, Shields recounts the adventures, tragedies, and travels of a woman who can, and does, turn the ordinary act of cutting the lawn into a bold statement about the shallowness of contemporary culture and the stagnation of art and humanity within the rising middle class.

AUTHOR BIOGRAPHY

Carol Shields (née Warner) was born on June 2, 1935, in Oak Park, Illinois, the third of three children to Robert and Inez Warner, who already had twins named Barbara and Robert. Her mother was a schoolteacher, and her father, whom she described as a remote and quiet man, worked in an office. Following graduation from Oak Park High School, Shields set off for Hanover College, in Indiana, where she studied for two years. Receiving a United Nations Scholarship in 1955, she crossed the Atlantic to study English literature at Exeter

Shields won the 1998 Orange Prize for Fiction.
(© *AP Images / Adrian Dennis*)

The Shields family had five children: John Douglas was born in Toronto in 1958, Anne Elizabeth in Toronto in 1959, Catherine Mary in Manchester in 1962, Margaret Lorin in Toronto in 1964, and Sara Ellisyn in Ottawa in 1968. Shields was both an involved mother and active academic, teaching English at the University of Manitoba (1982–2000), as well as serving as chancellor of the University of Winnipeg (1996–1999).

To call Shields a prolific writer would be an understatement. Working throughout her writing life as a novelist, poet, and playwright, she produced a list of titles that spans over several literary forms and cultural decades. A list of her best-known titles includes *Small Ceremonies* (1976), *The Box Garden* (1977), *Happenstance* (1980), *A Fairly Conventional Woman* (1982), *Various Miracles* (1985)—containing "Mrs. Turner Cutting the Grass"—*Swann: A Mystery* (1987), *The Orange Fish* (1989), *The Republic of Love* (1992), *Coming to Canada* (1992), and *Thirteen Hands* (1993). What are arguably her two most acclaimed books were published within five years of each other: *The Stone Diaries* (1993) and *Larry's Party* (1997).

Throughout her career Shields won an impressive and eclectic catalogue of awards for her poetry, stories, and plays, including the Arthur Ellis Award for the Best Canadian Mystery of the Year for *Swann: A Mystery* (1988), France's Prix de Lire for *Larry's Party* (1998), and the Charles Taylor Prize for Literary Nonfiction for *Jane Austen* (2002).

Much loved and appreciated in her adopted country, Shields was named an Officer of the Order of Canada (1998) before being promoted to Companion of the Order of Canada in 2002. Carol Shields passed away on July 16, 2003, at the age of sixty-eight after an extended battle with breast cancer.

PLOT SUMMARY

"Mrs. Turner Cutting the Grass" opens dramatically, with an exclamatory "Oh" as the narrator reacts to the "sight" of Mrs. Turner cutting her grass on a June afternoon. It is a scene that obviously causes some consternation amongst her neighbors, the Saschers, as they pass judgment on almost everything about Mrs. Turner, from her choice of clothing to

University, in England. She returned to Hanover in 1956 to complete her degree in history and education, graduating magna cum laude in 1957. She would add a master's degree in English from the University of Ottawa in 1975.

Upon graduation, she married Don Shields, a Canadian engineer she had met during her stay in Exeter. The couple immediately relocated to Vancouver, British Columbia, where her new husband worked. Although Carol would not take full Canadian citizenship until 1971, the couple moved throughout the country often, relocating variously to Toronto and Ottawa (both in Ontario) and back to Vancouver before settling in Winnipeg, Manitoba, in 1980. (Their Canadian travels were interrupted by a three-year stay in Manchester, England, in the early 1960s). The couple lived in Winnipeg for twenty years, before relocating to Victoria, British Columbia, in 2000. (Winnipeg would appear frequently as a primary setting in much of Shields's writing, as it does in "Mrs. Turner Cutting the Grass," which is set in the River Heights neighborhood of the city.)

the fact that she does not use a catcher to collect the lawn clippings; she also deploys apparently vast amounts of the herbicide Killex on her dandelions. The narrator recounts the similar reactions of the unnamed high-school girls passing judgment on Mrs. Turner's cellulite as they walk past her house as part of their own daily routine.

Having focused on the physical appearance of Mrs. Turner, the story shifts next to an emphasis, marked obviously by the exclamatory narrator, on Mrs. Turner's intellectual state. The reader is informed that she knows nothing of popular music, despite the fact that "the folk-rock recording star Neil Young" attended the high school just around the corner from her house. While the girls are "shuddering over her display of cellulite" they are unaware that Mrs. Turner "possesses a first name," Geraldine, and a rich, colorful history of her own.

The story turns back in time to recount Geraldine's history in Boissevain, Manitoba, where she was known as "Girlie Fergus, the youngest of the three Fergus girls and the one who got herself in hot water." The reader learns that while her sisters, Em and Muriel, led relatively quiet lives, the nineteen-year-old Geraldine was caught in a hotel room with a local, married farmer. Unwilling to endure the small-town humiliation that came with such an indiscretion, she left the farm in the summer of 1930, heading initially for Winnipeg but ultimately for New York City. What she recognizes on the long bus trip eastward becomes crucial to her maturation and evolving understanding of the world: that there are "hundreds and hundreds of towns" scattered across the landscape, all of which could be defined by the same oppressiveness as the one she left behind.

In New York, Geraldine is wholly immersed in the "immense and wonderful, dirty, perilous and puzzling" world of the city. Despite her occasional longing for "a sight of real earth," she is enthralled by the bustle of humanity that surrounds her and, implicitly, by the freedom that comes with the anonymity associated with it. Taking a job "as an usherette in the Lamar Movie Palace in Brooklyn," she finds a place in which she feels very much at home.

It is at the Palace that she meets Kiki, a man whose skin is "black as ebony" and whose good-heartedness is of little support when the

unmarried couple has a baby son. He leaves Geraldine fifty dollars and flees from the city. Unable to care for the child on her own, Geraldine contemplates following Kiki but soon realizes the futility of that path. With few options available to her, she decides on "a murderously hot night…when the humidity was especially bad" to wrap "him in a clean piece of sheeting" and leave him in "a beautiful wicker baby carriage" that she finds parked on the porch of a house in Brooklyn Heights. Unaware of what happened to either her son or the man who fathered him, Geraldine moves forward with her life believing that "she did the best she could under the circumstances."

A year later, Geraldine returns to Boissevain by train, bringing "with her all her belongings, and also gifts" for her sisters, including "boxes of hose, bottles of apple-blossom cologne, phonograph records." Her second departure is less dramatic. Newly wed to Gordon Turner, she moves to Winnipeg, finally settling in a "little house in River Heights just around the corner from the high school" that Neil Young attended. Her husband is loving, attentive, and caring, their life together apparently quiet and peaceful.

Following Gordon's death, Geraldine begins to travel with her sisters. They visit Disneyland and Disney World, take "a sixteen-day trip through seven countries" of Europe, and journey south to see "the famous antebellum houses of Georgia, Alabama, and Mississippi." Following a trip to Mexico, where they "took pictures of Mayan ruins and queer shadowy gods cut squarely from stone," the sisters do what "they swore they'd never have the nerve to do": take a trip to Japan.

The story shifts at this point to focus on this particular trip, which starts in Tokyo, commencing by bus to Osaka and then venturing to Kyoto, where the focus narrows even more to a day spent visiting the Golden Pavilion. It is here, amidst the photo taking and general excitement, that readers are introduced to one particular tour member, "the one they all referred to as the Professor." A balding man with a trim body and penchant for "Bermuda shorts, sandals and black nylon socks," he is indeed a small-town academic and also a frustrated (and one might assume only mildly talented) poet.

Replete with reasons for his failure as a poet, the Professor believes that in the "crowded, confused country" of Japan, he experiences a creative "catharsis" that allows him to connect with a sense of "simplicity and order and something spiritual, too, which he recognized as being authentic." The trip to Japan does wonders for the Professor, and the "solid little book of poems" that comes out of the experience is received well enough for the Boston publisher to send him on a university and college reading tour. The most frequently requested poem on this tour is "A Day at the Golden Pavilion," a poem that becomes his "crowd pleaser." The Professor plays a role whenever he reads this poem, making sure to speak "in a moist, avuncular amateur actor's voice, reminding himself to pause frequently, to look upward and raise an ironic eyebrow."

The topic of this particularly popular poem is not the day at the temple itself, but the Professor's scathing representation of Geraldine and her sisters, whom he obviously spent much time observing during the tour. The poem casts the sisters in the role of the "three furies" or "three witches" whose "vulgarity and tastelessness formed a shattering counterpoint" to the Professor's self-declared (and poetically appropriate) "state of transcendence" during the trip. His most acerbic words are reserved for Geraldine. The audience inevitably applauds loudly, its members turning to each other in a kind of conspiratorial judgment of "such unspeakable tourists."

The story shifts smoothly in its final section to juxtapose Geraldine's reflections on her travels and the current state of the sisters' lives with the much-sought-after success that has come to the Professor for his book of poems about the Japanese tour. The story ends somewhat quietly, focused back on Mrs. Turner cutting her grass, greeting her neighbors, living her life fully and oblivious to the judgment around her.

CHARACTERS

Em Fergus

Em Fergus is Mrs. Geraldine Turner's sister and one of the Professor's "three furies" of "vulgarity and tastelessness." Growing up in the small town of Boissevain, Manitoba, she trains as a teacher early in life. Em joins Geraldine on her travels following the death of Gordon Turner, Geraldine's husband. By the story's end, Em has "retired from school teaching and is a volunteer in the Boissevain Local History Museum," to which she has donated a number of items, including a pair of Geraldine's underwear from circa 1918.

Geraldine Fergus

See Mrs. Geraldine Turner

Muriel Fergus

Muriel Fergus is Mrs. Geraldine Turner's sister and one of the Professor's "three furies" of "vulgarity and tastelessness." Following high school, she goes "to Brandon to work at Eaton's" and eventually joins Geraldine on her travels following the death of Gordon Turner. By the end of the story, Muriel is celebrating the successes of her children, "a son in California and a daughter in Toronto," and sharing photos of her grandchildren with anyone who will take the time to listen.

High-School Girls

An unnamed cluster of teenage girls who pass Mrs. Turner's house as part of their daily routine, the high-school girls represent the next generation of townspeople who will ridicule the Mrs. Turners of the world without ever pausing to reflect on the possibility that there might be an interesting history behind the gaudy clothes and aging body. Though relatively minor in terms of the space awarded them in the story, the girls do serve an important role as a reminder of the inevitability of aging.

Kiki

With skin as "black as ebony," Kiki is a man whom Geraldine meets while working at the Lamar Movie Palace in Brooklyn. Goodhearted and generally kind, he provides no real support for Geraldine when she gives birth to their child, a baby boy. Instead, he leaves her fifty dollars and returns "to Troy, New York, where he'd been raised." His presence in the story is underplayed as a means of emphasizing Mrs. Turner's ability to move through the challenges in her life with an ease that is, at times, unsettling.

The Professor

Introduced during the section of the story dedicated to the adventures at Kyoto's Golden

Pavilion, the Professor is a bald man with a trim body and penchant for "Bermuda shorts, sandals and black nylon socks." The professor may come across as a petty, dissatisfied, self-important man. He provides a powerful foil to Geraldine, whose obliviousness to external judgment run counter to the Professor's annoyance with the sisters' casual tourism. When the Professor does find success as a poet it is due largely to "A Day at the Golden Pavilion," a poem that takes Mrs. Turner as its subject. The success of his poem highlights the shallowness of contemporary audiences, who seem to find great pleasure in character attacks disguised as poetry.

Roy Sascher

Roy Sascher is the husband and father of the family that lives next door to Mrs. Turner. Whereas his wife, Sally, is irritated by their neighbor's carelessness with lawn clippings, he is "far more concerned about the Killex that Mrs. Turner dumps on her dandelions." Not one inclined to such an easy chemical fix, Roy is "patient and persistent," a man obviously keen on acquiring knowledge, whether pertaining to "knowing exactly how to grasp the coarse leaves in his hand" when weeding dandelions or to his experiments in domestic use of dandelion greens. With his wife, he stands as a symbol of middle-class attitudes and values.

Sally Sascher

Sally Sascher is the wife and mother of the family that lives next door to Mrs. Turner. Like many other members of the community, she seems to feel morally and aesthetically superior to her neighbor, as "Mrs. Turner's carelessness over the clippings plucks away" at her middle-class sensibilities. Rather than leaving her clippings to deteriorate naturally in the lawn, Sally leads her family in a campaign to "make compost, which they hope one day will be as ripe as the good manure that [her] father used to spread on his fields down near Emerson Township." The emphasis in this sentence is important, marking Sally as a woman whose relationship with the land (her lawn) has been dislocated from her family's farming roots despite the fact that the farming life lingers in her memories. Collectively, the Saschers represent a middle-class view of the world that celebrates order, planning, and a reassuring sense of routine.

Mrs. Geraldine Turner

The protagonist of the story, Mrs. Geraldine Turner is a colorful presence in a community that judges her wholly by her garish clothes, seemingly limited intellect, and propensity for public display. What the people of the town never recognize, or take the time to learn, is that Mrs. Turner's life has been one filled with indiscretions, travel, adventure, and difficult decisions. She has been publicly humiliated for an affair with a married man, elected to abandon a child born out of wedlock, and has inspired poetry. She has traveled extensively, been loved deeply by her husband, and mastered the art of moving through life with an openness that is unthinkable to the middle-class world around her. In the context of the story, Mrs. Turner pushes readers to think about such perpetually troublesome issues as guilt, authenticity, identity, self-awareness, and creativity, to name but a few.

Gordon Turner

Geraldine's husband from Boissevain, Manitoba, Gordon Turner is a gentle but perpetually "tongue-tied man" whose love for his wife is matched only by his love for the house they buy in the River Heights neighborhood of Winnipeg. His presence in the story is very much in the background, although his influence on the story is significant, given that Mrs. Turner is free to travel because of the financial security he brought to her life. He is also an important counterpoint to Kiki, whose relationship with Geraldine left her vulnerable and instigated a series of troubling decisions.

THEMES

Epiphanies

Shields's stories are often defined by epiphanies (powerful moments of insight or transcendence) that not only punctuate the lives of her characters but speak more broadly to a worldview that Shields is determined to explore throughout her work. Like James Joyce before her, Shields uses the epiphany in two ways: as a moment of personal revelation and a literary technique that reinforces her creative mandate to give seemingly ordinary events or things deeper meaning.

Thought of another way, Shields's use of epiphany in "Mrs. Turner Cutting the Grass" is

TOPICS FOR FURTHER STUDY

- A number of critics have compared Shields's representation of everyday events and items to the work of such visual artists as American Andy Warhol or fellow Canadian Mary Pratt, both of whom "also blurred the distinctions between the kitchen and the art gallery," as Marta Dvorak notes in her essay "Carol Shields and the Poetics of the Quotidian." Not surprisingly, "Mrs. Turner Cutting the Grass," like so many of Shields's best stories, focuses on capturing the elusive patterns of life that are, as Jenny Uglow puts it in her review in the *Independent*, "grasped in flickering glimpses beyond words, like patterns on the inner eye-lid before sleep." Imagine that you have been asked to select a piece of art for the cover of a new edition of stories that is designed to highlight this particular aspect of Shields's fiction. Using the Internet, find an image that you feel captures the major themes or ideas of the stories. Present this image along with a well-written justification for your selection that draws on the stories for evidence in support of your case.

- Mrs. Turner is positioned as an outsider in her neighborhood, despite the fact that her life is rich with color and stories. Read Jerry Spinelli's *Stargirl* (2000), which recounts the story of another unconventional young woman, Susan "Stargirl" Caraway, as she transitions from outsider to role model without ever losing her senses of creativity, individualism, and eccentricity. Create a poster or multimedia presentation that represents the central message of *Stargirl*: that people are different, and difference should be accepted and celebrated within any community. Be prepared to share this presentation with your class.

- In a 2002 interview, Shields shared a secret affinity for adverbs, those *-ly* ending words that tend to modify verbs: adverbs "situate us in space," she explains; "they situate us in a narrative, they call upon other parts of the language. I think they should be kept in a little box all by themselves over in a corner of the tool box, and when you need one of them, you just reach for it." Select a major word group—noun, verb, adjective, or adverb—and create a multimedia presentation in which you explore the power of that particular part of speech in "Mrs. Turner Cutting the Grass." You can make a traditional, paper-based collage, for instance, or choose to explore the language of Shields's story through a program like Wordle, Prezi, or even Instagram. Be prepared to share your creation with your class and explain what you discovered during the building of this project.

- As "Mrs. Turner Cutting the Grass" comes to a close, the reader finds out that Em Fergus, Mrs. Turner's sister, has "retired from school teaching and is a volunteer in the Boissevain Local History Museum," to which she has donated a number of items, including "a white cotton garment labeled 'Girlie Fergus's Underdrawers, handmade, trimmed with lace, circa 1918.'" In the next sentence, Shields's narrator notes that "if Mrs. Turner knew the word *irony* she would relish this." In a well-structured and well-considered essay, discuss how the presentation of Mrs. Turner's underwear in a glass case at the Boissevain Museum can be considered an ironic artifact. What are the implications of this irony in the broader context of the story? How might it relate to such other artifacts in the story as the Professor's book of poems or suburban lawns, for instance?

both psychological and artistic, and both forms are embedded deeply in the domestic routines that define the story. When a young Geraldine looks out the bus window on her journey to New York City, for instance, she sees "hundreds and hundreds of towns whose unpaved

As a young woman, Mrs. Turner abandoned her baby in a carriage on the porch of a nice house.
(© *Elzbieta Sekowska | Shutterstock.com*)

streets and narrow blinded houses made her fear some conspiratorial, punishing power" that could take control of her future unless she herself took control. The result: she embraces the immensity and wonder of the city with such a depth of feeling that she is changed forever. Her sudden understanding is not a lightning flash but a quiet realization deep in her soul that her life and her future are far away from the narrow-mindedness and parochialism of a small town. Wherever she lives, Geraldine is determined to make the place her own and to live openly and without fear "that anyone would wish her harm."

In contrast to Joyce's use of the epiphany as an organic and wholly individualized experience, Shields shows how the concept of the epiphany has been reconfigured within middle-class culture into a commercialized experience. When the Professor embarks with the tour group in Japan, he brings with him a desire for an experience that will lift his creative spirit (and his poetry) out of the ordinariness in which it has settled. His tour of Japan is used

to generate a spontaneous discovery of something spiritual, creative, and emotional. The result is not entirely art, one might argue, but includes a moral kind of anger that sells well to undergraduate audiences largely because of the attacks on other members of the middle class (in this case, Geraldine and her sisters).

Rather than appearing at the end of the story, as is often the case with traditional epiphanies, Shields's moments of revelation are more often embedded in the body of the story. This positioning is a challenge to the traditional story structure, which emphasizes a recognizable closure in the final paragraph, sentence, or even word, repositioning the revelation so that it is forced to brush up against the realities that build on both sides of its moment.

Shields's epiphanies, then, are illuminations that burst forth as part of the usual routine of life, not as sudden and dramatically transformative moments that linger unchallenged at the end of the story. Her epiphanies not only find their source in everyday moments and experiences but remain firmly embedded in those experiences. Transcendent moments rub up against everyday ones, allowing for a kind of creative and spiritual cross-pollination to occur. In her interview "Art Is Making," Shields explains that she has "always believed . . . that each of us is given a number of these moments of transcendence" in our lives. The problem, she continues, is that

> they're very difficult to shape into language that doesn't sound utterly insane. I think this is why we don't always recognize them, let alone share them. We don't know what brings them about; usually it's a strange combination of things that come together, but I think they should be savoured so that we can call on them in moments that are less than transcendent.

Middle-Class Values

"Mrs. Turner Cutting the Grass" is at many levels a satiric probe of middle-class values, especially of those values that allow middle-class people to shape their lives through a sense of moral and intellectual superiority that is linked more to their powers as consumers than their qualities as human beings. The neighboring Saschers' obsession with lawn clippings (and by extension, with the aesthetics of lawn care), for instance, speaks to a profound dislocation from the community's agricultural past, while the reactions of the high-school girls who find Mrs. Turner's aging body repugnant mark a disturbing devaluation of the elderly within predominantly middle-class generations. The Professor, determined to create art, seems to try to buy his way to insight and inspiration during a guided tour of Japan.

Shields is quick, too, to underscore the passivity that informs her imagining of middle-class values. Rather than confronting Mrs. Turner over what they decry as her "abuse of the planet," despite the fact it makes them "morose and angry," the Saschers choose instead to say nothing. Opting for silence and stagnation over engagement and activity, they wait, "hoping she'll go into an old-folks home soon or maybe die," at which time "all will proceed as it should."

STYLE

Foil

Geraldine is, in many ways, a foil to the entire world of the story, but she contrasts most sharply with the Professor, the frustrated poet whom she

encounters during a tour of Kyoto's Golden Pavilion. Perhaps guided by an unquestioned sense of superiority, the Professor finds Geraldine's loud behavior (with camera in hand) as a personal affront to his poetic sensibility and to his own self-proclaimed "state of transcendence."

The starkest point of contrast between the two is in their approach to the challenges that life presents. Whereas Geraldine has shown resiliency, the Professor is a man with ready excuses to explain away his lack of production and limited success as a poet. Geraldine lives her life unencumbered, despite having suffered various humiliations, abandoning a child, and losing a husband, but the Professor is quick to lay blame externally for the "paltry, guarded, nut-like thing that was his artistic reputation." "His domestic life had been too cluttered," he laments, and "there had been too many professional demands" to allow him the time and space he needed to capture his brilliance in verse. And, of course, there was always "the political situation in America," which "had drained him of energy." In the end, the Professor is rewarded with some international praise for a poem he wrote, ironically, about Geraldine, a woman who is wholly satisfied that "all she's done is live her life."

Irony

"Mrs. Turner Cutting the Grass" is rich with both obvious and subtle ironies that underscore the hypocrisy and shallowness of a middle-class world that defines itself, in part, on its determined attempts to purchase (and consume) knowledge, experience, and happiness. Shields points, for instance, to the Saschers' loathing of grass cuttings left to rot organically on a lawn and to their determination to create a rich compost out of the same rotten cuttings. She recounts, too, the long tradition within the town of touching "the incised letters" on Neil Young's old desk in order to bring luck on an exam, "despite the fact that the renowned singer wasn't a great scholar." Shields engages the character of the Professor to illuminate perhaps the greatest irony of all: that the most popular art of his career is generated through his experiences with what he sees only as symbols of the "vulgarity and tastelessness" energizing the world of the banal and trivial. In a description that delivers its satiric punch with both grace and velocity, Shields allows the Professor to expose his own limitations as a creative and constructive presence in the story: "He felt as though a flower, something like a lily, only smaller and tougher, had unfurled in his hand and was nudging along his fountain pen."

The ironies exposed in the story underscore a deep sense of dislocation and disconnectedness that permeates so much of "Mrs. Turner Cutting the Grass." There is a sadness to the realization that the Saschers are hoping for the death of their neighbor in order to rid themselves of the irritants of grass clippings and herbicide. There is a sense of cultural loss in the fact that the high-school girls put such value in "the spiritual scent, the essence, the fragrance, the aura of Neil Young" but remain ignorant of the fact that Mrs. Turner "possesses a first name" and a deep, often pitiful history that reaches far beyond the River Heights neighborhood in which they all live.

Omniscient Narrator

When asked by Eleanor Wachtel about the seemingly experimental turn that distinguished the stories collected in *Various Miracles* (1985), Shields answered with direct attention to a new commitment to explore the contours and possibilities of narrative voice: "I discovered the old storyteller's voice, the omniscient narrator," she explained:

> I'd never tried it before and I wanted to. I thought I would write a book of short stories, because you're not bound to one particular voice. I could tell stories from close up or from far back.

Told from the point of view of an omniscient (all-knowing) narrator, who can move freely across time and space as well as into the minds of characters to capture their thoughts and feelings, "Mrs. Turner Cutting the Grass" is a master class in point of view. Allowing Shields to move her plot effortlessly across decades and continents, the point of view allows her the creative freedom to build textures across the emotional geographies of the story. Although certain elements remain under-narrated (Geraldine's relationship with Kiki, for instance), others are raised to detailed positions of prominence (the Professor's reflections on the day at the Golden Pavilion).

Despite the effective omniscience of the narrator, readers are never allowed a true sense of the depth of Geraldine's grief upon abandoning her infant son following Kiki's disappearance. The reader never truly understands whether she actually feels any grief, which might shift one's understanding of her dramatically. Shields's subtle manipulation of point of view effectively invites readers to answer these questions for themselves, filling in blanks and expanding upon moments left undescribed. Shields positions readers as cocreators of the story of Mrs. Turner, making every reading of the story an act of creation in itself.

HISTORICAL CONTEXT

Canada in the Trudeau Era

With the exception of a very brief period (June 1979 to March 1980), the decades in which "Mrs. Turner Cutting the Grass" primarily takes place saw Canada under the leadership of Prime Minister Pierre Elliott Trudeau, a vibrant and colorful politician whose outspokenness and liberal views set the tone for the entire country. In contrast to the United States, where the president is limited to being elected to a maximum of two four-year terms, the Canadian political system stipulates no fixed term of office. Once appointed and sworn in by the governor-general, a prime minister remains in office until he or she is defeated in a federal election, resigns, is dismissed from office, or dies.

Catapulted into the Canadian consciousness by an unprecedented level of personal popularity among voters, which came to be known as Trudeaumania, Trudeau was arguably responsible for negotiating some of the most influential cultural shifts in Canadian history. With an emphasis on participatory democracy (by which all members of a population participate in meaningful decision making), Trudeau was a very vocal and active supporter of making Canada a more "Just Society." What this meant in practical terms was that he defended universal health care and expanded programs that would support regional development, especially in such areas as Winnipeg (where Mrs. Turner lives) and similar midsized cities across the country. He was also a political force in ensuring that Canada would remain a bilingual country (Quebec has a large French-speaking population), would embrace multiculturalism, and would continue to expand its role in global affairs.

At times perceived as arrogant, overly intellectual, and out of touch with the growing middle

COMPARE
&
CONTRAST

- **1980s:** Technology is obviously absent from "Mrs. Turner Cutting the Grass," especially in the section of the story involving the high-school girls, none of whom seem to be carrying the hottest new piece of technology of the day: the portable Walkman, which plays audiocassettes.

  Today: The same group of girls today would likely be carrying an assortment of technologies that could capture Mrs. Turner's image digitally and share it immediately through a variety of social media and digital video outlets.

- **1980s:** Designated as a National Special Historic Site and a National Special Landscape, Kyoto's Temple of the Golden Pavilion is already one of Japan's most visited monuments. A reconstruction of the original temple, which was lost to arson in 1950, the historic site that Mrs. Turner and her sisters visit is a remarkable copy that includes some of the gold-leaf coating salvaged from the original. Even in the mid-1980s, as Mrs. Turner notes, the temple is in some need of further restoration, especially when it comes to the "soft old flaky gold" adorning the wooden structures.

  Today: The Temple of the Golden Pavilion looks very different, having undergone an extensive treatment of re-lacquering and re-gilding using a much thicker gold leaf than visitors in the mid-1980s would have seen. Additionally, the interior of the building has been totally restored, as has the dramatic roof design.

- **1980s:** Mrs. Turner's neighbors, the Saschers, represent a new wave of middle-class suburban homeowners whose environmental concerns would likely have been fueled by Rachel Carson's 1962 classic *Silent Spring*, which explores the impact of DDT and related pesticides on the environment. By the late 1970s, more engaged readers are devouring James Lovelock's *Gaia Hypothesis*, which argues for a reimagining of the Earth as a single, fragile organism. The environmental activism of Greenpeace has expanded from its inception as a small, west-coast operation to become a global presence.

  Today: Environmentalism is still a topical issue, having become gradually more segmented into groups focusing specifically on such areas of concern as water usage, wetland degradation, local food security, sustainable land management, and global ice conservation, to name but a few. Perhaps ironically, the turf-grass and lawn-care industry has grown exponentially since the 1980s, with annual economic impact figures running into the billions of dollars annually.

---

class of the country, Trudeau lost power briefly in the summer of 1979 before regaining it in 1980. Curiously, his return to office marked a clear and sharp geographical divide in Canada: his Liberal Party won no seats west of Mrs. Turner's Manitoba. Interestingly, Trudeau was a lifelong fan and practitioner of the Japanese martial art of judo, which he began practicing in the 1950s. During one of his many official trips to Japan, he took the opportunity to complete the requirements for his first-degree black belt.

The Canadian Short Story
Appearing initially in Shields's 1985 collection *Various Miracles*, "Mrs. Turner Cutting the Grass" was recognized almost immediately as an important addition to an already vibrant period of story writing in Canada. It is a period that is generally seen as a time of balanced paradoxes, when Canadian writers continued to tell powerful stories but did so with an expanding sophistication of style and technique. Regionalism was still influential (Shields,

Mrs. Turner traveled with her sisters to Japan and saw the Golden Pavilion in Kyoto, where their behavior inspired the scornful poetry of the Professor. (© Pigprox | Shutterstock.com)

for instance, sets many of her stories clearly in Winnipeg, Manitoba), while at the same time Canadian story writers were increasingly garnering international attention and praise. Alistair MacLeod's acclaimed collection *Lost Salt Gift of Blood* (1976) focuses singularly on the lives and people of Cape Breton and Newfoundland; Nobel Prize winner Alice Munro established herself as the voice of Ontario with such collections as *Who Do You Think You Are?* (1978) and *Moons of Jupiter* (1982); and Mavis Gallant and Mordecai Richler made the streets and stories of Montreal their own.

Increased attention to story writers fed into a kind of renaissance of the story form during this period as well. Hundreds of collections came to market in the 1980s, and multiauthor anthologies appeared regularly, in part to feed the growing interest in Canadian literature in high schools, colleges, and universities. Although still present in Canadian stories, such traditional themes as the complexities of love affairs, the struggle of individuals within a community, and the power of evil were joined by more direct questions about

what it means to be Canadian (especially for writers, like Shields, who were born elsewhere), how one might understand the expansive and dangerous geography of the country, and how language shapes the reality in which humans live. Also, although a modernist perspective still held sway, with its focus on realistic characters, well-structured linear plots, and firm resolutions, many writers, Shields included, began to explore postmodern techniques that often saw time and space bend freely within a story as questions (not answers) and uncertainties (not clarity) added texture.

CRITICAL OVERVIEW

Marta Dvorak summarizes elegantly in "Carol Shields and the Poetics of the Quotidian" (2002) that Shields's international reputation has been built "on her uncanny ability to re/present the details of everyday life, to anatomize the mundane" or what Shields herself calls "the texture of the quotidian." Dvorak goes on to note that Shields's writing, however "rooted in everydayness" it might appear at first, "is profoundly metaphorical." It is this focus on the extraordinariness of everyday objects and events that reviewers return to often in discussions of Shields's short fiction generally and of "Mrs. Turner Cutting the Grass" specifically. An anonymous writer for *Kirkus Reviews*, noting the story's first appearance in *Various Miracles* (1985), observes how the powerful "contrast between the poet's career and Mrs. Turner's unexceptional decency makes for an exquisite little dissertation—thoughtful, quiet, full of literary turns." Writing for the London *Observer* in 2004, Tim Adams picked up on this sense of the fullness to be found in Shields's stories, remarking that they "are full of tiny leaps of faith, made in order to give a shape and purpose to things."

This focus on enhancing the meaningfulness of the ordinary is a fine balancing act, as Josh Rubins of the *New York Times* points out in his 1987 review, but one that Shields manages with aplomb: "Avoiding cuteness on the one hand and pomposity on the other," he notes, she "frequently succeeds in twirling fragmentary daydreams and peculiar anecdotes into tiny fictions of sizable impact." The result is a "dainty, full-hearted brand of minimalism—not unlike a short-fiction equivalent of haiku—[that] manages to extract the shrewdest details, the most intriguing implications, from modestly inventive notions."

As Jenny Uglow adds in her 1994 review of *Various Miracles*, Shields's stories are not simply about expanding the meaning of things. They are also stories about people in various stages of completing their own journeys and stories. Many of "Shields's favourite characters," Uglow points out,

> do not even know they have stories. They just live. Thus, a jolly mid-western widow is blithely unaware that her weed-killer horrifies her ecological neighbours, that her sagging thighs strike terror into schoolgirls, that she is the star of a poem about ignorant tourists in Japan. But Mrs. Turner has her own rich, raucous history, her own worldview. When she travels she sees sameness, as well as difference.

Where others might miss the glorious complexities unraveling around them, this story, like so many others in the collection, focuses on capturing the most elusive truths about

life—truths that, in Uglow's words, "are grasped in flickering glimpses beyond words, like patterns on the inner eye-lid before sleep." Adams iterated this point in 2004, noting that "Shields gave her characters things to hold on to, rarely leaving them to cope alone. She loved foibles, distinguishing marks, habits that make people seem odd even to themselves."

Elke D'Hoker pushes this emphasis further still with her conclusion that

> although Shields is interested in personal stories and individual lives, her short stories betray an even greater interest in the relationships between people: not just the visible ties of blood, love, or friendship, but also the hidden, coincidental connections.

Clara Thomas, revisiting "Mrs. Turner Cutting the Grass" in her review of *The Collected Stories* in 2004, summarizes this uncanny ability aptly with her celebration of Shields's "final wondering perception of the intricacy, difficulty, and radiance of lives lived in the midst of the vast civilization beyond our view."

Further testament to the enduring appeal of the story is its selection for such compilations as *Canadian Short Stories: Fourth Series* (1985), *More Stories by Canadian Women* (1987), and *The Cosmopolitan Book of Short Stories* (1995). It is a story, too, that invites interpretations that push outwards (and across) the disciplinary borders, as with Benoit Léger's foray into structuralist literary theory in "Traduction littéraire et polyphonie dans 'Mrs. Turner Cutting the Grass' de Carol Shields" (1995; "Literary Translation and Polyphony in Carol Shields's 'Mrs. Turner Cutting the Grass'") and Dvorak's numerous journeys into the semantic complexities of Shields's short fiction.

CRITICISM

Klay Dyer

Dyer is a writer for a number of publications, specializing in the arts, innovation, and technology. In the following essay, he examines the intersection of performance, authenticity, and value in Shields's "Mrs. Turner Cutting the Grass."

The title of Carol Shields's "Mrs. Turner Cutting the Grass" echoes that of a painting by Johannes Vermeer (as in "Girl with a Pearl Earring"). It is a story that explores the cultural and

WHAT DO I READ NEXT?

- Given Shields's love for the novels of Jane Austen, Diana Peterfreund's *For Darkness Shows the Stars* (2012) is a great choice for young-adult readers. Inspired by Austen's *Persuasion*, it is a fast-paced romance set in a postapocalyptic world ruled by a Luddite nobility that has outlawed most technology.

- Irish writer James Joyce's *Dubliners* (1914) is a seminal collection of short stories that explore middle-class struggles and values during times of great change and uncertainty. These stories were instrumental in establishing the Joycean epiphany as a kind of standard by which all other writers would be measured.

- Eleanor Wachtel's *Random Illuminations: Conversations with Carol Shields* (2007) is more than a book of interviews and conversations. It is a glimpse into a literary and personal friendship that evolved across decades, across cities, and across artistic and health challenges. Given Wachtel's reputation as one of Canada's preeminent interviewers, it is not surprising that her letters and discussions with one of the country's most accomplished writers sparkle with intelligence, insight, and humor.

- Annie Dillard's *The Writing Life* (1989) remains an important and eminently readable book about one of the most tortuous and rewarding activities available to humans: writing. Moreover, it is both a book that Shields herself appreciated deeply and an exploration of a topic that she enjoyed discussing.

- Shields's *The Stone Diaries* (1993) was one of her most celebrated works, winning the Pulitzer Prize for Fiction in 1995. The novel also won Canada's Governor General's Literary Award (1993) as well as the National Book Critics Circle Award (1994), the McNally Robinson Award for Manitoba Book of the Year (1995), and the Canadian Booksellers Association Prize (1995). A subtle and multilayered novel, *The Stone Diaries* recounts the life and spiritual growth of its protagonist, Daisy Goodwill Flett, as told from the perspectives of multiple narrators and a variety of letter writers.

- Also from Shields, *Larry's Party* (1997) is probably her most experimental, and in many ways most rewarding, novel. Focusing on a character whose life is defined by a growing obsession with mazes, Shields builds an intricately connected sequence of fifteen chapters, each dedicated to a particular period in Larry's life and each flashing backward and forward in time with dizzying but controlled quickness.

- Canada has produced an abundance of internationally acclaimed short-story writers, including Margaret Atwood, Margaret Laurence, Alistair MacLeod, and Mavis Gallant, to name but a few. Alice Munro, however, would be at or near the top of every list. Winner of the Nobel Prize in Literature (2013), Munro creates worlds, like Shields, in which lives that seem defined only by surfaces and smallness unfold before a reader into complex layers of love and betrayal, desire and forgiveness, and undeniable beauty. Munro's *Selected Stories* (1997) provides a powerful overview of her vision and voice.

---

social dynamics of what is known as performativity, which means the capacity to use speech and gestures to construct and maintain an identity. In contemporary terms, think of any number of musicians or professional athletes who have created popular and marketable identities through their performances on stage or on a sports field. More specifically, Shields's story is about how the complex dynamics of three activities—seeing, watching, and being seen—can

> WHAT SHE IS WATCHING, IN THE END, IS
> A LIFE LIVED OPENLY, AUTHENTICALLY, AND
> WITH A SPIRIT THAT IS AT ONCE RAUCOUS,
> RESILIENT, AND READY ALWAYS FOR THE SIGN
> TO TAKE THE STAGE."

not only create a reality but can, as in the case of Mrs. Turner, create an incomplete or, in a worst case, unfair representation of the rich inner life of the individual captured in performance.

In the case of Mrs. Turner, performativity is inherently and deeply problematic. Rather than reinforcing a stable and knowable relationship between inner and outer life (body and emotion, for instance), performative actions and gestures complicate, and at times undermine, her relationship within the larger social contexts through which she moves. In the end, Mrs. Turner is defined (mistakenly) by those around her not in terms of who she is and the life she has led, but through the contours of her body and the actions she rehearses in public.

"Mrs. Turner Cutting the Grass" opens with the omniscient narrator in her role of audience, as she remarks with exclamatory flair at the performance that she is fortunate to witness: "Oh, Mrs. Turner is a sight cutting the grass on a hot afternoon in June!" The emphasis in this sentence on the word "sight" is important, introducing a world in which how things appear to the eye (are seen) is the most powerful determinant of their reality, their value, and their place in the system of middle-class values that define the communities through which this character travels. In Mrs. Turner's case, performance is a profoundly physical event, as she goes on display, as it were, in an "ancient pair of shorts and ties on her halter top and wedges her feet into crepe-soled sandals and covers her red-gray frizz with Gord's old golf cap." Joining the narrator in the audience is a cross-section of River Heights, including Mrs. Turner's neighbors, the Saschers, who pass judgment from the safe and appropriately distant vantage point of their front porch, and the high-school girls, who get a front-row seat as they walk

by "on their way home in the afternoon." Afraid that they see in Mrs. Turner a glimpse of their own futures, the girls bury fear in a generalized but momentary sense of being "repelled by the lapped, striated flesh" openly in view "on her upper thighs."

As the narrator begins to slowly pull back the curtain on Mrs. Turner's life, readers should not be surprised to find that her past, when she was known variously as Geraldine and Girlie Fergus, was also defined by a kind of lurid theatricality. Caught "one night—she was nineteen—in a Boissevain hotel room with a local farmer, married," she was forced to endure the humiliation of having a private moment suddenly translated into a public one as her affair was thrown openly onto the stage of the small town for all to judge. The elements of her now-public performance read like a litany of transgressions, from the staging (in a hotel room) through the casting (with a married man) to physical elements of the setting (night, in a small prairie town). With her private (interior) life fully exposed (made exterior) by no fault of her own, Geraldine/Girlie follows the path taken by so many humiliated women and aspiring actresses before her: she heads for the bright lights of New York City.

What Geraldine recognizes on the long bus trip eastward becomes crucial to her maturation and evolving understanding of the world: that there are "hundreds and hundreds of towns" scattered across the landscape, all of which could be defined by the same oppressiveness as the one she left behind. For Geraldine, there is no longer even the option of going back, of reinventing herself as a small-town girl. For her, the only future is to move forward to her next performance somewhere in the "immense and wonderful, dirty, perilous and puzzling" world before her. Appropriately, her response to this new opportunity is to find herself a job in the one place where performance would feel most natural: the theater.

As the narrator observes, "For eight and a half months she was an usherette in the Lamar Movie Palace in Brooklyn." She fits right into this world of "furry darkness," "plum-colored aisle carpet," and dramatic "streams of light." Her costume here, not unlike the one with which the story opens, is dramatic, colorful, and part of the broader spectacle of the theater. She especially loves the very public display of costume and physicality, noting happily the way the "perky maroon uniform...fit on her shoulders" and how "the strips of crinkly gold braid outlined her figure."

Gradually, and not surprisingly, she begins to feel part of the illusion itself, lifted from the role of viewer/usherette to performer: "She felt after a time that" the resonant "voices from the screen" talked directly to her and that the "tender replies" were for her alone. When the theatricality of romance collides dramatically with the realities of unwed motherhood and a doubled act of abandonment (Geraldine by Kiki, and their son by his parents), she returns to Boissevain for a temporary stay. Her return includes, not surprisingly, a suitcase full of the accoutrements of the city and of a life lived brightly and boldly: "boxes of hose, bottles of apple-blossom cologne, phonograph records."

The years of Geraldine's marriage are barely mentioned, perhaps because her performativity is set backstage temporarily, as she transitions from Girlie Fergus to Mrs. Turner, wife of Gord, suburban homeowner, and the classic character from all great romances: the woman with the troubled past. Following Gord's death, however, Mrs. Turner is free to step back onto the grand stage. Appropriately, her travels become a complex mixture of sightseeing, grand but wholly fake theatricality (Disneyland and Disney World), and equally grand but more authentic signs of cultures long past (antebellum houses and Mayan ruins).

Given the theatricality that has come to define Geraldine's life, it is also wholly appropriate that Kyoto's Golden Pavilion becomes the stage for one of the more critical performances in the story. A "three-storied temple... made of wood," with "a roof like a set of wings" and "painted a soft old flaky gold," the temple itself is an architectural representation of the dramatic spirit. It is here, where a crazed monk once set blaze to the most sacred temple in his country, that Geraldine confronts, albeit unknowingly, her most venomous critic.

Introduced during the section of the story dedicated to the adventures at Kyoto's Golden Pavilion, the Professor is himself a sight of some distinction: bald with a trim body, he has a notable penchant for "Bermuda shorts, sandals and black nylon socks." He is a familiar figure in Shields's short stories: a caricature of an academic who highly overestimates his own importance. More importantly, he is a man

"without a camera" and therefore a man to whom Geraldine's visual performances would be particularly disorienting.

Scribbling madly in his notebook, he struggles to make sense of his world and to capture with the artistry and profundity he so desires the words through which he can express the wonder of what he sees, feels, and experiences. His words, however, trip over themselves when confronted with the larger-than-life performance of Mrs. Turner and her sisters. "Angered" and "half-crazed," the Professor is unable to maintain the facade of "simplicity and order and something spiritual" that he claims to have discovered. Stripped of its pretense, his verse collapses into a vicious, petty attack on Mrs. Turner and her siblings, depicting them, ironically, in terms appropriate for the classical and Shakespearean stage: "They were the three furies, the three witches, who for vulgarity and tastelessness formed a shattering counterpoint to the Professor's own state of transcendence."

In spite of, or perhaps because of, Mrs. Turner's presence at the temple, the trip to Japan does wonders for the Professor. The "solid little book of poems" that comes out of the experience is received well enough for the Boston publisher to send him on a university and college reading tour. The most frequently requested poem on this tour is "A Day at the Golden Pavilion," which he thinks of as a "crowd pleaser." Playing to his audience, the Professor himself is perfectly willing to make the most of the part demanded by the poem, taking to his own stage now with the necessary commitment to read it "in a moist, avuncular amateur actor's voice, reminding himself to pause frequently, to look upward and raise an ironic eyebrow."

Sadly, Mrs. Turner's life of performativity has little impact on the middle-class world of the story. Rather than open a conversation with her about the dangers of herbicide use or alternative methods for dealing with noxious weeds, the neighboring Saschers withdraw into a static, isolating world that leaves them hoping not for an encore but for a radical decline in her health or even her death: "[Roy] and Sally so far have said nothing to Mrs. Turner...because they're hoping she'll go into an old-folks home soon or maybe die." Similarly, the high-school girls who are "repelled" by the performance they witness "on their way home in the afternoon" leave the

Mrs. Turner mows her lawn the way she plows through life: oblivious to the disapproval of others.
(© Bochkarev Photography / Shutterstock.com)

viewing untouched and unchanged, firm in their belief that their queasiness is due to the sight of "the lapped, striated flesh of her upper thighs" rather than a very authentic preview of their own futures. Only the narrator, whose exclamations opened the story, has shifted her perspective enough to realize that what she is watching, in the end, is a life lived openly, authentically, and with a spirit that is at once raucous, resilient, and ready always for the sign to take the stage: "Oh, what a sight is Mrs. Turner cutting her grass, and how, like an ornament, she shines."

Source: Klay Dyer, Critical Essay on "Mrs. Turner Cutting the Grass," in *Short Stories for Students*, Gale, Cengage Learning, 2015.

Faye Hammill

In the following excerpt, Hammill characterizes Shields as a Canadian writer, despite her American birth.

In an essay on tradition in Canadian women's writing, Carol Shields describes her childhood reading material: "it was mainly the books of my mother that I read, four of them in particular, two of which were Canadian (not that I noticed at the time) [...] *Anne of Green Gables, A Girl of the Limberlost, Helen's Babies*, and *Beautiful Joe*." She says of Anne that she "reshuffled the values of society by a primary act of re-imagination [...] Her sense of herself as heroine gives *Anne of Green Gables* the shading and grace that *A Girl of the Limberlost* never achieves." Later in her life, Shields read each published volume of L.M. Montgomery's journals avidly, and wrote a glowing review of the fourth volume, describing it as "a literary treasure" which "records [...] the transcendent and healing possibility of art." In her novel *The Republic of Love* (1993), Shields includes a conversation between two of her characters about "the biography of Lucy Maud Montgomery." She also considered writing a doctoral thesis on Sara Jeannette Duncan's work, and wrote in a letter: "I loved *The Imperialist* and can't understand why it isn't better known here [in Canada]." All this reveals Carol Shields's awareness of Montgomery and Duncan as Canadian

> CAROL SHIELDS'S AMERICAN ORIGINS
> NOTWITHSTANDING, HER WORK COULD BE SAID
> TO FIT RATHER NEATLY INTO THE VERY
> CATEGORY WHICH HER NOVELS SEEK TO
> QUESTION: THE CATEGORY OF 'CANADIAN
> LITERATURE.'"

predecessors, even though for Shields (as for Margaret Atwood), the dominant figure from the Canadian literary past is Susanna Moodie.

Carol Shields's responses to Canada's literary achievements and opportunities are, in several ways, comparable with Duncan's and Montgomery's. In general terms, *The Imperialist* and the "Emily" books share with Carol Shields's novels a preoccupation with the possibility of national signatures in literature. Shields also echoes Montgomery's interest in the influence of an artist's home background and national allegiances on her work. The texts I will discuss—*Small Ceremonies* (1976), *The Box Garden* (1977), *A Celibate Season* (1991) and *Swann: A Mystery* (1987)—all include poets and writers among their casts of characters, and explore many aspects of English Canada's literary culture in the late twentieth century.

"SASKATCHEWAN IN POWDER FORM": *SMALL CEREMONIES* AND *THE BOX GARDEN*

Judith Gill, the protagonist of Carol Shields's first novel, is working on a biography of Susanna Moodie, and is simultaneously preoccupied with the personal history of her novelist friend Furlong Eberhardt. Judith's investigation of the lives and writings of Moodie and Eberhardt exposes many of the assumptions and myths involved in the production and valuation of Canadian art. The insights offered cohere into a sceptical analysis of the Canadian literary establishment of the 1970s, and of its mission to isolate themes and images that distinguish Canadian texts from other literature in English or French. Thematic interpretations of literature are repeatedly deconstructed in *Small Ceremonies* and their distorting, homogenizing tendencies are revealed.

The discourse of Canadian thematic criticism is parodied in a scene in which Roger, an academic, discusses Eberhardt's novels:

> "take his use of the Canadian experience. Now there's a man who actually comprehends the national theme. [...] Which is shelter. Shelter from the storm of life [...] the hail is a symbol. He makes it stand for the general battering of everyday life."

Roger's simplistic equation of hail with the battering of life (hardly a peculiarly Canadian experience), together with his unequivocal definition of "*the* national theme," recall Atwood's pronouncement that "The central symbol for Canada [...] is undoubtedly survival." The plan for Roger's PhD thesis on Eberhardt is entirely consonant with the aims of thematic criticism:

> His design, as outlined in the Preface, was to survey the texts of Furlong's first four novels, collate those themes and images which were specifically related to the national consciousness—which were, in short, definitively Canadian—all this in order to prove that Furlong Eberhardt more or less represented the "most nearly complete flowering of the national ethos in the middle decades of this century."

Roger's verdict is confirmed by a reviewer who describes Eberhardt as "one who embodies the national ethos," an opinion that is ridiculed by Judith's husband, Martin. Martin points out that Furlong's inadvertent scheduling of his book-launch party on Grey Cup day shows him to be "fairly casual about the folkways of his country"—in other words, he is distanced from the true preoccupations of the Canadians around him.

Judith's view is that the supposedly Canadian elements of Furlong Eberhardt's books are contrived and formulaic. Without having read his latest novel, she discusses it with her daughter, Meredith, who is a devotee of Furlong's work: "He opens, Chapter One, to waving wheat. Admit it, Meredith, Saskatchewan in powder form. Mix with honest rainfall for native genre." The predictability of Furlong's scenery suggests a potential circularity: from the corpus of literature written in Canada, thematicists distil various images of the country that allegedly mark the writing as Canadian; but those images are subsequently incorporated into new books by writers such as Eberhardt who are, in effect, following the critics' recipe for an 'authentically' Canadian work. Meredith attempts to defend Furlong by saying that he grew up in Saskatchewan. Judith's reply underlines the discrepancy between Furlong's lived experience of Canada and his representation of Canadian life in his novel: "But he doesn't live there now. [...] For twenty years he's lived in the east. And he isn't a farmer. He's a writer." The implication of Judith's comment is not that her friend shouldn't describe what he hasn't lived, but that his notion of Canadian experience is derived from books and from the hackneyed tropes found in literature about Canada, rather than from any unconditioned perceptions of his own. Meredith's next argument is that "it's not supposed to be real life. [...] It's a sort of symbol of the country." Meredith's comment clearly relates to 1970s critical orthodoxies, but such views were still being articulated in later decades—by Leon Surette, for example:

> An interesting twist to the formation of the Canadian canon in fiction is a consequence of the unsuitability of the bourgeois realistic novel to the task of forging an indigenous culture. Symbolic, allegorical, and mythopoeic or romance forms of prose fiction are much more suitable to the task.

But Shields emphasizes the inappropriateness of some of Canada's symbolic images of itself by drawing attention to the fact that Furlong, along with a large proportion of the Canadian population, lives in an urban area where fields of wheat are not a feature of the landscape. The images of Canada which critics suppose to be enshrined in the national consciousness are, Shields suggests, mere ciphers—lifted from the texts of an earlier age and no longer able to communicate anything beyond nostalgia. The cover of Furlong's book bears a photograph of the author, with "behind him a microcosm of Canada: a fretwork of bare branches and a blur of olive snow, man against nature." This design signals the continuity of the novel with its Canadian predecessors, and prescribes the established symbolic framework within which it may mean.

As the novel progresses, it becomes clear that Furlong has deliberately included a number of conventionally Canadian symbols in order to profit from government policies of cultural nationalism. The somewhat indiscriminate munificence of the Canada Council towards Canadian authors and critics is defended by Furlong's champion, Roger, who argues thus:

> Of course Canadian culture has to be protected. For God's sake, you're dealing with a sensitive plant, almost a nursery plant. And don't tell me I'm being chauvinistic. I had a year at Harvard, remember. I tell you that if we don't give grants to our writers now and if we don't favour our own publishers now, we're lost man.

The climate fostered by such literary politics is taken advantage of by Eberhardt, whose overtly 'homegrown' books guarantee him support from the establishment. The artificiality of the whole notion of national characteristics which define certain literary works as Canadian emerges strikingly through Judith's discovery that "Furlong Eberhardt, Canadian prairie novelist, the man who is said to embody the ethos of the nation, is an American." She locates documentary proof that Furlong was born and brought up in the USA and moved to Canada at a relatively late stage in his life. Evidently, the required Canadian flavour can easily be imitated by an outsider: Furlong is merely cashing in on a literary fashion or, as Judith puts it, "taking a free ride on the bandwagon of nationalism."

Eberhardt manufactures a supposedly typical prairie atmosphere, and is rewarded first by government grants and later by lavish publicity for his books. He does not, however, return the favour by insisting that a Canadian outfit should have the film rights to his latest novel, and he is attacked on this front by an interviewer: "Wouldn't you say, Mr Eberhardt, that it is enormously ironical that you, a Canadian writer who has done so much to bring Canadian literature to the average reader, must turn to an American producer to have your novel filmed?" Matters are, of course, far more ironical than the interviewer realizes, since Eberhardt represents the ultimate subtlety of American infiltration of Canadian markets, having himself profited from them deviously and unscrupulously. There is still another layer of irony in the fact that Carol Shields herself was born in Illinois and lived there until she was married, yet is now considered to be a major Canadian author.

Small Ceremonies destabilizes the whole concept of 'Canadian literature' and questions the underlying assumptions of the nationalist thematic approach. Carol Shields was among the first to do this. The year *Small Ceremonies* appeared, 1976, was also the year in which Frank Davey published "Surviving the Paraphrase"—widely recognized as the earliest denunciation of thematics. Much English-Canadian criticism in the years following Davey's article has "continued to serve the perceived social imperatives of a nation in perpetual adolescence," and the attitudes and policies that Shields satirizes have to a certain extent persisted into the present.

Shields's specific exploration of Canada's need for indigenous myth, which began in *Small Ceremonies*, resurfaces in its companion novel, *The Box Garden* (1977). The protagonist of *The Box Garden*, Charleen Forrest, is the sister of Judith from *Small Ceremonies*. Charleen was at one time a poet, but she says: "poetry is part of my past now [...] having written away the well of myself, there is nowhere to go. The only other alternative would be to join the corps of half-poets, those woozy would-bes [...] the band of poets I've come to think of, in my private lexicon, as 'the pome people.'" These writers have a marked tendency towards symbolic poetry, which Charleen attacks: "symbolism is such an impertinence, the sort of thing the 'pome' people might contrive. (God knows how easily it's manufactured by those who turn themselves into continuously operating sensitivity machines.)." The words "manufactured" and "machines" suggest the output of writing which is in some sense inauthentic and produced according to a formula. Charleen admits that her own poems were at first similarly contrived, and she says that her writing process involved "putting together the shapes and ideas which I shoplifted." This is the only sense in which she worked in a tradition—her images were not so much influenced by previous writers as directly borrowed from them. She acknowledges a heavy debt to one poet in particular, who, ironically, is not a Canadian but an American who became an Englishman: T.S. Eliot. Eliot is the one figure who can represent the immensity of the British and the American poetic heritages simultaneously, and thus it is by stealing bits and pieces from those bodies of literature that Charleen's supposedly Canadian poems are constructed:

> My first poems (pomes) were lit with a whistling blue clarity (emptiness) and they were accepted by the first magazine I sent them to. Only I knew what paste-up jobs they were, only I silently acknowledged my debt to a good

thesaurus, a stimulating dictionary and a daily injection of early Eliot [...] I, who manufactured the giddy, dark-edged metaphors, knew the facile secret of their creation. Like piecework I rolled them off. Never, never, never did I soar on the wings of inspiration.

This confession functions to debunk the idea of a 'national subconscious' from which images somehow surface and inspire truly Canadian poetry.

Charleen's work is eagerly accepted by Canadian magazines and publishing houses and she begins to command the attention of several critics. None of the critics, however, perceives a distinction between her early "tinkering" and the poems she produces after her husband has left her, which are described by Charleen herself in an entirely different way: "poetry became the means by which I saved my life. I discovered that I could bury in my writing the greater part of my pain and humiliation." She comments: "To these critics my work was one [....] seamless whole." Surely there are parallels here, again, with the real-life nationalist critics who, at the time when *The Box Garden* was published, were engaged in developing schemas and keys which might be applied to the whole of Canadian literature. Their tendency was to discover continuity and uniformity, and they were also busy praising and promoting Canadian writing in almost all its manifestations, with little regard for traditional standards of originality and merit, or, indeed, for saleability.

Charleen's creative potential is hemmed in on three sides: first, by her fear of becoming like the deluded "pome" people; secondly by her narrowly practical Ontario background, where literary interests were frowned upon:

> All the other girls in the neighbourhood were going on to secretarial school or studying to be hairdressers [...] Our mother alone had been cursed with strange daughters: Judith [...] bookish and careless, and I with [...] my books of poetry. The neighbours' children hadn't dismayed and defeated and failed their mothers.

Both Judith and Charleen publish books, but their mother (like Emily's relatives in Montgomery's New Moon trilogy) takes no pride in this and is not interested in reading them. Thirdly, Charleen continues, as an adult, to encounter a rather philistine incomprehension when people discover what her profession is.

Her account of her first meeting with her lover, Eugene, includes the following exchange:

> "Merv says you're a poet," he said to me later [...]
>
> "Yes," I said knowing that he was about to tell me he never read poetry.
>
> "I can't pretend to know much about poetry," he said [...]
>
> "That's all right," I say socially. "It's a sort of minority interest. Like lacrosse."

It is these difficulties, and not Charleen's poems, which are presented as peculiarly Canadian in *The Box Garden*.

...Carol Shields's American origins notwithstanding, her work could be said to fit rather neatly into the very category which her novels seek to question: the category of 'Canadian literature.' This is true precisely by virtue of Shields's preoccupation with the contours of Canada's national culture, particularly with its literary output. She shares this preoccupation with Margaret Atwood. Although Atwood was herself a prominent thematic critic and nationalist writer in the 1970s, in her 1991 short-story collection *Wilderness Tips* her perspective is much closer to that of Carol Shields, and exhibits a similar tendency to parody and question certain assumptions about Canadian art and literature.

Source: Faye Hammill, "Influential Circles: Carol Shields and the Canadian Literary Canon," in *Literary Culture and Female Authorship in Canada, 1760–2000*, Rodopi, 1994, pp. 115–22, 132–33.

SOURCES

Adams, Tim, "The Consolation of Words," in *Observer* (London, England), July 18, 2004, http://www.theguardian.com/books/2004/jul/18/fiction.carolshields (accessed February 23, 2014).

D'Hoker, Elke, "Moments of Being: Carol Shields's Short Fiction," in *Studies in Canadian Literature*, Vol. 33, No. 1, 2008, pp. 151–68.

Dvorak, Marta, "Carol Shields and the Poetics of the Quotidian," in *Journal of the Short Story in English*, Vol. 38, Spring 2002, http://jsse.revues.org/203 (accessed March 1, 2014).

Eagleton, Mary, "What's the Matter? Authors in Carol Shields' Short Fiction," in *Canadian Literature*, No. 186, Fall 2005, pp. 70–84.

Léger, Benoit, "Traduction littéraire et polyphonie dans 'Mrs. Turner Cutting the Grass' de Carol Shields," in *Studies in Canadian Literature*, Vol. 20, No. 1, 1995, http://journals.hil.unb.ca/index.php/SCL/article/view/8207 (accessed February 23, 2014).

Nishik, Reingard M., ed., "The Canadian Short Story: Status, Criticism, Historical Survey," in *The Canadian Short Story: Interpretations*, Camden House, 2007, pp. 1–40.

Review of *Various Miracles*, in *Kirkus Reviews*, January 1, 1985, https://www.kirkusreviews.com/book-reviews/carol-shields/various-miracles/ (accessed April 20, 2014).

Rubins, Josh, "They All Want a Piece of the Legend," in *New York Times*, August 6, 1989, http://www.nytimes.com/1989/08/06/books/they-all-want-a-piece-of-the-legend.html (accessed February 23, 2014).

Shields, Carol, "Mrs. Turner Cutting the Grass," in *The Collected Stories*, Random House, 2004, pp. 29–39.

Thomas, Clara, "The Collected Stories of Carol Shields," in *Books in Canada*, November 2004, http://www.booksincanada.com/article_view.asp?id=3794 (accessed February 23, 2014).

Uglow, Jenny, "Accidents at the Heart of Life," in *Independent* (London, England), October 2, 1994, http://www.independent.co.uk/arts-entertainment/book-review–accidents-at-the-heart-of-life-various-miracles-carol-shields- fouth-estate-999-pounds-1440337.html# (accessed February 23, 2014).

Wachtel, Eleanor, *Random Illuminations: Conversations with Carol Shields*, Goose Lane Editions, 2007, pp. 47, 92, 98, 103, 149.

York, Lorraine, "Carol Shields," in *Encyclopedia of Literature in Canada*, edited by W. H. New, University of Toronto Press, 2002, pp. 1037–38.

FURTHER READING

Besner, Neil K., *Carol Shields: The Arts of a Writing Life*, Prairie Fire Press, 2003.

> A diverse and deeply moving collection of essays, memoirs, and interviews written by critics from around the world, as well as by friends and family, this book includes a contribution by Shields's daughter Anne. Importantly, it also includes an original essay by Shields herself titled "About Writing," in which she adds substance to a subset within her broader body of work: meditative and critical reflections on the challenges and rewards of leading a life dedicated to and defined by writing.

Goertz, Dee, and Edward Eden, *Carol Shields, Narrative Hunger, and the Possibilities of Fiction*, University of Toronto Press, 2003.

> Focused primarily on Shields's longer fiction, this collection of well-written though at times difficult essays sheds light on many of the themes and techniques that she carries over

to her short stories as well. Collectively, the essays raise some fascinating questions about Shields's interest in the dynamics of fictional autobiography, her use of disrupted or ruptured narratives, and allusions to other works of literature and film in her writing.

Ramon, Alex, *Liminal Spaces: The Double Art of Carol Shields*, Cambridge Scholars, 2009.
Focusing on Shields's powerful but subtle manipulation of liminal spaces (thresholds between two places, conditions, or states of mind), Ramon presents a provocative rereading of Shields's works as a determined questioning of such topics as change, memory, and creativity.

Shields, Carol, "The Same Ticking Clock" and "Arriving Late, Starting Over," in *How Stories Mean*, edited by John Metcalf and J. R. (Tim) Struthers, Porcupine's Quill, 1993, pp. 88–89, 244–51.
A lifelong teacher as well as writer, Shields was adept at writing about the creative process and the discipline of writing. These two short essays are among her most insightful examinations of the complexities of the creative process.

Van Herk, Aritha, and Cornelia Janneke Steenman-Marcusse, *Carol Shields: Evocation and Echo*, Barkhuis, 2009.
This collection of international responses from critics and fellow writers reflects the deep and lasting influence that Shields's writing has had both on her contemporaries and on writers of later generations.

SUGGESTED SEARCH TERMS

Carol Shields

Mrs. Turner Cutting the Grass AND Carol Shields

Canadian literature

Carol Shields AND short story

Carol Shields AND Various Miracles

Carol Shields AND Collected Stories

middle class AND short story

Canada AND short story

quotidian AND short story

epiphany AND short story

liminal AND short story

postmodern AND short story

New Boy

RODDY DOYLE

2007

"New Boy" is a story by Irish writer Roddy Doyle that appeared in his short-story collection *The Deportees and Other Stories* (2007). Doyle is best known for his earlier authorship of *The Barrytown Trilogy*, which consists of the novels *The Commitments* (1987), *The Snapper* (1990), and *The Van* (1991), all of which were made into feature films. Those stories are set in a Dublin neighborhood based on the one where Doyle grew up. He later returned there to work as a teacher. The characters he has created come to life because he *knows* them—they are his family, friends, and neighbors.

The approach of the twenty-first century, however, brought changes to Dublin. Indeed, all of Ireland experienced an unprecedented influx of immigrants. The population was changing, and to some, it seemed to happen overnight. In the foreword to *The Deportees and Other Stories*, Doyle relates, "I went to bed in one country and woke up in a different one." In 2000, Doyle was asked to write a series of stories exploring the social fallout resulting from this wave of new people. The stories originally appeared in eight-hundred-word segments in the multicultural newspaper *Metro Éireann*.

"New Boy" is one of these newspaper serial stories, which were later published together in Doyle's 2007 collection. "New Boy" describes the experiences of Joseph, a nine-year-old African immigrant boy, on his first day in school in

Roddy Doyle is an Irish novelist, dramatist, and screen writer. (© Colin McConnell | ZUMA Press, Inc. | Alamy)

Ireland. With simple language and a deft touch of humor—and a few pointed words of profanity—Doyle captures Joseph's uncertainty and his bravery and portrays the reactions, both good and bad, of his classmates.

AUTHOR BIOGRAPHY

Doyle was born on May 8, 1958, in Dublin, Ireland. He grew up with two sisters and a brother in Kilbarrack, a Dublin suburb that would serve as the inspiration for the fictional Barrytown in several of his novels. Doyle attended University College, Dublin, where he contributed to the undergraduate newspaper. He graduated with a bachelor's degree in English and geography and then continued his studies in education at University College Dublin. In 1980, Doyle started work, teaching English and geography at a school in Kilbarrack.

In 1981, Doyle began his efforts to write seriously while continuing his work as a teacher. His first novel, *The Commitments*, was published in 1987 by his own publishing company, which he formed with a college friend. The same year, his first play, *Brownbread*, was produced. In 1989, Doyle married Belinda Moller, with whom he has two sons and a daughter: Rory, born in 1991; Jack, born in 1992; and Kate, born in 1998.

The Snapper, the sequel to *The Commitments*, was published in 1990. The following year brought *The Van*, the final book in what is now called *The Barrytown Trilogy*, which was published in one volume in 1995. Film adaptations of *The Commitments* and *The Snapper* premiered at the Cannes Film Festival in 1991 and 1993, respectively. The success of these movies and the popularity of his novels prompted Doyle to retire from teaching in 1993.

Doyle has published several other novels, including *Paddy Clarke Ha Ha Ha* (1993), for which he won the Booker Prize, and *The Guts* (2013). He has also written five children's books, including *The Giggler Treatment* (2000), his first, which he dedicated to his three children. In 2003, Doyle ventured into nonfiction, publishing *Rory and Ita*, a memoir about his parents. Doyle has also branched out into screenplays: he wrote a four-part television series called *Family*, which aired on the BBC in 1994, and adapted his own novel *The Van* into a screenplay. Doyle also formed his own production company, Deadly Films, which produced *The Van* in 1996.

In 2000, Doyle began writing a series of stories for a multicultural newspaper, *Metro Éireann*, exploring the cultural effects of the influx of immigrants to Ireland at the time. These stories, which include "New Boy," were originally published in eight-hundred-word segments. They were later collected in the volume *The Deportees and Other Stories* (2007). As of 2014, Doyle still lives and works in Dublin.

PLOT SUMMARY

1. He Is Very Late

It is Joseph's first day of school in Ireland. He feels uncertain and thinks of himself as "late"—five years late. He does not understand why some of the other students are laughing. Joseph cannot remember the teacher's name—the students call her "Miss." She introduces Joseph to

MEDIA ADAPTATIONS

- In 2009, "New Boy" was adapted into a short film directed by Steph Green and starring Olutunji Ebun-Cole as Joseph. Produced by Bord Scannán na hÉireann, Radio Telefís Éireann, and Zanzibar Films, the film is available on YouTube at http://www.youtube.com/watch?v = FdeioVndUhs &list = TL2l6ercd2K4w.

the class. When the class gets too rowdy, the teacher instructs them to put their hands in the air, a command she repeats often throughout the story, whenever the students get out of hand.

Seth Quinn, one of the other boys in the class, is accused of throwing someone else's book out the window. Although he denies having done it, the teacher sends him out to fetch the book.

The class begins a lesson on long division. Joseph does not find the problems difficult and seems relieved.

The boy sitting behind Joseph leans forward and calls him "Live-Aid." Joseph tries to ignore him, but the boy keeps poking him. The teacher notices the disruption, and when she scolds the boy, Joseph learns his name: Christian Kelly. However, Joseph will not admit that the boy was bothering him. A girl tattles on Christian. Christian tells Joseph, "You're dead."

2. The Finger

Joseph tries to figure out exactly what Christian meant by his threatening remark. Doyle gives the first hint of Joseph's background when Joseph thinks to himself, as the narration relates, "All boys must grow and eventually die—Joseph knows this; he has seen dead men and boys." However, he quickly realizes that Christian did not mean the threat literally. Joseph marvels that he must find a way to protect himself from a boy he has not yet even seen. Then there is a second

detail about Joseph's past: "He did not see the men who killed his father."

After Joseph has finished his math problems, Christian asks for solutions. Joseph tells him a couple without any argument. Because many of the other students are still working on their math, Joseph has a few minutes to look around. He notices another black boy in the class, as well as one black girl.

The teacher calls Hazel O'Hara, a girl with glasses, up to the board to do the first math problem for the class. Hazel is pleased by the attention. Christian bothers Joseph again, but this time Joseph stands up for himself. He grabs Christian's finger and pulls, jerking him to the floor. The teacher intervenes.

3. You're Definitely Dead

Christian complains loudly about his finger, claiming that Joseph broke it. The teacher examines him and decides he is not truly hurt. She asks Joseph to apologize to Christian, and Joseph obeys, but he will not agree that he did not mean to hurt Christian. To avoid further mischief, the teacher separates the boys, moving Joseph to sit next to Hazel. She blushes, and one of the other girls points it out to the class. The teacher tells Joseph to stay inside during the little break (a short recess) and calls Seth up to the board.

4. Milk

Seth is reluctant to go up to the chalkboard. He does not know how to solve the math problem, and Joseph wishes he could tell him the answer. The teacher allows Seth to return to his seat and says she hopes they have "less guff out of Seth for a while." Hazel explains the expression to Joseph and is taken aback when he politely thanks her.

The teacher dismisses the other students for the little break. Joseph stays behind as instructed, but he will not explain his behavior. The teacher expresses sympathy for Joseph and tells him she hopes he will do well here. She does, however, insist that she cannot allow the kind of behavior Joseph displayed when grabbing and twisting Christian's finger. Then she dismisses him for the last few minutes of the break.

Joseph finds his way out to the crowded school yard. After he opens the door and steps outside, something scrapes by his cheek and smacks into the window behind him. It is a milk carton, which bursts open, splashing milk all over Joseph. He is wet and cold, but he pulls off his sweatshirt. The crowd of students watching parts, and Joseph sees Christian Kelly, and right behind him is Seth Quinn.

5. The Bell

The crowd taunts the boys, pushing them into a fight. Then the verbal encouragement turns physical: the crowd starts pushing the boys toward each other. Joseph can see that Christian is frightened and understands that Christian does not wish to fight any more than he does, but they are all trapped now. Christian gives Joseph a shove, and Joseph grabs his hand, much like he did in the classroom.

As the boys are inching toward a fight that neither of them wants, Joseph remembers details about his past; the narrative shifts back and forth between the school yard and Joseph's memories. He remembers the day soldiers came into his village and took the bell from the schoolhouse. Joseph could hear gunfire and people screaming. One soldier rang the school bell and then dropped it. Another soldier fired his gun at the bell. Once the soldiers left, Joseph was too frightened to move for a long while. When he was finally able to move, he found his father's body behind the school. He could not bring himself to look at his father's face, but he recognized his trousers. Finally, Joseph remembers how he ran away.

The bell rings and the students start to walk away from the squabble, getting in line, ready to return to class. The teacher sees Joseph, Christian, and Seth. Joseph still has a hold on Christian's finger. She is angry to find them fighting again.

6. Robbing a Bank

The teacher ushers all of the other students back into the classroom, leaving Joseph, Christian, and Seth in the hall. She gives the class an assignment in their Gaeilge (Gaelic, or Irish) textbooks and returns to confront the boys. Joseph does not think she looks angry.

All three of the boys refuse to explain what happened. The teacher waits, and as the three boys stand there in stubborn silence, a change comes over them: they "become united.... They do not like one another but this does not

matter." Because they are united against the teacher, they are no longer enemies.

Hazel comes to the classroom door and tries to tell the teacher what she saw in the schoolyard, but the teacher sends her back into the room. Hazel complains to her classmates. The teacher goes to scold her and again orders the class to put their hands in the air. In the hall, Seth jokes that she "thinks she's robbing a . . . bank," and the boys cannot stop laughing, even when the teacher returns. She is not angry, however. She calls them the "three musketeers" and sends them back into the classroom.

CHARACTERS

Joseph

Joseph is the protagonist in "New Boy," and the story is told from his point of view. Having come to Dublin from Africa, Joseph finds himself in a different world. The smart-mouthed Irish students seem like alien creatures to him. The school schedule is unfamiliar, and he does not understand their local slang.

Joseph is an intelligent boy. He finds the math problems in his new class to be fairly easy. He pays attention to everything that is going on around him, trying to figure out his new home. Joseph is quiet, although it is difficult to determine whether he is quiet by nature or whether he decides to be quiet because at least that way he will not say anything wrong.

Through Joseph's memories, the reader learns why he immigrated to Ireland: violence in his homeland. Soldiers came to his village, and his father was taken out of the school and shot. No information is given about what other family Joseph has in Ireland or back in Africa. His background has made him brave.

Joseph does not tattle when Christian starts bullying him, but neither does he back down. Both in the classroom and in the schoolyard, Joseph stands up to Christian. It seems to make Christian have a bit of respect for him, so that in the end, when their resistance to the teacher unites them, the reader is fairly certain there will be no more bullying, even if it seems doubtful that Joseph and Christian will become the best of friends.

Christian Kelly

Christian is the troublemaker of the story. Almost as soon as Joseph sits down at his desk, Christian is poking him and saying, "You're dead." Doyle seems to be having a bit of fun with the character's name: treating others in a proper "Christian" way would not include bullying and name calling. Instead, someone acting in a truly Christian manner would follow Jesus's teachings about loving one another and turning the other cheek.

Christian calls Joseph "Live-Aid" and calls Hazel "Specky." He seems to pick the most obvious feature about a person to mock (such as Joseph's race and Hazel's glasses). Like many bullies, Christian is a coward. Before Joseph learns Christian's name, he thinks of him as the "dangerous boy," but when they are out in the school yard and everyone is expecting a fight, Joseph "looks at Christian Kelly. He knows. This is not what Christian Kelly wants. Christian Kelly is frightened." Christian assumes that if he bullies quiet Joseph, Joseph will scurry away or cower in fear. When Joseph stands up to him, Christian is forced into a confrontation he did not expect and does not want.

Miss

All of the students in the class call the teacher "Miss." Her name is not disclosed. Although she introduces herself to Joseph when he first arrives, he immediately forgets her name in his nervousness. He sometimes thinks of her as "teacher-lady."

The teacher seems overwhelmed by the class when they misbehave. She has the students lift their hands in the air to restore order, a trick that Joseph quickly picks up on. When she is completely exasperated, she says, "God give me strength." She alternates between being kind and stern. For example, she keeps Joseph behind in the classroom during recess to scold him for his behavior, though she surely suspects that Christian provoked him. Once the other students have gone outside for their break, she asks, "What have you to say for yourself?" When Joseph does not answer, it might be expected that she would become angry, but instead, she smiles and says, "I wish they were all as quiet as you."

Hazel O'Hara

Hazel is one of Joseph's classmates. Christian calls Hazel "Specky" because she wears spectacles, or glasses. Joseph marvels at Hazel's hair, which is so blonde it "is almost white." Hazel appears to be the class informer; it may be her who first tells the teacher that Christian is bothering Joseph. It seems she has taken a liking to Joseph, as her smile at him, Christian's teasing, and her blushing might indicate. Hazel likes to be the center of attention, whether because she is willing to report others' behavior or because she can properly solve a math problem. Hazel tries to help Joseph, telling him, "Don't listen to that dirt-bag," when Christian tries to bother him. She also explains slang terms to Joseph. At the end of the story, Hazel tries to tell the teacher what really happened out on the playground and becomes angry when the teacher will not allow her to talk about it.

Pamela

Pamela is one of the few other black students in the class. Because she and Joseph are of the same race, some of the children say that Joseph should sit next to her when the teacher wants to separate him from Christian. For whatever reason, Pamela objects.

Seth Quinn

Seth is described as "a small, angry boy." Like Christian, Seth is a troublemaker in the classroom. When another student accuses Seth of throwing a book out the window, Joseph is confused. He is not sure if throwing books out the window is an Irish custom or if Seth did something wrong. Seth is unable to solve a math problem when the teacher calls him to the board. Clearly the teacher knows that Seth will not be able to do the problem, and Joseph does not understand why the teacher would purposely embarrass Seth like that. Seth's discomfort makes Joseph want to tell him the answer to the problem. Along with Christian Kelly and Joseph, Seth is scolded by the teacher at the end of the story but refuses to explain what happened. This unites the three boys, if only for that moment.

THEMES

Immigrant Life

Because "New Boy" is told from the point of view of Joseph, a young African boy experiencing his first day of school in Ireland, the reader gains insight into what it might be like to be an

TOPICS FOR FURTHER STUDY

- Read Terry Farish's *The Good Braider* (2012), which tells the story of Viola, a young girl whose family flees political turmoil and violence in South Sudan to live with her uncle in Portland, Maine. Like Joseph in "New Boy," Viola feels out of place in her new school. Imagine that Viola and Joseph become pen pals. Think about how they might support each other and help each other navigate their hugely changed lives. Write several letters in which they describe their experiences both in their homelands and in their new countries.

- Doyle has said that he deliberately devotes little text to descriptions of setting. Conduct research in print and online sources to find pictures of African villages like the one where Joseph lived and of Irish neighborhoods like the one where the story takes place. Include images of schools, houses, and the people who live in these places. Create a PowerPoint presentation about setting in "New Boy," and share it with your class.

- Do some research about bullying. You might find print sources in your school library, or look at websites such as http://www.stopbullying.gov/index.html or http://www.thebullyproject.com/. Also, look into what policies your school has about bullying. With a partner or a small group from your class, put together a website that can be a resource for your community. Include information about where kids can get help locally and links to other useful websites.

- Read one of the other tales in the collection *The Deportees and Other Stories*. Also considering "New Boy," write an essay comparing the points of view of two characters, oncentrating specifically on opinions about the increase in immigration to Ireland at the time. For example, you might compare the thoughts of the teacher or Christian in "New Boy" with the father in "Guess Who's Coming for the Dinner," Ray Brady in "57% Irish," or the narrator in "Black Hoodie."

---

immigrant—someone who looks different from everyone else, who finds local traditions foreign, and who does not understand everyday expressions, even if he happens to speak the local language. Joseph has a lot to figure out in his new life, because everything is different from what he knew before.

Like many immigrants who sought asylum in Ireland in the 1990s and the earliest years of the twenty-first century, Joseph left his homeland because of dangerous conditions. Soldiers came into his village, frightening everyone and killing Joseph's father, the town's schoolteacher. This violent experience sets Joseph apart from his classmates, who have likely never undergone that kind of trauma or known that kind of fear.

Joseph feels like he has a disadvantage compared to his classmates, most of whom grew up in the neighborhood and have known each other since starting school. The first section of the story is called "He Is Very Late" because Joseph feels like he has come late to this way of life: "five years late. And that is very late, he thinks." Because he does not share the same background as the rest of the children, he feels like he has to catch up.

The simplest things are new to him. When the teacher scolds Seth Quinn for throwing another student's book out of the window, Joseph is not able to determine whether this is normal behavior: "It is not a custom he had expected, throwing books out windows. Are people walking past outside warned that this is

Joseph feels out of place as the new boy in school because he is stared at by the other students.
(© *Kiselev Andrey Valerevich* / *Shutterstock.com*)

about to happen? He does not know. He has much to learn." Joseph is smart, however, and even before coming to school he has strategies for figuring out what is going on. When the teacher asks him to stay behind in the classroom "at little break," Joseph is confused: "What is this little break? Joseph does not know. The other boys in the hostel did not tell him about a little break." Even though he is not familiar with this portion of the school day, it is obvious that he is clever enough to have asked questions of the other immigrant students in the hostel where he is staying, so that he could learn as much as possible.

Change

As an immigrant coming from a small African village to a neighborhood in Dublin, Joseph experiences huge changes in his life. He has been forced to leave his home and come to a place where everything is unfamiliar. The school bells represent the great shift in Joseph's life. When he thinks of the bell at his school at home, he recalls how he "loved its peal, its

beautiful ding. He never had to be called to school." He was happy and enjoyed attending the school where his father was the teacher.

When the soldiers came to the village, frightening everyone and killing Joseph's father, they also shot at the school bell. This represents the moment when Joseph's life changed forever. The lovely sound of the hand-rung bell at home contrasts with the bell that rings at the new Irish school, "a harsh electric bell" that represents the new, harsher world that Joseph must now learn how to navigate.

It is clear, however, that change can also be positive. Just as Joseph's life changed in a few moments when the soldiers came into his town, things change quickly for Joseph at his new school when he, Christian, and Seth refuse to explain to the teacher what happened in the school yard:

> She says nothing, for three seconds. These seconds, Joseph thinks, are important. Because, in that time, the three boys become united.... They are united in their silence. They do not like one another but this does not matter.

In those few seconds, their relationship changes. They may not become friends, but it seems they will no longer be enemies.

Prejudice

Christian bullies Joseph, it seems, because he is prejudiced. It is not clear precisely why Christian is prejudiced. It could be because Joseph is black. It is apparent that the students notice race, because some of them assume Joseph should sit next to Pamela simply because they are both black. Christian might also be prejudiced against Joseph because he is not Irish. He calls Joseph "Live-Aid," referring to a 1985 concert held to raise money to benefit those suffering from a famine in Ethiopia. Perhaps Christian assumes that anyone coming from Africa must be poor and starving, or perhaps he simply latches on to this insult as the most obvious—the first association that comes to mind when he thinks of Africa. Maybe Christian would mock anyone new or different or unfamiliar.

A lack of understanding is a common cause of prejudice: it is easier for people to fear those they do not understand. Bullying usually arises out of fear—fear of the unknown, fear of feeling powerless. Because Christian feels afraid or uncertain, he lashes out at Joseph. Joseph sees that Christian is afraid in the school yard when Joseph meets his gaze rather than cringing in fear himself. Christian wants to make himself feel stronger by bullying Joseph but fails because Joseph stands up for himself.

STYLE

Simplicity of Language

Throughout all of his writing, Doyle uses a simple style. The structure of his sentences is not complex, and he chooses words that anyone would recognize. Doyle's use of simple language has led some to question whether his work is truly literary. As Caramine White states in *Reading Roddy Doyle*, "because Doyle's work is so popular and accessible, the inevitable debate over his value as a serious writer rages."

However, it is clear that Doyle does not use his simple style because he is unable to write in a more formal or embellished style or with a wider or more complicated vocabulary. His writing style is a conscious choice. White explains that Doyle "purposely avoids the multisyllabic vocabulary that appears in many canonized texts," preferring writing that, in his own words, "is simple, straightforward, and serves the characters." In addition to the simple language, Doyle does not include much description or narration in the author's voice in his writing. His characters' thoughts, dialogue, and actions speak for themselves. White quotes Doyle from an interview in the *Sunday Correspondent*: "I deliberately didn't want descriptions, because I think they interfere."

These stylistic elements are evident in "New Boy." One only has to look at the first few sentences of the story to see Doyle's simple sentence structure and how effective that simplicity can be:

He sits.

He sits in the classroom. It is his first day.

He is late.

He is five years late.

And that is very late, he thinks.

The simple phrases and the repetition of words communicate the tension that Joseph is feeling. They also gives depth of feeling to Joseph's point of view, stressing how he breaks what he sees down into basics in an effort to understand what is, to him, an alien world. He is far from stupid, but everything is new for him, and he has a lot to learn. The simplicity of the sentences also allows the reader to pay attention to the deeper meaning. Obviously Joseph is not literally "five years late" for his first day of school. Rather, Doyle uses the idea of being late to class to portray Joseph's feeling of needing to catch up to his classmates in experience and understanding in this environment. With a few simple words—most consisting of only one syllable—Doyle accomplishes a lot.

Point of View

"New Boy" is told in third-person limited narrative mode. In third-person narration, the narrator refers to the characters as "he" and "she" but is not a part of the action of the story. The narration here is from a limited perspective because the story is told closely from Joseph's point of view; the reader learns what Joseph is thinking and feeling, but the narrator does not explain what other characters are thinking—only what Joseph guesses about them from their words and actions.

Third-person limited narration is particularly well suited to this story, because by seeing the story from the perspective of the title character, the reader experiences his uncertainty. Any kid on his or her first day at a new school is going to be confused about some things, and telling the story from his limited perspective allows the reader to share that confusion.

Doyle is also able to subtly give hints of Joseph's history, which would be hard to explain if the story were told from another person's point of view. For example, if "New Boy" were told from the teacher's perspective, it would reflect an adult's distance from the classroom's juvenile politics. She would likely understand what Joseph is going through and explain everything more quickly, and the story would not have its careful progression of events as Joseph comes to find connection with his classmates.

The teacher's point of view also would rob the story of much of its emotion, such as when the reader learns of the murder of Joseph's father. There are many subtle details that Joseph remembers, such as the sounds he heard on that day—the peal of the school bell, the screams of the frightened townspeople, and the soldier's laughter—that would be absent if the story was told from any other character's point of view. Any explanation of Joseph's past would have had to be just a recitation of the facts rather than the subtle but strong hints of emotion that Doyle conveys through Joseph's eyes and mind.

HISTORICAL CONTEXT

Immigration in Ireland

Ireland has always seen more emigration (people moving out of the country) than immigration (people moving into the country). Since the potato famine in the 1840s forced hundreds of thousands of people to leave Ireland, emigration has been a big part of Irish culture. Throughout the second half of the nineteenth century and the first half of the twentieth, Ireland's population decreased because of adventurous people leaving to seek their fortune in other parts of the world. There were far fewer people moving into the country, and Ireland's population is still smaller than one might expect when comparing countries of similar size.

World War II slowed Irish emigration, and in the second half of the twentieth century, immigration into Ireland slowly increased. The 1990s, however, brought huge changes. Although economic problems such as unemployment meant that Irish citizens were emigrating to places like the United States and the United Kingdom to look for work, there was an unprecedented increase in those seeking asylum because of political turmoil in their homelands: there were 39 applications for asylum in 1992, compared with 4,630 in 1998. During this time, the Irish government granted asylum to people from many countries, with the greatest numbers coming from Nigeria, Romania, the Democratic Republic of the Congo, Libya, and Algeria.

This great flood of immigration meant that the population of Ireland changed. The immigrant population increased further by 143 percent between 2002 and 2011. Approximately 11 percent of people living in Ireland today were born abroad, whereas ten years ago only 6 percent of people were born outside Ireland. Approximately two hundred nationalities are represented, and more than five hundred thousand people, out of over 4.5 million, speak a language other than Irish or English.

Having such a high percentage of immigrants is a new phenomenon for Ireland, and some native Irish people are prejudiced against their new countrymen and women. For example, according to the article "One-in-Nine People Living in Ireland Were Born Abroad," from the *Irish Examiner*, some believe that new immigrants are uneducated and unqualified to hold jobs. However, the Irish Central Statistics Office confirms that one in three immigrants has earned an academic degree. According to a report from the Irish Quarterly National Household Survey, approximately 24 percent of "non-Irish nationals feel they have been discriminated against," which is more than twice the rate of discrimination reported by Irish-born people. Immigrants felt that they experienced discrimination in relation to looking for a job, finding housing, getting service in shops or restaurants, and receiving financial services. Immigrants who were black were most likely to report experiencing prejudice.

Christian bullies Joseph in the classroom and on the playground, but Joseph does not back down.
(© EggHeadPhoto | Shutterstock.com)

In 1998, because of the sudden increase in Ireland's immigrant population, the United Nations High Commissioner for Refugees (UNHCR) began working with Irish authorities to help people seeking asylum, and in 2005, Ireland formed the Irish Naturalisation & Immigration Service. The UNHCR works not only to get people safely into the country but to make certain they can live and work without discrimination and contribute to their community and their new home.

CRITICAL OVERVIEW

Critical reception of *The Deportees and Other Stories* was mixed. While critics often praise Doyle's humor and his skill at rendering realistic dialogue, some object to the way the conflicts in the stories are sometimes wrapped up with too much ease. Tom Deignan's review in *America* is an example of mingled criticism and praise. Although Deignan points out that "some characters (particularly several of the noble new immigrants to Ireland) seem shallow or stereotypical," he also assures readers, "you can turn to Roddy Doyle for hilarious, acidic observations about 21st-century Ireland."

Starr E. Smith, in *Library Journal*, responds positively to the collection, asserting that "every selection reflects the author's mastery at creating authentic dialog and a realistic sense of place; readers will find themselves drawn into the sounds, sights, and highly charged atmosphere of contemporary Dublin." The reviewer for *Publishers Weekly* praises "Doyle's immense talent as a writer," which "is neatly showcased throughout," adding that "his sharp wit adds a richness to every tale." However, the reviewer also points out, "There are some abrupt endings that veer toward the convenient, though this may be an unavoidable consequence of their serial origins." Other critics also point to the original format as the cause of the stories' faults. A review in *New York* magazine explains as follows:

> These stories, serialized in thin slices for a Dublin newspaper, are all about the spots where old and new Ireland meet. As a result, they're rather petite pop observations, packed with playful and funny language. They're also strongly plotted, with tidy endings, and aren't the sort of thing that'll win him more literary prizes.

The reviewer for *Kirkus Reviews* expresses a similar view, that "what might have been entertaining as a newsprint monthly series seems slight in book form," and asserts that the collection "holds more socio-cultural than literary interest." Cressida Connolly, in *Spectator*, also objects to what she sees as endings that are too neat. She feels that in these short stories, even issues as difficult and complex as racism are "as soon overcome as a case of the hiccups." Acknowledging that Doyle usually handles such challenging themes more deftly, Connolly insists, "It matters if a writer as good and observant and witty as Doyle is disingenuous or facile; if he sacrifices uncomfortable truth for feel-good liberalism." In spite of this suggestion of rather harsh criticism, she ends with an apt summary of the general reaction to this collection:

At his best, Doyle writes some of the sharpest dialogue in current fiction and he can make you bark with laughter. *The Deportees* may not be Doyle at his very best, but it's still a highly enjoyable read.

CRITICISM

Kristen Sarlin Greenberg

Greenberg is a freelance writer and editor with a background in literature and philosophy. In the following essay, she examines Doyle's portrayal of the teacher in "New Boy."

It is a mark of Roddy Doyle's skill as a writer that on a first quick reading of his story "New Boy," the reader might not pay all that much attention to the teacher. She is the butt of the students' jokes, and her actions and words help to move the plot along, but she does not seem to be terribly important. However, upon careful examination of her behavior, one can trace a subtly portrayed, complex character with a clear motivation that explains why she treats her students in the way that she does.

At first, the teacher is a laughable character— a combination of stern authority figure and comic relief. She tries to enforce the rules, but she appears a bit foolish, and it seems that she cannot control her students. Her warnings to her class increase in severity from "Now, now," to "Now" to "Now!" in just the first two pages of the story. She has one student, Seth Quinn, who throws textbooks out the window, and another, Christian Kelly, who pokes at Joseph, the new student, and calls him names. Many of the students, even the goody two-shoes Hazel, talk back to the teacher and use inappropriate language. At times the situation in the classroom is so chaotic, the teacher can only stare into space and say, "God give me strength."

When Christian provokes Joseph past his breaking point so that he grabs him, the teacher must step in and pull the boys apart. This seems to be the point at which she completely loses control of her classroom, with Christian insisting that Joseph broke his finger and Joseph refusing to say much of anything. The other children are all clamoring to get a look at Christian's injured finger, and one student (Joseph thinks it might be Seth) whispers that he caught a glimpse of the teacher's underwear. It seems like a teacher's nightmare.

> THE TEACHER PLAYS THE ROLE OF THE DISAPPROVING AUTHORITY FIGURE, WHICH ALLOWS THE BOYS TO KEEP THEIR COMMON ENEMY AND STAY UNITED."

Her reaction to this dreadful situation is interesting. When she confronts Christian, he insists, "I didn't do anything." After all of the problems the students have caused that morning, one might assume that she will completely lose her temper when the boys break out in physical violence and lie about it, but she smiles at Christian. This smile could perhaps be seen as showing her exasperation—a sarcastic smile at his obvious falsehood. However, a few moments later, when another, uninvolved student interrupts this tense situation to point out that Joseph should look directly at Christian while apologizing, the teacher laughs.

Her laughter is followed by one of Doyle's brilliant, simple touches: "This surprises Joseph." This little, three-word sentence draws particular attention to the teacher's reaction, which also likely surprises the reader. It seems more likely that such an interruption would irritate her. Instead, she laughs and then admits that the interrupting student is right. This is where the teacher shows that she is better at her job than her classroom-management skills up to this point might suggest—she sees an opportunity to teach a lesson and to foster a better relationship within her class and takes time to try to do it correctly. She does not want Joseph and Christian at each other's throats for the rest of the school year.

Joseph, however, surprises the teacher in turn. She assumes that Joseph was merely reacting to Christian's taunting. After Joseph apologizes, she tells Christian, "He didn't mean to hurt you." Then Joseph responds with "That is not correct." The teacher's reaction to Joseph's admission that he did indeed intend to hurt Christian is ambiguous. She is obviously upset: her face turns "extremely red." Most of the students assume that she is angry at Joseph. One says, "He's in for it now." The teacher tells

WHAT DO I READ NEXT?

- Kimberly Newton Fusco's young-adult novel *Beholding Bee* (2013) tells the story of an orphan girl, Bee, who travels with a carnival, living on the edge of society. She feels even more like an outsider because of a birthmark on her face, which other children tease her about mercilessly. The book explores some of the same themes that Doyle tackles in "New Boy": bullying, prejudice based on appearance, feeling like an outsider, and the strength of community.

- Auggie Pullman, the hero of R. J. Palacio's *Wonder* (2012), wants to fit in with the other kids. He has been homeschooled, and his first experience in a regular classroom is made all the more difficult by a physical deformity. Palacio explores the themes of bullying, identity, and prejudice in this fascinating young-adult novel.

- Like Joseph in "New Boy," Sarah Darer Littman's protagonist in *Life, After* (2010) loses a beloved family member to political violence. Her family then emigrates from Argentina to the United States, where the young girl must learn to cope with a new home, a new school, a new language, and new problems. The novel is emotionally weighty, but Littman injects occasional humor as well.

- In *Integration and Social Cohesion in the Republic of Ireland* (2012), Bryan Fanning explores the recent wave of immigration to Ireland. Fanning has done extensive research, and the book provides a detailed portrait of immigrant life in Ireland, as well as discussions of politics, discrimination, and economic issues.

- Doyle's second short-fiction collection, *Bullfighting: Stories* (2011), shows the same talented ear for dialogue that has been praised by critics. The stories in *Bullfighting* are bittersweet, often dealing with themes of loss, but they also highlight Doyle's trademark sense of humor.

- Lila Quintero Weaver's *Darkroom: A Memoir in Black and White* (2012) describes her childhood in the 1960s. When Weaver was five years old, her family moved from Argentina to Marion, Alabama. While witnessing the turbulent events of the civil rights movement, Weaver struggled on a more personal level to find her place in the world as a Latina girl in the Deep South.

Joseph to get his bag, and the other students guess that she is going to kick him out of the class, but instead, she moves him to another seat. When Joseph looks at her, he does not seem to see anger there. She says, "We'll have to see about this," and Joseph thinks, "Her meaning is not clear."

It is not until Joseph and the teacher are talking during the little break, when all of the other students are outside, that more information emerges about what she might be thinking. The teacher tells Joseph that she knows a bit about his past, and one may assume that by this she means his father's murder and the violence in his village.

From this, we can see a possible explanation for her red face other than anger: perhaps she was embarrassed at being caught in a situation where she suddenly realized there was more going on than just schoolroom politics.

Up to that point, everyone has been treating Joseph as just another student. He is so quiet and polite that it would be easy to forget what he has gone through. Joseph has had experience with violence that the children in a Dublin suburb, even a habitual bully like Christian Kelly, have never known. The teacher realizes that she must make it clear that violent retaliation is not acceptable in the school, even when provoked, but she is kind to Joseph when she explains this. She recognizes that he is surely traumatized by what he experienced at home, likely still afraid of the things he saw, and harboring a lot of anger about his feelings of helplessness and loss. Violence means something different to him than to the other children and to her, and the conflict with Christian has forced the teacher to realize that she must pay more attention to this aspect of Joseph's past than his calm, courteous manner might at first suggest.

Perhaps the most telling moment about the teacher is the final scene in the story. In some ways, the scene is very funny. The teacher runs through all of her classroom tricks, shouting "Now!" and telling the students to put their hands in the air. Even her anger at Hazel's back talk is amusing—she is back to being the butt of the joke. However, unlike at the beginning of the story, a careful reader can see that here at the close, the teacher is well aware of what she is doing.

Clearly the teacher is conscious of the present shift in the boys' relationship, and she understands the significance of the moment. She recognizes that she is seeing the first indication that Joseph is truly interacting with his classmates, that he is something other than an outsider or a victim. She decides to protect Joseph's fragile new status in the complicated social structure of the class. This is illustrated by her unwillingness to listen to Hazel's tattletaling. Several times the teacher seems to appreciate being told what is going on because it helps her keep order in her classroom, but in this instance, she immediately sends Hazel back into the classroom.

It is particularly unfair that Hazel calls the teacher an unpleasant name when she is showing the most kindness of any character at any point in the story by not punishing the boys. If she listened to Hazel and if all of the students knew that she was aware of the fight, she would likely feel obligated to discipline them in some way. So she lets herself be laughed at, to be the bad guy. The teacher plays the role of the disapproving authority figure, which allows the boys to keep their common enemy and stay united.

Some reviewers have criticized Doyle for the endings of the tales in *The Deportees and Other Stories.* The critics say that while the stories worked in their original form—published serially in the newspaper—the resolution of the topics

raised in the stories seems too simplistic when gathered in a book. With the ending of "New Boy," one can see the point of these critiques. It seems unlikely that Joseph, Christian, and Seth will become fast friends because they giggle over their teacher's temper, quirks, and predictability. Will Christian stop bullying new students? Will Seth never again throw another student's book out the window? Will Joseph easily recover from his feelings of loss and anger over his father's death? This seems least likely of all. But does this make the ending false or superficial—too easy a fix for the serious issues the story hints at?

It does seem that the teacher hopes the boys will start to forge a friendship. She certainly nudges them in that direction, calling them "the three musketeers." With the story's final lines, Doyle seems to encourage the reader to think that this moment of unity might indeed be the beginning of a friendship, with the boys following one another back into the classroom. Doyle is too talented a writer to suggest that this one moment will be the end of prejudice against immigrants or bullying in school. But he can show that, with an everyday experience like this, Joseph is no longer set apart—he files back into the classroom between Christian and Seth, just another student in the class. Joseph's thoughts in their moment of silence explain it all: "They do not like one another but this does not matter." They have found a way to connect, however fragile, and that is a kind of progress.

Source: Kristen Sarlin Greenberg, Critical Essay on "New Boy," in *Short Stories for Students,* Gale, Cengage Learning, 2015.

Dermot McCarthy

In the following excerpt, McCarthy examines the themes of Irishness and nationalism in Doyle's work.

... The absence of explicit reference to matters of Irishness and Irish identity in Doyle's fiction until the explicitly anti-nationalistic *A Star Called Henry* situates Doyle's writing in the context of the "crisis of narratives" (McCarthy, 2000: 33) that has made Irish social, cultural, literary and political discourse over the past twenty years so lively. Along with writers like Dermot Bolger, Joseph O'Connor, and Fintan O'Toole, Doyle broke the quiet, stirred the pot, set in motion the dialogue in fiction and criticism about contemporary

The boys start to bond when their teacher scolds them for their behavior. *(© auremar / Shutterstock.com)*

Ireland, bursting the balloon, in a sense, of the hucksters and flunkies of "Ireland's ersatz modernity" (McCarthy, 2000: 18). Doyle's characters represent a class that feels no connection to the nationalist or colonialist versions of Ireland, Irish history, and Irish identity through which it is expected to see itself and understand its position in Irish society. If *The Commitments* (1987) did not begin the wave of new Irish writing in the late 1980s and early 1990s, a wave that was "characterised by an intense re-examination of what it might mean to be Irish in the late twentieth century" (Smyth, 1997: 66), it was part of the beginning and Doyle's novels and films since *The Commitments* have both reflected and contributed to the complex processes of socio-cultural introspection which have distinguished Irish writing and film in recent decades.

Joseph O'Connor offers an eloquent defence of Doyle's fiction (and implicitly of his own) when he asserts that "Naming the world ... describing it with faith and precision

and affection ... and in that process changing the world. Surely this is the real purpose of art, to change the world. But if you want to change the world, the first thing you do is change the way people see it. We really do need to do that in Ireland ..." (O'Connor, 1995: 141). This is what Gordan recognises when she begins her review of *The Woman Who Walked into Doors* by describing Doyle as the contemporary Irish novelist who has contributed "a new set of images for the Ireland of the late 20th century" (Gordan, 1996: 7). Doyle himself, however, seems uncomfortable discussing the political dimensions of his writing:

> I ... see myself as being socially committed and politically engaged—I always have done. At the same time, I would not inflict it on a writer. To me, one of the greatest enemies of writing is political correctness and it's only going to get worse, I suspect. It's the refusal to acknowledge satire. It's important to upset and outrage people. (Costello, 2001: 91)

"I do what I want to do. My novels come from within me" (Gerrard, 2001): thus Jimmy Rabbitte Jr and The Commitments may be a version of Paul Mercier or John Sutton and Passion Machine, but Jimmy is also a mask for Roddy Doyle.... Doyle belongs to a generation of writers that emerged from adolescence with an irreverent, sceptical, ironic attitude towards authority, institutions, traditions and conventions. The real critical issue is how Doyle relates to the new self-consciousness and self-interrogation of contemporary Ireland. A healthy democracy needs writers who question and satirise, but it also needs them to contribute constructive images of a renewed civil society to replace those that have been debunked and rejected. Does Doyle's fiction make a *positive* contribution to contemporary Ireland? If it helps to free it from the drag of the past, does it also help to move it forward?

O'Connor has summarised Irish critical response to Doyle's fiction as "snobbish, elitist and class-obsessed garbage":

> They say his work is clichéd and full of stereotypes. They says it's childish, moronic, sentimental, too full of dialogue, that it's mawkish and leans too heavily on a certain outmoded "gas" approach to Dublin life. They say— with some force—that if it had been written by an English writer, Doyle's work would be accused of being racist. (O'Connor, 1995: 139)

**WHETHER IT IS JAMES BROWN, MAN.
U, HOLLYWOOD FILMS OR AFRICAN REFUGEES,
DOYLE WRITES TOWARD A 'NEW IRELAND' THAT
WILL BE A SOCIETY AND CULTURE INCREASINGLY
OPEN TO ALTERITY, BUT MORE IMPORTANTLY,
LESS AND LESS THREATENED OR MADE
INSECURE BY DIFFERENCE."**

But for O'Connor, the point is that "it isn't written by an English writer. And surely Roddy Doyle is as entitled as any other Irish novelist to expose what he sees as the country's shortcomings in his own way, and on his own terms" (O'Connor, 1995: 139). Doyle's great value to his culture is the awkwardness and embarrassment he represents to those Irish who would rather appear to themselves and to the world in a different light altogether, and his writing does make a positive contribution to a new imagining of "Ireland" if, rather than focusing on Doyle's rejection of a traditional Irish nationalism and the narrow range of identity it validated (O'Mahony and Delanty, 1998: 181), we recognise his representation of the diversity of contemporary Irish society, not only in his representation of urban, working-class men and women but, most recently, of contemporary urban Ireland's changing racial composition.

Doyle describes the script for his recent film, the romantic comedy *When Brendan Met Trudy* (2000), as "portray[ing] the new multi-racial society we're living in"; likewise, in his recent children's books and short stories, "I bring black and white people together or Irish and Romanian. I get people to meet in the fictional sense and to come away knowing but not necessarily liking each other" (Costello, 2001: 92). This is a repetition in racial terms of what Doyle set out to achieve with his first five novels in class terms. Where his early career set out to bring into literary visibility the world and culture of the urban working-class, now he writes to acknowledge "the existence of these people and to make sure that visually they are

included and that eventually you can reach a point where you can like or dislike a person but the colour of the person won't matter" (Costello, 2001: 93); "Now I am writing about Nigerians and I am forcing Irish people to come up to Nigerians and to shake hands with them, their first black hand" (Costello, 2001: 97).

This new theme in Doyle's writing goes along with his active support of *Metro Éireann*, a Dublin-based multi-cultural newspaper started by two Nigerian journalists, Abel Ugba and Chinedu Onyejelem, in April 2000. Since May of that year Doyle has written three short stories for the paper: "Guess Who's Coming for the Dinner?," "The Deportees" and "57% Irish," all dealing with issues of race, ethnicity and identity. He has also served as patron and judge for its annual Media and Multiculturalism Awards. "Guess Who's Coming for the Dinner?" was also published as "The Dinner," in *The New Yorker*, and turned into a play which premiered at the Andrews Lane Theatre in Dublin in October 2001.

. . . Doyle seems liberated more than threatened by the possibilities of a postmodern, post-national "Ireland" and the basis of his security, like that of his aesthetic—and of his own personal identity—seems to be what the American poet, William Carlos Williams, called "a local pride" (Williams, 1963: 2) or what the Irish poet, Patrick Kavanagh, called "parochialism" (see Kavanagh, 1988: 204–6). Gerry Smyth understands the latter as "Kavanagh's solution to the aesthetic and personal dilemma caused by modern Ireland," and as what Kavanagh himself described as the need "to find some substitute for the national loyalty, some system to take the place of the enslaving State" (Smyth, 1998: 107). Doyle's Dublin-centred oeuvre represents his aesthetic and personal negotiation with late-twentieth-century Ireland, not only in the sense that it expresses *his* need to fill the vacuum caused by a discredited nationalism and disrespected State, but in the sense that it is a response to the crisis in urban identity caused by the blurring of urban-suburban distinctions with the growth of Dublin since the 1950s. Kevin Whelan has theorised an identity-crisis at the "townland" level in Ireland as a consequence of the challenge to regional "economic and social solidarity" that has ensued since EC membership: "The townland level is the 'neighbourhood level' or the practical farmland community size, which in the past shared farm work, tools, and equipment" (Jeffers, 2002: 14; see Whelan, 1993: 7–12). Perhaps Doyle's fiction—and that of others—should be read less in terms of the rural/urban, traditional/modern binaries in Irish discourse than in terms of an increasingly fractured urban identity which subsumes "old" and "new" within its own sense of a local history more central to its identity than the national story.

In 1962, Sean O'Faolain argued that "The lesson of our time is that Irish writers cannot any longer go on writing about Ireland, or for Ireland, within the narrow confines of the traditional Irish life-concept; it is too slack, too cosy, too evasive, too untense. They must, or perish as regionalists, take as writers everywhere do, the local (since they know its detail most intimately) and universalise it, as Joyce did" (O'Faolain, 1962: 746). Doyle's "local pride" or "parochialism," like Kavanagh's, is "a capacity to hold the local and the universal in fructifying tension" (Smyth, 1998: 108), but his aesthetic is perhaps better theorised as a literary form of what Kenneth Frampton, discussing postmodern architecture, has called "Critical Regionalism": "The fundamental strategy of Critical Regionalism is to mediate the impact of universal civilization with elements derived *indirectly* from the peculiarities of a particular place.... Critical Regionalism depends upon maintaining a high level of critical self-consciousness" (Frampton, 1983: 21). Doyle practises a form of literary critical regionalism in his co-option of American "soul" in *The Commitments*.

But more generally, his hallmark reliance on "Dub" dialect in his fiction is the keystone of a critical regionalism that mediates not only between "local" Irish and non-Irish cultural signifiers, but *within* the Irish national discourse, between his "local" north Dublin sense of place-identity and the Irish version of "standard" English that ghosts all Irish literary discourse. Furthermore, in this latter sense, it is important to recognise that the "mediation" that Doyle's use of dialect practises is itself "critical" of the homogenising, identity-subjecting drag not only of "standard" Irish English but also of the middle-class literary culture that regards such dialect as "infra dig."

Doyle has asserted that "I have no manifesto or agenda myself" (Paschel, 1998: 153) and has said he is "wary" of Ferdia MacAnna's

notion of a "Dublin Renaissance" because the writers MacAnna discusses "don't have much in common" (Paschel, 1998: 149; see also Sbrockey, 1999). Doyle has suggested that the 1990s saw "the beginning of something new" rather than a "renaissance" (Paschel, 1998: 149) and the critical regionalism that his work—as well as that of the Raven Arts writers and Passion Machine—represents, is perhaps better understood in terms of what Frampton theorises as an "*arrière-garde* position" rather than as the delusions of a *faux* or failed oppositional avant-garde (McCarthy, 2000: 135–64). Speaking in architectural terms, Frampton describes an "*arrière-garde* position" as

> one which distances itself equally from the Enlightenment myth of progress and from a reactionary, unrealistic impulse to return to the architectonic forms of the preindustrial past. A critical *arrière-garde* has to remove itself from both the optimization of advanced technology and the ever-present tendency to regress into nostalgic historicism or the glibly decorative.... Only an arrière-garde has the capacity to cultivate a resistant, identity-giving culture while at the same time having discreet recourse to universal technique. (Frampton, 1983: 20)

Doyle's novels and films of contemporary Ireland *do* "cultivate a resistant, identity-giving culture while at the same time having discreet recourse to universal technique" by giving expression to a distinctive and recognisably "Irish" experience, while also acknowledging that an important contributor to that experience is Ireland's participation in a postmodern global economy. Whether it is James Brown, Man. U, Hollywood films or African refugees, Doyle writes toward a "new Ireland" that will be a society and culture increasingly open to alterity, but more importantly, less and less threatened or made insecure by difference.

Doyle's openness reflects the security that his "local pride" instils in him. When asked if contemporary Ireland possesses a "soul," he replied: "my patch does. Having said that, I don't know what it is. When I walk around my patch, in north-east Finglas, I feel it. I hope it's not too bubble-like. I hope it's open to change and not a closed sealed community.... We are opening ourselves to different cultures. The possibilities are fantastic and I would like to think that these possibilities aren't just cultural but social too" (Costello, 2001: 98).

Doyle is, of course, in the middle of his career and any discussion of his work in relation to contemporary Ireland should end interrogatively, not conclusively. Will the rest of Doyle's career be as critically reflective of Ireland in the coming years as it has been of the Ireland of the past twenty years? Will "The Last Roundup"—the work-in-progress—achieve the coherence and scope of a major work of fiction? Will Doyle's recent turn to issues of race affect Henry's journey through America? In *A Star Called Henry*, by re-siting his signature themes of class and family in the sacred matter of nationalist Ireland, Doyle seems to posit that the roots of the contemporary malaises his earlier fiction explored are to be found in the birth of the "first" modern Ireland. The current pressures and strains on Irish society and culture are as much the continuing consequences of history as the supervention of completely novel issues. How the rest of the trilogy unfolds is crucial here because, depending on the upward or downward direction of the spiral form which the remaining novels will complete, an overall comic or tragic vision may emerge.

Dominic Head claims that in the second half of the twentieth century, the English social novel became "the privileged form of moral discourse in a secular world" (Head, 2002: 251). My reading of Doyle's work has been framed by the view that, by the end of the twentieth century in Ireland, the novel and film had become the most important forms of popular moral discourse in an increasingly secular Irish society and that Doyle played a major role in that development during the 1990s. For all their humour, Doyle's novels—like Graham Greene's, a writer he much admires—are seriously *moral* entertainments. At their deepest level of inspiration, they emerge from the passionate and optimistic commitment to human community that is Doyle's response to his profound sense that "we are on our own, but we are together. We sustain ourselves" (Costello, 2001: 99). If "The novel, with its imaginative range, and its freedom from 'factual' codes . . . [is] . . . an important focus for the society's alternative, redemptive, and connective thought" (Head, 2002: 251), one must hope that Roddy Doyle will continue to write novels that will focus, in such affective and provocative ways, the effects on individuals of the competing visions of an "Ireland" that can only ever be "new" to those who, like Doyle, are passionately committed to its moral and social well-being.

Source: Dermot McCarthy, "Conclusion: 'We Are on Our Own, but We Are Together. We Sustain Ourselves,'" in *Roddy Doyle: Raining on the Parade*, Liffey Press, 2003, pp. 228–32, 236–40.

Caramine White

In the following excerpt, White explains Doyle's popular and critical success and considers him "one of the world's best novelists."

Roddy Doyle is one of the brightest stars on the Irish literary scene today. His first six novels have all been well received, both critically and popularly. The literati have praised him: in his most signal accomplishment, Doyle won Britain's prestigious Booker Prize in 1993 for his fourth book, *Paddy Clarke Ha Ha Ha*—after *The Van*, his third novel, was short-listed for the prize in 1991. More generally, although he has on occasion been "condescended to as merely entertaining, just popular and funny" (Shepherd 1994, 164), the reviews of his work have been consistently good. He has been called "the laureate to a generation of thirty-somethings now ready to reconsider that experience [of growing up in Irish housing projects in the 1960s] . . . Doubtless, *Paddy Clarke* will soon be included on school syllabuses, as Salinger and Twain before it" (Kiberd 1994, 24). And Doyle keeps getting better: "Each novel bears distinct resemblance to but is arguably better than its predecessor" (Shepherd 1994, 163).

Doyle is also a commercial success. His first two novels have been turned into popular movies, and a film version of the third was completed in 1996. *Paddy Clarke* has become the biggest seller of all the Booker Prize winners and has been translated into at least nineteen languages. Although his next two novels, *The Woman Who Walked into Doors* and *A Star Called Henry*, have not won any awards thus far, they have been well received critically and have sold enormously well. His most recent four novels have also been made into books-on-tape. In acknowledgment of his popularity, in 1993 the BBC gave Doyle carte blanche to write something for television; he created *The Family*, a four-part miniseries about a family in turmoil, which was widely viewed and discussed by its Irish audience. Moreover, the author does not stand aloof: Doyle's earringed and bespectacled visage is seen on numerous Irish magazine covers, and he periodically makes the international talk show circuit. Stephen Frears, the director of the movie versions of *The*

> DOYLE'S ART SEEMS EFFORTLESS—THE
> DIALOGUE FLOWS EASILY—AND YET THE READER
> CAN SENSE HIS EARNESTNESS AND PERSONAL
> STRUGGLES."

Snapper and *The Van*, says of Doyle, "He's the only Irish writer I know of who's actually read by the kids he writes about in Dublin. You don't see them walking around with *Ulysses*" (Christon 1994, 5). In addition to his novels, Doyle has also written two plays: *Brownbread*, written and produced in 1987, a farcical comedy about three unemployed working-class youths who kidnap a bishop; and *War* (1989), a disturbingly dark comedy that counterpoints scenes in a pub (in which characters fiercely compete against each other in quizzes) and scenes of unhappy family life at the protagonist's home (see Doyle 1992). Both enjoyed local success and gave Doyle the reputation of being the most commercially successful playwright in Dublin since Sean O'Casey. Considering his popularity today, it seems almost absurd that he initially had to publish *The Commitments*, his first novel, at his own expense.

One key to the popularity of Doyle's novels can be found in their accessibility. He wants his work to be entertaining and readable: "Firstly, from my point of view, it's very important that they [his novels] be entertaining. We can talk then about what we mean by entertaining. I don't mean that it has to be escapist, though there's nothing wrong with escapism. A set of essays . . . is going to be entertaining, but not in the same way as *The Snapper*, but both have to be entertaining or no one will read them" (Fay 1993, 6). Doyle himself reads widely: "I don't see why I can't read Salman Rushdie's new work and Elmore Leonard's new work. I don't see any real difference, except that one's more self-consciously literary than the other. They're both good literature. . . . So I've never liked the division between the high and the low, between the literary and the popular." Doyle's own books are lively, realistic, engaging, and hilarious, featuring characters with whom one can

sympathize. Instead of the "thematic lumber which bolsters your average Booker winner" (Shone 1993, 48), Doyle provides for us simple, immediate themes couched in simple, immediate forms. He purposely avoids the multisyllabic vocabulary that appears in many canonized texts: "There's a school of writing which, though it may be unfair to summarize this way, has a lot to do with writers showing us how big their brains are. Like Anthony Burgess, who wants to show us that he has the biggest vocabulary in the world. . . . The type of writing I prefer is simple, straightforward and serves the characters. I like writers like Elmore Leonard, Anne Tyler, Raymond Carver and Richard Ford, where you tend to forget you're reading" (Christon 1994, F9). Doyle succeeds in achieving an unobtrusive literary style by using common, everyday language, which includes a great deal of profanity and slang, little description of any sort, and almost no authorial commentary—as he puts it, a "reflection of working-class life" (Fay 1993, 6).

Because Doyle's work is so popular and accessible, the inevitable debate over his value as a serious writer rages: "Why were the literary establishment so divided over Doyle? Elevated by some commentators as a social guru of enormous significance, other critics have objected to the unrelenting bad language which dominated the first three novels. Some questioned the authenticity of the life he described" (Battersby 1993, 10). Doyle has been accused "of playing up a professional Irishness for England and holding the Irish up to ridicule" (Bradshaw 1994, 129); according to one critic, "he simply serves up the foibles and patois of the working-classes for the patronising approval of the literary types" (Nolan 1991). Moreover, Doyle's craft has been disputed: "There's an over-reliance on incessant wise-cracking, funny incidents, and teed-up punchlines" (McFarlane 1991). Predictably, many people object to his profanity and refuse to read his work because of the frequent use of vulgar language: "[E]arthiness is a great tool to flush prudes, but too many sexual and scatological references can send the situation down into wearisome schoolboy vulgarity and a tool becomes a crutch" (ibid.). Doyle says he has been criticized for "the bad language in my books—that I've given a bad image of the country" (Turbide 1993, 50). His lack of descriptive writing has also received criticism: "No significant effort is expended on physical description of character or locale.... There were unkind thoughts that this department was being left to some cinematographer fellow in California with dark specs and a ponytail" (McFarlane 1991).

Stephen Frears counters: "Roddy's a deceptive writer. On the surface the work seems simple, but it's really very sophisticated, and very funny. He creates an entire world" (Christon 1994, F9). Doyle himself commented in 1996 that his works

> were on the list for books to be taught in schools, but they're off the list now because the Minister of Education decided they weren't literary. It's utter drivel... the idea that they are less literary because they use the vernacular—I don't agree. The decision to use the vernacular is a literary decision. The decision to use the word "f—" is a literary decision. It's a decision of rhythm... to use images from television instead of books, to use advertising jingles and such—it's a literary decision.

In this book, part of my aim will be to demonstrate that Doyle is indeed a serious artist. His novels are not simply entertaining, as a Brendan O'Carroll book is; although Doyle might cringe at my saying so, his works have literary merit and worth.

... Doyle is a wonderful writer who has the Dickensian gift of appealing to the uneducated and the educated alike. His novels, even at their most hilarious, contain serious messages. Doyle is as forgiving of his readers' limitations as he is of his characters' and does not demand that his readers spend as much time with his work as he has spent. Any reader will find humor, an engaging story, and the unforced exploration of important human issues. One can easily sympathize with his likable and realistic characters. Doyle's art seems effortless—the dialogue flows easily— and yet the reader can sense his earnestness and personal struggles. His work is extremely contemporary in its characters and situations, cutting-edge with its language, yet old-fashioned in its values and conclusions. At an early age, Doyle has become one of the world's best novelists.

Source: Caramine White, Introduction to *Reading Roddy Doyle*, Syracuse University Press, 2001, pp. 1–4, 23–24.

SOURCES

"About Roddy Doyle," Roddy Doyle website, http://www.roddydoyle.ie/?page_id=5 (accessed February 17, 2014).

Cionnaith, Fiachra, "One-in-Nine People Living in Ireland Were Born Abroad," in *Irish Examiner*, October 5, 2012, http://www.irishexaminer.com/ireland/one-in-nine-people-living-in-ireland-were-born-abroad-209895.html (accessed March 2, 2014).

Connolly, Cressida, "To Know Him Is to Love Him, Usually," in *Spectator*, Vol. 305, No. 9344, September 15, 2007, p. 51.

Deignan, Tom, "In Dublin's Fair City," in *America*, Vol. 198, No. 9, March 17, 2008, p. 35.

Doyle, Roddy, Foreword and "New Boy," in *The Deportees and Other Stories*, Viking, 2007, pp. xi, 78–99.

"Ireland," in *Worldmark Encyclopedia of the Nations*, 13th ed., edited by Timothy L. Gall and Derek M. Gleason, Gale, 2012.

"Is This Book Worth Getting? A No-Frills Guide to New Books by Writers Who've Won Big Awards in the Past," in *New York*, Vol. 41, No. 3, January 21, 2008, p. 94.

McCarthy, Dermot, "Chronology," in *Roddy Doyle: Raining on the Parade*, Liffey Press, 2003, pp. xiii–xvii.

"Overview: Fostering Integration in Ireland," United Nations High Commissioner for Refugees website, http://www.unhcr.ie/our-work-in-ireland/overview (accessed March 2, 2014).

Review of *The Deportees and Other Stories*, in *Kirkus Reviews*, October 1, 2007, https://www.kirkusreviews.com/book-reviews/roddy-doyle/the-deportees/ (accessed March 2, 2014).

Review of *The Deportees and Other Stories*, in *Publishers Weekly*, Vol. 254, No. 38, September 24, 2007, p. 41.

Russell, Helen, Emma Quinn, Rebecca King O'Riain, and Frances McGinnity, "The Experience of Discrimination in Ireland: Analysis of the QNHS Equality Module," Equal Authority and Economic and Social Research Institute, http://www.equality.ie/Files/The%20Experience%20of%20Discrimination%20in%20Ireland.pdf (accessed March 2, 2014).

Smith, Starr E., Review of *The Deportees and Other Stories*, in *Library Journal*, Vol. 132, No. 18, November 1, 2007, p. 62.

"Welcome to INIS—Irish Naturalisation & Immigration Service," Irish Naturalisation and Immigration Service website, http://www.inis.gov.ie/ (accessed March 2, 2014).

White, Caramine, Chronology and Introduction to *Reading Roddy Doyle*, Syracuse University Press, 2001, pp. xi–xiii, 3, 9.

FURTHER READING

Bazelon, Emily, *Sticks and Stones: Defeating the Culture of Bullying and Rediscovering the Power of Character and Empathy*, Random House, 2013.

In her *New York Times* best seller, Bazelon defines bullying and explains why intervention is essential. With deep research and through the stories of three teens, Bazelon shows the potentially serious effects of bullying, both personal and legal.

Cormier, Robert, *The Chocolate War*, Pantheon Books, 1974.

Considered by some to be the first true young-adult novel, *The Chocolate War* starts with a simple premise: boarding-school freshman Jerry refuses to participate in a fund-raising candy sale. His decision has dramatic results, however, when students and faculty take sides. Cormier's classic provides a realistic portrait of bullying in schools.

Doyle, Roddy, *The Barrytown Trilogy*, Penguin Books, 1995.

The Commitments, *The Snapper*, and *The Van*, the novels that made Doyle's reputation, were published in this single volume in 1995. Some of the characters who appear in the stories of *The Deportees and Other Stories* first appeared in this trilogy.

McCarthy, Dermot, "Introduction: Raining on the Parade, the 1990s, and the Myth of the 'New Ireland,'" in *Roddy Doyle: Raining on the Parade*, Liffey Press, 2003, pp. 1–20.

McCarthy's essay analyzes Doyle's writing in terms of style and intent. McCarthy also explores Doyle's depiction of Ireland, especially the people of Dublin.

SUGGESTED SEARCH TERMS

Roddy Doyle AND film

Roddy Doyle AND New Boy

Roddy Doyle AND Metro Eireann

Roddy Doyle AND Irish literature

Roddy Doyle AND The Deportees and Other Stories

contemporary Irish literature

Ireland AND immigration

Ireland AND discrimination

A River Runs through It

A River Runs through It, a novella by the American author Norman Maclean, originally appeared in his 1976 collection titled *A River Runs through It, and Other Stories*. (*Novella* is a term that resists precise definition; it refers imprecisely to a work of prose fiction longer than a short story but shorter than a typical novel.) The story is highly autobiographical and has many of the features of a memoir based on the author's experiences growing up and later working in Montana in the early decades of the twentieth century. At the same time, the work adopts some of the conventions of fiction, particularly by condensing the events of several summers into that of one year, 1937. What many observers see as remarkable is that Maclean wrote *A River Runs through It*, his first book and the only one published during his lifetime, after he turned seventy years old. In this regard, the narrator of the novella is to be regarded as an elderly man looking back on his life. Interestingly, the book was never advertised; it achieved almost cult status principally through word-of-mouth.

On the surface *A River Runs through It* is a story about fly fishing. Fly fishing, however, and the concept of a river running through the story are metaphors for a wide variety of themes, including brotherly love, friendship, family bonds, coming of age, the role of religion in a person's life, and the link between nature and human spirituality. The novella relies heavily on lyrical descriptions of the natural world,

NORMAN MACLEAN

1976

The story takes place in Montana in 1937. (© *Galyna Andrushko | Shutterstock.com*)

and its lovingly detailed descriptions of fly fishing, along with a highly regarded 1992 film version of the novella directed by Robert Redford and starring Brad Pitt, helped boost the popularity of the sport. At bottom, however, the novella is an elegy for Maclean's younger brother, Paul.

AUTHOR BIOGRAPHY

Norman Fitzroy Maclean was born on December 23, 1902, in Clarinda, Iowa, to a strict Scottish Presbyterian family. His father, a minister, was John Norman Maclean; his mother was Clara Davidson. In 1909 the family relocated to Missoula, Montana, where the Reverend Maclean was appointed pastor of the First Presbyterian Church. The elder Maclean, a strict disciplinarian, supervised the education of Norman and his brother, Paul, dividing each morning into three hour-long sessions, with emphasis on economy and precision in the use of the written language. During the afternoons,

Norman and Paul often went fishing and hunting or otherwise explored their western Montana surroundings. When Norman was ten years old, truant officers found him hunting and enrolled him in an elementary school. During his teenage years, Maclean worked for the U.S. Forest Service, an opportunity afforded him by the absence of so many men during World War I.

In 1920 Maclean traveled east to attend Dartmouth College, where he received a bachelor's degree with a major in English in 1924 (and where he took a writing seminar with the poet Robert Frost). In a historical footnote, he was succeeded as editor of the college's humor magazine, the *Dartmouth Jack-O-Lantern*, by Theodor Geisel, better known as Dr. Seuss. After two years as a teaching assistant at Dartmouth, Maclean returned to Montana to work for the US Forest Service. In 1928, he enrolled in the graduate program at the University of Chicago, and in 1931 he gained an appointment as an instructor at the university; that year, too, he married Jessie Burns. A key event in his life, one that figures prominently in *A River Runs through It*, was the murder of his brother, Paul, in an apparent robbery in a Chicago alley in 1938.

In 1940, "Bull" Maclean, as faculty and students called him, completed his doctorate at the University of Chicago, where he remained until his retirement in 1973. When World War II broke out, he declined a commission in the Office of Naval Intelligence, electing instead to remain at the university as dean of students, acting director of the university's Institute of Military Studies, and director of naval recruitment. Beginning in 1963, he was William Rainey Harper Professor of English at the university, where he taught primarily Shakespeare and the English Romantic poets and produced scholarly articles that were highly regarded, if small in number. During the summers, Maclean usually returned to Montana and his family's cabin on Seeley Lake. As of 2013, a hiking trail connecting Missoula and Seeley Lake, the Norman Maclean Trail, was almost complete.

It was only after his retirement that Maclean began to write fiction, claiming that he did so at the urging of his two children, who wanted to know what his life was like when he was young. *A River Runs through It, and Other Stories*, published in 1976, was the first—and for a long time, the only—work of original fiction ever published by the University of Chicago Press. In 1977 the book was short-listed for the Pulitzer Prize in Fiction. The selection committee recommended it as the winner, but the judges that year concluded that no work of fiction was worthy of the prize, so none was awarded. Interestingly, one New York publisher rejected the book because, according to Maclean in the acknowledgments to the book, "these stories have trees in them." Maclean obtained a measure of posthumous redemption when his *Young Men and Fire* won the National Book Critics Circle Award for Nonfiction in 1992. Maclean died on August 2, 1990, in the Hyde Park neighborhood of Chicago, of unspecified natural causes.

PLOT SUMMARY

A River Runs through It is not divided into chapters or parts but rather consists of a single uninterrupted narrative. It opens in Missoula, Montana, with the unnamed narrator commenting on his Scottish Presbyterian family, which includes his father, who is a minister,

MEDIA ADAPTATIONS

- In 1992, Columbia Pictures released a film version of *A River Runs through It* starring Craig Sheffer as Norman, Brad Pitt as Paul, and Tom Skerritt as the Reverend Maclean. The film was directed by Robert Redford and produced by Patrick Markey. Allied Filmmakers and Wildwood Enterprises were the production companies. Maclean cowrote the screenplay with Richard Friedenberg. The running time is 123 minutes.

- In 2010, HighBridge released an audiobook version of *A River Runs through It and Other Stories* read by David Manis. The running time is just over eight hours.

and his brother, Paul. He discusses the centrality of fly fishing to the men in the family. Given that the novella is based heavily on the author's life, it is reasonable to refer to the narrator as Norman, though only far into the novella is the name Maclean even mentioned. In particular here, Norman comments on the relationship between his father's Calvinist theology and the art of fly fishing. He also details some of the techniques of fly fishing, particularly the four-count rhythm of casting, and notes that he regards Paul as the better fisherman.

The narration evolves into discussion of the differences between the two brothers. Norman is the solid one, with goals and ambitions and with his feet on the ground; Paul is the reckless one, and the reader learns early on that he drinks to excess and likes to gamble and fight—although at the same time he is handsome and likable. During World War I, Norman worked for the U.S. Forest Service beginning at age fifteen; Paul, three years younger, remained at home. Norman notes that later Paul became a reporter for a newspaper in Helena, the capital of Montana. Norman describes a fight with his brother, which his mother had to break up.

The reader learns that events recorded to this point took place in the narrative past; the narrative present of the novella is the summer of 1937, when the boys are in their early thirties. Norman has since married Jessie and lives with his wife's family in Wolf Creek, Montana. Mention is made of his mother-in-law, Florence, and his wife's brother, Neal, who is described as a stylish, F. Scott Fitzgerald–like character who lives in California and earns Norman and Paul's scorn because he is a bait fisherman. The narrator describes a fishing trip he and Paul took on the Elkhorn River, affording him an opportunity to describe the geological history of the region and to provide further details about the art of fly fishing.

Indications that Paul is headed for trouble come when he is detained by the police for being drunk and for knocking teeth out of a man who insulted his girlfriend, a half Indian named Mo-nah-se-tah ("the young grass that shoots in the spring"). Neal arrives from California, and Norman takes him to a seedy bar called Black Jack's, where he describes some of the regulars, including Old Rawhide, described as a prostitute, and Long Bow, who tells tall tales about his ability as a hunter. Despite Neal's hangover, he, Paul, and Norman go fishing on the Elkhorn River the next day, although Neal insists on bait fishing. Norman uses the occasion to explain further details about the art of fly fishing. The outing ends with a heavy rainfall as the party returns home.

Norman and Paul take some time off to stay at the family cabin at Seeley Lake. Old Rawhide and Neal arrive, and Neal asks Norman and Paul to take him fishing. Norman breaks away and fishes by himself, providing an opportunity to comment further on the techniques of fly fishing, with emphasis on the flies themselves and on reading the water to find the best spot to fish. He reconnects with Paul, and on their way back to the car, they come across Neal and Old Rawhide asleep and sunbathing (and getting badly sunburned) in the nude apparently after having a sexual encounter. Norman and Paul return to town, where Old Rawhide bolts from the car and runs home while the boys take Neal home to be tended by Jessie, Florence, and Dorothy, who are angry at Norman and Paul for allowing Neal to get sunburned.

Norman and Paul agree to fish the Blackfoot again, but on the way they decide to stop in Missoula and visit their parents. Norman describes a fishing trip he and Paul take with their father the next day. Norman and his father watch as Paul demonstrates particular artistry in finding, hooking, and landing a big fish, the last one they would ever see him catch. The following May, Norman is awakened by a police officer and told that Paul has been beaten to death and his body dumped in an alley. He and the officer drive along the Blackfoot River to inform his parents. In subsequent years, Norman and his father do not talk of Paul, but Paul is always present in their conversations. Norman now indicates that he is old and not much of a fisherman, but he still finds meaning and understanding in the river, the rocks, and the four-count rhythm of fly fishing.

CHARACTERS

Dorothy

Dorothy is the wife of Kenny, Norman's brother-in-law. She is a nurse by profession.

Florence

Florence is Jessie's mother and therefore Norman's mother-in-law. She, Dorothy, and Jessie form a kind of chorus of tight-lipped Scottish women who look after the men in their lives and keep them on the straight and narrow but are kept apart from masculine activities.

Jessie

Jessie is Norman's wife.

Kenny

Kenny is Jessie's brother. He lives in Wolf Creek and is described as able to do anything with his hands.

Long Bow

Long Bow is the name of a seedy man Norman and Neal encounter in Black Jack's bar. The name is derived from the expression "he shoots a long bow," referring to the tendency to tell whoppers about one's hunting prowess.

Mr. Maclean

The narrator's father is of Scottish heritage and is a Presbyterian minister in Missoula, Montana. He is an avid fly fisherman, and like his sons, he has contempt for those who fish using bait. When his sons, Norman and Paul, are young, he educates them at home and teaches them to fly fish. He believes that the beauty and skill of fly fishing contribute to salvation and a oneness with the natural world. Like Norman, he loves Paul but does not entirely understand him or know how to help him.

Mrs. Maclean

The wife of the Reverend Maclean is the affectionate mother of Norman and Paul. She is described as a stereotypical Scottish woman who keeps her emotions under wraps. She tends to favor Paul, perhaps sensing that Paul needs her affection more than the steady Norman does.

Norman Maclean

The narrator of the novella, who can be thought of as Norman, functions primarily as an observer and reporter. Only later does the reader learn that he is narrating the events of his life up to and including 1937 from the perspective of old age. Norman is the son of a Scottish Presbyterian minister and his wife. He has spent virtually his entire life in Montana, close to nature and in tune with the rhythms of the rivers, where he fishes with his father and especially with his brother, Paul. Norman particularly admires his brother's artistry as a fly fisherman. He knows that his brother needs help with his addictions to alcohol and gambling, but he is uncertain how to provide that help. In the end, he feels as though he let his brother down by failing to provide the help Paul needed.

Paul Maclean

Paul is the narrator's younger brother. He becomes a writer-reporter for a newspaper in Helena, the capital of Montana. He is an expert fly fisherman, and Norman frequently comments on his skill and artistry in fishing Montana's rivers. At one point, Paul takes up with Mo-nah-se-tah, a half-Indian woman, and he gets himself into trouble with the police when he brutally punches a man he believes has insulted her. While Norman is the steady, reliable son, Paul is reckless and a bit of a prodigal—although he is also described as the "beautiful" son who wins love by who he is rather than what he does. Paul's alcoholism interferes with his life, he gambles, and he gets into fights; one scene depicts a fight he has with Norman. In the end, Paul is beaten to death in what appears to have been a robbery, or perhaps just an alley fight.

Mo-nah-se-tah

Mo-nah-se-tah is a half-Indian woman who lives on the outskirts of Helena, Montana. Early in the novella she is described as Paul's girlfriend. Her name means "the young grass that shoots in the spring." When she is insulted by a man they walk by in a café, Paul strikes him, knocking out a couple of his teeth. Mo-nah-se-tah is described as enjoying having men fight over her.

Neal

Neal is Norman's brother-in-law, the brother of his wife, Jessie. He lives in California and is described as stylish and not much of an outdoorsman. Norman and Paul hold him in contempt because he fishes with bait rather than flies. He dresses elegantly and fancies himself as resembling an international tennis star. He goes on fishing trips with Norman and Paul, but he is more of an impediment than a companion. Later in the novella, he goes fishing with the pair but ends up drinking their beer and sunbathing in the nude with Old Rawhide. Put simply, Neal violates all the codes of behavior, especially with regard to fishing, that Norman and Paul live by.

Old Rawhide

Old Rawhide is the name given to a woman whom Neal and Norman encounter at Black Jack's bar. She was a former trick horseback rider. She is referred to as a "whore," but implications are that she takes up with one man at a time (in the winter, at least). Norman and Paul spot her and Neal sleeping in the sun in the nude during a fishing trip. Along with Mo-nah-se-tah she represents a kind of threatening, potentially overpowering feminine principle.

THEMES

Family

A key theme in *A River Runs through It* is family and family relationships. The novella is not driven by plot; its parts are linked by the various fishing trips that the characters take and which establish the relationships between them. Beneath the concern with fishing is the fragility of family relationships, as Maclean explores the fears and hopes that the members of the extended Maclean family have for one

TOPICS FOR FURTHER STUDY

- Mark Isham composed the soundtrack for the 1992 film version of *A River Runs through It*. A remastered version, released by Milan Records in 2005, is available as an audio CD, and the individual songs are available as MP3 downloads. Procure the soundtrack and play selections from it for your classmates. In an oral report, describe how the music complements Maclean's story.

- A work that is often paired informally with *A River Runs through It* is Jim Harrison's *Legends of the Fall*, a novella first published in *Esquire* magazine in 1979. The pairing likely results from the fact that both works are set in Montana in the early twentieth century, and just two years after the film version of Maclean's story was released, Harrison's was also turned into a major motion picture—also starring Brad Pitt. Read *Legends of the Fall*, then prepare an oral report for your classmates indicating what the two works have in common and how they differ.

- Read Gary Paulson's 1997 young-adult novel *Grizzly*, part of his World of Adventure series. Write an essay in which you compare and contrast *Grizzly* and *A River Runs through It*, focusing on the vision of life in Montana created by the two authors.

- Investigate the history of Presbyterianism in North America. What were its origins? How did the religion find its way to Canada and the United States? What are its major doctrines? What does Presbyterianism have in common with Calvinism, and how might Calvinist doctrine have played a role in Maclean's life and thus in *A River Runs through It*? Summarize your findings in a written report.

- Investigate the geological history of western Montana, northern Idaho, and eastern Washington with emphasis on the geological events that shaped the landscape during the Pleistocene epoch some twelve thousand years ago. The Glacial Lake Missoula and the Ice Age Floods website (http://www.glaciallakemissoula.org/virtualtour/index.html) might be a good place to begin. Share the map at this site, or a similar one that you find, with your classmates using PowerPoint or a similar presentation application and explain how Maclean's description of the geology of the area is reflected by the map.

- Conduct research into relations with American Indians in Montana during the 1930s. What tribes were prevalent in the state? Where did they live? What impact might the 1934 Indian Reorganization Act have had on relations between whites and Indians in Montana? Present the results of your findings in a written report.

- Locate a copy of *Black Nature: Four Centuries of African American Nature Poetry* (2009), edited by Camille T. Dungy. Select one or more of the poems from the anthology that you believe bears themes or stylistic elements in common with *A River Runs through It*. Read a poem aloud to your classmates and be prepared to comment on how it might enrich a reader's understanding of Maclean's novella.

- If you fly fish, or if a member of your family or someone you know fly fishes, bring in tackle to display for your classmates. (Be sure your teacher supervises and that no one is injured by any of the gear, especially the hooks on the flies.) If you have expertise, show your classmates how a fly fisherman might tie his or her own flies. Weather and the school's landscape permitting, you might even take your classmates outdoors and demonstrate how a fly is cast. Explain to your classmates the difference between wet-fly fishing and dry-fly fishing.

another. The Reverend Maclean, for example, is motivated by a need to convey to his sons the divine spark to be gained through mastering the beauty, precision, and discipline of fly fishing. Norman's wife, Jessie, and his mother-in-law, Florence, are concerned about the welfare of Neal. Most important, however, is the relationship between Norman and Paul. Throughout, Norman ponders the extent to which he is his brother's keeper. At one point, he reflects: "I tried to find something I already knew about life that might help me reach out and touch my brother and get him to look at me and himself." Norman remains frustrated by his inability to do so, and he notes at one point:

> Sunrise is the time to feel that you will be able to find out how to help somebody close to you who you think needs help even if he doesn't think so. At sunrise everything is luminous but not clear.

Yet Norman remains troubled by his inability to extend to Paul the help he needs, and after Paul's death, he and his father wonder aloud to each other whether they could have done anything to save Paul.

Nature

A River Runs through It is set amid the natural beauty of western Montana, which is laced with rivers, streams, canyons, and ravines and which in many places is heavily forested. Through fishing expeditions on the rivers or just roaming the hills, the Maclean men establish a close bond with nature. The reverence they hold for the natural order is part and parcel of their religious convictions. This connection between nature and the divine is established in the novella's first sentence: "In our family, there was no clear line between religion and fly fishing." Later, Norman says this about his minister father: "My father was very sure about certain matters pertaining to the universe. To him, all good things—trout as well as eternal salvation—come by grace and grace comes by art and art does not come easy." Mastering the intricacies of fly fishing, the art of tying flies, and the obscurities of the rivers is a form of discipline that contributes to one's spiritual salvation. In contrast, a writer such as Izaak Walton (1593–1683), author of *The Compleat Angler* (1653), is not considered respectable because he was a bait fisherman (and an Episcopalian), that is, one who fished with worms, minnows, and the like as bait. In a similar vein, Neal earns the scorn of the Maclean brothers because

Norman takes Paul on a fishing trip to help him get back on the right track.

(© Russell Shively | Shutterstock.com)

he is a bait fisherman who has abandoned Montana for the artificialities of California.

As part of this abiding love of nature, Maclean provides the reader with information about the geological history of western Montana. Some twelve thousand years ago, during the Pleistocene epoch, western Montana, along with northern Idaho and eastern Washington, was covered by an immense glacial lake that quickly drained when the ice dam holding it in place broke. The river, then, not only runs through the lives of the characters but also runs through vast stretches of time. As Norman notes on the novella's final page,

> Eventually, all things merge into one, and a river runs through it. The river was cut by the world's great flood and runs over rocks from the basement of time. On some of the rocks are timeless raindrops. Under the rocks are the words, and some of the words are theirs."

Critics debate the antecedent of "theirs."

Addiction

The driving force behind *A River Runs through It* lies in Paul's various addictions. Paul is the reckless member of the family. He is not mean-spirited or unlikable—quite the contrary—but he is an alcoholic and a gambler, and he could be said to be addicted in a way to fighting. These vices interfere with his work and his personal life, but Norman and his parents are unsure how to help him overcome these addictions, and Paul refuses to ask for help. Ultimately, these weaknesses appear to lead to Paul's violent death, a death that is perhaps foreshadowed by the fights he gets into with his brother and with the man he believes has insulted his Indian girlfriend.

STYLE

Point of View

A River Runs through It is narrated in the first person by a man named Maclean, with a presumption that he is equivalent to the real-life Norman Maclean. Although Norman plays a prominent role in the novella, he does not function as a protagonist, or main character. Rather, he is more of an observer and reporter of events. Further, it becomes clear that he is reflecting on these events after the passage of many years. He quickly sums up his childhood with Paul in the opening pages, then zeroes in on the events of the summer of 1937 leading up to Paul's death in the spring of 1938. To the extent that the novella is based largely on fact, and given that the book was published in 1976, it is apparent that the narrator is in his seventies, providing a retrospective view of his early life. Norman is regarded as a reliable, trustworthy narrator whose observations and insights are to be taken as accurate, for he is open about his own fears and uncertainties.

Personification

One literary technique used frequently in *A River Runs through It* is personification, or the attribution of human characteristics to objects or abstractions. One example is Norman's personification of fear early in the novella, when he observes: "It is also interesting that thoughts about fishing are often carried on in dialogue form where Hope and Fear—or, many times, two Fears—try to outweigh each other." The narration continues by presenting this dialogue. Later, Norman personifies the Blackfoot River:

> The voices of the subterranean river in the shadows were different from the voices of the sunlit river ahead. In the shadows against the cliff the river was deep and engaged in profundities, circling back on itself now and then to say things over to be sure it had understood itself. But the river ahead came out into the sunny world like a chatterbox, doing its best to be friendly.

Symbolism

The central literary technique Maclean exploits in *A River Runs through It* is symbolism, particularly the symbolism of the river. Rivers dominate the landscape of the novella, from the second sentence—"We lived at the junction of great trout rivers in western Montana"—to the final sentence, "I am haunted by waters." Much of the power of the novella comes from the way Maclean describes the rivers and their effects on the humans who inhabit their environs. The river is associated with the flow of experience. Rivers can be dangerous and threatening, but they can also be a source of peace and restoration. Rivers, however, are inchoate; they can be hard to read. In this sense, the rivers become like the flow of words that the characters use to try to tame and make sense out of the flow of life and the tragedies that well up from it.

HISTORICAL CONTEXT

A River Runs through It makes no significant reference to historical events. Early in the novella, the narrator mentions that as a teenager he worked for the U.S. Forest Service because so many men were off fighting in World War I. But the bulk of the novella is set in the summer of 1937, when the United States was still mired in the Great Depression and the clouds of war were gathering over Europe and Asia. Maclean makes no reference to these developments.

Relevant to an understanding of the novella, however, are changes that were taking place in the state. Montana was at the time the nation's third-largest state, consisting of about 147,000 square miles; only Texas and California were larger. (Alaska became the largest state when it was admitted to the nation in 1959.) During the late 1930s, the state's population was sparse, with about 3.7 people per

COMPARE
&
CONTRAST

- **1937:** During Maclean's lifetime to this point, the population of Montana has grown from about 240,000 to roughly 550,000.

  1976: The population of Montana continues to grow and is more than 700,000.

  Today: The population of Montana has grown to just over one million, contributing to the westward shift of the mean center of population in the United States.

- **1937:** So-called pocket communities of "landless Indians" gather around Montana's cities, including Helena, during the early decades of the twentieth century; the state's Indian population is about 15,000.

  1976: Montana's Indian population stands at over 30,000.

Today: About 66,000 Montanans are Indians; a large majority live on the state's seven Indian reservations.

- **1937:** Early environmental movements in Montana focus on Yellowstone National Park, Glacier National Park, and the dangers of mining operations, including those conducted by the Anaconda Copper Mining Company; the New Deal's Civilian Conservation Corps carries out reforestation and fire-hazard reduction projects.

  1976: Montana's new constitution, created in 1972, guarantees environmental preservation and protection.

  Today: The Blackfoot River, featured prominently in *A River Runs through It*, is part of a major Superfund cleanup site because of pollution caused by the hard-rock mining industry.

---

square mile, compared to about 41.3 for the nation as a whole. Because people were so spread out, they regarded a hundred-mile drive to a neighboring town as unremarkable, particularly since after about 1925, the state was developing a network of modern roads, like those that the characters in *A River Runs through It* take in traveling back and forth between Missoula, Helena, and Wolf Creek.

Montana was seen as falling into two major portions. The western third of the state comprises the forested eastern ranges of the Rocky Mountains, including the Continental Divide, alluded to in Maclean's novella. Its geological history created large numbers of lakes, rivers, and streams. The eastern two-thirds of the state are flatter. Western Montana's economy was driven by logging, minerals, and hard-rock mining (particularly for copper and, in earlier generations, gold), and the economy of eastern Montana was driven by agriculture, although agriculture was significant in western Montana as well. But western Montana was where people

took vacations, often to fish. Many regarded semiarid eastern Montana as somewhat drab and colorless, with nothing but wheat farms and stubble fields. As the state grew and its population increased, people such as the Macleans might have felt that their idyllic world was disappearing under the onslaught of modernity. Maclean hints at this sense of change when Norman and Paul catch Neal and Old Rawhide sunbathing in the nude: "If you tried something like that on the Blackfoot River these days, half the city of Great Falls would be standing on the shore waiting to steal your clothes when you went to sleep."

Because of the state's immensity, bigger became better. Montana was dominated by big farms and big mining operations. Exploiting the economic opportunities of the state, its population more than doubled during the early decades of Maclean's life. During the 1930s, farming operations became more mechanized. Meanwhile, the tourist trade and dude-ranch operations were expanding, making the state in many

The story is ostensibly about fishing and the beauty of nature, but also explores some of life's deep questions. (© *Sandra Cunningham / Shutterstock.com*)

respects a recreational playground. While Helena, the state capital, was dominated by politics, cities such as Missoula, Great Falls, and Billings were agricultural centers, and Butte was the center of the state's mining operations, although in time much of that mining would cease and attention would turn to environmental cleanup. During the 1930s, the state retained its reputation as part of the Wild West and as a cultural backwater, but the University of Montana tried to change that image by publishing *Frontier and Midland*, a journal of regional literature that fostered writing by Northwest authors, including Montanans such as Maclean.

CRITICAL OVERVIEW

Since its publication in 1976, *A River Runs through It* has achieved almost cult status and is widely regarded as a minor classic in American western fiction. Many critics have focused their attention on the artistry of the novella's prose. In

a review in *Sewanee Review*, George Core states: "Maclean incorporates strong dimensions of ritual (the rituals of nature and religion) into the story, and the rhythms of the natural world are embodied in the cadence of his prose." In a similar vein, John G. Cawelti, in a review published by the *New Republic*, observes:

> Underneath the richness of particular details, there runs a wise and compassionate understanding of life and art forged through a lifetime of experience and learning and embodied in a prose that is richly colloquial yet highly controlled and which sometimes rises to extraordinary eloquence.

Similarly, Walter Hesford, in *Rocky Mountain Review of Language and Literature*, describes the novella's "piscatory prose" (prose about fishing):

> It is a generous prose, one that reflects and fosters a love for its subject, one that will not be hurried as it circles toward the synthesis of contemplation and action, piety and practice, and beauty and power which...is the hallmark of genuine art and genuine religion.

In an article for *Western American Literature*, Harold P. Simonson examines the religious underpinnings of *A River Runs through It*. He observes that "somewhere deep in Paul's shadowy inner world is chaos that the four-count rhythm of casting has not disciplined, a hell that grace has not transformed." Simonson continues:

> Clearly, Paul lives in a world more profoundly fallen than that represented even by Neal's damned messiness. Confirmation of this fact comes in the manner of Paul's death . . . this, the death of a dry-fly fisherman whose rod was a wand of magical power and beauty, and who, when inhabiting this river-world, embodied laughter and discipline and joy.

Mary Clearman Blew focuses on the female characters in *A River Runs through It*. She concludes in "Mo-nah-se-tah, the Whore, and the Three Scottish Women":

> For Maclean, . . . drawing as he does from the powers of the trout rivers as well as those of blood and custom, the story is a fiction—that is, a story that is true, a way of understanding the truth.

Blew continues:

> And it is a comedy—a healing, a reconciliation, a wholeness achieved through the love of trout rivers and the love of family, an integration completed by the Northern Cheyenne girl, Old Rawhide, and the three Scottish women.

Still other critics have examined the mythic aspects of *A River Runs through It*. In an essay titled "On the Sublime and the Beautiful: Montana, Longinus, and Professor Norman Maclean," Glen A. Love explains:

> At least two sets of literary contrasts are at work . . . : the contrasts between West and East, country and city, nature and civilization on the one hand, and those between youth and age, heart and head, energy and wisdom, naïveté and tragic awareness on the other.

Love goes on to note that "Maclean's work gathers interest and complexity from another set of opposites, that is from the extremes of time which it encompasses." In "Casting Flies and Recasting Myths with Norman Maclean," Helen Lojek outlines the mythology that underlies the novella:

> There are, of course, several mythic American Wests. . . . But heroes in fictional portrayals of all of these Wests have generally shared a cluster of personal characteristics. Tight-lipped, powerful, independent loners governed by a "code" of fair but assertive behavior, they are uncomfortable with the structures and conventions of encroaching civilization.

Lojek concludes, "It is that category of western hero into which Maclean's brother Paul fits."

CRITICISM

Michael J. O'Neal

O'Neal holds a PhD in English. In the following essay, he examines the religious themes that underlie A River Runs through It.

Fly fishermen concern themselves with surfaces and depths. They know, or at least hope, that fish lurk in the depths of rivers and lakes. The goal of fly fishing is to persuade those wily fish to rise out of the depths to the water's surface. The art of fly fishing is the art of duping the fish with a fly that looks like food without scaring the fish off by revealing the line and leader.

A River Runs through It is a novella about surfaces and depths. On the surface, it seems to be largely about fly fishing, and in fact, the first review of the book was published in a fly-fishing magazine. Considerable attention is given to the art and techniques of fly fishing: the handling of the rod, the tying of flies of various sorts and sizes, the rhythm of casting, the adjustment of the cast when circumstances demand it, the reading of the water to find fish, and the techniques of hooking and reeling in a fish without losing it. But for many readers, fly fishing is really a symbol of a much deeper reality that Norman Maclean explores. In this sense, fly fishing is what literary scholars often refer to as an *objective correlative*, defined as an object, a situation, or a sequence of events that symbolizes or objectifies an emotion and is used in literature to evoke an emotional response in the reader.

That fly fishing is an objective correlative symbolizing religious or spiritual truth is established in the novella's first sentence: "In our family, there was no clear line between religion and fly fishing." The first paragraph goes on to note that the narrator's father was a Presbyterian minister who tied his own flies and "told us about Christ's disciples being fishermen, and we were left to assume, as my brother and I did, that all first-class fishermen on the Sea of

WHAT DO I READ NEXT?

- Maclean's *Young Men and Fire* (1992) tells the harrowing and tragic story of the Mann Gulch forest fire in Montana, where most of the members of an elite crew of US Forest Service firefighters lost their lives on August 5, 1949. The book won the National Book Critics Circle Award in 1992. The event is alluded to in *A River Runs through It*.

- The other two stories in the 1976 collection that includes *A River Runs through It* are "Logging and Pimping and 'Your Pal, Jim,'" which recounts Maclean's experiences in 1928 working as a logger for the Anaconda Company at a camp on the Blackfoot River, and "USFS 1919: The Ranger, the Cook, and a Hole in the Sky," which describes his experiences as a seventeen-year-old working for the US Forest Service in wilderness later added to the Clearwater National Forest. A twenty-fifth-anniversary edition of the collection was published in 2001.

- Izaak Walton's *The Compleat Angler* was first published in 1653. Like Maclean's novella, it is in large part a celebration of fishing. In the modern world, it continues to play a role in the debate between proponents of fly fishing and those who prefer natural bait such as worms and even frogs.

- One of the most famous novels about fishing is Ernest Hemingway's *The Old Man and the Sea* (1952), which tells the story of an aging fisherman who hooks and battles a giant marlin.

- A. B. Guthrie's novel *The Big Sky* (1947) survives as a chronicle of the settlement of the American West, prominently including Montana. The novel is the first in a series of six that Guthrie wrote dealing with the development of Montana.

- James Welch, a founding author of the Native American Renaissance, is the author of *The Death of Jim Loney* (1979), a tragic novel about a solitary, brooding Native American who lives on the margins of society near a small Montana town.

- Walter Dean Myers, a prominent author of young-adult fiction, is the author of *Autobiography of My Dead Brother* (2005), a novel about the blood-brother bond between two African American teens in contemporary Harlem, New York.

- David James Duncan is the author of *The River Why* (1983), a coming-of-age story narrated by Gus Orviston, who tires of the bickering between his bait-fishing mother and fly-fishing father and moves to a cabin in the hills, where he learns that fishing is not all that life has to offer.

- Tom Mulvaney is the editor of *Helena* (2008), an entry in the Postcard History series. The book reproduces numerous postcards with photographs of Montana from its early days. Readers can browse the collection and form a picture of the Montana in which Maclean grew up and lived.

- Some mystery surrounds the real-life death of Maclean's brother Paul. Martin J. Kidston discusses the mystery in "The Other Maclean," which was published by the *Missoulian* on July 16, 2000, and is available at http://missoulian.com/uncategorized/the-other-maclean/article_cf560cd6-1523-5985-99f0-e2138939c090.html.

Galilee were fly fishermen." The narration then immediately turns to the family's religious life: the father's Sunday-morning sermons as pastor of his church, the boys' participation in Christian Endeavor (an organization for Protestant youth), evening services, and study of *The Westminster Shorter Catechism*. The catechism is a series of 107 questions and answers first compiled in 1646 and 1647 by the Westminster Assembly, a synod formed to standardize

BY REVEREND MACLEAN'S LOGIC, PAUL'S

PERFECTION OF THE ART OF FLY FISHING LEADS

TO GRACE, WHICH IN TURN LEADS TO ETERNAL

SALVATION. PAUL HAS LEARNED THE RHYTHMS

OF GOD, SO THE IMPLICATION IS THAT HE WILL

BE ABLE TO ENJOY GOD FOREVER, DESPITE THE

FLAWS IN HIS CHARACTER."

Presbyterian doctrine. The shorter catechism is a condensation of a longer work and was compiled for children and those of so-called weaker capacity. The most important of these questions and answers is the first, which teaches that the chief end of man is "to glorify God, and to enjoy Him forever."

When Norman begins to describe the principles of fly fishing, it is no accident that he begins by referring to his father as "a Scot and a Presbyterian." In this brief phrase, the author sums up hundreds of years of religious and cultural history. The Scots have historically been somewhat stereotyped as dour, thrifty, cautious, rugged, and detail oriented, but stereotype or not, these words describe the Reverend Maclean. The Presbyterian Church (or Church of Scotland) places considerable emphasis on independence, individuality, and the virtues of education. As a product of the Protestant Reformation, the Presbyterian Church, along with Reverend Maclean, "believed that man by nature was a mess and had fallen from an original state of grace"—a central tenet articulated in *The Westminster Shorter Catechism*. Norman goes on to note that his father believed that "only by picking up God's rhythms were we able to regain power and beauty." Norman adds:

> So you too will have to approach the art [of fly fishing] Marine- and Presbyterian-style, and, if you have never picked up a fly rod before, you will soon find it factually and theologically true that man by nature is a damn mess.

The discussion of the theological underpinnings of fly fishing continues:

> Well, until man is redeemed he will always take a fly rod too far back, just as natural

man always overswings with an ax or golf club.... Then, since it is natural for man to try to attain power without recovering grace, he whips the line back and forth making it whistle each way.

Later, Norman sums up: "My father was very sure about certain matters pertaining to the universe. To him, all good things—trout as well as eternal salvation—come by grace and grace comes by art and art does not come easy." Note the distinctions between nature and art, between fallen man and redeemed man, between mess and discipline.

Within this spiritual and theological framework, the attention shifts to Paul and his relationship with his brother, Norman. Under conventional religious beliefs, perhaps, Norman, the steady, well-behaved brother, would achieve redemption through his actions. Paul, on the other hand, is the black sheep, the prodigal son of biblical tradition. He drinks to excess. He is addicted to gambling, and he would like to place bets on seemingly everything. He gets into fights. Ultimately, he meets an untimely end in an alley, and while the narration does not explain why he was beaten to death, the reader suspects that he ran afoul of gamblers, or perhaps he picked a drunken fight with the wrong person. Had he adopted a steadier, more disciplined life, showing the discipline he exemplified on the rivers, he would not have run afoul of a man with a revolver and would not have been killed.

Paul, however, is described as the "beautiful" son. A halo seems to surround him, and he is often seen as a prototypical western hero: tall, handsome, muscular, brave. The rod in his hand is like a magic wand. As can often be the case, his parents, especially his mother, seem to prefer him to his brother, perhaps believing that given his weaknesses, he needs a parent's love more than Norman does. Further, Paul is the better fly fisherman. He is the one who has perfected the art (although he announces late in the novella that he believes he needs three more summers to learn to think like a fish). By Reverend Maclean's logic, Paul's perfection of the art of fly fishing leads to grace, which in turn leads to eternal salvation. Paul has learned the rhythms of God, so the implication is that he will be able to enjoy God forever, despite the flaws in his character.

This belief is in keeping with the Calvinist doctrines that form the foundation of Presbyterianism.

One doctrine is the belief in total depravity, meaning that people have fallen from grace through original sin and are unable to save themselves from sin; bait fishermen, by the way, are irredeemably fallen in the Macleans' view. A second doctrine is unconditional election, meaning that God calls sinners to himself not on the basis of their acts or virtues but on the basis entirely of his mercy. A third is limited atonement, or the belief that Christ shed his blood to redeem only the elect. Finally, the doctrine of irresistible grace means that people are unable to resist the grace that God provides to produce faith. Although *A River Runs through It* does not explicitly outline these theological principles, they are implicit in the reader's sense that Paul, despite his manifest failings, despite being fallen, achieves grace and therefore salvation, and his skill as a fly fisherman is a reflection of this achievement. On the waters of the rivers, he is baptized and thus a recipient of God's grace.

Near the end of the novella, one final fishing scene is depicted. Norman and Paul are paying a visit to their parents in Missoula. The next day, the three men take a fishing trip on the Blackfoot. After he catches his limit, Norman joins his father, who is on the riverbank reading his New Testament. Norman catches a glimpse of the open Bible and concludes that what he sees is the beginning of the Gospel of John, which says, "In the beginning was the Word, and the Word was with God, and the Word was God." Immediately, a connection is established between creation, God, and the words that reflect Norman's struggle to capture the essence of Paul. As the scene progresses, Norman and his father watch Paul, who suddenly is referred to as "the man," suggesting that he is now not simply Paul but a representative of all fallen humans who can experience God's grace. During this extended scene, Paul exhibits particular skill and artistry. He makes difficult casts and expertly lands a fish. Tellingly, Norman remarks that this was the last fish they ever saw him catch and that "we never saw the fish but only the artistry of the fisherman." Just pages later, Paul has been murdered. Paul, the reader suspects, has achieved a kind of apotheosis, an ascent to a spiritual realm, where his grace and skill earn him salvation in the eyes of the reader, his parents, and his brother.

" I THINK THAT PARAGRAPHS SHOULD HAVE A LITTLE PLOT, SHOULD LEAD YOU INTO SOMETHING STRANGE AND DIFFERENT, TIE THE KNOT IN THE MIDDLE, AND AT THE END DO A LITTLE SURPRISE AND THEN ALSO PREPARE YOU FOR THE NEXT PARAGRAPH."

Source: Michael J. O'Neal, Critical Essay on "A River Runs through It," in *Short Stories for Students*, Gale, Cengage Learning, 2015.

Nicholas O'Connell

In the following interview excerpt, Maclean discusses fly fishing and how he learned to tell stories.

When did you start fly-fishing?

I was about six when we came to Montana, and almost immediately we started going on these vacations and my father started teaching me to fly-fish. My father was a Presbyterian minister and always had at least a month off in the summer. We would camp out for a month on some big river, the Bitterroot or the Blackfoot.

Do you still fly-fish?

No, I don't. I hope that's a temporary answer. A couple of years ago I hurt my hip and I haven't been able to work very well since then. I quit fishing but I'm getting better. I hope I'll still be able to fish a little before I quit for good. It's hard though. I don't think I'll ever be very good at it again. I've lost my sense of balance, and I can't stand up on those big rocks and I can't fish that big hard water. And that's the only fishing I like to do, fishing the big rivers. If you want big fish, you fish big water.

I miss it a lot. I suppose I get some second-hand pleasure by writing about it.

What has fly-fishing taught you about the nature of grace?

It's taught me many, many things about grace. I think it's one of the most graceful things an individual can do out in the woods.

It's a very difficult art to master. My father thought it had the grace of eternal salvation in it.

In "A River Runs Through It," you wrote, "Good things come by grace, grace comes by art and art does not come easy." Is that true of writing?

Oh, yes. It's conceivable that someone could find it smirky and pleasurable on some kind of level, but I think it's a highly disciplined art. It's costly. You have to give up a lot of yourself to do it well. It's like anything you do that's rather beautiful. Of course some people can do it seemingly by genes and birth, but I don't think nearly as often as one would think. I think it always entails terrific self-discipline.

Why did you start writing fiction so late in life?

I can't answer that, but I'll make a couple of stabs. There will be a certain amount of truth to them, but no one ever knows why he tries something big in life.

One stab is that in the literary profession, which was my life profession, it was always said that no one began serious writing late in life. That was kind of a challenge. I thought, "As soon as I retire, I've got some serious things I'd like to write, and I think I know enough about writing to do them well. We'll see how they come out."

Just the fact that you would ask me such a question is part of the reason why I started. I wanted to answer it. But it must have been deeper than just showing off.

When you teach literature, you're so close to it, and yet in some ways so far. If you don't have a lot of extra energy, you don't have time to do what a lot of teachers claim they always want to do but seldom do, and that is both write and teach. I suppose I said it too, but being Scotch I was thick-headed and so I tried it.

It's very costly to start writing when you're so old as I am. You don't have any of the daily discipline built up. Some writers get up every morning and it's like shaving to them. They can do it without thinking.

In "A River Runs Through It," you talked about God's rhythms. I wondered what you meant by that.

One of my fascinations about my own life is that every now and then I see a thing that

unravels as if an artist had made it. It has a beautiful design and shape and rhythm. I don't go so far as some of my friends, who think that their whole life has been one great design. When I look back on my life I don't see it as a design to an end. What I do see is that in my life there have been a fair number of moments which appear almost as if an artist had made them. Wordsworth, who affected me a great deal, had this theory about what he calls "spots of time" that seem almost divinely shaped. When I look back on my own life, it is a series of very disconnected spots of time. My stories are those spots of time.

Did you feel a real need to write about these spots of time?

I've given up everything to write them. I'm now getting so old I don't know whether I can write much more. I knew when I started, of course, that starting so late I wouldn't get much done, but I hoped to get a few things done very well. It's been very costly, though, and I don't know whether I would recommend it. I've sacrificed friends. I've lived alone. I work on a seven-day-a-week schedule. I get up at six or six-thirty every morning. I don't even go fishing up here any more.

When you're this old, you can't rely on genius pure and undefiled. You've got to introduce the advantages of being old and knowing how to be self-disciplined. You can do a lot of things because you can do what the young can't do, you can make yourself do it. And not only today or tomorrow, but for as long as it takes to do it. So it's a substitute, alas maybe not a very good one, for youth and genius and pure gift. And it can do a lot of things, but it's very, very costly. Sometimes I wish that when I retired I'd just gone off to Alaska or Scotland and played croquet on the lawn.

Do you want to write many other things?

I'm too realistic to entertain such thoughts. Even when I began, which was right after I retired, I knew I could never become a great writer, if for no other reason than I didn't have time. When I started, I agreed to myself that I would consider I'd accomplished my mission if I wrote several substantial things well. And I haven't lost that sense of reality; in fact it deepens as I grow older and see I was right.

I am now trying to finish a second long story based upon a tragic forest fire. I've been on that for some years, and I hope within the next six or seven months to have it completed. But I have been hoping that for some years now. I'm being enticed into making a movie of "A River Runs Through It." If I do those two fairly big things, then I won't try anything very big again.

Do you write every morning?

I don't write every morning, but I keep my writing schedule. I'm the only one who keeps me alive now. I don't have a family living with me any more. I have two homes, here and Chicago. I have a lot of accounting and just plain housework to keep both those places going.

And even when you just make a small success, there are many people who want to see you. So I spend more time than I should seeing people and writing letters. I still go on four to six talking tours each year.

Your book has only three stories in it, but because they're so well written, it's made you more renowned than writers with four or five novels.

Yes, I would grant that, but there are probably a variety of reasons for that. To some at least, the book is a kind of model of how to begin a story and how to end a story, and it is taught as such. When people are good enough, they try to teach it as an example of prose rhythms. It has a special appeal to teachers of writing, and of course it has a great appeal to fly-fishermen, for many of the same reasons: it seems expert at what it is doing. I've had biologists write me and tell me it's the best manual on fly-fishing ever written.

Did you enjoy writing it?

I don't know how to answer that. Writing is painfully difficult at times, and other times I feel like I have a mastery over what I'm trying to do, and of course there's no greater pleasure than that. But when you feel that words still stand between you and what you want to say, then it's a very unhappy business.

Where did you learn to tell stories?

When I was young in the West, most of us thought we were storytellers. And of course we all worshipped Charlie Russell, partly for his painting, but also because he was a wonderful storyteller. I feel I learned as much about storytelling from him as I did from Mark Twain or Wordsworth or any professional writer. The

tradition behind that of course was the old cowboy tradition—coming into town with a paycheck, putting up in a hotel, and sitting around with a half a dozen other guys trying to out-tell each other in stories. Whoever was voted as telling the best story had all his expenses paid for the weekend.

The storytellers' tradition is a very, very deep one in the West. It probably doesn't exist very much any more, but then you don't have the great sources of stories. You don't have bunkhouses for loggers and cowpunchers any more. They live in town with families. They don't sit around at night and tell lies to each other. So part of it has been lost.

I learned as much, even technically, about storytelling from Charlie Russell's stories as I did, say, from Hemingway. He [Russell] was still alive and kicking until I was in my twenties. He was an idol of Montana, much more so than now. He's an idol now of course, too, but then we worshipped him, and with good cause. His stories are only two to ten pages long, but if you want to learn how to handle action economically and just have every sentence jumping with stuff, take a look at him. Marvelous storyteller.

A volume of his called *Trails Plowed Under* is just a miraculous piece of narration. Good title, isn't it? That title pervades not only his paintings, but all of his stories. All the time he was writing and painting he had this feeling that "the West that I knew is gone." There's always a nostalgia hanging over his paintings and stories.

When you were writing your stories, how did they change as you turned them into fiction?

They changed long before I started writing them. I'm not sure that after a few years I could tell what happened from what I say happened, which is fortunate if you want to be a storyteller. I had a drenching of storytelling in all the years when I was in the Forest Service and logging camps, and so it's easier for me to tell a story about what happened than telling it exactly as it happened. They became stories long before I told them.

Did you have to make them longer when you wrote them down?

No. From the time my father gave me my first lessons in writing to the end of my training in writing, I always had teachers whose chief criterion was literary economy—use of the fewest words possible.

When you were writing your stories, did you write them down all at once, or bit by bit?

I know pretty well ahead of time what I'm going to do in the whole story, and often I come home after going for a walk in the afternoon and take a bath before dinner; in the bathtub I sit in the hot water till it gets cool, trying to figure out what I'm going to write the next day. The next day I'm concerned with saying it. That's probably highly individual. A lot of guys when they sit down don't know where they're going. They even use the act of writing to make them find out what they're going to write about.

Do you work over the stuff that you've written a number of times?

Yes, three or four times.

Sentence by sentence, paragraph by paragraph?

I suppose so, but that would vary. I'm a great believer in the power of the paragraph. I can't say that I always write by paragraphs, but I often do. I think that paragraphs should have a little plot, should lead you into something strange and different, tie the knot in the middle, and at the end do a little surprise and then also prepare you for the next paragraph.

Why did you choose to write those particular stories?

The title story, "A River Runs Through It," was the big tragedy of our family, my brother's character and his death. He had a very loving family, but independent and fighters. We were guys who, since the world was hostile to us, depended heavily upon the support and the love of our family. That tends often to be the case with guys that live a hostile life outside.

There was our family which meant so much to us, and there was my brother who was a street fighter, a tough guy who lived outside the mores of a preacher's family. We all loved him and stood by him, but we couldn't help him. We tried but we couldn't. There were times when we didn't know whether he needed help. That was all and he was killed. I slowly came to feel that it would never end for me unless I wrote it.

The others? Well, they're all spots of time. Spots of time become my stories. You get that very openly in the Forest Service story. That's

the plot. They go out and it's spring, and the things that they do and their order are determined by the job. There's no human preference indicated. The first thing you did was clear out the trails from the winter, dead trees and all that fallen-down stuff. Then you made some new trails, then pretty soon fire season came and you fought fires. It was determined by the seasons and the nature of the job.

The plot starts that way and then things begin to happen in such a way that human decisions are determining and changing this natural order of things. It's the change in the causes that order the events which is the story.

I'd had a good training when I was young in the woods. My father didn't allow me to go to school, kept me home for many years until the juvenile officers got me, and as a result I had to work in the morning, but the afternoons were mine. All the guys my age were in school, so I went out in the woods alone. I became very good in the woods when I was very young. I trained myself, both in the logging camps and in the sawmills. I was going to know the wood business from the woods to board feet.

When World War I came along they were looking for young guys or old men to take the place of the foresters who were getting grabbed up as soldiers. So I was in the Forest Service when I was fourteen. And it became a very important part of my life. I almost went into it; I thought until I was almost thirty that I was going to go into the Forest Service as a life profession.

All these things are important to me: my family, the years I spent in the logging camps, the years I spent in the Forest Service.

Why are these stories about your life in Montana, rather than about teaching in Chicago?

I've written many things about Chicago and teaching, some of my best things in articles, stories, talks, discussions about teaching. I wrote a story about Albert Michelson, who measured the speed of light and was the first American scientist to win the Nobel Prize. Strangely, when I was quite young I came to know him intimately. I was just a kid from Montana, a half-assed graduate student and teacher in English, and I was knocking around with this guy who was regarded as one of our two greatest scientists (Einstein being the other). Now I suppose Nobel Prize winners are a dime a dozen, but in those days we had only two in the whole country; he was one of them, and Theodore Roosevelt was the other. I was very touched, as a young boy from Montana, to be trusted with the acquaintanceship of such an outstanding, strange and gifted man. I think my story about him is one of the best things I ever wrote....

Source: Nicholas O'Connell, "Interview with Norman Maclean," in *The Norman Maclean Reader*, edited by O. Alan Weltzien, University of Chicago Press, 2008, pp. 166–72.

Harold P. Simonson

In the following excerpt, Simonson examines religious themes in Maclean's work.

...Norman Maclean, the third Montana regionalist, makes religion an explicit component in his novella, *A River Runs Through It* (1976). Although sharing with Ivan Doig and James Welch a regional consciousness, best described as psychological (thus giving personal meaning to a sense of place), Maclean uses orthodox Christian theology to add typological dimension as well. To say this does not imply that Doig and Welch lack spiritual perceptiveness; Doig is broadly humanistic in his, Welch is tribal and cultural. But the challenge Maclean poses is a regional consciousness that combines Judeo-Christian and mythical perspectives, the one affirming a God of history and the other venerating a gentle paganism with its celebration of soil, fertility, vegetation and the seasons. Through these perspectives Maclean discerns places—specifically Montana's Big Blackfoot River—as charged with special sacredness. Moreover, he uses the New Testament concept of *caritas* to bring out this same quality in human beings. The river is not only a place where he once fished with his beloved father and brother, but a place where boredom, cynicism, anxiety and the world's horror give way to the transcendent magnificence toward which the river as both symbol and type flows.

Thus on a level that is only implicit in Welch and even less suggestive in Doig, Maclean addresses questions that twentieth-century literature asks with special urgency. Critic Lionel Trilling writes, "It asks us if we are content with ourselves, if we are saved or damned—more than anything else, our literature is concerned with salvation." Trilling cites such writers as Yeats and Eliot, Joyce, Proust and Kafka, Lawrence, Mann, and Gide. The

> IN TRUTH, THE MONTANA RIVER RUNS THROUGH HIS MIND AND CONSCIOUSNESS, LANGUAGE AND LIFE. BUT SOMETHING ALSO RUNS THROUGH THE RIVER ITSELF, SOMETHING THAT IS IN IT BUT NOT OF IT, SOMETHING MORE ELEMENTAL THAN WATER."

point, says Trilling, is not that these writers are "actually religious," but that they manifest a "special intensity of concern with the spiritual life which Hegel noted when he spoke of the great modern phenomenon of the secularization of spirituality." What Havre is for Welch, Helena is for Maclean—a world not only messy and corrupt but damned, totally secularized. The distance from this world to that of the Big Blackfoot River is the journey Maclean's narrator takes. For the author himself, an emeritus professor of English at the University of Chicago, the novella evokes the home he once left and has returned to.

"In our family, there was no clear line between religion and fly fishing." The analogy Maclean creates in this arresting opening sentence takes on intriguing resonances that include the questions Trilling names, and leaves the reader sharing the feeling expressed in the novella's closing sentence: "I am haunted by waters."

Christ's disciples were fishermen, those on the Sea of Galilee were *fly* fishermen, and Maclean's favorite, John, had to be a *dry-fly* fisherman. This was the logic Maclean as a boy learned from his father's Presbyterian sermons. Yet for all the sermons preached and heard, and all the hours the boy and his brother Paul studied *The Westminster Shorter Catechism*, what really restored their souls, including that of their clergyman father, was to be in the western Montana hills where trout rivers run deep and fast. Ernest Hemingway had said in "Big Two-Hearted River" that swamp fishing was a "tragic adventure"; for Maclean, fishing the Big Blackfoot River was a redemptive one, thanks not only to divine grace but to self-discipline. The theology is sound Calvinism: God does all, man does all.

As for human nature, theologically speaking, just try to use a fly rod for the first time and, says the author, "you will soon find it factually and theologically true that man by nature is a damned mess." Again, Calvin couldn't have said it better. Only the "redeemed" know how to use it. Until such a time, a person "will always take a fly rod too far back, just as natural man always overswings with an ax or golf club and loses all his power somewhere in the air." Natural man does everything wrong; he has fallen from an original state of harmony. And he will continue to be a mess until through grace and discipline he learns to cast "Presbyterian-style." The great lesson the father taught his two sons was that "all good things—trout as well as eternal salvation—come by grace and grace comes by art and art does not come easy."

All this theological business is not as heavy-handed as it sounds. Indeed, Maclean transforms it into characterization, metaphor, humor and fine detail. He also transforms memories of his father and brother into Rembrandt portraiture edged in darkness and tragedy but also pervaded by the light of a haunting presence, a prelapsarian truth associated with sacred origins, the divine *logos*. Maclean would have us see fishing as a rite, an entry into "oceanic" meanings and eternities compressed into moments, epiphanous "spots of time," the *mysterium tremendum*. Entering the river to fish its dangerous waters is to fish eternity and to unite in love with those few persons who also obey the exacting code. None obeyed the code more religiously than brother Paul who, when entering the river, made fishing into a world perfect and apart, a place where joy comes first in a perfect cast, then in a strike that makes the magic "wand" jump convulsively, and finally in a big rainbow trout in the basket—in all, a performance of mastery and art.

Narrator Maclean remembers his brother Paul as a master dry-fly fisherman, indeed as a true artist when holding a four-and-a-half-ounce rod in his hand. But more, Paul was one for whom the river in its sacrality held answers to questions, and for whom fly fishing was the search for those answers. That, Paul said, was what fly fishing was, and "you can't catch fish if you don't dare go where they are." Paul dared, and he showed his brother and his Presbyterian father, both expert fishermen too, how to dare. On what was to be their last fishing trip together, before Paul's murder and the father's later death, all things seemed to come together—the river, the fishing, the father and two sons. Sinewing the union was love, and in the union the powerful Big Blackfoot River spoke to them. It is truly a redemptive moment, caught and held secure in Maclean's memory and in his narrative art. The story is equal to anything in Hemingway and a good deal more courageous theologically.

Support for this assertion needs to include Maclean's theological doctrine of man. Maclean says that man is a "damned mess." Maclean's courage comes not in asserting this doctrine, which Hemingway, Mark Twain and number-less other writers have had no trouble with, but in juxtaposing it with a doctrine of salvation. Without the juxtaposition, damnation is no less a bromide than is salvation. The courage comes in one's affirming a larger context of reality in which the juxtaposition both is and is not reconciled. To change the image, we might imagine a world where a river runs *through* it but is not *of* it. The test of courage is to embrace the paradox.

As for the messiness unto damnation, Maclean's story does not equivocate. The world is a fallen one, people are liars and cheats, family entanglements ruin the most blessed vision. When the narrator's brother-in-law steps off the train at Wolf Creek, we see Neal, genus *phonus bolonus*, dressed in white flannels, a red, white and blue V-necked sweater over a red, white and blue turtleneck sweater, and elegant black and white shoes. At Black Jack's Bar his big talk with oldtimers and the town whore, Old Raw-hide, shows him in his true element. The family picnic the following day on the Elkhorn River shows him disgustingly out of it. He fishes not with flies but worms and gets nothing; he whimpers from his hangover and feigns sickness to avoid picnic chores. A genuine bastard, he deserves neither solicitude nor Montana. Neal violates everything that is good, including the code of fishing. On a subsequent trip he violates a trust by stealing beer that the brothers have left to cool in the river—and in *this* the Big Blackfoot River. Even worse, he has brought not only a coffee can of worms for bait but also Old Raw-hide, and has "screwed" his whore on a sand bar in the middle of "our family river." The brothers find the two asleep, naked and sunburned. On the cheeks of her derriere they see the tattooed letters: LOVE. The river sanctuary has been defiled; never again will the brothers throw a line here at this hole.

Close as narrator Maclean appears to be to his brother Paul—both reverencing the river whose secrets only the best dry-fly fishermen can hope to touch—a vast gulf nevertheless separates them. If they both find the river an enigma where answers lie hidden in watery shadows, the narrator finds his brother an enigma as well.

That Paul seeks answers in fishing leaves his brother wondering about the questions being asked. Somewhere deep in Paul's shadowy inner world is chaos that the four-count rhythm of casting has not disciplined, a hell that grace has not transformed. Yet Paul seeks no help either from brother or father. Only the visible things show—namely, that he drinks and gambles and fights too much, that gambling debts translate into enemies, that his job as reporter on a Helena newspaper confirms a world full of bastards, and, finally, that he wants no help, asks for none, expects none except what the hard-driving river can bring. Clearly, Paul lives in a world more profoundly fallen than that represented even by Neal's damned messiness. Confirmation of this fact comes in the manner of Paul's death: beaten with the butt of a revolver, nearly all the bones of his right hand (his fighting hand) broken, and his body dumped in an alley—this, the death of a dry-fly fisherman whose rod was a wand of magical power and beauty, and who, when inhabiting this river-world, embodied laughter and discipline and joy.

Wherein, then, is saving grace? In the water? In the words that the father reads in his Greek New Testament? In the Word (the *logos*) from the Fourth Gospel that the father seeks to interpret as the two of them, father and son, wait on the riverbank to watch Paul catch his final big fish? "In the part I was reading," the father explains, "it says the Word was in the beginning, and that's right. I used to think water was first, but if you listen carefully you will hear that the words are underneath the water."

Now comes the crucial distinction.

"If you ask Paul," the son says, "he will tell you that the words are formed out of water."

"No," the father replies, "you are not listening carefully. The water runs over the words. Paul will tell you the same thing."

Of course, Paul never tells, and we suspect he has never found out. Neither his brother nor his father knows the truth about him. Yet the distinction deserves close attention together with the images that Maclean allows to arise from his memory, images that come out of the past to bear new meanings, joining the past and the present in the image and the image bearing the truth.

Watery images bring forth fish seen sometimes as "oceanic," with their black spots resembling crustaceans. The river itself flows from origins shaped by the ice age, the rocks by more elemental forces emanating "almost from the basement of the world and time." The rain is the same as "the ancient rain spattering on mud before it became rock...nearly a billion years ago." Whereas in the sunny world where the river-voice is "like a chatterbox, doing its best to be friendly," in the dark shadows where the river "was deep and engaged in profundities" and where it circled back on itself now and then "to say things over to be sure it had understood itself"—in these primal depths the voice issues from a "subterranean river" where only the most courageous ever venture and where only *real* fishing takes place.

Through such imagery Maclean takes us to foundations antecedent to water. From these foundations the father in the narrative hears words—words beneath the water, words before the water. The distinction between words formed out of water and words formed out of foundations beneath the water is the distinction between mystical pantheism and the Christian *logos*. The distinction is between the *unity* of creator and creation on one hand and their *separation* on the other. Again, the distinction is between the saving grace found in one's merging with nature, and that found in one's belonging to the God antecedent to nature, the God in nature but not of nature, immanent yet transcendent. And whatever the word spoken in the pantheistic unity, it is not the same as that spoken in the separateness, spoken in the *logos*, spoken from under and before the timeless rocks.

Maclean, the author, is involved in more than mere theological dialectic. What he is saying comes not from such abstractions but from memory and images, from time past when he and his father and brother were one in love if not in understanding. And now those he loved but did not understand are dead. "But," he adds, "I still reach out to them." Something of this love he still hears in the waters of the river and in the foundations beneath. Perhaps he hears the Word itself as did John of the Fourth Gospel. This is what his father must have heard too and what his brother Paul did not. Whether the words come from water or from the deeper foundations, they are words his memory translates into those of father and brother, words that spoke of love. In their words he has his epiphany, yes his redemption, and thus he can say, "I am haunted by waters."

Maclean's story is a classic, deserving a place in the pantheon not only of Montana but of American literature. Putting aside such matters as structure and tone, characterization, imagery and a hundred other elements that subtly harmonize (whether the art be that of Maclean's fiction or his fishing), one finds something else, something identifying the river as symbol and type.

As for symbol, all the age-old meanings associated with living waters—one immediately thinks of purification, fertility and renewed life—are predicated upon a perceiving mind and a symbolic mode of perception. The argument here concerns more the act of perception than the object, more the perceiver than the perceived or percept. In short, the perceiver as symbolist finds significance through the interaction of experience and imagination, whereas the perceiver as typologist finds significance through a sacred design that is prior to, greater than and independent of the self. The mode of perception makes all the difference, and in this analysis the two modes are radically different. Symbolism results in a direct interpretation of life, whereas typology relates to history, prophesy, teleology. The symbol is created in the womb of the perceiver's imagination, whereas the type is revealed within the perceiver's faith. Again, the symbolist possesses a special quality enabling him to fuse object and meaning; the typologist possesses a special but different quality allowing him to see what has already been fused and now revealed but is separate from and independent of him. Finally, the symbolist enters the river, as it were, and is redeemed by the waters which his imagination transforms into purification and renewal. But the typologist enters what has already been transformed or, more accurately, what flows from a sacred design, purpose, or destiny, made visible through the regenerate eyes and ears of faith.

In Maclean's story the two modes of perception show the river as both symbol and type. When attention is upon Paul's marvelous artistry, validating the halo of spray often enclosing him, we see by means of the narrator's imagination not only a transformed fisherman but a river metamorphosed into a world apart. Fishing becomes a world apart, a world perfect, an imagined and sinless world fusing person with vision. For Paul, when he steadied himself and began to cast, "the whole world turned to water." The narrator shares in the imagined oneness of his brother's world.

But the narrator does not lose himself in it. He also hears his father's words bespeaking a separate design, revealed as the *logos* or Word that was in the beginning—before the river and before human imaginings. More than speech, this Word is divine action—creating, revealing, redeeming. That the father carries his Greek New Testament along with his fishing rod is a fact not lost upon the author as narrator. Through his father's faith the son reaches out to hear this other Word. No wonder he is haunted by waters.

In truth, the Montana river runs through his mind and consciousness, language and life. But something also runs through the river itself, something that is in it but not of it, something more elemental than water. Call it the Word, the ultimate synthesis, where the abode of all passing things resides.

Source: Harold P. Simonson, "Three Montana Regionalists: Ivan Doig, James Welch, Norman Maclean," in *Beyond the Frontier: Writers, Western Regionalism, and a Sense of Place*, Texas Christian University Press, 1989, pp. 162–69.

SOURCES

Blew, Mary Clearman, "Mo-nah-se-tah, the Whore, and the Three Scottish Women," in *Norman Maclean*, edited by Ron McFarland and Hugh Nichols, Confluence Press, 1988, pp. 190–200.

Cawelti, John G., "Norman Maclean: Of Scholars, Fishing and the River," University of Chicago Press website, 2008, http://www.press.uchicago.edu/books/maclean/maclean_cawelti.html (accessed January 28, 2014).

————, Review of *A River Runs through It, and Other Stories*, in *New Republic*, Vol. 174, No. 18, May 1, 1976, pp. 24–26.

"Center of Population and Territorial Expansion, 1790–2010," US Census Bureau website, February 7, 2013, http://www.census.gov/dataviz/visualizations/050/ (accessed February 3, 2014).

Connors, Philip, "A Tough Flower Girl: On Norman Maclean," in *Nation*, March 30, 2009, pp. 30–33.

Core, George, "Wanton Life, Importunate Art," in *Sewanee Review*, Vol. 85, No. 1, Winter 1977, pp. ii–x.

"Demographics," Table 3-2, "Population and Growth Rate of Montana Indians," Fort Peck Tribes website, p. 3-3, http://www.fortpecktribes.org/asrwss/pdf/vol1/demographics.pdf (accessed January 29, 2014).

Federal Writers' Project, *The WPA Guide to 1930s Montana*, University of Arizona Press, 1994, pp. 3–30.

Fraser, C. Gerald, "Norman Maclean, 87, a Professor Who Wrote about Fly-Fishing," in *New York Times*, August 3, 1990, http://www.nytimes.com/1990/08/03/obituaries/norman-maclean-87-a-professor-who-wrote-about-fly-fishing.html (accessed January 28, 2014).

Hesford, Walter, "Fishing for the Words of Life: Norman Maclean's *A River Runs through It*," in *Rocky Mountain Review of Language and Literature*, Vol. 34, No. 1, Winter 1980, pp. 34–45.

Lojek, Helen, "Casting Flies and Recasting Myths with Norman Maclean," in *Western American Literature*, Vol. 25, No. 2, August 1990, pp. 145–56.

Love, Glen A., "On the Sublime and the Beautiful: Montana, Longinus, and Professor Norman Maclean," in *Norman Maclean*, edited by Ron McFarland and Hugh Nichols, Confluence Press, 1988, pp. 201–12.

————, "Revaluing Nature: Toward an Ecological Criticism," Western Literature Association Presidential Address, October 1989, in *Western American Literature*, November 1990, pp. 201–15, http://www.westernlit.org/pastpresadd1989.htm (accessed February 1, 2014).

Maclean, Norman, *A River Runs through It*, University of Chicago Press, 1989.

Montana Indians: Their History and Location, Montana Office of Public Instruction, Division of Indian Education, April 2009, http://www.opi.mt.gov/pdf/IndianEd/Resources/MTIndiansHistorylocation.pdf (accessed February 5, 2014).

"Norman MacLean Trail Route Almost Complete," ABC Fox–Montana website, June 10, 2013, http://www.abcfoxmontana.com/story/22299229/norman-maclean-trail-route-almost-complete/ (accessed January 31, 2014).

"125 Montana Newsmakers: Norman F. Maclean," in *Great Falls Tribune* online, http://www.greatfallstribune.com/multimedia/125newsmakers3/maclean.html (accessed January 28, 2014).

Simonson, Harold P., "Norman Maclean's Two-Hearted River," in *Western American Literature*, Vol. 17, No. 2, August 1982, pp. 149–55.

Slick, Matthew J., "The Five Points of Calvinism," Calvinist Corner, 2012, http://www.calvinistcorner.com/tulip.htm (accessed February 2, 2014).

"State and County QuickFacts: Montana," US Census Bureau website, http://quickfacts.census.gov/qfd/states/30000.html (accessed January 29, 2014).

"Upper Blackfoot Mining Complex CECRA Facility (UBMC)," Montana Department of Environmental Quality website, 2013, http://deq.mt.gov/statesuperfund/ubmc/default.mcpx (accessed January 29, 2014).

Weltzien, O. Alan, Introduction to *The Norman Maclean Reader*, University of Chicago Press, 2012, pp. vii–xxiv.

Westminster Shorter Catechism, Reformation Scotland, 2007, http://www.reformation-scotland.org.uk/confessions/shorter-catechism.html (accessed February 2, 2014).

Wright, Russell O., *A Twentieth-Century History of United States Population*, Scarecrow Press, 1996, p. 83.

FURTHER READING

Hillerman, Tony, ed., *The Best of the West: Anthology of Classic Writing from the American West*, Harper-Collins, 1991.

> This volume is a collection of classic and contemporary fiction and nonfiction with a focus on the spirit of the American West and its people. Among the 142 entries are those by such authors as Edward Abbey, Wallace Stegner, Owen Wister, N. Scott Momaday, J. Frank Dobie, Meriwether Lewis, and Helen Hunt Jackson.

Holmes, Krys, *Montana: Stories of the Land*, Montana Historical Society Press, 2008.

> This volume is a comprehensive history of Montana. Chapter 18 details the condition of the state during the 1930s. The book includes a large number of maps, photos, time lines, charts, and sidebars to provide a lively portrait of the state.

Kittredge, William, and Annick Smith, eds., *The Last Best Place: A Montana Anthology*, University of Washington Press, 1995.

> This massive volume contains more than 200 stories, poems, reminiscences, reports, tall tales, essays, and journal entries from 150 men and women, from (Meriwether) Lewis and (William) Clark and John James Audubon to more recent authors such as Rick Newby and Bill Hoagland. The collection is also noteworthy for containing a number of Native American stories and myths as related by Jerome Fourstar, James White Calf, and Pete Beaverhead, among others.

McFarland, Ron, and Hugh Nichols, eds., *Norman Maclean*, Confluence Press, 1988.

This volume is a collection of scholarly essays about Maclean and his writings, along with interviews and previously uncollected writings by Maclean. It helps to establish the author as a uniquely western writer whose work is a product of a recognizable western tradition.

SUGGESTED SEARCH TERMS

A River Runs through It

fly fishing

Helena Montana AND history

Izaak Walton AND Compleat Angler

Little Blackfoot River

Montana AND geography

Montana AND geology

Montana AND history

Norman Maclean

Presbyterianism

Reverend John Norman Maclean

western authors

Signs and Symbols

VLADIMIR NABOKOV

1948

Vladimir Nabokov (1899–1977) is widely acknowledged as being among the greatest writers of the twentieth century. According to his biographer Brian Boyd, in 1948 Nabokov "produced one of the greatest short stories ever written, 'Signs and Symbols,' a triumph of economy and force, minute realism and shimmering mystery." In "Signs and Symbols" Nabokov tells the story of a family very much like his own, a family that had fled the Russian Revolution to the relative safety of Weimar Germany only to have to flee again from the Nazi dictatorship. Now elderly and living in America, the parents' lives revolve around the needs of their mentally ill son. Through the lens of the son's delusions, Nabokov encodes another story beneath the surface of the text, a much larger account of the tragedy of the Holocaust. That symbolic structure was misunderstood by Nabokov's editor when the story was published in the *New Yorker*. Her changes to the text seriously damaged its meaning, an episode that Nabokov commented upon in his novel *Pnin*. Nabokov had to restore the original text of the story when he was later to republish it under his own editorial control in *Nabokov's Dozen* (1958) and later anthologies.

AUTHOR BIOGRAPHY

Vladimir Vladimovich Nabokov was born in St. Petersburg, Russia, on April 22, 1899, into

Russian novelist Vladimir Nabokov
(© Everett Collection Historical | Alamy)

a prominent aristocratic family. His great-uncle had been on the military tribunal that condemned Fyodor Dostoyevsky to death, and his uncle was among the Russian admirals signing the peace treaty that ended the Russo-Japanese War (1904–1905); his image can be seen in the murals commemorating that event in the American Museum of Natural History in New York. His grandfather and father both served as minister for justice (the equivalent of the US attorney general) in Russia. Nabokov's father, Vladimir Dmitrievich, was a champion of Western liberal democratic reform of the Russian government and, when the Bolshevik Revolution of 1917 forced him to flee with his family to Germany, continued to promote those ideas among the exile community. In 1922, Vladimir Dmitrievich was killed while preventing an assassination attempt on a colleague by right-wing nationalist Russian émigrés who were closely aligned with the Nazi Party.

Nabokov grew up speaking both English and Russian, since he was raised by English governesses, as was the fashion among the Russian elite classes. He considered his privileged

childhood idyllic, and after the revolution he was able to take a degree from Cambridge University, in England. Nabokov then returned to Germany and supported himself by teaching within the émigré community. He married a Russian woman of Jewish descent. Accordingly, Nabokov and his family (his son Dmitri was born in 1934) were forced to flee to France in 1936 and then to the United States in 1940. His and his family's movements in the face of persecution by the Bolsheviks and the Nazis closely parallel those of the family in "Signs and Symbols." Nabokov secured a teaching post in comparative literature at Wellesley College, in Massachusetts, but he split his time with doing volunteer work in the lepidoptera (butterfly) collection at the American Museum of Natural History. His summers were spent butterfly collecting, mostly in the Southwest. He became a prominent entomologist and considered his work in that field to be as important as his writing.

During his time in Germany, Nabokov had begun to publish fiction in Russian, and in the 1940s he began to publish in English. He would write in the evenings during his entomological fieldwork each summer. "Signs and Symbols," published in the *New Yorker* magazine in 1948, was one of his first English short stories. It was accepted with a host of editorial changes, as is usual in fiction publishing. Nabokov refused to allow any changes except the most minor, but the published version nevertheless contained four seemingly small alterations that Nabokov insisted destroyed the meaning of the text. (The changes were the alteration of the title to "Symbols and Signs," the deletion of the numerical division into three sections, the combination of two short paragraphs into one, and the correction of the misspelled "beech plum" to "beach plum.") Since then, the story has always been reprinted in anthologies controlled by Nabokov and his estate without those alterations. In 1955, the success of his novel *Lolita* (widely regarded as one of the greatest works of literature ever produced) made Nabokov independently wealthy. He retired to Montreux, Switzerland, where he was able to devote himself full-time to writing and entomology. His works from this period include his memoir *Speak, Memory* (1967) and the novels *Pale Fire* (1962) and *Pnin* (1957), in which he evidently addresses the publication of "Signs and Symbols." He died in a hospital in Montreux on July 22, 1978, of pneumonia, a complication of an underlying infection.

PLOT SUMMARY

1

An elderly Jewish couple have a son who is schizophrenic and who has been hospitalized for four years. In their son's distorted perception, almost everything seems evil and threatening. The parents are having a hard time finding a birthday present for him that he will not believe is a threat, and they decide that a selection of jellies would seem safe.

The parents are refugees who have been living in the United States for many years. Although the husband had been a successful businessman in the old country (Russia) before the revolution, in America they are supported by his brother Isaac, called "the Prince."

To reach the sanitarium (hospital) where their son lives requires a long trip across the city. (The city is never named, but it is most likely New York.) The subway loses power, leaving them stranded for a time in the tunnel, and their connecting bus is late. When they arrive, it is raining, and an unpleasant nurse tells them their son made another suicide attempt the night before, and a visit now would only upset him. Waiting for the bus to return, the couple notice a baby bird that has fallen in the storm and is drowning in a puddle.

The son had once been saved from a previous suicide attempt when "an envious fellow patient thought he was learning to fly—and stopped him." The nature of the son's delusions is so unusual it was the subject of a paper in a psychology journal. He suffers from "referential mania," believing that the whole inanimate universe around him is constantly engaged in describing him, discussing him, and communicating with him, using a system of signs and symbols that only he can decipher. The trees spend their nights discussing his inmost thoughts, coats in the store windows conspire to lynch him, and the mountains in the distance sum up the ultimate truth of his being.

2

When the couple exit at their subway stop, the husband takes the basket of jellies back to their apartment while the wife goes to buy fish for dinner. However, he realizes that he gave her his keys earlier in the day and so must wait for her, sitting on the steps.

After she returns, he removes his uncomfortable dentures; without them, he can only eat soft foods. The wife realizes her husband is too upset to talk during dinner. After the husband goes to bed, the wife looks over old photo albums. The family had fled the Russian Revolution after 1917 and settled for a time in Leipzig, Germany, where their son was born in 1927. The family came to America when the son was ten years old. Other pictures show relatives who remained in Germany and were murdered in the Holocaust. While the son had at first seemed a gifted child, making weird, surreal drawings, his behavior eventually became odd enough (filled with irrational fears of random things like wallpaper and pictures in books) that he was sent to a special school in America, and then committed to institutional care as he finally became detached from reality.

The mother accepts all this because, she realizes, "living did mean accepting the loss of one joy after another, not even joys in her case—mere possibilities of improvement." Although the world is filled with tenderness, that tenderness "is either crushed, or wasted, or transformed into madness."

3

After midnight, the wife is still going over the family photos when her husband wakes up, greatly agitated. He has decided that they must bring their son home from the sanitarium. He says, "Otherwise we'll be responsible. Responsible!" His wife agrees enthusiastically. They eagerly discuss the details of bringing their son home while drinking tea, but they are interrupted by a phone call. It is a girl asking to speak with a certain Charlie. The wife asks her the number she wanted and confirms it is a wrong number. A few seconds later, the phone rings again and it is the same girl. The wife tells her: "I will tell you what you are doing: you are turning the letter O instead of the zero." As the couple go on talking, the father looks at the various jellies they had bought for their son's birthday: "apricot, grapes, beech plum, quince...crab apple." Then the phone rings again.

CHARACTERS

Herman Brink

Herman Brink is the psychiatrist who has written a professional article about the son and his referential mania. Although the description of referential mania given in "Signs and Symbols," presumably reflecting Brink's article, is substantially identical to the real diagnosis of *ideas of reference*, Brink is a fictional character and does not appear to be based on any particular historical psychiatrist.

Doctor

A doctor is briefly mentioned; he had discussed one of the son's previous suicide attempts with the mother and father. Although the reader does not learn precisely what happened, the doctor demonstrated remarkable insensitivity in calling the attempt "a masterpiece of inventiveness."

Father

Like most of the characters, the father goes unnamed. Though he was once well able to support his family through his business in pre-revolutionary Russia, his ability to do so has continuously declined, and since they have come to America, he must depend on the charity of his brother Isaac. He is in a sense fading away and becoming more and more superfluous in the life of his family and indeed in his own life. He indicates this near the end of the story, when he says that he is dying; surely no immediate medical crisis is meant. His life is becoming ever more marginal. He has false teeth but they do not fit, a sign that he no longer has any place to fit in with the world. His being locked out of his apartment and having to sit on the stairs to wait for his wife's return is another sign that he no longer has any place. If there is any rationale in the surface narrative of the story for his sudden inspiration to bring his son home from the hospital, it is that the new arrangement will give new meaning and purpose to his life, a prospect that fills him with the first happiness he has known in years.

Girl

At the end of the story, an unnamed girl twice dials a wrong number to the father and mother's phone. In the surface narrative, this mistake is seemingly random and unconnected. It therefore invites the reader to look more deeply into the symbolic narrative inside the story.

Isaac

Just as the father was a successful businessman in Minsk, his younger brother Isaac came to America, probably sometime before the

Revolution, and made a fortune. During their ten years in America, the father and mother have lived on Isaac's charity, and he also pays the no doubt substantial fees for keeping their son in the sanitarium. It seems he must also have paid the considerable sums (including bribes) that would have been necessary to get a Jewish family out of Germany in 1937. Yet they are resentful of him and mockingly call him "the Prince." Despite his obvious generosity, they imagine that Isaac is stingy and will agree to their plan of bringing their son out of the hospital to live with them at home because in the long run it will be cheaper for him. This irrational resentment probably arises over the mother and father's feelings of guilt and shame at having no way to repay his kindness.

Mother

Although it is difficult to identify the protagonist, or main character, of "Signs and Symbols," many critics see the mother in this role. The narrative presents a much clearer view of her inner life than her husband's, and the story is told more from her viewpoint than his. Much of the story is devoted to her memories and interpretations. Her son was born very late in her life, probably when she was close to being forty years old. Her recollection of her son's life in Germany through examining the family photos of that time introduces the theme of the Holocaust, an important motif and linkage within the story. Her marriage is untouched by any ideas of feminism: she does the cooking and shopping and devotes herself to the household and to family history. Nevertheless, her husband seems to treat her as his equal. Given their circumstances, with the husband's profession long since gone, he indeed seems dependent on her in many ways, and she has a nearly motherly role toward him. Her life for the last thirty years has been filled with increased suffering, to which she is resigned. She has learned that living consists of losing one joy after another, or in her case losing "mere possibilities of improvement." She has lost her community, her extended family, and, in a way, her son, but these setbacks have not destroyed her ability to see the world as filled with tenderness and compassion. Nevertheless, she sees that the world inevitably destroys such feelings.

Nurse

When the mother and father arrive at the sanitarium to visit their son on his birthday, a nurse announces to them that he tried to kill himself the night before and that any visit would be unwise. The parents decide not to leave the gift of the basket of jellies with her; they believe the gift would inevitably be lost because of the confusion in the sanitarium's administration caused by understaffing. They may have reason to believe that the nurse is too incompetent to keep track of the gift. The parents know the nurse and dislike her, perhaps because she has interposed herself between them and their son before. The parents' whole experience of the medical profession seems to consist of encounters with thoughtless and uncaring doctors and nurses.

Aunt Rosa

Though she is one of the few characters to have a name, the story gives no clue as to whose aunt she was, presumably either the mother's or the father's. The mother comes across her picture in the family album and recalls "Aunt Rosa, a fussy, angular wild-eyed old lady, who lived in a tremulous world of bad news, bankruptcies, train accidents, cancerous growths—until the Germans put her to death, together with all the people she had worried about." This means that she was a victim of the Holocaust. This is the only clear mention of that event in the story, forming a bridge to the story hidden inside the narrative. Rosa's life was not noticeably different from the mother and father's except in one important detail: they escaped and survived, while Rosa did not.

Son

The son is twenty years old on the day "Signs and Symbols" takes place. On the surface he is not dissimilar from many young men, "his poor face botched with acne, ill-shaven, sullen, and confused." Because of a history of suicide attempts and serious mental illness, he is hospitalized in a private sanitarium. Perhaps the most engaging and intriguing element of "Signs and Symbols" is the description of the son's psychological condition, diagnosed as "referential mania." For the son, the entire inanimate world is alive and intelligent. Moreover, every part of the world is intently focused on him as the center of attention and locked in eternal conversation about him: "Clouds in the staring sky transmit to one another, by means of slow signs, incredibly detailed information regarding him. His inmost thoughts are discussed at nightfall, in manual alphabet, by darkly gesticulating trees." The world is hostile to him. Department store mannequins plot to murder him, and storms slander him. All of the son's attention is focused on decoding the malevolent conversations forever going on around him. His suicide attempts follow logically from these patterns of thought: "What he really wanted to do was to tear a hole in his world and escape." On the one hand, this suggests that when readers think a story is filled with metaphors and analogies, they are descending into a similar "mania," but on the other hand, it suggests that that is the only satisfactory way to read this text as a whole. The reader is drawn to consider the story that Nabokov has hidden within the surface narrative.

Son's Cousin

Nabokov had a habit of repeating characters from work to work, sometimes briefly referring to the main character of one story in another story. The brief mention here of the cousin provides enough details—he is a Russian Jew who becomes a great chess master in Germany—to suggest that he is Aleksandr Luzhin, the protagonist of Nabokov's early Russian-language novel (translated in 1964) *The Defense.* Luzhin commits suicide at a young age, as is suggested of the son in "Signs and Symbols." The novel also shares many of the short story's themes of mental obsession and suicide, and it ends just as ambiguously.

THEMES

Symbolism

Nabokov calls attention to the importance of the signs and symbols in his story in its very title. In this case, the word *sign* and the word *symbol* are very nearly synonyms, both referring to an image (including a verbal image) that stands for something other than itself. A stop sign, for instance, is a painted piece of flat metal on a pole, but it communicates the idea of stopping an automobile by conventional understanding of its meaning. Language itself is a system of symbols. It consists of series of sounds or figures (letters) that refer to objects, actions, and

TOPICS FOR FURTHER STUDY

- Charles Weaver Cushman was a highly skilled amateur photographer who documented his travels around the world from 1938 to 1969. He donated his collection of more than four-teen thousand Kodachrome color slides to the University of Indiana, which has posted the images online (http://webapp1.dlib.indiana.edu/cushman/index.jsp). Thousands of the photos document life in New York during the 1940s. Make a PowerPoint presentation illustrating the trek across the city by the mother and father in "Signs and Symbols" using Cushman's photos. Assume they start in Brooklyn and end at the sanitarium north of Washington Heights in Manhattan.

- The phrase "referential mania," Nabokov's version of the psychiatric diagnosis *ideas of reference*, has taken on a life of its own. Search the Internet (using, in particular, specialized search tools such as Google Books and Google Scholar) to document its use in contexts unrelated to "Signs and Symbols." Present an analysis of your findings in a brief paper.

- There are many accounts of the Holocaust derived from the diaries of young people who either died in or survived the death camps, including not only the well-known *The Diary of a Young Girl* (1947), by Anne Frank, but others such as *We Are Witnesses* (1995), edited by Jacob Boas; *I Am a Star: Child of the Holocaust* (1986), by Inge Auerbacher; and many others. Write your own short story based on one of these diaries.

- Ariel Dorfman's poem "Hope" describes the dilemma of two parents in Chile during the dictatorship of Augusto Pinochet. Their son has been kidnapped by the secret police. The parents' hope comes from a report they had from another young man, recently released from prison, who saw their son being tortured, which would at least mean he was still alive. Write a comparison between "Hope" and Nabokov's "Signs and Symbols."

qualities but that have no necessary connection to those things. The relationship of words to the things and actions they name is metaphorical. The *New Yorker* publication of Nabokov's story reversed the title, calling it "Symbols and Signs." Nabokov rejected this decision because it loses resonance with phrases like *signs and symptoms* (referring to the problem of medical diagnosis in the story) and the Biblical *signs and wonders* (suggesting a transcendent meaning for the story).

The story is filled with symbols. Perhaps the most obvious is seen when the couple are waiting for the bus to start the journey back home from the sanitarium: "A few feet away, under a swaying and dripping tree, a tiny half-dead unfledged bird was helplessly twitching in a puddle." The reader will have no difficulty in identifying this as a symbol of the son's life and condition. He too is young ("unfledged," which refers to a young bird before it is able to fly) and hopeless.

In any sophisticated work of literature, the use of such symbols is commonplace. But imagine for a moment that "Signs and Symbols" is a newspaper article rather than a fictional story. In that case, the parents might still see the doomed bird, but what relationship would it have to their son? None at all. It would be a random and meaningless event. To imagine that it had any objective meaning specific to the lives of the people who see it would be to succumb to the son's mental illness of referential mania. Many critics have interpreted this to mean that Nabokov is calling into question the whole symbolic structure of fiction as a kind of madness, but there are other possibilities. Referential mania is a real psychological diagnosis, though it is usually called *ideas of reference*. A main point in the criticism of psychiatry that developed during the twentieth century is that such ideas of reference might actually have real-world correspondences. In particular, ideas of the world as an agent of persecution often seem to have a basis in reality, and in fact the entire life of the family in "Signs and Symbols" has been shaped by fleeing from very real persecution, the same as with the Nabokov family. Nabokov was an outspoken critic of psychiatry, especially of psychoanalysis, so he may in fact be suggesting that the psychiatric profession is too quick to dismiss ideas of reference as delusional.

A statue honors Nabokov in Montreux, Switzerland. (© *InnaFelker | Shutterstock.com*)

1940s

"Signs and Symbols" was published in 1948. Nabokov purposely provides no clues about when or where the story takes place, but there is little doubt that it is meant to be contemporary and to take place in New York City. It must in any case take place after the end of World War II, since it looks back on the Holocaust as something that is over. However, through the narrative that underlies the surface narrative of "Signs and Symbols," Nabokov indicates symbolically that the year it takes place is 1947. One of the four changes introduced when the story was published in the *New Yorker* was the collapsing of two short paragraphs into one. Nabokov must have had a good reason for rejecting this and changing the text back to his original version in subsequent republications under his control. The change altered the number of paragraphs in the third section from nineteen to eighteen. The first section has seven paragraphs, while the second has only four. If these total are arranged together in reverse order,

they become 1947. The reason why Nabokov found it so important that the story take place in 1947, rather than 1946 or 1948, is less clear. It may be too personal ever to recover, or it may be revealed by further interpretative analysis of the story. Nabokov had mapped out the surface plot of the story in his mind as early as 1943, though he did not write it down until just before submitting it for publication in 1948. The story must have evolved in his imagination throughout the 1940s, in parallel with the course of the war.

STYLE

Postmodernism

Although "modern" suggests a more recent period, *modernism* was a literary and artistic movement of the late nineteenth and early twentieth centuries. Some writers of that era viewed history as an advance into a future of boundless prosperity and improvement, with learning, science, and industry constantly making the world better (in contrast to the random, destructive character of the world in "Signs and Symbols"). This kind of optimism came to an end during the twentieth century when civilization itself was endangered by the two world wars and the Holocaust, by the failure of capitalism in the Great Depression, by the failure of imperialism, by the failure of Communism (exposed by Soviet leader Joseph Stalin's atrocities, not yet by the collapse of the Soviet Union), by the failure of science and industry in the environmental degradation produced by modern society, and by the failure of all the systems working together in producing nuclear weapons and the Cold War. A human race threatened with nuclear annihilation, and the clear evidence that supposedly civilized states were all too ready to commit genocide, had left little room for optimism.

The realism and faith in progress of modernist literature gradually came to seem terribly naive. T. S. Eliot, a late modernist poet, saw the world as a place of mourning for the ruins of civilization. Postmodernists, such as Jorge Luis Borges, Joseph Heller, Kurt Vonnegut, and Thomas Pynchon, regarded the heaps of broken ruins as a playground. Dark, irreverent humor is a hallmark of postmodernism, and there is no greater master of such satire than Nabokov, though it is entirely lacking in "Signs and

COMPARE
&
CONTRAST

- **1940s:** The Jewish community in Europe is threatened with extinction by the Holocaust during World War II (1939–1945) but is given shelter from such persecution in the future through the creation of the state of Israel (1947).

  Today: The state of Israel is an established regional power in the Middle East and is frequently accused of carrying out oppressive policies against the Palestinian population within Israel.

- **1940s:** Psychoanalysis (of which Nabokov was critical) is the primary form of psychological treatment and provides the back-ground for the referential mania in "Signs and Symbols."

  Today: Psychoanalysis is an embattled minority field within the psychiatric profession and is not generally considered useful in treating paranoia, which is now recognized as an organic brain disease.

- **1940s:** New York is the largest city in the world and is generally considered the world leader in economic and cultural terms.

  Today: Though still a large and vital city, New York has lost its unquestioned first place in culture and dynamism among the world's cities.

Symbols." Nevertheless, the story is thoroughly postmodern in its paranoid, even schizoid, character. By Nabokov's own account, the text tells two stories, of which the narrative about the old couple and their mentally ill son is the less important. Yet the story's main narrative is nearly invisible for being buried under a heap of its own signs and symbols. It is told through obscure puns and strange numerological devices, and two generations of scholarly digging have not succeeded in excavating it entirely. Only a postmodern author would play with the reader in this way, hiding his meaning under a secondary narrative.

Autobiography
Few authors can avoid putting some details of their own lives into their work, but Nabokov especially delighted in basing his stories on his own history, particularly in twisted, satirical versions, even making them play out in parallel universes (as in his novel *Ada*). In "Signs and Symbols," the parallels between the lives of the story's characters and Nabokov's own life are more prosaic. Nabokov's family fled the Bolshevik Revolution and traveled around Europe before settling for many years in Germany.

Nabokov, with a Jewish wife, later had to flee Nazi persecution, first to France, and then during the war to the United States. There Nabokov had to scramble to find a job—his appointment at Wellesley perhaps derived from a feeling that America should help refugees from European tyranny. His brother, who remained in Germany, eventually died in the Holocaust. The couple in "Signs and Symbols" also fled the Bolsheviks, traveled around Europe before settling in Germany, and eventually fled the Nazis to the United States, where they live on the charity of the father's brother, Isaac. They left behind many relatives who died in the Holocaust.

HISTORICAL CONTEXT

The Holocaust
Whether or not "Signs and Symbols" is at a deeper level ultimately concerned with the Holocaust, that tragedy is firmly embedded even in the plainest level of its surface story. The family in the story fled Germany to escape persecution, and many friends and family members who did not are revealed to have died in the Holocaust as

The old couple worries about their mentally ill son. *(© Aletia / Shutterstock.com)*

the mother goes through the family photo albums. Nabokov had his own personal connection to the Holocaust. His brother Sergey was incarcerated for homosexuality and died in the Neuengamme camp in 1945.

Anti-Semitism is the irrational hatred of Jews, a form of bigotry with a long history. In Roman antiquity, Jews were considered suspect because they did not share the religious practices of their neighbors. Anti-Semitism rose to new levels in Europe during the Middle Ages. Christian communities generally forced Jews to live in segregated neighborhoods called ghettos that were kept under lock and key. Christians often acted as though the Jews living in their towns were the ones responsible for the death of Jesus in the biblical narratives. Jews were frequently massacred, especially at Easter. In 1348, Germans in particular blamed local Jewish communities for causing the Black Death by poisoning the wells, resulting in a general massacre as well as the flight of many German Jews to Poland and Russia, establishing what would become large and prosperous Jewish communities in those countries.

After the defeat of Germany in the First World War, the aspiring politician Adolf Hitler latched on to popular hatred of the Jews (still common in Germany, as it was in Europe and the United States generally) as a unifying principal for his political movement National Socialism (Nazism), irrationally blaming the Jews for the nation's defeat. Hitler became dictator of Germany in 1933, and in 1936 he began to enact his anti-Semitic principles into law. Under the Nuremberg Laws, Jews were denied the most basic civil rights in Germany, and rioting against Jewish communities was encouraged and aided by the government. Vast amounts of private wealth owned by Jews in the form of businesses and artworks were stolen and transferred to corrupt Nazi officials. Eventually, those Jews who did not flee Germany were rounded up by the government and forced to live in concentration camps such as Theresienstadt and Buchenwald. Although these camps were at first touted as utopian communities where Jews could live in peace separated from Germans, the inmates were actually treated as slaves. At the same time, the Nazi government quietly began a policy of murdering individuals of German descent whom they nevertheless considered to be racially impure, including homosexuals, those with congenital diseases, and the mentally ill. As these systematic murders increased in frequency, they were transferred from hospitals to the camps.

Once World War II began and Germany acquired vast new territories in eastern Europe with millions more Jews, the Nazis devised what they called the final solution to the Jewish question. They built a vast new system of camps in Poland, with the administrative center at Auschwitz, where they transported millions of Jews and others who were considered undesirable. The inmates were worked as slaves, but the main purpose of the new camps was to commit murder on an industrial scale, with gas chambers and special crematoria designed to recover chemicals from the bodies of the victims for use in the war effort. Including the camps in Germany and Poland, the Nazis murdered more than ten million civilians, of whom six million were Jews. Buchenwald, near the city of Weimar, was the first death camp liberated by Western Allied forces, which began to make clear the barbarity of the Nazi régime. The German atrocities were labeled the *Holocaust*, from a Greek word for a burnt offering to the gods, in an effort to impose some sort of meaning on the Nazi crimes.

CRITICAL OVERVIEW

"Signs and Symbols" is one of Nabokov's most widely critiqued works, with a vast number of articles usually commenting on one aspect, or one layer of meaning, of the story, which has been slowly built up into a number of interpretive schemes over the years. One of the earliest commentators, William Carroll, in "Nabokov's Signs and Symbols" (1974), offers what may be taken as a reader's first response, namely, that Nabokov is inflicting upon the reader the same referential mania that afflicts the son in the story. Any work of fiction is built up of metaphors and other symbols that connect the elements of plot and character. In reality, seeing a dying baby bird has no connection with anything else, but the same event in the story must be connected to the character of the son if the text there is to have any meaning. Thus, Nabokov leaves the reader with a choice between denying any meaning in his story or recognizing

that artistic creation—along with the artistic re-creation that the reader must accomplish to follow the writer—is a form of madness (an insight that goes back to the literary criticism of the ancient Greek philosopher Plato). This view is followed by Brian Boyd in his 1991 biography of Nabokov. Carroll also points to Nabokov's use of the double meaning of "cipher." In the story, the word occurs in the sense of a system of secret writing, in the description of the son's referential mania, but *cipher* can also mean zero—the cause of the misdialed phone at the end of the story. This contributes to Carroll's interpretation of the story as a choice between meaning and non-meaning. Mary Tookey, in a 1988 article in *Explicator*, refines this reading of the wrong number and suggests that the substitution of zero (nothing) for the letter *O* (a symbol of unity and even of god) relates to the loss of faith and meaning in Western intellectualism over the twentieth century.

John V. Hagopian, in the essay "Decoding Nabokov's 'Signs and Symbols'" (1981), offers an important counterpoint to Carroll's reading. He rejects the idea of meaninglessness or madness in the story and asks, given the miserable facts of human existence (exemplified in the parents' lives as well as the son's), "Is it necessarily paranoid to feel that nature and the universe are the enemies of man?" In Hagopian's interpretation, the third telephone call is from the sanitorium announcing the son's suicide, but this should be seen as liberation from a paranoid reality. Michael Wood, in *The Magician's Doubts: Nabokov and the Risks of Fiction* (1994), takes up Hagopian's reading and interprets the three telephone calls as evidence of some hostile force in the world torturing the mother and father. The 2012 anthology *Anatomy of a Short Story: Nabokov's Puzzles, Codes, "Signs and Symbols"* collects a number of old and new perspectives, two of the most important of which are in the articles by Alexander Dolinin and Alexander N. Drescher. Both try to find meaning in the story through the second narrative that Nabokov claimed to have embedded in the story, which they find to be about the Holocaust. Dolinin sees the technique of the hidden narrative as derived from nineteenth-century Russian literary criticism, which distinguishes the relationship between the plot of the story and the *fabula*, the totality of meaning created in the story by the interconnection of its events and characters. Drescher finds a specific context for the paranoid worldview suggested by Hagopian in the plight of European Jews in the Holocaust; he also offers a persuasive analysis of the many symbols embedded in the story through numerology and other techniques.

CRITICISM

Rita M. Brown

Brown is an English professor. In the following essay, she explores what Nabokov called the "second story" or "inside" meaning that is hidden under the surface story of "Signs and Symbols."

Katherine A. White, the *New Yorker* editor who published "Signs and Symbols," rejected a later story by Nabokov, "The Vane Sisters." On March 17, 1951, Nabokov wrote her a letter that has been published in *Vladimir Nabokov: Selected Letters*. In the letter, he talks about the structure of the story: "Most of the stories I am contemplating (and some I have written in the past—you actually published one with such an "inside"—the one about the old Jewish couple and their sick boy) will be composed on these lines, according to this system wherein a second (main) story is woven into, or placed behind, the superficial semitransparent one." Nabokov suggests here that the whole surface story of "Signs and Symbols" is only a veil covering over another, indirectly stated story that is hidden inside the text. The surface narrative of the story is itself a large symbol, or system of symbols, that tells a different story that must be deciphered. Nabokov is a skilled and subtle writer; even the smallest detail can be considered significant, and nothing is left to chance. Very little work has been done by scholars to get at the second story inside the first. The most important effort along this line is Alexander N. Drescher's article "Arbitrary Signs and Symbols," which is partly followed in the reading offered here.

"Signs and Symbols" takes place in 1947. The date is encoded in the number of paragraphs of the three sections: seven, four, and nineteen. The change in the *New Yorker* of the last section from nineteen to eighteen paragraphs was one of the alterations that Nabokov corrected in later editions. Nabokov alludes to this event in his 1957 novel *Pnin*. There the character Timofey Pnin discusses his having

> THE SURFACE STORY CONCERNS THE HISTORY OF THE UNNAMED FAMILY DURING THOSE THREE DECADES, BUT THE INSIDE STORY CONCERNS THE LARGER EVENTS OF THOSE YEARS, NAMELY, THE HOLOCAUST."

checked out the wrong book with a female library clerk:

"I requested on Friday Volume 19, year 1947, not 18, year 1940."

"But look—you wrote Volume 18. Anyway, 19 is still being processed..."

"Eighteen, 19," muttered Pnin. "There is not great difference! I put the year correctly, that is important!..."

They can't read, these women. The year is plainly inscribed.

This is his public rebuke to his editor White for her tampering. The year 1947 is important because it makes the story cover exactly thirty years, from the earliest event mentioned in the text, the 1917 Russian revolution, until the day described in the story. This also divides the arc of the story into three ten-year periods. The first period is the ten years when the couple lived in Germany. At the end of the first decade, in 1927, their son was born. They left Germany in 1937, when the son was ten years old.

The surface story concerns the history of the unnamed family during those three decades, but the inside story concerns the larger events of those years, namely, the Holocaust. This is mentioned outright in regard to the Aunt Rosa who died in the German death camps, but many other details of the story refer to the Holocaust obliquely.

The symbols in the story can begin to be analyzed with a reference to Nabokov's own life at that time. At age six, which is to say in 1933, the son "drew wonderful birds with human hands and feet." These are the sirens of Greek mythology. The pen name that Nabokov used when he published his Russian-language literature in Germany in the 1930s was Sirin, the

WHAT DO I READ NEXT?

- Angela Gluck Wood's *Holocaust* (2007) is a history of the Holocaust for young-adult readers that relies heavily on first-person narratives of survivors.

- Nabokov published various excerpts from and translations of his memoirs throughout his life, creating a text that was constantly shifting and being revised. The last version was *Speak, Memory: An Autobiography Revisited* (1967).

- The Argentinean writer Jorge Luis Borges deals with the postmodern theme of the union between the observer and the observed in, for example, his short stories "The Zahir" and "The Aleph," available in his *Collected Fictions*, translated in 1998 by Andrew Hurley. Similarities can be seen to the referential mania suffered by the son in "Signs and Symbols."

- Set in Poland during the Second World War, Morris Gleitzman's young-adult novel *Once* (2010) tells the story of a young Jewish boy hidden in a Catholic orphanage. He has the habit of interpreting everything he sees in the world as a sign trying to communicate with him. When these signs lead him to escape from the orphanage to search for his parents, he discovers a world that he did not know was at war and in the midst of the Holocaust.

- Buchenwald was the first concentration camp liberated by American forces, and it became the center for American intelligence services to gather information on the camp system, drawn from captured records and from interviews with inmates and guards. The amount of information compiled about Buchenwald far exceeds that about any other camp. The official report on Buchenwald was long thought to be lost but was discovered and republished in 1997 as *The Buchenwald Report*, translated and edited by David A. Hackett.

- Andreas Feininger was a photographer for *Life* magazine who extensively documented scenes of New York in the era during which "Signs and Symbols" takes place. A large collection of his photos was published in *New York in the Forties* (1978), with textual commentary by John von Hartz.

- The first academic biography of Nabokov was written by Andrew Field: *Nabokov: A Life in Part.* At first, Nabokov eagerly cooperated with the project, but eventually he came to feel that Field was presenting a distorted and unrecognizable picture of his life and his writing. Nabokov sued to stop publication but only succeeded in delaying it until 1977. Nabokov also responded with his own parody version of his life, a fictional biography of the Russian American author Vadim Vadimovich N., published in 1974 as *Look at the Harlequins!*

- The most accessible sampling of Nabokov's entomological work is contained in *Nabokov's Butterflies: Unpublished and Collected Writings*, edited in 2000 by Brian Boyd, with several Russian articles translated by Dmitri Nabokov.

Russian spelling of the same monstrous bird-like creatures. At the same time, though, the son "suffered from insomnia like a grown-up man." What anxiety disturbed his sleep? The Nazis came to power in 1933. When the son was eight years old, in 1935, he grew "afraid of a certain picture in a book which merely showed an idyllic landscape with rocks on a hillside and an old cart wheel hanging from the branch of a leafless tree." In the same year, the anti-Semitic Nuremberg Laws were passed in Germany, laying the foundation for the Holocaust. Drescher has pointed out that Nabokov frequently used a Renaissance painting, *The*

Triumph of Death, by Pieter Brueghel the Elder, as a symbol for the Holocaust in his work. That seems to be the painting hinted at here. To describe the picture in more pointed detail, it shows a barren landscape in which animated skeletons kill people in a variety of ways. (The SS, the Nazi paramilitary organization responsible for carrying out the Holocaust, used a skull and crossbones, also known as a death's head, as its symbol.) In the painting, one person is being beheaded with a sword, another is being thrown down a cliff, and some are being hung from scaffolds. Several are crucified on wheels attached to the top of poles. Other corpses are being burned in great bonfires (suggesting the Auschwitz crematoria). Although the large death camps in the Auschwitz system generally executed their prisoners with poison gas, in the early days of the Holocaust, hanging and crucifixion were common in camps in Germany such as Dachau. The "merely" and "idyllic" in the mother's recollection of this hellish image are ironic.

When the son was ten years old, the family finally left Germany for the United States. It is unlikely that a relatively poor and obscure Jewish family would have been allowed to leave Germany in 1937. That the father and mother and their son did so suggests that bribes must have been paid to corrupt officials. The only person who would have been in a position to pay such bribes would have been the father's brother, Isaac. He is also responsible for supporting the family in America, in particular paying what must be the large fees to keep the son hospitalized. In view of this, the family's rather hostile and condescending attitude toward "the Prince" seems strange. They owe him so much, but, having no way to pay him back, they respond with hostility rather than gratitude. Unpleasant as it is, this is a common human response to the kind of shame the couple must feel in the face of their absolute dependence on Isaac's charity. Since they can never repay him, they can never forgive him. This is in contrast to the victims of the Holocaust whom the world did nothing to rescue when they could have. Throughout the 1930s, Western countries, including the United States, routinely turned away Jewish refugees, even the few who could get out of Germany, unless they were prominent intellectuals or had relatives or sponsors to receive them.

The most striking element of "Signs and Symbols" is the description of the son's "referential mania." In this delusion, he imagines himself to be the center of a universe in which the very land and sky, the clouds and trees, are in constant conversation with him and about him. Indeed, they are constantly conspiring against him. Everything the son sees he believes is spying on him and plotting to kill him: "Some of the spies are detached observers, such as glass surfaces and still pools; others, such as coats in store windows, are prejudiced witnesses, lynchers at heart." It is hard not to see all the reflective imagery in those lines as a reference to *Kristallnacht* (the Night of Breaking Glass), so named after the countless shards of glass lying in the street on the morning of November 10, 1938, after the Nazi paramilitary SA and thousands of German civilians attacked, looted, and destroyed the majority of Jewish businesses and synagogues in Germany, as well as countless Jewish homes, killing nearly a hundred Jews (at the time a shockingly large number) and sending thirty thousand to the concentration camps, beginning the Holocaust. More generally, however, this reading calls into question the delusional status of the son's referential mania. If it refers instead to the position of German Jews after 1938, then there is no delusion involved. Their world did conspire to destroy them, and the referential mania is no more than an acceptance of reality. Finally, some of the spies persecuting the son are seen as "hysterical to the point of insanity, have a distorted opinion of him, and grotesquely misinterpret his actions." This refers to the anti-Semitic myth that fueled the Holocaust, the entirely false belief that Jews were involved in an effort to control and destroy Western civilization and therefore deserved to be exterminated. This indeed is the clinical delusion of the Holocaust, not the Jews' quite warranted fear of persecution.

Another curious point that cries out for interpretation is the father's sudden resolution that they have to bring their son home, expressed in his shouting, "Otherwise we'll be responsible. Responsible!" If they are talking about their mentally ill son who is in a sanitarium under the care of doctors (who, whatever their failings, have already prevented at least two suicide attempts), it is hard to see how the parents would be responsible for anything

The story ends with a third phone call, but the reader does not learn who is calling.
(© vita khorzhevska | Shutterstock.com)

worse happening to their son if they left him in medical care. This seems more like an expression of guilt. They feel they are not doing enough to help their son because it is impossible to do enough. This suggests survivors' guilt, the self-recrimination for still being alive after others have perished. It was a common feeling among Holocaust survivors.

Nabokov calls attention to another detail through the reversions he made from the *New Yorker* text of the story. Among the jellies named toward the end of the story, the *New Yorker* printed *beach plum*, which is the correct name of a fruit. But Nabokov insisted on the misspelling *beech plum*, as if the harried father with his limited knowledge of English made a mistake in the spelling (although, in fact, he is reading it). But this misspelling allows Nabokov to make a very meaningful pun. The German name for the beech tree is *Buchen*; the word for a beech forest, *Buchenwald*. This was the name of one of the Nazi concentration camps, and not coincidentally, the first one to be liberated by the Allied forces at the end of World War II. Coming at the end of the story—the end of the inside story as well as the outside story—it signals the end of the Holocaust. This gives some support to those readers who interpret the last phone call as coming from the son announcing he has escaped from the sanatarium. It means that the victims of the Holocaust, at least those who survived, are now free. The year 1947, when Nabokov indicated that the story takes place, also saw the foundation of the state of Israel. The girl who misdials the phone and dials the letter *O* should be dialing the number zero because the cyclical time of the story has been completed and must be reset at a new beginning. Alternatively, the final phone call, much debated by critics, perhaps means that the son has succeeded in leaving the hospital, only through a successful suicide attempt. But his death is to the world, and is also a rebirth into a new world, a world in which the parents who stand for the old world of the persecuted can have no part (hence the father describing himself as "dying").

Source: Rita M. Brown, Critical Essay on "Signs and Symbols," in *Short Stories for Students*, Gale, Cengage Learning, 2015.

Gennady Barabtarlo

In the following excerpt, Barabtarlo discusses "Signs and Symbols" as a masterfully rich story told in relatively few words.

... It is worthy of note that "Signs and Symbols" (May 1947; May 1948) is the only English short story Nabokov wrote in regular third person—in a quiet, compassionate, but firm voice originating outside the story. None of his short stories has commanded nearly as much attention of some of the most astute Nabokov students as this one. Nabokov's biographer considers it "one of the greatest short stories ever written ... a triumph of economy and force, minute realism and shimmering mystery." Economy indeed: in the course of 118 uncharacteristically short sentences that make up the story Nabokov carefully avoids naming any one of the three principal characters—a difficult feat that he had already attempted in the vaster space of "The Enchanter." Moreover, the main personage never appears on stage. He is the only son of two elderly Russian émigrés, a young man of twenty, who for the last four years has been kept in a mental asylum. His peculiar insanity, called *mania referentia*, consists in relating outside objects and phenomena to his person in a menacing way, as if he were a focal point of continuous and hostile ecological scrutiny and machinations. He had attempted, not for the first time, to take his life on the eve of his parents' visit on his birthday, so that they were not allowed to see him and had to take back with them the present they had brought—ten little jars of assorted fruit jellies. Around midnight that very Friday, after they have decided to bring their son home next day, a sudden telephone ring, then another, grips their old hearts with fright. In each case, the same girl has misdialed, it appears. They sit down to their late tea, and as the father is reading the jelly labels, the phone rings for the third time, and the curtain falls. But the hushed audience lingers: Has the young man finally torn "a hole in his world and escaped"? Or perhaps, as one acute interpreter has recently suggested, the reader is invited to imagine "a moment of panic prolonged to infinity, with the telephone still ringing and the mother's hand still stretching towards the receiver"? Several others have cleverly argued that Nabokov mesmerizes the reader into seeing the disaster beyond the story's boundary by infecting him with exactly the sort of referential mania that clouds the young man's mind, so that the sharper and more attentive the reader the surer he is enmeshed. For all its magnetic ingenuity, this line of argument discounts the importance of evidence pointing to the tragic end which comes about through a chain of secret signals and not by force of a crafty syllogism. The title once again carries a double load, meaning as a set phrase a chart of referential codes appended to an atlas. Not only does Nabokov shirr the length of the story with a series of omens but he also tells the reader that the signs are all mapped and coordinated. Some of them are trivial (it's a Friday; the subway train suddenly loses its "life current") or obvious (an attempt at suicide on a birthday; father's twitching hand resembling the half-dead, twitching bird fallen out of a nest and seen a moment earlier), others are vague (the "kind shock" at the sight of a girl weeping on the bus) and tenuous (the letter O that Charlie's girlfriend erroneously dials for the zero; incidentally, this o–zero, the ovoid emblem of a void, appears later in *Lolita* and *Pale Fire*), but together they all unite to confer a designative value on themselves. One signpost tends to be underestimated although its value increases greatly for the fact that it is the very first *and* the very last item in the series of the story's internal references: if nothing else, Nabokov's propensity for rounded structures alone should warrant our redoubled attention to the set of jelly jars. But it is not simply a frame. When the woman hands her husband the basket with the jellies but not the keys to their flat, thus making him wait on the stair-landing for her return, the incident seems to be more than yet another mishap of that sad Friday: it assumes in retrospect a queer symbolism, as though that undelivered gift *were*, in another dimension, a key to the invisible over-plot. In the last sentence, the old man is halfway through the labels on the jars when the final call comes, and the reader should not fail to realize that the jellies are arranged in the order of increasing astringency, from pungent-sweet to tartish to tart. The five flavors somehow answer the five photographs of her son that the woman examined an hour earlier; and those pictures recorded the five stages of the incremental occlusion of his mind (baby, then aged four, six, eight, and ten). The gift had been selected as a "dainty and innocent trifle," one that would not frighten the young man by an evil reference, as any "man-made object" inevitably would. Instead, the old couple decides not to leave it in the sanitarium and brings home the basket of jars that perhaps is charged with ominous reference to other signs and ultimately to the tragic outcome their concordance predicts.

Nor is the double entendre of the title an "innocent trifle," nor even the curious string of uniradical names of otherwise unrelated marginal characters, the Soloveichiks—Dr. Solov—Mrs. Sol, that may imply that the pre-charted coincidences are not "man-made." Or does it imply more? For instance, that the doctor and the neighboring lady are of Russian extraction and may even be related to the Soloveichiks (their names being typical New World dockings of long Slavic names, this one meaning "little nightingale") whom the old lady recalls in a spasm of compassion, in the depth of her own grief? Whether leading to a secret passage or a cul-de-sac, these signals can hardly be taken for a word game or a reference-hunt game, in a story welling with pain, love, and gentle sympathy, a story bemoaning the waste of "the incalculable amount of tenderness contained in the world." Nabokov later would single out "Signs and Symbols" as an example of a story with a second plane "woven into, or placed behind, the superficial semitransparent one" (*SL* 117). The "superficial" story paints an unforgettable picture of piercing sadness. Here is how the invisible *main* story envelops the obvious: "From within the parents' world, their son's death seems simply more jagged glass on the pile of miseries that makes up their life. But from outside their vantage point, we can see that *if* the boy has died, then the story bears the mark of a tender concern that shapes every minute detail of a world that from within seems unrelieved, meaningless tragedy. The final blow of death, in one light so gratuitous, in another seems the very proof of the painstaking design behind every moment of their lives." One can see here a scantling of the concentric pattern that all of Nabokov's English novels would reproduce to much larger scale. . . .

Source: Gennady Barabtarlo, "English Short Stories," in *The Garland Companion to Vladimir Nabokov*, edited by Vladimir E. Alexandrov, Garland Publishing, 1995, pp. 109–11.

SOURCES

Boyd, Brian, *Vladimir Nabokov: The American Years*, Princeton University Press, 1991, pp. 115–19.

Carroll, William, "Nabokov's Signs and Symbols," in *A Book of Things about Nabokov*, edited by Carl R. Proffer, Ardis, 1974, pp. 203–17.

Dolinin, Alexander, "The Signs and Symbols of Nabokov's 'Signs and Symbols,'" in *Anatomy of a Short Story: Nabokov's Puzzles, Codes, "Signs and Symbols,"* edited by Yuri Leving, Continuum, 2012, pp. 257–69.

Drescher, Alexander N., "Arbitrary Signs and Symbols," in *Anatomy of a Short Story: Nabokov's Puzzles, Codes, "Signs and Symbols,"* edited by Yuri Leving, Continuum, 2012, pp. 83–94.

Hagopian, John V., "Decoding Nabokov's 'Signs and Symbols,'" in *Studies in Short Fiction*, Vol. 18, No. 2, 1981, pp. 115–19.

Koogan, Eugen, *The Theory and Practice of Hell: The German Concentration Camps and the System behind Them*, Farrar, Strauss and Giroux, 2006, pp. 25–59.

Nabokov, Vladimir, *Pnin*, in *Novels, 1955–1962*, Library of America, 1996, p. 350.

———, "Signs and Symbols," in *The Stories of Vladimir Nabokov*, Alfred A. Knopf, 1995, pp. 594–99.

———, *Vladimir Nabokov: Selected Letters 1940–1977*, edited by Dmitri Nabokov and Matthew J. Bruccoli, Harcourt Brace Jovanovich, 1989, p. 117.

Tookey, Mary, "Nabokov's 'Signs and Symbols,'" in *Explicator*, Vol. 46, No. 2, 1988, pp. 34–36.

Wood, Michael, *The Magician's Doubts: Nabokov and the Risks of Fiction*, Princeton University Press, 1994, pp. 66–73.

FURTHER READING

Cherry, Vivian, *Helluva Town: New York City in the 1940s and 50s*, Powerhouse Books, 2007.

Cherry was a photographer for the Underwood and Underwood News Service. This volume presents a portrait of New York City in the 1940s through her photographs.

Gilbert, Martin, *The Boys: The Story of 732 Young Concentration Camp Survivors*, Holt, 1998.

The English historian Gilbert here reports the interviews he conducted with hundreds of male youths who all survived their experience of the Nazi concentration camp and all of whom were sixteen years old or younger at the time of liberation in 1945.

Nabokov, Vladimir, *Pale Fire*, G. P. Putnam, 1962.
This novel consists of a 999-line poem by the fictional poet John Shade and several hundred pages of commentary by the equally fictional academic Charles Kindbote. The plot of the novel arises out of the interaction between the two texts.

Proffer, Ellendea, *Vladimir Nabokov: A Pictorial Biography*, Ardis, 1991.
This biography of Nabokov makes extensive use of the Nabokov estate's collection of family photos, dating back to Nabokov's idyllic childhood in czarist Russia.

SUGGESTED SEARCH TERMS

Vladimir Nabokov

Signs and Symbols AND Nabokov

postmodernism

Holocaust

Buchenwald

referential mania

ideas of reference

New York AND 1940s

The Triumph of Death AND Pieter Brueghel the Elder

The Suitcase

CYNTHIA OZICK

1971

"The Suitcase" is a story by the American writer Cynthia Ozick. It was published in 1971 in Ozick's short-story collection *The Pagan Rabbi and Other Stories* and reprinted in Ozick's *Collected Stories* (2007). "The Suitcase" is set in the 1960s in a New York art gallery where an exhibition is being held. At the exhibition, the artist's father, Mr. Hencke, a German who has long lived in the United States, is subject to the ire of Genevieve, a married Jewish woman with whom Gottfried, the artist, is intimately acquainted. Genevieve dislikes all Germans and taunts Mr. Hencke with allusions to the Holocaust. The situation intensifies when something is stolen. The story raises the issue of whether ordinary Germans can be thought to bear some responsibility for the Holocaust, an issue that is balanced by the issues of Jewish victimhood and revenge, as embodied in Genevieve.

AUTHOR BIOGRAPHY

Ozick was born on April 17, 1928, in New York City, to William and Celia (Regelson) Ozick. Her parents were Russian Jewish immigrants who ran a pharmacy. Ozick was a voracious reader as a child and soon developed a desire to become a writer. She attended Hunter College High School, in Manhattan, and in 1946

Cynthia Ozick (© *AP Images / Gerald Herbert*)

enrolled at New York University. She graduated in 1949 with a bachelor of arts degree and went immediately to Columbus, Ohio, to pursue a master's degree in English literature. She graduated in 1950, writing her thesis on the work of Henry James.

Ozick married Bernard Hallote, a lawyer, in 1952, and they had a daughter, Rachel. Ozick worked briefly as an advertising copywriter in Boston in the early 1950s. But her main activity during the early and mid-1950s was writing a long philosophical novel that she abandoned after several years' work. She also made extensive study of the literature and philosophy of Judaism. In 1957, Ozick began writing another long novel and labored on it until 1963. It was eventually published as *Trust* in 1966 and received positive reviews. Ozick's first collection of short stories was *The Pagan Rabbi and Other Stories* (1971), which includes "The Suitcase." The collection won the B'nai Brith Jewish Heritage Award, the Edward Lewis Wallant Award, and the Jewish Book Council Award for Fiction.

Bloodshed and Three Novellas followed in 1976 and received the Jewish Book Council Award for Fiction.

After *Levitation: Five Fictions* (1982), Ozick published *The Shawl* (1989), which consists of one story set in a Nazi concentration camp and a novella. This is one of her best-known and highly regarded works. Her *Collected Stories* was published in 2007, and another collection of short stories, *Dictation: A Quartet*, appeared in 2008. Ozick's novels include *The Messiah of Stockholm* (1987), *The Puttermesser Papers* (1997), *Heir to the Glimmering World* (2004), and *Foreign Bodies* (2010). Ozick has also published many collections of essays, including *Art and Ardor* (1983), *Metaphor & Memory* (1989), *Quarrel & Quandary* (2000)—which won the National Book Critics Circle Award—and *The Din in the Head: Essays* (2006). The Jewish Book Council honored Ozick with its 2010 Lifetime Achievement Award. Ozick has also been a visiting lecturer at many colleges and universities. As of 2014, she lives in New York City.

PLOT SUMMARY

As "The Suitcase" begins, Mr. Hencke, a German architect in his late sixties who has lived most of his life in the United States, arrives at an art gallery in New York City, where his son Gottfried is exhibiting his work. The gallery is located in a loft of Gottfried's. Catherine, Mr. Hencke's daughter-in-law, tries to persuade him to stay at their house, but Mr. Hencke prefers to stay at a hotel. He tells Genevieve, a married woman with whom Gottfried is having an affair, that he thinks Gottfried is not entirely comfortable in the house when his father is in it, so he prefers to stay at a hotel. It emerges from his conversation with Genevieve that Mr. Hencke does not think highly of Gottfried's work as an artist and does not really regard it as work. He thinks Gottfried should have an actual job. He does not need to, however, because his wife Catherine is wealthy. Genevieve and Catherine insist to Mr. Hencke that Gottfried works hard as an artist. Genevieve makes remarks to Mr. Hencke that he realizes are meant to antagonize him. She makes reference to the Holocaust, for example, and he knows she dislikes Germans and regards him as a Nazi sympathizer. Mr. Hencke was living in the United States during World War II. His main memory of the war is that his sister lost her home and her eleven-year-old daughter in a British bombing raid on the German city of Köln (Cologne). He becomes exasperated at her provocative remarks and says defensively that he has never harmed anyone or destroyed anything.

A crowd of people has arrived. They are anticipating a lecture by the famous literary and cultural critic Creighton MacDougal. The pretentious MacDougal gives his talk, titled "His Eye's Mind: Hencke and the New Cubism," and afterward Mr. Hencke engages him in conversation, rambling on about his experience as a World War I aviator. Mr. Hencke then talks to Gottfried and asks to be taken to his studio. Gottfried is surprised, because his father never asks to see his work. In fact, Mr. Hencke has noticed Gottfried and Genevieve arranging to meet later that night and is trying to forestall it, although it takes a while before Gottfried realizes this. The two men speak roughly to each other, and Gottfried accuses his father of wanting to break up his affair with Genevieve,

which has been going on for eighteen months. Mr. Hencke expresses sympathy for Catherine.

Genevieve comes up to Mr. Hencke and Gottfried and speaks playfully but disrespectfully to Mr. Hencke. Then she harangues him with the details of her life married to a certified public accountant, Lewin. She emphasizes that Lewin is a Jew. She also mentions that she has four daughters, all under twelve, and they are all highly intelligent. She tells Mr. Hencke more about herself and then switches the subject to him. She wants to know more about his brother-in-law who is a shampoo manufacturer in Cologne. What ingredients did he use in his shampoo during the war, she asks. Was it "Jewish lard"? This is a reference to the allegation that the Nazis used the corpses of their Jewish victims to make soap and other products. Gottfried tells Genevieve, "Leave my father alone." Genevieve, who is aware that Mr. Hencke has been trying to prevent her and Gottfried from meeting later that night, kisses Mr. Hencke on the cheek, makes another cutting remark about Germany and World War II, and goes away.

Mr. Hencke retains his self-control and professes to admire the Jews. He mentions Corbusier and says he may be a "secret Jew." This is a reference to Le Corbusier (1887–1965), a well-known twentieth-century architect who was born in Switzerland and later became a French citizen. Mr. Hencke obviously admires him. Then Mr. Hencke asks his son whether he enjoys Genevieve and whether she is bossy. Gottfried says she is not. Gottfried is angry with his father and accuses him of breaking up his affair with Genevieve.

The visitors are beginning to leave, but the band is playing and Catherine asks her father-in-law to dance. She reproaches him for his negative view of Gottfried, insisting that the artist works very hard. Their conversation is interrupted by a scream. Genevieve's purse has been stolen. She had left it on a chair covered up by her coat. Catherine and Gottfried think it must have been stolen by one of the truckmen who had been setting up the chairs for the lecture, and Mr. Hencke agrees. He says that Genevieve must be given some money in compensation before she goes home. Genevieve says it is all her fault and fears what her husband will say. Gottfried tells his father that he will not give her any money. Eventually he says that Catherine should do it.

In conversation with Mr. Hencke, Genevieve admits to being bored with New York but will not agree with his provocative remark that she is bored with Gottfried. She says she regrets losing the purse, although it is not the loss of money that concerns her. It is more a matter of loss of dignity.

Mr. Hencke picks up his suitcase and places it at her feet. He says that the next morning he will be visiting Sweden. He likes Scandinavia because it reminds him of the Germany of his youth. He tries to ignore yet another provocative remark from Genevieve that alludes to the Holocaust. He confesses that he did not have the heart to let Gottfried know that he was just passing through New York on his way to somewhere else rather than especially visiting him. Genevieve continues her provocation, saying she thinks he is really going to Germany, not Sweden. He denies it and adds that the Swedes were innocent in the war. They saved many Jews. Then he thinks once more of the robbery, saying that the truckmen were responsible for it. He opens his suitcase and displays the contents, eager to prove his own innocence, even though no one has accused him of theft.

Catherine approaches and hands Genevieve a check, saying that Gottfried insisted that she write it, and invites her to stay the night if there is not enough time for her to catch her flight. Genevieve takes the check and departs after declining the offer to stay. Catherine asks Mr. Hencke why the suitcase is open and the contents rumpled up. She wonders whether he has been the victim of thieves as well. Her final remark, that they have been harboring criminals without knowing it, unwittingly sounds like something Genevieve would say in one of her remarks about the guilt of all Germans.

CHARACTERS

Catherine Hencke

Catherine Hencke is Gottfried's wife. They have a two-year-old son. Her father-in-law, Mr. Hencke, loathes her because of her superficiality, ignorance, and lack of intelligence, and he finds her company depressing. Catherine's main advantage in life is that she comes from a wealthy Chicago family and has plenty of money to spend. She is described as a "beautiful girl, long-necked, black-haired, sweetly and irreproachably mannered, with a voice like a bird." She lives a mostly idle life, since she has little to do. She employs a cook, a maid, and a governess for the child. She is friends with Genevieve, without realizing that Genevieve and Gottfried are having an affair. She naively believes that Gottfried is a hard worker, protesting against Mr. Hencke's negative perception of him, but she does not realize that when Gottfried goes to his studio, it is often to entertain his mistress rather than to work.

Gottfried Hencke

Gottfried Hencke is Mr. Hencke's thirty-seven-year-old son. He is a Yale-educated artist whose work has been attracting attention in the art world—or at least a secluded corner of it—although he seems to have little talent. People come to the gallery more to hear the great critic MacDougal than to view Gottfried's work. Gottfried is able to devote his life to art because he has married a wealthy woman, Catherine, and he also relies on the superior intellect of his lover, Genevieve, to explain the nature of his work. His father regards him as an idiot and a lazy man who does not have a proper job. Gottfried and his father therefore have a rather distant and sometimes hostile relationship. During the evening, Gottfried tries to persuade Genevieve to agree to a romantic tryst later that night at his studio, where he is used to meeting her, but he tells his unsuspecting wife that he wants to go to the studio to work.

Mr. Hencke

Mr. Hencke is a sixty-eight-year-old retired German architect and traveler. He flew warplanes for Germany in World War I and was once shot down and wounded. He is proud of his military service and recalls it vividly. After the war, he immigrated to the United States. He now lives in Virginia and does not consider himself very German any more. He is a widower and has not spoken German since his wife died. Mr. Hencke does not get along with his son, whom he regards as unintelligent and lazy, nor does he like Gottfried's wife, Catherine, whom he regards as stupid. He does not understand Gottfried's art and has little patience with it. He is visiting his son while en route to Sweden, although he allows Gottfried to believe that he is making a special visit just to see him. Mr. Hencke is taunted by Genevieve, who tries to make him feel guilty about the Holocaust.

Genevieve Lewin

Genevieve Lewin is a Jewish woman who is married with four young daughters. She is having an affair with Gottfried, and they try to keep the affair secret. Gottfried's wife seems to suspect nothing, and she and Genevieve are fine friends. Genevieve lives in Indianapolis, where her husband is a well-off certified public accountant. Genevieve is intelligent and well educated, with a degree from Smith College. She is far more intelligent than Gottfried, and it is she who supplies him with the quotations used in the leaflet describing the program for the art exhibit and lecture. Genevieve dislikes Germans and makes provocative remarks to Mr. Hencke about the fact that he is German. She regards him as a Nazi sympathizer and keeps bringing up the Holocaust, implying that all Germans, including Mr. Hencke, must share the guilt. When Genevieve's purse is stolen, she fears that her husband will be angry and blame her for being careless. She says he has warned her in the past about this.

Creighton MacDougal

Creighton MacDougal is a famous literary and cultural critic from the *Partisan Review* who gives a lecture on Gottfried's art at the gallery. He is bearded, and Catherine thinks he looks like God. MacDougal charges a high fee for his services and is presented in satirical fashion as an academic who is very involved in his own theorizing, which nonetheless sheds little actual light on what he is talking about. His talk seems to be more about himself than Gottfried's art.

THEMES

Guilt

In her interactions with Mr. Hencke, Genevieve tries to implicate him in the Holocaust and make him feel guilty about it. She does this solely because he is German, even though he played no part in World War II. Her first allusion to the topic comes when she refers to the crowd at the gallery as they stare at the paintings as resembling people in a "concentration camp.... Everybody staring through the barbed wire hoping for rescue and knowing it's no use." Then, deliberately trying to provoke Mr. Hencke, she refers to Gottfried's art as "shredded swastikas." Later she tries to quiz Mr. Hencke about whether the shampoo manufactured by his brother-in-law in Germany

during the war was made out of the fat of Jewish victims. Not letting up, she kisses him and declares, "Your cheek is like barbed wire. Your cheek has the ruts left by General Rommel's tanks." (Rommel was a German commander during World War II, although he was not associated with any war crimes.) Her final reference to the Nazis and the Holocaust is made after she has been robbed of her purse. When Mr. Hencke tells her that Germany now is all factories and chimneys, unlike the pastoral landscapes he remembers from his boyhood, Genevieve retorts, "Don't speak to me about German chimneys.... I know what kind of smoke came out of those damn German chimneys." She is referring to the burning of the Jewish corpses during the Holocaust. It is clear that Genevieve believes in collective guilt. She appears to blame all Germans for the Holocaust and rejects anything German. As Mr. Hencke puts it, "She was the sort who, twenty years after Hitler's war, would not buy a Volkswagen."

For his part, Mr. Hencke, the architect, is keen to protest his innocence. "I have harmed no one," he says. "I have built towers. Towers!... I have never destroyed." However, it is notable that Mr. Hencke carefully avoids the topic of who was responsible for the Holocaust. It seems he does not want to think about the German destruction of the Jews. He will not attribute it to Hitler and the Nazis but only to some inexorable historical process, apparently under no one's control: "Who could be blamed for History?" he thinks to himself, as "History was a Force-in-Itself, like Evolution." He thereby suggests that no one (and certainly not himself) should carry any blame or guilt for it. It is the same when it comes up in conversation that the famed psychologist Carl Jung is not Jewish. That fact explains, says Genevieve, "why he went on staying alive." When Catherine says she thought Jung was dead, Mr. Hencke responds with the banal generality, "Everybody dies," as if no one is ever responsible for the death of another. However, Mr. Hencke's reaction following the theft of Genevieve's purse shows that he has been rattled by her accusations. He is anxious to establish that he is traveling the next day not to Germany but to Sweden, saying, "The Swedes were innocent in the war, they saved so many Jews." And the fact that he opens his suitcase and displays the contents to prove he did not steal the purse also shows his defensiveness, which has been brought on by Genevieve's aggressive attitude, since no one present believes that he is the thief.

TOPICS FOR FURTHER STUDY

- Research the topic of anti-Semitism today and give a class presentation. Is anti-Semitism on the rise? If so, in what countries or regions, and why? What can be done to end anti-Semitism? A good place to start your research is online at the United States Holocaust Memorial Museum website with the article "Anti-Semitism: The Longest Hatred," at http://www.ushmm.org/confront-antisemitism/anti semitism-the-longest-hatred. Another useful source is the November 2013 *New York Times* article "Jews in Europe Report a Rise in Anti-Semitism," available from http://www.nyti mes.com/2013/11/09/world/europe/jews-in-eu rope-report-a-surge-in-anti-semitism.html?_r = 0 and written by Andrew Higgins.

- Reread "The Suitcase," and then write an additional section to the story in a blog. In the section, imagine Mr. Hencke in his room at the hotel that night after his visit to the gallery and his disturbing encounter with Genevieve. What thoughts are going through his mind? Does he regret opening his suitcase when it did not seem necessary? Is he angry with Genevieve? Does the thought of who is responsible for the Holocaust enter his head? Send the blog entry to your classmates and invite them to comment.

- In "The Suitcase," Genevieve keeps bringing to Mr. Hencke's attention Germany's extreme anti-Semitism during the Nazi era. However, Genevieve and her husband, both Jewish, have been very successful in the United States, and it seems they have faced no discrimination. In this they may be typical. Although Jews have been persecuted for centuries in many countries around the world, especially in Europe, their experience in America has been different. Why is this so? What has been the history of the Jews in the United States? Have Jews faced discrimination at any time in the history of the United States? Write an essay in which you discuss this topic.

- In "The Suitcase," Mr. Hencke makes no comment on the Holocaust, but he does mention the bombing by the British Royal Air Force (RAF) of the German city of Köln (Cologne), in which his sister lost her home and her daughter died. Cologne was bombed many times by the Allies during World War II. The most devastating raid was conducted on the night of May 30, 1942. It was called the thousand-bomber raid. At https://www.youtube.com/watch?v = Xfe0vEkz3lI watch the news report "The First Thousand-Bomber Raid, Cologne," made by the British at the time. Conduct further Internet research on the raid, and give a multimedia class presentation about it. What was the intent of bombing Cologne? What did the British hope to achieve? Was the raid successful?

- Read *Tell Them We Remember: The Story of the Holocaust* (1994), by Susan D. Bachrach, which is an account of the Holocaust for young readers that contains many photographs. What do you learn about the Holocaust from this book that you did not know before? Does reading this book make you see "The Suitcase" differently? How does it alter or refine your reading of the story? Write a blog entry in which you express your thoughts.

Revenge

If Mr. Hencke can be seen as unwilling to engage the issue of the Holocaust, Genevieve might be seen as bent on revenge against the Germans for the destruction of the Jews. She identifies herself with the victims and seeks to make her point even in an inappropriate setting, at an art gallery and with a German man who did not fight in World War II and was not even in Germany at the time. There is an irony

Mr. Hencke meets his son's mistress, Genevieve, at the art show. (© Semisatch | Shutterstock.com)

in her position because she herself appears to have suffered no discrimination on account of being Jewish, and neither, it would seem, has her successful husband in Indianapolis, who occupies a respected place in society. She harbors feelings of resentment on behalf of the Jewish people as a whole and plays the role of victim. This, at any rate, is how Mr. Hencke sees her. When he hears her scream after discovering that her purse has been stolen, he likens it to "A Biblical yell, as by the waters of Babylon." This is a reference to Psalm 137, in which the Israelites in exile envision revenge on their captors.

Mr. Hencke is not averse to some revenge himself. Although he controls himself in Genevieve's presence, he likely resents her attitude toward him. When he tells Gottfried to give Genevieve money after the theft of her purse, there is a suggestion that he regards her, because of her affair with Gottfried, as a prostitute who must be paid off. The payment would therefore be a humiliation. (Earlier, he resents what he interprets as her suggestion that he is likely to entertain prostitutes in his hotel room.) The fact that he harbors notions of revenge against Genevieve is confirmed by the thoughts he has when he hears her scream. He "envisioned wounds. In his heart, she bled, she bled."

STYLE

Point of View

"The Suitcase" is told by a limited third-person narrator from the point of view of Mr. Hencke. This means that the narrator knows the thoughts and feelings of Mr. Hencke but not those of the other characters, who are revealed only by their own words and actions and Mr. Hencke's reactions to them. Occasionally the narrator does reveal information about the other characters that Mr. Hencke might not know (such as the fact that when Gottfried is in his studio, he can hear the sound of the cuckoo clock in the neighboring apartment), but these are minor exceptions. Much of the story is told through dialogue, and the characters are given many opportunities to reveal themselves fully through their words. Also, during the course of the story, the narrator offers up many of Mr. Hencke's detailed observations of his son, his daughter-in-law, and Genevieve (almost none of which are flattering or positive) and reveals much of his own inner world.

Imagery

"The Suitcase" contains rich and varied imagery, much of it in the form of similes. A simile is a comparison, usually using "like" or "as," between two unlike things made in such a way as to bring out some underlying similarity. Many examples can be found. Mr. Hencke's mouth when seen in the context of his whole face is "like a slipped thread in a linen sack." Mr. Hencke describes the literary critics from *Partisan Review* as having "faces like a mackerel after it's been caught, with the hook still in its mouth"; Genevieve offers a self-description using a simile: "Nose thin and delicate, like a Communion wafer" (there is irony here in the Jewish woman describing herself with the aid of a Christian image). Catherine's laugh "broke like a dish." The critic Creighton MacDougal "snapped his heels like a Junker officer" (the Junkers were Prussian landowning nobility in the nineteenth century, and Prussia later became the dominant region in the unified German state). Gottfried, after stubbornly refusing to give Genevieve any money, "resembled a pretty little spotted horse spitting disappointing hay."

The imagery often gives insight into character. In the case of Mr. Hencke, it reveals the extent to which the memory of his military service in World War I has remained with him nearly a half century later. He loved the airplanes he flew, and the way he describes the Rumpler-Taube converts a plane that served as both fighter and bomber into an image of peace and beauty: it "resembled a lovely great dove." This is the description he gives to Creighton MacDougal when he speaks to the critic after his lecture. All Mr. Hencke talks about to MacDougal are those World War I planes. It is thus not surprising that military metaphors come naturally to him. When the saxophone starts playing, he hears that "a saxophone opened fire," identifying a saxophone with a gun. When Genevieve screams he "envisioned wounds," and "the saxophone machine-gunned him in the small intestine." The violence of the imagery suggests the violence of his feelings against Genevieve, despite his courtly and polite manner toward her.

HISTORICAL CONTEXT

The Holocaust

Although the setting of "The Suitcase" is in a New York art gallery in the mid-1960s, the story cannot be fully understood without knowledge of the Holocaust. The Holocaust refers to the murder of approximately six million Jews in Nazi concentration camps during World War II (1939–1945). The Jews were exterminated because the Nazis believed they were an inferior race and a threat to German racial supremacy. During the Holocaust, nearly two out of every three European Jews died.

ATTITUDES TOWARD THE HOLOCAUST IN AMERICA

In the late 1940s and throughout the 1950s and well into the 1960s, the Holocaust was not a major topic of discussion in American public life, according to Peter Novick in his book *The Holocaust in American Life*. Only a few books dealt with it. Even *The Diary of a Young Girl* (1947), by Anne Frank—a Dutch Jewish teenager who perished in the Holocaust before the diary was found—was not much read at the time, although it went on to sell millions of copies. Even high-school and college textbooks contained only brief references to the Holocaust, and some did not mention it at all.

Novick explains that the Holocaust was neglected because the global political situation had changed. After the war, Germany was divided into two independent countries. East Germany became part of the Communist eastern bloc, but West Germany became a US ally, and the Soviet Union replaced Nazi Germany as the main enemy and threat to US security. The atrocities of the Nazis, including the Holocaust, tended to fade into the background in this situation.

Most American Jews during this period, however, according to Novick, likely retained considerable anti-German sentiment. Some of them boycotted German products, rejecting Volkswagen cars and Grundig radios, for example. (As Mr. Hencke points out in "The Suitcase," Genevieve is one of those Jews who refuses to buy a Volkswagen.) American Jews also conducted an informal and not scrupulously observed boycott of travel to Germany. Despite these private anti-German feelings, however, American Jews were reluctant to display their sentiments in public for fear of being seen as out of step with the mainstream of American life, which might have raised the risk of producing a wave of anti-Semitism in the United States. At this time, in the late 1940s and early 1950s, there was still some negative perception of Jews among Americans generally, and Jews were also often associated with Communism, although Jewish organizations worked hard to neutralize that perception during the 1950s and into the 1960s. They lobbied movie producers, for example, to make sure that Hollywood films did not present Jewish characters in a bad light or associate them with pro-Communist sympathies.

Novick points out that another reason the Holocaust did not figure prominently in American life in the 1950s was that the postwar years were very optimistic. Anti-Semitism diminished rapidly as the 1950s went on, and during that decade American Jews felt there were no barriers to what they could achieve. Novick points out that three-quarters of American Jews were American born. They therefore perceived themselves, and were perceived by others, as less foreign, and were more integrated into the mainstream of American life. (In "The Suitcase," the successful Genevieve Lewin and her husband are examples of this.) Novick writes, "The upbeat and universalist postwar mood...muted

COMPARE & CONTRAST

- **1960s–1970s:** Jewish American literature becomes part of mainstream American literature. Saul Bellow wins the Nobel Prize in Literature in 1976. Isaac Bashevis Singer, Bernard Malamud, Philip Roth, Grace Paley, and Ozick all produce notable works that are critically well received and commercially popular. Singer wins the Nobel Prize in Literature in 1978.

  Today: Prominent Jewish American novelists include Nicole Krauss, the author of *Man Walks into a Room* (2002) and *Great House* (2010); Jonathan Safran Foer, who is married to Krauss and the author of *Everything Is Illuminated* (2002) and *Extremely Loud and Incredibly Close* (2005); and Michael Chabon, the author of *The Mysteries of Pittsburgh* (1988), *The Yiddish Policeman's Union* (2007), and *Telegraph Avenue* (2012).

- **1960s–1970s:** In the United States during the 1960s and beyond, artists experiment with new forms, including pop art, minimalism, and color-field painting. Prominent artists include Robert Rauschenberg and Jasper Johns.

  Today: There is a rich diversity in twenty-first century American art. No one style or movement dominates, and fresh ideas flourish. American art attains international recognition.

- **1960s–1970s:** In contrast to the 1950s, when the Holocaust is not widely discussed in public by American Jews, these decades mark a turn. Remembering the Holocaust becomes a more significant part of Jewish American identity. This coincides with a period when American Jewish leaders fear the rise of a new anti-Semitism that makes American Jews feel more vulnerable and therefore more ready to identify with the Jewish history of victimization.

  Today: Knowledge and remembrance of the Holocaust are firmly embedded in the United States and globally. In Washington, DC, the United States Holocaust Memorial Museum receives an average of 3.6 million visitors per year. International Holocaust Remembrance Day, established by the United Nations General Assembly in 2005, falls on January 27 each year.

discussion of the Holocaust." American Jews did not want to identify themselves as victims.

CHANGING PERCEPTIONS

During the 1960s, the reluctance of American Jews to identify themselves as victims began to change, according to Novick, as a few key events forced the Holocaust into the American consciousness. First, in 1962 Israel captured the war criminal Adolf Eichmann (1906–1962) in Argentina and took him to Israel to face trial. During the war Eichmann was one of the chief organizers of the Holocaust. He was convicted in court and executed by hanging in 1962. (Eichmann is mentioned in "The Suitcase" when Mr. Hencke observes that Genevieve regards him as an anti-Semite, an Eichmann-type figure.) The trial of Eichmann received wide publicity in the United States and around the world, raising public awareness of the Holocaust.

Another key event was the Six-Day War of 1967, between Israel and a coalition of Arab states. When the war broke out, American Jews were at first anxious that another Holocaust might be about to unfold in the Middle East as Arab leaders boasted about annihilating Israel. Israel's quick victory alleviated those fears, but they resurfaced more acutely during the Arab-Israeli War of 1973 (the Yom Kippur War). In that war, Israel suffered serious early reversals, and US assistance was vital in securing its ultimate victory. During this period,

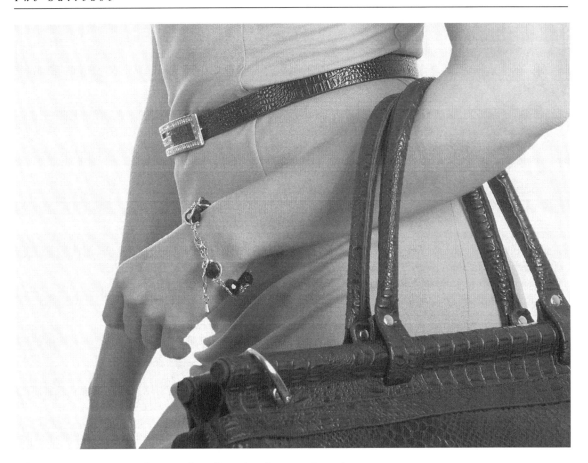

The story comes to a climax when Genevieve's purse is stolen. (© sergei telegin / Shutterstock.com)

American Jews felt keenly the isolation and precarious position of Israel in the Middle East and Jews in the world generally. Ozick wrote a polemical essay, published in *Esquire* in November 1974, titled "All the World Wants the Jews Dead."

In the wake of the 1973 war, Jewish leaders in the United States adopted the notion that the reason for Israel's isolation was that the Holocaust had been forgotten. A new generation had emerged knowing little or nothing about the mass murder of the Jews by the Nazis that had taken place only thirty or so years before. During the 1970s and continuing into the 1980s, 1990s, and beyond, the need to remember the Holocaust became more central to American Jews and Americans generally than it had ever been before. "In the 1970s, American Jews' anxiety about Israel's security, and their viewing Israel's situation within a Holocaust framework, was the single greatest catalyst of the new centering of the Holocaust in American Jewish

consciousness," writes Novick. In terms of "The Suitcase," Genevieve Lewin can be seen as an early representative of this new Jewish assertiveness about the Holocaust, since she brings it up again and again in the unlikely setting of an art show in New York sometime in the mid-1960s. She makes it abundantly clear that the Holocaust is not something to be forgotten or airbrushed away. She also seems to insist on general German guilt for the atrocity. In this she not only reflects the anti-German sentiment common among American Jews in the 1950s but also expresses a view close to that advanced by Daniel Jonah Goldhagen in his book published in 1996, *Hitler's Willing Executioners: Ordinary Germans and the Holocaust.* Goldhagen argues that anti-Semitism had permeated German society for generations and that the Holocaust could not have taken place without this general hatred of the Jews in Germany. Goldhagen's book was a best seller, but his thesis has proved controversial.

CRITICAL OVERVIEW

The Pagan Rabbi and Other Stories was highly praised by reviewers upon publication in 1971. In a laudatory review in *Newsweek*, Peter S. Prescott declares that three of the seven stories in the collection "are among the best written by Americans in recent years." Although Prescott does not include "The Suitcase" among those three stories, his later comment about the collection as a whole might well be applied to "The Suitcase":

> Miss Ozick plays with wisecracks and with ironies. Nothing happens in her stories that is not bound up into the whole. Nearly all of them, for all their wit and their absurdities, turn out to be both funnier and sadder than we expected at the start.

In the *New York Times Book Review*, Joanna Kaplan was equally enthusiastic. She describes Ozick as "a kind of narrative hypnotist. Her range is extraordinary; there is seemingly nothing she cannot do. Her stories contain passages of intense lyricism and brilliant, hilarious, uncontainable inventiveness—jokes, lists, letters, poems, parodies, satires."

Later critics have commented directly on "The Suitcase." Josephine Z. Knopp, in "Ozick's Jewish Stories," argues that of the two adversaries, Genevieve is the guilty one, and by the end of the story it is Mr. Hencke "who is victimized, reduced from strength and self-assurance to uncertainty and tearful guilt." Knopp continues:

> Humiliated, guilty for reasons which are at best obscure, he may be considered a victim of Jewish revenge, a revenge that brings an unwelcome awareness of his implication, the implication of the world, in distant atrocities, and an awareness too that Genevieve, though a victim herself, "was not innocent."

In *Understanding Cynthia Ozick*, Lawrence S. Friedman argues against the interpretation of the story that would see Mr. Hencke as a victim, pounced on by Genevieve. On the contrary, Mr. Hencke's "compulsive show of innocence...is the guilty reflex of a man whose innate Germanness has just been exposed." Friedman continues, "To see Mr. Hencke as a victim is to conspire with him in obliterating the history he would prefer to forget or at least subtly to revise." Genevieve, according to Friedman, "forces upon Mr. Hencke the awareness of his implication in the atrocities."

Victor Strandberg, in "The Art of Cynthia Ozick," notes that at first the two main characters, Genevieve and Mr. Hencke, "seem totally assimilated into the larger American society." But when they meet, "their layers of assimilation rapidly peel away, exposing the ethnic granite at the core of each personality." For Strandberg, it is Genevieve who gets the better of their encounter, because she forces Mr. Hencke into "compulsively prov[ing] himself innocent.... It is a paradigm of his much larger and unanswerable need for innocence."

For Elaine Kauvar, in *Cynthia Ozick's Fiction: Tradition and Invention*, as the story progresses, Mr. Hencke "becomes more German" and Genevieve "becomes more Jewish." In the contest between them, Kauvar, like Strandberg, regards Genevieve as the victor because Mr. Hencke is made to feel guilty for "his dreams and his German thoughts."

CRITICISM

Bryan Aubrey

Aubrey holds a PhD in English. In the following essay, he examines the conflict between father and son in "The Suitcase."

"Cynthia Ozick is never in danger of saying too little as a writer," states Thomas R. Edwards in a review of Ozick's *Bloodshed and Three Novellas* from the *New York Review of Books* in 1986. Edwards's comment might well be applied to the stories in *The Pagan Rabbi and Other Stories*, including "The Suitcase." In "The Suitcase," Ozick revels in her clever and exuberant use of language as she paints the portraits of her characters and develops her themes, piling up layers of description and presenting unusual images and metaphors. Her wicked sense of humor finds an outlet in her highly satirical presentation of the pretentious critic from the *Partisan Review*, Creighton Mac-Dougal, and in Mr. Hencke's jaundiced and emphatic views of his son and daughter-in-law. Still, Ozick is able to suggest with some subtlety the underlying dynamics that exist between the four characters presented: Mr. Hencke; his son, Gottfried; Gottfried's wife, Catherine; and Gottfried's lover, Genevieve. In this respect, the story continues to reveal itself even after several readings.

WHAT DO I READ NEXT?

- *The Holocaust: The World and the Jews, 1933–1945* (1992), by Seymour Rossel, is an account of the Holocaust for young-adult readers. The book describes the rise of anti-Semitism in Europe, the murder of Jews in the Holocaust, Jewish resistance, and the trials of Nazi war criminals that followed the war. Rossel makes use of primary documents such as memoirs and journals, and there are many black-and-white photographs.

- "The Shawl" is one of Ozick's most powerful short stories. Only about two thousand words in length, it is about Rosa, a young Jewish woman in a Nazi concentration camp during World War II. Rosa has an infant daughter, Magda, who in the climax of the story is thrown against an electrical fence by a camp guard. "The Shawl" was first published in the *New Yorker* in 1980. It was reprinted, along with a longer story, "Rosa," in the volume titled *The Shawl* in 1989. "Rosa" focuses on Rosa thirty years later. She is living alone in Florida, dealing with the memory of what happened to her and her daughter.

- *A Cynthia Ozick Reader* (1996), edited by Elaine M. Kauvar, contains a representative selection of Ozick's work, including poems, short stories, novel excerpts, and essays.

- *The Complete Stories* (1997), by Bernard Malamud, edited and introduced by Robert Giroux, contains fifty-five stories by one of the leading American short-story writers of the twentieth century. Ozick wrote in the same tradition as Malamud (1914–1986), who belongs to an earlier generation of Jewish American writers.

- Ozick is sometimes compared to Flannery O'Connor (1925–1964), an important Southern American twentieth-century writer known for her thirty-one stories and two novels. O'Connor's *The Complete Stories* (1971) is a testament to her achievement.

- *Elijah Visible: Stories* (1999), by Thane Rosenbaum, comprises nine interlinked stories in which a character named Adam Posner appears in various guises and experiences what it is like to be the son of Holocaust survivors. Rosenbaum is a New York City lawyer whose own parents were Holocaust survivors, and this debut collection of stories was critically well received.

Ozick knows when not to be subtle. For example, when Genevieve quite deliberately taunts Mr. Hencke with the facts of the Holocaust, it is as if she is actually striking him with a heavy, blunt instrument. "What were its secret ingredients?" she asks about the shampoo that Mr. Hencke's brother-in-law made in Germany during World War II; "Whose human fat? What Jewish lard?" It is in this uncompromising way that Ozick brings up and develops her main themes of German guilt and Jewish revenge. Genevieve challenges Mr. Hencke because she nurses a deep sense of victimization, and under her relentless pressure, Mr. Hencke finds that he is by no means as free of his original Germanness as he likes to believe. There are deep and raw emotions at work here.

Another theme in the story, less explosive perhaps but nonetheless keenly felt, is the conflict between father and son. Mr. Hencke and Gottfried do not get along with each other. The first indication that the relationship between them has broken down, seemingly irretrievably so, comes in the first paragraph, when Mr. Hencke reveals that he regrets naming his son after himself. If he could do it over again, he would call his son John, not Gottfried. This suggests that when Gottfried was born, his father, not unnaturally perhaps,

> MR. HENCKE'S ART, HE WOULD ARGUE,
> HAS RESULTED IN SOMETHING TANGIBLE THAT
> IS ALSO USEFUL AND FULFILLS A SOCIAL NEED.
> NOT SO FOR GOTTFRIED, AT LEAST AS FAR AS
> MR. HENCKE SEES IT."

had high hopes for his son and wanted him to follow in his footsteps. Like many fathers who expect their sons to be virtual copies of themselves, he has been badly disappointed. Mr. Hencke is a sophisticated man who appears to have led a rather successful life. He flew warplanes for Germany in World War I, and after the war immigrated to the United States and became an architect. He is also a world traveler. In contrast, Gottfried, at the age of thirty-seven, appears in his father's eyes to have done very little in life so far. Mr. Hencke expresses contempt for his son when he thinks that while he himself is retired, his son "could never retire because he had never worked."

Yet the two men do have things in common. They are both artists of a kind, although as an architect Mr. Hencke was a very different kind of artist than his son has turned out to be. Mr. Hencke's art, he would argue, has resulted in something tangible that is also useful and fulfills a social need. Not so for Gottfried, at least as far as Mr. Hencke sees it. Mr. Hencke has no understanding of his son's art, and little patience with it. This is his description of his son's offerings:

> His canvases were full of hidden optical tricks and were so bewildering to one's routine retinal expectations that, once the eye had turned away, a whirring occurred in the pupil's depth, and the paintings began to speak in their afterimage.

Not for the only time in the story, there is a hint here of a generation gap that is a common theme in modern literature. As life rapidly changes, the older generation is baffled by the new ideas and tastes of the young and is ready to dismiss them as worthless. In a telling image, Mr. Hencke sees his son's work as a kind of senseless playing around with something that might have been of value had it been used properly, namely, an architect's plan (like the no doubt numerous plans he himself drew up during his career):

> Everything was disconcerting, everything seemed pasted down flat—strips, corners, angles, slivers. Mr. Hencke had a perilous sense that Gottfried had simply cut up the plans for an old office building with extraordinarily tiny scissors.

Mr. Hencke thus implicitly contrasts his own, useful art with the apparent triviality and worthlessness of the work produced by his son. The generation gap can be seen again in the fact that Mr. Hencke admires what he calls the "old school," which he remembers as being embodied in his father and his teachers. This attitude toward life emphasized hard work, strictness, and discipline. "Boys nowadays don't stand for that," he tells Creighton MacDougal.

Mr. Hencke does recognize that he and his son share an artistic sensibility, but it is notable that Gottfried works for the most part only in black and white, whereas Mr. Hencke has a particular fondness for a certain color, yellow, and this color is associated with him throughout the story. He lives in a yellow-brick house, Catherine has placed yellow curtains in the room she expects him to stay in, and when she mentions this, he remembers an image from his childhood: "the yellow buttercups on the slope below the millhouse." He also reexperiences in dreams the incident in World War II when his niece was killed in a Royal Air Force bombing raid. He sees her lying dead, covered by her yellow hair. It seems that for some reason, the color yellow opens up for him deeper aspects of his own being. Gottfried, by contrast, seems to be more shallow, at least in his father's eyes, and also lacking in courage. When Gottfried tells Mr. Hencke that he has finally plucked up the courage to start working with colors—he mentions blue—Mr. Hencke remarks pointedly, "I am always glad to look at any evidence of my son's courage." It is a cruel remark that is not lost on Gottfried.

Although Gottfried is seen mostly through the eyes of his disapproving father, the facts of his life do not offer much to redeem him from his father's censure. He seems weak and self-indulgent, a nobody, as the name of his gallery, Nobody's Gallery, implies. (The name is meant

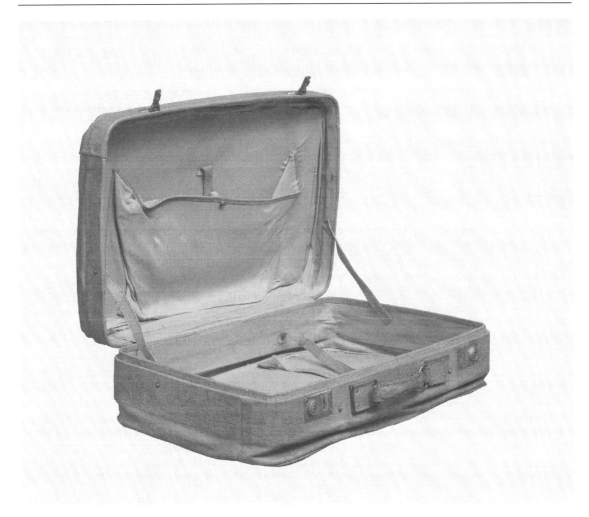

Mr. Hencke, feeling accused by Genevieve, opens his suitcase to prove his innocence.

(© aboikis | Shutterstock.com)

to be an ironic joke.) Gottfried has had the opportunity for an elite education, at Yale University, but seems to be coasting through life with the help of the women to whom he has become attached. It is Catherine, from a Chicago old-money family, who supplies him with the financial security to pursue his art. And it is his lover, Genevieve, a woman of superior intellect, who is willing to comb through the works of the likes of Beethoven, Goethe, and Thomas Mann to find appropriate quotations for the art exhibit program that appear to give intellectual heft to Gottfried's otherwise inconsequential art. Mr. Hencke's verdict on Gottfried's dependence on his women is a damning one: "he was two parts Catherine's money to one part Genevieve's brain, and too cowardly altogether to stir the mixture."

Adding to the negative portrait of Gottfried is his willingness to deceive his wife, who thinks that because he spends so much time at his studio, he works hard, when in reality he is using it as a place to meet with Genevieve. Mr. Hencke is aware of this, of course, and seems in that regard to know his son well. He also knows that his son sometimes frequents prostitutes. Given all this, it is not surprising that father and son are always at loggerheads. Mr. Hencke does not even like to stay at his son's house. He disapproves of Gottfried's liaison with Genevieve and does his best to sabotage it, which arouses Gottfried's anger.

Seen in this light, the story becomes as much about family dysfunction as it is about a clash of viewpoints regarding the Holocaust, and in the course of the story, there is no movement toward familial reconciliation or rapprochement. The father makes a call on his son more out of duty than pleasure, and the two men fall into their apparently well-established pattern of quarreling. Meanwhile, there are a deceived, empty-headed wife—a woman who is held in contempt by her father-in-law—and, outside the family but pressing in on it, a Jewish woman who is not frightened of irritating and challenging her lover's father. It is a toxic brew, into which Ozick carefully places her bombshell themes of Holocaust remembrance and guilt.

Source: Bryan Aubrey, Critical Essay on "The Suitcase," in *Short Stories for Students*, Gale, Cengage Learning, 2015.

Dara Horn

In the following essay, Horn describes the collection The Pagan Rabbi and Other Stories, *which includes "The Suitcase," as the first book she ever truly loved.*

Your first love touches you like no other love ever will. Even if later loves linger, the first leaves its fingerprints on your body and brain, the impressions that every later love will have to fill. For most people, that soul-shaping love arrives in human form. Mine came, when I was 14, in the form of a book. It was *The Pagan Rabbi* by Cynthia Ozick.

I had been haunted since childhood by the possibility of stories as a kind of gash in the fabric of the universe, a rip in the veil that hung between the mundane and the real, through which one could glimpse the purpose that animated the world. I had gotten this idea from reading the Torah, whose angry and evil and utterly normal characters loved and lashed out at God as though they were teenagers confronting a disappointed parent. These characters felt the presence of this purpose as though no veil had ever existed. This puzzled and pained me. What caused that veil to fall between the creator and the created? And might it be possible to brush that veil aside?

When I tried to find modern literature with the power to tear through the veil, I came up empty. I was directed to books by Philip Roth—in which it appeared, to my teenage mind, that the most compelling purpose in life had something to do with hating one's mother. This got old fast. Someone else directed me to Chaim Potok, but the world in his books was so

distant from mine that I might as well have been reading about the patriarchs: people to whom the ineffable was available in a way it would never be for me.

And then I discovered *The Pagan Rabbi*, a book of stories, set in modern times, about idolatry. Yes, idolatry: that most irrelevant of biblical sins that preoccupies so much of the Torah and would appear to be no more meaningful to contemporary life than the sacrifice of goats. In Ozick's work, idolatry is not only an animating force in the contemporary world, but the weight and fabric of the veil itself. Yet Ozick is no preacher. She is an artist deeply involved in the practice of idol-worship that is contemporary literature. Her work is entwined with the sins and suffering that idolatry spawns: the seduction of status, "originality," youth, quests for immortality, what Ecclesiastes called *hevel*—vanity, vacuity, breath.

The title story is almost too explicit in its enactment of the lure of the temporal. It concerns a brilliant rabbi's suicide after his descent into a love of nature, to the neglect of his moral obligations. Yet I was astounded to find a real writer who cited the Mishnah—the Mishnah!—and cited it as though it mattered. Even the most seemingly casual description was infused with a subtle moral alertness so alien to American letters that it seemed like it ought not be allowed. Felled trees in a city park, in Ozick's language, did not merely evoke neglect, but became an evocation of an alien natural world whose ephemeral quality rendered it strangely worthless: "Their moist inner wheels breathed out a fragrance of barns, countryside, decay."

This was a mere prelude to what are the shining stars of this astounding book: two novella-length stories, "Envy, or Yiddish in America" and "Virility." The former is the story of two American Yiddish writers. One feeds the crowd "subversive" stories of a dead Jewish life that they yearn for; his work is adulated and translated into every language. The second writer, from whose perspective the story emerges, is a real poet, untranslated and forgotten and crippled by envy of the other writer's success. (Ozick has denied that this story is a roman à clef, though no reader aware of Yiddish literature can avoid thinking of the rivalry between Isaac Bashevis Singer and the brilliant and never-translated Polish-born American poet Yankev Glatshteyn.) A lesser artist might have made this into a sob story, but in Ozick's hands, this setup is the stage for a story about idolatry: the debilitating quest for fame, how irresistible the seduction of adulation is for the person who doesn't have it, and, by the story's end, how weird and painfully difficult Judaism has always been for setting itself against it—for insisting that we are but dust and ashes even if the world was created for us, that our creativity is limited, that nothing we can do as artists can ever come close to creating or redeeming the world. It is the story of the existential impossibility of being a Jewish writer. "Virility" is about a famous poet whose renown comes from a source that makes the whole idea of fame, of art, of transcendence itself into a kind of cosmic pun. By the time the reader reaches this story at the collection's end, it's impossible not to get the joke.

These stories could not pull away that veil that hangs before our eyes today, and now that I have become a writer myself, its presence continues to haunt me. But Ozick's stories showed me what that veil was made of—and taught me how to see beyond it.

Recently I spoke with a religious man, a Jewish writer who has nobly won his own struggles against the seductions of fame. He called Cynthia Ozick holy. Ozick herself would surely reject this description as idolatrous. Perhaps it is the pagan urge within me, but I agreed with him. One cannot help but feel that way about one's first love.

Source: Dara Horn, "Idolatrous First Love," in *Moment*, Vol. 35, No. 1, January–February 2010, p. 77.

Lawrence S. Friedman

In the following excerpt, Friedman points out the "reverse victimization" in "The Suitcase."

... Genevieve is the lone Jew in the radically different setting of "The Suitcase": the New York art world. The confrontation between Jew and Gentile—and their respective ethos—confined to a single telephone conversation in "Envy," makes up the central action of "The Suitcase." Edelshtein's bitter exchange of epithets with the anti-Semite is anticlimactic in the sense that it confirms what was already known; Genevieve's politely destructive exchange with Mr. Hencke is climactic in the sense that it reveals what was only suspected. Like Edelshtein, Genevieve is cast as representative Jew—but one whose victimization is less immediately apparent than his. Although Mr. Hencke, a former pilot in the Kaiser's air force, has lived in America so long that he "no longer thought of himself as a German," he is forced by Genevieve into a role as symbolic as her own. Mr. Hencke correctly interprets her comparison of the people crowded together at Gottfried's exhibit to concentration camp victims and of Gottfried's paintings to "shredded swastikas" as an attempt to label him a "Nazi sympathizer even now, an anti-Semite, an Eichmann." If it is true that Genevieve tries to make of Mr. Hencke the stereotypical German, it is equally true that he makes of her the stereotypical Jew—"the sort who, twenty years after Hitler's war, would not buy a Volkswagen, ... full of detestable moral gestures." It seems to Mr. Hencke that Genevieve's "detestable moral gestures" are misdirected and that he, a man who has "harmed no one," is a victim of Jewish revenge.

To accept Mr. Hencke's point of view is to read "The Suitcase" as a study in reverse victimization: "Genevieve as Jew is a victim, but in the story it is Mr. Hencke who is victimized, reduced from strength and self assurance to uncertainty and tearful guilt." But this is to confuse revelation with victimization. Only in the narrow sense of being prodded into an unconscious admission of guilt can Mr. Hencke be regarded as a victim. His compulsive show of innocence—when Genevieve's purse is stolen he throws "open his suitcase with so much wild vigor that it quivered on its hinges"—is the guilty reflex of a man whose innate Germanness has just been exposed. His extravagant denial—"Please, I swear it"—of a petty crime against a Jew, which of course he did not commit, is actually a denial of his complicity as a German (and possibly an anti-Semite) in the massive crimes committed against all Jews. Mr. Hencke insists to Genevieve that his suitcase is packed for Sweden, not for Germany—"I swear it"—juxtaposing the innocence of the Swedes, who "saved so many Jews," with his own innocence as regards the missing purse. It is largely by means of such ironic juxtapositions, clustering together in the last few pages of "The Suitcase," that Mr. Hencke in protesting too much aligns himself with the victimizers. And it is impossible to read Catherine's joke about the "criminals we've harbored unawares!"—which "sounded exactly like a phrase of Genevieve's"—as anything but a shatteringly ironic reference to Mr. Hencke.

To see Mr. Hencke as a victim is to conspire with him in obliterating the history he would prefer to forget or at least subtly to revise. As a Jew, Genevieve can condone neither his amnesia nor his revisionism. She therefore strips away the American veneer to expose the German foundation of Mr. Hencke's identity. For him the Holocaust was perpetrated not by Germans but by the impersonal forces of history: "Who could be blamed for History?" which "was a Force-in-Itself, like Evolution." "A horrible tragedy," he calls his sister's loss of home and daughter of eleven in an R.A.F. raid on Cologne. Yet he is silent about the infinitely more horrible tragedy of the Holocaust that engulfed six million Jews. Aside from that suffered by his sister, the only other "tragedy" he sees fit to mention is the damage sustained by the Cologne cathedral. To Genevieve's remark that if Jung were a Jewish psychiatrist (as Catherine had mistakenly thought) he would have been murdered by the Nazis, Mr. Hencke replies, "Everybody dies." This bland rejoinder, effectively equating natural process and genocide, is among the most striking of Mr. Hencke's evasive strategies. By successively exposing—and exploding—these strategies, Genevieve forces upon Mr. Hencke the awareness of his implication in the atrocities. To dismiss, to depersonalize, to universalize those atrocities is to commit further atrocity oneself. Toward the end of "The Suitcase" Holocaust imagery—smoke from German chimneys, coat "scorched into gray"—invokes history to override Mr. Hencke's pleas of innocence. No Eichmann, Mr. Hencke nonetheless reveals symptoms of what the distinguished Jewish political philosopher Hannah Arendt saw revealed in that infamous Nazi war criminal: the banality of evil. . . .

Source: Lawrence S. Friedman, *"The Pagan Rabbi and Other Stories,"* in *Understanding Cynthia Ozick*, University of South Carolina Press, 1991, pp. 81–83.

Vera Emuna Kielsky

In the following essay, Kielsky discusses the conflicting viewpoints of the two main characters in "The Suitcase."

A very impressive attempt to juxtapose History and Nature, to depict the two opposite approaches to life, is the story "The Suitcase." It is a witty presentation of a confrontation between a Jewish woman and her Gentile adversary, rich in allusions, metaphors and satire, and

> ON THE ONE HAND ALL ARE EXALTED BY THE CRISIS AND REJOICE IN THE CRIME; ON THE OTHER, ALL ARE APPREHENSIVE. IN THE URGE TO BE REGARDED INNOCENT, EACH TRIES TO PUSH THE SUSPICION AWAY FROM HIMSELF AND ON TO THE OTHERS."

always accompanied by two symbols—a suitcase and a purse. The suitcase, as the title implies, plays the pivotal part in this story, but its subject matter would be lost without the other symbol, the purse, a pocketbook that mysteriously disappears during a party. The ensuing embarrassment gives the author the opportunity to reveal the weakness of human nature in a critical situation, and to spotlight the feelings of guilt in both antagonists.

As so often in her other stories, Cynthia Ozick chooses for "The Suitcase" two controversial but not unlikeable characters, and places them in a suitable background. The scenario gives them all the opportunity they need to react appropriately upon each other and therewith to present the author's views. The two colliding forces of the story are Genevieve, the Jewish mistress of the amateur painter Gottfried, and his father, Mr. Hencke, a retired architect who "had flown a Fokker for the Kaiser," and later was "raising towers" in America. The setting of their confrontation is a party given at Gottfried's first exhibition.

Genevieve comes to the party to help promote her lover's painting career, and Mr. Hencke, who is on the way to a vacation in Europe, shows up to bid farewell to his son. The suitcase he brought with him is "heavy as some icon" and makes him perceivably uncomfortable—he seems hesitant about what to do with it.

The antagonists distrust each other for different reasons. However, they cannot keep out of each other's way. They act like two magnets which at one and the same time attract and repel the other. "I have nothing against you, believe me," Mr. Hencke assures his adversary. "I admire you very much, Genevieve. I have absolutely no animus." But, although drawn by Genevieve's appearance ("A beautiful complexion, beautiful eye-lashes"), he disapproves of her "Jewish" worldliness and envies his son ("Do you enjoy her, Gottfried?") and her influence on him: "does she boss you much?" He is particularly distressed by her unforgiving attitude towards the past ("'Genevieve invokes History always,' Mr. Hencke said"), and the part the Germans played in it: "She was the sort who twenty years after Hitler's war, would not buy a Volkswagen." He feels her disdain for him, but is reluctant to comprehend the reason behind her scorn:

> "Gnädige Frau," he said—and dropped his suitcase to the floor in a kind of fright.... — "What do you want from me?" he appealed. "I'm a man of sixty-eight. In sixty-eight years what have I done? I have harmed no one. I have built towers. Towers! No more. I have never destroyed."

He has been in America so long that he "no longer thought of himself as a German. He did not have German thoughts, [and even] was sorry he named his son after himself," and had not given him an American name: "If he had it to do over again he would have called him John."

Genevieve scorns Mr. Hencke not so much for being a petty bourgeois, a man with a "conventionally gossamer soul" or for trying to break up her liason with his son ("Gottfried's papa wants to get rid of me"), but mostly because he is German ("Your cheek is like barbed wire. Your cheek has the ruts left by General Rommel's tanks") and because of his behavior: "I hate people of principle. All the persecutors of the world have been people of principle." She scorns him particularly because "she thought him a Nazi sympathizer even now, an anti-Semite, an Eichmann." At the same time she is determined to listen to him and by "provoking him" to prove him wrong and refute his *Anschauung*.

Their incompatible views trigger a discourse between the two which subsequently leads to the disclosure of their true selves. Although both seem fully assimilated in American society and had known the war in Europe merely from the snugness and security of America ("only a little sugar rationed"), they feel affected by history in totally opposite ways; their comprehension and feelings towards the past are poles apart. And so are their reactions.

The prelude to the confrontation and the indication of its direction is the short but pregnant conversation between Genevieve and Catherine, the wife of the painter, with Mr. Hencke understanding the situation accurately. It already foreshadows the future events. Catherine mistakes the famous Swiss-German psychologist Carl Gustav Jung for a Jew. "A Chicago blueblood," educated in the exclusive "Miss Jewett's Class," Catherine brought with her the conviction that psychology is a typically Jewish profession; ergo, a famous psychologist must be Jewish: "another Jewish psychiatrist persecuted by Nazis." Corrected by Genevieve who says "Jung isn't Jewish," she wonders:

> "Isn't? Don't you mean wasn't? Isn't he dead?"
>
> "He isn't a Jew," Genevieve said. "That's why he went on staying alive."
>
> "I thought he was dead."
>
> "Everybody dies," Mr. Hencke said.

For the simple-minded, unbiased Catherine as for the sophisticated Genevieve, to be a German Jew is synonymous with being dead. Not so for Mr. Hencke, who refuses to accept this historical fact. For him to be dead is a natural occurrence, something inevitable, which has nothing to do with history: "Everybody dies," Jew or not Jew, with or without Hitler.

For Mr. Hencke the war in Europe was just another war in a long unavoidable chain of armed conflicts with nobody particularly responsible for it, as "Who could be blamed for History? It did not take a philosopher... to see that History was a Force-in-Itself, like Evolution." He was moved by the war personally as far as his remaining family in Germany was concerned. And only so far. Anyhow, the Jews were not the sole victims in the war: Germans were also afflicted. His compassion was directed entirely towards

> his sister, an innocent woman, an intellectual, a loyal lover of Heine [the Jew] who could recite by heart *Der Apollogott* and *Zwei Ritter* and *King David* and ten or twelve others, [who] lost her home and a daughter of eleven in an R.A.F. raid on Koeln.

This he perceived as "a horrible tragedy," particularly because "Even the great Cathedral had not been spared." But he never blamed the English for that and could not comprehend why Genevieve "was full of detestable moral gesture, and against what?"

Mr. Hencke clings to his vision of the country of his origin. It was formed by his memories: he "remembered Germany from boyhood," and still saw it with the eyes of his youth. Nothing could distort the sentimental picture of a "field furry with kummel, a hairy yellow shoulder of a field shrugging at the wind." It was a pleasant and sometimes serene picture which he plainly savored. It appeared in a

> recurring dream, in which he always rode naked on a saddleless horse, holding on to its black moist mane and crying "Schneller, Schneller." With the slowness of anguish they glided over a meadow.... past the millhouse, into a green endlessness hazy with buttercups.

In such a placid picture atrocities and brutality have no place.

Genevieve seemed to associate Germany with less idyllic images. Her vision had nothing to do with sentiments and dreams:

> "Your brother-in-law the shampoo manufacturer... He was making shampoo in Cologne all the while you were an American patriot architect, raising towers, never destroying. Please discuss your brother-in-law's shampoo. What were its secret ingredients? Whose human fat? What Jewish lard?"

Like Cynthia Ozick herself, for whom "Jewish blood cries from that ground," she probably dreamed about German fields pierced with graves of innocent people rather than furry with kummel; about meadows marked with the striped extermination camp attire of Jews driven like cattle by black uniformed SS butchers to the slaughterhouses of Auschwitz and Dachau, rather than hazy with flowers. In her vision the fields were not yellow, but grey, covered with human ashes that the wind blew from the chimneys of the crematoriums: "'Don't speak to me about German chimneys,' Genevieve said. 'I know what kind of smoke came out of those German chimneys!'" And for her, the fields smelled not of caraway, but of the burned flesh of men, women, and children, while the yell "hurry, hurry" was aimed not at a horse but at the endless line of people to move "*Schneller, Schneller*" into the gas chambers.

For Genevieve the genocide against Jews was in no way an inevitable "Force-in-Itself," but a terrible crime, a cold-blooded undertaking to carry out the Final Solution of the "Jewish problem," the elimination of six million people—all her sisters and brothers—in the name of the idea of superiority of one human race over another. She suspected that feelings of racial superiority were not strange to Mr. Hencke. And rightly so, as his "admiring" remark about her indicates: "When *they* turn up a blonde type you can almost take them for *our* own" [my stress].

To underscore her thesis that a non-Jew and a Jew are unable to look upon the world in one and the same way, Cynthia Ozick very pointedly juxtaposes the antagonists' views of Gottfried's paintings. Mr. Hencke was not excited by the art of his son: "Mr. Hencke had a perilous sense that Gottfried had simply cut up the plans for an old office building with extraordinarily tiny scissors." He looked down on his activity as not appropriate to a man ("Papa thinks Gottfried should have a job") and did not understand his kind of art: "he himself did not know what to think of Gottfried's labors." But while he did not accept it, he also did not disapprove of it. Not so Genevieve. Though she was the one who encouraged her lover to paint, inventing the "Nobody's Gallery," organizing the exhibition, and even delivering comments from Beethoven, Goethe and Mann for its program, she treated Gottfried's art with contempt. "You know what Gottfried's stuff reminds me of?" she challenges Mr. Hencke. "Shredded swastikas, that's what," she announced. "Every single damn thing he does. All that terrible precision. Every last one a pot of shredded swastikas...."

More obvious are the conflicting views of both adversaries in the scene where they both look into the crowd, which "had taken the form of a thick ragged rope and was wandering slowly past the long even array of Gottfried's paintings." For Mr. Hencke it was "a zoo crowd... peering into each one as though it were a cage containing some unlikely beast." For Genevieve, however, it was "Like a concentration camp.... Everybody staring through the barbed wire hoping for rescue and knowing it's no use. That's what they look like."

The confrontation scenes, particularly the last one, serve Cynthia Ozick to establish the two perspectives of History: on the one hand, of a quasi-unengaged spectator, who is aware of all the occurrences without feeling emotionally involved, and on the other—of the affected sufferer. But instantly she shows that such a distinction is inadequate, more—it is often misleading: it does not answer the decisive questions who is the guilty one, and who is free of guilt; who is the victim, and who is the victimizer?

Though the motif of guilt wriggles through all the story, it rises to prominence only at its end: shortly before the discovery of the disappearance of Genevieve's purse and more so after it. From the beginning of the story it is obvious that both antagonists, despite their ostensible self-confidence, feel quite uneasy with themselves. Mr. Hencke is clearly uncomfortable with the atmosphere of the house, which "he...despised," and with the exhibition. He disdained his son, whom he regarded as a parasite, living off his wife's money ("You don't see any of the Rockefellers idle. Every Rockefeller has a job"), and he "hated his daughter-in-law." And last but not least, he was disturbed by the unavoidable confrontation with his son's Jewish mistress. His categorical refusal to stay overnight with his family ("for family peace I prefer the hotel—") and his conspicuous hesitation about what to do with his suitcase (he compulsively feared being separated from it, though he asked again and again: "Where am I to put my bag?") indicate his inner unrest. Genevieve's provocations intensify his emotional split and draw him nearer to acknowledging, though not yet to confessing, his part in the guilt. So he reluctantly admits to himself he is not completely without blame in the death of his niece in Cologne:

> Sometimes he dreams he was in his sister's city, and the bomb exploded out of his own belly, and there rolled past him, as on a turntable in the brutalized nave, his little niece laid out dead, covered only by her yellow hair.

Genevieve was also not free from vexation and doubts in her role as a Jew and a mistress of a Gentile. The heat of her passion for Gottfried first blocks the comprehension of her situation. She reacts more than acts: her initial remarks in the conversation, as cynical as they may sound, spring more from her endeavor for clarification than from a wish to hurt. For sure, her reprimands are directed not so much towards her audience as at herself. But in the course of the confrontation, she comes to realize the fact of her displacement; she grasps that nothing associates her with her lover and his "satiated paintings," nor with all the other people at the party including Mr. Hencke and his "evil sweated dreams." All the humiliations and disillusions that have accumulated in her Jewish

heart over countless generations have come free. She begins to act by denouncing her relationship with Gottfried ("Goodbye. I'm going back to Nora Lewin, Bonnie Lewin, Andrea Lewin, Celeste Lewin and Edward K. Lewin, all of Indianapolis, Indiana") and by confessing her insincerity: "I'm a deceiver." She has deceived her family and herself because she could not resist the temptation. She threw away her body for an illusion, and her heritage for a short-lived enjoyment. Seeking an absolution she sees no other alternative but to expose herself physically and spiritually.

Genevieve reveals herself physically in a double figurative sense by stripping the "satiated paintings" of her lover in which she was "wrapped" till now, and by baring her beauty to the public:

> "First let me describe myself [she cried into the crowd]. Tall. Never wear low heels. Plump-armed. Soft-thighed. Perfectly splendid young woman. Nose thin and delicate, like a communion wafer. Impression of being both sleek and amiable. Large healthy, indestructible teeth. Half a dozen gold inlays.... My gold inlays click like castanets manufactured in Franco Spain. My breasts are like twin pomegranates. Like twin white doves coming down from Mount Gilead."

This self-portrait depicts exactly her state of mind, her disunity, the inner conflict between the two worlds in her. On the one hand, she uses markedly Gentile allusions like "Communion wafer," but on the other, she reaches to her roots paraphrasing the "Song of Solomon."

She undoubtedly feels herself a victim of the circumstances, of her foolishness. However, her awakening conscience teaches her that her thoughtlessness had long ago turned her into a victimizer. The feelings of guilt dictate her spiritual expose. It is in a way a proselyte's praise of the traditional values, of family and heritage, lit up by a glimmer of hope:

> "My husband is an intelligent and prospering Certified Public Accountant. His name will not surprise: Lewin. A memorable name. Kagan would also be a memorable name, so too Rabinowitz or Robbins, but his name is Lewin. A model to youth. Contributor to many charities. Vice-president of the temple. Now let me tell you about our four daughters, all under twelve. One is only in kindergarten. But the two older ones! Nora, Bonnie. At the top of their grades and already reading *Tom Sawyer*, *Little Women*, and the *Encyclopaedia*

Britannica. Every month they produce a family newspaper of one page on an old Smith-Corona in the basement of our Dutch Colonial house in Indianapolis, Indiana. They call it *The Mezuzzah Bulletin*—the idea being that they tack it up on the doorpost. They all four have the Jewish brain."

By this she reveals that she has finally understood that her spiritual home is not in the barren desert emptiness of the Henckes and their towers and their paintings, but in the fertile oasis of Lewins and "The Mezuzzah Bulletin." She got lost, but now she again found her way.

Just as Genevieve was ready to forsake her present involvements, she noticed that her purse was missing. Catherine had aptly marked the border of her intent, saying: "'she didn't even leave yet,... she was just starting to go,'" and then continuing

> "Someone's stolen Genevieve's pocketbook!....
> She had it lying just like that on a chair, only
> it was covered with her coat, and there was
> this hundred dollars in it, and her driver's
> license, and the plane ticket, and a million
> other things like that."

She is shaken. Her confidence is shattered not so much because of the significance of the purse and its contents ("Ed'll kill me"—) but because she has trusted the people around her—she has felt at home here. Moreover, the purse was seemingly protected by Gottfried's personality: the coat, like all her clothes was shaped in its image "with all that black-and-white geometry all over it." She conceives that it is not so simple to let all be forgotten and forgiven, to leave all behind her without a sore. She begins to realize the paradox of her situation—she was saved and destroyed at the same time. Atonement claims its price: "a scream leaped out of the bowl of apples," (an allusion to Eve in Paradise after the Fall). Nostalgia caught up with her and her voice was coarse, "the voice of the bass fiddle? A Biblical yell, as by the waters of Babylon" (an allusion to the lost home(land)).

Mr. Hencke is the only one who is able to immerse himself in Genevieve's situation. Such a desperation was not strange to a man who hid feelings of guilt in his subconscious mind, feelings which he refuses to acknowledge and is not willing to admit. "Always horrible tragedy for the innocent," he recognizes. But he not only "envisioned wounds. In his heart she bled, she bled." He also "suspected what wounds." He

discovers that "She was not innocent." But all others are not innocent either.

In the circumstances of a general consternation everybody feels suspected and loses his self-assurance. On the one hand all are exalted by the crisis and rejoice in the crime; on the other, all are apprehensive. In the urge to be regarded innocent, each tries to push the suspicion away from himself and on to the others. A situation emerges, well known to Jews, in their long history of persecution, in which unsubstantiated suspicion strikes the most innocent, the uninvolved:

> "Gottfried thinks it must have been one of the
> truckmen," Catherine said....
>
> "Absolutely it was the truckmen," Mr.
> Hencke assented.
>
> "There was no one else here like that."
>
> "The barman?"
>
> "The barman perhaps," Mr. Hencke once
> again agreed.
>
> "But it couldn't be the barman, the barman's
> still *here*...."
>
> "Then the truckmen," Mr. Hencke said. "The
> truckmen without question."
>
> "All right, but you know what *I* think, papa?"
>
> "No."
>
> ..."Well, the way that weird man [the famous
> critic] *argued* about his fee when we hired
> him...so what *I* think...is Mr. MacDougal
> decided to raise his own fee, hook or crook!"
>
> "It was the truckmen," Mr. Hencke said with
> the delicacy of finality.

As so typical in such situations, the belief emerges that one can buy peace of mind and dispose of a painful embarrassment by offering money as compensation. Obviously it is no one else but Mr. Hencke who realizes that "Nothing comes free in this life," and he suggests:

> "Genevieve must be given some money to go
> home with." and again:
>
> "Tell Gottfried to give her some money," and
> again:
>
> "I want you to give Genevieve money," and
> again:
>
> "For Genevieve. It's the least you can do,
> Gottfried."

But not money, nor his repeated assurance that "The most logical ones were the truckmen. I swear it," can appease Genevieve. Her concession ("I suppose it *was* the truckmen"—) is half-hearted and does not free him from the feeling of guilt in Genevieve's predicament. He is disturbed:

> In his tenuously barbule soul, for which he had ancestral certitude, the father of the artist burned in the foam of so much kummel, so many buttercups, so much lustrous yellow, and the horse's mane so confusing in his eyes like a grid, and why does the horse not go faster, faster?

In order to regain his self-confidence, he has to win her trust ("You understand, hah, Genevieve?") by owning up to his original deception: "I have the one bag only to mislead. I confess it, purposely to mislead. In my hotel room already there are four other bags." He opens the door to confessing what really weighs heavily on his mind—the feeling that he is not as free of guilt as he wishes to appear. But he immediately closes it again: instead of unburdening himself, he washes his hands in innocence. He has nothing to hide; he has no dirty washing; his conscience is as clean as the contents of his suitcase:

> "Look, look, Genevieve, I'll show you," he said, "just look—" He turned the little key and threw open his suitcase with so much wild vigor that it quivered on its hinges. "Now just look, look through everything, nothing here but my own, here are my shirts, . . . my new underwear. Only socks, see? Socks, socks, shorts, shorts, shorts, all new."

Any old or dirty washing that he had, he discarded long ago. The past does not count. He has turned a new leaf. All he can show now is pristine: "I like to travel with everything new and clean, . . . see for yourself—"

However, he could not convince anyone. Even the obtuse Catherine, for whom the implications of the confrontation remain obscure, inadvertently discovers the truth: "'Tonight what criminals we've harbored unawares!'—it sounded exactly like a phrase of Genevieve's."

Source: Vera Emuna Kielsky, "The Suitcase," in *Inevitable Exiles: Cynthia Ozick's View of the Precariousness of Jewish Existence in a Gentile Society*, Peter Lang, 1989, pp. 31–45.

SOURCES

"About the Museum," United States Holocaust Memorial Museum website, http://www.ushmm.org/information/about-the-museum (accessed January 18, 2014).

"American Art in the 1960s," Michael Blackwood Productions website, http://www.michaelblackwoodproductions.com/arts_americanartsinthesixties.php (accessed January 24, 2014).

Cole, Diane, "Cynthia Ozick," in *Dictionary of Literary Biography*, Vol. 28, *Twentieth-Century American-Jewish Fiction Writers*, edited by Daniel Walden, Gale Research, 1984, pp. 213–25.

Edwards, Thomas R., "Bloodshed," in *Cynthia Ozick*, edited by Harold Bloom, Bloom's Modern Critical Views, Chelsea House, 1986, p. 31; originally published in *New York Review of Books*, April 1, 1976.

Friedman, Lawrence S., *Understanding Cynthia Ozick*, University of South Carolina Press, 1991, pp. 82–83.

Goffman, Ethan, "The Golden Age of Jewish American Literature," ProQuest Discovery Guides, March 2010, http://www.csa.com/discoveryguides/jewish/review.pdf (accessed January 18, 2014).

"Introduction to the Holocaust," United States Holocaust Memorial Museum website, http://www.ushmm.org/wlc/en/article.php?ModuleId = 10005143 (accessed January 18, 2014).

Kaplan, Joanna, Review of *The Pagan Rabbi and Other Stories*, in *New York Times Book Review*, June 13, 1971, p. 14.

Kauvar, Elaine, *Cynthia Ozick's Fiction: Tradition and Invention*, Indiana University Press, 1993, pp. 65–66.

Knopp, Josephine Z., "Ozick's Jewish Stories," in *Cynthia Ozick*, edited by Harold Bloom, Bloom's Modern Critical Views, Chelsea House, 1986, p. 25; originally published in *Studies in American Jewish Literature*, Vol. 1, No. 1, Spring 1975.

Marter, Joan, ed., Introduction to *The Grove Encyclopedia of American Art*, Vol. 1, Oxford University Press, 2011, p. xxix.

Novick, Peter, *The Holocaust in American Life*, Houghton Mifflin, 1999, pp. 114, 168.

Ozick, Cynthia, "The Suitcase," in *The Pagan Rabbi and Other Stories*, Dutton, 1983, pp. 103–27.

Prescott, Peter S., "Looking for Life," in *Newsweek*, May 10, 1971, p. 114.

Strandberg, Victor, "The Art of Cynthia Ozick," in *Cynthia Ozick*, edited by Harold Bloom, Bloom's Modern Critical Views, Chelsea House, 1986, p. 107; originally published in *Texas Studies in Literature and Language*, Vol. 25, No. 2, Summer 1983.

FURTHER READING

Lowin, Joseph, *Cynthia Ozick*, Twayne's United States Author Series No. 545, Twayne Publishers, 1988.

This concise survey of Ozick's work up to the late 1980s includes a chronology, a biographical sketch, an annotated bibliography, and analysis of Ozick's short stories, novels, and essays.

Pinsker, Sanford, *The Uncompromising Fictions of Cynthia Ozick*, University of Missouri Press, 1987.

This chronological overview of six works by Ozick, from *Trust* to *The Cannibal Galaxy*, traces the evolution of Ozick's work in her novels, short stories, and essays and places her work in the context of other Jewish American writers, such as Philip Roth, Bernard Malamud, and Saul Bellow.

Rosenbaum, Ron, *Those Who Forget the Past: The Question of Anti-Semitism*, Random House, 2004.

In this collection of forty-nine essays on anti-Semitism, especially as it has arisen in the early years of the twenty-first century, contributors discuss the possibility of a second Holocaust, in the Middle East, and how anti-Semitism differs from anti-Zionism, among many other topics. Ozick contributes an afterword.

Walden, Daniel, ed., *The World of Cynthia Ozick*, Vol. 6, Studies in American Jewish Literature, Kent State University Press, 1987.

This collection of essays discusses Ozick's work, including many of her short stories.

SUGGESTED SEARCH TERMS

Cynthia Ozick

Ozick AND The Suitcase

Holocaust

Ozick AND Holocaust

anti-Semitism

Ozick AND anti-Semitism

assimilation

German AND guilt

Year of the Big Thaw

MARION ZIMMER BRADLEY

1954

"Year of the Big Thaw" is a science-fiction story by Marion Zimmer Bradley. It was first published in the magazine *Fantastic Universe* in May 1954. The story is set on a farm in Connecticut not long after the Civil War. A farmer, Mr. Emmett, tells a clergyman, Reverend Doane, the story of the origins of his son, Matt, who is now of an age when he is ready to go to college. Mr. Emmett explains that Matt is not actually his biological son. There was a huge blizzard one winter, followed by a thaw that flooded the valley, including Mr. Emmett's pasture. He saw something unusual in the sky and heard a great crash. Upon investigation, he discovered some kind of spaceship in the flooded river. The story is a simple one, with an amusing twist near the end, and it shows Bradley's concern, in this early work, with the notion of unconditional family love.

"Year of the Big Thaw" is available in a number of different books, including *The Early Works of Marion Zimmer Bradley*, published in 2010, and *The Science Fiction Megapack: 25 Science Fiction Stories by Masters*, published in 2011. The story has also been published as both a printed book and an e-book, in 2011. A version of the story is available for free online at Project Gutenberg: http://www.gutenberg.org/ebooks/28650.

Mr. Emmett reminds Reverend Doane about a huge blizzard that hit the area years ago.
(© marevos imaging | Shutterstock.com)

AUTHOR BIOGRAPHY

Bradley was born on June 3, 1930, in East Green-bush (near Albany), New York. Her parents were Evelyn Parkhurst Conklin and Leslie Raymond Zimmer. Zimmer was a farmer, and as a girl Bradley regularly did farm chores. She did not begin her schooling until 1937, when she was at last big enough to walk a mile though snowdrifts to and from the school bus stop. At school, Bradley soon developed an interest in reading and writing. She particularly loved reading the Arthurian legends. At the age of fourteen, she began writing a novel set in Roman Britain. Sometimes she skipped school and went instead to the library of the New York State Department of Education, where from 1944 to 1945 she read all ten volumes of *The Golden Bough*, a classic work about mythology and comparative religion by Sir James George Frazer. She also developed an interest in science fiction.

Bradley graduated from Columbia High School in New York in 1946 and began college in Albany. She had already written a novel, which was never published. In 1949, she left college and married Robert A. Bradley and

moved to Texas. The following year her first son, David Stephen, was born. In 1953, her first science-fiction stories, "Women Only" and "Keyhole," were published in the magazine *Vortex Science Fiction*. The following year, "Centaurus Changeling" appeared in the *Magazine of Fantasy and Science Fiction*, and "Year of the Big Thaw" was published in *Fantastic Universe*. During the remainder of the decade, more of Bradley's short stories were published, and in 1961, her first science-fiction novel, *The Door through Space*, appeared. Bradley returned to college, enrolling at Hardin-Simmons University, in Abilene, Texas, from which she would graduate in 1964 with a triple major in English, educational psychology, and Spanish literature. In 1962, Bradley separated from her husband. The couple divorced in 1964, and Bradley married Walter Breen. Her second son was born that year, and a daughter followed in 1966. The family divided their time between Berkeley, California, and New York City.

In the 1960s, Bradley published many novels, including *The Sword of Aldones* (1962), which was nominated for a Hugo Award, and *The Bloody Sun* (1964), one of the central novels in her science-fiction/fantasy series set on the planet of Darkover. *Star of Danger*, another Darkover novel, appeared the following year. During the 1970s, Bradley continued to publish prolifically, including twelve Darkover novels or short stories, the science-fiction novels *Hunters of the Red Moon* (1973) and *Endless Voyage* (1975), and *Drums of Darkness*, a gothic fantasy (1976). In 1977 *The Forbidden Tower* was nominated for the Nebula Award, and the book won the Hamilton-Brackett Memorial Award in 1979. *The Catchtrap*, a mainstream novel, followed in 1979, the science-fiction novel *The House between the Worlds* in 1980. In 1983, *The Mists of Avalon*, an Arthurian fantasy novel, was published by Knopf and became an immediate *New York Times* best seller. It remains Bradley's most well-known and successful book. From 1988, she edited *Marion Zimmer Bradley's Fantasy Magazine*, fifty issues of which were published between then and 2000, when the magazine closed.

In all, there are more than forty novels and collections of short stories set on Darkover. Many of these, especially from the mid-1990s, when Bradley was in ill health, were written with coauthors. Several Darkover novels have been published posthumously, based on work in progress at the time of Bradley's death. Coauthors include Deborah J. Ross, as in *The Alton Gift* (2007). After some years of ill health following a series of strokes, Bradley died of a heart attack on September 5, 1999, aged sixty-nine, in Berkeley. In 2000, she was given a posthumous World Fantasy Award for lifetime achievement.

PLOT SUMMARY

The story is set on a farm in Connecticut a few years after the Civil War. Mr. Emmett, a farmer, is in conversation with a clergyman, the Reverend Doane, who is looking over an application for a scholarship that Mr. Emmett's son is applying for. Mr. Emmett confirms that the boy, who works on the family farm, is his own son. He is a good son, the farmer says, adding that he will miss the boy if he gets the scholarship he has applied for, but that he needs more education than he is getting at the local school.

Reverend Doane then brings attention to the fact that, on the form he has filled out, he

MEDIA ADAPTATIONS

- "Year of the Big Thaw" is available for free audio download at the LibriVox website, at https://librivox.org/author/819?primary_key =819&search_category=author&search_ page=1&search_form=get_results. The story is read by Gregg Weeks.

---

has written "birthplace unknown" in reference to his son, whose name is Matt. Mr. Emmett admits that although he and his wife, Marthy, think of Matt as theirs, he is not really their natural, biological son.

He then tells his story. It happened twelve years before the war, which would put it about 1849. Mr. Emmett was living and farming in New Hampshire at the time. This was before he moved to Connecticut. It was a terribly cold winter, and during one blizzard, even the Hudson River at Albany (southwest of New Hampshire) froze. When the thaw came, the snow melted off Scuttock Mountain, and some of the surrounding farmland in the valley went underwater. On Mr. Emmett's land, there was a foot of water in the cowshed. The swimming hole turned into a deep, fast-flowing stream fifty feet across that covered the pasture. He tied his cow, calf, and horse in the woodshed behind the house where they would be safe. He went to get the milk pail, but then suddenly he heard a tremendous screeching sound. He saw Marthy in the yard, pointing up at the sky. He looked up and saw a trail of fire in the sky over Shattuck Mountain and what seemed like a rocket the size of a house. He and his wife were scared. Their daughter, Liza Grace, came out of the house, saying that the soup was burning, and Marthy returned inside. Mr. Emmett decided that the rocket must have been a shooting star and got on with the milking.

However, as they sat down to supper, there was a huge crash, apparently coming from their back pasture. Mr. Emmett saddled up his horse, Kate, and rode out to investigate. He reached the top of a hill and looked down at a watery scene. It was still raining. When he reached the pasture, Kate started to get very agitated. Mr. Emmett smelled something burning. Then he saw "the contraption." It was long, thin, and shiny, with two red rods sticking out of it and a globe at the top. It was turned on its side and stuck in the mud. He realized that the contraption must have flown across the mountain and then crashed, thus explaining the loud noise he had heard. He saw a door on the craft, hanging by its hinges. As he investigated further, he heard someone shouting. He looked down and saw a man in the water, flailing around. Mr. Emmett waded into the rushing stream and pulled the man out.

The man was like no other that Mr. Emmett had ever seen. He was dressed in bright red, shiny clothes that were dry, in spite of the man's immersion in the water. There was also blood on his clothes, and his chest had been crushed. Mr. Emmett realized that the man must have been dying. The man opened his greenish-yellow eyes, and Mr. Emmett felt as if the man were reading his mind. The man then spoke to him in English, albeit in an odd kind of way, telling him to get his baby, who was in the ship.

Mr. Emmett plunged into the river to rescue the baby. He managed to struggle across the river and reach the contraption, which he refers to as "some flying dragon kind of thing." He climbed into it and found some dead people in the cabin, including a man, a woman, and an animal like a bobcat, though smaller. He heard a whimper and discovered a baby boy about six months old. The baby was crying. He was in pain because in the crash his arm got twisted under him. Mr. Emmett looked around for something to cover the naked baby, then gently pulling a cape off the dead body of the woman. He believed that she was the boy's mother.

Mr. Emmett managed to bring the baby back to the man, the baby's father, who opened his eyes and asked Mr. Emmett to take care of the baby. Mr. Emmett said he would, and he also said he would try to get the man to the house, where his wife could treat him. The man said not to bother, because he was dying. He explained that he came from another planet and crashed. Mr. Emmett held him and promised that he would look after the man's son until his own people could come to fetch him. Mr. Emmett recited the Lord's Prayer and saw when he finished that the man was dead.

Mr. Emmett wrapped the baby in the cape and took him home. The next day he buried the dead man, and shortly after that he and Marthy had the boy baptized and christened Matthew Daniel Emmett. They raised him just like they raised all their other kids.

Reverend Doane asks Mr. Emmett if he ever found out where the ship came from. Mr. Emmett replies that the man told him it came from a star. Mr. Emmett consulted someone whom he refers to as "the Teacher," who told him that one prominent scientist has seen canals on a certain planet through his telescope. Mr. Emmett cannot remember the name of the planet; it is "March or Mark or something like that." (Obviously he is referring to Mars.) Mr. Emmett concludes that if creatures on that planet are able to build huge canals, there is no reason why they could not build flying machines, too. (Some astronomers in the late nineteenth century believed in the existence of a network of canals on Mars, based on their observations.)

Mr. Emmett then continues his story. He returned the next day to see if he could bury the dead bodies, but the flying machine had disintegrated and been washed away. He then says that his wife still has the cape he wrapped the baby in. They never told Matt the story of his origins, however. They did not want him to think he was not really theirs.

Reverend Doane wonders whether anyone had asked them where they got the baby from. Mr. Emmett acknowledges that people were curious, especially given the fact that Marthy was not pregnant at the time, but people just minded their own business. He told Liza Grace, his young daughter, that he had found her a new brother out back, which happened to be the truth.

Reverend Doane asks if Matthew is any different from other children. Mr. Emmett says there is no difference that anyone would notice. Matt is a very smart boy. Then he adds, "when he were about twelve years old he started reading folks' minds, which didn't seem exactly right." He would tell his parents what they were thinking. He would tease his sisters, Liza Grace and Minnie, telling them what their boyfriends were thinking about and also telling the boys what the girls were thinking. Mr. Emmett, realizing that Matt was only teasing, nonetheless disapproved, and he took Matt to the woodshed and whipped him. After that, Matt stopped his teasing.

CHARACTERS

The Dead Woman

Mr. Emmett thinks that the dead woman on the spacecraft is likely the mother of Matt and the wife of the man who dies soon after. Mr. Emmett takes her long cape so he can wrap the baby in it.

Reverend Doane

Reverend Doane is looking over the application that Mr. Emmett has filled out for a scholarship for his son, Matt. Mr. Emmett is not an educated man, so it is likely he has asked the Reverend Doane to make sure he has done everything correctly. It is the reverend's question about Matt's place of birth that prompts Mr. Emmett to tell his story. As he is telling it, Reverend Doane asks him various questions, which enable Mr. Emmett to bring out the story more fully.

The Dying Man

The man from outer space is Matt's father. He and his family, as well as some other unidentified travelers, fly in their spacecraft to Earth but crash on Mr. Emmett's property. The man, who is tall and thin, is severely injured and dies soon after Mr. Emmett discovers him. Before dying he asks Mr. Emmett to look after his baby boy. Mr. Emmett feels that the man is able to read his mind.

Liza Grace Emmett

Liza Grace is one of Matt's sisters. She is older than Matt. She married a boy named Taylor.

Matthew Daniel Emmett

Matthew Daniel Emmett is the full name of the boy known as Matt. When the story begins, Matt is likely about seventeen or eighteen years old, and his father is helping him to apply for a scholarship so he may continue his studies. All that is known about Matt is what his father tells Reverend Doane about him. Matt is in fact an alien from outer space, perhaps the planet Mars. He was in a spacecraft that crashed, and his birth parents were killed. Mr. Emmett adopted him, and he and his wife raised Matt as if he were their own. When he was about twelve or thirteen, he wanted to join the US Navy and serve with Admiral Farragut. (Admiral David Farragut commanded the USS *Hartford* in the Civil War.) This was just after the Civil War began. Neither his father nor his mother wanted him to go, so he stayed at home on the farm.

Matthew is very smart and seems in all respects exactly like a human boy, except for the fact that he is able to read people's minds. He has a mischievous sense of humor, and when he was about twelve he would use this unusual skill to tease his sisters. After receiving some corporal punishment from his father, he stopped doing that. Mr. Emmett regards him as a good boy and a good son.

Mr. Emmett

Mr. Emmett is a farmer in Connecticut during the 1860s, when the story takes place. Before that, he lived in New Hampshire, where his father farmed. He was born and raised there. Mr. Emmett is a family man, with a wife and three children, including two daughters, Liza Grace and Minnie, and an adopted son, Matt, who began his life on an alien planet. Mr. Emmett lives a normal, conventional life, apart from the fact that one astounding thing happened to him. One day he discovered a crashed spaceship and the little alien who was about to become an orphan. The farmer is a decent man who did not think twice before promising the baby's dying father that he would look after the baby. Mr. Emmett appears to be a religious man, too. As the alien man died, Mr. Emmett recited the Lord's Prayer. He and his wife went on to raise the child as if he were their own.

Mrs. Marthy Emmett

Mrs. Marthy Emmett is Mr. Emmett's wife and the adoptive mother of Matt. Like her husband, she immediately accepts Matt as part of the family.

Minnie Emmett

Minnie is one of Matt's sisters.

The Teacher

Mr. Emmett is curious about Matt's origins, so he consults someone he calls "the Teacher," who tells him about Mars and about scientists seeing what look like canals on its surface.

THEMES

Familial Love

The story presents two different families, both bound together by love. Love is the primary value, which transcends all differences, even those between humans and alien beings. The

TOPICS FOR FURTHER STUDY

- In 2013, a Dutch company announced plans to send four people to colonize Mars sometime in the 2020s. These pioneers would live the rest of their lives on Mars. By December 2013, 200,000 people had expressed an interest in taking the trip. Write a letter (which you do not have to actually mail) to the company in which you state your interest in being on the first flight. Say why you want to go to Mars and also what conditions you expect to find there. You can start your research by reading the CNN article "200,000 People Apply to Live on Mars," available at http://www.cnn.com/2013/12/10/tech/innovation/mars-one-plan/.

- In "Year of the Big Thaw," Matt has the ability to read people's minds. Investigate the phenomenon of telepathy. What is telepathy? Does it exist? Is it real or a fiction? If it is possible, how might it be explained? Give a class presentation in which you define telepathy and discuss the results of your investigation.

- *The Year's Best Science Fiction and Fantasy for Teens* (2005), edited by Jane Yolen and Patrick Nielson Hayden, contains eleven stories published in 2004 in a variety of science-fiction and fantasy subgenres. Pick one of the stories you like, and write an essay in which you compare it to "Year of the Big Thaw." Are there any similarities between the two stories? If not, what are the major differences between them?

- Imagine that a movie is to be made based on "Year of the Big Thaw." Go to Glogster.com, and create a poster that might be used to advertise the movie.

possibly Martian creatures, though distinguished from their human counterparts by their dress, the color of their eyes, and their telepathic abilities, are nonetheless very similar to a human family. There is a man, a woman, and a child, and the dying father is concerned not for himself but only for the life of his baby son, whom he clearly loves. The family bond is therefore presented as something that would apply to alien life as well as that of humans.

Mr. Emmett grasps this immediately. He does not get caught up in thoughts of the strangeness of the situation or the fact that he is dealing with creatures from another planet. A devout as well as a practical man, he instinctively observes his Christian duty to show kindness to strangers, even strangers as unusual as these. His first action is one of compassion. He takes his coat off and puts it around the dying man to comfort him. After the man tells him there is a baby in the ship, Mr. Emmett is conscious only of the need to rescue the helpless infant. He also has the presence of mind to assure the dying father that his baby will be safe. "Don't worry, mister," he says. "I'll take care of your little fellow until your folks come after him. Before God I will." This is a solemn promise, and he makes it without thinking much about it; he simply knows what has to be done, and he is determined to do it.

After Mr. Emmett gets the baby back to his house, the need to provide a loving home for a forlorn creature, an orphan, is paramount in his mind. He and his wife offer unconditional acceptance and love for the new arrival, showing that the bonds of family can unite living beings across different worlds and, quite literally, across different planets. Matt, the alien, responds well to being in a loving human family and grows up just like a human boy (with the exception, of course, of his mind-reading capabilities, which he learns to keep in check). Familial love is thus shown to be a universal value.

Science Fiction

The story presents a theme common in science fiction: contact between humans and creatures from a different planet or galaxy. In this case, the contact is with visitors possibly from Mars. Few details are given about these aliens, although they do appear to be benevolent rather than hostile. Mr. Emmett never finds out what their purpose was in visiting Earth. For her story Bradley chose not to make much attempt to build on known scientific facts or provide rational explanations (other than the fact that some people in the late nineteenth

When the snow from the blizzard thawed, it caused the creek to rise over its banks, flooding the fields.
(© bluecrayola | Shutterstock.com)

century, based on erroneous interpretation of astronomical observations, thought that Mars was inhabited by intelligent beings).

In this story, the differences between the humans and the Martians are superficial. For example, the Martians wear unusual clothing that stays dry even when immersed in water, and they have greenish-yellow eyes. Other than that and their telepathic abilities (something commonly attributed to aliens in science fiction), they appear to be much the same as humans, in appearance, emotions, and values. They even speak English. The close similarities between the humans and the Martians are in fact essential to the story Bradley has to tell, because there is no other way that the alien Matt could grow up and attend school in Connecticut without attracting attention to himself. The author uses the science-fiction framework in order to offer a commentary on what she presents as an important aspect of human life: the need for unconditional love, extended to every creature who needs it, regardless of origins.

STYLE

Dialogue and First-Person Narration
The story is presented in the form of a dialogue between Mr. Emmett and the Reverend Doane. However, the clergyman's role is merely to ask a few short questions—five in all, none longer than a sentence—that act as prompts for Mr. Emmett to tell his story. Thus for the most part, the story is a first-person narrative, in which Mr. Emmett tells of what happened one winter's day about eighteen years or so prior to his current meeting with the Reverend Doane.

Dialect
Mr. Emmett tells his story in colloquial language using many words that belong to a regional dialect. "Tarnal," for example, is New England dialect for *damned*. "Quare" is a dialect variant of *queer*, meaning strange or remarkable. "Crick" is a variant of *creek*, and "yander" is a dialect variation of *yonder*. The use of dialect grounds the story in a particular region, thus giving it some realism, which

stands in contrast to the fantastic nature of the tale. The rustic, simple nature of the narrator, as shown by his colloquial expressions and use of dialect, helps to persuade the reader to accept the authenticity of the story, suspending disbelief and entering into the world the author has created.

"First Contact" Science Fiction

Science fiction has numerous subcategories, and "first contact," though not a subcategory in its own right, is a frequent theme in science fiction. "Year of the Big Thaw" is a first contact story. In this context, *first contact* means the first time humans encounter beings from somewhere other than Earth. H. G. Wells's *The War of the Worlds* (1898) is a first contact story. Wells's Martians, merciless and bent on killing and conquest, are very different from the gentle aliens who appear in "Year of the Big Thaw." James White, in his collection of linked stories *Hospital Station* (1962), describes first contacts that arise when humans treat sick aliens in a space hospital. A more recent example of such fiction is *Learning the World: A Novel of First Contact* (2005), by Ken MacLeod.

HISTORICAL CONTEXT

Mars and Science Fiction

Given the popularity of Mars in science fiction, it is not surprising that the extraterrestrials in "Year of the Big Thaw" are suggested to come from that planet. Martians have been a staple of science fiction since H. G. Wells published *The War of the Worlds* in 1898, about an invasion of Earth by Martians. For many decades, beginning in the late nineteenth century, Mars was considered by many scientists to be the planet most likely to contain intelligent life. It was thought likely to have vegetation and water.

In 1877, an Italian astronomer, Giovanni Schiaparelli (1835–1910), observed through a telescope a network of what he called *canali* on Mars. The word literally means "channels" but was often translated as "canals," spurring the inevitable conclusion that the canals had to have been constructed by intelligent beings. (This is the theory that Mr. Emmett in "Year of the Big Thaw" is dimly aware of, although his belief is slightly anachronistic, since the story is set about ten years before Schiaparelli's

observations.) An American astronomer, Percival Lowell, in a series of books including *The Canals of Mars* (1906), expounded his belief that Mars was inhabited by beings who had built a civilization, but that the planet was now cooling and drying out, so the Martians had built the canals to try to offset the effects of the deteriorating climate.

Many of the early science-fiction stories about Mars feature, as does "Year of the Big Thaw," a Martian visiting Earth. One example is *The Man from Mars* (1891), by Thomas Blot. Edgar Rice Burroughs's *The Mastermind of Mars* (1928) is set on a civilized Mars and is one of a number of similar adventure stories of the period. Early science-fiction pulp magazines from the 1930s to the 1950s frequently featured stories set on Mars. (Pulp magazines were named after the cheap paper they were printed on.) Notable among these is the work of Leigh Brackett in the 1940s and 1950s, including stories such as "Martian Quest," which appeared in *Astounding Science Fiction* in February 1940, "Shadow over Mars" (1944), "Queen of the Martian Catacombs" (1949), "The Ark of Mars" (1953), and many more. Some of these stories were later expanded and published in book form.

Science Fiction in the 1950s

The period from the end of the 1930s to the end of the 1950s is known as the golden age of science fiction. The period roughly began with the publication of the pulp magazine *Astounding Stories* in 1937, which changed its name to *Astounding Science Fiction* in 1938. The magazine was edited by John W. Campbell, who gained a reputation for encouraging high-quality fiction and discovering such writers as Robert A. Heinlein and Isaac Asimov. *Astounding Science Fiction* remained the most important outlet for science fiction throughout the 1940s. In the 1950s, the number of magazines grew, including the *Magazine of Fantasy and Science Fiction* and *Galaxy Science Fiction*. As M. Keith Booker and Anne-Marie Thomas state in their introduction to *The Science Fiction Handbook*, the number of magazines published is evidence that "the short story continued to be a vital form for the exploration of new sf ideas."

The 1950s also featured the rise of the science-fiction novel. These developments, as Robert Silverberg notes in "Science Fiction in the 1950s: The Real Golden Age," produced "a

COMPARE
&
CONTRAST

- **1850s–1860s:** Scientists speculate about Mars. In 1854, the English philosopher of science William Whewall declares that Mars has green seas, red land, and maybe life forms as well. In 1862, Sir Joseph Norman Lockyer of the Royal College of Science in London makes drawings of Mars. He believes that Mars possesses oceans.

  1950s: In 1956, there is a dust storm on Mars. The storm begins in August and covers the entire planet by the middle of September.

  Today: After many unmanned missions to Mars, such as Mars Exploration Rover (2003), Mars Reconnaissance Orbiter (2005), and Phoenix (2007), scientists believe that although Mars is cold, dry, and inhospitable to life, there was once water on the planet, and water may still exist in large quantities as ice beneath the surface.

- **1850s–1860s:** Science fiction does not yet exist as a recognized genre. Some will later regard Mary Shelley's *Frankenstein* (1818) as the first work of science fiction. Readers in the United States in the 1850s might also be aware of "The Unparalleled Adventure of One Hans Pfaall," a short story by Edgar Allan Poe published in June 1835 about a man who makes a trip to the moon in a balloon.

  1950s: During what is known as the golden age of science fiction, Ray Bradbury publishes *The Martian Chronicles* in 1950, which is mainly a collection of previously published stories. Isaac Asimov, another groundbreaking science-fiction writer, publishes three novels about the Galactic Empire, *Pebble in the Sky* (1950), *The Stars, Like Dust* (1951), and *The Currents of Space* (1952).

  Today: Science fiction continues to flourish in a variety of forms. Among the notable science-fiction works of the twenty-first century are *Player of Games* (2008), by Iain M. Banks; Marcel Theroux's *Far North* (2009); and *Zoo City* (2011), by Lauren Beukes.

- **1850s–1860s:** In the United States in 1850, the average number of people in each household is 5.39. In 1860, it is 5.16.

  1950s: In 1950, the average number of people in each household is 3.38. This figure falls to 3.29 by the end of the decade. The decline is caused not by a fall in the birth rate but by fewer relatives such as grandparents living under the same family roof.

  Today: In 2010, the average number of people in each household in the United States is 2.58. Family structures are changing, and there is an increase in the number of households headed by single parents.

---

grand rush of creativity, a torrent of new magazines and new writers bringing new themes and fresh techniques that laid the foundation for the work of the four decades that followed." Silverberg mentions such writers, in addition to Bradley, as Jack Vance, Poul Anderson, Damon Knight, Arthur C. Clarke, Ray Bradbury, Philip K. Dick, and James E. Gunn.

Barry N. Malzberg, in "The Fifties," also notes the explosion of interest in science fiction during the 1950s: "In 1953 there were forty or fifty times the outlets for science fiction that had existed five years earlier." By the mid-1950s, according to Malzberg, there were forty science-fiction magazines and several hundred science-fiction novels being published every year. He notes that one book editor, Donald A. Wollheim at the publisher Ace, "was publishing more science fiction in a month than had appeared in all of 1943." Given this favorable publishing environment, it is not surprising that Bradley was able to find many outlets for her early work in the 1950s.

Mr. Emmett went to check out what he thought was a shooting star and found a spacecraft.
(© pixelparticle / Shutterstock.com)

Women Science-Fiction Writers in the 1950s

In Kingsley Amis's book, *New Maps of Hell: A Survey of Science Fiction* (1960), which was based on lectures Amis gave in the spring of 1959, he estimated that at the time no more than 2 percent of published science fiction was by women. He also pointed out that according to surveys, readers of science fiction were mostly male, by a proportion that ranged from five to one to fifteen to one, although he noted that the disparity was likely decreasing. Lisa Tuttle and Helen Merrick, in "Women SF Writers," explain further that

> as a commercial genre, sf was formed chiefly by the men who edited, wrote for and read the US pulp magazines of the 1920s and 1930s. For decades the belief that most readers were adolescent males imposed certain restrictions on subject matter and style—women, and women's supposed interests, were sentimentalized or ignored.

Tuttle and Merrick point out, however, that in those early days up to the 1950s, women both read and wrote science fiction, and sometimes they did so "under androgynous bylines." Examples include Leigh Brackett, C. L. Moore, and Andre Norton. Other women science-fiction writers prior to the 1960s included Marion Zimmer Bradley, Miriam Allen deFord, J. Hunter Holly, Lilith Lorraine, Margaret St. Clair, Evelyn E. Smith, and Thea von Harbou.

Jane L. Donawerth and Carol A. Kolmerten, in their introduction to *Utopian and Science Fiction by Women: Worlds of Difference*, write that in the 1950s, female authors

> who wrote near-future dystopias or space operas with macho male heroes for the paperback market, did not much change the literary conventions of science fiction but they made a secure place for women writers in the science fiction publishing industry.

Donawerth and Kolmerten also note that women writers continued to influence science fiction in the 1960s, leading to the development of a "women's tradition," to which Bradley made a contribution, in which the "traditionally feminine trait of empathy" is presented as a "special power."

CRITICAL OVERVIEW

As a relatively minor story in the catalog of Bradley's work, "Year of the Big Thaw" has not attracted much critical comment, although the fact that it has been reprinted several times in the twenty-first century, over fifty years since its first publication, suggests that some regard it highly.

Rosemarie Arbur, in *Marion Zimmer Bradley*, describes the story as "a monologue, in dialect . . . 'first contact' as it might have happened among nineteenth-century rural folk who mind their own business." Further, Arbur states that Bradley's earliest works are "about 'family' in the most profound sense of the word." She argues that stories such as "Women Only" (1953), "Centaurus Changeling" (1954), and "Year of the Big Thaw" make up "an examination of the parent-offspring bond which may fairly be said to define the concept of 'family.'" "Year of the Big Thaw," writes Arbur, "extends the concept of 'family' to persons who are 'parents' not only to their own progeny but to the young who may belong to another human (sub)species." These stories, according to Arbur, can therefore be understood as early examples of the goal Bradley had as a writer throughout her career of presenting "increasingly detailed explorations into human nature."

Other critics who have examined Bradley's oeuvre have mainly commented on her later work. For example, Janice C. Crosby, in "Feminist Spirituality," declares Bradley to be

> a groundbreaking author who used feminist spirituality in a variety of ways, in different genres and subgenres. Due to her prominence, Bradley introduced many authors and readers to the potential of feminist spirituality in literature of the fantastic.

According to John Clute's entry on Bradley in *The Encyclopedia of Science Fiction*, "Her work has had an electrifying effect on a very large readership; and at her best she spoke with the rare transparency of the true storyteller."

CRITICISM

Bryan Aubrey

Aubrey holds a PhD in English. In the following essay, he discusses "Year of the Big Thaw" in terms of its form, its realistic and science-fiction

> 'YEAR OF THE BIG THAW' MAY BE A SLIGHT STORY, THE APPRENTICE WORK OF A YOUNG WRITER, BUT IT MAKES ITS POINT NONETHELESS, AFFIRMING THE VALUE OF LIFE AND LOVE IN THE MOST UNUSUAL OF CIRCUMSTANCES."

elements, how it differs from earlier depictions of Martians, and its theme of unconditional love.

Marion Zimmer Bradley was a prolific writer over a career that spanned forty years. "Year of the Big Thaw" was one of her earliest efforts. In fact, it was among the first half-dozen stories that Bradley published. Bradley, it is fair to say, was a born writer, and she was fortunate that the early part of her career coincided with the period known as the golden age of science fiction, when publishing opportunities in the flourishing pulp magazines of the 1950s were plentiful.

In her introduction to *Jamie and Other Stories: The Best of Marion Zimmer Bradley*, Bradley explains her emergence as a writer while still quite young. In August 1946, at the age of sixteen, she was riding home on a train in New York, and for the first time in her life found herself with money in her pocket, earned from her summer vacation job. At the train station, she bought a copy of *Startling Stories*, a pulp science-fiction magazine, and read in it the novel *The Dark World*, by Henry Kuttner (which she attributes to his wife and collaborator Catherine Moore Kuttner), and several short stories. Bradley writes, "By the time my journey was finished I knew not only that I wanted to be a writer but that I wanted to write science fiction." That summer Bradley typed the first draft of a novel she had written the previous summer, which was to become *The Sword of Aldones*, published in 1961.

Bradley's inclinations were always toward the novel rather than the short story. She preferred the freedom of developing characters and plots at length rather than laboring in the more constricted field of the short story. As a writer, she has always been known more for her novels

WHAT
DO I READ
NEXT?

- *The Mists of Avalon* (1983), Bradley's most well-known novel, is a well-researched Arthurian fantasy that centers on Morgaine, King Arthur's half-sister, and the other women who were close to the men of the Round Table and wielded influence behind the scenes.

- *Fourth Planet from the Sun: Tales of Mars from the Magazine of Fantasy and Science Fiction* (2005), edited by Gordon Van Gelder, is a collection of twelve stories about human expeditions to Mars. Authors represented include Ray Bradbury, Philip K. Dick, Arthur C. Clarke, and Leigh Brackett.

- *Twenty-First Century Science Fiction* (2013), edited by David G. Hartwell and Patrick Nielson Hayden, is an anthology of thirty-four science-fiction stories published between 2003 and 2011 by both established writers and newcomers.

- In *Broken Symmetry: A Young Adult Science Fiction Thriller* (2013), by Brian Rix, sixteen-year-old Blaire Adams has to come to terms with her father's mysterious disap-

pearance and death. She finds out that he had a rare chromosomal disorder that she has inherited and that may kill her. She is also haunted by nightmares of a murderer who lures his victims to suicide.

- David Seed's *Science Fiction: A Very Short Introduction* (2011) is a concise, 144-page introduction to the genre that shows how it evolved to become popular in the twentieth century. Seed examines drama, poetry, and film as well as prose narratives.

- Science fiction in the twentieth century was dominated by white writers, but toward the end of the century, the African American writer Octavia Butler made a major contribution to the field. Butler, a feminist, used her novels to subvert the ways in which male-dominated science fiction had dealt with issues of race and gender. In her Xenogenesis trilogy, in the wake of a nuclear holocaust, the alien Oankali try to save humanity by creating human-alien hybrids. Unwilling to adapt, the humans resist. The trilogy comprises *Dawn* (1987), *Adulthood Rites* (1987), and *Imago* (1989).

---

than her short stories. Later in her introduction to *Jamie and Other Stories* she gives some insight into her preferences. She writes, "I never felt much at ease writing short stories; my natural feeling is to write novels, the longer the better." She then describes the process of writing a short story as she experienced it: "the great majority of them [are] impulses—I would wake up with an idea, juggle the plot a bit, and sit down and write it on a sustained impulse, not stopping till I finished it."

This, one may suppose, is how "Year of the Big Thaw" was conceived. It is a slight, whimsical story of no more than about three thousand words, notable as much for its touch of humor near the end—something that science

fiction is often said to lack—and its message of all-inclusive love as for its science-fiction content. The story is unusual in the sense that it is set not in the future, unlike the vast majority of the science fiction that appeared in the American pulp magazines of the 1950s, but in the past, and not a vague past but a rather precisely defined time in American history, as well as in a particular locality.

The form of the story is also a little unusual, since the Reverend Doane, who sets the story in motion, is a disembodied questioner who is not described at all in terms of his age, physical appearance, position in the community, or anything else. He interacts with Mr. Emmett only by asking him a few short

---

questions at various intervals, which are designed simply to keep the story moving. It is not even clear where their conversation takes place, because no setting is given. Presumably, it occurs on Mr. Emmett's farm, but it could just as well be at Reverend Doane's church, for all the reader knows. Perhaps this was simply the form in which the story first came to Bradley (in the manner in which she describes above), and she just decided to stick with it, although it would not have been difficult to refine it and integrate the clergyman more into the narrative.

What is noticeable about the way the story develops is how carefully Bradley establishes a realistic setting as a prelude to her fantastic tale. Almost the entire first half of the story is taken up with this background, as Mr. Emmett recalls a little of Matt's early life, recounts his own family history, including the fact that he was raised on his father's farm in New Hampshire, and then tells the story of the great blizzard, complete with geographic detail: "I heard tell it spread down most to York. And at Fort Orange, the place they call Albany now, the Hudson froze right over, so they say." This is followed by vivid, realistic details of the flooding caused by the great thaw and then eventually the strange sight in the sky, the loud sound of the crash, and the discovery of the "contraption," the spaceship that has transported beings from Mars, perhaps, to Earth. It is here that the story takes its turn from realism into science fiction, although there is more fiction in it than science—a fact that raises interesting questions about the definition of science fiction.

During the mid-twentieth century most definitions of science fiction emphasized that actual science, or at least scientific method or development, was an essential part of science fiction. However, Kingsley Amis, in *New Maps of Hell: A Survey of Science Fiction*, states that the genre "is not necessarily fiction about science or scientists, nor is science necessarily important in it." Amis offers the following definition:

> Science fiction is that class of prose narrative treating of a situation that could not arise in the world we know, but which is hypothesized on the basis of some innovation in science or technology, or pseudo-science or pseudo-technology, whether human or extraterrestrial in origin.

In "Year of the Big Thaw," Bradley gives her story the faintest veneer of scientific validity by setting it in the past, when some astronomers were suggesting the possibility of intelligent life on Mars. Based on observations by telescope, this is the sort of innovation in technology that Amis refers to, upon which an alien civilization is hypothesized, although of course such a hypothesis was based on incorrect interpretation of the data and has long since, even by Bradley's lifetime, been discarded. Beyond that, Bradley feels little need to be even remotely scientific. The spacecraft in which the aliens arrive has a cartoonish quality; it is, according to Mr. Emmett,

> long and thin and as shiny as Marthy's old pewter pitcher her Ma brought from England. It had a pair of red rods sticking out behind and a crazy globe fitted up where the top ought to be.

The reference to the color red here, with the fact that the clothes the Martians wear are also bright red, seems to be a nod by the twenty-four-year-old writer to the fact that Mars has a reddish hue and is sometimes known as the red planet.

Bradley's Martians, when Mr. Emmett discovers them, are quite different from what a reader of science fiction at the time might have expected. Aliens, whether from Mars or anywhere else, had often been depicted as bug-eyed monsters, a descriptive term that was commonly abbreviated to the acronym BEM. The origin of the BEM tradition may go back to H. G. Wells and *The War of the Worlds* (1898), which depicts an invasion of Earth by Martians whose appearance is the stuff of nightmares:

> Those who have never seen a living Martian can scarcely imagine the strange horror of its appearance. The peculiar V-shaped mouth with its pointed upper lip, the absence of brow ridges, the absence of a chin beneath the wedgelike lower lip, the incessant quivering of this mouth...the extraordinary intensity of the immense eyes...were at once vital, intense, inhuman, crippled and monstrous.

BEMs were still appearing on the covers of the science-fiction magazines in the 1930s and into the 1940s, when the teenaged Bradley was eagerly devouring them. But the BEM is not for Bradley. In "Year of the Big Thaw," she has an altogether different idea in mind: a kinder, gentler Martian. Apart from the unusual color of their eyes, their strange clothes, and the fact that Mr. Emmett feels that the surviving Martian is reading his mind, these Martians are about as close to humans as makes no difference. The dead female he describes as "a right pretty woman," for example, and Mr. Emmett feels no fear at all in encountering these alien life forms.

Nor is Bradley deterred by the obvious problem of communication that Kingsley Amis identifies: "If aliens are to be introduced... the problem of communicating with them is likely to arise.... Talking to an alien... presents difficulties that are literally insurmountable." Bradley happily skips over this problem as if it did not exist, because her Martian speaks perfectly intelligible English: "My baby—in ship. Get—baby," he tells Mr. Emmett. Mr. Emmett cannot quite place the accent ("not like Joe the Portygee sailor or like those tarnal dumb Frenchies up Canady way, but—well, funny"), but that does not seem to matter much. Later, after Mr. Emmett returns with the baby, the dying Martian says—not quite managing the correct verb form but otherwise doing pretty well for an alien: "I dying.... We come from planet—star up there—crash here—" Bradley has thus created one of the few English-speaking Martians in the entire field of science fiction, and she has done so because at this point in her story she is not much interested in science fiction, per se, but wants only to convey her main theme, which, to put it simply, is love—unconditional love, given unquestioningly wherever it is needed, even to alien life forms. By saving the alien baby and pledging to look after him, Mr. Emmett does his duty by his God, and he thinks nothing much of it. An unassuming man, he probably thinks that anyone in his position would have done the same thing.

In this story, then, the simple, God-fearing Connecticut farmer shows himself to have a loving heart that never thinks to exclude an unknown, strange being from love or regard it as "other," that is, disturbing because it is different. He sees the need and fills the need, no questions asked. "Year of the Big Thaw" may be a slight story, the apprentice work of a young writer, but it makes its point nonetheless, affirming the value of life and love in the most unusual of circumstances.

Source: Bryan Aubrey, Critical Essay on "Year of the Big Thaw," in *Short Stories for Students*, Gale, Cengage Learning, 2015.

Robert Sabella

In the following excerpt, Sabella characterizes Bradley as a writer whose popularity increased gradually.

Some science fiction writers burst into prominence, their very first stories shouting the author's importance to the entire world. Robert A. Heinlein, John Varley, and Lucius Shepherd are examples of this. Others start slowly, almost anonymously, gradually building a reputation while they perfect their craft. And yet, at some point the science fiction community realizes that, yes, there is another major writer in their midst.

Marion Zimmer Bradley is a prime example of the latter category. Her first published story "Centaurus Changeling" caused little stir in 1954. Nor did her first novel *The Door Through Space* or her 1962 Ace Double *The Planet Savers* backed with *The Sword of Aldones*.

But that Ace Double was the first step in Bradley's growing importance as a science fiction writer. It introduced the world Darkover, a feudalistic society whose technology is based on psionics rather than on physical science. Isolated for centuries, Darkover has suddenly been contacted by the Terran Empire which wishes to absorb it into its union.

The Darkover novels are typical Bradley: mostly action SF with a good deal of swashbuckling, often touching on sword and sorcery, though always with a recognizably SF rationale.

And yet there is much more to a Marion Zimmer Bradley story than simple adventure. Beneath the surface story Bradley examines such serious issues as the relationship between the technological Terran Empire and the feudalistic Darkover; the traditionally repressed role of women on Darkover; and the need for telepaths to repress their sexuality in order to perform their function in society. In all cases, Bradley does not take sides. She presents all positions fairly, allowing her readers almost complete freedom to decide which is the more humanly practical decision.

Marion Zimmer Bradley has written nearly twenty Darkover novels since 1962. In the process she has built up the world of Darkover with a richness of detail comparable to that of J.R.R. Tolkien's Middle-Earth or Frank Herbert's world Dune.

The series reached its peak in the 1970s with such acclaimed novels as *The Heritage of Hastur*, *The Shattered Chain*, and the Hugo-nominated *The Forbidden Tower*. In recent years her interest in the series seems to have waned. Although she wrote thirteen Darkover novels between 1970 and 1984, there have been few since then.

Instead Bradley has written several acclaimed historical fantasies. Her Arthurian fantasy *The Mists of Avalon* was a national bestseller. Although far removed from Darkover in both setting and era, it addresses some of the same issues: the clash between the old mystical Pagan religion and the new Christian conquerors, and the role of women in English society.

Her next bestseller was *Firebrand*, a novel about the Trojan War told from the point of view of the female participants. While not as popular as *The Mists of Avalon*, it too told a solid story while examining serious issues.

Bradley has also lent her popularity to help new science fiction and fantasy writers get published. Several volumes of short stories set on her Darkover world have been published, all written by "the friends of Darkover," a fan group. She also publishes *Marion Zimmer Bradley Fantasy Magazine*, one of the most professional quality outlets for pure fantasy short fiction.

Very quietly Marion Zimmer Bradley has become one of the very best science fiction writers whose novels entertain as well as raise serious issues. Her Darkover series was one of the first ongoing science fiction series. Its serious nature wrapped in a fantasy-like adventure package influenced many of the popular series currently dominating the genre....

Source: Robert Sabella, "Marion Zimmer Bradley," in *Who Shaped Science Fiction?*, Kroshka Books, 2000, pp. 221–22.

Marion Zimmer Bradley

In the following excerpt, Bradley explains the positive effects that fandom has on science-fiction literature.

I have a great deal in common with such science-fiction "greats" as Harlan Ellison, Isaac Asimov, Ray Bradbury, Robert Silverberg and Donald Wollheim—and others too numerous to mention: I came up through the ranks of fandom to become a pro writer. My first works, like theirs, were published in the letter columns of the old pulp magazines; later, in the pages of hectographed or mimeographed fanzines published by other young science fiction or fantasy fiction enthusiasts. Many of these fans, like myself, aspired to be professionals, and many of them actually made it; those I have mentioned, and many more. So many of these science-fiction and fantasy professionals came from the ranks of fandom, back in the days when science fiction was still a rather minor genre, that I once lightheartedly quipped that reading the 1965 membership list of the Science Fiction Writers of America (SFWA) was like reading the 1955 membership list of the Fantasy Amateur Press Association (FAPA).

That's not nearly as true as it used to be. In the years since 1966 or so, more and more writers are entering the ranks of science fiction and fantasy who have never had anything to do with fandom, and who tend, in fact, to be a little scornful of organized fandom, even when they attend its conventions and accept its awards. Writers such as Samuel R. Delany, Ursula Le Guin, and Joanna Russ, clinging to their intellectual credentials from academia, are often gracious to fans when they must interact with them, but they do not, as do I and most of the others mentioned above, recognize their origins in fandom; and such writers as Gene Wolfe and Stephen King, while they may use fandom for publicity purposes, are occasionally snide or sarcastic about it. Fewer and fewer fans aspire to become professionals in any field—or if they do, it is harder to get in touch with their fellows.

Partly this is a matter of sheer *size*. When science fiction and fantasy were lumped together in the forties or thereabouts, there were, it was estimated, fewer than three hundred active fans who formed a loosely connected network of enthusiasts. There were fewer than half a dozen magazines published, and most of them had letter columns in the back pages, where potentially active fans could find the names and addresses of other fans, and could write to them and swap letters, friendship, and their own little magazines or fanzines. Many book collectors claimed that they bought literally everything published in either fantasy or science fiction in a given year—and could still do it without being millionaires, on the modest salaries of postal clerks or shoe salesmen.

THOSE WRITERS WHO HAVE NEVER THEMSELVES BEEN FANS HAVE BEEN RATHER BEMUSED BY AND OCCASIONALLY RESENTFUL OF THIS PHENOMENON. SOME LOVE IT; SOME HATE IT; OTHERS SHRUG AND MATTER-OF-FACTLY ACCEPT IT AS A GODSEND FOR PUBLICITY PURPOSES."

I published my first fanzine on a pan hectograph which cost me five dollars, paying a dollar for a ream of paper, thirty cents for a special hectograph ribbon, and about a dollar for thirty three-cent stamps to mail it out with; and I joined in the cry of rage when paperback books went up to thirty-five cents, certain that no one would ever pay that much for them. (Just to keep perspective, a stamp is now twenty cents, paper is about ten dollars a ream, and my latest novel is advertised to sell at $3.50. The newest Montgomery Ward catalogue doesn't even advertise hectographs for sale anymore, and the cheapest mimeograph I've seen is about three hundred dollars instead of the $21.95 model I bought way back when. But then, the minimum wage has risen from fifty cents an hour to about $3.65. And wages have gone up to about six or seven times what they were then, but the price of publishing supplies, etc., has risen nearly ten times. Even with so-called teenage affluence, it costs more for the young enthusiast to start a fanzine, while the pulps, with their ready lists of names and addresses of fellow fans and other fanzines, are gone forever.)

Science fiction, of course, is now more respectable. It's easier to find other fans, the reader is not so isolated. Probably half of your graduating class has read Tolkien, Ursula Le Guin, Anne McCaffrey, and the latest Heinlein or Frank Herbert. They have watched *Star Trek* on television, played Dungeons and Dragons or some science-fiction video game, stood in line to see the latest Lucas *Star Wars* epic or Steven Spielberg saga, and watched the moonshots and the space shuttle takeoff.

But this kind of fandom is not what it used to be—a refuge for young people who love *reading* above all things, a very specialized form of reading which isolates them from the other interests of the young people they know. Early fans were readers, compulsive readers of their chosen fiction, and often compulsive writers who, when they wanted to go and write the kind of thing they loved, couldn't get it published in their high-school magazine or college creative writing class without getting a lecture about wasting their good minds on trash. Or maybe even get hustled off to a school counselor to be brainwashed into taking more interest in what they called "healthy" reading: *Sports Illustrated* or *Good Housekeeping*, depending on your sex.

In those days, if you liked science fiction, there was no government space program, no NASA, no L-5 societies grabbing headlines, to reassure you that your interest in space was normal or even praiseworthy. A poll taken in 1952 or thereabouts showed no fewer than 10 percent of the public believed we would ever get to the moon, and of that 10 percent, almost none believed it would be before the year 2000. If you liked fantasy or horror you were even worse off. In the movies it was either Dracula or Disney, and psychologists were talking about how unhealthy it was to have any interest even in fairy tales. "Magical thinking" was the nasty epithet applied to anyone who was not completely materialistic. Nowadays about half of best-selling novels and more than half of popular movies have some supernatural or horror element; but back then anything to do with fantasy was rare and difficult to find.

So, in those days, when you met another fan, you were instant friends—even instant family in many cases. Behind all the rather childish feudin' and fussin', the immature name-calling in fanzines and silly teapot tempests, there was a very strong sense of togetherness. You were a member of a minority, and it created strong bonds. Even if you were, for instance, a devotee of *Weird Tales*, and the fan who lived across the city in the next town was dedicated to joining Rocket Societies and wanted to work in Space Technology, you were still under the blanket umbrella of fandom. You knew at least some of the same people. The two of you could talk without the ghastly left-out sense you felt at school, or at work, when it seemed the only subjects of mundane conversation were (for women) hair styles, fashions and dates for the Senior Prom, or (for young men) cars, baseball and girls.

Fandom, of course, still remains as a support group. It goes even further; at the last World Science Fiction Convention there were, I think, eight thousand fans, all of whom had at least *something* in common—they all cared enough about *some* aspect of the convention to buy a ticket and come to the hotel. That's very reassuring. Of course, there were a lot of them who also were interested in such peripheral fannish items as comic books, *Star Wars* games or Dungeons and Dragons game pieces, horror films, video games, L-5 colonies, or the Society for Creative Anachronism, costumes and the masquerade...you name it. There is still a hard core of fans interested in science-fiction writing, and in professional aspirations; but you can no longer walk up to any fan at a convention and assume that he or she shares your desire to work professionally in the field. Even if she wants to turn pro some day, she just might want to work as a lights technician for George Lucas instead of selling a story to *Analog*.

Many writers now, even those who came up through fandom, have very little to do with fandom as such. There is, for instance, a great difference, or so it seems to me, between the people who came into fandom through *Star Trek* and those who came in back in the days of the old pulps.

There is at least some good reason to think that it was *Star Trek* that made the difference. Those of us who were old-time fans and still dearly loved the television program quickly found out that *Star Trek* fandom was quite different from ordinary fandom. In 1962, for instance, when the Big Names were people like Isaac Asimov, Leigh Brackets, Ed Hamilton, Robert Heinlein, Poul Anderson, and Tony Boucher, a young writer just up from fandom could (as I did) get invited to a party in Chicago where all these living idols were sitting together in a single room and were willing to talk to you informally as a fellow writer or just as a human being who shared interests in common. You could sit on the same sofa, share a drink, and chat casually with these people, with no sense that there was a Great Fixed Gulf between you and the object of your interest. There was little, if any, sense that he was a Great Big Important Superstar and that you were a member of the

Great Unwashed from whom the Star must be protected. Granted, even then there were teenage fans who made nuisances of themselves, demanded to tell the Big Names the details of their unwritten novels or the stories of their lives, and it became a rather rueful joke that some of the pro writers would hang out down in the bar (where teenagers, of course, would not be admitted) to get away from the more wearying and juvenile of their admirers.

But even the "down in the bar" attitude of some of the writers was a very far cry from the way gulfs were fixed between *Star Trek* Big Names and their fans. Granted that it is easier for thirty writers to relate to two hundred or even five hundred fans than for five or six film actors to relate to twenty thousand fans. But whatever the good reasons for the security surrounding the film and TV actors, it is *different*. The seventeen-year-old fan who had a chance for ten minutes of conversation, as I did with Leo Margulies and Sam Merwin, in 1947, could literally have her life changed. One does not reach that kind of metamorphosis by listening to a TV star or lining up for his or her autograph. I was deeply moved and inspired when I heard Mark Lenard of *Star Trek* speak, and I am sure that the appearances, and the role models presented by Nichelle Nichols and Grace Lee Whitney—to say nothing of Nimoy and Shatner—have raised the self-awareness and even perhaps the creativity of the fans who heard them. But it is a *different* inspiration. Only the tiniest minority, and then mostly those few who were working in security or guest liaison, ever had the opportunity to get to know these people as human beings like themselves, or to feel that what these people had done maybe they themselves could do. Many *Star Trek* fans, accustomed to meeting their celebrities only along the roped-off barricades of a thousand-person-long autograph line, were surprised and delighted when they found that a writer such as Poul Anderson or myself was a person who would sit and drink soda pop or beer and answer casual questions about their work in a casual way.

Please understand that I am in no way criticizing the celebrities of *Star Trek*, who with a few exceptions have been wonderful, charming people, making themselves accessible to their fans far above and beyond the call of duty; and despite all the unkind things people can and do say about actors, they too, like writers, are only human and mostly well-meaning. Whenever they dare to relax the façade of wariness (and having once been literally mobbed by fans at a huge convention, to the point where I feared for my physical safety, no one can blame, say, Leonard Nimoy for his caution in venturing unescorted on to a hotel floor), they are wonderful people. Once when I appeared as guest writer at a convention where Grace Whitney ("Yeoman Rand") was the *Star Trek* guest, she and I enjoyed a couple of hours of very pleasant conversation. And I remember with great affection an episode where George Takei ("Sulu") expressed interest in meeting A. E. van Vogt; I sat by, deeply moved and charmed by the interplay of mutual admiration and courtesy between the older writer and the younger actor. But there are so many *more* of their fans that they simply cannot get to know each and every one of them on a personal basis; while in the smaller and more intimate old-time fandom, based on books and magazines before the expansion of science fiction (in a larger sense) into the media, there was always a chance that any fan could meet, and get to know, almost any writer. That situation simply does not exist any longer and there is no way to bring it back. Even at science-fiction conventions, Robert Heinlein has had to show a certain caution in going out on the floor without someone to protect him against the well-meaning but almost dangerous adoration of his fans.

This being so, the question naturally arises as to whether fandom still has any uses for the writer and the would-be writer. Granted, science-fiction fandom—whether the fan is interested in standing in line to see yet another *Star Wars* epic, or in collecting different Dungeons and Dragons game pieces—is a wonderful hobby on any level. Collectors of comic books share the same kind of camaraderie as, say, Bela Lugosi fans. Those fans interested in "filk singing" gather in hotel rooms, lobbies and late-night party rooms to the point where the tone-deaf or the serious musicians have been known to protest that filk-singing, like sex, should be done in private by consenting adults. A word about "filk singing," actually, "folk singing"—but ever since a printing error in a program book, fandom adopted this new term. Where once there were two or three fantasy-oriented amateur press associations (apas) there now must be twenty or thirty, including one for

Women's Studies, one for gays and lesbians, one for pagans, one for psychedelic experimenters, several for *Star Trek* and *Star Wars* fans, one highlighting pornography, and one for almost every big-city science fiction club...as well as probably a dozen others I don't even know about!

There are fanzines which run all the way from the two-page "personal-letter-mimeographed-for-a-few-close-friends" in the various apas, to highly professional fiction magazines with two-color covers and printed literary journals of serious criticism, many of which pay for material accepted and consider themselves all but prozines (magazines for professionals). There is no longer even a common base of assumed interest among all fanzine lovers or even all fanzine editors; the readers of an L-5 Society Newsletter cannot be automatically assumed to have anything in common with a fanzine of *Star Trek* amateur fiction. But almost every lover of the larger field which now takes in science fiction—not only printed books and magazines, but all the media—can find some recreational interest within the field, be his interest serious or frivolous.

Science fiction is one field where writers have always been able to get feedback. From the days of the old pulps—whose letter columns, unlike those written to, say, Western magazines, were filled with highly articulate commentary both from a scientific and a literary standpoint—science-fiction writers in general have known that they ignore the fans at their peril. Those writers who have never themselves been fans have been rather bemused by and occasionally resentful of this phenomenon. Some love it; some hate it; others shrug and matter-of-factly accept it as a godsend for publicity purposes. Some old-time fans have come very far from their origins and honestly don't like being reminded of them, such as Bob Silverberg. Some have turned on fandom; Harlan Ellison, especially, is given to caustic outbursts. Pragmatically, producers of *Star Trek* and *Star Wars* and such things have welcomed the active publicity among their fans; everybody knows the story of the writing campaign, kicked off by Bjo Trimble, which kept *Star Trek* alive for an extra season. Other writers, like myself, retain close sentimental ties with fandom and keep their connection with it very much alive. Jacqueline Lichtenberg and Katherine Kurtz, as well as myself, have found something very like a small cult fandom organizing around their work; I can't speak for any of the others (though I know that Anne McCaffrey, at least, has very mixed feelings about the desperate and often-articulated desire for her fans to *partici-pate* in the Dragon/Pern universe by dressing in their clothes, speaking the language, writing amateur fiction).

Apart from the perfectly obvious benefits to sales—and before anything else, we must acknowledge that the Dorsai filksongs and fandom certainly benefit Gordon Dickson, that the Darkover fanzines create a ready-made market for new books for DAW, that Jacqueline Lichtenberg's crew of Sime/Gen fans and their fanzines probably play a part when an editor decides whether or not a new book will be bought—does organized fandom really have anything to offer the would-be professional writer?

At this point I could be accused of setting up a straw man, for a quick and pat answer, which says, Oh, yes, fandom is invaluable, that is established, it deserves absolute support, a writer can hardly do better than getting into fandom. If this were my only point, I could single out writer Susan Schwartz, who made her first bow in Darkover fandom, such artists as Alicia Austin and Hannah Shapero and George Barr, who made their reputations illustrating fanzines until they began to sell professionally, and point out the obvious, that such fanzines as *Algol* and *Fantasiae* and *Shayol* serve as training grounds for writing and editorial skills. Fandom has certainly proved its worth; not only the "old" style of fandom, producing greats in the field such as those I listed in the first paragraph, but the "new" style of fandom has supported the rise of many professional talents.

If it were only for this, fandom would have, I think, definitely established its worth. But there are, after all, other roads into professional accomplishment. Harlan Ellison, in one of his speeches, has attacked fandom for attempting to stereotype any writer as forever after somehow "belonging" to them, as if the writer had a duty to continue to write what his fans wanted. This is one of the very real dangers, and must be respected. The fact that I have chosen to remain attached to fandom as a part of my "roots" does not imply that Harlan must

consider himself bound in honor to do the same; and there is something to be said for an attitude of total indifference to one's admirers, especially where the alternative is to remain bound by their wishes and desires. I have been pressed often to write sequels to certain books and I admit I have sometimes wondered whether I have been pressured to write books which perhaps should have remained unwritten, out of a desire for the security of a guaranteed following and assured popularity at least among my own personal fandom. I suppose this can be said of everyone who writes a series, from the followers of Darkover to the followers of Lord Peter Wimsey or Travis McGee. There is a telling passage in one of Louisa May Alcott's books where the writer Jo speaks of the insatiable demands of her fans and the desire at the end of *Jo's Boys* where the author speaks of the temptation to conclude her books with an earthquake which will sink Plumifield to the depths of the earth so that she could never be tempted to resurrect those characters and scenes. Conan Doyle threw Sherlock Holmes over the Reichenbach Falls, but was forced to resurrect him. . . .

Source: Marion Zimmer Bradley, "Fandom: Its Value to the Professional," in *Inside Outer Space: Science Fiction Professionals Look at Their Craft*, edited by Sharon Jarvis, Frederick Ungar Publishing, 1985, pp. 69–76.

Rosemarie Arbur

In the following excerpt, Arbur discusses Bradley's psychological approach to science fiction.

. . . As a beginning science-fiction writer, Bradley had to play by the rules: science fiction was supposed to be fiction based on probable results of extrapolation from known sciences, and thus her earliest published works—most of them in the form of short stories—are crafted carefully to avoid blatant violations of what contemporary scientists said was true or probable. Once she had made a name for herself, Bradley paid increasing attention to the less certain extrapolations that psychology makes possible. Although Bradley herself feels that anything she wrote earlier than the mid-sixties is not worth serious consideration, critics and careful readers are best served by D. H. Lawrence's advice: "Never trust the teller; trust the tale." More recently, Ursula K. Le Guin simultaneously urges the same caution and celebrates disregard for it: "I am an artist, too, and therefore a liar. Distrust everything I say.

IN THESE VERY EARLY WORKS, MZB BEGINS
TO EXPLORE THE THEMES THAT BECOME DOMINANT
IN *ALL* HER SCIENCE-FICTION AND FANTASY
WRITING."

I am telling the truth." Despite what Bradley says, readers of her early short fiction will find much worth considering quite seriously.

Bradley's progress as a writer had and has the goal of increasingly detailed explorations into human nature. Her earliest published works—the stories mentioned here as well as most that she published within the next several years—are about "family" in the most profound sense of the word. There is in "Women Only," "Centaurus Changeling," and "Year of the Big Thaw" (1954) an examination of the parent-offspring bond which may fairly be said to define the concept of "family." The first story suggests that a vital aspect of being human inheres in the loving acceptance and nurturance of the being(s) to whom one gives birth. The second suggests that another requisite for humanity is the risk-taking and trust involved in human reproduction, a trust that includes parents and offspring, yes, but that also includes other adults who in various ways make society a macrocosm of the family. And the "Year of the Big Thaw," like "Centaurus Changeling," extends the concept of "family" to persons who are "parents" not only to their own progeny but to the young who may belong to another human (sub)species.

Her second major published work, "The Climbing Wave" (1955), shows a sensitivity to gender-related uses of language that is at least a decade ahead of its time. More important, the story is an inquiry into a really fundamental aspect of the human condition. The novella is the tale of the descendants of the first interstellar voyage; after much preparation on their dim-lighted homeworld, a group of young people make the triumphant trip back to Earth. They know that their grandparents' mission will be, because of the temporal effects of relativistic travel, mere history. In part because of this,

they expect to be welcomed to an Earth that is technologically superior even to their starship's "culture." They are doubly disappointed.

Those pioneers who left Earth for the Centaurus system are known to the contemporary Earthpeople as "Barbarians"; worse, the inhabitants of Earth use such demeaning expressions as "wife," as if a woman were not the equal of her mate. And, most shocking of all, they find that the homeworld of humanity is scarcely technological at all: the most complicated form of government is the village which, when it grows too large, "fissions" like a protozoon into two smaller ones.

It is important—for literary record-keeping if nothing else—that MZB endows the children of a star-traveling culture with revulsion for sexist-seeming words like "wife" in 1955. It is even more important that the thematic focus of this early novella is the question: "Why should human beings *work?*"

Twenty-five years later, with the Darkover novels well established as a "text" from which one can draw conclusions about the "technomania" of the Terrans and the "technophobia" of the Darkovans, Bradley was still exploring the same question. In this early novella, though, the question is central and simply but cogently presented. The answer is also simple: human beings should work to ensure the well-being of themselves and of other human beings. The viewpoint character of the novella finds this simple answer difficult to understand and, repeating "the climbing wave" in its original context (the poem "The Lotus Eaters"), thinks that the Earthfolk are like the original lotus eaters of the *Odyssey*, content to exist placidly and comfortably, without questing after new knowledge or applying current knowledge in novel situations. The Earthfolk in this novella, as far as the viewpoint character can see, have little ambition and even less "scientific curiosity," and he finds these attitudes to be wrong.

MZB has purposely made this character a rigid technocrat so that readers will not identify too strongly with his attitudes, but for the greater part of the novella readers, too, find something lacking in the Earthfolks' very simple lives. There is no *technology* in evidence! By the conclusion of the narrative, readers and the protagonist discover the technology that does exist and discover too why it is so clearly relegated to a secondary position in the culture.

The Earthfolk have electricity, and radio, and airplanes, and almost everything technical that one would want, but they do not build electric generators to have more electricity than they need. Frobisher, one of the leaders of the Earthfolk in his region, explains how, in the "Barbarian Ages," people did not use the radio to talk to one another but instead to entertain, how they kept building things they did not need and then began relying on their unnecessary technology to keep themselves alive. In other words, Frobisher's ancestors were barbarians not because they had an advanced technology but because they allowed technological—or materialist—values, not human ones, to dominate their lives.

In brief, "The Climbing Wave" presents a Utopian vision of the future, in certain respects oversimplified yet overall—for 1955—an admonitory and entertaining one. People ought not to work, MZB seems to imply, for any other good than that which benefits individual persons. If a family wants a rug and cannot make one, they are best served by locating someone who can make just what they'll like. There is no need for a factory to produce one hundred rugs a day that no one needs or wants. If a sewage-disposal plant for a village is inadequate, it is most unlikely that one that is merely larger will be better. This thematic emphasis on the use of humanity's tools and constructs is not new, but as MZB's authorial habits evolved, increasingly she concentrated on the false progress of material production at the cost of humankind's "spiritual" or nonmaterialistic values.

In these very early works, MZB begins to explore the themes that become dominant in *all* her science-fiction and fantasy writing. There is the quest for family, demonstrated by "Women Only" in the genetically-engineered provisions for the future of our species; this same theme is less obviously embodied in the rigid technocrat of "The Climbing Wave," for the young man is lost and is seeking a human group to which he can truly belong. There is also the exploration of the nature of human intimacy—or any sapient intimacy—in "Centaurus Changeling," as the pregnant human woman's behavior strains the relationship between her and her husband and as she comes to know better than any other Earth-human the people on whose homeworld she is to bear her child. All these stories touch upon another of MZB's themes: the meaning of being a woman. As they do, they bring a fourth theme into her literature, since being a woman is often being a second-class, sometimes not-recognized-as-human, organism: the theme of tolerance. Finally, as Bradley's career has developed, her fifth major theme—one might call it a kind of anti-materialism—has emerged with increasing strength and frequency. . . .

Source: Rosemarie Arbur, "Themes and Techniques: The Science Fiction," in *Marion Zimmer Bradley*, Starmont Reader's Guide No. 27, Starmont House, 1985, pp. 68–72.

SOURCES

Amis, Kingsley, *New Maps of Hell: A Survey of Science Fiction*, Harcourt, Brace, 1960, pp. 18, 20, 59–60.

Arbur, Rosemarie, *Marion Zimmer Bradley*, Starmont Reader's Guide No. 27, Starmont House, 1985, pp. 69, 109.

Booker, M. Keith, and Anne-Marie Thomas, eds., Introduction to *The Science Fiction Handbook*, Wiley-Blackwell, 2009, p. 7.

Bradley, Marion Zimmer, Introduction to *Jamie and Other Stories: The Best of Marion Zimmer Bradley*, Academy Chicago Publishers, 1993, pp. viii, x.

———, "Year of the Big Thaw," in *The Early Works of Marion Zimmer Bradley*, Douglas Editions, 2010, pp. 205–10.

Clute, John, "Bradley, Marion Zimmer," in *The Encyclopedia of Science Fiction*, 3rd ed., edited by John Clute and David Langford, http://www.sf-encyclopedia.com/entry/bradley_marion_zimmer (accessed February 2, 2014).

Crosby, Janice C., "Feminist Spirituality," in *Women in Science Fiction and Fantasy*, Vol. 1, edited by Robin A. Reid, Greenwood Press, 2009, p. 246.

"Definitions of SF," in *The Encyclopedia of Science Fiction*, 3rd ed., edited by John Clute and David Langford, http://www.sf-encyclopedia.com/entry/definitions_of_sf (accessed February 8, 2014).

Donawerth, Jane L., and Carol A. Kolmerten, eds., Introduction to *Utopian and Science Fiction by Women: Worlds of Difference*, Syracuse University Press, 1994, p. 10.

Gibson, Campbell, "Households and Average Household Size for the United States: 1790 and 1850 to 2010," in *American Demographic History Chartbook: 1790–2010*, http://www.demographicchartbook.com/Chartbook/images/figures/fig6-1.pdf (accessed February 12, 2014).

Langford, David, and Peter Nicholls, "First Contact," in *The Encyclopedia of Science Fiction*, 3rd ed., edited by John Clute and David Langford, http://www.sf-encyclopedia.com/entry/first_contact (accessed February 2, 2014).

Malzberg, Barry N., "The Fifties," Library of America website, http://www.loa.org/sciencefiction/why_malzberg.jsp (accessed January 31, 2014).

"Mars," in *The Encyclopedia of Science Fiction*, 3rd ed., edited by John Clute and David Langford, http://www.sf-encyclopedia.com/entry/mars (accessed February 5, 2014).

"Mars Chronology: Renaissance to the Space Age," NASA website, http://www.nasa.gov/audience/forstudents/9-12/features/F_Mars_Chronology_prt.htm (accessed February 6, 2014).

Silverberg, Robert, "Science Fiction in the 1950s: The Real Golden Age," Library of America website, 2012, http://www.loa.org/sciencefiction/why_silverberg.jsp (accessed January 31, 2014).

Tuttle, Lisa, and Helen Merrick, "Women SF Writers," in *The Encyclopedia of Science Fiction*, 3rd ed., edited by John Clute and David Langford, http://www.sf-encyclopedia.com/entry/women_sf_writers (accessed February 5, 2014).

Wells, H. G., *The War of the Worlds*, Lancer Books, 1967, pp. 28–29.

the fiction that female writers produced and how it differed from the work of male writers.

Larbalestier, Justine, ed., *Daughters of Earth: Feminist Science Fiction in the Twentieth Century*, Wesleyan University Press, 2006.

This is a collection of eleven essays, each of which explores a single science-fiction story by a female author. The publication dates of the stories range from 1927 to 2002.

Pyle, Rod, *Destination Mars: New Explorations of the Red Planet*, Prometheus Books, 2012.

Pyle discusses the projects being developed at NASA and the European Space Agency to explore Mars further. Four new missions are being planned for the 2010s and early 2020s.

Roberts, Adam, *The History of Science Fiction*, Palgrave Macmillan, 2007.

Roberts traces the history of science-fiction literature from earliest times to the present, also covering cinema, television, graphic novels, and other manifestations of science fiction in contemporary society.

FURTHER READING

Davin, Eric Leif, *Partners in Wonder: Women and the Birth of Science Fiction, 1926–1965*, Lexington Books, 2005.

Davin examines women's contributions to early science fiction. He identifies over two hundred female authors who collectively published over one thousand stories in science-fiction magazines between 1926 and 1965. Davin gives brief biographies of over one hundred of these writers and supplies an extensive bibliography. He also explores the nature of

SUGGESTED SEARCH TERMS

Marion Zimmer Bradley

Year of the Big Thaw

first contact AND stories

Martians AND science fiction

Mars AND canals

science fiction AND golden age

science fiction AND women writers

science fiction AND aliens

Glossary of Literary Terms

A

Aestheticism: A literary and artistic movement of the nineteenth century. Followers of the movement believed that art should not be mixed with social, political, or moral teaching. The statement "art for art's sake" is a good summary of aestheticism. The movement had its roots in France, but it gained widespread importance in England in the last half of the nineteenth century, where it helped change the Victorian practice of including moral lessons in literature. Oscar Wilde and Edgar Allan Poe are two of the best-known "aesthetes" of the late nineteenth century.

Allegory: A narrative technique in which characters representing things or abstract ideas are used to convey a message or teach a lesson. Allegory is typically used to teach moral, ethical, or religious lessons but is sometimes used for satiric or political purposes. Many fairy tales are allegories.

Allusion: A reference to a familiar literary or historical person or event, used to make an idea more easily understood. Joyce Carol Oates's story "Where Are You Going, Where Have You Been?" exhibits several allusions to popular music.

Analogy: A comparison of two things made to explain something unfamiliar through its similarities to something familiar, or to prove one point based on the acceptance of another. Similes and metaphors are types of analogies.

Antagonist: The major character in a narrative or drama who works against the hero or protagonist. The Misfit in Flannery O'Connor's story "A Good Man Is Hard to Find" serves as the antagonist for the Grandmother.

Anthology: A collection of similar works of literature, art, or music. Zora Neale Hurston's "The Eatonville Anthology" is a collection of stories that take place in the same town.

Anthropomorphism: The presentation of animals or objects in human shape or with human characteristics. The term is derived from the Greek word for "human form." The fur necklet in Katherine Mansfield's story "Miss Brill" has anthropomorphic characteristics.

Anti-hero: A central character in a work of literature who lacks traditional heroic qualities such as courage, physical prowess, and fortitude. Anti-heroes typically distrust conventional values and are unable to commit themselves to any ideals. They generally feel helpless in a world over which they have no control. Anti-heroes usually accept, and often celebrate, their positions as social outcasts. A well-known anti-hero is Walter Mitty in James Thurber's story "The Secret Life of Walter Mitty."

Archetype: The word archetype is commonly used to describe an original pattern or model from which all other things of the same kind are made. Archetypes are the literary images that grow out of the "collective unconscious," a theory proposed by psychologist Carl Jung. They appear in literature as incidents and plots that repeat basic patterns of life. They may also appear as stereotyped characters. The "schlemiel" of Yiddish literature is an archetype.

Autobiography: A narrative in which an individual tells his or her life story. Examples include Benjamin Franklin's *Autobiography* and Amy Hempel's story "In the Cemetery Where Al Jolson Is Buried," which has autobiographical characteristics even though it is a work of fiction.

Avant-garde: A literary term that describes new writing that rejects traditional approaches to literature in favor of innovations in style or content. Twentieth-century examples of the literary avant-garde include the modernists and the minimalists.

B

Belles-lettres: A French term meaning "fine letters" or" beautiful writing." It is often used as a synonym for literature, typically referring to imaginative and artistic rather than scientific or expository writing. Current usage sometimes restricts the meaning to light or humorous writing and appreciative essays about literature. Lewis Carroll's *Alice in Wonderland* epitomizes the realm of belles-lettres.

Bildungsroman: A German word meaning "novel of development." The *bildungsroman* is a study of the maturation of a youthful character, typically brought about through a series of social or sexual encounters that lead to self-awareness. J. D. Salinger's *Catcher in the Rye* is a *bildungsroman*, and Doris Lessing's story "Through the Tunnel" exhibits characteristics of a *bildungsroman* as well.

Black Aesthetic Movement: A period of artistic and literary development among African Americans in the 1960s and early 1970s. This was the first major African-American artistic movement since the Harlem Renaissance and was closely paralleled by the civil rights and black power movements. The black aesthetic writers attempted to produce works of art that would be meaningful to the black masses. Key figures in black aesthetics included one of its founders, poet and playwright Amiri Baraka, formerly known as Le Roi Jones; poet and essayist Haki R. Madhubuti, formerly Don L. Lee; poet and playwright Sonia Sanchez; and dramatist Ed Bullins. Works representative of the Black Aesthetic Movement include Amiri Baraka's play *Dutchman*, a 1964 Obie award-winner.

Black Humor: Writing that places grotesque elements side by side with humorous ones in an attempt to shock the reader, forcing him or her to laugh at the horrifying reality of a disordered world. "Lamb to the Slaughter," by Roald Dahl, in which a placid housewife murders her husband and serves the murder weapon to the investigating policemen, is an example of black humor.

C

Catharsis: The release or purging of unwanted emotions—specifically fear and pity—brought about by exposure to art. The term was first used by the Greek philosopher Aristotle in his *Poetics* to refer to the desired effect of tragedy on spectators.

Character: Broadly speaking, a person in a literary work. The actions of characters are what constitute the plot of a story, novel, or poem. There are numerous types of characters, ranging from simple, stereotypical figures to intricate, multifaceted ones. "Characterization" is the process by which an author creates vivid, believable characters in a work of art. This may be done in a variety of ways, including (1) direct description of the character by the narrator; (2) the direct presentation of the speech, thoughts, or actions of the character; and (3) the responses of other characters to the character. The term "character" also refers to a form originated by the ancient Greek writer Theophrastus that later became popular in the seventeenth and eighteenth centuries. It is a short essay or sketch of a person who prominently displays a specific attribute or quality, such as miserliness or ambition. "Miss Brill," a story by Katherine Mansfield, is an example of a character sketch.

Classical: In its strictest definition in literary criticism, classicism refers to works of ancient Greek or Roman literature. The term may also be used to describe a literary work of recognized importance (a "classic") from any time period or literature that exhibits the traits of classicism. Examples of later works and authors now described as classical include French literature of the seventeenth century, Western novels of the nineteenth century, and American fiction of the mid-nineteenth century such as that written by James Fenimore Cooper and Mark Twain.

Climax: The turning point in a narrative, the moment when the conflict is at its most intense. Typically, the structure of stories, novels, and plays is one of rising action, in which tension builds to the climax, followed by falling action, in which tension lessens as the story moves to its conclusion.

Comedy: One of two major types of drama, the other being tragedy. Its aim is to amuse, and it typically ends happily. Comedy assumes many forms, such as farce and burlesque, and uses a variety of techniques, from parody to satire. In a restricted sense the term comedy refers only to dramatic presentations, but in general usage it is commonly applied to nondramatic works as well.

Comic Relief: The use of humor to lighten the mood of a serious or tragic story, especially in plays. The technique is very common in Elizabethan works, and can be an integral part of the plot or simply a brief event designed to break the tension of the scene.

Conflict: The conflict in a work of fiction is the issue to be resolved in the story. It usually occurs between two characters, the protagonist and the antagonist, or between the protagonist and society or the protagonist and himself or herself. The conflict in Washington Irving's story "The Devil and Tom Walker" is that the Devil wants Tom Walker's soul but Tom does not want to go to hell.

Criticism: The systematic study and evaluation of literary works, usually based on a specific method or set of principles. An important part of literary studies since ancient times, the practice of criticism has given rise to numerous theories, methods, and "schools," sometimes producing conflicting, even contradictory, interpretations of literature in general as well as of individual works. Even such basic issues as what constitutes a poem or a novel have been the subject of much criticism over the centuries. Seminal texts of literary criticism include Plato's *Republic,* Aristotle's *Poetics,* Sir Philip Sidney's *The Defence of Poesie,* and John Dryden's *Of Dramatic Poesie.* Contemporary schools of criticism include deconstruction, feminist, psychoanalytic, poststructuralist, new historicist, postcolonialist, and reader-response.

D

Deconstruction: A method of literary criticism characterized by multiple conflicting interpretations of a given work. Deconstructionists consider the impact of the language of a work and suggest that the true meaning of the work is not necessarily the meaning that the author intended.

Deduction: The process of reaching a conclusion through reasoning from general premises to a specific premise. Arthur Conan Doyle's character Sherlock Holmes often used deductive reasoning to solve mysteries.

Denotation: The definition of a word, apart from the impressions or feelings it creates in the reader. The word "apartheid" denotes a political and economic policy of segregation by race, but its connotations—oppression, slavery, inequality—are numerous.

Denouement: A French word meaning "the unknotting." In literature, it denotes the resolution of conflict in fiction or drama. The *denouement* follows the climax and provides an outcome to the primary plot situation as well as an explanation of secondary plot complications. A well-known example of *denouement* is the last scene of the play *As You Like It* by William Shakespeare, in which couples are married, an evildoer repents, the identities of two disguised characters are revealed, and a ruler is restored to power. Also known as "falling action."

Detective Story: A narrative about the solution of a mystery or the identification of a criminal. The conventions of the detective story include the detective's scrupulous use of logic in solving the mystery; incompetent or ineffectual police; a suspect who appears guilty at first but is later proved innocent; and the detective's friend or confidant—often the narrator—whose slowness in interpreting clues emphasizes by contrast the detective's brilliance. Edgar Allan Poe's "Murders in the Rue Morgue" is commonly regarded as the earliest example of this type of story. Other practitioners are Arthur Conan Doyle, Dashiell Hammett, and Agatha Christie.

Dialogue: Dialogue is conversation between people in a literary work. In its most restricted sense, it refers specifically to the speech of characters in a drama. As a specific literary genre, a "dialogue" is a composition in which characters debate an issue or idea.

Didactic: A term used to describe works of literature that aim to teach a moral, religious, political, or practical lesson. Although didactic elements are often found inartistically pleasing works, the term "didactic" usually refers to literature in which the message is more important than the form. The term may also be used to criticize a work that the critic finds "overly didactic," that is, heavy-handed in its delivery of a lesson. An example of didactic literature is John Bunyan's *Pilgrim's Progress.*

Dramatic Irony: Occurs when the reader of a work of literature knows something that a character in the work itself does not know. The irony is in the contrast between the intended meaning of the statements or actions of a character and the additional information understood by the audience.

Dystopia: An imaginary place in a work of fiction where the characters lead dehumanized, fearful lives. George Orwell's *Nineteen Eighty-four,* and Margaret Atwood's *Handmaid's Tale* portray versions of dystopia.

E

Edwardian: Describes cultural conventions identified with the period of the reign of Edward VII of England (1901–1910). Writers of the Edwardian Age typically displayed a strong reaction against the propriety and conservatism of the Victorian Age. Their work often exhibits distrust of authority in religion, politics, and art and expresses strong doubts about the soundness of conventional values. Writers of this era include E. M. Forster, H. G. Wells, and Joseph Conrad.

Empathy: A sense of shared experience, including emotional and physical feelings, with someone or something other than oneself. Empathy is often used to describe the response of a reader to a literary character.

Epilogue: A concluding statement or section of a literary work. In dramas, particularly those of the seventeenth and eighteenth centuries, the epilogue is a closing speech, often in verse, delivered by an actor at the end of a play and spoken directly to the audience.

Epiphany: A sudden revelation of truth inspired by a seemingly trivial incident. The term was widely used by James Joyce in his critical writings, and the stories in Joyce's *Dubliners* are commonly called "epiphanies."

Epistolary Novel: A novel in the form of letters. The form was particularly popular in the eighteenth century. The form can also be applied to short stories, as in Edwidge Danticat's "Children of the Sea."

Epithet: A word or phrase, often disparaging or abusive, that expresses a character trait of someone or something. "The Napoleon of crime" is an epithet applied to Professor Moriarty, arch-rival of Sherlock Holmes in Arthur Conan Doyle's series of detective stories.

Existentialism: A predominantly twentieth-century philosophy concerned with the nature and perception of human existence. There are two major strains of existentialist thought: atheistic and Christian. Followers of atheistic existentialism believe that the individual is alone in a godless universe and that the basic human condition is one of suffering and loneliness. Nevertheless, because there are no fixed values, individuals can create their own characters—indeed, they can shape themselves—through the exercise of free will. The atheistic strain culminates in and is popularly associated with the works of Jean-Paul Sartre. The Christian existentialists, on the other hand, believe that only in God may people find freedom from life's anguish. The two strains hold certain beliefs in common: that existence cannot be fully understood or described through empirical effort; that anguish is a universal element of life; that individuals must bear responsibility for their actions; and that there is no common standard of behavior or perception for religious and ethical matters. Existentialist thought figures prominently in the works of such authors as Franz Kafka, Fyodor Dostoyevsky, and Albert Camus.

Expatriatism: The practice of leaving one's country to live for an extended period in another country. Literary expatriates include Irish author James Joyce who moved to Italy and France, American writers James Baldwin, Ernest Hemingway, Gertrude Stein, and F. Scott Fitzgerald who lived and wrote in Paris, and Polish novelist Joseph Conrad in England.

Exposition: Writing intended to explain the nature of an idea, thing, or theme. Expository writing is often combined with description, narration, or argument.

Expressionism: An indistinct literary term, originally used to describe an early twentieth-century school of German painting. The term applies to almost any mode of unconventional, highly subjective writing that distorts reality in some way. Advocates of Expressionism include Federico Garcia Lorca, Eugene O'Neill, Franz Kafka, and James Joyce.

F

Fable: A prose or verse narrative intended to convey a moral. Animals or inanimate objects with human characteristics often serve as characters in fables. A famous fable is Aesop's "The Tortoise and the Hare."

Fantasy: A literary form related to mythology and folklore. Fantasy literature is typically set in non-existent realms and features supernatural beings. Notable examples of literature with elements of fantasy are Gabriel García Márquez's story "The Handsomest Drowned Man in the World" and Ursula K. Le Guin's "The Ones Who Walk Away from Omelas."

Farce: A type of comedy characterized by broad humor, outlandish incidents, and often vulgar subject matter. Much of the comedy in film and television could more accurately be described as farce.

Fiction: Any story that is the product of imagination rather than a documentation of fact. Characters and events in such narratives may be based in real life but their ultimate form and configuration is a creation of the author.

Figurative Language: A technique in which an author uses figures of speech such as hyperbole, irony, metaphor, or simile for a particular effect. Figurative language is the opposite of literal language, in which every word is truthful, accurate, and free of exaggeration or embellishment.

Flashback: A device used in literature to present action that occurred before the beginning of the story. Flashbacks are often introduced as the dreams or recollections of one or more characters.

Foil: A character in a work of literature whose physical or psychological qualities contrast strongly with, and therefore highlight, the corresponding qualities of another character. In his Sherlock Holmes stories, Arthur Conan Doyle portrayed Dr. Watson as a man of normal habits and intelligence, making him a foil for the eccentric and unusually perceptive Sherlock Holmes.

Folklore: Traditions and myths preserved in a culture or group of people. Typically, these are passed on by word of mouth in various forms—such as legends, songs, and proverbs—or preserved in customs and ceremonies. Washington Irving, in "The Devil and Tom Walker" and many of his other stories, incorporates many elements of the folklore of New England and Germany.

Folktale: A story originating in oral tradition. Folk tales fall into a variety of categories, including legends, ghost stories, fairy tales, fables, and anecdotes based on historical figures and events.

Foreshadowing: A device used in literature to create expectation or to set up an explanation of later developments. Edgar Allan Poe uses foreshadowing to create suspense in "The Fall of the House of Usher" when the narrator comments on the crumbling state of disrepair in which he finds the house.

G

Genre: A category of literary work. Genre may refer to both the content of a given work—tragedy, comedy, horror, science fiction—and to its form, such as poetry, novel, or drama.

Gilded Age: A period in American history during the 1870s and after characterized by political corruption and materialism. A number of important novels of social and political criticism were written during this time. Henry James and Kate Chopin are two writers who were prominent during the Gilded Age.

Gothicism: In literature, works characterized by a taste for medieval or morbid characters and situations. A gothic novel prominently features elements of horror, the supernatural, gloom, and violence: clanking chains, terror, ghosts, medieval castles, and unexplained phenomena. The term "gothic novel" is also applied to novels that lack elements of the traditional Gothic setting but that create a similar atmosphere of terror or dread. The term can also be applied to stories, plays, and poems. Mary Shelley's *Frankenstein* and Joyce Carol Oates's *Bellefleur* are both gothic novels.

Grotesque: In literature, a work that is characterized by exaggeration, deformity, freakishness, and disorder. The grotesque often includes an element of comic absurdity. Examples of the grotesque can be found in the works of Edgar Allan Poe, Flannery O'Connor, Joseph Heller, and Shirley Jackson.

H

Harlem Renaissance: The Harlem Renaissance of the 1920s is generally considered the first significant movement of black writers and artists in the United States. During this period, new and established black writers, many of whom lived in the region of New York City known as Harlem, published more fiction and poetry than ever before, the first influential black literary journals were established, and black authors and artists received their first widespread recognition and serious critical appraisal. Among the major writers associated with this period are Countee Cullen, Langston Hughes, Arna Bontemps, and Zora Neale Hurston.

Hero/Heroine: The principal sympathetic character in a literary work. Heroes and heroines typically exhibit admirable traits: idealism, courage, and integrity, for example. Famous heroes and heroines of literature include Charles Dickens's Oliver Twist, Margaret Mitchell's Scarlett O'Hara, and the anonymous narrator in Ralph Ellison's *Invisible Man.*

Hyperbole: Deliberate exaggeration used to achieve an effect. In William Shakespeare's *Macbeth,* Lady Macbeth hyperbolizes when she says, "All the perfumes of Arabia could not sweeten this little hand."

I

Image: A concrete representation of an object or sensory experience. Typically, such a representation helps evoke the feelings associated with the object or experience itself. Images are either "literal" or "figurative." Literal images are especially concrete and involve little or no extension of the obvious meaning of the words used to express them. Figurative images do not follow the literal meaning of the words exactly. Images in literature are usually visual, but the term "image" can also refer to the representation of any sensory experience.

Imagery: The array of images in a literary work. Also used to convey the author's overall use of figurative language in a work.

In medias res: A Latin term meaning "in the middle of things." It refers to the technique of beginning a story at its midpoint and then using various flashback devices to reveal previous action. This technique originated in such epics as Virgil's *Aeneid.*

Interior Monologue: A narrative technique in which characters' thoughts are revealed in a way that appears to be uncontrolled by the author. The interior monologue typically aims to reveal the inner self of a character. It portrays emotional experiences as they occur at both a conscious and unconscious level. One of the best-known interior monologues in English is the Molly Bloom section at the close of James Joyce's *Ulysses.* Katherine Anne Porter's "The Jilting of Granny Weatherall" is also told in the form of an interior monologue.

Irony: In literary criticism, the effect of language in which the intended meaning is the opposite of what is stated. The title of Jonathan Swift's "A Modest Proposal" is ironic because what Swift proposes in this essay is cannibalism—hardly "modest."

J

Jargon: Language that is used or understood only by a select group of people. Jargon may refer to terminology used in a certain profession, such as computer jargon, or it may refer to any nonsensical language that is not understood by most people. Anthony Burgess's *A Clockwork Orange* and James Thurber's "The Secret Life of Walter Mitty" both use jargon.

K

Knickerbocker Group: An indistinct group of New York writers of the first half of the nineteenth century. Members of the group were linked only by location and a common theme: New York life. Two famous members of the Knickerbocker Group were Washington Irving and William Cullen Bryant. The group's name derives from Irving's *Knickerbocker's History of New York*.

L

Literal Language: An author uses literal language when he or she writes without exaggerating or embellishing the subject matter and without any tools of figurative language. To say "He ran very quickly down the street" is to use literal language, whereas to say "He ran like a hare down the street" would be using figurative language.

Literature: Literature is broadly defined as any written or spoken material, but the term most often refers to creative works. Literature includes poetry, drama, fiction, and many kinds of nonfiction writing, as well as oral, dramatic, and broadcast compositions not necessarily preserved in a written format, such as films and television programs.

Lost Generation: A term first used by Gertrude Stein to describe the post-World War I generation of American writers: men and women haunted by a sense of betrayal and emptiness brought about by the destructiveness of the war. The term is commonly applied to Hart Crane, Ernest Hemingway, F. Scott Fitzgerald, and others.

M

Magic Realism: A form of literature that incorporates fantasy elements or supernatural occurrences into the narrative and accepts them as truth. Gabriel Gárcia Márquez and Laura Esquivel are two writers known for their works of magic realism.

Metaphor: A figure of speech that expresses an idea through the image of another object. Metaphors suggest the essence of the first object by identifying it with certain qualities of the second object. An example is "But soft, what light through yonder window breaks? / It is the east, and Juliet is the sun" in William Shakespeare's *Romeo and Juliet*. Here, Juliet, the first object, is identified with qualities of the second object, the sun.

Minimalism: A literary style characterized by spare, simple prose with few elaborations. In minimalism, the main theme of the work is often never discussed directly. Amy Hempel and Ernest Hemingway are two writers known for their works of minimalism.

Modernism: Modern literary practices. Also, the principles of a literary school that lasted from roughly the beginning of the twentieth century until the end of World War II. Modernism is defined by its rejection of the literary conventions of the nineteenth century and by its opposition to conventional morality, taste, traditions, and economic values. Many writers are associated with the concepts of modernism, including Albert Camus, D. H. Lawrence, Ernest Hemingway, William Faulkner, Eugene O'Neill, and James Joyce.

Monologue: A composition, written or oral, by a single individual. More specifically, a speech given by a single individual in a drama or other public entertainment. It has no set length, although it is usually several or more lines long. "I Stand Here Ironing" by Tillie Olsen is an example of a story written in the form of a monologue.

Mood: The prevailing emotions of a work or of the author in his or her creation of the work. The mood of a work is not always what might be expected based on its subject matter.

Motif: A theme, character type, image, metaphor, or other verbal element that recurs throughout a single work of literature or occurs in a number of different works over a period of time. For example, the color white in Herman Melville's *Moby Dick* is a "specific" motif, while the trials of star-crossed lovers is a "conventional" motif from the literature of all periods.

N

Narration: The telling of a series of events, real or invented. A narration may be either a simple narrative, in which the events are recounted chronologically, or a narrative with a plot, in which the account is given in a style reflecting the author's artistic concept of the story. Narration is sometimes used as a synonym for "storyline."

Narrative: A verse or prose accounting of an event or sequence of events, real or invented. The term is also used as an adjective in the sense "method of narration." For example, in literary criticism, the expression "narrative technique" usually refers to the way the author structures and presents his or her story. Different narrative forms include diaries, travelogues, novels, ballads, epics, short stories, and other fictional forms.

Narrator: The teller of a story. The narrator may be the author or a character in the story through whom the author speaks. Huckleberry Finn is the narrator of Mark Twain's *The Adventures of Huckleberry Finn.*

Novella: An Italian term meaning "story." This term has been especially used to describe fourteenth-century Italian tales, but it also refers to modern short novels. Modern novellas include Leo Tolstoy's *The Death of Ivan Ilich,* Fyodor Dostoyevsky's *Notes from the Underground,* and Joseph Conrad's *Heart of Darkness.*

O

Oedipus Complex: A son's romantic obsession with his mother. The phrase is derived from the story of the ancient Theban hero Oedipus, who unknowingly killed his father and married his mother, and was popularized by Sigmund Freud's theory of psychoanalysis. Literary occurrences of the Oedipus complex include Sophocles' *Oedipus Rex* and D. H. Lawrence's "The Rocking-Horse Winner."

Onomatopoeia: The use of words whose sounds express or suggest their meaning. In its simplest sense, onomatopoeia may be represented by words that mimic the sounds they denote such as "hiss" or "meow." At a more subtle level, the pattern and rhythm of sounds and rhymes of a line or poem may be onomatopoeic.

Oral Tradition: A process by which songs, ballads, folklore, and other material are transmitted by word of mouth. The tradition of oral transmission predates the written record systems of literate society. Oral transmission preserves material sometimes over generations, although often with variations. Memory plays a large part in the recitation and preservation of orally transmitted material. Native American myths and legends, and African folktales told by plantation slaves are examples of orally transmitted literature.

P

Parable: A story intended to teach a moral lesson or answer an ethical question. Examples of parables are the stories told by Jesus Christ in the New Testament, notably "The Prodigal Son," but parables also are used in Sufism, rabbinic literature, Hasidism, and Zen Buddhism. Isaac Bashevis Singer's story "Gimpel the Fool" exhibits characteristics of a parable.

Paradox: A statement that appears illogical or contradictory at first, but may actually point to an underlying truth. A literary example of a paradox is George Orwell's statement "All animals are equal, but some animals are more equal than others" in *Animal Farm.*

Parody: In literature, this term refers to an imitation of a serious literary work or the signature style of a particular author in a ridiculous manner. A typical parody adopts the style of the original and applies it to an inappropriate subject for humorous effect. Parody is a form of satire and could be considered the literary equivalent of a caricature or cartoon. Henry Fielding's *Shamela* is a parody of Samuel Richardson's *Pamela.*

Persona: A Latin term meaning "mask." Personae are the characters in a fictional work of literature. The persona generally functions as a mask through which the author tells a story in a voice other than his or her own. A persona is usually either a character in a story who acts as a narrator or an "implied author," a voice created by the author to act as the narrator for himself or herself. The persona in Charlotte Perkins Gilman's story "The Yellow Wallpaper" is the unnamed young mother experiencing a mental breakdown.

Personification: A figure of speech that gives human qualities to abstract ideas, animals, and inanimate objects. To say that "the sun is smiling" is to personify the sun.

Plot: The pattern of events in a narrative or drama. In its simplest sense, the plot guides the author in composing the work and helps the reader follow the work. Typically, plots exhibit causality and unity and have a beginning, a middle, and an end. Sometimes, however, a plot may consist of a series of disconnected events, in which case it is known as an "episodic plot."

Poetic Justice: An outcome in a literary work, not necessarily a poem, in which the good are rewarded and the evil are punished, especially in ways that particularly fit their virtues or crimes. For example, a murderer may himself be murdered, or a thief will find himself penniless.

Poetic License: Distortions of fact and literary convention made by a writer—not always a poet—for the sake of the effect gained. Poetic license is closely related to the concept of "artistic freedom." An author exercises poetic license by saying that a pile of money "reaches as high as a mountain" when the pile is actually only a foot or two high.

Point of View: The narrative perspective from which a literary work is presented to the reader. There are four traditional points of view. The "third person omniscient" gives the reader a "godlike" perspective, unrestricted by time or place, from which to see actions and look into the minds of characters. This allows the author to comment openly on characters and events in the work. The "third person" point of view presents the events of the story from outside of any single character's perception, much like the omniscient point of view, but the reader must understand the action as it takes place and without any special insight into characters' minds or motivations. The "first person" or "personal" point of view relates events as they are perceived by a single character. The main character "tells" the story and may offer opinions about the action and characters which differ from those of the author. Much less common than omniscient, third person, and first person is the "second person" point of view, wherein the author tells the story as if it is happening to the reader. James Thurber employs the omniscient point of view in his short story "The Secret Life of Walter Mitty." Ernest Hemingway's "A Clean, Well-Lighted Place" is a short story told from the third person point of view. Mark Twain's novel *Huckleberry Finn* is presented from the first person viewpoint. Jay McInerney's *Bright Lights, Big City* is an example of a novel which uses the second person point of view.

Pornography: Writing intended to provoke feelings of lust in the reader. Such works are often condemned by critics and teachers, but those which can be shown to have literary value are viewed less harshly. Literary works that have been described as pornographic include D. H. Lawrence's *Lady Chatterley's Lover* and James Joyce's *Ulysses.*

Post-Aesthetic Movement: An artistic response made by African Americans to the black aesthetic movement of the 1960s and early 1970s. Writers since that time have adopted a somewhat different tone in their work, with less emphasis placed on the disparity between black and white in the United States. In the words of post-aesthetic authors such as Toni Morrison, John Edgar Wideman, and Kristin Hunter, African Americans are portrayed as looking inward for answers to their own questions, rather than always looking to the outside world. Two well-known examples of works produced as part of the post-aesthetic movement are the Pulitzer Prize–winning novels *The Color Purple* by Alice Walker and *Beloved* by Toni Morrison.

Postmodernism: Writing from the 1960s forward characterized by experimentation and application of modernist elements, which include existentialism and alienation. Postmodernists have gone a step further in the rejection of tradition begun with the modernists by also rejecting traditional forms, preferring the anti-novel over the novel and the anti-hero over the hero. Postmodern writers include Thomas Pynchon, Margaret Drabble, and Gabriel Gárcia Márquez.

Prologue: An introductory section of a literary work. It often contains information establishing the situation of the characters or presents information about the setting, time period, or action. In drama, the prologue is spoken by a chorus or by one of the principal characters.

Prose: A literary medium that attempts to mirror the language of everyday speech. It is distinguished from poetry by its use of unmetered, unrhymed language consisting of logically related sentences. Prose is usually grouped into paragraphs that form a cohesive whole such as an essay or a novel. The term is sometimes used to mean an author's general writing.

Protagonist: The central character of a story who serves as a focus for its themes and incidents and as the principal rationale for its development. The protagonist is sometimes referred to in discussions of modern literature as the hero or anti-hero. Well-known protagonists are Hamlet in William Shakespeare's *Hamlet* and Jay Gatsby in F. Scott Fitzgerald's *The Great Gatsby*.

R

Realism: A nineteenth-century European literary movement that sought to portray familiar characters, situations, and settings in a realistic manner. This was done primarily by using an objective narrative point of view and through the buildup of accurate detail. The standard for success of any realistic work depends on how faithfully it transfers common experience into fictional forms. The realistic method may be altered or extended, as in stream of consciousness writing, to record highly subjective experience. Contemporary authors who often write in a realistic way include Nadine Gordimer and Grace Paley.

Resolution: The portion of a story following the climax, in which the conflict is resolved. The resolution of Jane Austen's *Northanger Abbey* is neatly summed up in the following sentence: "Henry and Catherine were married, the bells rang and every body smiled."

Rising Action: The part of a drama where the plot becomes increasingly complicated. Rising action leads up to the climax, or turning point, of a drama. The final "chase scene" of an action film is generally the rising action which culminates in the film's climax.

Roman a clef: A French phrase meaning "novel with a key." It refers to a narrative in which real persons are portrayed under fictitious names. Jack Kerouac, for example, portrayed various friends under fictitious names in the novel *On the Road*. D. H. Lawrence based "The Rocking-Horse Winner" on a family he knew.

Romanticism: This term has two widely accepted meanings. In historical criticism, it refers to a European intellectual and artistic movement of the late eighteenth and early nineteenth centuries that sought greater freedom of personal expression than that allowed by the strict rules of literary form and logic of the eighteenth-century neoclassicists. The Romantics preferred emotional and imaginative expression to rational analysis. They considered the individual to be at the center of all experience and so placed him or her at the center of their art. The Romantics believed that the creative imagination reveals nobler truths—unique feelings and attitudes—than those that could be discovered by logic or by scientific examination. "Romanticism" is also used as a general term to refer to a type of sensibility found in all periods of literary history and usually considered to be in opposition to the principles of classicism. In this sense, Romanticism signifies any work or philosophy in which the exotic or dreamlike figure strongly, or that is devoted to individualistic expression, self-analysis, or a pursuit of a higher realm of knowledge than can be discovered by human reason. Prominent Romantics include Jean-Jacques Rousseau, William Wordsworth, John Keats, Lord Byron, and Johann Wolfgang von Goethe.

S

Satire: A work that uses ridicule, humor, and wit to criticize and provoke change in human nature and institutions. Voltaire's novella *Candide* and Jonathan Swift's essay "A Modest Proposal" are both satires. Flannery O'Connor's portrayal of the family in "A Good Man Is Hard to Find" is a satire of a modern, Southern, American family.

Science Fiction: A type of narrative based upon real or imagined scientific theories and technology. Science fiction is often peopled with alien creatures and set on other planets or in different dimensions. Popular writers of science fiction are Isaac Asimov, Karel Capek, Ray Bradbury, and Ursula K. Le Guin.

Setting: The time, place, and culture in which the action of a narrative takes place. The elements of setting may include geographic location, characters's physical and mental environments, prevailing cultural attitudes, or the historical time in which the action takes place.

Short Story: A fictional prose narrative shorter and more focused than a novella. The short story usually deals with a single episode and often a single character. The "tone," the author's attitude toward his or her subject and audience, is uniform throughout. The short story frequently also lacks *denouement*, ending instead at its climax.

Signifying Monkey: A popular trickster figure in black folklore, with hundreds of tales about this character documented since the 19th century. Henry Louis Gates Jr. examines the history of the signifying monkey in *The Signifying Monkey: Towards a Theory of Afro-American Literary Criticism*, published in 1988.

Simile: A comparison, usually using "like" or "as," of two essentially dissimilar things, as in "coffee as cold as ice" or "He sounded like a broken record." The title of Ernest Hemingway's "Hills Like White Elephants" contains a simile.

Socialist Realism: The Socialist Realism school of literary theory was proposed by Maxim Gorky and established as a dogma by the first Soviet Congress of Writers. It demanded adherence to a communist worldview in works of literature. Its doctrines required an objective viewpoint comprehensible to the working classes and themes of social struggle featuring strong proletarian heroes. Gabriel García Márquez's stories exhibit some characteristics of Socialist Realism.

Stereotype: A stereotype was originally the name for a duplication made during the printing process; this led to its modern definition as a person or thing that is (or is assumed to be) the same as all others of its type. Common stereotypical characters include the absent-minded professor, the nagging wife, the troublemaking teenager, and the kindhearted grandmother.

Stream of Consciousness: A narrative technique for rendering the inward experience of a character. This technique is designed to give the impression of an ever-changing series of thoughts, emotions, images, and memories in the spontaneous and seemingly illogical order that they occur in life. The textbook example of stream of consciousness is the last section of James Joyce's *Ulysses*.

Structure: The form taken by a piece of literature. The structure may be made obvious for ease of understanding, as in nonfiction works, or may obscured for artistic purposes, as in some poetry or seemingly "unstructured" prose.

Style: A writer's distinctive manner of arranging words to suit his or her ideas and purpose in writing. The unique imprint of the author's personality upon his or her writing, style is the product of an author's way of arranging ideas and his or her use of diction, different sentence structures, rhythm, figures of speech, rhetorical principles, and other elements of composition.

Suspense: A literary device in which the author maintains the audience's attention through the buildup of events, the outcome of which will soon be revealed. Suspense in William Shakespeare's *Hamlet* is sustained throughout by the question of whether or not the Prince will achieve what he has been instructed to do and of what he intends to do.

Symbol: Something that suggests or stands for something else without losing its original identity. In literature, symbols combine their literal meaning with the suggestion of an abstract concept. Literary symbols are of two types: those that carry complex associations of meaning no matter what their contexts, and those that derive their suggestive meaning from their functions in specific literary works. Examples of symbols are sunshine suggesting happiness, rain suggesting sorrow, and storm clouds suggesting despair.

T

Tale: A story told by a narrator with a simple plot and little character development. Tales are usually relatively short and often carry a simple message. Examples of tales can be found in the works of Saki, Anton Chekhov, Guy de Maupassant, and O. Henry.

Tall Tale: A humorous tale told in a straightforward, credible tone but relating absolutely impossible events or feats of the characters. Such tales were commonly told of frontier adventures during the settlement of the west in the United States. Literary use of tall tales can be found in Washington Irving's *History of New York,* Mark Twain's *Life on the Mississippi,* and in the German R. F. Raspe's *Baron Munchausen's Narratives of His Marvellous Travels and Campaigns in Russia.*

Theme: The main point of a work of literature. The term is used interchangeably with thesis. Many works have multiple themes. One of the themes of Nathaniel Hawthorne's "Young Goodman Brown" is loss of faith.

Tone: The author's attitude toward his or her audience maybe deduced from the tone of the work. A formal tone may create distance or convey politeness, while an informal tone may encourage a friendly, intimate, or intrusive feeling in the reader. The author's attitude toward his or her subject matter may also be deduced from the tone of the words he or she uses in discussing it. The tone of John F. Kennedy's speech which included the appeal to "ask not what your country can do for you" was intended to instill feelings of camaraderie and national pride in listeners.

Tragedy: A drama in prose or poetry about a noble, courageous hero of excellent character who, because of some tragic character flaw, brings ruin upon him- or herself. Tragedy treats its subjects in a dignified and serious manner, using poetic language to help evoke pity and fear and bring about catharsis, a purging of these emotions. The tragic form was practiced extensively by the ancient Greeks. The classical form of tragedy was revived in the sixteenth century; it flourished especially on the Elizabethan stage. In modern times, dramatists have attempted to adapt the form to the needs of modern society by drawing their heroes from the ranks of ordinary men and women and defining the nobility of these heroes in terms of spirit rather than exalted social standing. Some contemporary works that are thought of as tragedies include *The Great Gatsby* by F. Scott Fitzgerald, and *The Sound and the Fury* by William Faulkner.

Tragic Flaw: In a tragedy, the quality within the hero or heroine which leads to his or her downfall. Examples of the tragic flaw include Othello's jealousy and Hamlet's indecisiveness, although most great tragedies defy such simple interpretation.

U

Utopia: A fictional perfect place, such as "paradise" or "heaven." An early literary utopia was described in Plato's *Republic,* and in modern literature, Ursula K. Le Guin depicts a utopia in "The Ones Who Walk Away from Omelas."

V

Victorian: Refers broadly to the reign of Queen Victoria of England (1837-1901) and to anything with qualities typical of that era. For example, the qualities of smug narrow-mindedness, bourgeois materialism, faith in social progress, and priggish morality are often considered Victorian. In literature, the Victorian Period was the great age of the English novel, and the latter part of the era saw the rise of movements such as decadence and symbolism.

Cumulative Author/Title Index

Cumulative Nationality/Ethnicity Index

Cumulative Nationality/Ethnicity Index

Subject/Theme Index

C

Calvinism
 A River Runs Through It: 203,
  218–219
Canadian culture
 Mrs. Turner Cutting the Grass:
  168–170, 175–179
Censorship
 A Logic Named Joe: 157
Change (Philosophy)
 New Boy: 187–188
Chaos
 The Dunwich Horror: 116
 A Logic Named Joe: 148–149
 A River Runs Through It: 220
Characterization
 A Bush League Hero: 26, 30–33,
  36–41
 The Cold Equations: 58
 Dance in America: 79
 The Dunwich Horror: 109, 118
 Geraldine Moore the Poet: 139, 140
 Mrs. Turner Cutting the Grass: 174
 New Boy: 191, 194, 198, 199
 The Suitcase: 247–248, 251
Charity
 Signs and Symbols: 236
Childhood
 Dance in America: 78
Christianity
 A River Runs Through It: 220
Comedy
 A River Runs Through It: 211
Coming of age
 Geraldine Moore the Poet: 141
 A River Runs Through It: 201
Communication
 Dance in America: 79
 Year of the Big Thaw: 277
Community
 A Bush League Hero: 25–26
Compassion
 The Cold Equations: 42
 Year of the Big Thaw: 269
Computers
 A Logic Named Joe: 143–145,
  152–158
Conflict
 A Bush League Hero: 38
 The Dinner Party: 83, 91
 The Suitcase: 252–255, 259–260
Confusion
 New Boy: 189
Connectedness
 Dance in America: 79
 New Boy: 193
Conscience
 The Suitcase: 262
Contempt. *See* Disdain
Contrast
 Mrs. Turner Cutting the Grass: 167
 The Suitcase: 253

Courage
 The Cold Equations: 47
 The Dinner Party: 85, 93
 The Dunwich Horror: 116
Cowardice
 The Suitcase: 254
Creativity
 The Boy Who Drew Cats: 5,
  12–14
 Mrs. Turner Cutting the Grass:
  164
Cruelty
 Mrs. Turner Cutting the Grass: 174
Culture
 Dance in America: 65
 A Logic Named Joe: 157

D

Daily living
 A Bush League Hero: 30
 Mrs. Turner Cutting the Grass:
  170–171
Dance
 Dance in America: 61, 64, 65
Danger
 The Cold Equations: 45
 New Boy: 186
Death
 The Cold Equations: 46, 47, 49–50,
  55, 59
 Dance in America: 61, 65, 66, 74, 77
 A River Runs Through It: 208, 217,
  219–221
 Signs and Symbols: 239
Decay
 The Dunwich Horror: 102–103,
  118, 119
Deception
 The Suitcase: 254, 260
Decline. *See* Decay
Defiance
 Dance in America: 75, 78
Delusions
 Signs and Symbols: 226, 236
Dependence
 A Bush League Hero: 32
 The Suitcase: 254
Destruction
 The Suitcase: 256
Details
 A Bush League Hero: 20, 27, 30
 The Cold Equations: 57
 Geraldine Moore the Poet: 135
Dialect. *See* Language and
  languages
Difference
 Geraldine Moore the Poet: 139
Disappointment
 The Suitcase: 253
Disapproval
 The Suitcase: 258

Discipline
 A River Runs Through It: 213, 215,
  219
 The Suitcase: 253
Disdain
 The Suitcase: 253, 258, 260
Disease
 Dance in America: 78
Disillusionment
 Geraldine Moore the Poet: 141
 The Suitcase: 260
Displacement
 The Boy Who Drew Cats: 13–14
 The Suitcase: 260
Dissatisfaction
 Mrs. Turner Cutting the Grass: 164
Domesticity
 A Bush League Hero: 36
 The Dinner Party: 92
Doubt
 The Suitcase: 260
Duty
 Year of the Big Thaw: 269, 277
Dysfunctional families
 The Suitcase: 254–255

E

Education
 The Dunwich Horror: 117, 118
 A River Runs Through It: 213
Embarrassment
 New Boy: 192
Emotions
 Dance in America: 77, 78–79
 Geraldine Moore the Poet: 126,
  134
 New Boy: 188, 189
 A River Runs Through It: 211
 The Suitcase: 252, 260
Empathy
 Dance in America: 81
Endurance
 Geraldine Moore the Poet: 141
Epiphanies
 Mrs. Turner Cutting the Grass:
  164–167
Experience
 A River Runs Through It: 208

F

Fairy tales
 The Boy Who Drew Cats: 1, 4, 7,
  11
Faith
 A River Runs Through It: 221
Familial love
 A River Runs Through It: 217
 Year of the Big Thaw: 264, 268–269
Family
 Geraldine Moore the Poet: 140

John C. Hart Mem Lib (Shrub Oak)

3 1030 15438685 8

RECEIVED AUG 1 2 2015